Lenscrafters	http://www.lenscrafters.com/	Reebok	http://www.reebok.com/
Levi Strauss & Co.	http://www.levi.com/	Renault	http://www.renault.com/
Lincoln Electric	http://lincolnelectric.com/	Republic Pictures	http://www.republic-pictures.com/
L. L. Bean	http://www.llbean.com/		
Lockheed Martin Corporation	http://www.lmco.com/	Revlon	http://www.revlon.com/
Logic Works	http://www.logicworks.com/	Rubbermaid	http://home.rubbermaid.com/
Lotus Development Co.	http://www.lotus.com/	Ryder System	http://ryder.com/
L. R. Nelson, Inc.	http://www.lrnelson.com/	Saab	http://www.saabusa.com/
3M	http://www.3M.com/	SAS Institute, Inc.	http://www.sas.com/
Mary Kay Cosmetics	http://www.marykay.com/	Sears Roebuck	http://www.sears.com/
Matsushita	http://www.mei.co.jp/	Siemens	http://www.siemens.com/
Mattel, Inc.	http://www.mattelmedia.com/	Smith Barney	http://www.smithbarney.com/
Maytag	http://www.maytag.com/	Southland Corporation (7-Eleven)	http://www.7-11.com/
May Department Stores Company	http://www.maycompany.com/	Sony	http://www.sony.com/
		Southwest Airlines	http://www.iflyswa.com/
Mazda	http://www.mazda.com/	Square D	http://www.industry.net/squared
McDonald's	http://www.mcdonalds.com/	State Farm Insurance	http://www.statefarm.com/
The Medicine Shoppe	http://www.harb.net/the medicineshoppe/	Steelcase	http://www.steelcase.com/
		Stride Rite	http://www.striderite.com/
Mercedes-Benz	http://www.mercedes-benz.com/	Subaru	http://www.subaru.com/
Merck	http://www.merck.com/	Sumitomo Steel	http://www.sumikin.co.jp/
Merrill Lynch	http://www.ml.com/	Sun Microsystems	http://www.sun.com/
Microsoft	http://www.microsoft.com/	Sybase Inc.	http://www.sybase.com/
Mobil	http://www.mobil.com/	Symantec, Inc.	http://www.symantec.com/
Montgomery Ward	http://www.mward.com/	Target	http://www.targetstores.com/
Moody's Investor Services	http://www.moodys.com/	Texaco	http://www.texaco.com/
Motorola	http://www.motorola.com/	Texas Instruments	http://www.ti.com/
Moto Photo	http://www.motophoto.com/	Toshiba	http://www.toshiba.com/
Mitsubishi	http://www.mitsubishi.com/	Toyota	http://www.toyota.com/
Nabisco	http://www.nabisco.com/	TWA	http://www.twa.com/
NEC	http://www.nec.com/	Unilever	http://www.unilever.com/corporate/
Neiman-Marcus	http://www.neimanmarcus.com/		
Nestle	http://www.nestle.com/	United Airlines	http://www.ual.com/
Nike	http://www.nike.com/	United Way	http://www.unitedway.org/
Nissan	http://www.nissanmotors.com/	United Parcel Service (UPS)	http://www.ups.com/
NKK	http://www.nkk.co.jp/	US Air	http://www.usair.com/
Northwest Airlines	http://www.nwa.com/	U.S. Postal Service	http://www.usps.gov/
Nordstrom Inc.	http://www.npta.com/	USX	http://www.usx.com/
Novell Inc.	http://www.novell.com/	ValuJet	http://www.valujet.com/
Olivetti	http://www.olivetti.it/	Viacom Inc.	http://www.viacom.com/
Oracle Corp.	http://www.oracle.com/	Visa	http://www.visa.com/
Oticon	http://www.oticon.com/	Volkswagen	http://www.vw.com/
Packard Bell	http://www.packardbell.com/	Volvo	http://www.volvo.se/
PepsiCo	http://www.pepsico.com/	Walgreens	http://www.walgreens.com/
Peterbilt	http://www.peterbilt.com/	Wall Street Journal	http://www.wsj.com/
Peugeot	http://www.peugeot.com/	Wal-Mart Stores	http://www.wal-mart.com/
Play It Again Sports	http://www.playitagainsports.com	Wendy's	http://www.wendys.com/
		Westinghouse Electric	http://www.westinghouse.com/
Proctor & Gamble	http:www/pg.com	Xerox	http://www.xerox.com/
Raytheon	http://www.raytheon.com/	Yamaha	http://www.yamaha.com/
Red Lobster	http://www.redlobster.com/	Zenith	http://www.zenith.com

Business

An Integrative Framework

Business

An Integrative Framework

FRED L. FRY

Bradley University

CHARLES R. STONER

Bradley University

RICHARD E. HATTWICK

Western Illinois University

Irwin McGraw-Hill

Boston   Burr Ridge, IL   Dubuque, IA   Madison, WI   New York   San Francisco   St. Louis
Bangkok   Bogotá   Caracas   Lisbon   London   Madrid
Mexico City   Milan   New Delhi   Seoul   Singapore   Sydney   Taipei   Toronto

Irwin/McGraw-Hill

A Division of The **McGraw·Hill** Companies

Icon logos courtesy of Motorola, Inc., Southwest Airlines, and Brinker International.

BUSINESS: AN INTEGRATIVE FRAMEWORK

This book is printed on acid-free paper.

1 2 3 4 5 6 7 8 9 0 DOW/DOW 9 0 9 8 7

ISBN 0-256-23612-7

Vice president and editorial director: *Michael W. Junior*
Publisher: *Craig S. Beytien*
Senior sponsoring editor: *John E. Biernat*
Senior development editor: *Maryellen Krammer*
Senior marketing manager: *Katie Rose Matthews*
Project manager: *Jim Labeots*
Production supervior: *Scott Hamilton*
Senior designer: *Crispin Prebys*
Senior photo research coordinator: *Keri Johnson*
Compositor: *Precision Graphics Services, Inc.*
Typeface: *10/12 Times Roman*
Printer: *R. R. Donnelley & Sons (Willard)*

Library of Congress Cataloging in Publication Data
Fry, Fred L.
    Business: an integrated framework/Fred L. Fry, Charles R. Stoner, Richard E.
  Hattwick.--1st ed.
        p.   cm
    ISBN 0-256-23612-7
    Includes index.
        1. Industrial management--Case studies.   I. Stoner, Charles R.   II. Hatwick,
  Richard E.   III. Title
  HD31.F79   1998
    658--dc21   97-32432
http://www.mhhe.com

Contents in Brief

Contents

CHAPTER 3   *Decision Makers and Decision Making*   61

CHAPTER 4   *The Links Between Business and its Stakeholders*   90

PART

Two   *The Impact of
External Forces*   122

CHAPTER 5   *Diversity and Social Patterns*   124

CHAPTER 6   *Economic Forces*   156

CHAPTER 7   *Global Influences*   185

CHAPTER **8**   *The Impact of Financial Markets and Processes*   214

CHAPTER **9**   *The Impact of Legal and Regulatory Forces*   240

PART

Three   *Providing Excellence in Goods and Services*   304

CHAPTER **17**   *Promoting Change and Renewal*   512

APPENDIX **A**   *Preparing a Business Plan*   543

Preface

Business: An Integrative Framework represents a new approach to teaching the Introduction to Business course. While covering the most important topics found in traditional introductory books, we present you with a book whose approach is *truly integrative*. This framework captures how businesses really work in today's world and how contemporary colleges and universities will teach the Introduction to Business course.

Rationale for the Book

The idea behind *Business: An Integrative Framework* arose in 1994 when Bradley University reconfigured its curriculum in light of new AACSB guidelines that strongly suggested the need for a more integrative curriculum. It seemed ironic to us that while most Colleges of Business espoused the virtues of an integrative curriculum, the sole effort at meaningful integration was reserved for the final capstone course in Business Policy and Strategic Management. We vowed to rectify this inconsistency by building an integrative focus throughout our curriculum. Logically, it seemed that the launching point of this new curricular thrust should be the initial course in Business. Accordingly, a required, integrative Introduction to Business course was proposed and added to our curriculum at the freshman level.

Our move to a more integrative curriculum and toward writing this text was certainly motivated to some extent by AACSB. A greater influence, however, was the realization that this is increasingly how successful businesses work. Today's businesses are eliminating barriers between functional departments and are seeking to be boundaryless organizations. They are using cross-functional teams and self-directed teams. They are operating on a much more customer-centered basis. They are focusing on the big picture and discouraging functional autonomy.

Accordingly, students of business need to understand how the whole business works and how the parts fit together. They need to understand how the business environment, such as financial markets, global competition, the legal and regulatory system, and the industry in which the firm operates, affect business decisions and actions. They need to realize that quality, teamwork, and technology apply across the board. For example, quality is no longer the job of quality control specialists buried within the production department. Technology is changing the way entire departments or companies operate. And teams are the way to implement these changes.

We are convinced that *Business: An Integrative Framework* is truly the most integrative book on the market. We use the term *framework* to capture a different approach to teaching the Introduction to Business course.

The Development of the Book

Business: An Integrative Framework has received far more input and involvement of faculty, students, and reviewers than first edition books typically do. Because we were breaking new ground, Irwin/McGraw-Hill was especially careful in soliciting feedback regarding the prospectus and sample chapters. The development process began with a number of concept meetings held with the authors and representatives from Irwin/McGraw-Hill. Creative ideas were plentiful and the discussions were spirited and exciting. Through these discussions, the authors' initial work, and countless hours of author reflection at the local coffee house, the framework for this book began to unfold. Sample chapters were prepared, and a panel of faculty members from 15 colleges and universities reviewed the initial materials. Representatives of this panel were brought together in a focus group to discuss the project in detail and to offer input and direction. Overall, the focus group feedback was quite positive and the suggestions were relevant and meaningful.

We completed a first draft of the text which was sent out to eight instructors across the country for intense review. Additionally, the first draft was used in Bradley University's new Contemporary Business course. This pilot effort allowed us to test the product on the firing line. With five different professors teaching various sections of the course, we were able to see what worked and what needed refinement. A focus group, conducted by Irwin/McGraw-Hill with Bradley students was held to solicit their opionions of the first draft, and valuable feedback was gained.

Results from the reviews commissioned by Irwin/McGraw-Hill, our colleagues' use of the manuscript, and the student focus group guided the development of the second draft. This draft was sent out to an additional panel of ten instructors for more intense scrutiny. Based on their responses, additional changes were made—some very substantial—and the final manuscript was completed, resulting in the book you have in your hands.

Our Goals for this Book

Our goals in writing this book were the following:

- Write a book that helps students see how business really works. Increasingly, businesses work in teams and are breaking traditional boundaries that have restricted creativity and efficiency. Foremost, we wanted a book that helped students understand the dynamic way in which today's businesses must operate.
- Write a book that is as integrative as possible rather than discussing material in terms of functional silos. Experienced instructors will immediately notice differences in the Table of Contents, particularly in Parts I, III, and IV.
- Write a book that has a clear customer orientation. The need to focus on the customer is the dominant driving force behind company restructuring and changes in philosophy. You will note this customer orientation throughout the book. Chapter 1 discusses meeting customer needs as one of the indicators of business success. Chapter 12 discusses providing value for customers. Chapter 16 discusses measuring performance from a customer perspective. The need for customer sensitivity appears throughout the text.
- Write a book that is theoretically based, yet highly readable by students. Our students have assured us that we have indeed accomplished this even though they were reading the first draft which was often missing relevant charts and photos.

- Write a book that captures the excitement of business, while making business an approachable and engaging course of study. We are convinced that one way to accomplish this is to use examples that students understand and find interesting. It also means taking the mystery out of business. We use many entrpreneurial examples so students can see themselves in business roles. We spend considerable time in Part I discussing the ways businesses form, the key players, and the key stakeholders so students can see the personal side of business.

- Write a book that captures the positive nature of business, including significant sections on ethics and social responsibility, diversity, international issues, quality and technology, and the use of teams. We include significant coverage on these topics both within designated chapters and throughout the text.

- Write a book that uses focus examples throughout to illustrate how businesses address key issues. Do this in such a way that students are not bored with a single continuous case, but still have the continuity provided by the easily identifiable focus examples. We have chosen three companies—Motorola, Southwest Airlines, Brinker International (parent company of Chili's, Romano's Macaroni Grill, and other restaurant chains) and the entire mountain bike industry—to be our focus examples. Each of the companies is well known and respected, and the bicycle industry allows us to feature smaller manufacturers and associated retailers. Each time we use one of the examples, we indicate it with either a company logo or a bicycle icon.

- Write a book that addresses the business environment in terms of impacts on business, recognizing that businesses can seldom influence their environments but are heavily influenced by them. The entire Part II addresses the impacts of the environment on businesses. Note, for example, how we treat economics. Throughout that chapter, the focus is on how economic theories and issues *impact the business*. Similarly, the chapter dealing with financial markets focuses on how those markets impact how a business operates and competes rather than on a simple discussion of banks and the Federal Reserve system.

- Do all of this while still including most of the salient content found in traditional books and providing the same complement of ancillaries that instructors have grown to expect. We have carefully compared our text with traditional texts. We feel strongly that we have covered the key issues in business that students need to know. We trust you will agree.

Our Approach and Philosophy

As we began the development of *Business: An Integrative Framework*, we did so with two guiding philosophies in mind. The first was that the book has to be integrative. It has to do a good job of bringing functions and processes together. To the extent possible, we wanted to illustrate to students the complexities of managing a business. We wanted to show that decision making in a business is not done in a vacuum, that the actions in one part of a business affect other parts. This is illustrated in Chapter 13, Acquisition and Use of Resources, in which we discuss four different kinds of resources that businesses use. We highlight the interaction among those four kinds of resources and the tradeoffs that can occur by using more of one resource instead of another. Chapter 12, Providing Value For Customers, covers many of the topics normally found in the marketing section of traditional books, but we also cover product development and how cross-functional teams work to develop products that provide value. And we emphasize communicating with customers both as part of market research and as part of customer service. Chapter 16, Measuring Performance, discusses the measurement from a financial perspective, but it also discusses measurement from a customer, a quality, and an employee perspective. As you can see, we integrate the discussion of topics across functional areas more so than discussing them *within* functional areas.

The second guiding philosophy was that *Business: An Integrative Framework* should take an objective, but positive view of business. With the business and popular press highlighting the unethical behavior, strategic mistakes, and bad management practices of companies, we felt it was important to illustrate good business practices and how to encourage employees to act ethically. For example, our two largest focus companies—Motorola and Southwest Airlines—have been listed in Levering and Moskowitz's *The 100 Best Companies to Work For In America*. Motorola was the first recipient of the Malcolm Baldrige Award for quality, and *Business Week* recently ranked it second among large companies in family-friendly policies. We also use examples of other companies throughout the book to illustrate socially responsible behavior, commitment to the customer, and the infusion of quality into products and services.

Special Features of This Book

We have included features throughout *Business: An Integrative Framework* that we feel provide an optimal learning experience for students. Each of these is a significant improvement over traditional books. We highlight some of these here.

Read Me First!

We think it is important to capture the attention and interest of students at the outset. Accordingly, we have developed a prologue which highlights the excitement and challenge of business. We then introduce our four focus examples so the readers will understand our point of view and have an idea of what is to come later.

An Integrative Model

We developed a model which guides students throughout the entire book. We feel that this model helps integrate the material throughout the book and shows how the different aspects of a business and its environment interrelate. In order to maximize the effect of the model, we build the model piece by piece in Chapter 1 and then illustrate it with a Trek bicycle example. We then repeat the model at the beginning of each part to remind readers of and reinforce the integrative nature of business. The model helps students tie concepts together.

The value of the integrative model is seen from the beginning to the end of the book. Discussions throughout the text refer back to the model. In addition, Chapter 16, Measuring Performance, uses measurement perspectives that parallel the indicators of business success found in Chapter 1.

Shorter Text

Student feedback and faculty focus groups have consistently noted the need for a shorter introductory book. The integrative approach allows us to cover key topics necessary for introductory business courses while keeping the material within 17 chapters and under 600 pages.

Internet Addresses and Exercises

The internet addresses of virtually every business referenced in the text, along with those of other well-known businesses, are included on the inside covers of the book. Students will find it interesting to visit company websites. Exercises at the end of each chapter include at least one internet exercise to encourage students to explore and learn from this important resource. We encourage students to use the world wide web to gather information for this course and, therefore, become accustomed to using this valuable source of information.

Customer Focus

By design, this book takes a strong customer focus. In our integrative model, we demonstrate the significance of knowing customer needs and continually moving the business to fully meet those needs. This customer focus is emphasized throughout the text. Indeed, Chapter 16 includes an entire section on measuring performance from the customer perspective.

Diversity Focus

No other Introduction to Business text allocates an entire chapter to diversity and diversity management. We want students to understand the changing face of the workforce and marketplace. We also want them to understand the impact that these changes hold for businesses. Finally, we want them to understand the complexities of managing diversity.

Change and Innovation Focus

Today's business students must view innovation and change as a necessity of business competitiveness. This theme is introduced in Chapter 1 and emphasized throughout the text. Departing from other texts, we devote an entire chapter to the issues of creativity, innovation, and change.

Focus on Technology

Technology is revolutionizing the business world. While devoting special chapter material to address key technology themes, we emphasize the role of technology throughout the text. We want students to recognize that technolgy is a tool that encourages better business practice and enhances competitiveness across all business areas.

International Focus

It is easy and rather trite to tell students that today's businesses compete in a global marketplace. We are committed to helping students understand the opportunity and complexity of that statement. Although we devote a separate chapter to global forces, we emphasize international and global issues throughout the text. For example, we help students see why many of today's businesses must view thier operations from a global perspective. We help students understand how a business might actually become a global player. We help students see the cultural and operational complexity that global activities can bring to the business. It is our hope that students will have a much fuller and richer sense of the dynamics of the global marketplace after studying this text.

Focus on Teams

Today's businesses are increasingly moving toward team empowerment and team decision making. We agree with this trend and have integrated the team concept throughout the book. In addition to treating teams in a number of different chapters, the applications and exercises at the end of each chapter include assignments involving teams. We think it is imperative that students learn to work in teams at this early stage in their academic career.

Quality Focus

Contemporary businesses focus heavily on quality. We have also adopted this as a key issue. In fact, quality is so important that we discuss quality in-depth a number of times in addition to highlighting its importance throughout the text. We include quality as one of the indicators of business success (Chapter 1), a key part of strategy (Chapter 11), part of developing quality products (Chapter 12), and then cover it in its own part of Chapter 15.

Ethical Focus

This book contains the most thorough coverage of business ethics available from any introductory text. Chapter 4 includes detailed discussion of moral dilemmas and ethical decision making. Students will recognize why ethical practice makes sense. They will learn how businesses encourage ethical behavior. They will learn how decision makers must deal with tough options to make the proper choices. We visit ethics throughout the text including a discussion of ethics in the global arena and ethics compared with government regulation. We want students to understand that ethical decisions are the responsibility of people in all areas and at all levels of the business.

Entrepreneurship Focus

We focus on entrepreneurship and small business issues throughout the book. Many of our examples deal with smaller businesses where we feel students can gain exposure to this important part of the economy. As part of our integrative approach, we purposely do not have a separate, stand alone chapter on small business. Rather, we include the significance of small business in Chapter 2, The Scope of Business Today, and in Chapter 3, Decision Makers and Decision Making. We also highlight small businesses regularly in other chapters. In addition, we have included an Appendix on how to do a business plan which is especially useful for those students thinking about starting their own business.

Appendix on Business Plans

Recognizing that instructors use a variety of approaches and areas of focus in the introductory course, we have included the development of a business plan in an appendix for those who want to emphasize this important tool. The appendix discusses the use of the plan and outlines the process necessary to develop the plan. A sample business plan is then presented to show what a business plan really looks like.

Appendix on Careers

Since it is never too early for students to begin thinking about their careers, this appendix will be valuable as a tool for helping students in their career thinking. We emphasize the dynamics of the career search process, drawing attention to campus career centers, and the use of the internet. We also discuss career possibilities to help students see some of the exciting career options that can be expected for those who study business.

Conversational Writing Style

We have written this book to be direct and engaging for students. We have kept the writing conversational in tone. Student feedback has encouraged and offered strong support for this approach. Students have commented that the book is highly readable. We have been careful to write a book that is theoretically sound, yet able to hold the attention of students.

Pedagogical Features

We have included a number of pedagogical features that you will appreciate. These will facilitate learning and retention of material. Some of these, including the appendix on business plans, were suggested by reviewers. Special features include:

Learning Objectives

It is important to begin each chapter with an understanding of the goals of the chapter. Thus, we introduce the chapter with a brief vignette and then introduce five or more learning objectives. These objectives guide the presentation of the material. A learning objective is provided for each major heading of the chapter.

Integrative Summaries

The chapter summaries are linked to the learning objectives introduced at the beginning of each chapter. Students are provided responses that highlight the key themes and serve as a check for their learning.

Opening Vignettes

Each chapter begins with an opening example which serves to introduce some of the key dimensions of the chapter. We have chosen business examples that are interesting, thought-provoking, and contemporary. Many feature small businesses or entrepreneurial ventures.

Cross-Referencing System

Key concepts are identified and cross-referenced throughout the book. This enhances the integrative themes of the book. For example, students learn that outsourcing affects strategy decisions, resource decisions, operational and production decisions, and is a key factor in efficiency and cost control. They see that teams affect decision making, impact the design of organizations, and have motivational influences on the people of the organization. The cross-referencing system helps students see where the major discussion of a key concept occurs. Whenever students encounter a key concept, they will be alerted to where they can turn to see a fuller discussion. This system helps students as they study the topics and use the book to its fullest potential.

Key Terms

Important terms in each chapter are bolded in the text. Definitions of key terms are included in the margins to highlight them. They are repeated at the end of the chapter to enable students to easily identify and study terms. Finally, each key term is included in the glossary at the end of the book.

Developing Your Critical Thinking Skills

At the end of each major topic within a chapter, students are asked a series of critical thinking questions. Although these questions are related to the material covered in the text topic, the questions are designed to be expansive and thought-provoking. These encourage thinking beyond the printed material, helping students understand how the material fits together, and how it can be applied to business situations. These questions are also good discussion generators in the classroom.

Real World Examples

Students will appreciate the vast array of real world examples in this book. We have selected examples to show the range and complexity of business. Small, mid-sized, and large businesses are all represented, as are nonprofit organizations. We have chosen companies students will enjoy reading about and those they will recognize. These examples not only enhance the readablity of the text, but are wonderful ways of demonstrating important points so students can relate to and remember the themes being stressed.

Focus Examples

Faculty reviewers and students alike have indicated an interest in a continuous case or example to illustrate concepts throughout the text. At the same time, focusing on a single company becomes tedious and boring. We have captured the benefit of a continuous case without the boredom by using four focus examples. We selected three easily recognizable companies—Motorola, Southwest Airlines, and Brinker International (the parent company of Chili's, Romano's Macaroni Grill, and others)—and the entire mountain bicycle industry. These examples highlight the application of material, provide continuity, and pique the interest of the students.

Exercises and Applications

Each chapter concludes with a series of exercises and applications that relate to the material presented in the chapter. Some of the exercises and applications are to be done in teams. Some require individual research or reflection. Some suggest a brief writing assignment. Each chapter contains an internet exercise. The exercises and applications were carefully designed to encourage further exploration of the chapter themes, to draw on student experiences, to move the student beyond the textbook and encourage interaction with the business community, and to generate some fun.

End of Chapter Case Vignettes

Each chapter concludes with a brief case that speaks to some area that is discussed in the chapter. These cases, drawn from a variety of businesses, allow students to think further about the issues of the chapter. Each case includes a set of questions asking students what they think, how they would respond, or how the business should act. Through this mechanism, we hope to build decision-making perspective and skill within our student readers.

Meet the Authors

Fred L. Fry is a Professor of Management in the Foster College of Business Administration at Bradley University. His Ph.D. is from Oklahoma State University. He has taught a variety of business classes including Contemporary Business, Introduction to Business, Entrepreneurship, Small Business Management, Management of the Nonprofit Organization, and Strategic Management.

Dr. Fry's research has centered around entrepreneurship and small business management. He has published over forty articles and papers in journals such as *Business Horizons*, *Journal of Small Business Strategy*, *Journal of Small Business Management*, *Business Forum*, *Personnel*, and *Journal of Behavioral Economics*, and at national and regional professional conferences. He has written three books, *Entrepreneurship: A Planning Approach* (1993), *Strategic Planning in New and Small Businesses* (1995), and *Strategic Planning in the Small Business* (1987). The last two of these were co-authored with Charles Stoner.

Charles R. Stoner is the Robert A. McCord Professor of Executive Management Development at Bradley University. He is also chair of the Management Department in the Foster College of Business Administration at Bradley University. His D.B.A. is from Florida State University. He has published over forty articles and papers in journals such as the *Journal of Occupational Psychology*, *Journal of Business and Psychology*, *Journal of Applied Business Research*, *Business Horizons*, *Journal of Small Business Management*, *Journal of Services Marketing*, *The Journal of Marketing Management*, and the *International Journal of Management*. His research has focused on diversity management, women in management, team and interpersonal dynamics, telecommuting, and small business management. He co-authored *Strategic Planning for the New and Small Business* (1995) and *Strategic Planning in the Small Business* (1987) with Dr. Fry. His course teaching includes Contemporary Business, Organizational Behavior, Leadership and Interpersonal Dynamics, Management Theory, and Strategic Management. Dr. Stoner has won numerous teaching awards and has done extensive consulting in the areas of team dynamics, organization culture, conflict resolution, leadership, and family business. Much of his consulting has been with CEOs of large and mid-sized companies.

Richard E. Hattwick is a Professor of Economics in the College of Business and Technology at Western Illinois University. He teaches a variety of courses for majors in both business and economics. Dr. Hattwick holds a Ph.D. in Economics from Vanderbilt University. He has taught economics to business and economics students at the University of Houston, University of Colorado, State University of Guanabara (Brazil), and Vanderbilt University in addition to teaching at Western Illinois University. For 23 years he served as director of the Center for Business and Economic Research at Western Illinois University.

Dr. Hattwick is the founder and current editor of the *Journal of Socio-Economics*. He is also the founder and president of the Illinois Business Hall of Fame and serves as the current president of the American National Business Hall of Fame. Dr. Hattwick is the author of numerous business leadership articles and is a frequent guest lecturer on business ethics and business history at various universities.

Acknowledgments

In a project as comprehensive as a first edition integrative text, it is nearly impossible to recognize all those who have contributed. Yet, we want to offer our thanks to some of the special people who have helped make this book through their encouragement, talented insights, and support.

First, we thank our editors. John Biernat, our senior sponsoring editor at Irwin/McGraw-Hill, had the insight and courage to back a new, innovative approach to the Introduction to Business course. John demonstrates the creative thinking and the teamwork we have espoused throughout this text. Others at Irwin/McGraw-Hill have played valuable roles. Maryellen Krammer, Development editor, and Rose Hepburn, Supplements coordinator, gave us excellent input and support on the text supplements. Jim Labeots was our production editor and shepherded the project through critical editing and production phases. We really appreciate their efforts.

We especially thank all of the faculty who reviewed this manuscript. Their names and school affiliations are noted below. We were impressed with the careful and thoughtful reading these reviewers did. Some reviewers were extremely thorough, and their comments were thought provoking. Their ideas and suggestions are reflected throughout the book. Our product is far better, thanks to them.

We owe a special thanks to the students and professors at Bradley University. In particular, Professors Mitch Griffin and Patty Hatfield graciously used an early draft in their Contemporary Business classes. Associate Dean Doan Modianos not only used the manuscript in his own class, but also team taught the class with the Bradley authors. Doan has provided a number of helpful ideas, important and honest criticism, and has been fully supportive of our entire project. He also modeled, through his teaching, how exciting the material can be. We have also asked questions and sought advice from a number of colleagues. We offer special thanks to Professors Richard Hartman, Larry Weinzimmer, Ross Fink, Matt McGowan, Larry Cornwell, Sandra Perry, Rob Baer, Ed Sattler, Ray Wojcikewych, Amy Morgan, and Phil Horvath. The unusually large number of Bradley faculty represent virtually every department in the Foster College of Business Administration and are indicative of the effort to create an integrative text. Dean James Lumpkin has provided encouragement and understanding. At Western Illinois University, Mary Sherwood and Esther Grimes provided valuable assistance.

The Bradley students who participated in the inaugural year of Contemporary Business provided considerable feedback and encouragement. Bradley students Christina Bogoyavlenskaya, Heidi Maurer, Catherine Danz, Brian Baker, and Peigen Tao provided special help. Finally, Sharon Rochester, our department secretary, provided help and assistance in countless ways. She helped check websites, did great work in preparing tables, formatting, copying, and other special manuscript preparation tasks, and she tolerated our idiosyncrasies during particularly stressful times on the project. To say thanks for secretarial support would fail to capture the range and extent of what she did.

Finally, we are grateful for the moral support provided by our wives, Lois, Julie, and Nazareth. You each tolerated our schedules, our long phone conversations, and provided highly valuable input and feedback throughout our project. We appreciate you more than you know.

Stephanie Bibb
Chicago State University

John McCreary
Western Carolina University

Julie Giles
DeVry–DuPage

Teresa Palmer
Illinois State University

Sherry Hockemeyer
IUPU–Ft. Wayne

Kenneth Sousa
Bryant College

Phil Kemp
DePaul University

Carl Stem
Texas Tech University

Carolyn Mueller
Ball State University

Charles Stubbart
Southern Illinois University

Cathy Parkison
Indiana University–Kokomo

David Ketcham
Bryant College

Frank Pianki
Taylor University

Elaine LeMay
Colorado State University

David Vollrath
Indiana University–South Bend

Reg Foucar-Szocki
James Madison University

Donna Blancero
Arizona State University

Linda Anglin
Mankato State University

Shawn Carraher
Indiana State University

Robert Senn
Shippensburg University

Luther Denton
Georgia Southern University

Thomas Morrisey
SUNY at Buffalo

Nancy Dittman
Bloomsburg University

Gunther Boroscheck
University of Massachusetts–Boston

Jeff Klivans
University of Maine

Mary Meredith
University of Southwestern Louisiana

Bob Markus
Babson College

Cindy Lengnick-Hall
Wichita State University

Bradley University Focus Group

Todd Gilsdorf

Kurt Meyerhoff

Kevin Graham

Rahul Sandhu

Becky Hubick

Justin Waldsmith

Read Me First

Business is dynamic and exciting! It is competitive and challenging. It can be rewarding, both from a financial and psychological perspective. It sometimes requires risky, tough decisions, where careful analysis and logic are keys. Quite important, though, business can be fun.

The Excitement of Business

So what makes business exciting and challenging? Consider the following information, taken from a recent *Inc.* magazine, a magazine targeting those who own or would like to own a business.[1] The second annual *Inc.*/Gallup poll of American workers uncovered the following information.

- There are approximately 134 million people employed in the United States.
- They work in over six million businesses, the vast majority of which are small.
- Seventy-two percent of those surveyed said they were extremely satisfied or satisfied with their current job. The numbers were even higher for those who own or work for small companies.
- Eighty-four percent said their work included opportunities for learning and development.
- The median salary is over $25,000 and increases approximately four percent per year.
- Job growth in the past five years is especially rapid in most service industries.
- Job growth is significant in small companies (under twenty employees).
- Over 1.3 million new businesses are started each year.
- Businesses are increasingly using the internet and World Wide Web to interact with customers and to make internal operations more efficient.

Still not convinced that business is exciting? Consider some of the award winners of the 1997 Industrial Design Excellence Awards. How about a bright yellow TV set marketed toward kids? Perhaps you would like a Kodak Fun Saver Sports Camera designed for bikers, hikers, boaters, or beach volleyball players. It is bright blue with a rubberized case to survive rough use, and it is a one-time-use camera (better known as disposable). Then, there is John Deere's Gator, an off-road vehicle which is used by farmers, contractors, and sports teams. The *Green Bay Packers* use one to haul around equipment and transport injured players to the locker room. The U.S. Army finds it to be more versatile than their own Humvee and at one-eighth the cost. How about the space-conserving new charcoal gray Aptiva computer from IBM which is designed to capture the home computer market? It has only a slim console on the desktop that holds the CD-ROM, diskette holder, and power switch. The rest of the box is underneath the desk. And when not in use, the keyboard sits on top of the console, underneath the monitor which is perched high enough to clear the console and keyboard. Need a birthday present for someone who works in an office? How about a stapler that stands up instead of laying down on the job. Your tool-oriented buddies are sure to like Shrade's Tough Tool™ which boasts twenty-one tools in one.[2]

Not all products are as exciting as the IDEA award winners. But product design is but one of many interesting and challenging areas of business. You may be more interested in marketing products, arranging financing for the expansion of manufacturing facilities, or working in human resources to hire and train employees. Maybe a challenge for you is to become known as the owner of the best restaurant in town or to create the most innovative advertising on television. (Who created all those milk mustache and "Got milk?" advertisements?) Yes, it's no overstatement to say that business can be exciting. Now consider some of the trends in business.

Trends in Business and the Economy

The business environment is evolving today with changes coming at record speed. (Does it seem possible that the best use for an eight-year-old computer is as a book shelf?) Changes are making businesses more productive, more customer focused, more globally oriented, and more sensitive to innovations in production and information technology. Look at some recent trends.[3] Although some of the terms presented below may be new to you, they will be discussed in depth in the chapters that follow. You will also find their definitions in the glossary at the end of the text.

- As of 1997, the U.S. economy has had six years of expansion in a row. Most analysts predict that this will continue.
- Many companies downsized in the 1980s and early 1990s and now outsource much of their production and administrative procedures—making them much more efficient.
- Information technology has always been important to businesses, but the advent of the internet and other related information technology developments has had a major impact on how businesses operate and compete.
- Gains from downsizing, outsourcing, and information technology have considerably increased productivity compared with earlier years.
- Jobs are plentiful for well-trained individuals. Unemployment is now around five percent, the lowest it has been in years.
- Those groups with historically high unemployment rates have experienced significant growth in employment in recent years—10.1 percent increase in employment among Hispanics, almost six percent among black teenagers, and almost five percent among women heads of households.

Opportunities in Business

The changes impacting business today create both challenges and opportunities for businesses. Among the opportunities that we see for the near future are:

- Opportunities for small companies to supply goods and services to large companies that are moving toward outsourcing. Some companies are moving toward virtual corporations, requiring only a skeleton staff and outsourcing everything.
- Anything dealing with quality. Quality is the name of the game now and will continue to be in the future.
- Opportunities dealing with customer service. This is related to quality and is a must for the future. Increasingly, customers expect and demand excellence in customer service.

- International opportunities. Our world is shrinking as communications and transportation allow and encourage global commerce.
- Technology-related opportunities. Technology is the key to efficient operations in most businesses and is a criteria for survival in many.
- Ethics in business practices. Society expects ethical decisions from business. Those firms whose management follow and encourage this philosophy will benefit.

We hope you agree from our brief discussion above that business is indeed dynamic. Changes, challenges, risks, and opportunities abound. Astute people who understand the marketplace of business are poised to capture the returns offered in today's business environment. As you will learn from many of the examples in this book, some of the best and most creative business ideas have come from those who have carefully studied the dynamic nature of business.

The Nature of the Book

So how does this book bring the world of business to you? *Business: An Integrative Framework* provides you, the student, with a broad view of business that allows you to see how businesses operate within our contemporary society. We will introduce a model in the first chapter that will guide much of the discussion throughout the text. We will return to our model numerous times to illustrate how the many activities and functions of business interact.

Throughout this text, we focus on the interrelated nature of business. What does this mean? We are careful to discuss topics and issues any time they are relevant. This may mean that the same themes are discussed at various places throughout the text. This overlap and redundancy is by design. Students of business must recognize the ways in which topics and issues link with and do overlap with each other. For example, teams are discussed when we talk about decision making. They are also discussed when we talk about building quality. They are again discussed when we discuss building an environment of employee commitment. You should come away with the notion that teams really affect businesses in a lot of ways. This is exactly what we want. We believe this helps reinforce the building and integrative focus that is so critical to successful business activity.

Websites

Throughout this book, you will get brief looks into a vast array of companies as we use them to illustrate important concepts. We encourage you to delve further into many of the companies we highlight. By doing so, you will learn more about their products and their financial situations and perhaps even uncover information that will suggest whether they might be a company you would someday like to join. In order to assist you, we have provided the world wide website address for virtually every company we mention plus a number of other large or interesting companies and organizations. These website addresses are provided on the inside covers of this book.

We have visited all of the websites listed. Each provides good information about the companies and their products or services. Almost all provide the latest annual reports. But in addition to being informative, some of the websites are downright entertaining.

Incidentally, Irwin/McGraw-Hill, also maintains a website specifically for this book. We will add information to the site from time to time to help you stay current. In particular, we will add new website links for companies that are in the news or that we think you might like to visit. Check it out at http://www.mhhe.com.

Learning Objectives

We begin each chapter of this book with a set of learning objectives. These are the key concepts which we feel you should master upon reading the chapter. Note that these objectives are action oriented. In other words, we feel that you should be able to do something with the information rather than just absorb it. Focusing on these objectives as you read the chapter material will help you remember it and also see how it relates to your experiences.

Developing Your Critical Thinking Skills

We think it is important that you be able to apply the information you read in your text book. To assist you with that, we include questions or assignments for you to consider near the end of each major section of the chapters. We encourage you to pause for a moment and ponder the questions. Can you really do what the question asks of you? Does the information make sense for your particular situation? Does the information integrate well with the material found elsewhere in the chapter or the book? Giving thought to these assignments or questions will help you develop your analytical abilities. In addition, thinking beyond the pages of a book is one way to develop the analytical skills that are necessary for success in business.

Entrepreneurship and Business Plans

One of the trends in America is that more and more people are working for small- and mid-sized companies. In addition, over a million new businesses are started each year. Because of this growing tendency toward small business and entrepreneurship, we include an appendix that discusses how to develop a business plan of your own. We discuss the analysis necessary to do the plan and a format to use in developing a plan. We even show you a completed plan that is based on an actual business plan that a group of students prepared for a venture as part of a class project.

Exploring Career Opportunities

Research tells us that about half of you have made up your minds to major in some business field. That is good. But our experience also tells us that many of you are taking this class as perhaps the only business class you will ever take. Some of you are currently undecided about your intended major and are shopping around. We think this book will be of interest to each one of you. In order to assist you in reaching decisions about majors and careers, we include an appendix on careers at the end of the book. Your instructor may also have a number of videos, available from Irwin/McGraw-Hill, that are oriented toward careers and how to get a job. We also include, near the end of each chapter, a few words about how the chapter points toward other business courses you may choose to take regardless of your major.

Cross Referencing System

In order to assist you in integrating the material in *Business: An Integrative Framework*, we provide a cross-referencing system throughout the text. As you will note, many topics are discussed in more than one chapter. Each time we mention a topic which is discussed in more depth elsewhere in the book, we will provide a symbol indicating where the major discussion can be found. This will help you look forward or backward in the text to either learn more about a topic or to review and study its basic discussion.

Focus Examples

One of the features of *Business: An Integrative Framework* is that it is, well, integrative. That means that we show how the pieces of business work together. We show how business as a whole is impacted by external forces and how teams work together to produce and deliver quality products and services to customers. We will provide numerous examples throughout each chapter of businesses and other organizations in order to illustrate to you just how businesses work within a contemporary environment.

As part of these examples, we will focus on three specific businesses and one entire industry. We will include short examples of these periodically throughout the book. This will give you a feel for how firms deal with many different issues they face. We have chosen to highlight three companies which are well known and well respected in the business world. One manufactures products you will instantly recognize, one is a service business, and one is the parent company of a number of restaurant chains. In addition, we have chosen one entire industry in order to give examples of small- and medium-sized businesses and how they interact and compete.

The manufacturer is Motorola, which produces pagers, cellular phones, satellite communications, and computer components. It is an internationally-known firm which competes in a number of different markets within the electronics industry. It is a high-tech firm and experiences all the challenges and frustrations of that kind of industry. (Its stock prices in 1997 ranged from $45 a share to over $90.) The service firm is Southwest Airlines, an airline which is best known for its discount fares but is also known as a fun place to work. It is a fast-paced business and is in the news often with its emphasis on quality, efficiency, and employee-oriented policies. Finally, we have chosen the parent company of a number of restaurant chains, Brinker International, whose restaurants include Chili's, Romano's Macaroni Grill, On the Border, Cozymel's, and others. The industry example we use is the bicycle industry. Here, you will see companies such as Trek, Cannondale, and Specialized as well as some unique niche companies and some retailers of bicycles. We even create our own bicycle company in one place just to show you how an organization's structure develops.

We set the stage for our four focus examples in this prologue by briefly discussing each. We will include company logos and a bicycle logo in these introductory vignettes. You will see the logos throughout the book each time one of the focus examples is used. This will be your cue to think about how the particular example used fits the material that is being discussed. We are careful not to overdo this, so you won't get bored reading about our examples. But we think you will agree that these continuous examples will make the material come alive for you.

Motorola, Inc.

Paul Galvin began a small company called Galvin Manufacturing Corporation in 1928. Its first product was a "battery eliminator," allowing consumers to operate radios directly from household current instead of the batteries supplied with early models. Galvin had a lot of experience in running a business and the perils associated with owning one's own business. Three previous businesses had gone bankrupt. Just as his company seemed on the verge of failing again, he invented a new product—a radio for cars. He created the name Motorola, which was a combination of the concepts of sound and motion.

On a trip to Europe in the 1930s, Galvin became convinced that a war of major proportions was about to develop. From this, Galvin saw a need for mobile communications. His company then developed what is commonly called the Walkie-Talkie which became one of the military's greatest strengths during the war—the ability to communicate over radios while on the move. By the time of Galvin's death in 1959, Motorola was a leader in military, space, and commercial communications, had built its first semiconductor facility, and was a growing force in consumer electronics.

Bob Galvin, Paul's son, took Motorola into international markets during the 1960s and began to shift the focus away from consumer electronics. The television business which had been launched after World War II was sold in the mid-1970s as Motorola moved more and more into electronics and communication. By 1990, Motorola had become the premier worldwide supplier of cellular telephones.

Motorola has consistently been at the forefront of technological development. Its move into wireless communications continues. In 1995, Motorola was granted 1,016 patents, up from 613 in 1991. Expenditures in research and development alone in 1996 totaled almost $2.4 billion, an increase of almost twenty percent over 1994. It is now heavily involved in satellite communications. One of its most recent enterprises is as one of several consortium members of IRIDIUM, a company which will develop worldwide wireless communications. Based upon sixty-six satellites circling the earth in Low Earth Orbits (LEOs), IRIDIUM will allow voice, data, fax, or paging communications from one cellular phone to another in any spot on earth, possibly without going through a single telephone line.

Motorola's commitment to quality and to its employees has been legendary. Its culture is clearly one of quality as a norm. It is well known for producing products that virtually never fail. This commitment to quality allowed Motorola to win the first Malcolm Baldrige Quality Award in 1988. The Baldrige Award is the most coveted award for quality given in the United States. Motorola is consistently listed as one of the best companies to work for in the United States.

Motorola now has 142,000 employees and maintains sales, service, and manufacturing facilities throughout the world. Only slightly more than a third of its sales were in the U. S. in 1995. Its current product lines include wireless communications, semiconductors and advanced electronic systems, components and services, cellular telephone, two-way radio, paging and data communications, personal communications, automotive, defense and space electronics, and computer components. In 1997, Chris Galvin, grandson of Paul Galvin and son of Robert, became Chairman and CEO of Motorola.

Southwest Airlines

Southwest Airlines is known for many things. It is known for its on-time performance. It is known for the quickness of its turnaround time at a gate. It is known for its discount fares and limited frills, no-meals service. It is known for its first-come, first-served seating. Because of all of this, Southwest Airlines has had twenty-four consecutive years of profit when many of its competitors and the airline industry as a whole have lost billions of dollars. It has won the Triple Crown Customer Service award for five consecutive years. It is now the eighth largest airline, flying to fifty-one cities in twenty-five states. It is known for many things, but among its 25,000 employees, it is best known as a fun place to work. It has been recognized as one of the Nation's top ten places to work, in the book *The Best Companies to Work For in America.*[4]

Herb Kelleher and a partner started Southwest Airlines as an intrastate airline in the state of Texas. They were forced to overcome numerous challenges from other airlines who resisted an intruder into their markets. Much of the initial funding they arranged was spent in arguing legal cases before a variety of court venues in order to gain the right to fly, first within Texas and later from Texas to other points. Even today, they are restricted in the routes they can fly because of legislation that was passed specifically to limit their strategies.

In spite of their early travails, Herb Kelleher set the tone that an airline need not be a stodgy place to work. His sense of humor helps make up for the long hours that his employees work. You don't even need to get on a Southwest plane to get a feel for the culture. Simply call their reservation number and listen to the messages if you are put on hold. See if the following Kelleher comment gives you a clue to their corporate culture. "We started back in 1971 with three planes serving three Texas cities. In the short-haul markets, most people will drive those distances instead of fly. A lot of people figured us for road kill at the time. But today we've got over 240 airplanes in 50 cities. We like mavericks—people who have a sense of humor. We've always done it differently. You know, we don't assign seats. Used to be we only had about four people on the whole plane, so the idea of assigned seats just made people laugh. Now the reason is you can turn the airplanes quicker at the gate. And if you can turn an airplane quicker, you can have it fly more routes each day. That generates more revenue, so you can offer lower fares."

Even as Southwest has grown into a nationwide airline, employees still feel a family culture and are quick to say that they are convinced that there is no better airline to work for than Southwest. Flight attendants and reservationists often state that they know people who work for other airlines who do not have the advantage of Southwest's culture.

Why is Southwest Airlines continuously profitable? They make money in a number of ways. They fly a single model of airplane, the Boeing 737, which eases maintenance. Their employees willingly work long hours, often twelve hours a day (except for pilots who are limited in the number of hours they can fly by government regulations). They are the model of efficiency in loading passengers onto an airplane and also in reducing paperwork. This limits their time at the gate and on the ground. It adds to the efficiency that Southwest enjoys.

Because of the dedication of its employees and its unwavering focus on efficiency, Southwest Airlines has the lowest cost per seat-mile of any airline (based on an average domestic trip length) and is the only airline to remain profitable throughout its existence.[5]

Brinker International

You may not know the name Brinker International, but you probably recognize one or more of the restaurants that are included in this business—Chili's Grill & Bar, On The Border Cafe, Romano's Macaroni Grill, Maggiano's Little Italy, Cozymel's, Corner Bakery, and Eatzi's. Odds are that you have eaten at one of these restaurants if you live in a large- or medium-sized city.

The restaurant industry is a fast-paced and exciting one. Competition is fierce, and the demands are great. The overall formula for success in this industry is not dramatically different from other industries, but the emphasis may be. Since restaurants provide a service and consumers typically have a number of options from which to choose, customers are always the key. Businesses in this industry have to stay focused on the customers and their ever changing dining preferences and habits. Within this challenging and competitive environment, Brinker International restaurants have not only succeeded, they have experienced meteoric growth over the last fifteen years. In fact, Brinker's systemwide sales have increased from $32 million in 1983 to over $1.8 billion today.

To get a flavor of Brinker restaurants, let's look at the company's chairman and driving force, Norman Brinker. Norman Brinker is a classic entrepreneur and a legend in the restaurant industry. For example, in the 1960s, he noticed an interesting gap in the restaurant industry. There were fast food restaurants and there were fine (expensive) dining establishments, but little in between. Brinker recognized an opportunity. He started Steak and Ale which introduced quality dining at affordable prices. Today, we know this as the casual dining segment of the restaurant business. Within ten years, Brinker grew Steak and Ale from a single Dallas location to a chain of over 100 restaurants. Along the way, he started another new restaurant, Bennigans. Eventually, Steak and Ale and Bennigans were both sold to Pillsbury which also owns Burger King, and Brinker joined the Pillsbury organization.

After a stint as President of The Pillsbury Restaurant Group, Norman Brinker's entrepreneurial spirit sparked him to look for new challenges. He found that challenge in a small chain of 22 restaurants, known as Chili's. Brinker has worked his magic on Chili's and the other restaurants in the Brinker family. Today, there are nearly 600 Chili's and the other chains are also growing. There are over 700 restaurants in all, employing over 75,000 people. Brinker International is a global operation with restaurants in sixteen different countries. New concepts and new restaurant ideas are always being explored. This will be a fun business to follow!

The Bicycle Industry

The bicycle industry is a nearly four billion dollar a year industry. Over twelve million bicycles are sold annually, and more than thirty million adults ride bikes at least once a week. The bicycle industry is really two industries in one. On one side are the bicycles that are manufactured for sale through mass merchandising chains such as Sears, Toys "R" Us, and Wal-Mart. These bicycles typically sell for $79 to $179. They tend to be low-end bicycles which customers buy primarily based on price. About seventy-five percent of all bicycles are sold through this distribution channel. The other part of the bicycle market is the high quality bicycles which are typically sold through one of the 6800 independent bicycle shops. These bikes may cost from $200 to thousands of dollars, with an average of around $300. These bicycles are typically lighter, more durable, fit properly, are assembled properly, and are matched to the individual rider's needs. Although mass-merchandised bicycles account for seventy-five percent of all units sold, approximately half of the dollars spent on bikes is through specialty bicycle shops because of their higher price. Virtually all of the parts and service on bicycles is through the independent shops.

Some manufacturers build a full line of bikes which includes a selection of mountain bikes. Fuji and Schwinn are examples. Other businesses have built their reputations on specializing in bikes that will appeal to serious riders. Some of these businesses are well known, such as Trek, Specialized, Cannondale, and Giant. Other businesses appeal to special groups or segments of riders. For example, Gary Fisher produces a range of bikes, some of which sell for thousands of dollars. Only serious or competitive riders are likely to buy a high-end Fisher. Terry Precision Bicycles for Women are uniquely designed to provide the best fit, comfort, and precision for women riders. Their business seems to be strong, as the demand for a Terry has grown a great deal.

One of the manufacturers which we will note frequently is Trek. Trek Bicycle Corporation started as a five-person operation in 1976. In those days, the company built bikes in a rented barn in the small farming community of Waterloo, Wisconsin. Today, Trek is one of the world's leading full-line manufacturers of high quality bicycles. Over the years, Trek has earned a reputation for its excellent craftsmanship and careful quality focus. It now has approximately 1800 employees—not small, but considerably smaller than Motorola, Brinker International, or Southwest Airlines. Many of our examples will key on Trek.

Another manufacturer in the mountain bike industry is Cannondale. Cannondale recently celebrated its twenty-fifth anniversary, having been started in a loft over a pickle factory. It is located in Bedford, Pennsylvania, and boasts the finest bicycle frame and components testing facility in the industry. Cannondale's founder and president, Joseph Montgomery, is proud that Cannondale maintains its small company atmosphere. Included in their philosophy is caring about customers, innovative products, continuous improvement, concentration on detail, distribution to only the finest dealers in the world, and a commitment to what is just and right. Cannondale's F1000 bike was named 1997 bike of the year by *Mountain Biking* magazine.

REFERENCES

1. Michael Hopkins and Jeffrey L. Seglin. "Americans @ Work." *Inc.*, May 20, 1997, pp. 77–85; and Elyse M. Friedman. "The New-Economy Almanac." *Inc.*, May 20, 1997, pp. 108–121.

2. Various authors. "Annual Design Awards," *Business Week*, June 2, 1997, pp. 92–111.

3. Michael Mandel. "How Long Can This Last?" *Business Week*, May 19, 1997, pp. 30-34; Peter Coy, "The Best Kind of Affirmative Action," *Business Week*, May 19, 1997, p.35.

4. Levering and Milton Moskowitz. *The 100 Best Companies to Work for in America*. New York: Plume, 1994, p. 318.

5. *Southwest Airlines Annual Report, 1996*.

PART One

The Integrative Nature of Business

MODEL OF THE PATH TOWARD A SUCCESSFUL BUSINESS

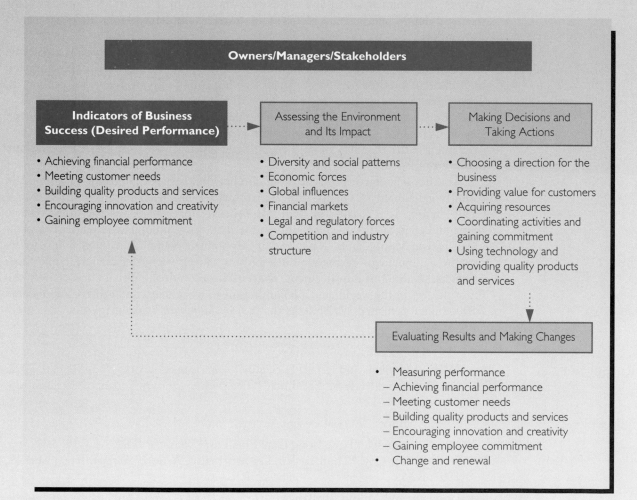

Owners/Managers/Stakeholders

Indicators of Business Success (Desired Performance)

- Achieving financial performance
- Meeting customer needs
- Building quality products and services
- Encouraging innovation and creativity
- Gaining employee commitment

Assessing the Environment and Its Impact

- Diversity and social patterns
- Economic forces
- Global influences
- Financial markets
- Legal and regulatory forces
- Competition and industry structure

Making Decisions and Taking Actions

- Choosing a direction for the business
- Providing value for customers
- Acquiring resources
- Coordinating activities and gaining commitment
- Using technology and providing quality products and services

Evaluating Results and Making Changes

- Measuring performance
  - Achieving financial performance
  - Meeting customer needs
  - Building quality products and services
  - Encouraging innovation and creativity
  - Gaining employee commitment
- Change and renewal

In Part One of this book, you are introduced to the world of business and the integrative nature of business activity. The four chapters in Part One are devoted to helping you better understand the landscape, key players, and important decisions that help shape business in our contemporary world.

Chapter 1 presents and briefly discusses our model of the path toward a successful business. Here, you will recognize the key outcomes a business must achieve if it is to succeed over time. You will be introduced to areas of study that are important for business decision makers as they grapple to make the right choices in an increasingly competitive international environment.

Chapter 2 helps you understand the scope of business. You will learn that businesses come in an array of sizes and forms. You will recognize the attraction of small business ownership. You will understand some of the opportunities that a business achieves only as it grows. You will understand the advantages and risks of various forms of business ownership. This chapter describes some of the complexity of business ownership and thereby provides an important foundation for further study.

Chapter 3 introduces you to the various decision makers who affect businesses. You will learn the role that each plays in helping the business. You will also learn about the logical process of business decision making that successful business people follow. In addition, you will recognize how creative decision making can be encouraged. You will be introduced to the power of team decision making and to the nature of creative decision making.

Chapter 4 introduces you to the idea of stakeholders—those people or groups who have some claim on or expectation about how the business should operate. You will recognize how business tries to properly carry out its responsibilities to these stakeholders. In Chapter 4, you will also study business ethics. You will recognize how businesses help their people determine the right thing to do. You will understand that ethics is a foundation of decisions and actions for healthy and successful businesses.

Many of the topics discussed in Part One will appear throughout the text. As you read the text and study the business examples presented, recognize the excitement and opportunity that a career in business holds. Think and enjoy.

1 The Nature of Business

As a boy growing up in Minnesota, Scott Olson was truly an ice-skating fanatic. During the winter months, he skated everywhere, covering miles on ice-covered roads and sidewalks. He dreamed of skating wherever he went. Unfortunately, when the spring thaws came, he knew that his favorite activity would once again be put on hold until the following winter. One day, while browsing through a Bloomington, Minnesota, sporting-goods store, he saw a strange pair of roller skates hanging on the wall. These skates had wheels set in a line rather than the traditional parallel style. Olson says, "I immediately fell in love with it. I knew right away what it meant. I had a mental vision. It was like my dream."

Scott Olson did not invent in-line skates. But his vision spawned the in-line skating craze. He bought several pairs of the skates, and he and his brothers soon made a critical design change. Working out of their basement and garage, they put in-line wheels and frames on ice-hockey boots. Soon ice-hockey players from the Minneapolis region began using the boots for summer training—and a business was born. The year was 1980. Today Olson's business, Rollerblade, Inc., is the leader in the billion-dollar in-line skating industry.[1]

Scott Olson realized that there was a demand for his visionary product, and he built a major company around that idea. He took some risks as he launched his new venture. He made some tough decisions. His decisions helped his company to grow rapidly and become successful. He soon had competitors in the industry, and decisions became more and more complex.

The path of Olson's company is not unusual. Businesses are complex. They require ideas, an understanding of customer needs, and the ability to satisfy those needs. Businesses operate in a competitive environment that heavily influences decision making at all levels in the organization. Managers must study that environment to make the most appropriate decisions that allow them to compete successfully.

This chapter sets the stage for the rest of the book. It lays out a model of what businesses strive to achieve, the types of information managers must seek and consider, and the decisions they must make. After studying this chapter, you should be able to:

1. Write and apply the definition of business and explain the nature of a successful business.

2. Recognize and explain the indicators of business success.

3. Identify the external forces that affect business success.

4. Explain the decisions and actions necessary to achieve business success.

5. Recognize how measurement and change enable a business to improve performance.

6. Describe a complete model of the decisions and processes that put a business on the path to success.

The study of business is both exciting and challenging. Each of us encounters the products and services of business organizations as we move through the day. Yet an understanding of how these businesses work often seems hard to grasp. In fact, the complexity of business sometimes strains even seasoned managers' powers of comprehension.

For example, how is it possible for companies like General Motors and IBM to build such power and scope that they are recognized and respected throughout the world? Even more amazing, how could these same giants of industry so dramatically misstep that their competitive foundations were threatened? Why did these businesses have to engage in the painful process of reducing their massive workforces by the thousands? How were they able to make the changes needed to turn their companies back toward profitability?

The answers to these questions are not simple. Yet the answers must come from managers and other employees working in a business. They must do what you will be doing throughout this book. They must learn how to analyze the conditions and factors affecting their businesses. They must learn how to put all the pieces together to make decisions. They must understand the business system and be willing to take action.

Business decision making is not magical. Sometimes decisions are highly judgmental. Sometimes history proves some decisions to be less than ideal. Business is not a precise science. Issues are not always clear. Rarely is enough information available. Sometimes managers are bombarded with conflicting information that makes it hard to come to definitive conclusions. Alternative interpretations abound. However, in any organization, from General Motors to the corner hardware store, managers try to understand business events. They work to make decisions that they believe will create a healthy, successful business organization. That task is never easy, but it is always exciting and challenging.

Consider, for example, Blockbuster Entertainment in Profile 1–1. Blockbuster is an excellent example of both the excitement of a highly competitive business and the importance of key decisions made by a firm's leaders.

P R O F I L E   1 – 1   *Blockbuster Entertainment: Entertainment Center or Back to Basics*

●

vision p. 310>

One of the fastest-growing and most profitable businesses in the early 1990s was Blockbuster Entertainment. Blockbuster was founded in 1985 by David Cook, but it really took off in the late 1980s when H. Wayne Huizenga became the chief executive officer. In a seven-year period from 1987 to 1994, Huizenga grew Blockbuster from three stores to over 4,000 retail locations. His accomplishment came from savvy business leadership. First, he understood where technology was headed and what consumers wanted. His vision of a family-oriented store captured the needs of video customers. He built a talented team of managers. In order to maintain the creative focus of the company, Blockbuster recruited employees with an entrepreneurial spirit. This contributed to an open sharing of new ideas, facilitating the fast growth of the business.

Blockbuster made critical marketing decisions, many patterned after the success of McDonald's. Convenient locations, fast service aided by state-of-the-art computer networks, national advertising (a first among video retailers), wide selection of titles (as many as 8,000 titles per location), and value decisions (no X-rated movies) were just some of the day-to-day marketing decisions the managers made. They also made some important longer-run business decisions. For example, Blockbuster used a strategy of acquiring competitors, buying other businesses such as Major Video (a West Coast chain) and Applause Video (a Midwest chain) to foster growth.

Clearly, the decisions Huizenga and his managers made enabled the explosive growth and success Blockbuster enjoyed. They took risks, but each was a calculated business risk based on an understanding of the complex forces affecting the

Blockbuster videos is one of the fastest growing businesses today. Yet, Blockbuster is having an identity crisis in the 1990s. Are they just a video store, or should they also be in movie production, music videos, and chains of music stores?

business. Their decisions for the most part seemed to be on the mark. Sales exceeded $2 billion each year and Blockbuster became one of the most profitable businesses in the United States.

But success does not stop the uncertainties. Nor does past success minimize the need for careful, responsive decision making on an ongoing basis. Moving into the 1990s, Blockbuster faced new challenges. The videocassette rental business was reaching its peak. While video rentals had provided about 90 percent of profits in the early 1990s, Blockbuster realized that picture was changing. It projected that rentals would soon provide only about 60 to 70 percent of operating profit. The biggest reason for this decline would probably be the growth in pay-per-view TV.

Blockbuster needed to understand the changing entertainment environment, and it needed to act. New markets had to be explored and new ventures tested. Blockbuster began to move into the music retail business. It also began to move into film production and distribution by buying interests in Republic Pictures and Spelling Entertainment. It explored a number of other options too. Producing music CDs and video CDs and adding a chain of music stores could all be good moves. Further, Blockbuster reasoned that if cable TV was its biggest threat, maybe it should start its own cable channel. Many of these strategic options fell into place in 1994 when Blockbuster was acquired by the entertainment giant Viacom, Inc.[2] Blockbuster engaged in vigorous advertising to convince customers that it was not just a place to rent videos. It was "their neighborhood entertainment center."[3]

By mid-1997, the new strategy appeared questionable as competition grew and Blockbuster's profits slipped. Change was needed once again. The company has now gone back to basics, refocusing on video rentals. As Viacom executive Tom Dooley says, "We want people to think of Blockbuster as the place to go to rent tapes."[4]

This is the dynamic nature of business. Blockbuster managers, like all successful managers, must assess and understand the changing environment, evaluate their options, and act in a way that makes the most sense given all their readings and judgments. In short, these managers must be students of business, just like you.

Definition of Business

Business
Any organization that strives for profits by providing goods and services that meet customer needs.

A **business** is any organization that strives for profits by providing goods and services that meet customer needs. Although this definition is basic, you will soon see how rich and complex it really is. Recognize that business really deals with a fundamental exchange, an exchange of products and services for money. Now understand how fragile this exchange can be. The business must produce and offer products and services that customers need and desire. If it doesn't, customers will not exchange their dollars for these products and services. In the same light, the business must receive a fair and reasonable amount of money for its products and services. If it doesn't, it will see little value to be gained through the exchange. So a business is really an *integrated* process of exchanging value between a business organization and its customers.

Successful business
Any business that excels over a long period of time.

We define a **successful business** or healthy business as one that *excels over time*. A business that happens to make a lot of money in a short time period but then falls far short of its objectives later is not successful. Neither is a business that makes great financial returns but only at the expense of low morale, uncommitted workers, shoddy products, or unethical behavior. In order to be truly successful, a business must excel, and it must excel over the long run.

Many organizations exist that do not have the goal of making a profit. Known as not-for-profit or *nonprofit organizations,* they share many of the characteristics of businesses. For example, the American Red Cross, YWCA, Boy Scouts, and your college or university are all nonprofit organizations. We will discuss these organizations in more depth in Chapter 2.

Developing Your Critical Thinking Skills

1. Consider a small business in your home town. Now consider any one of our focus companies: Motorola, Southwest Airlines, or Brinker International. Look at our definition of business. Does the definition apply as well to the small company as it does to the focus company?

2. Why is it important for a business to concentrate on excelling over time, as opposed to in the short run?

The Path to a Successful Business

How does a business get started, and how does it become successful? What is the path toward business success? To an extent, each business takes its own unique path. Yet there are some themes that all successful businesses have in common. These themes and the way they fit together are the focus of this book. Consider this example from one of our focus companies. In the early 1970s, the airline industry was highly regulated, which meant that the government had to approve both airline routes and fares. The U.S. airline industry was dominated by large companies such as American Airlines, TWA, Delta, and United Airlines. There was not much competition, and existing airlines had little incentive to lower fares or offer different routes.

Typical airline customers were either business travelers or people wealthy enough to afford luxury travel. An entire group of potential customers was not being served. How could an airline convince the typical traveler to fly rather than drive or take a bus for short trips, say from Dallas to Austin, Texas?

Against this backdrop, Southwest Airlines was started. The owners understood customers and how they think. Southwest reasoned that if fares were low enough, routes were convenient, quality of service was high, and on-time arrival was consistent, large numbers of customers would choose flying over other travel options. This is exactly what Southwest did. Its approach was innovative. It also offered employees a fun place to work and made them feel part of the team.

Today, 25 years later, Southwest Airlines is one of the country's most successful businesses. How did this happen? The company understood its customers. It recognized the changing nature of its environment. It controlled costs. It assured customers of quality service. It innovated. It created a motivating culture. Most importantly, it has been consistently profitable. In short, Southwest successfully integrated its decisions and actions to build a healthy business.

Like Southwest Airlines, managers in every business must make decisions based on careful consideration of what it takes to be successful and the environment the business faces. We present now a process that businesses use to achieve success. Figures 1–1 through 1–5 show pieces of the path to a successful business. The model

FIGURE 1–1   The Participants in Business

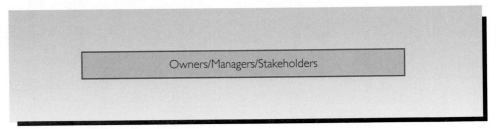

Owners/Managers/Stakeholders

in Figure 1–6 will pull all those pieces together. Follow the model carefully; it forms the basis for the rest of the book.

The Participants in Business

Owners
People who have invested money into the business with hopes of receiving a return for their investment.

Managers
The decision makers of a business.

Stakeholders
People or groups who have some claim on or expectation of how the business should operate.

Before we explore the process, it is important to realize who the participants are in business. Figure 1-1 shows them. **Owners** are those people who have invested money into the business and hope to receive returns for their investment. **Managers** are the decision makers for the business. These managers may or may not be owners. The third group of participants are called **stakeholders**. They are people or groups who have some claim on or expectation of how the business should operate. These three groups influence the decisions made by the business.

Indicators of Success

financial performance p. 481>
innovation p. 522>
creativity p. 522>

Decision makers in business must begin by looking at the desired results, or indicators of success. Figure 1–2 shows five major indicators, the outcomes managers strive to achieve. Decisions are made with these indicators in mind. Each indicator is important; a business cannot be truly successful unless it achieves adequate results in all five areas.

The five indicators of success we have selected are, in our opinion, the most important indicators for businesses in general. But keep in mind that specific types of businesses will emphasize some indicators more than others. Our five indicators are *financial performance, customer needs and values, quality of products and services, innovation and creativity,* and *employee commitment.* We will discuss each of these later in the chapter. We will refer to these indicators throughout the text and will focus on them in more detail in Chapter 16 when we discuss measuring performance.

Assessing the Environment and Its Impact

Once the indicators of success for a particular business have been determined, the next step in the process is to research and study the firm's environment. This step is shown in Figure 1–3. It gives the managers the information they need to make good decisions. The **environment of business** consists of those factors or influences that affect the business but over which the firm has little control. Decision makers must understand the

FIGURE 1–2   Indicators of Success

Environment of business
Factors or influences that affect the business but over which the firm has little control.

nature of the environment in which their business operates. They must be aware of critical forces in the environment and recognize the shifts and patterns that occur.

Managers must not only be aware of environmental forces but be able to assess the potential impact of forces on the business. A business that lacks this environmental sensitivity is severely handicapped. It is unlikely to be able to make good decisions and continue to survive.

FIGURE 1–3   Assessing the Environment and Its Impact

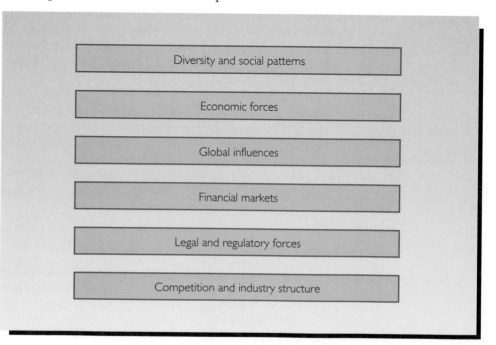

Six key environmental forces influence business decisions. They are so important that a separate chapter is devoted to each environmental force. We will begin by looking at *diversity and social pattern*s. Then we'll move to *economic forces, global business influences, financial markets, legal and regulatory forces*, and *competition and industry structure*. These chapters together form Part II of the book.

diversity p. 125>

Decision Making and Actions

Once decision makers have a sense of the business environment, they can begin the process of making decisions and taking actions. This next stage of the model zeroes in on what the business will do and what approaches it will pursue. These sets of activities and decisions must be performed to get things done and keep the business moving toward the indicators of success. This process is shown in Figure 1–4.

Managers must begin to *establish a sense of direction for the firm*. A strategic direction does not just happen. For the successful business, this direction follows a careful analysis of the environment, with one eye always on the indicators of business success. This process of strategic thinking and planning is developed in Chapter 11.

With the strategic direction in mind, managers are ready to begin the process of *creating value for their customers*. They must be keenly aware of customer needs and develop products and services that meet those needs. This can be an involved and complex process. Developing products requires knowing your customers. A business must continually study its customers (as well as potential new customers) to find out what consumers in the marketplace really want and need.

teams p. 71>

Once the customers are identified, the business must actually develop products or services that meet those needs. Product development is one of the most integrative of all activities in a business. Cross-functional teams from marketing, accounting, engineering, and production often work together to create products that meet customer needs while providing a profit to the company. These actions will be discussed in Chapter 12.

FIGURE 1–4   Decision Making and Actions

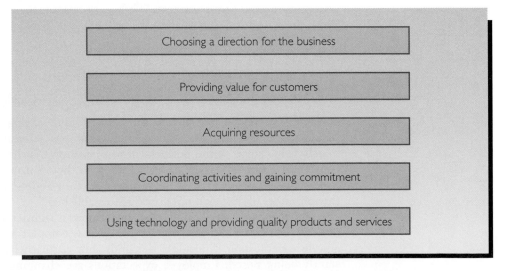

To grow, a business must *acquire the resources* necessary to produce products or provide services. Generally, businesses are concerned with four types of resources: human, physical, financial, and information. These resources become the inputs needed to produce the products and services that customers desire. Economists refer to these input resources as the *factors of production* since they are the critical factors needed to produce things. Human resources are the people needed to get things accomplished. Physical resources refer to the land, buildings, equipment, and raw materials that the business uses in producing the product or service. Financial resources are needed to acquire the other types of resources and ensure that the business can continue to operate. Information is needed to coordinate, plan, and measure the performance of the firm. The complexity of acquisition decisions is discussed in Chapter 13.

Once resources have been secured, they must be properly organized and managed in order to provide high-quality goods and services in a timely manner. This is the basis of *coordinating activities and gaining employee commitment.* Even the best resources can be squandered if they are not properly managed. Decisions must be made about how the business will be organized, that is, how the resources will be put together to get the best results possible. Further decisions involve how the various jobs will be designed and how managers attempt to build commitment within the workforce. These decisions and actions are presented in Chapter 14.

We emphasize throughout this book the importance of *continuous quality improvement* for a competitive business. Many of the actions taken and decisions made by managers focus on quality issues. Approaches to achieving quality are constantly evolving, so today's student of business must grasp recent thinking on quality. These issues will be discussed in Chapter 15.

One key issue of quality management is the *use of technology*, which is changing at breakneck speed. The prevailing technology in an industry may be obsolete within a few years. If a business is going to succeed, it must remain technologically competitive. This means it must not only be aware of technological changes, but be constantly updating. Technology falls into two broad categories, information technology and production technology. Both are necessary for the business to operate effectively and efficiently. Contemporary views of technology will be discussed in Chapter 15.

These five chapters make up Part III of the text. They deal with key decisions and actions of the successful business. While each chapter focuses on special areas of decisions, these decisions are related. You will enjoy learning about the actions that business managers take.

human resources p. 374>

acquisition p. 322>

information technology p. 456> production technology p. 463>

Evaluating Results and Making Changes

A business can be successful over time only if its managers carefully evaluate performance results and make necessary changes to improve these results and meet new demands. This stage of the business process is shown in Figure 1–5. Managers must constantly know how they are performing so they can take corrective action when necessary. This demands that the business monitor and *measure its performance* against the indicators of success it has previously established.

Sometimes a manager finds that the business is right on target with the success indicators. However, the business environment is complex and changing. Competitors are always adjusting. Consumer demands shift regularly. Quality standards are constantly being raised. Employee expectations are changing. As a result, adjustments

FIGURE 1–5   Evaluating Results and Making Changes

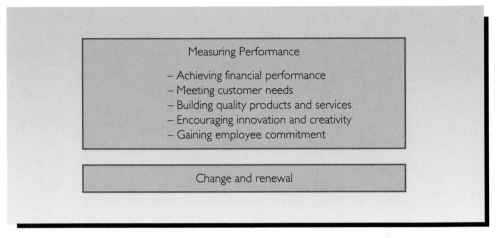

often must be made. Measurement is important because it pinpoints where adjustments are needed. Measurement issues will be discussed in Chapter 16.

If properly done, measurement focuses the business toward needed *change and renewal.* Yet that does not mean that change occurs easily. One of the key challenges facing any business is to convert the need for change into action. The healthy business must be willing and able to renew itself. This is difficult. There is often resistance involved.

training p. 379>
Accordingly, the way the business approaches change is critical. Successful businesses invest in ongoing training and development to facilitate positive change. They encourage creativity and innovation. They understand that change is a process. They approach planned change as a serious set of activities for which management must assume responsibility. Issues of change and renewal are discussed in Chapter 17.

The Complete Model of the Path Toward a Successful Business

Now look at the entire model as it is presented in Figure 1-6. Note the arrows between groups of topics, especially the arrow from the Evaluating Results box back up to the Indicators of Success box. These arrows suggest that the actions in each successive box build on the previous one. For example, it is important to have the success indicators firmly in mind before studying the environment. It is important to know the environment well before developing strategies and actions for the firm. And it is important to have a firm grasp on the actions taken to create value before trying to measure performance.

But reality is more complex than a model, and it is important to understand that these are continuing processes. We are always studying the environment. We measure performance frequently, and we regularly update our approaches and improve our products and services. It is important to see the model of the path toward a successful business as a circular flow. Let's see how the model may be applied.

FIGURE 1–6   Model of the Path Toward a Successful Business

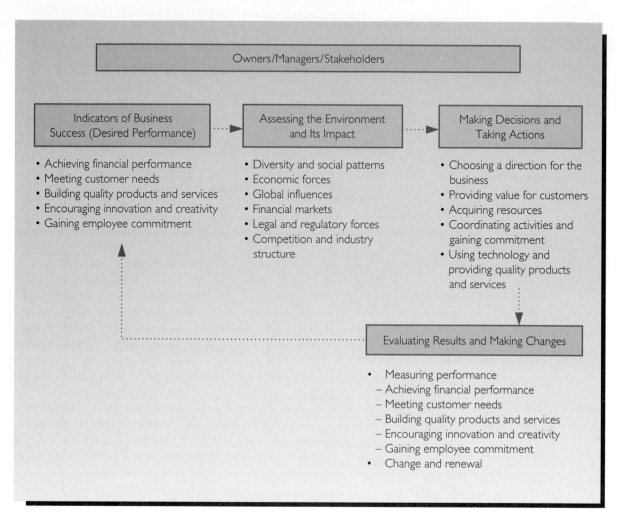

The Model in Action

In the following paragraphs we illustrate the model for this book, using Trek Bicycle Corporation as an example. As noted in the prologue, Trek is a manufacturer of high quality bicycles. Their bicycles sell at retail from below $300 to as high as nearly $5000. Keep in mind as you read, that some of the terms and concepts may be unfamiliar to you at this time. We will define and discuss them throughout the book, however.

Indicators of Success

Trek has many indicators of success, some of which are unique to the bicycle industry and to the firm itself. Yet, Trek certainly addresses the five key indicators emphasized in the model.

Trek, like all businesses, is concerned with *financial performance*. Trek managers study the company's financial indicators and financial reports to understand how successful their financial performance really is. Here, Trek managers study indicators such as total revenue from all sales, revenue from foreign sales, net profit, and return on investment. Further, they look at how these indicators change over time. One indicator, for example, is their percentage of international sales which began in 1987. International sales now account for 32 percent of their total sales. That is an important item of information for Trek managers to know. The company is doing well. It is profitable and it is growing. Yet, a key area of that growth is coming from the international arena.

Meeting customer needs and values is extremely important for a company like Trek. In order to cover the entire market, Trek has many basic styles and models of bicycles which a customer can customize with specifically requested components. The models range from kids' and BMX bikes to off road, multi-track, road, touring, and tandems. In an industry such as bicycles, it is critical for companies to be sensitive to their customers. This is especially true in the more expensive, specialty bikes designed for racing. In order to stay in touch with customers, Trek has developed an extensive website. It hears from thousands of customers through the site and receives up to 700 calls per day on its customer service line. These are wonderful mechanisms for staying in touch with customers.

customer service
p. 340>

Quality is the defining factor of Trek's success. It must constantly pay attention to both its own quality and the quality of competitors. Its bikes often carry premium price tags, so customers expect cutting-edge quality.

Innovation and creativity are keys at Trek. Many competitors are trying to appeal to the same target customers as Trek. The only way to stay on top is always to be looking for ways to build better bikes. What is the best bike? How can frames be made both stronger and lighter? How can the company design special features that bikers want while keeping prices competitive? Trek realizes that it must be at the forefront in answering these questions. Innovation is the route to competitive success.

Employee commitment enables Trek to produce high-quality bikes. This is another key indicator of success for Trek. Although parts may be manufactured abroad, most assembly is done in Wisconsin. When quality is of the essence, highly motivated workers are a must. Substantial empowerment of lower-level workers must occur to keep them motivated and committed.

empowerment p. 422>

Assessing the Environment

Each of the six areas of the environment is important to Trek, although some may be more critical than others. Trek recognizes the need for *diversity* in the workforce. It has an aggressive policy of hiring the best people. It is proud of its track record in hiring a number of disabled workers and of the quality of the work they do.

Economic forces affect Trek in many ways. Certainly the cost of components and the pricing of bikes are important; so are economies of scale and efficiencies of production. But Trek must study and understand the impact of what is happening in the general economy too. For example, if unemployment rates rise or inflation skyrockets, Trek needs to know how these factors will likely affect the sale of bikes.

Trek is involved in *global markets* on both the supply and the demand side. Some of its components are made abroad, and its bikes are exported through marketing subsidiaries and independent dealers in other countries. Trek must be aware of the impact of currency values, import and export rules, and international cultures.

financial markets
p. 215>

Financial markets have an impact on Trek. Interest rates may affect Trek's external financing. High interest rates may reduce sales of higher-priced bikes.

Legal and regulatory issues also affect Trek. In addition to issues faced by all firms such as taxes, employment regulations, and environmental laws—Trek is particularly aware of product liability issues due to the nature of its product.

Trek operates in the very competitive *bicycle industry*. Most producers today are extremely competitive, and Trek itself has purchased companies that were formerly suppliers or competitors. The dynamics of the industry and its products certainly keep Trek on its toes.

Making Decisions and Taking Actions

strategic decisions p. 77>

Trek managers, like those of any other firm, spend countless hours making both strategic and routine decisions. Much of their time is involved with *choosing a direction* and making strategic decisions regarding how best to compete. They have developed core competencies built around their high-quality bikes, with particular emphasis on the frames. There are many strategic decisions that have a big impact on the business. For example, Trek has to determine which components to outsource and which to build itself. Outsourcing occurs when Trek buys bike components from, say, Shimano rather than manufacture them internally. It might do this if Shimano provides good quality at a competitive cost.

Trek's focus on *providing value to customers* is legendary. As mentioned earlier, Trek maintains close contact with customers in a number of ways. One of these, of course, is through its own racing teams. There is no better way to assess and meet customer needs than to be your own customer. Trek not only knows its customers, it responds and builds bikes the customers want. Some customer expectations even extend beyond the traditional bike lines. For example, Trek has introduced a line of clothing and accessories designed by cyclists.

Resource acquisition is important. Human, physical, financial, and information resources must all be assimilated to produce bikes as efficiently as possible. As a privately held corporation, Trek relies on sales revenues and privately acquired financing to underwrite its operations.

efficiency p. 478>

Trek's 1,800 *employees* are located in three plants in Wisconsin. Because of this, Trek must coordinate its operations to ensure efficiency and quality performance. Trek works with its employees to develop a culture of *dedication to the company* and dedication to biking. Since many of the employees are also bikers, this is not difficult.

Trek has won numerous awards for its use of *technology* in the building of bikes. Its Y bike has won several coveted awards for product design, both domestically and internationally. It is also recognized as a top company for *quality*.

Evaluating Results and Making Changes

Because Trek is a privately held corporation, it does not share its measurements of *financial performance*. We do know, however, that sales reached over $400 million in 1995. That's not bad for a company started in a rented barn in 1976. In addition, the number of awards and recognition Trek has received suggests that its overall performance is exemplary.

Yet Trek does not rest on its laurels. It is willing to *change* to adopt new technology, develop new products, and find new ways to meet customer needs.

This example provides only a brief sketch of the parts of our model. However, you can already see how the themes of the model interrelate and how they affect decisions, actions, and the quest for success.

The model in Figure 1–6 is the basis for this entire book. The brief introduction of its parts is intended to show you how all the parts fit together to affect the success of a business. Throughout the book, each part of the model will be considered in more detail. We will often refer back to this model as we discuss different topics. Chapters 2 and 3 look more closely at the participants in businesses. The remainder of this chapter will focus on the indicators of success. The last three parts of the model are explained in detail in Parts Two, Three, and Four of the book.

Developing Your Critical Thinking Skills

1. Look again at the model in Figure 1–6 and consider our Trek example. If you were an executive at Trek, how would you respond if you learned that one of your main competitors was about to introduce a bicycle frame it claimed was stronger and lighter than yours?

2. In the early days of the auto industry, Ford cars were number one in the industry. Henry Ford refused to make his cars in any color except black. What impact do you think this decision had on the business? What part(s) of the model did Ford miss?

3. We mentioned the circular flow of the model as symbolized by the arrows. What does this really mean? How does each part of the model depend on other parts?

The Indicators of a Successful Business

As we explained in the preceding section, an understanding of the indicators of business success is critical. These indicators become both the performance targets that businesses try to achieve and the basis for measuring actual performance to determine if corrective action is needed. Today's businesses must be sensitive to these indicators. The five indicators we have stressed affect all businesses and even nonprofit organizations. Strength in each area is important for overall success. Therefore, we end this chapter by emphasizing the indicators in more depth.

Achieving Financial Performance

Perhaps the single most dramatic measure of organizational health and business success is financial performance. This is the *bottom line* we hear mentioned so often. Regardless of what else goes on in the business, if bottom-line performance is not good enough, the business will not survive.

The most direct indicator of financial performance is captured in the concept of profit or firm value. Indeed, the managers of successful businesses constantly strive to make a profit, thereby adding value to the firm. Let's explore what profit really means.

On the way to class today, you stopped at Natural Joe's Pushcart and bought one of Joe's special concoctions, his all-natural multifruit juice, to quench your thirst. The unique blend of strawberry, banana, papaya, and cherry seems to help you concentrate better in class. You paid Joe 90 cents for the drink. That 90 cents is revenue for Joe and his business. In other words, **revenue** is the amount customers pay for the goods and services they purchase.

Of course, that 90 cents does not represent a profit for Joe's business. Joe must pay out money in order to make his products and provide services to his customers. These

Revenue
The amount customers pay for goods and services they purchase.

Expenses
Money a business must pay out in order to make its products and provide its services.

Profit
The amount of money left over after the business records all its revenues and subtracts all its expenses.

Productivity
The ratio of goods and services provided to resources used.

payouts include the raw materials he uses in his drinks. He must buy strawberries, bananas, papayas, and cherry extract. He must also pay for the sugar he uses in each drink, as well as the biodegradable cups. He even has to pay the university a fee to rent pushcart space on campus. Stated concisely, the money a business must pay out in order to make its products and provide its services is known as **expenses**. It is only when revenues exceed expenses that the business realizes a profit or, in other words, makes money. Thus, **profit** is the amount of money left over after the business records all its revenues and subtracts all its expenses.

The example of Natural Joe's Pushcart offers some important business insights. First, it lets you see how important revenue is to business. A business needs revenue to survive. Consequently, businesses are always looking for ways to increase their total revenues.

Let's explore that idea of total revenue for a moment. What is Joe's total revenue for the day? Do you have enough information to know? Not really. You know he charges 90 cents for each drink. But you don't know how many drinks he sells in a day. Today, with students streaming by and the temperature pushing 90 degrees, Joe sold 500 drinks. So his total revenue for the day was $450. The price per drink (90 cents) times the quantity sold (500) equals the total revenue ($450). Businesses are always playing the price/quantity trade-off game. If Joe lowers his price, will he sell more drinks? If he raises his price, will he sell fewer? The answers and Joe's subsequent action are critical because they affect the total revenue that Joe's business will earn.

Businesses must always be concerned with expenses. They realize that if they can find ways to reduce expenses while still giving customers the desired products and services, they will make more money. This idea is fundamental, and it is a popular theme in business today. Businesses produce goods and services. Of course, it takes money and other resources to do so. A business converts its resources into goods and services that customers value enough to pay for them. The ratio of goods and services produced to resources used is known as the rate of **productivity** of the business. If a business can increase its level of goods and services offered without increasing the resources it uses, it is increasing its productivity. If a business can produce the same level of output while reducing the resources it uses, it is said to be operating more efficiently. Both actions, increased productivity and efficiency, should give the business a more favorable bottom line. Throughout the book, we will see some of the innovative ways businesses are trying to control expenses, operate more efficiently, and increase their productivity. The logic for this is simple: It is profitable to do so.

A final note on profits. Some people seem to have an impression that there is something sinister about a business seeking profits. Let's recognize right up front that there is nothing negative, manipulative, or corrupt about the firm's pursuit of profits. In fact, profit is the incentive for which individuals invest in a business. It is the reward for risking one's wealth and/or efforts in a venture. For example, Joe may have committed his life savings to getting his pushcart business started. He works hard, and he sacrifices for his business. Profit is a reasonable and fair incentive to encourage Joe's actions.

Profit may be taken out of the business for the owner's personal use, or it can be reinvested in the business. It can be shared with employees or invested in other ventures or donated to charitable causes. Profit is one of the key aspects of a capitalist society. The quest for profit drives innovation and efficiency.

Remember, profit is one of the primary measures of a firm's success. It certainly is not the only measure, but it is the most commonly accepted one. If a business fails to make a profit over time, it will ultimately go out of business.

Analyzing the overall financial performance of a business is, however, more complicated than simply looking at profits. In later chapters, you will learn that financial performance can be calculated from the financial statements and reports that the managers prepare. While these measures are objective and numerically based, you should exercise care in using and interpreting them.

For example, a relatively new business may not make much money. In fact, it may actually lose money each month that it operates. Yet it may be poised for growth. In essence, the business may be healthy given its situation. It just has not taken off yet.

In contrast, a business may appear to be in good financial condition and yet be far from healthy. Other measures of success may indicate that there are problems. It may take some time for the effect of inattention to these factors to appear on the bottom line. For example, the business may be making a lot of profit for its investors. Yet it may not be buying new equipment, updating its facilities, or investing in new technology. Therefore, even if the business seems to be financially successful, its failure to modernize may cast doubt on its longer-term success. Given this perspective, we will now look more closely at the nonfinancial indicators.

Meeting Customer Needs

Every business has customers, regardless of whether it produces a product or provides a service. The amount of profit a business makes is ultimately determined by how well it meets its customers' needs over the long run. There are many different kinds of customers. Some customers are other businesses. Some are individuals. Some purchase goods or services from the business only once. Others purchase often and repeatedly. Some purchase products costing a few pennies. Others spend thousands of dollars for a single product. They may be next door to the business or thousands of miles away. They may talk face to face with a sales representative or order via direct mail or the Internet. Whatever the nature of the customer, the key to business profits is satisfying customer needs over time.

Today, many experts feel that customers are the key indicator of business health and success. Note that rather than thinking of profits first, they think of customers first. They recognize that if customers are satisfied, the base for financial profitability is in place. Without customer acceptance, the business will not survive. If a business does not meet the needs of a customer, that customer will go to a competitor.

Many businesses recognize this relationship and focus their efforts on *customer satisfaction*. Many say they want to not only meet but exceed customer expectations. Some even talk about *delighting the customer*. Many organizations are quite creative about how they approach the customer and try to satisfy customer needs. Some organizations even "guarantee" customer satisfaction.

Consider a unique example at the University of Missouri at Rolla. The university realizes that students and prospective students are its customers. These students have a major demand, or need, from universities today. They ask, "Will I be able to get a job after I graduate?" This is what the customer wants. In response the university introduced the UMR promise: "If you don't find a job in your field within six months of graduation, the school will provide as much as a year of additional classes at *no charge*." Of course, the student must agree to maintain a minimum grade point average of 2.75 and stay involved in extracurricular activities. The message is clear. The university, to an extent, is guaranteeing customer satisfaction.[5]

How do we know if we are meeting customer needs? Ultimately, we know through the purchases and selections that customers make. However, that may be too late. A successful business keeps a watchful eye on two factors: (1) customer sensitivity and service and (2) timeliness. Let's look at each of these.

customer sensitivity
p. 493>

Compaq has done well in recent years by listening to its customers. What information would a computer manufacturer be able to get from its customers—both its retailers and its end customers?

Customer Sensitivity and Service

Customer sensitivity
The awareness of customer desires and needs.

Customer sensitivity is about awareness. **Customer sensitivity** means being aware of customer desires and needs and anticipating changes in customer preferences. Customer sensitivity leads to customer service, which is action oriented. **Customer service** is the set of actions a business takes to meet customer needs and preferences.

Customer service
Business actions taken to meet customer needs and preferences.

This approach to customers is *proactive* instead of reactive. Reactive businesses wait until customer shifts have occurred to change their patterns or approaches. They may be so out of touch with customer preferences that they are forced to change. That is, they face markets and customers that demand change if they are to survive.

For example, IBM revolutionized the computer industry with its personal computer in the early 1980s. However, it failed to remain attuned to customers. It didn't offer the range of software applications that customers came to desire by the late 80s. IBM became a rather stodgy and nonresponsive business, and it suffered at the hands of IBM clones and other market innovators. It soon found itself in a reactive mode, playing catch-up rather than leading. Today Compaq, not IBM, is the top PC maufacturer.

In customer service, a healthy business must be proactive. It must anticipate customer trends and respond quickly to new needs. Proactive businesses constantly look for new trends, new ways to serve customers, and new ways to operate more efficiently. They try to stay ahead of the game and anticipate what may be coming. Large businesses even have marketing research professionals and customer relations specialists to help them better understand and predict customer needs and how those needs are changing.

**customer service
p. 340>**

Customer service is an ongoing process, a goal that is never fully realized. As soon as customers' needs are met, their expectations rise. The bar on customer service is always being raised higher and higher. Clearly, a business without a proactive awareness of customers will not remain healthy for long.

Continental Airlines has weathered shaky financial performance that at one time resulted in a *bankruptcy filing*. Yet by the mid-1990s Continental was poised to take off. Part of its turnaround effort hinged on its emphasis on service. The airline doubled its customer service staff, began offering special customer attention, and responded quickly and decisively to customer concerns. Customer complaints fell and many fliers seemed willing to give Continental another chance.[6] Customer sensitivity and service became a foundation for building business health.

Timeliness

In today's volatile business environment, speed and response time are extremely important. A wonderful new product idea or a vision of a novel area of service is meaningless unless it can be delivered to would-be customers in a timely way. True, managers must analyze their decisions and carefully reflect on available information. This process of analysis is the backbone of effective decision making. Yet leaders must be action oriented. They must avoid the tendency to overevaluate decisions. Indeed, while they wait for more information and gain assurance that the risk is acceptable, a competitor may act. That competitor will have gained initial consumer acceptance, achieving *first-comer advantages*. The slow mover is then playing catch-up. The phrase "if you snooze, you lose," has real business implications. Consider the case of Fiat.

While Fiat is a relatively small Italian company, it has an international presence. Recently Fiat announced that it was developing a new small car to be targeted toward the developing nations of Latin America as well as India and China. If Fiat takes the risk of entering these markets before the major manufacturers do, it expects to earn a large initial share of what should be a massive market. Then, as the market grows, it will benefit from its strong market position. This formula has worked in the past. Fiat was an early entrant into both Poland and Brazil, and it has reaped the benefits as those markets grew. Timeliness appears to be a fundamental factor in Fiat's strategy for success.

Timeliness is a tough issue for many businesspeople. No one wants to rush to a decision without all the information necessary. No one wants to risk a premature entry into a new market without sufficient study. To do so would be foolish and irresponsible. But there is never as much information available as you would like. All decisions carry some element of risk. There is rarely time for study to answer all questions. Healthy businesses are always studying, anticipating, developing, and looking for new options—but they are poised to act. Indeed, their health and even their survival demand that they act with speed and conviction.

In addition to being a major issue in larger, more strategic actions of a business, timeliness is important in specific customer situations. Lands' End, a mail-order seller of quality clothes, prides itself on getting every order out within 24 hours. It ships by an express delivery service, so the package usually reaches the customer's door within three days after the order is placed. In recent years, banks have moved to almost exclusive use of ATMs because quick service has become more of a priority for customers than seeing a bank teller face to face. In later chapters, you will learn about *just-in-time delivery* in manufacturing, yet another example of how timeliness has become a key factor in business today.

Companies such as Lands' End and L.L. Bean are noted for their ability to get products to customers in the minimum time possible. Lands' End uses UPS. L.L. Bean uses Fed Ex. What would be the effect if either used regular delivery rather than express delivery services?

Building Quality Products and Services

Increasingly, today's businesses must focus on the quality and value of their products and services. Customers won't tolerate low quality unless low prices are more important to them than the quality of the product. The trend in recent years, however, has been to emphasize quality even if the cost is higher. In a competitive environment, customers will readily abandon any business that fails to meet their quality expectations. Some businesses may generate initial sales and revenues by offering low prices that lure customers to their products. But if quality is low, these customers generally do not return.

continuous improvement p. 448>

Continuous improvement

Efforts by a business to provide steadily higher quality throughout all phases of its operations.

Quality is a near obsession for many companies. In fact, *quality management* is the expected way of operating for most businesses today. Quality management is nothing more than a company's unique approach for addressing quality. The foundation of quality management is a philosophy known as **continuous improvement**, which refers to a company's efforts to provide steadily higher levels of quality throughout all phases of its operations. This means each step in the production process is examined and altered to make it better. This often results in more efficient and less costly ways

Trek is a good example of indicators of success. Their managers must look at all five indicators to see if their company is successful. Check out their website at http://www.trekbikes.com and see if you can find evidence of success or lack of success.

of making a product. Continuous improvement also means that the products and services provided to customers are getting better all the time.

Many companies have made quality the foundation for their future. Motorola, Ford, and Xerox are all large U.S. businesses that are recognized as quality leaders. In these companies, quality has been a key piece of the *competitive strategy*. They have formalized plans and programs for promoting and ensuring a quality focus. (Note that Motorola is featured throughout this book, partly because of its emphasis on quality.)

Consider the advertisement for Trek bikes that is presented above. Even from this ad, you get a sense of the attention paid to quality and continuous improvement. From *zero excess manufacturing* to ABT bonding, Trek stresses quality as a unique feature of its bikes.

competitive strategy
p. 317>

Kmart has made major strides recently in turning itself around. Much of the attempt at resurgence can be attributed to introducing Martha Stewart lines of products to Kmart shoppers. Many shoppers have gone to Kmart for their first time to browse the products inspired by Martha Stewart. How effective are celebrities like Michael Jordan, Jerry Seinfeld, or Martha Stewart in the success of products or companies?

Encouraging Innovation and Creativity

In today's volatile business setting, the only constant is change. Customer tastes and preferences are constantly changing. Employee demands are always shifting. Competitors are always searching for new ways to edge rivals out of the market. Organizations are always looking for methods of operation that will bring greater efficiency and productivity. New technologies are always being developed. The only way a business can stay on top and compete is to be creative and innovative. Without the ability to change, a firm's success will surely be short-lived.

Consider Kmart's success, fall, and attempts at revival. In the 1970s, Kmart revolutionized the retail industry by offering customers a discount alternative to traditional retailing. The company was on the leading edge in creating the contemporary discount-store chain. But by the late 1980s, Kmart had fallen to number two behind Sears in the industry. In 1992 it was overtaken by Wal-Mart Stores, Inc. Many argue that Kmart became comfortable with its success and even dismissed Wal-Mart as a real competitive threat. Today Kmart is trying to reinvent itself by updating its stores and its merchandise.

A fundamental way to think about creativity and innovation is to look at how the two terms are related. Creativity is a process; innovation is an outcome. This means that **creativity** is new and different patterns of thinking and behaving. **Innovation** is the result, or what is produced through these creative activities. Innovation deals with new approaches and options. In short, creativity leads to innovation.

Innovation is quite difficult because it requires a business to think about change and improvement even when things look quite good. Indeed, one of the biggest barriers to innovation is success. The argument goes, "Why should we change when the bottom line looks so good?"

Innovative businesses behave differently. For example, Ford redesigned its Taurus for 1996 even though it had been the best-selling car in America. This was an important proactive move because Ford knew that Toyota was redesigning the Camry for 1997. The reasoning is straightforward: while the business may be successful today, without appropriate innovation it will not be successful in the future. Profile 1–2 explores Ford's decision.

Creativity
New and different patterns of thinking and behaving.

Innovation
New approaches and options that are the result of creative activities.

PROFILE   1–2   *The Shape of a New Machine*

"Team Taurus constantly pitted quality and engineering refinement against cost. More often than not, engineering won out." This quote from *Business Week* typified the philosophy of Ford executives and designers as they designed the 1996 Ford Taurus. Designers were constantly encouraged to push the limit in innovation. Early designs were conservative and boxy, but Ford chair Alexander Trotman told designer Douglas Gaffka, "On a wow scale, this isn't there yet. Give us an absolute grabber."

Throughout the design process, Team Taurus conducted consumer research with both Taurus and Honda Accord owners to determine just what consumers wanted and where they felt the current Taurus was weak. For example, customers complained that the Taurus had a "cheap plastic" look. So the team used a more expensive process to give the one-piece molded dash a leatherlike appearance. It also designed the control panel, door handles, and even the rear window to match the elliptical shape of the exterior.

A key to innovation is support by top management. Indicative of this support was Trotman's carefully considered purchase of a $90 million stamping machine to improve the quality of the car. Trotman encouraged innovation because he wants Taurus to be the flagship of the Ford line well past the year 2000. And when it must compete head-on with the likes of the Honda Accord and the Toyota Camry, innovation is not a luxury.[8]

top management
p. 65>

learning organizations
p. 279>

Learning organizations
Organizations that adapt to change and creatively search for new and better ways to operate and meet the needs of their employees and customers.

Recently businesses have been encouraged to operate as learning organizations.[9] **Learning organizations** are ones that not only adapt to change but creatively search for new and better ways to operate and meet the needs of their employees and customers. A learning organization is highly proactive. It is ripe with creativity and is

Ford spent millions of dollars redesigning the Taurus even though it was the number one selling car. It spent considerable time researching consumers' needs and wants before completing the redesigned car. If Ford or GM asked your opinion, what would you tell them?

more likely to produce useful innovations. Increasingly, this focus must be present if a business is to be considered truly healthy.

Gaining Employee Commitment

A successful business is composed of employees who care about the jobs they do. They are proud of their work, and they feel a sense of commitment to their jobs and to the company. They are dedicated and concerned, not simply going through the motions. Committed employees are motivated to do the best job possible.

Progressive, healthy organizations invest considerable time and effort in finding ways to build greater employee commitment. Many have formal programs to provide more opportunities for employee participation and involvement in decision making. Many give employees opportunities for growth through company-supported training efforts. Many offer creative benefits and work options. Many give workers more discretion and more power to do things that were previously done only by their bosses. This process of giving more decision-making authority and responsibility to workers throughout the organization is known as **empowerment**.

One way to build commitment is to use the talents of the workforce to the fullest extent possible. Most employees want to feel needed in their work. Certainly, if people feel that they are asked to do more than they can, they become frustrated and dissatisfied. However, people also experience frustration and dissatisfaction if they feel that their talents and skills are not being used by the business. This condition is known as *under-utilization*. If the business does not provide employees the opportunity to use their skills and express their contributions, their sense of underutilization can be a major cause of stress. Healthy organizations encourage employees to contribute their talents.

Employee commitment comes when managers understand their workforce, are attuned to workers' needs, and make an effort to meet those needs. This area is so important that we will spend considerable time later in the text discussing the process of building commitment.

benefits p. 433>

Empowerment
The process of giving more decision-making authority and responsibility to workers.

Significance of the Critical Measures

We have briefly outlined five key indicators of a successful, healthy business. In many ways, these are the five outcomes a business hopes to achieve as it operates. More will be said about each of these outcomes as we move through the text.

Recognize that these outcomes are not independent of one another. In fact, they are interdependent. What happens in one area affects other areas. For example, attention to quality and sensitivity to customers should enable a business to foster operations and provide products and services that improve its financial performance. Innovation keeps the business on the cutting edge, assuring customer responsiveness and enhancing financial outcomes. Utilizing the workforce and gaining employee commitment builds a sense of drive and dedication that may promote quality, customer service, and innovative ideas. A focus on one piece of the success picture without attention to others would yield an incomplete picture and could endanger the long-term success of the business.

Developing Your Critical Thinking Skills

1. Think of a business you have worked for in the past or where you are working now. What does that business do to stay focused on the customer?

2. How does this same business attempt to be innovative?

SUMMARY

1. There are millions of businesses around the world. The prosperity of a country's economy is affected, to a large extent, by the success of its businesses.

    ■ What is a business?

    A business is any organization that strives for profits by providing goods and services that meet customer needs.

    ■ What is a successful business?

    A successful business is one that excels in all aspects of its operations over time.

2. A successful business produces several different kinds of desired results. The results are measured by indicators that managers strive to achieve.

    ■ What are the indicators of business success?

    Five critical indicators of business success are (1) achieving financial performance, (2) meeting customer needs and values, (3) building quality into products and services, (4) encouraging innovation and creativity, and (5) gaining employee commitment.

3. A business does not operate in a completely controllable environment. Numerous forces affect business success but are beyond the control of business managers. Managers must be aware of changes in those forces and must decide how to respond to those changes.

    ■ What are the external factors that affect business?

    Six key environmental forces influence business decisions. They are (1) diversity and social patterns, (2) economic forces, (3) global influences, (4) financial markets, (5) legal and regulatory forces, and (6) the nature of the firm's industry.

4. A successful business is one in which managers make good decisions and follow them with effective actions. Many different kinds of decisions must be made and this usually means that many different employees must be involved in the decision-making process. Even more employees are usually involved in taking the actions which implement the decisions.

    ■ What kinds of decisions and actions are required for business success?

    The five categories of decision making and actions are (1) choosing a direction for the business, (2) providing value for customers, (3) acquiring the resources needed to produce the planned goods and services, (4) coordinating activities and gaining commitment, and (5) using technology and providing quality products and services.

5. Business is both exciting and challenging precisely because most decisions involve uncertainty. Managers can never be sure that their actions will produce the results they expect. For that reason, every successful business must monitor the results of past actions and constantly look for ways to improve performance. That is, it must evaluate results and make changes.

    ■ Recognize how measurement and change enable firms to improve performance.

    Measurement permits the business manager to evaluate the results of operations in terms of the indicators of success that were previously established. Measurement should help the business identify where changes are needed. However, making needed changes is difficult. It requires overcoming resistance to change and involves ongoing training and innovation.

6. Managers of successful businesses engage in a never ending cycle of decisions and actions. In this chapter you read two short case studies of this process, the cases of Blockbuster Entertainment and Trek bikes.

    ■ Describe a complete model of the decisions and processes that provide a path toward a successful business.

    This consists of four steps that are continually repeated. First, management determines the indicators of success. Five indicators were presented in this chapter. Second, management assesses the environment. Six areas of environmental concern were identified. Third, management makes a variety of decisions, which are then translated into actions. Five categories of decisions and actions were discussed. Fourth, management evaluates the results of the decisions and actions. On the basis of the assessment, new decisions and actions are taken in order to produce necessary changes. The four steps are repeated over and over again, as illustrated in Figure 1–6.

Links to future courses

We introduce here a service that we include at the end of each chapter. This service will be helpful to both those who anticipate majoring in business and those who choose other majors. We list a number of courses where the themes introduced in this chapter are developed in more detail. For this introductory chapter, the themes will relate to virtually all the advanced courses in business, especially to core business courses such as:

■ Principles of economics   ■ Principles of finance
■ Principles of management   ■ Strategic management
■ Principles of marketing   ■ Organizational behavior

This chapter also introduces themes that you may encounter in nonbusiness courses such as:

■ Introduction to psychology   ■ Introduction to sociology

EXERCISES AND APPLICATIONS

1. Form teams of three to six people. Discuss the work experiences of each person. Do you think the places where you worked paid attention to the five indicators of success? Give examples of how your managers addressed or failed to address those indicators.

2. Assume you have just been given $500,000 to start a business. What business would you form? Justify why this business is a good choice, given today's business environment.

3. Go to the *Entrepreneurial Edge* Magazine website (http://www.edgeonline.com/). In the section "Companies on the Move," find a company that interests you. Write a one-page summary of the business and how it meets customer needs.

4. Form teams of three to six people. Have each person briefly discuss the business he or she researched in Exercise 3. Given what you have learned in this chapter, which business do you think will be most successful five years from now? Explain why.

CASE: PANASONIC

You are probably familiar with the Panasonic brand of consumer electronics products. But can you name the company that makes those products? The answer is the Japanese multinational firm Matsushita Electric, the world's leading consumer electronics firm. This firm introduced the VHS format for videotapes. It sells them and other products all over the world under such brand names as Panasonic, Quasar, Technics, Victor, and Japan.

A key to the company's success is the clear sense of business direction developed by the company's founder, Konosuke Matsushita. He started the company in his small home in 1918 with a $50 investment and two other employees (his wife and her brother). His early products included inexpensive lamps, batteries, radios, and motors. In every case he took products being made by others and found ways to both improve quality and reduce costs. His rule of thumb was that success required a 30 percent reduction in price and a 30 percent improvement in quality.

production p. 464>

To improve quality, he employed a variety of methods to find out what product features were most important to customers. To lower costs, he emphasized both large-scale production and a daily search for cheaper production methods. Matsushita Electric still uses those approaches.

From the beginning, Matsushita believed that his success depended on the cooperation of others, particularly his suppliers, his employees, and his distributors. Over time, he developed a number of practices that are prominent features of Matsushita Electric today. To increase employee satisfaction and productivity, he developed a mission: "to overcome poverty, relieve society as a whole from misery, and bring it wealth." To further increase employees' sense of participation and importance, he divided the company into divisions and the divisions into smaller units, each of which had substantial freedom to make decisions. To raise the skill level of decision making, he established a training and development program for employees. To further motivate workers, he adopted a policy of continuous pay increases (coupled with insistence on productivity increases that more than offset the raises).

Decision Questions

1. Matsushita specifically addressed employee commitment and motivation. This seems to work well with Japanese employees. Do you think this technique would be effective in a typical American company?

2. Matsushita believes in finding out what customers really need in terms of product features. What are some ways it might obtain such information?
3. How does Matsushita Electric's approach to business success compare with what you have read in this chapter?

SOURCES: John P. Kotter, *Matsushita Leadership Lessons from the 20th Century's Most Remarkable Entrepreneur* (New York: The Free Press, 1997); Patrick J. Spain and James R. Talbot, eds. *Hoover's Handbook of World Business: 1995–96* (Austin, TX: The Reference Press, 1995).

REFERENCES

1. Roger Thurow, "In Inventing Sports, U.S. Is a Winner." *The Wall Street Journal*, December 18, 1996, p. A10.

2. Todd A. Finkle, "Lessons Learned from Blockbuster Entertainment," *NBDC Report*, no. 175, June 1995, pp. 1–4.

3. Sally Goll Beatty, "Blockbuster Ads Will Play Down Video Rentals," *The Wall Street Journal*, December 30, 1996, B1, 2.

4. Eben Shapiro, "Blockbuster Rescue Bid Stars Viacom Top Guns," *The Wall Street Journal*, May 7, 1997, pp. B1, B7; and Stephanie Anderson Forest, "The Script Doctor is in at Blockbuster—Again," *Business Week*, July 28, 1997, pp. 101–103.

5. Carl Quintanilla, "A Special News Report About Life on the Job—and Trends Taking Shape There," *The Wall Street Journal*, July 12, 1996, A1.

6. Bridget O'Brian, "Continental Airlines is now Climbing toward a Profit," *The Wall Street Journal*, June 22, 1995, p. B4.

7. Audrey Choi and Maureen Kline, "Fiat's New World Car is Designed with Developing Nations in Mind," *The Wall Street Journal*, June 20, 1995, p. A18.

8. Kathleen Kerwin, "The Shape of a New Machine," *Business Week*, July 24, 1995, pp. 60–6.

9. Peter M. Senge, *The Fifth Discipline: The Art and Practice of the Learning Organization*. New York: Doubleday/Currency, 1990.

2

The Scope of Business Today

In the mid-80s, Georgena Terry began tinkering around with custom bicycle frames. Working out of her basement and prompted by her frustration with her own bike, Terry became convinced there was a market for her idea, a bicycle that was designed especially for women. As she explains, "The average woman is 5-foot-4, half a foot shorter than the average man. Because of the placement of muscle mass and the length of limbs, women like to sit more upright than men do." Riding a man's bike means that women have to bend over further than is comfortable. This increases the likelihood of neck, shoulder, and crotch pain. Terry became convinced that a redesign was needed.

She shortened the distance between the saddle (seat) and handlebars, providing a better fit, and the business took off. Terry Precision Bicycles for Women produces quality bikes selling from $600 to over $1,600. Staying in touch with her customers, Terry has modified the traditional saddle to make it more comfortable. The new design has a shorter nose and better fits a woman's body. Today, saddles account for nearly 30 percent of Terry's business. Other accessories and a line of clothing have followed. Her customers are happy, and Terry has the only company in the world with a product solely for women cyclists.[1]

When Georgena Terry left her job at Xerox and started her own business, it became one of the million-plus new businesses that are started each year. As you will learn in this chapter, however, there are many kinds of businesses. You need to understand the scope of business today. It is important to know some of the ways businesses differ. It is also important to understand the impacts of those differences. For example, you need to recognize that there are millions more small companies than large companies.

In terms of employees, however, almost half of all workers are employed by only about 15,000 firms. It is important that you know the different forms of businesses and the different ownership combinations that are possible in case you ever start your own firm or work for one of the millions of small firms in the nation. Once you have completed this chapter, you should be able to:

1. Explain the magnitude of business in our society.

2. Differentiate between a small business and a large business and describe the impact of each.

3. Define franchising and explain its advantages and disadvantages.

4. Explain the nature and impact of not-for-profit organizations.

5. Differentiate among sole proprietorships, partnerships, and corporations.

6. Identify the different types of owners of businesses.

In this chapter, you will learn the significance of business in today's world. That significance is, to a large extent, a function of the vast number of businesses and the great variation in their sizes and scopes. We begin our discussion by noting the number and sizes of businesses. We follow that with the impacts of large and small businesses and of not-for-profit organizations. We then note the most important legal forms of businesses today. Finally, we discuss who actually owns businesses. In our model of the path toward a successful business note that owners appear in the top box.

The Number and Size of Businesses

According to the Internal Revenue Service (IRS), there are over 21 million businesses in the United States. This number includes approximately 9 million people who have business income, but not as a result of their primary occupation. Examples of this might include one of your high school teachers who paints houses during the summer for extra income or your next-door neighbor who is a part-time Mary Kay Cosmetics representative. Even the authors of this textbook fall into this category, since all three of us are full-time professors in addition to writing this book. Of the remaining 12 million businesses, 7 million individuals own businesses in which they are the sole employee. These would include a carpenter who works for a variety of homeowners, a barber or hairstylist who rents space in a salon, and a novelist who writes murder mysteries as her only occupation.

Subtracting out the part-time business owners and the sole-employee owners leaves approximately 5 million businesses with employees.[2] Of those, over 4.5 million have fewer than 20 employees. In fact, less than 2 percent of all businesses employ over 100 workers. Only about 15,000 businesses have more than 500 employees. Figure 2–1 presents this rather dramatically by showing the percentages of all businesses by number of employees.

To realize the magnitude of business today, consider the following. The 5 million firms with employees represent a total of over 90 million workers, or 35 percent of the total U.S. population. If we consider that most of these employees have families or

FIGURE 2-1   Percentages of Businesses by Number of Employees

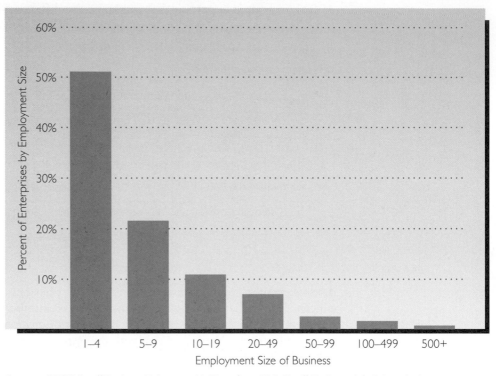

SOURCE: NFIB Small Business Primer, p. 11 (Data from U.S. Small Business Administration).

significant others who depend on them for part of their livelihood, the impact of business is certainly substantial.

Small business
Any business that is independently owned and operated, is not dominant in its field, and meets size standards that vary depending on the industry.

Most businesses are small. The U.S. Small Business Administration defines a **small business** as any business that is independently owned and operated, is not dominant in its field, and meets size standards that vary depending on the industry. A rule of thumb is that any business with under 100 employees is considered a small business, although that varies from industry to industry.

At the opposite end of the continuum are the large businesses. There are far fewer large businesses than there are small businesses. But their impact is tremendous. Further, we hear so much about large businesses that they are common knowledge to us.

Even large businesses vary greatly in size and number of employees. For example, General Motors employs almost 650,000 workers throughout the world. Motorola employs 142,000. Trek employs 1,800 in the United States. Although each of these is considered a large business, the differences among them are dramatic. The following two sections discuss the relative impact of large and small businesses. You may be surprised at some of the facts presented.

The Impact of Large Business

Here is a quick quiz for you. Name the following:

1. Three cereal companies
2. Four companies that produce cars in the United States (hint: Honda is one)
3. Three computer manufacturers

4.   Four retail chains
5.   Three oil companies

Chances are you listed large companies for most of your answers. In fact, you probably listed what would be called very large businesses—for example, companies such as General Mills, Chrysler, IBM, J.C. Penney, and Mobil Oil. Very large businesses have thousands of employees, earn billions of dollars in sales, and invest millions of dollars in advertising. This is why we hear so much about them. To illustrate the magnitude of large businesses, consider Table 2–1. It shows the 15 largest U.S. businesses in terms of sales. Most of them are household names. Companies like General Motors , IBM, and Sears have thousands of employees worldwide.

Note in Table 2–1 that the number of employees is not highly correlated with the amount of sales. There is a reason for this. Some businesses, such as oil companies, are very **capital intensive,** which means they depend heavily on equipment and machinery to produce their products. Other businesses, such as retail chains, are very labor intensive. People are the keys to the products and services in **labor intensive** industries.

Study Table 2–1 carefully. Note, for example, that the top fifteen firms in the country—only 15—have total sales of $1.1 trillion and employ about 3.4 million people. In addition, the 15,000 largest businesses account for 46.9 percent of the employees and 52.7 percent of the total payroll in the country. As you can see, the impact of very large businesses is tremendous if we consider only sales and employ-

capital intensive
p. 277>

Capital intensive
A business that depends heavily on equipment and machinery to produce its products.

Labor intensive
A business where people are key to supplying products and services.

TABLE 2 – 1   The Top 15 U.S. Companies in Sales

Rank	Company	1996 Sales ($ Billions)	Number of Employees
1	General Motors	$158	647,000
2	Ford	146.9	371,702
3	Exxon	116.7	79,000
4	Wal-Mart Stores	104.8	728,000
5	General Electric	78.5	239,000
6	IBM	75.9	240,615
7	Mobil	71.1	43,000
8	Philip Morris	69.2	154,000
9	Chrysler	59.3	126,000
10	AT&T	52.2	130,000
11	Texaco	44.6	28,957
12	Dupont	43.8	97,000
13	Sears Roebuck	38.2	335,000
14	Chevron	37.6	40,820
15	Proctor & Gamble	35.8	106,000

*SOURCE: Company Web Sites.

TABLE 2–2   GDP and Revenues of Selected Countries and Companies

	($ billions)
▪ Switzerland	$299
▪ Argentina	291
▪ Austria	228
▪ General Motors	158
▪ Denmark	148
▪ Ford	147
▪ Exxon	117
▪ Greece	108
▪ General Electric	78
▪ IBM	76
▪ Mobil Oil	71
▪ Peru	52

SOURCES: Company web sites; U.S. Department of Commerce.

information technology p. 456>

Diversified business
A business that is involved in more than one type of business activity.

Mergers and acquisitions
Two ways that one business combines with another business.

ment. Amazingly, as Table 2–2 shows, the revenues of the largest U.S. businesses exceed the total gross domestic product (GDP) of many *countries*. (The GDP is the total value of goods and services produced in a country. For information on how GDP is measured, see Chapter 6.)

Adding to the magnitude of large businesses is the number of industries in which they compete. You may be familiar with General Electric as a manufacturer of home appliances (even though it sold its small appliance division to Black & Decker). But did you know that G.E. also makes jet engines, plastics, lighting, electrical power generation equipment, medical equipment, and information technology equipment—and owns the NBC TV network? Johnson & Johnson makes baby oil and Tylenol, but it also makes Band-Aids, Imodium A-D, Reach toothbrushes, Neutragena skin and hair products, joint replacements, surgical instruments, and a host of prescription drugs. H.J. Heinz Company sells 50 percent of the ketchup in the United States, 48 percent of the frozen potatoes, 26 percent of the cat food, and 51 percent of the diet food. It sells eight brands of pet foods, including Kibbles 'N Bits and Gravy Train. Rubbermaid is the familiar maker of containers, but it also makes chair mats, floor sweepers, office furniture, playground equipment, lab coats, shipping containers, wheelbarrows, and workbenches.[3] There is an additional message here. Many large, easily recognized businesses are diversified. A **diversified business** is involved in more than one type of business activity.

Another indication of the size and scope of large businesses deals with **mergers and acquisitions,** which are ways one business combines with another business. Disney recently acquired Capital Cities/ABC, which gave it the TV networks ABC, ESPN, and A&E, as well as other properties. This is in addition to its theme parks, three movie production studios, and merchandise production. Clearly, Disney is a company of tremendous size and influence in the entertainment industry. Other megamergers include Boeing's recent purchase of McDonnell-Douglas. Boeing is the number one producer of commercial airliners; McDonnell-Douglas is one of two major producers of military planes. These corporations, huge before the merger, are now giants that can have substantial impact in the industries in which they operate.

Often larger businesses acquire smaller ones. This happened, for example, when Trek bought Gary Fisher Bicycles. The larger business, Trek, gained design expertise and considerable experience from the Fisher team. Fisher gained capital and other resources, which may allow it to lower the price of its bikes. It also gained access to Trek's distribution system. Sometimes a company makes an acquisition to extend its overall product line. This was the case when Brunswick, a manufacturer of sporting-goods equipment, bought Mongoose, which makes specialty bikes.[4]

acquisition p. 322>

The Impact of Small Business

The impact of large businesses comes from the sheer size of the individual businesses. Each business employs large numbers of people, and they contribute much to the overall economic productivity of the country. The impact of small business is different, but certainly no less dramatic. There are four special ways that small businesses affect society and the economy. Each deserves some attention.

The first impact of small businesses is economic and is due to the sheer number of small businesses that exist. As we discussed earlier, over 98 percent of the businesses in this country are technically considered small. Although each small business produces relatively few goods or services, when all small businesses are added together, the economic impact is substantial. For example, look at Figure 2–2, which shows the relative gross domestic product of major countries. Note that U.S. small businesses together rank just after Japan. Although our economy may be driven by giant businesses, the cumulative impact of small businesses is critical. American small business is an economic power.

The second impact of small businesses is seen in the number of people they employ. Over half of the U.S. private workforce is employed by small businesses.[5] In fact, small businesses have created more net new jobs in recent years than large businesses have. Almost half of the nation's business payroll is now provided by small businesses.[6]

The third small business impact comes from the technological innovations they contribute. Most new products are created in small businesses. One study found that half of all innovations and 95 percent of all radical innovations—those entirely new products—came from small businesses.[7] Following are some of the innovations that have come from small businesses.[8]

1. Photocopiers
2. Insulin
3. Vacuum tube
4. Penicillin
5. Zipper
6. Automatic transmission
7. Jet engine
8. Helicopter
9. Color film
10. Ballpoint pen

innovation p. 522>

In Chapter 1, we discussed why innovation is important to a business. Recognize that innovation is also important to a society. It is a sign of growth and progress.

FIGURE 2–2   Small Business as a World Economic Power

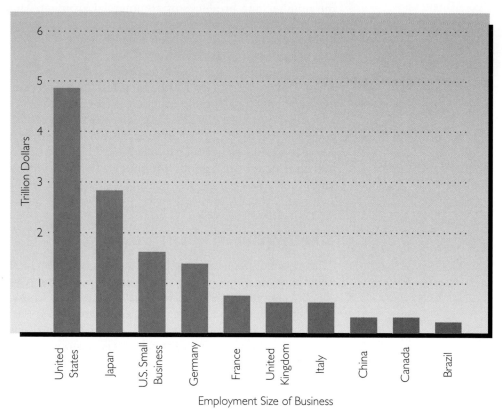

SOURCE: NFIB Small Business Primer, p. 9.

There are logical reasons why small businesses tend to be so innovative. They are often run with fewer restrictions and more flexibility than larger firms. Accordingly, it is generally easier to bring new ideas into focus. Also, there are fewer layers of bureaucracy to work through, so new ideas are less likely to get buried. Further, small businesses are often run by creative entrepreneurs, who feel comfortable taking risks and grasping new ideas. To a great extent, their businesses probably survive in the tough competitive environment because they operate in this manner. Creativity and innovation are part of the success formula for many smaller operations.

creativity p. 522>

The fourth and final small business impact is significant. Many small businesses serve special segments or *niches* of the market that larger firms choose to ignore. This is precisely what Terry Precision Bicycles, profiled at the beginning of this chapter, does. Georgena Terry realized that larger companies were not addressing the special needs of women bikers. It is this strategy of filling unmet customer niches that allows the smaller firm to compete and succeed. There is, of course, a broader outcome of such actions: consumers also win.

Some industries have more small businesses than others. In construction, for example, 88 percent of the firms have fewer than 500 employees and 72 percent have fewer than 100. More than half the companies in the retail trade are small businesses, as are 60 percent of service businesses. Mining, utilities, and manufacturing are somewhat less populated with small companies, but even they are over one-third small businesses.[9]

Small businesses, particularly new small businesses, tend to fail more often than large businesses do. However, the percentage failing is not nearly as high as might be expected. Most researchers now conclude that over half of all new businesses survive eight or more years.[10]

Small business can be an exciting and challenging career. Owning or working in a small business can be both personally gratifying and financially rewarding. Many of you may choose to work in a small business. Some of you will even own your own business. To assist in this possibility, we have included a discussion of business plans in Appendix 1 at the end of the book. It discusses the preparation needed and a format to use in writing a plan. It also includes a sample business plan.

Links between Small and Large Businesses

retailers p. 282>

In the preceding two sections, we discussed the impacts of large and small businesses. It is important to recognize the relationships between the two. Often small businesses are closely tied to larger businesses. In such instances, large businesses would not be able to operate as efficiently without the products and services provided by smaller businesses. Small businesses may serve as suppliers, distributors, and retailers for the products large businesses make. For example, Trek is a large business, but its products are sold by hundreds of retail outlets throughout the country. Any one of these bike shops may employ only a few people. Yet Trek's success depends on the effective sales efforts of these shops combined. One of these dealers is highlighted in Profile 2–1.

PROFILE 2–1   *The Best Dealers on Wheels*

While Trek is very proud of the bikes they make, one of their greatest assets is their family of dealers. Here's the way Trek describes it.

Day after day, in small towns and sprawling cities alike, they turn the world's best bikes into the world's best biking. Meet Elmer Sorenson. He's an old friend of ours, and a perfect example of the kind of commitment you'll find anywhere

Independent bicycle dealers such as Elmer and Pat Sorenson of Penn Cycle in Minneapolis can give excellent service for customers wishing to buy Trek bikes. The small business retailer is dependent on the larger manufacturer, but the manufacturer is also dependent upon the small retailer. How is each dependent on the other?

you see a Trek sign in the window. You'd be hard-pressed to find a bicycle dealer who has seen more than Sorenson, founder of Penn Cycle in Minneapolis. The former airline mechanic and avid fisherman opened his first bike shop in 1957, operating out of the alley behind his house. "It was extra money for minnows," he reminisces, "and fishing trips with my boys." Elmer has been with Trek since the very beginning as well, signing on as its first dealer in 1976. "There was need for a lightweight, advanced bike and Trek came through with it," he says, "and at a great price." Both companies have grown considerably over the years, as evidenced by the 1995 grand opening of Penn Cycle's fifth shop, a $1 million superstore in Eagan, Minn. The business is much larger now, and son Pat has become a partner and major contributor. Still, the Sorensons remain steadfast proponents of the guiding principle that got them here. "The number-one thing our customers should expect is to enjoy their bikes," the elder Sorenson proclaims. "When we sell a bike, it's a long-term relationship." Many customers have purchased more than 20 bikes from Penn Cycle, a fact that Elmer is very proud of. "You've got to start with a high-quality product and back it up with service. Only a dedicated bike dealer can do that for you."

SOURCE: 1996 Trek Catalog.

Franchising: A Hybrid of Large and Small Business

It is the day before the prom, and you are busily taking care of last minute preparations. You stop by Gingess Formalwear to pick up the tuxedo you rented and Budget Car Rental to get a clean late-model car. On the way home, you grab some chicken at KFC. Then you stop at Baskin-Robbins for some ice cream. You have just had exchanges with four businesses. All have provided a product or service, and all have something else in common. They are franchises, a special type of business arrangement that is increasingly popular.

Over 40 percent of all retail sales in the United States come from franchises.[11] Franchised sales are expected to reach $1 trillion by the year 2000. From Dairy Queen and Dunkin' Donuts to the Hair Emporium and the Medicine Shoppe, franchises dot the business landscape. Let's examine the attraction of this business arrangement in more detail.

Franchise
A business that grants the exclusive right to another individual or business to use its name and sell its products or services.

Franchising combines the advantages of both large and small businesses. In a **franchise**, a business that owns a service or trademarked product grants the exclusive right to another (individual or business) to use the franchise name and sell its products or services within a given location. There are two important designations here. The business that sells the franchise is known as the **franchisor.** The person or business that purchases the franchise is known as the **franchisee.**

Franchisor
The business that sells the franchise.

There are two different types of franchises. The first, and older, is called the *product and trade name franchise*. These companies have agreements with the franchisor to sell products under given trade names. Examples of these are car dealers, gasoline stations, and soft drink bottlers. This type of franchise is still the largest type of franchising in terms of sales. In 1992, product and trade name franchises accounted for $554 billion in sales.[12] The second kind of franchise is the *business format franchise*, in which the franchise agreement specifies exactly how the business will be operated. Examples here include fast-food restaurants, oil change shops, business services, and carpet

Franchisee
The person or business purchasing a franchise.

cleaning. This segment registered $249 billion in sales in 1992 and is now growing at over 12 percent per year.[13]

To understand the logic of franchising, let's explore the business basis for the franchise arrangement. Why would anyone want to operate a franchise? In other words, what does the franchisee get from the franchise relationship? Three outcomes are important. First, the franchisee gains the advantage of a proven business reputation. The franchising company or product name carries an earned reputation and guarantees instant customer recognition and positive regard. Much of the initial building of customer rapport that is so critical when a new business starts has already been done. The franchisee can count on immediate customer awareness and related sales. Second, franchisors provide franchisees with managerial assistance and training in how the business should be run to assure its success. Most franchisors have regional managers who help franchisees deal with the tough day-to-day decisions that must be made. Further, franchisors often offer advertising and provide accounting and reporting systems that help the franchisee stay on top of the operation. Third, the franchisee gains the rights to an exclusive territory. If you have the Red Lobster franchise for your city, the company assures you that no competing Red Lobster will enter your territory without you having the right to purchase the franchise.

While this picture looks quite favorable, there is a downside. The franchisee does incur some costs. A franchise fee is paid to the franchisor simply for the right to operate the business. The franchise fee may range from $10,000 to $50,000. A royalty, often 5 to 8 percent of gross sales, is paid to the franchisor on a continuous basis. Then there's the advertising fee. The franchisor typically handles the advertising for the entire chain. Each franchisee contributes an average of 2 percent of sales to underwrite those costs. The last fee is the investment in the actual building and equipment. This amount varies depending on the nature of the business. Even though the franchise fee itself is usually less than $50,000, the total investment in the franchise may easily exceed $500,000 and may reach $1 million for companies like McDonald's.

Beyond these direct monetary factors, there is another concern for the franchisee. The franchisee sacrifices some owner discretion as a result of the franchise relationship. The franchisor designates the products that will be carried, how items will be arranged or prepared, and how promotions will be run. Much of the independent discretion that some business operators enjoy is lost. This structure and control make sense from the franchisor's perspective. Burger King, for instance, wants to assure customers that they can expect the same quality and similar experiences whether dining at a store in Maine or Montana. Without that consistency, the franchise image looses its appeal. But this means an individual franchisee cannot add a special sauce or modify the way the fries are prepared even if local customers would love it. For some businesspeople, this sacrifice of individual discretion is troubling. It is important to understand both the advantages and disadvantages of the franchising arrangement before choosing this business option.

Franchising is experiencing continued growth both domestically and throughout the world. But keep in mind that it is only one of many kinds of business arrangements. An important issue is which kind of business situation appeals to you. Would you like to own your own business? Would you like to have a franchise? Or would you like to work for a large business with all its advantages? Read Profile 2–2 to get an idea for yourself. Which kind of career is best for you?

Should You Start Your Own Business?

There are four primary ways to enter the business world on your own. First, you can start your own business from scratch. Second, you can buy an existing business. Third, you can buy a franchise. Fourth, you can assume control of a family business. Each has its advantages and disadvantages. But should you do any of these? Or should you be content to work for someone else, perhaps in a large corporation?

You might want to own your own business for a number of reasons. The lifestyle is usually rewarding. You can structure the business however you like and operate it just as you want to (within the constraints of the community and the demand for your product or service). If you want the business to grow, you can make it grow. If you want it to stay small, you can do that too. Owning your own business offers you independence from the corporate world. In fact, virtually all studies of entrepreneurs show that a need for independence is one of the top two or three reasons for starting a business. Of course, owning your own business offers the opportunity to realize substantial profits if the business does well.

On the other hand, there are reasons why you may not want to start your own venture. One is the number of hours worked. Sometimes people quit a job to start a business, only to find that they are spending 80 hours a week operating the business. One owner reported that he often worked 100 hours per week in his firm, which recently went public. That works out to about 14 hours a day, seven days a week. An avid reader quit her job to open a bookstore, only to find she had less time to read than before. Second, entrepreneurs risk their own capital to start a business. If the business should happen to fail, they may lose their entire investment and even their savings. Third, being in charge of everything in the business can be very stressful. Some owners have difficulty juggling many balls at one time.

Clearly, owning a business is not for everyone. Research shows the following characteristics are typical among entrepreneurs.

1. They like freedom and independence.
2. They like challenges and like to see the evidence of what they have accomplished.

C.J. Harms worked for Vitesse Cycle shop for several years before he and his wife, Theresa, purchased the business and moved it to a better location. What are advantages of buying an established business rather than starting one from scratch? What are the disadvantages?

3. They are willing to take moderate risks.
4. They are optimistic.
5. They are able to tolerate uncertainty.

So having read this, what do you think? Are you willing to take the plunge into entrepreneurship? Do you have what it takes to be successful?

Not-for-Profit Organizations

In Chapter 1, we said the driving force of a business is to make a profit for its owners. We also noted that some organizations do not operate to make a profit, so they cannot, technically, be considered businesses. If an organization does not seek to make profits, what does it do and why does it exist? A **not-for-profit (or nonprofit) organization** exists to provide value to some set of constituents. Generally, nonprofits do this by providing a set of services. We encounter nonprofit organizations daily. Public schools, most colleges and universities, government agencies, social and human service organizations, some hospitals, religious organizations, and community theater and symphony groups are all nonprofit organizations.

Even though they are not driven by profits, nonprofits are extremely concerned with funds and money. They must rent or buy facilities, pay utilities, hire people, pay salaries, carry out valued programs, activities, or events, and pay a range of expenses in the process. Accordingly, they must find ways to generate enough revenue to allow them to cover expenses while meeting the needs of their constituents. Nonprofits generate revenues in a variety of ways. In some cases, constituents pay directly for all (or part) of the services they receive. You do this when you pay to skate at your community's park district skating rink or when you pay tuition to take classes at your college or university. In some cases, constituents pay indirectly for the services they receive. This is the case with public schools; every taxpayer contributes funds that are used to support the school's educational programs. Some nonprofits rely mainly on contributions and donations. This is the case with charities like the United Way and religious organizations. Other nonprofits rely on membership fees or ticket sales for at least part of their revenues. This is probably the case with your community symphony orchestra. In many cases, not-for-profit organizations rely on more than one type of revenue-generating activity. As you can see, money, *cash flow*, and careful *financial management* are critical to the very existence of nonprofits. In fact, most nonprofits of any size have full-time employees whose job is to figure out how to raise and distribute money for the organization.

Nonprofits have unique features that distinguish them from businesses. Their approach to getting funds is one. Another is their reliance on volunteers. Typically, a nonprofit organization has a number of unpaid workers who contribute their time and talents to the organization. Many nonprofits could not operate without these volunteers. This dependence on volunteers can make management of the nonprofit difficult. Finally, unlike businesses, nonprofits are exempt from paying income taxes.

Just as a business must understand its customers, a not-for-profit must seek to understand its constituents and their needs. One complication of operating a nonprofit is that there are usually many constituents, often with conflicting needs. Let's consider a nonprofit most of you know, public schools. They operate to provide a solid educational foundation for the young people within a community. To accomplish this goal, they receive funds from the government. Every taxpayer contributes to the school system. Who are the relevant constituents? The students, of course. But what about the

Not-for-profit organization
An organization that provides benefits to a set of constituents.

revenue p. 17>

The Ronald McDonald House is an example of a charitable not-for-profit organization. This particualr nonprofit organization has the support of a major corporation for much of its funding. Others depend on individual and group contributions as well as grants from companies, foundations, and the government. How has the role of nonprofit organizations changed over the past several years?

How do you convince a child with cancer to keep her chin up?

You do it with love, kindness and a safe haven for her to rest her head.

For 21 years, the Philadelphia Ronald McDonald House has been a home-away-from-home for families and their seriously ill children who are being treated at area hospitals.

What makes the Philadelphia Ronald McDonald House special is its caring environment where families can share experiences, find comfort among

each other and gain strength during the most difficult time in their lives.

And now with the addition of the new 24-bedroom US Healthcare Center at the Philadelphia Ronald McDonald House, 1,000 more children and their families will find a place to stay each year.

We appreciate your ongoing support as we open our House and our hearts to even more families from around the world.

Philadelphia • The First Ronald McDonald House
3921-3925 Chestnut Street, Philadelphia, PA 19104

parents, the taxpayers, the community, even society in general? If funds are to continue to flow to the school system, the needs of all these constituents must be balanced somehow.

This section has provided a brief introduction to not-for-profit organizations. Throughout the book we will refer to nonprofits and use them as examples. It is important that we do so, because nonprofits employ millions of people. Some of you reading this text will work for nonprofit organizations. Many of you will do volunteer work, and some of you will even provide leadership and managerial insights. Your business knowledge and background will be quite relevant.

Ties to Indicators of Business Success

In Chapter 1, we emphasized the indicators of business success. These indicators apply to all businesses, whether large, small, or franchised. Understanding customers, emphasizing quality, engaging in innovative behaviors, encouraging employee commitment, and achieving financial performance may be approached with different levels of sophistication in different sizes of business. However, the themes are important for businesses of any size.

financial performance p. 481>

The indicators of business success also apply to nonprofit organizations. In fact, such organizations are increasingly being encouraged to think in a business-oriented manner. Even when the nonprofit's financial goal is simply to operate within its existing budget, it must make many of the same operating decisions other businesses face. Concerns such as cost containment and operating efficiency are as relevant for nonprofits as they are for businesses. In fact, most of the ideas presented in this book apply to nonprofits as well as businesses.

budget p. 402> efficiency p. 478>

Developing Your Critical Thinking Skills

1. Think about your first job after you graduate from college. Would you rather work in a large business or a small business? What advantages do you see to your choice?

2. How can a small business compete with a large business in the same industry?

3. If you were going into the restaurant business, would it be wiser to start your own business or purchase a franchise? What do you see as the advantages and disadvantages of each option?

4. Look at the characteristics of entrepreneurs in Profile 2–2. Would you make a good entrepreneur?

Many small companies, such as this shoe repair shop, are sole proprietorships. Remember that the key to the form of business is not the number of employees, but rather the number of owners. A sole proprietorship has only one owner. What are the advantages of this form of ownership? What are the disadvantages?

Forms of Business Ownership

Every business is owned by someone and exists in one of a very few forms. There are three traditional forms of ownership and a few more specialized forms which are beyond the scope of this book. The three traditional forms are the sole proprietorship, the partnership, and the corporation. In addition, a new form of business, the limited liability company, is now becoming popular.

Sole Proprietorships

Sole proprietorship
A business that is owned by one person.

A **sole proprietorship** is a business that is totally owned by a single person. This is the most common form of business ownership. In the United States, nearly 70 percent of all businesses are sole proprietorships. One person owns not only the business but all the assets of the business. We encounter sole proprietorships daily. When the plumbing stops working in your house, you turn to the Yellow Pages and call Sam's Plumbing Service. Sam arrives later in the day. His truck is brightly painted with a giant plunger on the side. Sam enters your house with a rack full of special plumbing tools and equipment. Within an hour he has the problem remedied and you have his bill. As a sole proprietor, Sam owns his truck, tools, and equipment. His goal is to earn enough to cover the cost of these and other expenses and still make a profit.

Sole proprietorships do not have to be run by one person working alone. Instead of Sam's Plumbing, you might have called Royal Plumbing. Royal Plumbing is also a sole proprietorship, owned by Mike Royal. Mike has been in business for 15 years and has a much larger customer base than Sam's Plumbing. He provides 24-hour emergency service and has a staff of 20 plumbers. He has commercial contracts with a number of organizations in the community. He has a manager in charge of residential plumbing and a manager for commercial accounts. As long as Mike is the sole owner, the business is still a sole proprietorship, even though he employs 20 people and generates considerable revenue.

Let's look more closely at this form of ownership. Why is it so prevalent and what are the advantages and risks to this approach? The advantages help explain why this form is so popular. First, a sole proprietorship is easy to start. It requires little effort beyond getting locally required licensing and permits where you operate and reporting profits or losses on the owner's IRS 1040 form. Second, and quite significant, the owner receives all the profits of the business and does not have to share them with anyone else. The third advantage is a bit more involved. We call it *owner discretion*. Owners of sole proprietorships have complete control and discretion to do what they want. If Sam wants to take off on Mondays, he can. He calls the shots and makes the decisions. Many people like the freedom and independence this brings.

However, there are some risks and limitations involved with sole proprietorships. First, the owner is liable for the debts of the business. If the firm closes while it owes money or if it is sued, creditors can file a claim against the owner's personal assets. That means they can go after Sam's truck, his home, and even his personal savings. This, clearly, is the major risk to the sole proprietor.

Second, sole proprietorships are limited in the sources they can turn to for funds needed to run or expand the business. The owner has personal savings, perhaps gifts or loans from family and friends, and loans from lending institutions. That is a fairly limited source of funds. If the business is new and very small, lenders (banks) may be

TABLE 2–3　　Advantages and Disadvantages of Sole Proprietorships

Advantages	Disadvantages
It's easy to form	Owner is liable for debts
Owner has discretion	Funds are limited
Owner controls profits	Business ceases when owner dies

quite reluctant to extend much credit. Often the business is constrained by such a shortage of funds.

The final disadvantage is the lack of business continuity. When the owner dies, the business ceases to exist. These advantages and risks are highlighted in Table 2–3.

Partnerships

Partnership
A business owned by two or more individuals.

A **partnership** is a business owned by two or more individuals. Although less prevalent than sole proprietorships, partnerships do comprise about 10 percent of the businesses in the United States. The most common form of partnership occurs when family members or friends decide they want to pool their resources and start a business. The partnership may be formed because the partners have unique talents to offer, because the business venture needs more financing than one person can put together, or simply because two or more people want to work together. The financial motive is illustrated by the following example.

You're sitting in your dorm room one night when Dana, your neighbor across the hall, runs into your room full of excitement. Dana has a friend who can get a shipment of 100 sweatshirts at a rock-bottom price. Dana wants to emblazon the sweatshirts with a catchy slogan promoting the upcoming homecoming dance and sell them on campus. She says the cost of purchasing the sweatshirts and having them imprinted will be about $800. The sweatshirts can be sold for $15 each or $1,500 total. Accordingly, there is a $700 profit to be made for very little work. The problem, of course, is coming up with the initial $800. Dana knows that students have little extra money but wants to offer you a deal. She will invest $300 and is seeking five friends—including you—to invest $100 each. Each person will own part of the business and, of course, share in the windfall profits that are sure to come. Here, Dana is proposing a partnership with six partners.

Working partners
Business partners who play a role in day-to-day operations.

Although there are a number of distinctions that can be made regarding partnerships, there are basically two ways in which a partnership may function. First, each partner may play a role in the day-to-day operations of the business. Such partners are known as **working partners.** Second, some partners may work in the business while others do not. Partners who are not involved in the day-to-day operations of the business are known as **silent partners**. Typically, the silent partner contributes money to the business but does not want to get involved in its ongoing operations. In fact, that is exactly Dana's plan. She will do all the purchasing, printing, advertising, and selling of the sweatshirts. You need only contribute money and do nothing more. Dana is a working partner; you and the four other investors are silent partners.

Silent partners
Business partners who typically contribute money instead of being involved in day-to-day operations.

Partnership agreement
A document that prescribes the responsibilities and privileges of each business partner.

It is very important for the partners to establish a partnership agreement at the inception of the business. The **partnership agreement** is a document that prescribes the responsibilities and privileges of each partner. The agreement can be quite complex, but it should specify at least three things. First, the agreement should state the percentage of ownership of each partner. Second, it should state how the profits (and losses) will be divided. Often, profits are distributed based on percentage of ownership. However, this need not be the case. For example, Dana has contributed 37.5 percent of the funds for the sweatshirt business and thus has a 37.5 percent ownership share. However, because she is the working partner, she expects to get half of the profits, with the remaining 50 percent shared among the five silent partners. Such an arrangement may well be fair, but it should not be assumed. These expectations should be spelled out in the partnership agreement. Third, the agreement should state how the partnership can be dissolved. It should specify how partners can *buy out* other partners. More will be said about this provision shortly. The advantages and drawbacks to the partnership form of business are noted in Table 2–4. A major advantage is that it is relatively easy to form a partnership. A second advantage is the partners' claim to profits. As with a sole proprietorship, the partners claim all of the firm's profits and report them on their respective IRS 1040s in proportion to their ownership share. A third advantage is the range of backgrounds and skills the working partners bring to running the business. The fourth and probably most significant advantage of the partnership comes from the additional financing it makes available. Each partner brings their own monetary reserves to the business, and the presence of additional owners usually increases the business's capacity to borrow funds if needed.

Among the drawbacks to this form of ownership is financial liability. As with the sole proprietorship, creditors can file claims against the owners' personal assets. In fact, each partner is personally liable for the business's debts. A second disadvantage is that any partner can legally commit the entire business without other partners' consent. Third, if any partner dies, the business ceases to exist.

The fourth and final disadvantage is interpersonal conflicts that may arise between partners. A business between friends or family members that sounds great in the beginning may become quite contentious and strained as it struggles through the daily stresses of business life. These situations can get so difficult that work ceases to be enjoyable. This is why it is important to have buyout provisions written into the partnership agreement. Generally, if extensive conflict arises in the relationship, the partners need a way to dissolve their association and still keep the business intact.

TABLE 2–4   Advantages and Disadvantages of Partnerships

Advantages	Disadvantages
It's easy to form	Partners have financial liability
Partners have claim to profits	Partner's actions commit other partners
Additional talents help in running the business	Dissolves upon death of one partner
More sources of financing are available	Interpersonal conflicts between partners may arise

Some corporations, such as UPS, are publicly held. Others may be owned by only a few individuals. What are the advantages of being a publicly held corporation? Are there disadvantages?

Corporations

Corporation
A separate business entity owned by stockholders.

A **corporation** is a separate business entity owned by stockholders. Corporations make up almost 20 percent of all businesses. A corporation differs in a number of ways from both a sole proprietorship and a partnership. There are a number of advantages to forming a corporation. First, the corporation has an indefinite life. If one of the stockholders dies, the business continues. Second, and perhaps most important, there

TABLE 2–5   Advantages and Disadvantages of Corporations

Advantages	Disadvantages
Indefinite life	Double taxation
Limited liability	Laws and regulations
Ease of raising capital	

Limited liability
Business owners are liable for the firm's debts only to the extent of their investment in the business.

stock p. 216>

is **limited liability,** meaning owners are liable for the firm's debts only to the extent of their investment in the business. Therefore, their personal assets are protected. A third advantage is the ease of obtaining additional capital. If more money is needed to run the business, shares of stock can be sold to new investors. This is better than having individuals buy the company's assets, as in the case of sole proprietorships and partnerships.

There are also some disadvantages to the corporate form of ownership. The first deals with taxes. The earnings of the business itself are taxed. Then if those earnings—in the form of dividends—are paid to the stockholders, those dividends are taxed again as the stockholders' income. This is commonly referred to as double taxation. A second disadvantage is that the corporation is subject to more laws and regulations than either the sole proprietorship or partnership. The advantages and disadvantages of the corporate form are shown in Table 2–5.

Virtually all large companies are corporations. This allows them to be *publicly held* if desired, so they can have thousands of stockholders. This, of course, is important for growth. Consider the case of Southwest Airlines. When Southwest was formed, Herb Kelleher decided on the corporate form of ownership because he knew he would have to raise a lot of money to buy and maintain costly aircraft.

In many cases, the advantages of the corporation make it a desirable form of ownership. This is particularly true for those who choose the subchapter *S (sub s) corporation*, a variation on the corporate form of ownership allowed by the IRS that can be taxed as a partnership. The sub S corporation has the protection offered to a corporation without the double taxation, which makes it a very desirable form of ownership.

Limited Liability Company

LLC
A form of ownership that combines the advantages of partnerships and corporations without the limitations imposed by subchapter S.

A **limited liability company (LLC)** is a new form of ownership that combines the advantages of partnerships with the advantages of corporations without the limitations imposed by the subchapter S designation. There are many advantages that are making this an increasingly popular form of ownership. First, there are tax advantages. Since the limited liability company is a company, not a corporation, it is taxed as a partnership. Second, it receives the liability protection accorded corporations. The third advantage is the number and types of owners it can have. For example, a sub S corporation can have only 35 stockholders, but an LLC can have unlimited numbers of "members." Further, in the sub S corporation, the stockholders must be individuals, but the members of an LLC can be other companies or corporations. This is important because it gives the company much more flexibility. Having an unlimited number of owners makes it easier to raise capital.

TABLE 2–6   Advantages and Disadvantages of Limited Liability Companies

Advantages	Disadvantage
Taxed as partnership	Laws and regulations
Enjoys liability protection	
May have unlimited numbers and types of owners	

The tax provisions are a key to LLCs for both small and large companies. This is because a limited liability company's profits or losses can be reported on the owners' tax forms. Unlike a partnership, the owners may be either individuals or other companies. The LLC itself does not pay income taxes. If the owners are individuals, then the impact is shown on their personal taxes just as it would be in a partnership. If the owners are other companies, then the LLC's earnings or losses are reflected on their company tax forms. This is particularly important when the LLC may initially have significant losses.

There is only one major disadvantage of limited liability companies: the laws and regulations that must be followed in qualifying for and forming the LLC. The same type of registration is required for LLCs as for corporations. The limited liability corporation has now been approved by almost all states. Its advantages and the disadvantage are shown in Table 2–6.

An excellent example is Iridium LLC, recently formed by Motorola and several other investing corporations. Iridium is featured in Profile 2–3. Note the explanation of why Iridium was changed from a regular corporation to an LLC.

PROFILE 2–3   *Iridium: A Far-out LLC*

teams p. 71>

The Iridium system is a satellite-based, wireless personal communications network designed to permit any type of telephone transmission—voice, data, fax, paging—to reach its destination anywhere on earth, at any time. It will revolutionize communications for business professionals, travelers, residents of rural or undeveloped areas, disaster relief teams, and other users who need the features and convenience of a wireless handheld phone with a single number for use worldwide. The system is being financed by a private international consortium of telecommunications and industrial companies and will be operational in 1998. Motorola is the prime contractor.

Unlike conventional telecommunications networks, the satellite-based system will track the location of the telephone handset, providing global transmission even if the subscriber's location is unknown. An interconnected constellation of 66 Iridium satellites orbiting just above the earth will connect with ground-based gateways, allowing Iridium telephones to communicate with virtually any other telephone in the world.

Launching a system as complex as Iridium is extremely expensive and requires the input of many major companies worldwide. Iridium, Inc. was first formed as a corporation. Investors included North American-based companies

Iridium, LLC, a consortium of several large companies including Motorola is putting 66 satellites in low-earth orbits in order to offer world-wide cellular communications beginning in 1998. Why is an LLC a good choice for this kind of venture?

such as Motorola, Sprint Corp., Raytheon, Lockheed-Martin Corp., and Iridium Canada, as well as worldwide companies such as China Great Wall Industry Corp., Pacific Electric Wire and Cable Co. Ltd. of Taiwan, Korea Mobile Telecom, Nippon Iridium Corp., Thai Satellite Telecommunications Ltd., Iridium Africa Corp., and Iridium Middle East Corp.

To serve global investors better, Iridium, Inc., recently converted to a limited liability company, Iridium LLC. The most likely reason for the change to an LLC is that the Iridium system will not become commercial until at least 1998, but major investments and expenses are being incurred now. The short-term losses can be used by the investing companies to reduce their overall tax burden.

Developing Your Critical Thinking Skills

1. How would your decision regarding the form of ownership differ if you were starting a T-shirt business as opposed to a restaurant? Would liability be an issue?

2. Why are there fewer partnerships than there are corporations and sole proprietorships?

3. Some problems of sole proprietorships relate to the fact that there is only one owner. Some people argue that this can lead to a shortage of management talent. What types of problems might occur if there is a shortage of management talent?

Who Owns Businesses?

The preceding section discussed different types or forms of business ownership. In this section, we discuss who actually *owns* businesses. Some of the owners are obvious: only a single individual can own a sole proprietorship, and only two or more individuals can own a partnership. You may be surprised, however, at the different kinds of business owners that are possible.

There are at least five primary possibilities regarding the ownership of a business: single owners, partners, stockholders, employees, and other businesses. Keep in mind that our interest here is not on the forms of ownership but on *who* the owners are.

Stockholder
Any person who owns at least one share of stock in a corporation.

We mentioned earlier that one individual owns a sole proprietorship. Two or more individuals may own a partnership. However, the issue of who owns businesses becomes more complex when we consider corporations. In order to understand this better, let's look more closely at the concept of stockholders. A **stockholder** is any person who owns at least one share in a corporation. Corporations can have any number of stockholders, from one to perhaps millions. In some cases, a single person may own all the stock of a company even if the business is relatively large. This is the case with L. R. Nelson, discussed in Profile 2–4.

PROFILE 2–4

A Growth Spurt for L. R. Nelson

L. R. Nelson Corp. is wholly owned by David Ransburg. Ransburg earned an undergraduate degree in engineering at Purdue University and an MBA at Harvard. He then searched for a company to purchase. The one he found was L. R. Nelson Corp., a family business that had sold lawn sprinklers and related equipment for decades. The primary owner had died and the heirs chose to sell the company.

Ransburg bought L. R. Nelson and immediately began updating the company, which was still selling the original product that it had been selling for 40 years. He led the company to develop many new products and changed the primary material from metal to high-impact plastic. He substantially increased marketing and distribution, including selling to Wal-Mart (which sells the products under its own label). Even though the company has grown significantly over the past several years, Ransburg still owns all of the stock. L. R. Nelson is a corporation with all the stock held by one individual.

Privately held
A business that has a few stockholders and the stock is not open for public sale.

In some cases, a small number of stockholders may own all shares of the corporation and not wish to sell shares to anyone else. This is often the case in midsize businesses, where three or four family members may own all the stock and have no intention of extending stock ownership outside the family. This can also be the case when a handful of investors own a business and are quite comfortable with the arrangement. When there are only a few stockholders and the stock is not open for sale to the public, the company is known as a **privately held corporation.**

Publicly held
A business with stock that is open for public sale.

By contrast, there are many corporations with stock that is open for sale to the public. Such businesses are known as **publicly held corporations.** Publicly held companies, such as General Motors or Exxon, may have millions of stockholders. Each stockholder buys one or more shares in the company.

Employee stock ownership plan (ESOP)
An arrangement in which employees buy ownership in the company.

In recent years, a number of companies have moved toward employee ownership. Companies may become owned by their employees through an **employee stock ownership plan,** commonly known as an **ESOP.** An ESOP is an arrangement in which employees buy ownership in the company. For some companies, an ESOP takes the place of a pension plan or retirement plan. Instead of putting their money into a retirement account, the workers invest in their own company. This can be a powerful motivating device, since the employees know that their own performance can affect their future benefits. When employees retire, they can sell their shares either on the stock market if the company is publicly held or back to the company if it is privately held.

Three airlines became employee-owned in the 1990s. Northwest, TWA, and United are all partially owned by their employees. Profile 2–5 describes the experience of United Airlines.

PROFILE 2–5

The Employee–Owners of United Airlines

A banner above the ticket counter of United Airlines has the familiar "Fly the friendly skies of United," but "the" is crossed out and "our" written in. "Fly our friendly skies." This symbolizes the move to an employee-owned airline in July 1994. United Airlines, the world's largest airline, thus became one of the world's largest employee-owned companies. The results have been dramatic.

In 1994, United's workers (except flight attendants) took a 12 percent pay cut in exchange for 55 percent ownership in the airline and three of the 12 seats on its board of directors. The impact has certainly been felt at the board level, although the nature of the impact was not what people expected. The new employee–directors clearly have the airline at heart. But more importantly, the employees throughout the airline have changed their attitudes. Now it is their airline, and they work together to make sure it prospers.

Examples of the benefits of the new partnership abound. Teams saved the company $20 million a year by solving the problem of the expense of jet fuel wasted while planes idle at the airport dock. The solution: get longer ladders so the planes can be plugged into electricity. A shortage of pilots could have forced the airline to cancel some routes, but the owner–pilots agreed to fly a few more hours a week. The productivity of the airline's 83,000 workers increased, while the number of grievances plummeted. The price of United's stock more than doubled, leading to a 4-for-1 stock split in April 1996. A machinist union leader says some of his members can tell you the volume the airline does each day—unheard of before. Unionized ramp workers, making $38 an hour, recommended bringing in temporary workers at $7 an hour to unload skis during the winter in Salt Lake City. When the opportunity arose to buy USAir in 1996, CEO Gerald Greenwald consulted the union, which convinced him it was a bad idea. The increased productivity has allowed United to expand both its routes and its staff while outperforming rivals American and Delta.

SOURCE: Aaron Bernstein, "United We Own," *Business Week.* March 18, 1996, pp.96–102.

board of directors
p. 64>

A final category of ownership occurs when one business owns another business. For example, Time Warner, Inc., owns Warner Brothers, *Fortune* magazine, Six

Subsidiary
Any business that is
wholly or partially
owned by a parent com-
pany.

Parent company
Any company that owns
one or more subsidiaries.

Flags Entertainment, and Turner Broadcasting. These businesses are called subsidiaries, and Time Warner is called the parent company. A **subsidiary** is any business that is wholly or partially owned by a parent company. Conversely, a **parent
company** is any company that owns one or more subsidiaries. The parent company
provides capital to the subsidiaries just as stockholders would if the subsidiary were
publicly held.

The parent company may allow the subsidiary to function relatively independently, or the parent's managers may control the subsidiary very closely. Some
subsidiaries are wholly owned by another company. Others are only partially
owned by a parent company and partially publicly owned. Profile 2–6 illustrates
this.

PROFILE 2–6   *Ford and Mazda: Ford in the Driver's Seat*

production p. 464>

Ford Motor Co. is the largest producer of trucks in the world and the second
largest producer of cars and trucks combined. It has manufacturing plants in 34
countries and employed 337,800 workers in 1994. It has 87 plants in North
America and 41 in Europe. In 1995, Ford sold three of the eight best-selling cars
in Europe and five of the top 10 in the United States.

It is not uncommon anymore for car companies to own parts of other car
companies. One such example is Ford's increasing ownership of Mazda, Japan's
fifth-largest car manufacturer. For 16 years, Ford owned a 25 percent minority
share of Mazda of Japan. In fact, the two share production of Ford Probes and
Mazda models. Recently, however, Mazda has not performed well, especially
when compared with other Japanese firms such as Nissan, Honda, and Toyota. It
lost $732 million in two years and laid off 4,000 workers in three years, including
300 in its U.S. operations.

In April 1996, Ford increased its ownership of Mazda to 33.4 percent for
$480 million and took over its subsidiary's management. The move gave Ford
better access to Japanese auto markets as well as to considerable technical and
competitive information about Mazda that it could not get before. The move also
benefits Mazda, which had been so strapped for cash that it could not mount effective advertising campaigns or bring out new vehicles.

SOURCES: Lorraine Woellert, "Ford Boosts Stake, Takes Over Mazda; Move Opens Door to Sales in
Japan," *Washington Times*, April 13, 1996; Keith Naughton and Edith Hill Updike, "Why Ford Didn't
Junk Mazda," *Business Week*, April 29, 1997.

As you can see, many businesses are owned by other companies. In fact, most of
the Fortune 500 firms own other companies. For example, Keebler is owned by
Nabisco, which is part of RJR Nabisco.

In summary, a company may be owned by a single person, by two or more partners, by any number of stockholders, by employees, or by another company. Although
the general public seldom knows who the actual owner of a business is, it is important
for you to see these ownership distinctions. Ownership affects business control and ultimate decision making.

Developing Your Critical Thinking Skills

1. What is the significance of *who* owns a business compared with the *forms* of business ownership?

2. How would business decisions differ for a corporation owned by one major stockholder compared with one owned by thousands of stockholders?

3. What do you think are some of the benefits of an employee stock ownership plan?

SUMMARY

1. One way to appreciate the scope of business in American society is to look at the statistics about business.

   ■ What is the magnitude of business in our society?

   There are over 21 million businesses in the United States. This includes approximately 9 million people who report business income even though the business is not their primary occupation. It also includes 7 million businesses in which the owner is the sole employee. Of the remaining 5 million businesses, over 4.5 million have fewer than 20 employees.

2. A striking feature of the American economy is the coexistence of very large and very small businesses.

   ■ What is the difference between large and small businesses?

   The U.S. Small Business Administration defines a small business as any business that is independently owned and operated, is not dominant in its field, and meets size standards that vary depending on industry.

   ■ What are the impacts of large and small businesses?

   The impact of large businesses comes from their size. They employ many people and contribute greatly to the economic productivity of the country. In some communities, a single dominant large business may affect the quality of life.

   Small businesses affect the economy in four ways: (1) When all small businesses are taken together, they account for a large share of the American economy. (2) Over half the American workforce is employed by small business. (3) Many new products are created in small businesses. (4) Small businesses serve special market niches that larger firms ignore.

3. One interesting method of combining the advantages of large businesses and small businesses is franchising. In the last 40 years, franchising has virtually exploded and created a host of familiar names such as McDonald's, Pizza Hut, and Budget Car Rental.

   ■ How would you define franchising?

   A franchise exists when a business that owns a service or trademarked product grants the exclusive rights to another business or individual to use the franchise name and sell its products and services within a given location.

■ What are the advantages and disadvantages of franchising?

Advantages are that the franchisee gains (1) the advantage of a proven business reputation, (2) managerial assistance, and (3) the rights to an exclusive territory. Disadvantages are (1) the payment of a franchise fee and other costs and (2) the sacrifice of some owner discretion.

4. Society recognizes that there are some needed services that neither government nor business can appropriately supply. In these cases, society counts on volunteers and on not-for-profit organizations.

■ What is a not-for-profit organization?

Some organizations do not operate to make a profit, so they are not technically considered businesses. These not-for-profit organizations exist to provide services to some set of constituents. Even though they are not driven by profits, they are extremely concerned with attracting money to make their operations possible.

Nonprofits have three unique features that distinguish them from businesses: (1) their approach to fund-raising, (2) their use of unpaid volunteer workers, and (3) the fact that they are exempt from paying income taxes.

■ What is the impact of not-for-profit organizations?

We encounter nonprofits daily. Most schools, social and human service agencies, religious organizations, and artistic agencies operate on a nonprofit basis, as do some health care organizations. Thus, nonprofits make a valuable contribution to the quality of life of a community.

5. Although all businesses have owners, the legal form in which ownership is held can vary.

■ What are the basic forms of business ownership?

The three traditional forms of ownership are the sole proprietorship, the partnership, and the corporation. A relatively new form of ownership is the limited liability company.

6. The study of business ownership may involve more than merely examining the legal forms of ownership. When a corporation is involved, the issue of ownership becomes more complex.

■ Who owns the business?

There are five basic possibilities: (1) A company can be owned by a single person. (2) A partnership is owned by two or more individuals. (3) A corporation is owned by stockholders, who may number from one to millions. A privately held corporation has a small number of stockholders and the stock is not open for sale to the public. A publicly held corporation has a large number of stockholders and the stock is open for sale to the public. (4) In an employee-owned corporation, the majority of the stock is owned by employees. These are usually called employee stock ownership plans (ESOPs). (5) A business may be owned by another business.

Links to future courses

You will learn more about the themes in this chapter in the following business courses.

- Principles of management
- Small business management
- Entrepreneurship
- Legal environment of business
- Business law

EXERCISES AND APPLICATIONS

1. Consider the following resolutions for debate. Choose the resolution you support and prepare your arguments for debate.

   - Large businesses are more important to society than small businesses.
   - Small businesses are more important to society than large businesses.

2. Team with four other people who choose to support the same resolution as you. Discuss your arguments and arrive at a consensus of five key arguments.

3. Suppose you are one of three owners of a partnership. What might convince you to change the form of the business to a corporation?

4. Interview the executive director of a not-for-profit organization in your community. What challenges does that person face? How are these similar or different from what a business manager experiences?

5. Think about your career options. Would you prefer to work for a large business, a small business, or a nonprofit organization? Explain why.

6. Search the Internet for one of the following companies. Determine what its subsidiaries are.

   - General Motors
   - General Electric
   - PepsiCo
   - RJR Nabisco
   - Disney

KEY TERMS

Capital intensive, p. 35
Corporation, p. 49
Diversified business, p. 36
Employee stock ownership plan (ESOP), p. 54
Franchise, p. 40
Franchisee, p. 40
Franchisor, p. 40
Labor intensive, p. 35
Limited liability, p. 50
Limited liability company (LLC), p. 50
Mergers and acquisitions, p. 36

Not-for-profit organization, p. 43
Parent company, p. 55
Partnership, p. 47
Partnership agreement, p. 47
Privately held, p. 53
Publicly held, p. 53
Silent partners, p. 47
Small business, p. 34
Sole proprietorship, p. 46
Stockholder, p. 53
Subsidiary, p. 55
Working partners, p. 47

CASE: THE MARVING COLLINS STORY

continuous
improvement p. 448>
mission p. 310 >

One of the most inspiring human interest stories of the past few decades is that of a Chicago schoolteacher who singlehandedly showed the world how to provide a quality education to minority children living in low-income neighborhoods. The teacher's name is Marva Collins. Her secret was to focus on each individual student's talents and needs, to set high but achievable standards, to expect continuous improvement, and constantly to remind the students that their mission was to learn well enough to become successful, employable adults.

Collins developed her teaching practices while teaching grade school in the Chicago public school system. She found herself continually frustrated by administrative obstacles. The Chicago public school system was a not-for-profit organization, but it was a big not-for-profit and that meant that rules and regulations often made it difficult for good teachers to do good work.

After 14 years of this kind of frustration, Marva Collins decided that the only way to provide the quality of education she dreamed of was to start her own private school. In the fall of 1975, she opened Westside Preparatory School in a poverty-stricken area of Chicago. She used $5,000 from her pension fund to cover the costs of getting started and relied on volunteer help from her family and friends to construct classroom space on the second floor of her home. She planned to use tuition plus some volunteer help to cover the costs of operating her school. That was, to say the least, rather risky since her school was designed to serve low-income, minority children. The cost barrier was apparent in the beginning. Her first class had only eight students.

Enrollment expanded, however, and the school became an inspiring success because Marva Collins had found an important niche and filled it well. As she put it, "What were we doing at Westside Prep? Armed with a rigorous curriculum, nonstop personal caring, and a firm belief in the dignity and self-worth of each and every child, we were out to prove the naysayers wrong, that our children could succeed in school. Behind our walls, troubled children learned to read and reason, courtesy of Shakespeare, Plato, and Emily Dickinson. Children formerly labeled learning disabled went on to graduate magna cum laude from first-rate universities."

Within a few years, Marva Collins was running not only Westside Prep but also two Marva Collins Preparatory Schools (one in Chicago and one in Cincinnati). Over 13,000 students had graduated from her schools. She had been presented as a role model in the media nationwide, and a made-for-TV movie had showcased her success. In addition to teaching and running the schools, Collins gave lectures throughout the country. Her schools were funded through student tuition and the money she earned from lecturing. No federal funds or corporate grants were accepted.

Decision Questions

1. Marva Collins's success caused some private businesspeople to approach her with a proposal to set up a nationwide system of for-profit franchised Marva

Collins schools. She would probably have become quite wealthy from such a franchise operation, yet she turned down the offer. Why do you suppose she did so? If she had agreed to a franchise business, do you think she would have been successful?

2. Even though Marva Collins was running a not-for-profit organization, her success illustrates some of the principles of success in the for-profit sector. Can you identify those principles? (You may want to look back at Chapter 1 and the Prologue for some hints.) What aspects of the successful for-profit business model do not apply to the Marva Collins story?

vision p. 310>

3. Marva Collins had a vision of a better way to provide education. What ideas do you have? Do any of your ideas draw on principles that apply to successful businesses?

SOURCES: Marva Collins and Civia Tamarkin, *Marva Collins' Way* (Boston: Houghton Mifflin Co., 1982); Marva Collins, *Values* (Los Angeles: Dove Books, 1996).

REFERENCES

1. Gary Fallesen, "Women's Point of View." http://www.rochesterdandc.com/rec/biking/rb7087a.html, accessed 5/28/1997.

2. U.S. Census Bureau. http://www.census.gov/ Because the Census Bureau and Internal Revenue Service have different methods of collecting data, the numbers do not add neatly. The important issue is to note the approximate numbers and realize the magnitude of small businesses in today's economy.

3. Patrick J. Spain, and James R. Talbot, eds. *Hoover's Handbook of American Companies 1996.* Austin, TX: The Reference Press, 1995 (see citations for companies listed).

4. Richard A. Melcher. "Brunswick Wades into New Waters." *Business Week*, June 2, 1997, pp. 67, 70.

5. Justin G. Longenecker, Carlos W. Moore, and J. William Petty. *Small Business Management.* Cincinnati, OH: South-Western, 1997, p. 27.

6. William J. Dennis Jr. *A Small Business Primer.* The NFIB Foundation, 1993, p. 16.

7. Jeffrey Timmons, *New Venture Creation*, 4th ed. Burr Ridge, IL: Irwin 1994, p. 5.

8. Justin G. Longenecker, Carlos W. Moore, and J. William Petty. *Small Business Management.* Cincinnati, OH: South-Western, 1997, p. 29.

9. Longenecker et al., p. 27.

10. Longenecker et al., p. 35.

11. International Franchise Association Educational Foundation. http://www.entremkt.com/ifa/21qu.htm (accessed 7/30/97). Another interesting site is http://www.franinfo.com (accessed 7/30/97).

12. Ibid.

13. Ibid.

3 Decision Makers and Decision Making

Executives at Fox Broadcasting Co. recognized the impact of the decisions they were about to make. Although Fox was the fourth-rated television network, it had its best season ever in 1996. It had carried a very successful Super Bowl and boasted hit shows such as "The X-Files," "Melrose Place," and "The Simpsons." In fact, while rival networks were losing viewers, Fox had experienced a jump in viewership over the year.

This was great news, but also cause for question. The Fox executives wondered whether they should reshuffle the lineup for the fall 1997 season. After all, they had built their network reputation on always doing new and different programming. They had even been labeled "television rabble-rousers." Yet their lineup had been successful and their programs were already distinct. The decision was complicated by rumors that rival networks—NBC, ABC, and CBS—were all planning major overhauls of their programming. These networks' actions could reverse the previous year's results. A misstep would cost Fox millions of dollars and could be disastrous for the young, aggressive network.

Fox executives had gathered as much information as possible. They had compiled endless statistics and developed sophisticated projections. Now they had to step up and make decisions that would affect the future of their business. They had to confront the excitement and challenge of business decision making. While not all decisions are as dramatic as those faced by Fox, decision making is a constant that every business and every manager faces. Incidentally, Fox decided to make very few changes in the lineup, despite the moves of its competitors. As entertainment president Peter Roth noted, "The distinctiveness of our scheduling is our stability."[1]

In the first two chapters, we introduced you to the nature and scope of contemporary business. You have already seen that businesses differ by size and even by form of ownership. Yet you recognize that all businesses (and even not-for-profit organizations) strive to meet a fairly similar set of results that are necessary for success. Making decisions to ensure success is challenging, exciting, and tough. This chapter provides an introductory glimpse into the decision-making realm of the business world. This chapter is important for you because you will learn about both the process and key people involved in business decision making. Further, as you learn more about business throughout the text, this chapter will serve as a foundation. You'll begin to see if you would really like to be in one of the key decision-making positions of a business someday.

Specifically, when you have completed this chapter, you should be able to:

1. Identify major decision makers in an organization.
2. Understand the decision responsibilities of various people within a business.
3. Analyze and explain the benefits of teams in decision making.
4. Differentiate between decision making in large and small businesses.
5. Differentiate among the types of decisions managers make.
6. Understand and apply the basic decision-making process.
7. Use the creative decision-making model to generate solutions to problems.

strategic decisions p. 77>

As we saw in the Fox example, business is about decision making. Nothing can get done in a business without someone making a decision. Decisions range from major strategic decisions such as deciding a programming strategy or buying a subsidiary or possibly even selling the business itself to very mundane decisions such as buying office supplies for a department. But the decision-making process is essentially the same, regardless of the magnitude of the decision and the location of the decision makers in the organization.

This entire book is really about decision making in business settings. It is about people making decisions, gathering information, committing resources, deciding what products or services to provide to customers, and predicting how the business will perform. Managers have to consider the many factors that affect their decisions. They have to study how their decisions will be influenced by forces beyond their control. They have to set goals, and they have to collect information before making decisions. Managers of businesses must make sure their decisions maintain or improve the health of the business.

The significance of studying decision makers and decision making is apparent when you look at the model that is the basis of this book (Figure 1–6). Note that the top block contains three words: owners, managers, and stakeholders. We discussed owners in Chapter 2 and we will discuss stakeholders in Chapter 4. The key word of that block and of the model itself is *managers*. Managers make decisions in a business. The decisions the managers make determine how the business will perform when measured against the indicators of business success. Managers monitor the environment. They determine the direction of the company, provide value to customers, acquire resources, gain the commitment of workers, and assure that technology and quality are integrated into products or services. With this in mind, we'll look at who the decision makers are and how they make decisions.

Who Are the Decision Makers in Business

In Chapter 2, we discussed who owns businesses. In considering how businesses operate, knowing who manages them may be even more important. As you will see in this chapter, the decision makers are not always the same as owners. This section discusses the various decision makers that are important in the actual management of the company. These decision makers are shown in Table 3–1.

Stockholders

We noted in Chapter 2 that stockholders are the owners of corporations. It might seem logical that stockholders would also be actively involved in the management of the firm. However, this is seldom the case, especially for large corporations. Stockholders virtually never take an active role in a company. They buy and sell their stock, and they may vote (usually by *proxy*) on major issues at the annual meeting. They also elect members of the board of directors, although this is much more of a formality than one might expect. That is about all.

Thus, the role of stockholders is very limited in large corporations unless one person or group owns a significant proportion of the stock. This allows the key stockholder to play a major role in the selection of board members. The planning and management of the corporation are the responsibility of the board of directors and top management of the firm. In smaller, privately held corporations, stockholders may

TABLE 3–1   Decision Makers and Their Involvement

Stockholders	■ May vote on major decisions ■ Generally, involvement is limited
Board of directors	■ Approves major strategic decisions ■ Oversees general direction of the business
Top management	■ Makes major strategic decisions
Middle management	■ Implements top management decisions ■ Makes decisions within area of responsibility
Professional staff	■ Makes decisions in area of expertise
First-line supervisors	■ Implement higher-level decisions ■ Make day-to-day operational decisions
Nonmanagerial employees	■ Make decisions regarding performance of their individual jobs

play a role in managing the firm, but this is because they are also key managers or family members, not because they are stockholders.

Board of Directors

Board of directors
Individuals elected by the stockholders to oversee the management of the firm.

The **board of directors** is elected by the stockholders to oversee the management of the firm. The actual role the board members play depends on the company, particularly the size of the company. In small companies, the directors may be the owners of the firm, and they may be active in day-to-day management. In larger, publicly held companies, the directors perform a strategic role of helping top managers determine the overall direction of the company. However, it is the top managers who make most key decisions.

Boards of directors often meet monthly or quarterly. The meeting may last one or two days and may consist of hearing reports of top management and then discussing and voting on recommendations for major strategic items.

There are no requirements regarding how many board members a company should have. Many large companies have eight to 15 board members. Some of these members are *inside directors*, meaning that they are also employees of the company. The remainder are *outside directors*, meaning that they are not employed by the company. Often they are active or retired executives of other large but noncompeting businesses. Typically, they are paid (and often paid quite well) for serving on the board. Profile 3–1 shows the members of the board of directors for Motorola. Note that five are inside directors and 13 are outside directors.

PROFILE 3–1   *Motorola's Top Guns*

Motorola's board of directors is typical of large companies. The inside directors are five key top managers of the firm. Recall from the introductory vignette in the prologue that the company was founded by Paul Galvin. Now both Paul's son, Robert, and his grandson, Chris, are inside directors of the company.

Look at the 13 outside directors. These individuals are chosen to give the company expertise that may help in determining Motorola's strategic direction. Note that Ann Jones, formerly of the Federal Communications Commission, is on the board. The FCC is a government agency that oversees much of the communications industry, and having a former agency representative on the board is a real benefit. Other board members come from well-known companies and have vast experience in managing large firms. Motorola also has three university administrators, which gives it some ties to new developments in both business and engineering.

Board of Directors, Motorola, Inc.

Inside Directors

Gary L. Tooker, Chairman of the Board

Christopher B. Galvin, Chief Executive Officer

Robert L. Growney, President and Chief Operating Officer

John F. Mitchell, Vice Chairman of the Board

Robert W. Galvin, Chairman of the Executive Committee of the Board

Outside Directors

David R. Clare, Retired, formerly President, Johnson & Johnson

H. Laurance Fuller, Chairman of the Board, President, and CEO, Amoco Corp.

John T. Hickey, Retired, formerly Executive Vice President and CFO, Motorola, Inc.

Anne P. Jones, Consultant, formerly member of the FCC

Donald R. Jones, Retired, formerly Executive Vice President and CFO, Motorola, Inc.

Judy C. Lewent, Senior Vice President and CFO, Merck & Co.

Walter E. Massey, President, Morehouse College

Thomas J. Murrin, Dean of Duquesne University's School of Business Administration

John E. Pepper, Jr., Chairman of the Board and Chief Executive, Procter & Gamble Co.

Samuel C. Scott III, Corporate Vice President, CPC International, Inc.

Gardiner L. Tucker, Retired, formerly Vice President for Science and Technology, International Paper Co.

B. Kenneth West, Senior Consultant for Corporate Governance to TIAA/CREF

Dr. John A. White, Dean of Engineering, Georgia Institute of Technology

Regardless of the size of the company or the size of the board, the decisions it makes are of strategic significance. These decisions will affect the direction of the firm, its culture, and its goals. These decisions will be implemented at lower levels in the firm, but their impact is significant. In fact, some critics believe that boards of directors should take a more active role in the oversight of companies.[2]

Top Management

Top management refers to the officers of a business who make major decisions for the company and are responsible for the company's performance. The number of positions depends on the size of the firm. For example, a small business may have only one person in top management—the owner, who is also typically the president. Slightly larger firms may have a president (again, often the owner) plus a few vice presidents. Corporations may have a chair of the board of directors plus a president and some vice presidents. There are other titles that you should know. At the very top of most large companies are also three critical positions: chief executive officer (CEO), chief operating officer (COO), and chief financial officer (CFO). The **chief executive officer** is responsible for the long-range, strategic direction of the company. The **chief operating officer** is responsible for its internal day-to-day workings. The **chief financial officer** is responsible for its financial health and strategy. Increasingly, large firms have a *chief information officer* (*CIO*), who is in charge of policy relating to the gathering, use, and storage of the firm's information.

These top positions are not necessarily held by three or four different people. For example, the president may also be the chief executive officer. At Harley-Davidson, Inc., Richard Teerlink held both positions. Or the chair of the board

Top management
The officers of a business who make major decisions for the company and are responsible for the company's performance.

Chief executive officer
Individual responsible for the long-range, strategic direction of the company.

Chief operating officer
Individual responsible for a company's internal day-to-day operations.

Chief financial officer
Individual responsible for the overall financial health and strategy of a company.

Richard Teerlink at one time held the titles of both President and Chief Executive Officer for Harley-Davidson. In these positions, he was responsible for both the internal operations of the company and long-range strategic planning. He was successful in turning the company around from the brink of bankruptcy to a successful and profitable company. What are the differences between CEO, COO, and CFO?

may be the chief executive officer, as Joshua Smith is at Maxima Corp. In some cases, the president is also the chief operating officer. At Mattel, Inc., Jill Barad's title is president and COO. The titles indicate differences in duties and status for the particular company.

Regardless of the particular structure of top management, the people in these positions make decisions that are of major importance to the company. Examples include underwriting major new product introductions, acquiring or selling subsidiaries, issuing stock, and helping to set the strategic direction for the firm. All these decisions may involve millions of dollars of capital and equipment.

A **vice president** is a top manager who generally has responsibility for a specific area of the company. For example, a company may have vice presidents for marketing, finance, operations, and human resources. Other companies may have vice presidents in charge of particular products or geographic areas. It is common for the vice president of finance to be the chief financial officer of the business. Figure 3–1 summarizes the top management positions.

Vice president
A top manager who is responsible for a specific area of the company.

human resources
p. 374>

Middle Managers

Decision makers with positions of vice president and higher are typically considered to be top management. Managers who work at levels from just below vice president down to just above first-line supervisors are referred to as **middle managers.** These people have direct supervisory responsibility over other managers or employees and have significant decision-making authority.

Let's think for a moment about middle managers and what they really do. Middle managers are responsible for translating broad policies and strategies into doable tasks. They receive orders from their own superiors and then must divide those orders into parts for each of their subordinates to accomplish. They also report to their man-

Middle managers
Managers who work below the vice president down to just above first-line supervisors, responsible for translating broad policies into doable tasks.

FIGURE 3–1   Top Management Positions

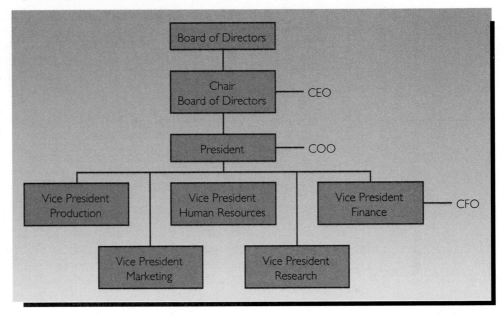

agers the results of previous actions. They discuss successes and failures and plans for the future. Profile 3–2 illustrates some of the duties of an actual middle manager in a midwestern firm.

PROFILE 3–2   *A Day in the Life of Ken Webster*

Ken Webster is a district manager with Ameritech Security Link in Minneapolis, Minnesota. The company sells a variety of security systems. A professional staff and several area managers report to Webster. The following is a day in his life before the company's recent purchase by Ameritech.

8:00 AM	Arrive at office, check my schedule and review in-basket.
8:15 AM	Review legal news. Look for bid opportunities and customers with credit problems.
8:30 AM	Review customer cancellation procedures with administrative assistant.
8:45 AM	Review purchase orders for approval.
9:00 AM	Meet with service manager. Discuss customer credits to be issued. Discuss and approve payment for services incurred by the service department. Discuss service problem with troublesome account.
9:35 AM	Discuss two customer problems with customer service rep.
9:45 AM	Document customer problems and create memos to direct problem resolution.

customer service
p. 340>

10:10 AM	Work on job cost and revenue projections.
11:00 AM	Staff meeting: Discuss inventory control, job cost control, cancellation tracking, and equipment removal procedures. Discuss staffing levels in installation and administrative departments. Discuss periodic fire alarm inspection delinquencies and corrective action. Discuss next year's vehicle requirements.
1:00 PM	Lunch
1:30 PM	Return phone call. MIS system administrator is looking for purchase approval on a few items.
1:35 PM	Return phone call. A long-term customer is upset, feels he was treated rudely by a sales rep.
1:40 PM	Return phone call. Boss wants to discuss presentation to potential investors next week.
2:20 PM	Discuss with the installation manager the addition of a management position to my staff. The new position will be in the installation department and will report to me. We will be splitting national account installation responsibilities away from the local branch structure. He is happy and relieved.
2:40 PM	Assign tasks related to next week's presentation to my administrative assistant. She will find a large van for us to rent that will accommodate the shuttle of potential investors to and from hotel and airport. We have most of the audiovisual equipment needed, and she will rent the rest. We review a proofreading step that I want her to add to the job approval process. I fill her in on the staff addition. She will prepare job posting, as I want to recruit from within.
3:20 PM	Meet with customer service rep to discuss strategy in preventing a large customer cancellation.
3:40 PM	Back to stack of paperwork that has accumulated in the in-basket: payment approvals, sales order approvals, and purchase order approvals.
3:55 PM	Receive another call from boss. He wants to discuss more details about the presentation next week.
4:05 PM	Discuss additional presentation requirements with administrative assistant. She tells me the same sales rep that the customer complained about created a problem with two members of the administrative staff who report to her.
4:10 PM	Discuss defective job paperwork with customer service rep.
4:15 PM	Meet with sales rep who caused customer and staff problems. We discuss the situation and he leaves to make the appropriate apologies.
4:30 PM	Return attention to in-basket.
5:00 PM	Return to revenue and cost projection project.
5:15 PM	Further discussion with administrative assistant concerning workload and department organization.

5:30 PM   Prepare report on May operating results for board meeting.

6:00 PM   Leave for home.

Middle managers sometimes find themselves in difficult situations, particularly in today's world. They depend heavily on those who work for them to achieve the goals that they and their superiors have set. But sometimes those goals were dictated to the middle manager because of the situation at hand—the competitive environment, the wishes of the company's top management, or pressure from outsiders. Middle managers are often held accountable for achieving challenging goals they did not have free rein in developing. At the same time, they may not have been given sufficient resources or have enough latitude in their authority to meet those goals. In addition, subordinates often have demands or requests that middle managers must consider.

Professional Staff

Professional staff
Employees who make decisions within their area of specialty that assist others in doing their jobs.

Accountants, market researchers, design engineers, computer consultants, and human resources representatives are a few of the hundreds of jobs that are categorized as professional staff. **Professional staff** make decisions within their area of specialty that provide information and advice so other managers and other employees can do their jobs. Staff positions illustrate the interrelated nature of most business jobs. The staff employee may spend considerable time interacting with customers, employees, and/or suppliers.

Consider two examples of staff positions. First is Pat, an apparel buyer for a major department store in Los Angeles. She must interact with managers to determine the types and quantities of goods to be carried in the store. She must also work with suppliers to make the needed purchases at the best price. Pat's decisions will affect the company's sales, expenses, and profits.

Second is Kelly, a staff employee in the marketing department of an electronics manufacturer. She has been charged with creating the marketing program for a newly developed camera. Kelly must interact with other marketing professionals to understand the scope of the marketing program. But she must work with her own manager to find out how much money is budgeted for the project. The human resources department will be involved, since more copywriters and artists may need to be hired. The production managers will need to give her input on unique features of the camera to include in her advertising. Both Pat's and Kelly's jobs can be done successfully only if they work with other key people who will affect their project.

First-Line Supervisors

First-line supervisors
The lowest level of management directly responsible for overseeing the work of employees.

First-line supervisors are the lowest level of management and are directly responsible for overseeing the work of employees who produce products or provide services. The specific titles of these managers vary broadly from industry to industry. In manufacturing businesses, duties of first-line supervisors include coordinating the arrival of component products, coordinating the flow down an assembly line, motivating workers to produce at their best, and completing paperwork necessary to inform higher managers. In service or retail businesses, the first-line supervisor may oversee the activities of the sales force, make sure inventory is ordered and properly displayed, and deal with special customer problems that other workers have trouble handling.

Supervisors are the direct link between the bulk of the workforce and higher management. Accordingly, they must be able to understand, talk with, support, motivate, and gain the confidence of the workers who are actually creating and selling products and services. Supervisors must also understand where their areas are headed and be able to represent their areas clearly and decisively with middle managers. Supervisors must be able to translate management directives to the workforce and translate workplace needs and issues to management. Supervisors are a key link between management and other employees and are considered by many to be pivotal people in the business.

First-line supervisors may be college graduates with advanced degrees, or they may have only a high school or trade school diploma. In their narrow area of expertise, they can provide valuable input to higher levels of management.

Nonmanagerial Employees

Nonmanagerial employees
Employees in a business who are actually involved in producing or selling products and providing services.

The employees in a business who are actually involved in producing or selling products or providing a service are referred to as **nonmanagerial employees.** They are the ones who have the most direct responsibility for the product or service. Their work is critical to the success of the company. Nonmanagerial employees may work on an assembly line or in an auto mechanic shop. They may work at a computer or travel extensively, selling products to retailers. They may perform highly skilled professional tasks, such as psychological counseling. Teachers in kindergarten, instructors in a community college, and professors in a university are all nonmanagerial workers because they directly provide a service to students.

As these examples show, the term *nonmanagerial* has nothing to do with an employee's skill or education. Nor is there any relationship among the tasks that different

Dennis Wickersham is a mechanic at Doyle Automotive, an independent car repair shop. He is well respected as an expert in analyzing problems with cars and making decisions regarding what is necessary to repair them. Yet, he is a nonmanagerial employee because he is not involved with the overall management strategy of Doyle Automotive. What kinds of decisions would he be making if he were a part of management?

nonmanagerial employees do. Both the auto mechanic and the teacher are nonmanagerial employees because they have direct responsibility for the product or service. There is also no relationship between pay rate or payroll method and whether or not the job is managerial. Some nonmanagerial employees are paid minimum wage on an hourly basis. Others are paid a monthly salary that may exceed $100,000 a year.

The reason nonmanagerial employees are so critical is that their decisions and actions directly affect the customer's future trade with the company. As the cliché has it, the nonmanagerial employees are "where the rubber meets the road." They can make the difference between a satisfied customer and a dissatisfied one. In a manufacturing company, they determine the quality of a given product regardless of top management's actions. In a hospital setting, they can be the key to patient comfort. In a university setting, they are the difference between high enrollment in a class and low enrollment. If the nonmanagerial employee does not do a good job, the customer is likely to go elsewhere.

You may not have thought of nonmanagerial employees as decision makers. However, as these examples show, they make important decisions every day that affect the business and its operations. Further, there is a movement in business today to give nonmanagerial employees more decision-making power. This movement, called **empowerment,** involves transferring decision-making authority and responsibility from management to employees at lower levels of the business. Logically, nonmanagerial employees are not empowered to make all decisions. Rather, they are given the chance to make decisions in areas where they have special experience and skill. In other words, these workers have the background they need to make decisions that contribute to the business in meaningful ways.

Empowerment
Giving employees the responsibility and authority to make decisions in areas where they have expertise and skill.

Developing Your Critical Thinking Skills

1. What kinds of problems do you think a business might encounter if the same person is the president, CEO, and chair of the board of directors ? What advantages might this arrangement provide?

2. We have noted that the first-line supervisor is in a pivotal position in the business. Why is this?

3. Consider the position of a neurosurgeon working in a large hospital. Obviously, the surgeon is highly educated and makes life-or-death decisions daily. Yet this surgeon is a nonmanagerial employee. Why?

Teams

Many companies have empowered nonmanagerial employees with decision-making rights by placing them in teams that make decisions about the work that is to be done. A typical example is seen in the manufacturing operations of a carmaker that has a team of workers build an engine. The team may be responsible for all assembly activities, including testing and verifying the quality of the engine once it is assembled.

Two types of teams are increasingly popular: self-directed work teams and cross-functional teams. In a **self-directed work team,** team members supervise their own work and are given broad discretion over the direction of their work. As you can see,

Self-directed work team
A group of employees who supervise their own work and are given broad discretion over the direction of their work.

Cross-functional team
A group of employees who are selected from various areas of the business and brought together to make collective decisions.

managers depend on and place high expectations on these teams. Team decisions can literally make or break the business.

In a **cross-functional team,** members are selected from various areas of the business and brought together to make collective decisions. They, too, may have wide decision-making discretion. Why is this form of team arrangement so relevant today? Because businesses are recognizing the importance of the same integrative themes we are stressing in this book. Many key decisions are not just production decisions or marketing decisions or engineering decisions or accounting decisions. Rather, they are complex decisions that should consider expertise and input from many areas and levels of the business. Bringing representatives from each area together to function as a team allows all members, through open discussion, to understand more clearly the needs and concerns of the other areas. Ideally, a better set of decisions will emerge and customers will be better served.

continuous improvement p. 448>

Consider the following example. Cummins Engine is the world's largest independent producer of diesel engines. It emphasizes a strong team approach to achieving quality and continuous improvement, an approach known as the Cummins Production System. Believing that some of the best ideas come from the people working on the production floor, Cummins brings them into teams with managers and other professionals. All are encouraged to offer their candid input based on their specific point of view. A few years ago, the company wanted to design a more efficient layout of the production floor in one of its plants. Rather than relying on a group of engineers to make the redesign decision, Cummins called on teams composed of engineers, supervisors, and production workers. They worked together, each offering their unique contributions. The result was a significant redesign that allowed the operation to produce engines more efficiently while maintaining quality.[3]

Teams are a very popular form of work arrangement today thanks to the advantages businesses can gain through the use of well-run teams. Let's consider just a few of the possible gains, as shown in Table 3–2. First, by bringing together talented people from throughout the business, the business can break departmental barriers and get action taken in a timely manner.

Second, by focusing on customer service and quality as their overriding goals, teams further these initiatives. In some businesses, team members are even rewarded for the team's contributions to service and quality.

Third, teams encourage and depend on employees getting involved in decision making. Workers recognize they have the chance to use their background and talents to make a difference. Often this helps build employee commitment.

TABLE 3–2   Advantages of Teams

- Brings together talented people from various areas of the business.
- Breaks departmental barriers, allowing quicker action.
- Focuses on customer service and quality.
- Promotes employee involvement and commitment.
- Provides excellent source of creativity and innovation.

creativity p. 522>
innovation p. 522>
empowerment p. 422>

Finally, teams are an excellent source of creativity and innovation. When teams are empowered to approach problems in ways that seem best to them, wonderful new approaches and ideas can emerge. As you can see, teams can be an excellent vehicle for fostering the indicators of a successful business.[4]

A good example of the use of teams and empowerment is seen at Motorola's cellular phone plant in Arlington Heights, Illinois. Here work teams are given wide ranges of flexibility, freedom, and responsibility. Rick Chandler, vice president at the plant, explains that Motorola wants to reduce dependency on managers and let the employees manage. He notes, "My workers are my managers. They manage my business, whether it's purchasing or production. . . . They determine when and how they should have a team, who goes in and who goes out."[5] At Motorola, this approach sparks excitement and enthusiasm in the workers, contributing greatly to meeting the goal of continual improvement.

Interrelationships among Positions

The interrelationships among positions in a business can be thought of as a giant spiderweb. Each position in the business is an intersection in that web. So any task accomplished by one person at one location in the web will affect and be affected by several other members of the organization.

Consider, for example, the position of the manager of product development, shown in Figure 3–2. This manager interacts directly with the vice presidents of marketing and research and, indirectly, with the president. There is also interaction with other vice presidents regarding issues affecting them. The manager has virtually constant interaction with clerical staff in the department, colleagues in the product design department, and assistants. But interaction also takes place with people in production, finance, marketing, and human resources, because the characteristics of a new product must be acceptable to those who will produce it, finance it, ship it, store it, and sell it. Assuming the product development is successful, the

FIGURE 3–2   Relationships among Positions

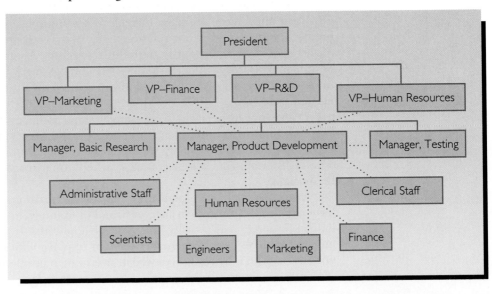

human resources department will be involved in hiring and training employees to produce and sell the product.

Note in Figure 3–2 that only a few of the lines represent *authority chains*, that is, the movement of official commands down through the hierarchy of the organization. The rest of the lines are *coordinative*. This means that individuals within product development must coordinate with those in marketing and production and others in order to produce a product that is best for the customer.

A product development manager is perhaps one of the best to illustrate the dynamic relationship among the different positions in a company. Yet all positions interact to some degree. Though positions at the very bottom of an organization rarely interact with those at high levels and the president of a large corporation rarely interacts directly with those several layers down, the impact of the president reaches throughout the organization. And even those on the lowest rung interact with their co-workers, their immediate supervisors, and various support staff.

Differences between Large and Small Businesses

The set of interrelated decisions that must be made become more complex as the business grows larger. For example, a large organization may have dozens of vice presidents. General Electric, for example, has 135 individuals with titles of corporate-level vice president or higher. Of those, 35 have the title of president of a division or regional unit. This does not include the vast number of vice presidents of units within divisions or subsidiaries. A medium-size business, however, may have only a handful of vice presidents, and a very small business may have none.

Let's look at the differences in the number of positions, using a midsize manufacturing company as an example. Morton Metalcraft makes sheet-metal housings for heavy-equipment manufacturers. Even though Morton Metalcraft employs over 800 people and has annual sales in excess of $59 million, the top management structure is quite lean. In fact, top management consists of Bill Morton, who is the president and chief executive officer, and only five vice presidents.

top management
p. 65>

In a large organization, a vice president may have a very specific set of responsibilities, such as vice president for customer relations. In a smaller company, a vice president may have multiple formal responsibilities, such as vice president of human resources and public relations. The actual tasks performed in small companies are often even broader than the title suggests. A person may be vice president of human resources but perform duties encompassing human resources, labor relations, customer service, public relations, and company representative to the local United Way.

Even top managers who have joined a small company with specific skills and talents find that their duties span a number of areas. Hence, the manager of, say, marketing needs to be reasonably well-versed in finance and human resources as well. This is different from a large company, where top managers are much more likely to be specialists.

A vice president of a small firm may also perform many of the duties that staff-level individuals would do in a larger firm. For example, in a small company, the VP of human resources may actually interview job applicants. In a large company, the VP of human resources has only general oversight responsibilities for recruiting and may be unaware of who is being interviewed or even which positions are being filled.

Construction is a good example of decision making by teams. Construction teams develop the ability to work together to make the pieces of a project fit together. They often have a keen sense of knowing what needs to be done and when, and can make decisions with a minimum of effort. What other examples can you think of where teams work so closely together that decision making seems effortless?

In smaller companies, a greater percentage of workers are considered nonmanagerial—that is, directly involved in providing the product or service. As a company grows, it tends to become more top-heavy, with more people in staff and management positions.

Finally, small businesses differ from larger ones in a very important way: how decisions are made. Large businesses tend to be very deliberative. They study issues carefully (sometimes for too long). Committees or teams or task forces are charged with investigating a problem or opportunity and reporting back to some higher level. Decisions often have to go through several layers of management. Small businesses tend to make decisions faster and with less study because they have fewer levels of management and fewer specialists in staff positions. This allows them to adapt quickly to changing environments. Of course, it also means that small business managers may make incorrect decisions sometimes because there has not been sufficient input nor analysis in the decision process.

Decision Makers in Nonprofit Organizations

The previous section discussed the various decision makers within a business and the interaction among them. Nonprofit organizations may have somewhat similar structures. Just as there are wide varieties of businesses, however, there are wide varieties of not-for-profit organizations. A large hospital may be nonprofit, as are most universities. The United Way and American Cancer Society are quite large organizations with many paid employees. At the opposite extreme is a local neighborhood development group with no paid employees at all.

board of directors
p. 64>
A primary difference between a business and a nonprofit organization is the ownership and top management. Businesses are usually owned by individuals, either directly or through stock. Not-for-profit organizations have no such ownership. No one "owns" a nonprofit. They do have top management in the form of a board of directors, although it is almost always a volunteer board. Large nonprofit organizations may have a president, a full set of vice presidents, and many paid staff employees.

Smaller nonprofits may have only an *executive director* and perhaps a secretary as paid staff. Volunteers handle all other work.

We now turn from decision makers to the process of making decisions. In particular, the following section will discuss the various factors that influence how decisions are made in businesses. We will introduce each factor here and then discuss them in more detail in later chapters.

Developing Your Critical Thinking Skills

1. There are many benefits from using teams. How large should a team be? If we use cross-functional teams, how do we decide which areas should be represented?

2. Decision making may be faster yet riskier in small businesses than in large ones. Explain why this is so.

The Decison-Making Process

So far in this chapter we have discussed who the decision makers are in an organization. We now turn to the process of making decisions. We look first at the types of decisions that are made in businesses and then at the actual decision-making process.

A strategic decision has a long run impact on the business. Unfortunately, sometimes that decision is to close the business. If owners conclude that revenues will not be sufficient to cover expenses in the forseeable future, closing the business may minimize losses. What other options might be available for a business which is losing money?

As we've said, business is about decision making. Indeed, much of every employee's time is spent making some kind of decision. Some decisions are of critical, long-term impact to the firm and are made only after months of careful study. Other decisions are fast and simple, like which kind of label to put on a carton before it is shipped.

Consider the following example of rapid decision making. A bar-coding facility for the U.S. Postal Service puts bar codes on letters whose zip code was not readable by scanners. An employee sits at a machine for hours at a time, looking at envelopes as they move through the machine at about one envelope per second. The employee's job is to look at the zip code, decide what it really is, and enter the code into the machine, which then applies a bar code to the envelope for mailing. Thus, the employee of the bar-coding facility makes one decision per second. These certainly are not high-level decisions, but they are nevertheless decisions.

Types of Decisions

Managers make many different types of decisions. We consider three types here: strategic, operational, and problem-solving decisions.

Strategic Decisions

Strategic decisions
Decisions that have a major impact on the general direction of the firm.

acquisition p. 322>

Strategic decisions are those decisions that have a major impact on the general direction of the firm. These decisions are often carefully considered and may involve millions of dollars of investment. They may change the way a business competes. They may involve the introduction of new products or the acquisition of another company. They may require hiring hundreds of employees or laying off thousands. Perhaps the most extreme of all is the decision to sell or close the business. The characteristics of strategic decisions are shown in Table 3–3.

TABLE 3 – 3   Characteristics of Strategic Decisions

- Have long-range impact.
- Require careful analysis of the firm and its environment.
- Are often the result of a strategic planning process.
- May involve millions of dollars.
- Are designed to capture opportunities or offset competitive weaknesses.
- Involve top management, including board of directors.

The most significant characteristic in Table 3–3 is that strategic decisions are long-range decisions made by top management. Others in the organization will have input, but the magnitude of the decision dictates that managers at the very highest level be involved. Strategic decisions involve a structured, analytical process that carefully considers as much information as can possibly be gained. These decisions are typically made slowly, after careful study.

For an example of a strategic decision, consider Southwest Airlines. Southwest was started as a regional airline flying point-to-point routes rather than using hubs. It grew slowly until it was flying to selected cities in the United States even though the key routes were still in the Southwest or connected to cities in the Southwest. Part of Southwest's strategy has always been to fly short hauls into the less-used airports of major cities, such as Love Field (Dallas), Midway (Chicago), Baltimore (Washington, D.C.), and Providence (Boston). Southwest Airlines recently made the strategic decision to offer coast-to-coast service for the first time. This decision has many risks. With its budget fare approach, Southwest may be able to take business away from other airlines. On the other hand, the decision may ignite airfare wars with other airlines. To reduce the chances of angering competitors, Southwest decided to move slowly on these long hauls and keep a relatively low profile.[6]

Operational Decisions

Operational decisions
Decisions that affect the day-to-day actions of the business.

Operational decisions are those that affect the day-to-day actions of the business. Characteristics of operational decisions are shown in Table 3–4. Operational decisions may or may not involve large amounts of capital, but they tend to deal with specific situations and are made by managers who have considerable experience in the area affected by the decision. Operational decisions might include the volume of products to be produced this month, the selection of a new supplier to replace one whose quality is unacceptable, the selection of new employees to replace those who have left the company or been promoted, the amount of money budgeted for maintenance of equipment, or the selection of TV stations on which to advertise.

Another characteristic is that operational decisions are frequently made within the boundaries of established policies and procedures. There are often *standard operating procedures (SOPs)* in place to guide the decision making. This structure eases the decision-making process. It means that managers do not need to do a significant study

TABLE 3–4   Characteristics of Operational Decisions

- May or may not involve large amounts of capital.
- Deal with specific situations within an organization.
- Are made by experienced managers in the area.
- Often have standard operating procedures available to guide decisions.
- Require less analysis than strategic decisions do.

of the situation each time a new decision must be made. Only those decisions that fall outside the purview of the SOP need substantial amounts of analysis.

Problem Solving Decisions

Problem solving
Decision making aimed at correcting an adverse situation that has developed.

budget p. 402>

Problem solving is decision making aimed at correcting an adverse situation that has developed. The orientation of problem solving is how to fix something that is wrong. Examples abound. A company whose die-stamping machine just blew up is in a problem-solving mode because it cannot use the machine. A key staff employee decides to leave the company abruptly, and the company is left with no one who knows how to do billing correctly. Two employees who previously were cooperative suddenly argue constantly. A firm's accountant presents a department manager with information suggesting that the department's telephone expenses were over budget by 25 percent.

The common element of each of these examples is that the situation is some adverse deviation from the norm. Table 3–5 shows some of the characteristics of problem solving. Problems to be solved are sometimes of crisis proportions and sometimes minor. The key to problem solving is to reach a decision somehow that leaves the organization in the best possible position, given the situation at hand. The task is to analyze the situation as carefully but quickly as possible and find a solution to the problem that is acceptable to all involved.

In some cases, there are no good solutions. Most experienced managers know that occasionally a situation arises that simply cannot be completely resolved. Here the manager must carefully decide which of a set of poor alternatives comes closest to solving the problem, knowing that not everyone will be happy. This is unfortunate, but it is the reality of the workplace. For example, suppose your company has a hiring freeze; top management has dictated that absolutely no new employees will be hired. One of your long-time workers decides to take early retirement. This will create a void in your department, and work will have to be spread among the remaining workers. But the reality is that you will not get a replacement and you must simply live with the problem.

Sometimes the best decision is to leave the problem unresolved for now in hopes that conditions may change. For example, suppose you work in a job that requires you to spend hours each day working on a computer. Your computer seems to be increasingly slow and locks up more often than it should. You report this problem to your supervisor, indicating your frustration with the computer.

TABLE 3–5   Characteristics of Problem Solving Decisions

- Situation is a deviation from normal operations.
- May be minor or of crisis proportions.
- Often need quick decisions to find solutions acceptable to all involved.
- There may be no easy solution.

The supervisor could turn in a repair request immediately to have your computer fixed, but your entire department is scheduled to get new computers in two months. Thus, it does not make sense to have your computer repaired. You are told to keep using it, back up files frequently, and hope it doesn't crash completely before the new computers arrive.

A Basic Decision-Making Model

Figure 3–3 shows a simplified model of the decision-making process. This model is essentially the same regardless of the type of decision being made. In some cases, the terminology may change, but the overall process is similar. This process entails six steps.

The first step is to *define the decision issue*. This can be more difficult than it may appear. Sometimes the real issue is hidden and must be uncovered. Generally, managers must spend a fair amount of time in this first step. Only when we really know what the issue is can we start to address it. Sometimes the decision issue has a strategic focus; sometimes the issue is to overcome a problem.

The second step is to *gather information about the issue* itself. If the decision is of a strategic nature, we need to gather as much information about the industry, the competitors, and other parts of the environment as possible. If it is a problem-solving decision, we must gather information about the situation in order to be objective.

The third step is to *gather information about the company and people involved*. We look at strengths or weaknesses of our firm before embarking on a new strategy. If we are dealing with a conflict, we try to gather as much information as we can about the problem, the people involved, and their motives. Sometimes the problem is more complex than it seems, and substantial study is required to ferret out the truth.

There is often a dilemma in the information-gathering stage. Most managers always want more information. This is logical—more information usually provides greater assurance that the right decision will be made. But gathering additional information takes time, effort, and perhaps money. Successful managers recognize that there must be a trade-off. Sometimes we have to step forward boldly and make the best decisions we can with the information available. Sometimes we can't wait for more information.

Once information is gathered, sifted through, and analyzed, managers are ready to begin the fourth step, *develop alternatives*. These alternatives may be strategies. They may be problem solutions. They may be choices of suppliers or a selection of advertising media or identification of which potential employees to bring back for additional interviews. Usually several alternatives are considered. Some will be better than others. Some may seem good but might create other problems.

Once we have a number of alternatives in hand, we must evaluate them and *select the best one*. Sometimes that choice is based on simple judgment, but often detailed analysis will create a number of criteria that must be considered. For example, a strategy to increase sales might seem very good—until we look at the cost of gaining the sales. If the cost of the strategy is as high as the revenues generated, then the strategy is not justifiable.

revenue p. 17>

FIGURE 3–3 Basic Decision-Making Model

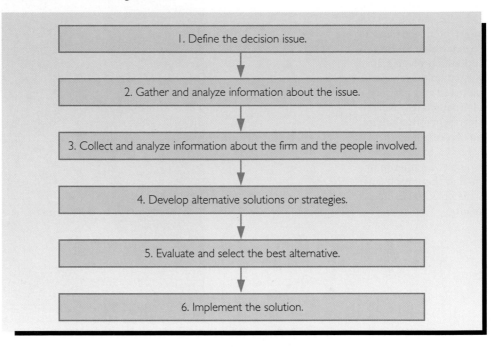

1. Define the decision issue.

2. Gather and analyze information about the issue.

3. Collect and analyze information about the firm and the people involved.

4. Develop alternative solutions or strategies.

5. Evaluate and select the best alternative.

6. Implement the solution.

An additional and important consideration in this evaluation stage is the ethical implications of each of the alternatives. Alternatives that violate the ethical standards and culture of the business should be rejected no matter how attractive they appear.

Finally, we must *implement the selected alternative.* If the problem is small, implementing the solution may be as simple as announcing the decision to all who are involved. For a major strategic change, implementing the solution may require selling additional stock or getting a large bank loan. Such complex actions will take considerable time to complete. Alternatives must be implemented as carefully as they were developed. Managers sometimes develop a great idea but then fail because they do a poor job of implementation.

stock p. 216>

A Decision-Making Example

Let's consider an example of a decision a manager may face. Lisa is the manager of the customer service department of a large upscale department store. Five customer service representatives report to her. She has just received reports that one of her people, Ken, has received an unusually high number of complaints. In fact, many customers have expressed dissatisfaction with the way Ken handles their problems. This affects the overall rating of Lisa's unit and could affect their bonuses. Clearly, Lisa has to get to the bottom of this problem.

What exactly is the problem? Lisa begins to investigate. First she looks at the situation to determine just how severe it is. In talking with other reps and with cus-

In technical areas, some decision making is quite complex and requires serious discussion in order to determine the best solution to problems. Information must be gathered and a variety of alternatives may be considered before reaching an agreement on the best solution. In what ways would you gather information about problems with a piece of equipment?

tomers she saw were unhappy, she determines that the problem is severe enough that the store might actually lose customers because of it. Further, the store's policy of quality customer service will not tolerate this magnitude of a problem.

Lisa then begins to study the people involved. Ken is 58 years old and has been with the company for over 25 years. He worked in the catalog department for many years and recently transferred into customer service. This is not the first time problems have surfaced regarding Ken in the six months he has been in Lisa's unit. Apparently he simply lacks the interpersonal skills needed to interact effectively with the public. The problem becomes clearer: Ken is receiving too many complaints because he has weak interpersonal skills.

What are the alternatives? First, Lisa could fire Ken. But that appears to be a drastic and perhaps even legally inappropriate approach for this worker. Although Ken has never been a star performer, he has always done acceptable work. Lisa doesn't think it would be fair or even ethical to dismiss a 25-year company veteran in this manner. Also, she doesn't want to risk his suing the company for age discrimination. A second alternative would be to invest in training to help Ken develop his interpersonal skills. Such training is expensive, and there is no assurance that Ken will change enough to work really well with customers. Finally, Lisa could transfer Ken back to the catalog area, where he did mostly data entry and did not interact directly with the public.

Lisa ponders these options and decides it might be wise to ask Ken what he thinks of the training and transfer options. To her surprise, Lisa learns that Ken does not really enjoy the customer service job; he took it only because he heard there was going to be some downsizing in the catalog area. Armed with this information, Lisa does some more checking. She finds that while reductions in the catalog area were considered at one time, catalog sales have grown substantially and no one will be let go now.

The solution is now evident to Lisa. She should transfer Ken back to the catalog area, where he did an adequate job. However, implementing that solution is not necessarily easy to do. First there has to be an opening. Further, she wants to find a good person to replace Ken in customer service. After a few days Lisa learns that Maria, who works in catalog sales, would like to transfer to customer service. She is an outgoing, personable young woman who should be quite successful interacting with customers. All the pieces are now in place and the switch is made.

This decision is a fairly simple example of the day-to-day sorts of issues that managers face regularly. Yet even here you can see that the decision process can become quite involved. The process is often even more complex than shown here. Keep in mind that regardless of the level of complexity, the decision-making process remains essentially the same.

A Model of Creative Decision Making

The decision-making model described in Figure 3–3 presents a structured, logical approach to making the kinds of decisions that managers regularly face. This basic approach is based on research, information, and careful evaluation of that information. Although the basic model is widely accepted, it has certain limitations. Sometimes the nature of the situation and the nature of the real problem are not clear. Sometimes managers do not possess enough information to evaluate alternatives logically. Sometimes obvious or available alternatives are simply not good enough. Sometimes totally new, unique, and unexpected solutions are needed. In short, today's business world is volatile and uncertain. Sometimes a business has to *break out of the mold* of basic decision making to get the edge on increasingly tough competition. In such cases, creative decision making is needed.[7]

Creative decision making
The process of developing new or different ways to solve problems or capture opportunities.

Creative decision making is a process of developing new or different ways to solve problems or capture opportunities. It requires a somewhat different pattern of thinking from rational decision making. The steps of creative decision making are shown in Figure 3–4.

The first stage of creative decision making is the *preparation stage*. Here we must recognize that the true problem may not be what appears at first blush. A decision maker may have to view a situation differently and look for new opportunities. This comes from careful and reflective study, but it also comes from being open to new perspectives. It is at this stage that new options, alternatives, and creative approaches are encouraged.

It is also important in this preparation stage to look for many possibilities and defer judgment and evaluation. A popular technique used during this stage is *brainstorming*, where a team of people look at a problem and generate as many alternatives as possible for addressing it. Free association is encouraged. Criticism is forbidden. The goal is to expand possibilities, not limit them.

In short, the preparation stage works when existing assumptions and thought patterns can be suspended and new possibilities can be generated. This step relies on the view that true creativity usually occurs when people take what is already known and look for new associations, new combinations, and new relationships.[8]

The second stage of creative decision making is known as the *incubation stage*. This stage requires the decision maker to take time to mull over what has been generated during the preparation stage. This process is subconscious mental activity. When a manager takes time simply to let all of the information and possibilities sit for a while, the

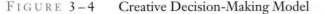

FIGURE 3 – 4   Creative Decision-Making Model

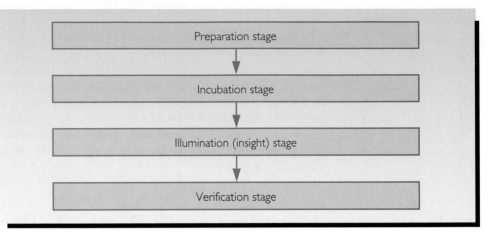

mind will rearrange and search for new linkages that make sense. Who knows what will emerge? This step cannot be programmed, nor can it be logically directed. This step is difficult for many managers. Given the fast-paced nature of business and business decision making, it's hard to allow enough time for incubation to occur.

The third stage is the *illumination* or *insight stage*. It is here that a creative or novel idea is recognized. These are the flashes of insight that strike a manager, often in quite unexpected ways. In these "aha" experiences, a solution pops up or an idea suddenly comes together, seemingly out of nowhere. Although illumination may appear to be a stroke of unexpected insight, it comes from nonjudgmental preparation and open incubation.

The final step is the *verification stage*. Here the decision maker takes the creative idea and tests it to see if it makes sense. This may involve talking through the solution with others or even conducting formal research to see if it has merit. It is probably impossible ever to feel completely sure that a creative idea will work, yet verification seeks to gain at least enough sense of acceptance that the manager is not going off the deep end with some wild scheme. This stage verifies that the risks involved in the decision are reasonable and acceptable.

Increasingly, businesses are becoming aware of the need for creative decision making. Motorola, 3M, and Hewlett-Packard are among the companies known for their encouragement of creative decision making.

Proposing novel solutions or alternatives may be exactly what the business needs in many situations. Yet formulating new and creative solutions is a difficult task. Many businesses realize that innovation demands thinking up solutions or alternatives that are *outside the box* and break from traditional alternatives. There are a number of ways such creativity can be encouraged. These will be addressed more fully in Chapter 17, when we discuss change and renewal.

Team Decision Making

We discussed earlier the trend in today's business toward empowerment, the moving of decisions to lower levels in organizations. These decisions are often made by teams.

teams p. 71>

Team decisions tend to take longer to make than individual decisions, but they are often better decisions. More information is brought into the process, and the decisions are better supported by the group once they are made. Team decisions, especially for cross-functional teams, also help assure that the decisions will reflect the broader background of team participants.

Selecting team members is an important task. Participants may want team members with whom they feel comfortable, but this should not be the guiding criterion. Members should be selected because they have talents and backgrounds that the team needs to make decisions. This may lead to differences of opinion and conflicts. A well-run team will use those conflicts to spark the creativity that leads to new approaches. This creativity is one of the things that make the team approach so special.

For people to work effectively in teams, they must understand team goals. Members must practice active listening and open communications with one another. Divergent views must be explored to see how they can be used to reach a *team consensus* that all members can support.

The primary disadvantage of team decision making is the time and effort required to make the decision. Some decisions simply do not need to be made by teams. Sometimes it's a good idea to have one person charged with making decisions for which there is likely to be little conflict. If the decision is not critical, the efficiency of individual decision making may outweigh the benefits of team decision making. As a manager, you must decide when a team effort is better than an individual decision.

Decision Making in an International Arena

We have discussed decision makers and decision making throughout this chapter. We presented a basic model of the decision-making process. These decision making tasks become even more complex as a business operates in the international marketplace. Customs, laws, customer needs, international currencies, and governmental and political influences are additional factors that require attention by skilled decision makers. At times, international decisions create challenges when the ethics of one country differ from that of another.

Return to the model we presented in Figure 3–3. Data gathering will be more difficult because of the distances between countries. Possible language barriers make interpreting information difficult. Analyzing the data is also more difficult because many additional points of view must be considered. We will discuss these complexities in more detail in subsequent chapters.

Developing Your Critical Thinking Skills

1. Consider your decision to attend the university where you are now studying. Use the basic decision-making model in Figure 3–3 to trace how you chose your university.

2. Now use the same model to think about potential career choices. What types of information do you need? What do you need to know about yourself as part of the model?

SUMMARY

1. Business is about decision making. Nothing can be done in a business without someone making a decision.

    ■ Who are the decision makers in business?

    The major categories of decision makers in business are stockholders, the board of directors , top managers, middle managers, members of the professional staff, first-line supervisors, and nonmanagerial workers.

2. Businesses are composed of individuals with varied responsibilities. It is important to understand the relationships among various decision makers in order for decisions to fit together for the benefit of the entire organization.

    ■ What are decision responsibilities of the various people within a business?

    Stockholders buy and sell stock. They may also vote (usually by proxy) on major issues at annual meetings. The *board of directors* may actively assist top managers in making strategic decisions. The board may also review various aspects of company performance and require corrective actions where necessary. Finally, the board selects some members of top management and often sets their compensation. *Top management* makes the major decisions for the company and is responsible for its performance. *Middle managers* are responsible for translating broad policies and strategies into doable tasks. *Professional staff employees* provide technical support and make decisions in specialty areas. *First-line supervisors* make decisions related to the direct management of nonmanagerial employees. *Nonmanagerial employees* make the hourly, daily, and weekly decisions needed in the process of actually producing the firm's product or service.

3. Sometimes decisions are made by a single individual. But in recent years, businesses have increasingly turned to team decision making at the level of nonmanagerial employees. This is done by forming teams and giving them broad guidelines and the authority to make and implement decisions.

    ■ What are the benefits of team decision making?

    There are four major benefits. (1) The business is able to break departmental barriers and get faster action. (2) Teams provide better customer service and higher quality. (3) Teams build employee commitment. (4) Teams are an excellent source of creativity.

4. Regardless of the size of a business, the basic decision-making process is the same, but the decisions differ depending on the size of the firm.

    ■ How does decision making differ between large and small businesses?

    There are four major differences. (1) Large businesses have many more decisions to make than do small businesses. (2) The interrelated decisions that have to be made by big businesses are more complex than those in small businesses. (3) Smaller companies tend to have a higher percentage of employees in nonmanagerial positions. (4) Decision making in large businesses tends to be very deliberative, whereas small businesses tend to make decisions more quickly and with less study.

5. Even though vast numbers of decisions are made in any business, it is possible to describe all decisions in terms of a few categories.

    ■ What are the main types of decisions that managers make?

Strategic decisions are those decisions that have major, long-range impacts on the general direction of the company. They are primarily made by top management. *Operational decisions* are those that affect the day-to-day operation of the business. These decisions are often made by people who have experience in the specific area. *Problem solving* is decision making designed to correct problems that have arisen. Sometimes the solutions to problems are limited.

6. Managers of successful businesses engage in a never-ending cycle of decisions and actions. Regardless of the types of decisions being made, a similar process of decision making is used.

   ■ Describe the basic decision-making model presented in this chapter.

   The model consists of six steps: (1) define the issue, (2) collect and analyze information about the issue, (3) collect and analyze information about the firm and the people involved, (4) develop alternative solutions or strategies, (5) evaluate and select the best alternative, and (6) implement the solution.

7. When normal decision making simply does not provide the kind of decision that is best for a situation, a creative decision-making approach may yield better solutions.

   ■ Describe and use the model for creative decision making.

   The creative decision-making model has four stages: (1) preparation, (2) incubation, (3) illumination, and (4) verification. Creative decision making often uses brainstorming to generate ideas. Teams can often produce unique and creative outcomes.

Links to future courses

The material covered in this chapter is quite basic to a study of business. Decision making is the emphasis of all business courses. In particular, decision making will receive more detail in the following courses:

■ Principles of management   ■ Managerial decision making
■ Principles of marketing   ■ Strategic management
■ Human resources management   ■ Operations management

EXERCISES AND APPLICATIONS

1. Refer to the Ken Webster example in Profile 3–2. What decisions could Ken have made to make his day less hectic?

2. Suppose you need to travel on business from Los Angeles to Miami with a stop for a one-hour meeting at noon at the airport in Tulsa, Oklahoma. Your boss wants you to choose the most economical route. Go on the Internet and decide which airline to take.

3. Form teams of five people each. Using the basic decision-making model, address the following problem:

   A team member in a manufacturing setting frequently calls in sick. You suspect that he is not ill but is spending time enjoying his new swimming pool. Your boss has become aware of the situation. You must resolve this problem.

4. In the same teams, turn to the model of creative decision making. For each of the following products, brainstorm uses that are not its normal use. Break away from old assumptions and look for creative possibilities. Do not make evaluations or judgments.

- Used tennis balls
- A brick
- A rubber band
- This textbook

KEY TERMS

Board of directors, p. 64
Chief executive officer (CEO), p. 65
Chief financial officer (CFO), p. 65
Chief operating officer (COO), p. 65
Creative decision making, p. 83
Cross-functional team, p. 72
Empowerment, p. 71
First-line supervisors, p. 69
Middle managers, p. 66

Nonmanagerial employees, p. 70
Operational decisions, p. 78
Problem solving, p. 79
Professional staff, p. 69
Self-directed work teams, p. 71
Strategic decisions, p. 77
Top management, p. 65
Vice presidents, p. 66

CASE: HIGH PAY FOR DECISION MAKING BY CEOs

Executive pay is a hot topic in America today. The ratio of compensation for top managers to that of the average worker is much higher than it used to be. And the gap seems to be growing. The April 21, 1997, issue of *Business Week* reported the phenomenon:

"For 1996, CEO pay gains far outstripped the roaring economy or shareholder returns. The average salary and bonus for a chief executive officer rose a phenomenal 39 percent, to $2.3 million. Add to that the retirement benefits, incentive plans, and gains from stock options, and the numbers hit the roof. CEOs' average total compensation rose an astounding 54 percent last year, to $5,781,300. That largesse came on top of a 30 percent rise in total pay in 1995—yet it was hardly spread down the line. The average compensation of the top dog was 209 times that of a factory employee, who garnered a tiny 3 percent raise in 1996. White-collar workers eked out just 3.2 percent, though many now get options, too ....

"As once-outsize options packages become the norm, many CEOs are taking the lion's share. Far smaller gains are going to managers and other key employees. The disturbing message: The CEO deserves nearly all the credit for the company's success."

Decision Questions

1.   In view of what you have learned about decision making in this chapter, do you think the high CEO pay in American business is justified by the importance of the decisions those people make?

2.   Suppose you are working as a middle manager in a large company and you have been given what you consider to be important decision-making responsibilities. Now suppose that you learn that the CEO of your company just received a 54 percent increase in pay while you have been granted a 10 percent increase. Under what circumstances would you consider the difference to be fair? Would the gap in pay increases have any effect on how hard you work?

3.   Suppose that through the action of stockholders or boards of directors there were a general reduction in CEO pay increases. Whenever a CEO received a 30 percent pay raise, most other employees in the company would receive the same percentage. What impact would such a policy have on the decision-making effectiveness of most American top managements?

4.   Do you believe that pay and pay increases should differ among managers based on the kinds of decisions they make? Should extra compensation be provided as a reward for good decisions?

SOURCE: Jennifer Reingold, "Executive Pay," *Business Week*, April 21, 1997, p. 59.

REFERENCES

1. Kyle Pope. "Fox's Fall Schedule Avoids Shake-ups Planned by Rivals," *The Wall Street Journal*, May 21, 1997, p. B8.

2. Richard Melcher. "The Best and Worst Boards." *Business Week*, November 25, 1996, pp. 82–98.

3. J. H. Boyett and H. P. Conn. *Workplace 2000: The Revolution Reshaping American Business*. New York: NAL/Dutton, 1991.

4. For an excellent overview of teams and their significance, see J. R. Katzenbach and D. K. Smith. *The Wisdom of Teams: Creating the High-Performance Organization*. Boston: Harvard Business School Press, 1993.

5. Robert Levering and Milton Moskowitz. *The 100 Best Companies to Work for in America*. New York: Plume, 1993.

6. Scott McCartney. "Scrappy Southwest Reaches Coast in One Stop." *The Wall Street Journal*, April 22, 1997, pp. B1, B2.

7. An excellent overview of organizational creativity is provided by Richard W. Woodman, John E. Sawyer, and Ricky W. Griffin. "Toward a Theory of Organizational Creativity." *The Academy of Management Review*, vol. 18, no. 2, April 1993, pp. 293–321.

8. Robert E. Quinn, Sue R. Faerman, Michael P. Thompson, and Michael R. McGrath. *Becoming a Master Manager: A Competency Framework*, 4th ed. New York: John Wiley & Sons, 1996, pp. 348–349.

4

The Links Between Business and its Stakeholders

Joe Camel, the cigarette-smoking cartoon symbol, was the focus of controversy. Cigarette manufacturer RJ Reynolds Tobacco Co. saw Joe as a successful advertising gimmick that appealed to a key target market of smokers in their early 20s. Others saw it differently. Industry critics argued that Joe's cool, somewhat irreverent image, coupled with his cartoon persona, was an intentional move on the part of the tobacco giant to lure kids into becoming smokers. These critics said such behavior was unacceptable and society in general was the loser.

Even the Federal Trade Commission (FTC) became involved. In fact, the FTC charged that the Joe Camel advertising campaign was so successful that Camel's market share among kids was greater than it was among adults. "Joe Camel has become as recognizable to kids as Mickey Mouse. Yet the campaign promotes a product that causes serious injury, addiction, and death. It is illegal and should be stopped," claimed the FTC's director of consumer protection, Jodie Bernstein. In June 1997, Joe Camel's influence decreased dramatically as the FTC and the tobacco industry reached tentative agreements which will ban billboard advertisements and ads with cartoon characters like Joe.

Clearly, there is more involved here than just the sale of RJR products. Many interested parties were involved. A lot of people had a stake in the outcome including consumer watch groups, the FTC, government officials and politicians (among them President Clinton), the court system, and youths who may become smokers. RJR could not afford to ignore these powerful and important groups.[1]

Businesses do not operate in a vacuum. Every decision that managers make and every action that an organization takes affects those around it. In a similar way, the business is affected by those who have contact with it. Some of the interactions are exciting, some are troublesome. Some are easily controllable, some are not. Some have limited impacts, some have significant long-run effects. With that in mind, when you finish this chapter, you should be able to:

1. Explain the concept of stakeholders and list the major categories of stakeholders in business.

2. Differentiate between the primary and secondary stakeholders for businesses.

3. Write an integrated definition of the term *business*.

4. Explain the responsibilities of a particular business to its stakeholders and how those stakeholders affect the business.

5. Describe the role of business ethics in contemporary business.

6. Define the concept of a moral dilemma.

7. Explain three methods of moral reasoning that can be used to resolve a moral dilemma.

8. Discuss how a business can build an ethical culture.

In Chapter 1, we discussed the definition of business. We presented a model for a successful business. In Chapter 3, we discussed the many different decision makers in a business and the process of decision making. However, business managers do not make decisions in isolation. Many groups both inside and outside the business affect and are also affected by the decisions it makes. In this chapter, we discuss the interactions between a business and those who have an interest in it. As part of our discussion, we emphasize the responsibilities of a business to each of its stakeholder groups. Finally, we discuss the role of managers in establishing ethical behavior in the organization. It is important, however, to begin these discussions with a concept that may be new to you, that of stakeholders in businesses.

The Concept of Stakeholders

You may not have realized that as a customer of a business, you are one of many key stakeholders of that business. As an employee you are another. If you become an owner of the business or one of many stockholders, you are yet another. As a resident of the community in which the business operates, you are still another stakeholder of the business, since you are affected either positively or adversely by the actions of the business. So what is a stakeholder anyway?

Stakeholder
A person or group that has some claim on or expectation of how a business should operate.

A **stakeholder** is a person or group that has some claim on or expectation of how a business should operate.[2] The model for a successful business shows how important stakeholders are. Stakeholders include founders and other owners, employees and retirees, customers, suppliers, other businesses, the government, the community, and even

FIGURE 4-1   Typical Business Stakeholders

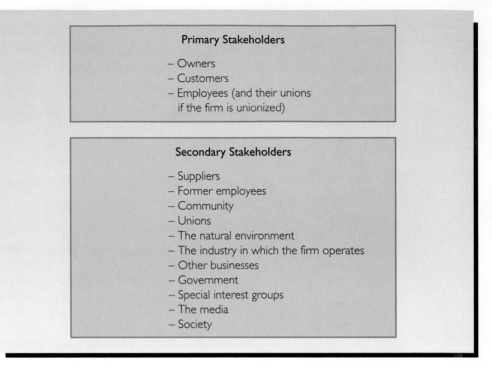

society in general. Each of these groups has expectations regarding how a given business should operate. Unfortunately, these stakeholder expectations are often contradictory. Managers must constantly be aware of the conflicting demands of stakeholders. Often, addressing the needs of one stakeholder disappoints another. For example, owners want as much profit as possible, but customers want the lowest possible price and highest possible quality. Providing a low price may conflict with the owner's expectation of a return for money invested. The leaders of a successful business must integrate and reconcile stakeholder expectations. Figure 4–1 lists typical stakeholders of businesses.

Primary stakeholders are those stakeholders whom a business affects and interacts with most directly. At least three stakeholders are commonly considered to be primary stakeholders: the owners of the firm, the firm's customers, and its employees. **Secondary stakeholders** are those whom the business affects in an indirect or limited way. These include suppliers, former employees, unions, the community, the environment, industry in which the firm operates, other businesses, various levels of government, special interest groups, the media, and society in general. Although the business may not have direct contact with secondary stakeholders on a day-to-day basis, managers must recognize the importance of those stakeholders' expectations.

unions p. 104>

Primary stakeholders
Those stakeholders whom a business affects and interacts with most directly.

Secondary stakeholders
Those stakeholders whom a business affects in an indirect or limited way.

Stakeholders as Part of the Business System

Recognizing the links between the business and its stakeholders is critical to understanding how the business system works. In fact, the idea that businesses and stakeholders interact and affect each other is a unique characteristic of a free market society.

Let's consider this point further. In a command economy, such as that of the former USSR, one stakeholder group—the government—dictates how a business operates. The government even decides production amounts and prices. For example, assume you lived in a command economy and wanted to buy a car. The government would determine how many car manufacturers there were, the number of cars produced, the number of models available, and the price of each. You as a consumer would have few options and might have to wait several years before you were authorized to buy a car.

In a free market society, however, the picture is dramatically different. Owners provide capital. Customers influence the volume, models, colors, and options that are produced. Competitors affect prices, designs, and distribution. Government is involved in product, employee, and environmental safety. Unions affect wages and working conditions. Suppliers affect costs and, in turn, prices. All these stakeholders interact to comprise the free market business system.

Primary stakeholders play the major role in how the business operates. The secondary stakeholders play a smaller role—unless a particular issue becomes vitally important to the company or the stakeholder. The importance of a particular stakeholder group varies with the company. A bank, for example, would probably have little interaction with environmental groups, but to a coal mine they might be important stakeholders.

The importance of considering stakeholders of business is seen in the recent General Motors strike discussed in Profile 4–1. Note that GM's primary stakeholders are owners, customers, employees, and, in this case, the United Auto Workers (UAW), the union that represents many of the employees. All primary stakeholders were clearly affected by the strike, as were many secondary stakeholders. Suppliers, communities, and other businesses were affected. The rest of the automotive industry was affected by the disruption in production.

PROFILE   4–1   *Seventeen Days at General Motors*

●......................

It lasted only 17 days. It happened at only two facilities in one community. Yet those 17 days had an amazing impact on stakeholders.

The United Auto Workers, representing GM's brake assembly plants, took its 3,000 members out on strike on March 5, 1996, partially to protest the company's use of outside contractors for some of the production. On March 22, 99 percent of the UAW members voted to ratify their new contract. As is typical in labor disputes, the two sides disagreed on who won and who lost. But consider the following stakeholders and the impact of the strike on them:

Dayton, Ohio, UAW members	3,000 people were out of work for 17 days
Other GM plants	Forced to close 26 plants because brake assemblies were not available; idled 178,125 workers
Caterpillar Inc.	Could not ship the truck engines it sells to GM for inclusion in medium-duty trucks
Ryder System (provides trucking services for GM)	Expected quarterly earnings to be down 30 percent
ITT Industries (makes parts for GM automobiles)	Expected earnings for the period to drop by $30 million

| GM stockholders | First-quarter net income was off by $900 million, although some was recovered later |

Some of the losses to some of the stakeholders will be recovered over time. But one 17-day strike disrupted the country like a stone being tossed into a quiet lake. Those stakeholders who were closest to the action were affected dramatically. Those who were not as closely connected were less affected but still felt the impact of the strike.

SOURCES: Rebecca Blumenstein and Nichole M. Christian, "Parts Dispute to Remain Despite GM–UAW Accord," *The Wall Street Journal*, March 25, 1996, p. A3; "GM Strike Means Drop in Earnings for Some Concerns," *The Wall Street Journal*, March 25, 1996, p. A8.

In the summer of 1997, UPS drivers went out on strike. Like the GM strike, this strike caused considerable disruption to companies such as Lands' End which ships 40 truckloads of merchandise each day. If you were the CEO of a direct-mail firm, how would you handle this disruption?

An Integrated Definition of Business

The short definition in Chapter 1 said a business strives for profits while meeting the needs of its customers. However, as we consider the nature of stakeholders, it becomes apparent that a broader definition is necessary to sufficiently integrate business with its various publics. Thus, with stakeholders in mind, we now provide an integrated definition of business. A **business** is an organization that strives for profits for its owners while meeting the needs of its customers and employees and balancing the impacts of its actions on other stakeholders. This definition captures better the interrelationships among the business and its various stakeholders.

Business
An organization that strives for profits for its owners while meeting the needs of its customers and employees and balancing the impacts of its actions on other stakeholders.

Developing Your Critical Thinking Skills

1. Choose a company with which you are familiar. Identify the stakeholders for that company. Which are primary and which are secondary?

2. How does the integrated definition of business differ significantly from the definition provided in Chapter 1?

Linking Business and Its Stakeholders: Expectations and Responsibilities

We have established that businesses have links to the stakeholders listed in Figure 4–1. The fact that a business affects and is affected by these stakeholders is an important, complex notion that needs to be discussed more fully. Stakeholders provide businesses with the *capacity* to operate. Think about that comment. Owners provide capital necessary for operations. Customers make the purchases that enable the business to generate revenue necessary for survival. Employees are the resources necessary to build products and offer services. Suppliers provide the inputs that allow the business to produce with quality and efficiency. Communities provide the atmosphere and facilities that help the business attract talented people and keep them happy. Without these stakeholders, the business would not have the capacity to do what it does.

But each of these stakeholders has certain *expectations* of the business. They realize that the business is at least to some extent dependent on them, so they find it reasonable to place certain demands or expectations on the business. Thus, owners expect profits or return on their investments. Customers expect quality products. Employees expect fair payment for their efforts. Suppliers expect favorable contracts and relationships. Communities expect business support of community programs. The business cannot ignore these expectations. If it does, the stakeholder groups may withhold their part of the capacity formula and make it very difficult for the business to survive.

Accordingly, the business must recognize its *responsibility* to address stakeholder expectations. Of course, not all the expectations of all the stakeholders can be met. Remember, we said that stakeholder expectations often conflict, so the business and its managers must reasonably address and balance the expectations of its various stakeholders. In essence, business decision makers are always looking at the "capacity—stakeholder expectations—business responsibility" framework and trying to determine how best to make it all fit together. In the following sections, we will consider the links between business and some of its key stakeholders. We explore both stakeholder expectations and business responsibilities. We see that management decisions are always subject to the scrutiny of stakeholders.

To start us on this process, consider the advertisements of Calvin Klein noted in Profile 4–2. This issue is tough. Do you think the ads are in poor taste? Are they socially offensive? Even if they are, does it matter as long as they are effective in capturing the intended target market?

PROFILE 4–2   *Calvin Klein's Ads*

Young men and women in suggestive poses. Provocative centerfold-type ads. A woman in a jeans vest touching her breasts. A topless female model. Welcome to the world of advertising at Calvin Klein. Welcome to the struggles of selling Calvin Klein jeans and fragrances in an increasingly competitive environment.

Is the Calvin Klein approach an example of creative advertising and good business? Is CK simply in touch with the young people who buy its products and who value an on-the-edge, challenging, unconventional approach to life? Or has Calvin Klein gone too far? Are these ads, as Janice Grossman of *Seventeen* magazine says, simply too blatant? Is this cool and adept marketing or is it just bad taste?[3]

These ads raise two important questions. First, is this approach really effective? That is, will the advertising appeal to the intended youth market and truly lead to increased sales for Calvin Klein? Second, even if these ads do enhance sales and lead to better financial performance, are they the right thing for a business to do? There is no definitive answer to this second question. It is a matter of opinion and of business philosophy. Each business and more specifically, its managers, must answer these questions. In part, the answer lies in what managers view as the ethical and social responsibilities of the business to the society in which it operates.

Developing Your Critical Thinking Skills

1. Look at a Calvin Klein ad. Who are the stakeholders that may be affected by the decision to run it?

2. What do you think each stakeholder expects in this situation?

3. How would you recommend that Calvin Klein act to balance stakeholder expectations? What is the responsible thing to do?

Owners and Investors

The owners of the firm are obviously primary stakeholders. They are the ones who underwrite the firm. They are the people and institutions who have risked their dollars and support so the business could operate. They have chosen to invest in business rather than pursue other opportunities. Surely they deserve to receive a return on their investment for taking such risks. In fact, this notion of a business providing returns to its owners and investors is fundamental to our free enterprise system. Without this focus, there would be no real incentive for anyone to take the risk of investment. Most people agree that a business has a responsibility to its owners and investors to assure a return on their investment.

The real sticking point is, how much return is proper? Some people argue that the most important (many would say sole) responsibility of a business is to maximize return to owners and investors. That means the firm provides the owners and investors as much money as it can. Therefore, managers should focus their energies on enhancing revenues, reducing expenses, and thereby gaining as much profit as possible. Advocates of this view believe that it is *not* the job of business to address social issues or problems. They think other institutions, such as government and nonprofit social service agencies, should deal with social concerns. Do not dismiss this perspective lightly. It is technically sound and is backed by some powerful and well-respected business and economic thinkers. Consider, for example, Profile 4–3.

PROFILE 4–3   **THE CONCEPT OF WEALTH**

The role of wealth creation is considered by many to be the essence of business. It is the very reason why entrepreneurs start businesses and why others invest in them. It is why venture capitalists invest in high-risk ventures. It is why owners of potentially successful businesses take their business public, selling their stock on one of the stock exchanges. It is why investment counselors are in high demand. Milton Friedman, an internationally acclaimed economist, even asserts that it is the social responsibility of business to increase its profits.[4] The following table shows the eight richest individuals in America. Virtually all of them made their money from owning a business. Note that Microsoft cofounder Paul Allen is only two slots below his better-known colleague Bill Gates, and Steve Ballmer is number six.

We do not intend to convey the message that the only reason for starting a business is wealth creation. Studies show that people also start businesses because they want independence, desire achievement or challenge, or even need an alternative to unemployment. But wealth creation is consistently in the top two or three reasons cited in surveys. Nor do we contend that everyone who either owns or invests in a business is concerned only with the pursuit of profits. Yet the lure of profit and wealth is a powerful incentive for both Bill Gates wannabes and individuals who have a few hundred dollars a year to invest for retirement.

The Eight Wealthiest Individuals in the United States		
1. William Henry Gates III	Microsoft	$39.8 billion
2. Warren Buffett	Berkshire Hathaway	$21 billion

3.	Paul G. Allen	Microsoft	$17 billion
4.	Lawrence Ellison	Oracle Corp.	$9.2 billion
5.	Gordon Moore	Intel Corp.	$8.8 billion
6.	Steven Ballmer	Microsoft	$8.3 billion
7.	John Werner Kluge	Metromedia	$7.8 billion
8.	Ronald Perelman	Investments	$6.5 billion

SOURCE: "Forbes Four Hundred," October 13, 1997, http://www.forbes.com, (accessed October 31, 1997).

Others argue that the profit maximization argument is too extreme and fails to recognize that business *does* and *should* have a broader role of responsibility to other stakeholders. Consider, for example, businesses' responsibility to their communities and to society in general. Advocates note that businesses exist in society and are part of society, so being socially responsible is the right thing to do. Because business is in a better position to address social issues than any other institution in our society, it is logical for business to assume this role. Anita Roddick, founder of the Body Shop, says, "Business is now entering centre stage. It is faster, it is more creative, it is more wealthy than governments. However, if it comes with no moral sympathy or honourable code of behavior, God help us all."[5]

benefits p. 433>

motivation p. 426>

Further, some people argue that in the long run, attention to social concerns does benefit the business on the bottom line. For example, if a business helps address public health issues, costs of benefits such as insurance may be reduced. If a business works to provide a less stressful work environment for its employees, they may demonstrate less absenteeism and more overall motivation toward the job. If a business focuses on community issues, it may be able to attract skilled workers to move to the community. If a business addresses important social issues, customers may view it more favorably. The arguments here can be compelling. In fact, one survey found that over three-fourths of its respondents preferred to buy from businesses that supported worthy causes.[6] The key here is that the business does derive benefits by addressing social issues, and sometimes those benefits are fairly direct. This seems to be the case with Starbucks, which is highlighted in Profile 4–4.

PROFILE 4–4   *Starbucks: Coffee with a Conscience*

Howard Schultz is the principal owner of Starbucks, a Seattle-based chain of coffee bars that's spreading faster than spilled coffee. His ideas on how to treat employees (known as "partners") are innovative. At Starbucks, every employee who works at least 20 hours a week is provided full medical benefits, including mental health coverage. Recently these part-time employees were even granted stock options, a perk typically reserved for top managers. While many businesses are cutting back, Starbucks intends to keep expanding benefits coverage; it just added vision care to the package. Starbucks is not legally obligated to do any of this. In fact, with 40 percent of its employees working more than 20 hours but less than 40 hours a week, the added costs are staggering.

Starbucks is recognized as an excellent company to work for and one whose managers respond to the needs of the workers. CEO Howard Schultz feels that this attention to employees' needs helps the bottom line. Do you think there is a relationship between profit and the concern for employee needs or other social issues for most companies? Is Starbucks unique?

Schultz is focused in his intent. He believes that these actions are not only morally right but also good business practice. He attributes Starbuck's phenomenal growth over the past six years to employees who take a personal interest in the business and in their customers. He says these policies give Starbucks a philosophical advantage as well as a competitive one. And they do seem to help the bottom line: net sales have grown sixfold over the past six years and employee turnover is less than 60 percent annually, about one-fifth the rate of the average restaurant business.

SOURCE: Don L. Boroughs, "The Bottom Line on Ethics," *U.S. News & World Report*, March 20, 1995, pp. 61, 66.

Today most business leaders accept that business does have social responsibilities beyond those to owners and investors. However, there should be no doubt that the *first* responsibility of the healthy business is to its owners and investors. They deserve a fair return on their investment. Attention to other stakeholders may require short-run trade-offs for the business. Even if businesses ultimately experience some benefits from these actions, there is still a cost involved. Therefore, the managers of the business must determine how much and how far they will move toward balancing stakeholder expectations. Not surprisingly, there is great variation from business to business.

Customers

Customers are a primary stakeholder since, without them, the business could not survive. Managers of successful businesses must be sensitive to their customers if they hope to compete. The business must provide consumers the products they want, when they want, at prices that they are willing to pay. However, many people argue that the business' responsibilities to its customers extends beyond this basic competitive focus. Customers' expectations of businesses include quality products and services, choice, communication, safety, and respect. Note as we discuss these expectations that there are trade-offs. Managers must always have an eye on the bottom line. They must ask, "What is the relationship between meeting customer expectations and making a profit?"

Product/Service Quality

Value/price relationship

A relationship in which customers get the best possible value from the products they purchase, given the price they pay.

Customers expect an adequate **value/price relationship** from a business. This means that they expect to get the best possible value from the products they purchase, given the price they pay. They also expect the products they purchase to be of good quality, performing as they are advertised and doing so with consistency and dependability. But let's think this through more carefully. As a customer, you would like to have the absolute top quality while paying bargain basement prices. A business simply cannot do this. It is important for managers as well as their customers to understand this value/price relationship.

The value/price relationship does not necessarily mean that the product or service must be of highest quality. Sometimes average quality is sufficient if the price is low enough. For example, customers at Kmart or Wal-Mart expect no more than average

Romano's Macaroni Grill allows customers to tell the table attendants how many glasses of wine they have drunk with their meal. Macaroni's management feels that the honor system is part of the quality of service and part of the ambiance of the restaurant. What are some other ways that a restaurant can provide quality service to its customers and still make money?

service in their shopping experience, but they expect the lowest possible price. But when those same customers shop at Nordstrom's, they expect top-quality personal service because that is what they are paying for. Two examples from our focus companies illustrate how companies can create expectations for quality service or products and then meet them effectively. Note that both companies do quite well financially because of those high expectations of quality.

At Brinker International's Romano's Macaroni Grill, table attendants bring a large bottle of house wine to the table soon after customers are seated. The customers simply drink as much wine as they want and, at the end of the meal, tell the attendant how many glasses they drank. The restaurant figures that customers underestimate by about 5 percent because of dishonesty or bad memory. Yet this amenity helps to create an atmosphere of quality and value—and Macaroni's more than makes up for any losses through the volume of wine consumed over an evening. In this case, Brinker International developed a policy that not only became part of the ambience of the Macaroni Grill restaurant but also brings in considerable income. Customer expectations are met, and the company profits.

Many of you own pagers or cellular phones, and about 70 percent of you who do own them carry Motorola brand equipment. Motorola focuses on quality. In fact, it is so confident about the quality of the equipment that it assures customers that virtually no pagers will fail for reasons associated with the manufacturing of the product. This, then, becomes your expectation, that your pager will never need repair unless you damage it or the battery causes problems. Logically, customers are willing to pay a premium for Motorola products. You can find cheaper alternatives, but not with the same quality assurance.

Choice

Another area in which customers have expectations is in competitive pricing and selection. Customers expect that companies will compete fairly both in terms of pricing and selection. For the free market to work effectively, companies must not collude in price-fixing and must respect patents and copyrights held by other companies. There are laws designed specifically to protect customers' freedom of choice. Some of these will be presented in Chapter 9.

Communication

Another set of customer expectations has to do with communications in both directions. First, customers expect that businesses will communicate with them. This may be in the form of labels on boxes, instructions enclosed with products, truthful lending terms, and complete information regarding what services will be provided and what the real cost is. This is always important, and no more so than in health-related products. Customers expect to know if there are side effects to drugs, how much fat or cholesterol is in food, and whether there are other risks.

The second issue regards communication back to the company. If customers have a problem or concern, they expect that someone will answer the phone and give them immediate attention. Some companies do extremely well here in providing hot lines or other mechanisms for contacting them. Others provide websites where customers can interact with the company.

Lands' End's policy of accepting returns without questioning shows great respect for customers. This is critical in a mail order business in order to get repeat business. Is the importance of respect for customers the same in all industries?

Safety

Consumers expect that products will be safe for normal usage. This is critical because consumers typically operate on a *presumption of safety*. Such expectations are reasonable since it is not feasible for consumers to test every product before using it. They assume that the business has done the appropriate tests.

However, the right to safety must be balanced with reality. If, for example, customers use products in a blatantly unsafe manner, it is unfair for them to hold the company liable in the case of accidents. Similarly, if customers have disabled products' built-in safety features, they should not expect remuneration if they are injured.

Respect

Customers expect businesses to treat them with respect. There are few things as frustrating as dealing with a business whose employees seem to feel that the customer is nothing but a necessary evil. This arrogance and insensitivity to customers and their needs risks driving them away. By contrast, customers appreciate businesses that treat them with care and consideration. Many businesses use their foundation of customer respect as a competitive edge that can pay dividends in terms of repeat sales.

Consider the example of Lands' End, a major catalog seller of high-quality clothing. The company has built its reputation on prompt, friendly service. It also adds another customer-friendly twist: an ironclad guarantee to give a total refund for any item the customer is dissatisfied with, whatever the reason, no questions asked.[7] This shows a high level of respect for customers and no doubt enhances the Lands' End image in a very competitive market.

We have focused here on customer expectations. Does this mean that businesses have an equivalent responsibility for each customer expectation? It means businesses have a responsibility to consider those expectations carefully. To the extent that they can meet customer expectations while maintaining or enhancing profits, they should make every attempt. In those cases where meeting customer expectations is just too expensive, managers must be cautious. They should analyze whether the customer expectations are indeed legitimate and if they can be met profitably.

Employees

Employees are a third primary stakeholder . Their claim on the business is meaningful jobs that pay an equitable wage or salary. They expect managers to treat them fairly. They expect the business to provide them with a safe place to work. They expect the business to give them sufficient training to do their jobs well. The role of employees as stakeholders is particularly significant if they belong to unions. Unions are generally secondary stakeholders due to the impact of unionism on the way the business world operates. But if a particular business is unionized, then the union becomes a primary stakeholder because of the direct interaction between the union and the firm. This is especially true if the union is a major national union that represents workers at several large manufacturing companies (for example, the UAW or Teamsters).

Businesses recognize these expectations. Yet businesses in today's competitive environment face extreme pressures to ensure that their labor force is as productive as possible. In today's era of downsizing, there is considerable controversy regarding the level and extent of a firm's responsibility to its employees. Certainly, some of the traditional employer/employee relationships and expectations appear to be changing. For example, most businesses believe their competitive situations are so fickle that they can no longer guarantee employee's long-term job security.

It is certainly in a company's best interest to treat workers with respect, give them adequate training, provide meaningful work, and pay them a fair wage. Responsibility to employees, however, goes beyond just those items that are directly in the best short-run interest of the firm. While Southwest Airlines CEO Herb Kelleher focuses on customers through discount fares, it is clear that his employees come first—even if it means dismissing customers. But aren't customers always right? "No they are not," Kelleher snaps. "And I think it is one of the biggest betrayals of employees a boss can possibly commit. The customer is sometimes wrong. We don't carry those sorts of customers. We write to them and say, 'Fly somebody else. Don't abuse our people.'"[8]

Exactly what are the business' responsibilities to its people? Four themes seem important. First, the business should operate so that *talent prevails*. This means that people who have talent and skills should be developed, promoted, and compensated regardless of their backgrounds or other differences. It means that companies must ensure that workers are not unduly harassed or coerced. This includes preventing sexual and racial harassment, of course, but it also means preventing the coercing of employees to falsify records, knowingly produce inferior products, or commit other unethical or illegal acts. Indeed, this is the focus of Chapter 5.

Second, businesses should ensure that employees operate in a *safe working environment*. Like other stakeholders, the government has an interest in safe working conditions. The *Occupational Safety and Health Administration* (*OSHA*) is charged with overseeing safety in businesses. The impact of OSHA regulations will be discussed further in Chapter 9.

Third, the business should make the work environment as *meaningful and rewarding* as possible. Employees spend a significant portion of their time and often the bulk of their productive efforts and energies at work. In return, the business should try to make that work experience as satisfying as possible.

training p. 379>

Fourth, the business should invest in the *training and development* of its people. No business today can guarantee the security of lifetime employment. However, if their skills are consistently being upgraded, employees should feel reasonably secure. They will know that they have talents the business needs. Of course, making sure its people retain marketable and competitive skills should help the business perform better.

Many companies go beyond the minimum. One that is noted for its employee orientation is Northwestern Mutual Life Insurance. Northwestern has a no-layoff policy, which works because of its commitment to training, education, and continual skills development. But there's more. For example, corporate headquarters houses a fitness center and an outstanding employee restaurant with a staff of chefs. About 2,500 employees eat lunch at that restaurant each day. And it costs those employees—nothing! Northwestern believes that the cost of these free lunches (about $3 million each year) is money well spent to support the desired family environment.[9]

Secondary Stakeholders

We listed in Figure 4–1 nearly a dozen groups that could be considered secondary stakeholders. The following paragraphs focus on a few of those to illustrate the links between businesses and these stakeholders. Included is a very broad category called responsibility to society, which encompasses many different elements.

Unions

Unions
Formally recognized organizations that represent a company's or industry's workers.

Unions are formally recognized organizations that represent a company's or industry's workers. Unions are typically considered to be secondary stakeholders because unionism in general affects how businesses operate. For example, wage rates in a community are affected by unions, even in companies that are not represented by a union. However, unions can succeed only if the business succeeds. If a company's costs are so high that it has trouble competing in global markets, unions may have to make concessions. The union and its members lose if the company is forced to downsize or close a plant.

outsourcing p. 279>

Union membership in the United States has been steadily declining over the last 40 years.[10] This is due in part to the growth in service industries, which typically are not unionized. Growth in part-time positions has also hurt the union movement, since part-timers are seldom unionized. Finally, part of the decline is due to technology and increased outsourcing, which have led to layoffs in unionized industries. Despite this trend, unions still represent about 16 percent of the workers in the United States.[11] A large, powerful union like the United Steel Workers can be a strong, primary stakeholder to which a company must pay attention. This interaction between the business and union becomes particularly relevant during times of *contract negotiation*. We will discuss unions in more depth in Chapter 9.

The Natural Environment

Environmentalism
Efforts and actions to protect the natural environment in which a business operates.

Environmentalism, or the *green movement*, has become a key public policy issue. **Environmentalism** refers to efforts and actions to protect the natural environment in which a business operates. Many people suggest that business must step forward and take a leading role in addressing global warming, landfill contamination, pollution, and other issues of environmental concern. But despite the importance of these concerns, remedies and responsibilities are tougher to establish.

A business can address environmental issues by its policies and actions. Particularly in the areas of air, water, and land pollution, businesses can make decisions and take actions that encourage care of our nonrenewable natural resources. A number of companies are known for their environmental philosophies and activities. Earlier we mentioned Anita Roddick and her Body Shop stores. The Body Shop has always made environmental protection a key priority and included it in the statement of core business values. For example, it emphasizes recycled paper and recycled plastic. Believing that the greatest opportunity for waste reduction is through minimal packaging, the business even has a refill policy so customers can reuse bottles.[12]

The Community

Many people believe businesses have a responsibility to the communities where they operate. That responsibility may be carried out in many ways. Often businesses support or even sponsor community events such as the symphony, opera, ballet, or special community festivals. These businesses commit their financial support to bring entertainment and cultural enrichment to their community. Many companies have matching gifts programs, in which the business matches employee contributions to charitable organizations.

Many businesses encourage their employees to be actively involved in their communities. It is not unusual to find businesspeople holding key positions as community volunteers. Most social organizations, from the United Way to the Boy Scouts, depend on such a cadre of volunteers to accomplish their goals. By and large, the business world accepts that volunteerism is important and needs to be encouraged. Often businesses even provide employees some scheduling flexibility so they can pursue both work and volunteer activities.

Some businesses support foundations that exist to promote social and community progress. For example, Ben & Jerry's Foundation awards funds to support research in the areas of children and families, disenfranchised groups, and the environment.

Businesses recognize that community involvement is both the right thing to do and good business. Consider the words of Norman Brinker, chair of Brinker International. He says one of his underlying leadership philosophies is "to give something back to the community. Getting involved both politically and philanthropically will repay you in a thousand ways you never even knew existed."[13]

Society in General

Society places broad expectations on the shoulders of business. The logic is direct and simple. Businesses that are prospering in a society should contribute back to the betterment of that society. Many businesses are doing this.

For example, some businesses are taking a lead in promoting and supporting public health issues. They may contribute funds for basic research aimed at finding answers to troubling health concerns. Corporate sponsorship of muscular dystrophy research (much of it through the very visible avenue of the Jerry Lewis Labor Day Telethon) has enabled important medical advances in dealing with this crippling childhood disease. Research into the most troubling social health concern of our day, AIDS, would be difficult without corporate backing.

Trek is a business that takes its responsibility to society seriously. Trek works to generate funds for cancer research. Its annual Trek 100 charity rides, in partnership with Midwest Athletes Against Childhood Cancer, have raised over $1.5 million since 1990.[14]

Trek's "Ride for Hope" brings in considerable funds for cancer research. At the same time, it builds comaraderie among Trek bikers. What effect will their sponsorship of the races have on their own profits?

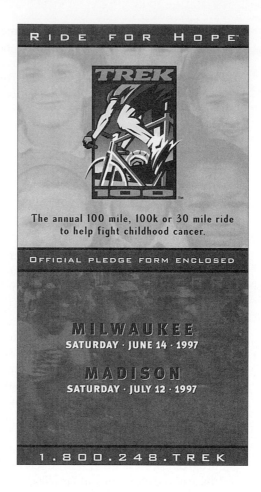

Some companies even make strategic business decisions that are guided by their interest in public health concerns. For example, the refusal of Harley-Davidson to continue allowing the name Harley to be used on cigarettes was based on clear evidence of the dangers of smoking. The company did not wish to support such harmful products.

Developing Your Critical Thinking Skills

1. Some people argue that unions have improved the working conditions of all employees over time. How is this so?

2. Can you think of a situation where attention to the interests of *secondary* stakeholders would improve the overall success of the company?

3. What is the benefit of thinking of customers as stakeholders rather than just customers?

4. When does a business know it has gone too far in investing in social causes?

Creating an Ethical Culture

Superimposed on the responsibilities to stakeholders is the need to act ethically in whatever the firm does. This need transcends everything else, and it influences how the firm's managers view their responsibilities to their various stakeholders. The remainder of this chapter discusses the role of ethics in decision making. It introduces the concepts of moral dilemmas and ethical cultures.

Why a Business Focus on Ethics?

There are many reasons why businesses emphasize the practice of ethical behavior. For many managers, it is simply the right thing to do and it reflects their personal values. But there are three additional reasons business ethics is important, reasons that are key ingredients in the formula of business success and competitiveness.

- Customers demand ethical behavior.
- Good ethics improves the work climate.
- Newly empowered workers need clear guidelines.

First, businesses must understand and meet the ethical expectations of their customers. Customers demand ethical action and increasingly support businesses' efforts to be good corporate citizens. Many customers are repulsed by businesses that fail to meet ethical standards. They are disgusted by the visible examples of poor ethical practice, from companies that pollute to those that practice discrimination to those that cut corners on safety. Whenever possible, these customers are likely to turn from such businesses.

High ethical standards and public trust are the essence of some businesses. When public trust is lost, the firm's competitive strength is also lost. This is the case with certified public accounting (CPA) firms, which must adhere to the highest levels of ethics. Reputations for ethical behavior are essential for the confidence clients place in these firms. The same is true for many independent consulting businesses.

Consider the case of Healthy Buildings International (HBI), an independent building inspection business. HBI provides a service to other businesses by inspecting their facilities and gauging the quality of the physical environment. For years, it has assured the public that smoking in well-ventilated buildings posed minimal health risk to the people working or living there. Recent findings may affect HBI's reputation. Apparently some of its research was funded by the Tobacco Institute, a trade group of the tobacco industry. Even though such an arrangement may be lawful, it calls into question HBI's independence. If this reduces the perceived credibility of its service, customers may stop relying on HBI for information and assessment.[15]

Second, clear ethical standards and direction foster more favorable and promising work climates. People know what to expect; they know what will and what will not be tolerated. They know that success is not secured at *any* cost. Often this knowledge makes them feel better about their employers and more committed to their work situations.

There is a third and quite significant reason why contemporary business emphasizes ethical behavior so strongly. As businesses become leaner and more streamlined, more and more discretion is being given to employees. The new, empowered workforce has been granted expanded decision-making authority. At the same time, there are fewer managers around to act as checks and balances. Increasingly, companies must trust employees to behave ethically on their own. In this environment, clear and consistent ethical standards and practices are fundamental. Empowered workers use these standards and practices as the basis for their actions and decisions.

It is unclear whether attention to ethical behavior does, in fact, result in higher profits. However, there is clear evidence that businesses that are exposed for corporate crimes such as bribery, tax evasion, and violation of government contracts see a negative impact on their stock prices. This effect is even stronger if the business was earlier accused of illegal actions.[16]

Defining Business Ethics

Business ethics
The search for and commitment to meet appropriate standards of moral conduct in business situations.

Ethics involves a search for standards of moral conduct. Therefore, **business ethics** involves the search for and commitment to meet appropriate standards of moral conduct in business situations. In simplest terms, business ethics means figuring out the appropriate way to act in different business settings. In practice, business ethics is concerned with two issues. First is the difficulty of determining what actions really are appropriate from situation to situation. Second is having the fortitude to carry out those ethical actions.

At this point, you may question why there is so much concern over ethics. Certainly, reasonable people know the difference between right and wrong. Further, behaving in ways you know are right is pretty straightforward. Figuring out what is appropriate behavior and acting accordingly just cannot be that difficult! But in fact the determination of what is appropriate is often quite complicated. And even if you know what should be done, there may be significant pressures nudging you to act in ways different from your personal inclinations. Let's explore these complexities further.

The Concept of Moral Dilemmas

On a recent episode of the popular TV show "ER," a young doctor named Dr. Benton was faced with a moral decision. He had accidentally discovered that a respected senior surgeon had been excluding certain patients from his research. These exclusions made the senior physician's pioneering surgical procedures appear to have stronger and more successful outcomes than actually was the case. They were inconsistent with the research parameters being touted and even raised questions regarding the overall effectiveness of the surgical procedure. Benton's personal moral standards told him that these discrepancies should be reported. But nearly everyone advised him to say nothing. These colleagues argued that the senior surgeon could destroy Benton's career. Also, the senior surgeon's well-earned reputation brought large financial contributions—contributions that were essential to the survival of one of the few hospitals that cared for patients who couldn't pay. What should be done? As in most real situations, the issues are cloudy and open to different interpretations. Further, the ramifications are perplexing and potentially costly. This story allows us to examine some of the dynamics of ethical decision making.

Moral dilemma
A conflict of interests involving ethical choices.

Dr. Benton is experiencing a **moral dilemma,** which exists when there is a conflict of interests involving ethical choices (see Figure 4–2). A moral dilemma exists because Benton's personal standards of what is right and appropriate conflict with the demands of the situation (strong pressures to say nothing). Like Benton, each of us has

Private morality
Our personal moral standards.

personal moral standards, which are known as our **private morality.** Our personal standards, or private morality, are learned. They are developed and refined throughout our entire lives. Like anyone confronted by a moral dilemma, Benton must decide how to act or respond to resolve this dilemma. Consider the possibilities. He may abide by his own sense of what seems to be right (private morality) and file a formal report outlining his charges. He may talk to the senior surgeon and attempt to change the surgeon's behavior. Or he may yield to the pressures of the situation and reason that it is less risky to just forget what he saw.

Whatever action he takes will produce consequences. If a formal report is filed, a surgeon's reputation will be tainted, hospital funding will probably be affected, many meaningful programs may be lost, and many people will be angry with Benton. If he takes a personal approach and talks informally with the surgeon, this action may clear his conscience, but it may be devastating to his career. Finally, if Benton does nothing, the lives of innocent patients may be affected. As you can see, identifying and understanding the possible consequences should play a major role in the decision-making process.

The decision that Benton makes—his enacted ethical decision—will contribute to the ethical environment of the organization (hospital) where he works. His decision will affect others' perceptions of him. His actions (or lack of action) may eventually even affect the reputation of the hospital. Ethical decisions have a way of affecting many more people (stakeholders) than might appear to be the case at first.

Many of our most pressing ethical concerns are affected by issues of *exploitation*, which involves taking advantage of someone or something for personal gain.[17]

FIGURE 4–2   Elements of Moral Dilemma

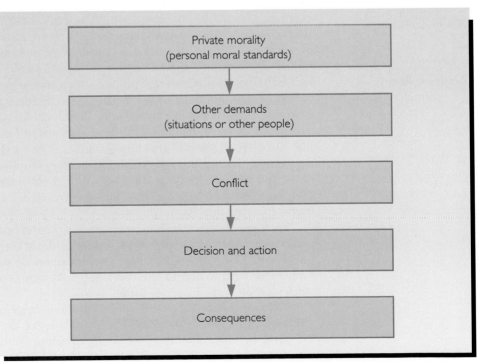

top management p. 65>

Although exploitation can occur in a number of ways, the question is tricky. When is an action just good hard-nosed business, and when is it taking advantage? Is, say, corporate downsizing an unethical and exploitative action? Consider a company that eliminates the jobs of thousands of middle managers. These managers may have given years of loyal performance to the business. They have done nothing wrong. In fact, it may be the strategic errors of top management that have pushed the business into financial disarray. Can it possibly be "right" to crush the lives of thousands who do not deserve it?

On the other hand, the business must survive and its costs must be curtailed. Only the most critical areas and positions can be protected. This is the nature of our contemporary competitive climate. As you can see, there is a conflict of interests. There is a moral dilemma. Whatever decision is made will have consequences that affect the lives of many.

Helping Employees Resolve Moral Dilemmas

Managers, as well as employees at every level, must make difficult choices and decisions that represent their best attempts to resolve the moral dilemmas they face. How do people make such choices and decisions? Even more important, how should they? To answer this question, we must consider some basics of moral reasoning and suggest some approaches for deciding what is the right thing to do.

Return to the question of downsizing. The downsizing decision affects not only the lives of hundreds of employees and their families but also the future competitiveness (perhaps even the survival) of the business. Some ethicists would propose an approach to this dilemma known as utilitarianism. Here is how it works. Decision makers (in this case business leaders) are asked to consider all possible parties who could be affected by the downsizing decision. These parties are stakeholders, since they have some stake in what happens. Leaders are asked to evaluate the impact of the decision for each of these relevant stakeholders. Sometimes this impact can be determined objectively. Usually it cannot, and a subjective impression must be used. In **utilitarianism,** a decision that produces the greatest good for the greatest number of stakeholders is a morally sound decision. Stated differently, an ethical decision should maximize benefits and minimize harms for stakeholders.

Utilitarianism
An approach to decision making that assumes decisions producing the greatest good for the greatest number of stakeholders are ethical.

In our example, the downsizing decision will affect the hundreds of workers who will lose their jobs. It will affect their families. Their reduced buying power may affect the communities where they reside. Remaining employees (survivors) may feel extra stress and pressure at their jobs. For all of these stakeholders—laid-off employees, their families, their communities, and even surviving employees—there are costs or harms from the downsizing decision.

Yet there are other stakeholders whose situations must be considered. If the company continues to lose competitive position and market share, even more workers will be laid off. The business may have to close a portion of its operations, which will be even more detrimental to the community. As competitiveness slips, the company's stock plummets and investors suffer.

A decision maker must consider all of these stakeholders and the likely impact of a downsizing decision on each. The advantages of downsizing may truly outweigh the costs, in which case the downsizing decision, from a purely utilitarian perspective, is ethically sound. Decision makers should exercise caution when approaching decisions as utilitarians. They must be careful to consider the full range of stakeholders that are involved. Further, they must be objective and thorough when weighing the real impact on each stakeholder.

Most business managers feel comfortable with the utilitarian approach. It is the kind of logical, cost/benefit style of decision making that makes sense to them. Yet there are times when a utilitarian-based decision may not be enough. It may fail to consider other important issues that should be part of ethical decision making. Therefore, two other methods of moral reasoning are typically emphasized: the theory of rights and the theory of justice.

Theory of rights

An approach to decision making that assumes there are certain individual rights that must always be protected.

The **theory of rights** approach to decision making argues that there are certain individual rights that must always be protected. If a decision violates or threatens these rights, it is not ethical. Return to our example of the young doctor faced with the dilemma regarding the senior surgeon. One might argue from a utilitarian view that saying nothing is the best way to maximize overall stakeholder benefit while minimizing stakeholder harm. But doesn't every person have the right to life and safety, the right not to be placed in a threatening situation without prior knowledge? By saying nothing, the doctor risks violating the rights of innocent patients. Even though the risks may be small, individual rights may be violated by a failure to disclose information, and patients' well-being may be endangered. Rights to safety, health, privacy, and truthfulness are held in high regard in the American culture. If a decision threatens these basic rights, its moral integrity is suspect.

Theory of justice

An approach to decision making that assumes decisions should be guided by equity, fairness, and impartiality.

The **theory of justice** states that decisions should be guided by equity, fairness, and impartiality. Using this line of reasoning, decision makers should try to be sure that both the benefits and the burdens that result from decisions are shared equitably by those involved.

For example, in recent years, a number of companies have received attention for the multimillion-dollar compensation packages their top executives receive. Is it fair for high-ranking executives to receive such lofty rewards? Is it fair for top executives like Robert Allen, who is profiled in Profile 4–5, to receive salary increases while they are downsizing the business and providing only average returns? Sometimes companies have even asked people lower in the organization to make concessions and cut spending to the barest of necessities. There have even been cases, in these same companies, where executives rewarded themselves after they gained a more favorable bottom line by extracting concessions from their employees. According to the theory of justice, these compensation decisions are of questionable morality since all parties are not sharing in the benefits and in the pain and trauma fairly.

Note that the key to the justice approach is *equity*, not equality. Nearly everyone agrees that the CEO deserves to make considerably more than a nonmanagerial employee. But how much more is fair and equitable? This points out a basic problem with both the theory of rights and the theory of justice: they are based on subjective impressions. When are rights really called into question? When is a discrepancy in pay really inequitable? Of course, there are no easy answers here. Today, most experts in business ethics suggest that decision makers should consider all three approaches when making decisions. In other words, does the decision appear morally sound when weighed against the standards of utilitarian, rights, and justice approaches? If the answer is yes, the decision is probably ethical. If the answer from any of the forms of moral reasoning is no, then further examination is needed. Again, this is never easy.

PROFILE 4–5   *How Much Is Too Much?*

In November 1997, Robert Allen retired at the age of 65 as chair of AT&T, one of the world's largest and most visible businesses. In the last few years of his tenure, he had been criticized for his personal compensation package. Here is why.

In 1995 AT&T eliminated 40,000 jobs and still barely broke even. For that year, Allen received a salary of $1.2 million. In addition, he received a bonus of $1.5 million, long-term incentive pay of $1.9 million, stock options, and other incentives. The entire compensation package carried a present value of nearly $11 million! Was he really worth that much? Even more puzzling, from an ethical perspective, was whether this lofty compensation package was fair.

Fairness is difficult to assess even when objective evidence exists. Consider the evidence. AT&T's performance under Allen has been decidedly average. Since he assumed the chairmanship in 1988, AT&T's stock price has kept pace with Standard & Poor's 500 average, but it has not excelled. Some see the massive and painful downsizing activities as evidence of poor use of investors' capital. Yet Allen was in the hot seat. He made tough decisions and boldly moved AT&T to change, which is never easy. For example, he moved the company away from its equipment and computer businesses and positioned it for growth in the telecommunications industry.

As with any values-based decision, there is no easy way to evaluate the ethics of Robert Allen's compensation. And as with any values-based decision, there are many advocates arguing strongly on both sides of this issue.

SOURCE: Roger Lowenstein, "Is Chairman Allen of AT&T Overpaid?" *The Wall Street Journal*, February 29, 1996, p. C1; AT&T press release, October 20, 1997.

Figuring Out What to Do

As the examples here show, it is often quite difficult to know what to do. Even weighing the perspectives of different moral theories helps only so much. However, businesses can guide their employees to determine what is right and proper.

mission p. 310>   Many businesses include their ethical intentions as part of their *mission statements*. For example, Hallmark specifies "ethical and moral conduct at all times and in all our relationships," Southland Corp. (7-Eleven stores) says it will "conduct its business in an ethical manner with the highest integrity," and AT&T states that "we are honest and ethical in all our business dealings."[18] While such statements are broad and general, they do signify that the practice of ethical behavior is fundamental to the business. This underscores the tone of ethics that the business believes is important.

Core values
Those specific beliefs that a business makes part of its operating philosophy.

Some businesses go a step beyond the mission statement by defining a set of **core values,** those specific beliefs that the business makes part of its operating philosophy. These statements of core values typically cover honesty, respect, trust, and the overall moral tone of the business. For example, giant advertising agency Leo Burnett provides employees with 10 core values, which it calls operating principles. Included is the principle of integrity, which extolls employees to operate at all times in an ethical and moral manner. Boeing and Kellogg both have integrity statements, which are shown in Profile 4–6. Such statements of core values are becoming increasingly popular. (More will be said about them later in this chapter.)

PROFILE 4–6   *Boeing's Integrity Statement*

Integrity is a fundamental part of Boeing history and the way we do business. Our commitment to integrity means that all of our actions and relationships are based on these uncompromising values:

- Treat each other with respect
- Deal fairly in all our relationships
- Honor our commitments and obligations
- Communicate honestly
- Take responsibility for our actions
- Deliver safe and reliable products of the highest quality
- Provide equal opportunity to all
- Comply with all laws and regulations

Kellogg's Statement on Integrity and Ethics

Integrity is the cornerstone of our business practice. We will conduct our affairs in a manner consistent with the highest ethical standards. To meet this commitment, we will:

- Engage in fair and honest business practice
- Show respect for each other, our consumers, customers, suppliers, shareholders, and the communities in which we operate
- Communicate in an honest, factual, and accurate manner

SOURCE: Patricia Jones and Larry Kahaner, *Say It and Live It: 50 Corporate Mission Statements That Hit the Mark* (New York: Doubleday, 1995), pp. 34–35, 147.

Code of conduct
A formal, written statement specifying the kinds of things a business believes should be done and those that should be avoided.

A popular way for many businesses to promote ethical behavior is through codes of conduct, sometimes referred to as codes of ethics. **Codes of conduct** are formal, written statements specifying the kinds of things that the business believes should be done and those things that should be avoided. The purpose of such a code is to tell employees how to approach and resolve difficult ethical issues. Usually the code tries to define and outline common ethical problems or dilemmas that are likely to arise. Codes of conduct can be quite specific. For example, they might tell employees to "accept no gifts from any dealers, suppliers, or associates with whom they do business." Presumably, such a directive is intended to reduce the risk of favoritism. Johnson & Johnson is well known for its ethics code, which helped guide the company through the Tylenol poisoning crisis of the early 1980s. Since the J & J code emphasizes public safety above all else, the extreme and costly decision to recall all Tylenol products was accepted as logical and reasonable.

While codes of conduct are important, they do not address the range of complex ethical situations managers encounter. In reality, they cannot. Codes of conduct deal with the most common issues and concerns and offer general guidance. They do not help much with the gray areas that are the most difficult struggles many managers face. However, codes of conduct do make positive, constructive statements regarding some areas of ethical intent and action.

Some companies provide more detailed policies and procedures than are contained in the code of conduct. For example, some companies use ethics booklets to offer specific guidelines for dealing with ethical questions that may arise in certain areas. These booklets are usually updated regularly to provide guidelines on how to respond to current ethical concerns. Texas Instruments is one company that generates some creative approaches for offering ethics advice, as shown in Profile 4–7.

PROFILE 4-7

Texas Instruments' Cornerstone Booklets

Although Texas Instruments (TI) has a well-regarded code of ethics, it has also developed other approaches to complement its code. For example, a series of ethics booklets known as Cornerstone Booklets provides more detailed ethical leadership for employees. Each booklet covers a unique area of concern. One booklet concentrates on gifts, travel, and entertainment, one on personal rights, and one on conducting business with the U.S. government.

It has also established online ethics menus, which provide documents from the ethics office on given ethics issues. There is an online ethics newspaper, with over 300 articles on a broad range of subjects. Employees who want personal, face-to-face advice can meet with officers from the ethics office and receive specific guidance. Those desiring more anonymity can call the ethics hot line. Confidential e-mail that doesn't disclose the message's point of origin is also available.

These plentiful options underscore TI's commitment to ethical practice. They want employees to have a variety of ways to access ethics materials and guidelines. To Texas Instruments, this is sound business practice.

SOURCE: Gillian Flynn, "Make Employee Ethics Your Business," *Personnel Journal* 7, no. 6, June 1995, p. 30(8).

Finally, many companies try to help their employees by providing formal ethics training. This training usually includes background on the utilitarian, rights, and justice approaches to moral reasoning and examples of how they can be used. Real-world business cases allow employees to practice making decisions in difficult ethical situations. The training also provides a detailed overview of the programs and approaches the business has available to provide guidance for handling ethical dilemmas.

Building an Ethical Culture

Business culture
A set of unwritten values and beliefs about what is proper, right, and appropriate in a business.

The idea of business culture is important to the study of business ethics. **Business culture** is a set of unwritten values and beliefs about what is proper, right, and appropriate in the business. These beliefs and values are generally well known and accepted by the members of the business. It is important to realize that a business culture develops slowly over time. A desired culture does not spring into existence full-grown because a leader dictates it. In order to nurture an ethical culture, business leaders must take certain steps. We emphasize three key steps for building an ethical business culture.

First, leaders must establish clear moral values for the business, removing as much doubt as possible regarding where the business stands on key moral values. In fact, business culture often reflects the personal values of its key managers. This is particularly true in small businesses, where the president of the company has a tremendously strong influence on the culture of the company. This culture is visible in the community in which the firm operates, and it is apparent to customers.

As noted earlier, businesses build culture through mission statements, statements of business philosophy, and statements of core values. Yet responsive leaders do more. They make sure company training efforts address moral values. The orientation programs for new employees feature the moral values of the business. Often there is open and regular discussion about ethical and moral concerns. In short, the leaders of the business go out of their way to elaborate and clarify moral values for their people.

The second step follows logically. Leaders must model the desired ethical standards and behavior. Actions really do speak louder than words. In business jargon, we say that leaders must "walk the talk." The best cue employees have as to how they should behave ethically comes from what they see people in positions of power and responsibility do. When leaders give ethical standards high priority and maintain them consistently, it sends a powerful signal to the rest of the employees.

The third step in this culture-building process may be the most difficult. The business must support and reinforce employees for adhering to ethical values. This shows most in the way it rewards employees. In general, people do what they are rewarded for doing. In other words, if the business consistently rewards ethical behavior and disciplines unethical behavior, employees learn how central ethical values are to the company. Logically, it is in their own best interests to practice ethical behavior.

Ethics as a Foundation of Business Practice

Ethics pervades every area of business. When salespeople promise customers delivery of products by certain dates, they are making ethical statements. When engineers design products to have the highest quality and safety controls possible, they are making an ethical statement. When internal accountants follow generally accepted practices without wavering, they are acting ethically. When managers treat their employees with respect and consideration, they are acting ethically.

Every employee in every area of the business is an ethical ambassador of the business. Of course, some employees are more visible than others. Some affect more people with their actions and decisions than others. However, as we have discussed in this chapter, the ethical nature of the business resides in the heart of the business. If an ethical philosophy is not felt and practiced by every employee at every level throughout the business, a true ethical culture will not exist. As a future business leader you must be an ethical role model within your business. Ethical considerations should be the foundation from which you start your decision-making process.

Developing Your Critical Thinking Skills

1. If you were Dr. Benton in the "ER" case, what would you have done? Why?

2. What do you think business leaders should do to promote the highest levels of ethical behavior in their organizations?

3. In your work experience, have you ever seen actions that you think were unethical? How should the business have responded to these actions?

SUMMARY

1. Businesses affect many different groups of people, and that fact presents a problem for ethical business managers. The problem is how to take into account the impact of the business on the affected groups or stakeholders.

   ■ What is a stakeholder?

   A stakeholder is a person or group that has some claim on or expectation of how a business should operate.

   ■ List the major categories of stakeholders.

   The major stakeholder groups are owners, customers, employees, suppliers, former employees, unions, the community, the natural environment, the industry in which the firm operates, other businesses, government, special interest groups, the media, and society in general.

2. Although the list of business stakeholders can be long, it can be divided according to how directly they influence the business.

   ■ Differentiate between the primary and secondary stakeholders for a business.

   Primary stakeholders are those stakeholders the business affects and interacts with most directly. The three stakeholder groups commonly considered to be primary are owners, customers, and employees.

   Secondary stakeholders are those whom the business affects in an indirect or limited way. These include all of the remaining stakeholder groups.

3. Some people view the business firm as having only one stakeholder (the stockholders). As a result, they tend to define or view business from a narrow perspective.

   ■ Give an integrated definition of the term *business*.

   A business is an organization that strives for profits for its owners while meeting the needs of its customers and employees and balancing the impacts of its actions on other stakeholders.

4. Stakeholders provide the business with the capacity to operate; in return, they expect something from the business.

   ■ What are the responsibilities of each stakeholder group to the business and what does each group expect in return?

   Owners provide capital and expect profits or return on their investments. Customers provide revenue and expect quality products. Employees provide labor and skills and expect fair pay and treatment. Suppliers provide needed inputs and expect favorable contracts and relationships. Communities provide the atmosphere and facilities that help the business attract talented people and keep them happy. In return, communities expect business to support community programs.

5. Underlying all the relationships between a business and its stakeholders is business ethics. This issue, which regularly appears in the media, has a major influence on business health.

■ What is the role of ethics in contemporary businesses?

There are many reasons why businesses emphasize ethics. Three important ones are these: (1) business must understand and meet the ethical expectations of its customers, (2) clear ethical standards and direction foster better work climates, and (3) clear and consistent ethical standards are crucial in the emerging environment of leaner organizations, where employees have to be trusted to know and do the right thing.

■ How would you define business ethics?

Business ethics involves a search for and commitment to meet appropriate standards of moral conduct in business situations.

6. In spite of its importance, addressing real ethical issues can be challenging due to the presence of moral dilemmas.

■ Define the concept of a moral dilemma.

A moral dilemma exists when there is a conflict of interests involving ethical choices.

7. Managers must have some foundation for reasoning through the moral dilemmas they face.

■ Explain three methods of moral reasoning that can be used to solve a moral dilemma.

One method is utilitarian reasoning, in which the morally best choice is that which produces the greatest good for the greatest number of stakeholders.

A second method is the theory of rights, which argues that there are certain individual rights that must always be protected. If a decision violates or threatens these rights, it is not ethical.

A third method is the theory of justice, which requires that decisions be guided by considerations of equity, fairness, and impartiality.

8. Given the importance of ethics, it is not surprising that many top managers devote substantial effort to helping employees act ethically. Those efforts consist of various specific practices and an attempt to create an ethical culture.

■ Describe some of the methods businesses use to help employees determine what is right and proper.

They may include the company's ethical intentions as part of the mission statement, define a set of core values, issue a code of conduct or a code of ethics, and/or provide formal ethics training for employees.

■ What is a business culture? What are the steps to building an ethical business culture?

A business culture is a set of unwritten values and beliefs about what is proper, right, and appropriate in the business.

Three key steps for building an ethical culture are these:

(1) Leaders must establish clear moral values for the business.

(2) Leaders must model the desired ethical standards and behavior.

(3) The business must support and reinforce employees for adhering to ethical values.

Links to future courses

This chapter is an important introduction to how business relates to its various stakeholders and how ethics plays a role in decision making. You may want to look at the following courses, both inside and outside of business, to deepen your learning.

- Philosophy and logic
- Business ethics
- Principles of finance

- Principles of marketing
- Strategic management/ business policy

KEY TERMS

Business (integrated definition), p. 95
Business culture, p. 114
Business ethics, p. 108
Code of conduct, p. 113
Core values, p. 112
Environmentalism, p. 104
Moral dilemma, p. 108
Primary stakeholders, p. 92

Private morality, p. 109
Secondary stakeholders, p. 92
Stakeholder, p. 91
Theory of justice, p. 111
Theory of rights, p. 111
Unions, p. 104
Utilitarianism, p. 110
Value/price relationship, p. 100

EXERCISES AND APPLICATIONS

1. Ask three professors to comment on which stakeholders are most important to a business. Select one professor from each of the following disciplines: finance or economics, management or marketing, and sociology or philosophy. Write a brief statement on how these professors agree and differ on the idea of stakeholders.

2. Go to the Ben & Jerry's website (http://www/benjerry.com). Look at the three-part mission statement. How does it include stakeholders?

3. Divide the class in half for a debate. One group is to assume, "The only relevant goal of a business is to maximize its profits and provide as much return as possible to its owners." The other group is to assume, "The successful business must balance the needs and concerns of a broad range of stakeholders, even if that means providing a lower rate of return to its owners."

4. Consider the following situations. For each, decide what you think is the proper course of action.

- You are the human resources director of a midsize business. You have just interviewed a candidate for an engineering job. While not the best candidate, he has an interesting background. He has spent the previous 10 years working in engineering and design for your top competitor and has indicated he knows many design secrets that he is willing to share with you and your business. Should you hire him?

- Your business has a strict policy that limits personal absence days to two days a year. However, it allows six sick days a year. You have already taken your two personal days for a ski trip to Vail but have taken no sick days. Last night, a close friend you have not seen in two years called to say he would be in town tomorrow and would like to spend the day with you. Will you call in sick?

- While going through some paperwork, you came across evidence that your company is dumping waste materials into the local river. You bring this to the attention of your supervisor. He tells you to forget you ever saw the documents and implies that your job may be at risk if you pursue this matter. You are young, have a new house in a nice neighborhood, and have just had your first child. Do you forget the event or report it?

5. Form teams of six students and discuss the three scenarios in Exercise 4. Reach a team consensus on what the appropriate action should be. What arguments presented during the team discussion were helpful in understanding and dealing with the issues at hand?

6. Moral dilemmas are tough to handle. As discussed in this chapter, there are always conflicting interests. Look again at the "waste in the river" scenario in Exercise 4. What is the moral dilemma here? Write a one-page analysis of this situation using each form of moral reasoning (utilitarianism, rights, and justice).

CASE: **BEN & JERRY'S GOES TO JAPAN,**
                              OR MAYBE NOT

Ben & Jerry's Homemade is featured throughout this book. The company makes high-quality ice cream, sorbets, and other products that are distributed nationwide. The key to the operation, however, is its social conscience. Founders Ben Cohen and Jerry Greenfield are adamant that businesses have a responsibility to help society. They contribute a far greater percentage of their profits to charities than do most corporations. Their three-part mission statement (product, economic, and social) is proudly displayed in their Waterbury, Vermont, headquarters. It receives considerable play in their annual reports and other publications. In fact, helping society is a key to everything they do.

In 1996, Ben & Jerry's was presented with the opportunity to expand to Japan. It had already opened a factory and Scoop Shop in Russia (although it has since been eliminated as part of the B&J strategy). The appealing thing about the potential move to Japan is the size of the potential market. There are no upscale ice-cream shops in Japan, and the Japanese have sufficient disposable income to make success there highly probable.

After studying the Japanese move carefully, Cohen and Greenfield hit a major problem: Japan had no readily identifiable social causes that were of interest to them. Clearly, the economic mission would be addressed favorably. The product mission would also be achieved. But there was no opportunity to further their social mission. Therefore, the key owners decided to forgo the Japanese opportunity.

Decision Questions

1. Ben & Jerry's is a publicly held company even though Cohen and Greenfield have a substantial amount of the stock. Should shareholders insist that it enter the lucrative Japanese market?
2. Should the social mission be as important for any company as it is for Ben & Jerry's? Who are the company's stakeholders?
3. Why would investors buy Ben & Jerry's stock? Is maximizing profits the only reason people invest in a company?

REFERENCES

1. Bruce Ingersoll. "Joe Camel Ads Illegally Target Kids, FTC Says." *The Wall Street Journal*, May 29, 1997, pp. B1, B6; Timothy Noah, "A Hit or Miss for Mr. Butts," *Newsweek*, June 30, 1997, p. 22.

2. Adapted from Archie Carroll. *Business and Society: Ethics and Stakeholder Management.* South-Western Publishing Co., Cincinnati, 1993, p. 60.

3. Kevin Goldman. "Calvin Klein Ad Rekindles Debate as It Runs in Youths' Magazine." *The Wall Street Journal*, July 10, 1995, p. B7.

4. Milton Friedman. "The Social Responsibility of Business Is to Increase its Profits." *New York Times Magazine*, September 13, 1970, p. 33, 122–126.

5. "Anita Roddick Speaks Out on Corporate Responsibility." *The Body Shop Lectures*, 1994.

6. Justin Martin. "Good Citizenship Is Good Business." *Fortune*, March 21, 1994, p. 15(2).

7. Lands' End Catalog. Vol. 34, No. 13, December 1997, p. 4.

8. Kevin Freiberg and Jackie Freiberg. *NUTS! Southwest Airlines' Crazy Recipe for Business and Personal Success.* Austin, TX: Bard Press, 1996, p. 268.

9. Robert Levering and Milton Moskowitz. *The 100 Best Companies to Work for in America.* New York: Plume, 1994.

10. For an excellent review see Raymond A. Noe, John R. Hollenbeck, Barry Gerhart, and Patrick M. Wright. *Human Resource Management.* 2nd ed., Burr Ridge, IL: Irwin, 1997.

11. Ibid.

12. The Body Shop Values and Vision 94, The Body Shop International PLC, 1994.

13. Norman Brinker and Donald T. Phillips. *On the Brink: The Life and Leadership of Norman Brinker.* Arlington, TX: Summit Publishing Group, 1996.

14. *The World of Trek,* Trek Bicycle Co., 1997.

15. Alix M. Freedman. *The Wall Street Journal,* February 15, 1996, pp. B1, B6.

16. Wallace N. Davidson III, Dan L. Worrell, and Chun I. Lee. "Stock Market Reactions to Announced Corporate Illegalities." *Journal of Business Ethics,* vol. 13, no. 12, December 1994, pp. 979–87.

17. Warren A. French and John Granrose. *Practical Business Ethics.* Englewood Cliffs, NJ: Prentice-Hall, 1995.

18. Patricia Jones and Larry Kahaner. *Say It & Live It: 50 Corporate Mission Statements That Hit the Mark.* New York: Doubleday, 1995, pp. 1, 117, 213.

Two 2

The Impact of External Forces

MODEL OF THE PATH TOWARD A SUCCESSFUL BUSINESS

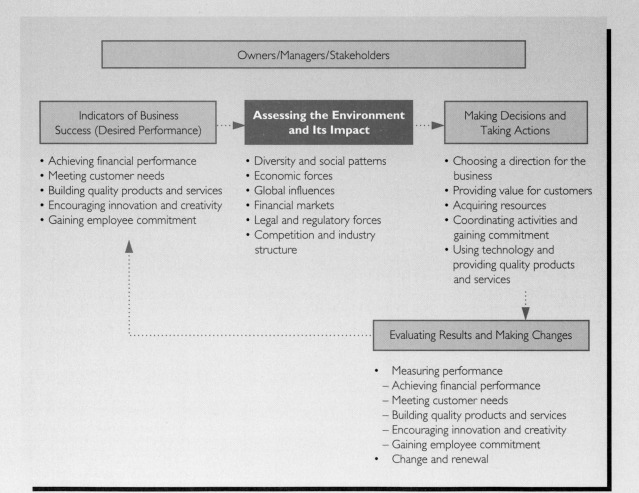

Owners/Managers/Stakeholders

Indicators of Business Success (Desired Performance)

- Achieving financial performance
- Meeting customer needs
- Building quality products and services
- Encouraging innovation and creativity
- Gaining employee commitment

Assessing the Environment and Its Impact

- Diversity and social patterns
- Economic forces
- Global influences
- Financial markets
- Legal and regulatory forces
- Competition and industry structure

Making Decisions and Taking Actions

- Choosing a direction for the business
- Providing value for customers
- Acquiring resources
- Coordinating activities and gaining commitment
- Using technology and providing quality products and services

Evaluating Results and Making Changes

- Measuring performance
  - Achieving financial performance
  - Meeting customer needs
  - Building quality products and services
  - Encouraging innovation and creativity
  - Gaining employee commitment
- Change and renewal

Part One of this book presented an overview of the path toward a successful business, explored the nature and scope of business, looked at the role of decision makers and the process of decision making, and addressed important links between business and its stakeholders. Part Two examines the impact of key external forces that affect the business and its operation. Business managers who understand these external forces and can devise approaches for capitalizing on the opportunities and minimizing the threats these forces pose will enjoy the greatest success.

Chapter 5 looks at the growing diversity that businesses face. This diversity presents both challenges and opportunities. We explore how business decision makers can manage diversity and build a supportive and inclusive business culture.

Chapter 6 explores the key economic forces affecting businesses. You will see how changes in the economy affect business and how knowledge of economic patterns can help business planning and decision making. Further, economics is the language of business. This chapter will help you understand the nature and meaning of key economic terms.

Chapter 7 examines global influences on business. You will learn why international business activity makes sense and why its influence has grown. You will also see some of the ways that businesses can participate in the global economy.

The chapter addresses some of the complexity that international activities can bring, such as dealing with cultural differences and sorting through a new range of ethical issues.

Chapter 8 examines the impact of financial markets and processes. Here, you will learn how financial markets affect the business firm. You will also gain sensitivity to the role of interest rates and the stock market.

Chapter 9 explores the impact of legal and regulatory forces. These establish the parameters within which businesses must operate. You will understand how laws and regulations both support and restrict business operations so the best interests of society can be served.

Chapter 10 examines the impact of industry structure and dynamics. You will gain a deeper understanding of the key industry sectors and understand some of the unique competitive features of each sector. This chapter provides an excellent foundation for understanding the unique competitive forces that are relevant for each business.

You will see from the chapters in Part Two that understanding external forces requires awareness, careful scrutiny, and solid skills of analysis. Such study provides the foundations that allow informed decisions and winning actions from the business. Understanding and responding to the external forces in Part Two are keys for building successful, competitive businesses.

5 Diversity and Social Patterns

She is only 27 years old. Yet Christina Jones has already achieved success in the business world. As cofounder of Trilogy Development Group of Austin, Texas, and founder of pcOrder.com, Inc., she has built a database service for computer resellers. Her service tracks prices and other specifications of over 150,000 hardware and software products. Her strong academic background (a degree in economics from Stanford) has no doubt been important in her career. Her commitment to staying on top of her field (she reads 10 computer-oriented magazines a week) helps fine-tune her skills and perspective. As Christina notes, "In the tech industry people don't care how old you are, what color you are, or what sex you are."

Donna Dubinsky would agree. She says the technology business is growing and changing so fast that competency is all that counts. Her business, Palm Computing, makes Pilot, an electronic organizer. Her business and its products were so successful that Palm Computing was recently bought by U.S. Robotics. The message from Christina and Donna is clear. In today's fast-paced world, talent is at a premium—and talent knows no racial, gender, or age limitations.[1]

We stated in earlier chapters that a successful business must understand its customers. It must also bring together talented people and keep them motivated to serve the needs of those customers. One of the biggest trends in today's business world is that both customers and the workforce are becoming increasingly diverse. As the model for a successful business shows, diversity is an important element of the environment in which a business operates. The chapter explores the nature of this diversity. It will help you recognize the challenges and opportunities diversity brings to a business. You will also learn how businesses need to respond proactively to diversity issues. More specifically, after reading this chapter, you should be able to:

1. Identify the dimensions of diversity.

2. Define workforce diversity.

3. Explain the major diversity challenges facing business and how those challenges affect business.

4. Formulate a definition of diversity management.

5. Identify and explain why a business should be concerned with diversity management.

6. Recognize the elements of a strong diversity management culture.

"No American is typical anymore. There is no average family, no ordinary worker, no everyday wage, and no middle class as we knew it. The state of the union can no longer be summarized in one sentence, because the body politic has become a motley crowd."[2]

You have probably heard and read about how our society is changing and becoming more diverse. In fact, that diversity is the hallmark of our society. Some societies are *homogeneous*, meaning that their members share a relatively uniform or standard set of values and backgrounds. Japan, for example, is a fairly homogeneous society. The United States, on the other hand, is a very **heterogeneous society.** That means it is composed of many dissimilar people with a varied mix of backgrounds, values, needs, and interests. Further, most evidence suggests that the United States is becoming more diverse all the time. Not surprisingly, our domestic workforce mirrors this growing diversity.

Heterogeneous society
A society composed of many dissimilar people with a varied mix of backgrounds, values, needs, and interests.

Diversity brings with it special issues and concerns, particularly for businesses trying to understand and respond to their environments. For example, it is hard to pinpoint trends. It is also hard to pinpoint emerging consumer interests and demands, since they may relate to only a small segment of the total market. Importantly, it is very difficult to manage all of the people in a business effectively. No single management style or approach will work. No given set of rewards will motivate all workers, since most businesses have a broad range of employees with unique and quite varied needs. Indeed, diversity and heterogeneity makes business a much more complex undertaking.

Yet we must remember that diversity offers many rich opportunities for businesses that understand the dynamics of change and are poised to act. Indeed, such understanding is essential for any business in today's competitive world.

In this chapter, we will explore the nature of these changes, discuss how they affect businesses, and look at some of the ways businesses must respond to them.

Dimensions of Diversity

One of the problems with studying diversity is that the concept itself is so complex. There are so many ways in which people can be different. Some of these differences, such as gender and race, are easy to recognize. Others are more subtle. To help us understand the range of diversity better, consider Figure 5–1.

The inner wheel of Figure 5–1 contains the areas of age, race, ethnicity, gender, physical abilities and qualities, and sexual and affectional orientation. These six areas are considered the primary dimensions of diversity. They are primary because they represent dominant ways of looking at differences in people. In fact, the authors of this model, Marilyn Loden and Judy B. Rosener, contend that these are the dimensions that shape our basic self-concept and are critical to the way we view and interact with the world.[3]

The outer circle includes work background, income, marital status, military experience, religious beliefs, geographic location, parental status, and education. These eight areas are considered the secondary dimensions of diversity. Unlike the primary dimensions, these areas can be acquired and changed. The model is certainly not all-inclusive, but it is helpful.

When dealing with the topic of diversity, it is important to avoid stereotypes. **Stereotyping** occurs when we place people in broad social groups, generalizing about and labeling them because they are part of a given group. Stereotyping ignores individual variation and difference. It is a shorthand way of categorizing people, but it ignores the uniqueness of each person.

Consider your peers in this class. Look at them as they enter the classroom. There are some obvious, primary dimensions of difference. There are both men and women. There are individuals from a variety of racial and ethnic backgrounds. Most of the students are probably about your age, but some are older. There may even be some obvious physical differences.

Sometimes we categorize people on the basis of a single area of difference, but this can be very misleading. To really understand, appreciate, and value any person, we have to look beyond the obvious elements of difference. For example, to say you are an 18-year-old college student tells us something about you. However, to say you are an 18-year-old Hispanic female who comes from a large family in Miami with professional parents and strong family values tells us a lot more. We begin to get a better sense of what a complex person you are. We begin to understand better the unique background and views you are likely to bring to the class discussion. We begin to see how you may be an important person to have on a class project team. By looking beyond the obvious, we get a richer sense of who you are.

Throughout this chapter, as we talk about differences, we encourage you to keep this beginning notion in mind. Recognize that although the topic of diversity may be studied in discrete sections, people do not fit into easy, simplistic categories. They are quite complex. Generalizations, while convenient, are often misleading. Given this cautionary note, we look at some key diversity themes in greater detail. We do this by dividing this chapter into two parts. In the first part, we look at some important diversity challenges and explore how these challenges are affecting today's businesses. In the second part, we discuss diversity management . How must a business begin to refocus its thinking to address the challenges and opportunities of diversity?

Stereotyping

Placing people in broad social groups, then generalizing about and labeling them because they are part of a given group.

Developing Your Critical Thinking Skills

1. Many social commentators argue that the United States is a richer, stronger society because of its heterogeneity and diversity. Do you agree? Why or why not?

2. Look around the classroom or another large group of people. How many areas of diversity can you identify?

FIGURE 5–1   Primary and Secondary Dimensions of Diversity

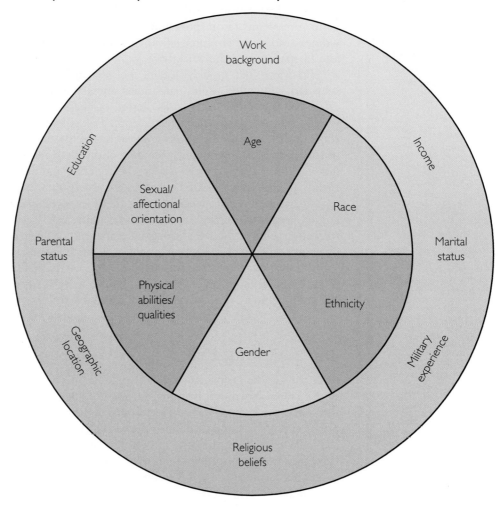

Primary and Secondary Dimensions of Diversity

SOURCE: Marilyn Loden and Judy B. Rosener, *Workforce America! Managing Employee Diversity as a Vital Resource* (Homewood, IL: Business One Irwin, 1991).

3. Some businesses do not employ a diverse group of people. What may be some of the reasons for this?

Diversity Challenges and Opportunities

In 1987, the Hudson Institute published a stimulating and provocative work entitled *Workforce 2000.*[4] This report predicted powerful changes that would be pervasive in our workforce as we moved through the 1990s, including a dramatic growth

Workforce diversity
The movement of
people from differing
demographic and ethnic
backgrounds and value
orientations into the
organizational mix.

in diversity. **Workforce diversity** simply refers to the movement of people from differing demographic and ethnic backgrounds and value orientations into the organizational mix. For most businesses, this translates to the inclusion of more women, older and younger employees, disabled people, African Americans, Asians, and Hispanics into the workforce.

Workforce 2000 quickly became a classic and a focal point of diversity insights. It spawned a flurry of additional studies, including a recent update entitled *Workforce 2020.*[5] Collectively, these works alerted business leaders and managers to some key human resource transitions. Further, they forced managers to begin thinking about some of the important business implications of these transitions. Today, after a decade of study, we recognize better the range of diversity and the complexity of the emerging workforce. Importantly, we also better understand the new set of workforce demands and realities that are beckoning for attention.

This section deals with some of these important diversity issues that confront contemporary businesses. These must be addressed. That means that businesses have to change some of their traditional assumptions and approaches in the face of growing diversity. You will recognize that these diversity issues can be both challenges and sources of opportunity for progressive and creative businesses. We will make no attempt to cover every diversity theme, but we will discuss seven of the most important ones. These themes or issues are shown in Table 5–1.

The Growing Presence of Women in the Workforce

Over the past half century, as shown in Table 5–2, there has been a steady and significant increase in women working outside the home. In 1950, about 33 percent of the women in the United States worked outside the home. By 2005, nearly two-thirds (63 percent) of U.S. women will be in the workforce.[6] Women now comprise about half of our workforce.[7] The majority of new jobs created in the 1990s were filled by women. Certainly, more work opportunities are available to women than in the past. Further, it has become common for women to pursue careers that were traditionally male dominated.

TABLE 5–1   Key Diversity Issues: Challenges and Opportunities

- Growing presence of women in the workforce
- Conflicts between work and family
- Growth in racial and ethnic minorities
- Impact on white males
- Age and generational influences
- Expanded global operations
- Impact of social trends

TABLE 5–2   The New Workforce

- Fewer new workforce entrants are native white males. They will be less than 40% of the U.S. workforce by 2005.

- Nearly 60% of U.S. women are in the workforce.

- The majority of married women with children are working.

- 20% of white children live with a single parent.

- Over half of black children live with a single parent.

- Racial minorities (male and female) will represent a growing proportion of the U.S. population and workforce in the years ahead. By 2050, minorities will comprise nearly half of the population.

- The population and workforce are aging. By 2020, almost 20% of the U.S. population will be 65 or older.

SOURCES: Richard W. Judy and Carol D'Amico, *Workforce 2020* (Indianapolis, IN: Hudson Institute, 1997); U.S. Department of Labor, Bureau of Labor Statistics, January 1996; Joseph H. Boyett with Jimmie T. Boyett, *Beyond Workplace 2000: Essential Strategies for the New American Corporation* (New York: Dutton, 1995).

There are countless ways this increased workforce participation among women affects society and its businesses. One obvious impact, the change in work and family patterns, will be addressed in the next section. At this point, though, let's consider another impact. The increased female presence in the business world creates a different workplace. Accordingly, the successful business must build a work environment where women (and all workers) can reach the full potential of their talents, where all employees can be comfortable and productive.

Women have made great corporate strides. In 1972, they held about 19 percent of the management positions in this country; today, they hold about 40 percent of all management positions. That represents significant movement and advancement. Yet most of those positions are at the lower levels of management. This means women typically are in management positions having less authority. In fact, women comprise only about 3 percent of the top management positions in the country.[8]

top management p. 65>

Such outcomes have led many to conclude that there may be systematic influences in some businesses that prevent women from rising in the organization. The **glass ceiling** is a barrier that is so subtle it is transparent, yet so real and so pervasive that it effectively blocks upward mobility.[9] That ceiling may be due to stereotypes, misdirected assumptions, or insensitivity to the unique needs women bring to the workplace. It may be due to underdeveloped career tracks. It may simply be due to a tendency of those in senior positions (usually men) to promote people quite similar to themselves (presumably men). In all likelihood, the reasons are complex, multifaceted, and usually not too clear.

Glass ceiling
A barrier that is so subtle it is transparent, yet so real and pervasive that it effectively blocks upward mobility.

What is more clear is the impact of the glass ceiling. The frustration of continually running into the glass ceiling leads many women to leave the company and seek opportunities elsewhere. This is especially troublesome when those who leave are among the most talented (and accordingly the most marketable) in the organization. The impact of the glass ceiling is so real and so problematic that a federal commission, known as the Glass Ceiling Commission, has addressed the topic.

Many women encounter barriers to advancement in companies. These barriers, often the result of stereotyping, cause frustration in careers and sometimes result in women leaving the company. What can responsive managers do to eliminate these barriers?

Often the demands women face as they progress in their businesses are formidable. Consider the case of Mary Rudie Barneby in Profile 5–1. These obstacles are not peculiar to the United States. As more women make advances in labor markets worldwide, more of them have experiences like Barneby's. In some countries, the patterns are even worse. In Mexico, it is not uncommon for women to be fired when their pregnancies become known.[10] In Japan, a society where a woman's traditional role was as a wife, not as a professional, feelings of alienation are widespread among career women. Not surprisingly, only 1 percent of Japan's working women are in managerial positions.[11]

PROFILE 5–1   *Mary Rudie Barneby*

She has been listed as one of America's 50 most powerful women managers. At 43, Mary Rudie Barneby has a staff of 20 and commands more than $250 million in pension assets from her Wall Street office. Her success on Wall Street is overwhelming. Yet it carried a big price tag. She drove hard to get to the top. In her early years, she pursued an MBA while working 70-hour weeks. Her personal sacrifices included a failed first marriage and time away from her young son.

Even today, after "making it," Barneby has to juggle a number of conflicting demands. For example, she assumes that child care responsibility for her nine-year-old son will fall to her, not to her husband. Business travel is difficult, again because of the time it takes from her family. There is a constant and conscious effort to balance work and family. Barneby says, "We can't work with total abandon. Our calendars and clocks are always in front of us."

She experienced the pressures of being female in a male-dominated business. Yet she doesn't look at the work environment as a glass ceiling. Rather, she suggests "a room divided by a one-way mirror, with the male executives on one side, talking among themselves and competing with each other. We can see them, but they can't see us." Barneby confirms what others have found. Often male executives assume that having a family reduces a woman's commitment to the job. They assume family responsibilities will interfere with or restrict after-hours meetings, travel, or challenging assignments. Accordingly, women may not be offered plum opportunities. This restricts their visibility and often limits their advancement in the business. These assumptions are frequently wrong and unfair, as the women in question have gone to great lengths to make family arrangements that let them meet their business commitments.

It's not easy, but women like Mary Rudie Barneby can make it happen. As she says, "The only thing I get upset about is when it's assumed that women can't make the commitment."

SOURCE: Paulette Thomas, "Success at a Huge Personal Cost," *The Wall Street Journal*, July 26, 1995, pp. B1, B12.

How can the glass ceiling be shattered and how can a gender-friendly workplace be structured? These are important questions. Some businesses offer mentoring programs and support groups to coach women in how to work through the political dynamics of the business. Others take active roles in developing career paths for promising women. This usually means that the business makes sure that women get access to the training and professional development they need. It also entails moving promising women into positions where they can gain the experience and the exposure necessary for promotion.

training p. 379>

In many cases, businesses must be more proactive in facing issues that affect women. One example is the area of sexual harassment. Most businesses of any size now have explicit sexual harassment policies designed to encourage a positive tone of interaction between genders in the workplace and avoid a hostile environment. The range of possibilities is endless. This movement really demands that businesses seek creative responses to better meet employee needs. More will be said about this later in the chapter, when we talk about how businesses can build cultures that embrace diversity.

Conflicts between Work and Family

Work/family conflict
The sense that work and family demands interfere with each other.

This challenge is an outgrowth of the fact that more women are in the workforce. However, **work/family conflict**—the sense that work and family demands interfere with each other—is not just experienced by women. For most of us, male or female, the two most important areas of our lives are work and family. Not surprisingly, these two areas do not exist independently. They spill over into each other, at least to some extent. The lines between work and family are becoming increasingly cloudy.

In the past, many women entered the workforce only after their children started school. But now it is common for women to combine career and family responsibilities. The traditional American nuclear family, where the father worked outside the home and the mother was a full-time homemaker, is largely a myth of the past. There are very few families today who meet this profile.

Dual-career household
Family in which both partners are actively pursuing full-time careers.

Currently, the majority of married women with children are working.[12] This workforce participation pattern is due in part to economic considerations. Many families need two incomes to afford the lifestyle they want. In many homes, both the husband and wife are actively pursuing full-time careers. These **dual-career households** are growing in number and in affluence. However, there is an interesting dilemma here. Most working mothers do not want to work full-time. Only half of all mothers believe they can adequately meet their family responsibilities when they work full-time.[13] This may be due to the fact that so many work the double shift—a full day at work plus most of the household chores when they come home.

Telecommuting offers the advantage of working while staying home at least some days of the week. Employees benefit by spending more time with their families and not having the stress and expense of a daily commute. This helps balance their work and family responsibilities. The downside of telecommuting is that employees have less interaction with others at work. Why is this a problem?

Telecommuting
Situation where workers spend part of each week working at home and communicating with the office via computer.

Flextime
Work arrangement that allows employees to adjust work hours, often to meet other responsibilities.

Job sharing
Work arrangement in which two employees share one job and split all the duties, responsibilities, and compensation of that job.

This change in family structure and the possible tension between work and family are issues of great significance for business. First, businesses have to address the potential conflicts between work and family. *Family leave policies, flexible work schedules,* and child care assistance may be solutions. When a business addresses diversity, it is concerned with all these issues. For example, the business may turn to flexible work schedules to attract more women and enable them to meet both work and family demands.

One approach that has become popular is **telecommuting.** Here, workers spend part of their time each week working at home and communicating with the office via computer. This reduces travel time and increases child care options. Of course, telecommuting will not work for every business, particularly where employees must be present to interact with customers. However, where appropriate, it lets employees be productive without being physically present.

More and more companies use **flextime,** which allows a worker to adjust work hours, often to meet other responsibilities. Basically, flextime gives employees discretion over when they start and end their workdays. Both men and women seem to appreciate the freedom to arrange part of their workday to better meet other responsibilities and needs.

Given that a number of parents prefer part-time work, some businesses have turned to a work approach known as **job sharing,** where two or more employees share one job and split all the duties, responsibilities, and compensation of that job. This means two workers can hold an important professional position. One may work from 8 AM to noon, handling all areas of the job. The other works from noon to 4 PM, continuing to carry out all the responsibilities of the job. Or one may work Mondays, Wednesdays, and Fridays while the other works Tuesdays and Thursdays. In job sharing both employees receive and share all the benefits, such as insurance plans, that go with the job. The job-sharing idea seems to be growing in popularity.

Some businesses recognize that quality child care is so important for working families that they go out of their way to support child care arrangements. Some have benefit packages that cover at least part of the cost of child care. Some have child care facilities on site, at the business. Johnson & Johnson, the world's largest maker of health care products, has a child care center at corporate headquarters with room for 200 children of employees. It also has centers at other J & J facilities throughout the country.[14] Proponents say that parents who know their children are being well taken care of and who can drop in on them during the workday are more productive employees.

Businesses support flexible work schedules and child care arrangements because these programs give businesses a better chance of employing talented workers who might otherwise find it difficult to be in the workforce or might go with a more understanding company. Also, employees who have more say over their lives and time feel better about their work, which may improve their morale and commitment toward their employer. Businesses hope that this will lead to better performance.

Changes in family structure also bring new opportunities for innovative entrepreneurs and their businesses. For example, KangaKab is a shuttle service that parents can hire to transport their preschoolers to and from day care centers.[15] The growth of dual-career families created this business opportunity. KangaKab and businesses like it are outgrowths of the changes in family structure.

Developing Your Critical Thinking Skills

**financial performance
p. 481>**

1. Our model of a successful business shows that financial performance is the prime indicator of a healthy business. How is the inclusion of more women in the workforce likely to lead to improvements in a business's financial performance?

2. What business opportunities can you think of that may come from the changing family structure and the increased spillover between work and family?

Growth in Racial and Ethnic Minorities

A potentially important impact of diversity for all businesses today relates to the dramatic changes in the racial and ethnic composition of our population. In 1994, Caucasians comprised nearly 193 million people, 74 percent of the domestic population. People of various racial and ethnic minorities, represented 26 percent of the population. Those numbers are changing for two reasons. First, the birthrate for minorities far exceeds that of whites. Second, though the United States has long been a land to which many diverse cultures immigrated, the rate of immigration is at record levels. The U.S. gained more immigrants during the 1980s, more than 7 million, than in any 10-year period since the first decade of this century. Asians are the fastest-growing minority group in the country.[16] By the year 2010, racial and ethnic minorities will comprise nearly one-third of the U.S. population. Projections indicate that by 2050, minorities will represent almost half of the domestic population.[17]

Between 1990 and 2050, the black population will grow 10 times faster than the white population. Yet blacks will not be the largest minority group. That distinction will soon be held by Hispanics. *Hispanics* is a term that encompasses various ethnic

TABLE 5–3   Population by Race and Ethnicity

	1990	1994	2000	2010	2050
White	75.6	74.0	71.6	67.7	52.5
Black	11.8	12.0	12.2	12.6	14.4
Asian	2.8	3.3	4.1	5.4	9.7
Native American	0.7	0.7	0.7	0.8	0.9
Hispanic	9.0	9.9	11.3	13.5	22.5

Numbers represent percentage of resident population.

SOURCE: Cheryl Russell, *The Official Guide to the American Workforce*, 2nd ed. (Ithaca, NY: New Strategist Publications, 1995), p. 323.

groups, including Mexicans, Puerto Ricans, Central and South Americans, and Cubans. While Hispanics comprise less than 10 percent of the population today, they will represent nearly 23 percent of the population by 2050. Table 5–3 offers a further look at some of these key population changes.

Although we have been discussing population dynamics from a broad national perspective, keep in mind that the population profile will be different for different regions and sectors throughout the country. For example, the influx of Hispanics may have little effect on a regional business in the Midwest (outside of Chicago). Yet growth in the Hispanic population will be acute for businesses with operations in California, Texas, and Florida. By the same token, inner cities typically have more minorities than do suburban areas. Businesses targeting city markets will want to respond accordingly.

Because of the growth in minority populations, many companies are trying to figure out strategies for reaching these markets. That often means being more understanding of and sensitive to their needs. Consider the following example. First Community Bank of BankBoston has been quite responsive to changes in market demographics. Recently, through ongoing research activities, it recognized an emerging and potentially important market in the Latino community. The bank took a number of specific actions to better serve this growing market. For instance, it became sensitive to translation within all aspects of the business. It created a toll-free phone line for Spanish-speaking people. It identified radio as an important advertising medium for this audience. It provided opportunities for Spanish-speaking employees. And the list goes on. The key is that First Community was willing to change because of the opportunities presented by a diversifying market.[18] Business opportunities and success come to companies that understand the uniqueness various population segments offer.

Businesses are coming to realize that racial and ethnic minorities increasingly represent the base from which they draw prospective employees. But there are still shortcomings in their efforts to include more minorities in the workforce. Let's look at two issues.

First is the reality of the glass ceiling. Although originally conceived to describe a lack of opportunity for women, the glass ceiling appears to be even more prevalent for ethnic and racial minorities. Minority employees are still quite uncommon in the managerial ranks. Yet it's dangerous to generalize. For example, black women are more likely to rise into the managerial ranks than are black men.[19]

Second, and quite significant, broad-based national studies show that members of racial minorities often feel they are victims of prejudice and discrimination in business.[20] The impact of such incidences is significantly affected by how the business chooses to respond. If it does not redress inequities, minority employees may reasonably feel frustrated and may seek to leave the organization.

Organizations can positively, aggressively, and firmly address these issues and concerns. One business that has done so is Xerox, which has been a leader in the diversity arena for over a quarter of a century. In 1984, Xerox initiated its "Balanced Work Force (BWF)" process. The goal of BWF was to change Xerox from a white male business to one that was fully diverse. Among other things, Xerox wanted equitable representation of women and minorities at all levels of the organization.

Caucus groups
Groups of employees who get together to address key concerns relating to members of their particular group.

One vehicle Xerox has used to further BWF has been caucus groups—for example, a women's caucus group and a black caucus group. These **caucus groups** are made up of employees who get together and address key concerns relating to members of their particular group. They then communicate these perspectives to upper management at Xerox. In addition to being a communication link, the caucus groups are a wonderful way for group members to network and offer support for one another. Thus, promising young African Americans can find role models and mentors through the caucus system. Importantly, Xerox has created a culture that is highly supportive of and responsive to these caucus groups.[21] This is one reason Xerox is recognized as a model of effective employee utilization.

Impact on White Males

White men, the foundation of our domestic workforce in the past, are no longer the typical workers. The explosive workforce growth among women, Americans of color, and immigrants means that white males are becoming a less dominant segment. By the year 2005, white males will represent less than 40 percent of the workforce.[22]

Yet this picture is complex and requires further consideration. While the overall workforce is becoming more diverse, white men still run corporate America. For example, nearly 92 percent of the officers and nearly 90 percent of the directors of U.S. businesses are still white males.[23] What does this tell you? First, it suggests that white men have a firm grip on positions of power. Second, many businesses must take special steps to encourage greater diversity into the top levels of the business. Third, those in power must understand the impact of a changing demographic mix. Finally, if change is to occur, the support of the white male power cohort must be gained.

Evidence suggests that some white men approach the issue of diversity with concern. They are becoming a minority, a status they have never experienced. Some white males fear that as businesses downsize, they are more vulnerable than other demographic segments. Some worry that as businesses move to develop and promote more women and minorities, they may be left behind. At the very least, white males will face more competition than before. Some experts have even suggested this may lead to a white backlash.[24]

Age and Generational Influences

In understanding and responding to diversity, businesses must consider age and generational influences. Profiling the population according to age leads to a better understanding of customer needs, as well as areas of business opportunity.

Baby Boomers

The generation of Americans born between 1946 and 1964 is known collectively as the **baby boomers.** Three out of every 10 Americans today are in this age group.[25] This generation has, since its arrival, been a major force for businesses, basically because it is such a significant proportion of the population. For example, in the 1970s and 80s, most baby boomers were in their 20s and 30s. As a group, they valued health and fitness. It was not surprising that entire industries, such as the home fitness industry, grew around the demands of this generation.

Today, as the boomers age, what influence will they pose? Businesses have to try to figure that out. For example, consider New Balance Athletic Shoe. Its business, the manufacture and sale of running shoes, flourished as the fitness and running movements took off during the 1980s. But research suggests that aging boomers are now changing from running to exercise walking. That represents a major threat for New Balance because a major segment of its market is switching preferences. It also represents a major opportunity. It signaled that a line of walking shoes would be a good addition to the business, and New Balance responded accordingly.[26]

As baby boomers move toward their 50s, demand for goods and services will reflect their new needs. Investment and retirement planning services should bene-

Baby boomers
The generation of Americans born between 1946 and 1964, comprising three out of every 10 people in the United States today.

Baby boomers often have three things that encourage companies like Smith Barney to develop websites for checking investments—money, good computer skills, and limited time. Many companies allow their clients to check their investments at their own convenience over the internet. How will this affect the financial world in the future?

fit. Vacation and travel services should grow. Products ranging from bifocals to electronic planners offer considerable sales potential. The possibilities are endless.

Young Adults

Apart from baby boomers, the generational group that has received the most recent attention is young adults in the 19–30 age group. This group is sometimes referred to as *Generation X*. While much has been written about the uniqueness of this generation, few generalizations can really be made. However, a few values and characteristics do seem to typify this group.

First, they are less sure than previous generations about stability in jobs, careers, and relationships. Growing up in an era where violence, divorce, and corporate downsizing are prevalent, they have a fundamental concern for security. Second, this generation seems to emphasize the value of education strongly. Third, many of these young adults are making a slower transition to adulthood than previous generations. Demographers note that this does not mean Gen Xers are overgrown children. Rather, they are probably hesitant to accept responsibilities where they have seen their elders fail. Finally, they seem to value diversity and are more accepting of different values and lifestyles than older generations.[27]

Again, the student of business must ask what is gained from understanding something about young adults and their values? Perhaps a lot. For example, a manager who is hiring a number of young college graduates knows that job security is quite important to them. These workers want challenging jobs, but they also want a sense of identity and stability from their jobs. Contrary to earlier negative assumptions about Gen Xers, a recent survey suggests that they value competition, have high levels of self-confidence, and tend to prefer to work on their own rather than for someone else. This may explain why they value entrepreneurship and starting their own business so highly.[28]

Matures and Baby Boomlets

Matures refers to the older generations of our population, generally those born before 1946. Matures, by their sheer numbers (over 68 million in the United States), are a presence that demands attention.[29] One question is who will care for them as they age. Indeed, as Profile 5–2 suggests, elder care is quite important. The effect on workers who shoulder the responsibility for care may be profound. The level, extent, and type of care are all issues. This affects baby boomers, who want elder care benefits for their parents. It also affects certain businesses, such as home health care, that focus primarily on the elderly.

The *baby boomlet* generation includes young people who are the children of the baby boomers. More than 20 million Americans were under the age of 5 in 1995. That is the largest number in that age group at one time since the baby-boom generation.[30] The business impact here seems significant. Children-related products and child care services are in strong demand.

Knowledge of population dynamics offers insights that can help businesses decide how markets may relate to their products and services. For example, matures are an interesting market. They are relatively substantial in number and relatively affluent. While they are obviously concerned about saving for retirement, they seem to be willing to spend freely. One area where they spend a lot is on their grandchildren. Think about the impact this can have for businesses like toy manufacturers. For one thing, it suggests that interesting toys can carry a higher price tag, because affluent grandparents may be paying for them.

PROFILE 5–2   *Elder Care*

Caring for an aged relative is a responsibility that more and more Americans are facing. Such care may be rather limited, such as helping with bills. Or it may involve intense personal care, such as bringing a loved one to live with you when he or she can no longer live independently.

As you might expect, care for parents is the most common form of elder care. The demographics here are staggering. By 2050, the ratio of parents needing support to people in their caregiving years will more than triple.

Caregiving responsibilities often contribute to increases in work absenteeism and turnover, as well as to employees being distracted at times. The personal costs, in terms of stress and worry, are significant. The business costs can be formidable. However, they are difficult to quantify. Surveys suggest that people caring for elders would comprise 18 percent of the workforce in 1998.

SOURCE: Sue Shellenbarger, "Study Tries to Lift Fog on Cost Employers Pay for Elder Care," *The Wall Street Journal*, July 19, 1995, p. B1.

The Aging of the Workforce

Another factor that is important for businesses is the aging (what some refer to as the "graying") of the workforce. The average age of the workforce is rising and the proportion of workers who are older is increasing. Part of this movement is driven by the demographics we've discussed. As the baby boomer generation ages, their sheer numbers mean more older workers as we move into the 21st century. Part of this phenomenon arises because people are living longer and simply wish to work longer.

There are a number of business implications to this trend and a number of open questions.[31] For example, some argue than an older workforce will be experienced and stable and thus more productive than a younger workforce. Others predict older workers may be less open to change, which may reduce their productivity. There is probably some merit to both views. Older workers do bring important backgrounds and experiences that can be extremely beneficial in business practice. Yet if their experiences are not relevant to the changing demands of contemporary business, they are of limited value. For this reason, we expect employee retraining to become even more important with an aging workforce. **Employee retraining** simply means regularly providing employees the education and training they need to expand their base of skills so that they meet the needs of businesses.

Older workers also raise competitive issues. Businesses are extremely concerned with reducing or controlling costs. They recognize that cost considerations are critical to their long-run competitiveness. In many ways, older workers do represent higher costs for the business. Since older workers have usually been with a business longer, their pay is often higher. They also represent higher health care costs and higher pension charges. Yet older workers represent talent and experience. Often the business has invested a lot of money in their development. They are important resources. It's a

Employee retraining
Regularly providing the education and training workers need to expand their base of skills so they can meet the needs of business.

dilemma. How should a business respond? What makes sense? What seems fair? There are no easy answers here. Some businesses offer incentives for older employees to take early retirement. But they must be cautious that they don't lose key talent in the process of reducing costs.

Expanded Global Operations

How can a business meet the challenges of operating in a globally diverse marketplace, where different cultures and values prevail? Actually, having a broad, diverse base of employees should help a company as it expands its operations globally. What better way to understand and respond to the diverse needs of different cultures than to have people from those cultures among the decision makers of the business. This view is confirmed by John E. Pepper, CEO of Procter & Gamble. He notes, "Our success as a global company is a direct result of our diverse and talented workforce. Our ability to develop new consumer insights and ideas and to execute them in a superior way across the world is the best possible testimony to the power of diversity any organization could ever have."[32]

Global operations create additional needs. For example, companies must understand the people, customs, and practices of the countries where they do business. American managers who serve in foreign countries should learn to appreciate the cultures of their host countries. There is probably nothing foreign customers and partners find more frustrating than Americans who are insensitive to their unique traits. It is seen as a sign of arrogance, and it is simply not good business.

Businesses need to train managers and employees to understand the customs, business etiquette, and expectations of foreign areas where they operate. For example, many Americans have little tolerance for small talk when they conduct business; they view it as a waste of time. But Middle Eastern businesspeople see the ritual of small talk as a way of building relationships. It would be rude to attempt to conduct business without having tea and a brief period of chitchat.[33] Misreading cultural cues can even lead to false conclusions. When Japanese smile and nod their heads, this is not necessarily a sign of agreement. It may simply mean that they have heard and understood what was said. In fact, they may firmly disagree!

Impact of Social Trends

It is extremely difficult and even a bit dangerous to try to suggest a finite set of social trends in a heterogeneous society. No list will be exhaustive or speak to the expectations of everyone and every group within the society. These trends represent changing values and ideas about what is important. Let us explore some social trends that seem to be prevalent in U.S. society.

Personal and Environmental Health

There seems to be an increasing concern for personal and environmental health. To a large extent, this concern arises because of the troubles and confusion facing our society. We live in an era of violence. Some are affected quite profoundly; for young black males, homicide is the leading cause of death. Others are affected less severely. Yet no one—regardless of race, ethnicity, or social status—can escape the impact of violence within our society.

As companies become more global, they have greater needs to move supplies and products from country to country. The U.S. Postal Service as well as other shipping companies are increasingly providing services that aid the movement of goods from one country to another. Why do companies need help in the international arena? How does this relate to diversity?

We also live in an era where AIDS, smoking, substance abuse, and shifting and uncertain health care provisions raise serious questions. We live in an era where many recognize that we must halt the continuing deterioration of our natural environment before we render our planet uninhabitable. There is some concern over our capacity to meet these modern challenges.

Businesses must respond to these issues. These challenges offer new business opportunities in industries like health care. Here, new forms of health care delivery, such as home care, seem poised to grow in significance.

mission p. 310>   The environment is part of the focus and mission of some businesses. An example of this is the Body Shop, founded by Anita Roddick. This cosmetics business, highlighted in Profile 5–3, is run with a constant eye toward environmentalism.

PROFILE 5–3   *Anita Roddick and The Body Shop*

Producing natural products for the hair and skin, Anita Roddick has built her business into a highly successful international chain. In the process, she has emerged as one of the world's foremost business activists. She even received the United Nations Environmentalist Award. She believes in the connection between good business and responsible citizenry. She says, "You don't have to lose your soul to succeed in business." These excerpts capture part of her philosophy:

In the Body Shop we believe, more fervently than any other company or multinational of which I am aware, that environmentalism will be the most important issue for businesses in the nineties. . . . Renewable resources have always been a company lodestone at the Body Shop, and we have run recycling and energy conservation schemes for years. . . . Body Shop bags are made from recycled polyethylene, which can be reused or recycled again and again. We introduced nonchlorine-bleached cotton bags stamped with the word "refillable" to encourage customers not to use carrier bags at all. . . . In 1990, the Body Shop became the first UK retailer to recycle its own postconsumer plastic waste. . . . Recycled paper is used throughout the company.

It is through dozens of schemes like this, continually monitored and updated, that we strive to limit our impact on the environment and also set an example to our staff, our customers, and other companies. We believe it is not enough, not nearly enough, to abide by existing environmental legislation—for the sake of future generations, business must take a lead.

SOURCE: Anita Roddick, *Body and Soul* (New York: Crown Publishers, 1991), pp. 242–243.

Anita Roderick believes strongly that companies should take an active role in protecting the environment while providing products to customers. Few company executives go to the extent that Roderick does—demonstrating against buring rainforests. Do you think executives should be involved in social issues and environmental causes? Do stockholders care?

A Learning Society

As we look toward the next century, all evidence is that continual, lifelong learning will be increasingly popular in our society. This trend is largely dictated by the pace of change. Skills that were mastered and relevant in the past may be useless in the future. Those who want to keep pace must keep studying, training, and seeking avenues of improvement.

information technology p. 456>

Perhaps this trend is felt no more acutely than in the area of information technology. Information systems change so quickly that those who fail to learn and update may lose their ability to communicate. In fact, one of the dilemmas of our society is what some have termed the growing schism between the info-rich and the info-poor.[34]

The response seems clear. We must widen the learning process and provide relevant education for all.[35] That is a challenge. It affects the ways businesses offer training and development for their employees. It also affects the business possibilities for many organizations. Universities, for example, recognize the opportunity that lifelong learning offers. Many have expanded their continuing education programs to meet the needs of a nontraditional student audience searching for new insights and skills.

Tolerance of Diversity

The theme of this chapter is the increasing tolerance of diversity. Our society must become more tolerant and accepting of our increasing diversity.

Many avenues of tolerance are important. But two themes seem to prevail. First is the need for better racial harmony. Despite the social movements for greater equality and rights over the last 30 years, racial tension remains. Because businesses operate within the society, they are not immune to this tension and its consequences. Second is the need for greater openness to lifestyle differences. This affects everything from society's sensitivity to lesbian and gay issues to concern over media censorship.

In all of these cases, we face dilemmas. These issues are not always clear and public sentiment is often fragmented. While the need for tolerance is apparent, the practice of tolerance is sketchy at best. An example is the recent scandal at Texaco, where senior executives were taped making disdainful and derogatory remarks about black employees.[36] Although Texaco formally apologized, the example points to an underlying problem in many businesses: While it is relatively easy to preach diversity, it is much harder to walk the talk. Changing attitudes and breaking cultural barriers are very difficult. Accordingly, society and businesses are likely to be torn between the need for greater sensitivity and concern over the implications of such change.

Although the path toward tolerance will not be smooth, we expect that successful businesses will lead the way in promoting tolerance and mutual respect. We will comment more on the business response in this area in the section of this chapter on diversity management.

Other Changes

Other workforce changes are worthy of attention. For example, in the future we are likely to see workers with a broader range of values and lifestyles. As businesses work teams p. 71> more in teams, we are more likely to see people with different professional backgrounds and interests working together. As we noted in Chapter 3, teams can spur

creativity p. 522> creativity. Often that creativity comes from diversity, but such diversity can lead to conflicts that must be managed. As businesses expand their operations to include a more global perspective, individuals with differing cultural values and expectations will be working together. Again, the need for understanding and management is heightened.

Many businesses are looking for specific skills and backgrounds that people just entering the workforce may lack. Jobs will require solid problem-solving and communication skills. For those who have these skills, challenging work and attractive compensation are likely. However, many new workers simply will not possess the basic skills needed to perform these jobs. Businesses will have increasing difficulty finding the qualified workers they need, so it will be a good investment for them to provide educational opportunities and other relevant training for their workers.

In the future, we are also likely to see more disabled workers. In fact, the *Americans with Disabilities Act* has required businesses to be more responsive to the unique needs of disabled workers. Progressive businesses have understood the talents that workers with disabilities can bring, so they have already made their work environments more accessible and accommodating.

Consider Trek as an example. About 16 workers with various hearing impairments build Trek bikes at their facilities in Waterloo and Whitewater, Wisconsin. In fact, many of these workers came to Trek because of their aggressive policy of hiring the best people, period. The company believes its program of hiring people with disabilities has been very successful. Other employees seem to appreciate and embrace

human resources p. 374> the program. Human resources director Gary Ellerman says that when Trek offered a course in sign language, all slots filled quickly. Ellerman points with pride to the program, noting that one of the hearing-impaired employees has been promoted with supervisory responsibilities for 10 other workers.[37]

A Sense of Impact

Businesses must understand these demographic and behavioral dynamics. Diversity efforts will probably be most effective when all parties, including white men, understand that diversity is about inclusiveness. It's about creating a business where all talent can be utilized and maximized. Diversity should not be seen as an agenda for any particular group. This progressive approach requires a mature understanding of diversity, a clear sense of the value and benefits to be gained by diversity movements, and a structured approach of how to proceed.

You now have some facts. You have seen some demographic profiles and projections. You have what we call an intellectual awareness of diversity. In other words, you have an educated sense of some of the key workforce changes that are occurring. But the big challenge of diversity has not yet been addressed. How do we convert what we know into meaningful organizational action? In other words, how do we manage diversity?

Today, most businesses are in the throes of exposing their people to the new demographic realities. Yet, as Susan Jackson notes in her superb book *Diversity in the Workplace*, there is a big difference between knowing what is changing and responding to the demands of change.[38] That is the challenge before us.

Developing Your Critical Thinking Skills

1. Have you ever been in a situation where you were a minority (in other words, where you were different from most of the people in that situation)? How did you feel? Did you want to leave?

2. Have you ever been in a situation where you felt as if you were being put down or discriminated against because of some difference? How did you feel? Did this motivate you to prove yourself or did it make you withdraw?

3. What difficulties is a business likely to face as it trains and retrains its workforce to deal with diversity?

Diversity Management

Motorola has been one of the most progressive and successful companies in this country in demonstrating a commitment to diversity. Some numbers will reveal the extent of this dedication. In 1989, Motorola had 350 vice presidents among its officers. Consistent with most of corporate America, only two of those vice presidents were women. Today, 38 women are vice presidents.[39] Similar gains have occurred with minorities. That sort of impressive change does not happen automatically. It requires diversity management .

Defining Diversity Management

Diversity management Putting together a well-thought-out strategy for attracting, motivating, developing, retaining, and fully utilizing the talents of competent people regardless of their race, gender, ethnicity, religion, physical ability, or sexual orientation.

Diversity management is putting together a well-thought-out strategy for attracting, motivating, developing, retaining, and fully utilizing the talents of competent people regardless of their race, gender, ethnicity, religion, physical ability, or sexual orientation. It is important to realize that diversity management moves beyond the traditional legislative approaches to workforce equity that have been in place in this country for years. These approaches were aimed largely at addressing discrimination in the workplace. You have probably heard of two of them. The *Equal Employment Opportunity (EEO) Act* specified that a business cannot deny a person a job because of race, gender, ethnicity, age, or sexual preference. Its well-known companion, *affirmative action*, directed businesses to take positive steps to hire and promote members of the classes noted in the EEO Act. These government efforts have been important.

Assimilation The assumption that women and minorities should blend in and learn how to work within the existing organization and its culture.

However, many of today's diversity leaders realize that these approaches have not gone far enough. In fact, EEO and affirmative action were based on a view of diversity known as **assimilation,** which presumes that women and minorities should blend in and learn how to work within the existing organization and its culture. It places the responsibility for changing and accommodating on the employee, not on the business. This approach loses much of the true value of diversity.

Diversity management is broader and more inclusive. Its goal is to create and maintain a culture where individual uniqueness is understood and valued. Further, diversity management helps build a culture where all workers feel welcomed and supported and have the opportunity to work up to their potential. This is how Motorola acted. The goal was to have a broader, more diverse group of executives. The company enacted carefully developed strategies to see that it happened. Do not be misled here. Diversity management does not mean that organizations capitulate on their goals in order to meet employee demands. It does mean businesses are more flexible and tolerant in how they go about meeting goals and achieving results.

Many companies have taken specific steps to attain meaningful diversity action. One common move in recent years has been the creation of a position known as *diversity manager*. Diversity managers have overall responsibility for coordinating all the efforts to help build a culture of diversity. Today, over half of the Fortune 500 companies have diversity managers. In some companies, these managers hold ranks as high as vice president.

Why Should a Business Be Concerned with Diversity Management?

There are good, logical, bottom-line reasons why businesses should be serious about putting a diversity management approach in place. Unless senior managers recognize and see value in diversity efforts, little meaningful diversity action is likely to occur.

acquisition p. 322>

There are seven basic reasons why diversity management makes sense. These arguments are shown in Table 5–4 and discussed here.

First is the *resource acquisition* argument. With needed skills in short supply, a business must do everything it can to attract the best and the brightest minds. Barbara (Bobbi) Guttman, vice president and director of human resources diversity at Motorola, speaks clearly to this issue. She says, "We're not interested in getting more blacks, more women, more Hispanics, per se. What we're interested in is taking away any barrier between us and the best minds in the country. And it just doesn't make sense to us that the best minds in the country all look the same."[40]

Businesses that are serious about diversity and have implemented a diversity management plan should be better able to attract some of the best minds from diverse groups of prospective employees. This just makes sense. For example, bright young women and African Americans will want to come to work for Motorola because they know the company will support their growth within the business.

TABLE 5–4   Arguments for Diversity Management

Resource acquisition	Needed skills are in short supply
Resource retention	Keep the talent of their workforce
Resource utilization	Build an environment where everyone can contribute fully
Customer sensitivity	Better understand and respond to broad base of customers
Innovation and creativity	Bring fresh ideas and novel approaches
Legal requirements	Respond to and avoid legal problems
Ethical stance	The right thing to do

Consider the case of Stride Rite Shoes. Stride Rite has been a leader in the diversity movement and was the first company in this country to offer on-site, company-supported child care. Arnold Hiatt, former chair of Stride Rite, explains that Stride Rite's progressive actions occurred in response to the needs it saw in the workforce, such as the need for child care. He says Stride Rite's diversity strategy enabled the business to attract capable, loyal employees in a region where good workers were in short supply. Whether these good workers are Hispanic or African American, disabled or mothers of young children, they are attracted to a company that appreciates them and is aggressively addressing key diversity issues.[41]

The second argument is *resource retention*. Attracting a diverse talent pool to a business is only part of the equation for success. To be competitive and successful, a business has to keep that talent. But turnover rates for women and minorities are typically higher than for white men, often twice as high.[42] That represents a drain of talent from the organization. It is also quite expensive. The business has to recruit, select, replace, and orient new people and bring them up to speed. All of that takes time—and a lot of money. Businesses that can avoid such costs gain a competitive cost advantage over rival firms.

Third is the *resource utilization* argument. This view asserts that in a global, competitive environment, a business must use its human resources as effectively as possible if it is going to be successful. Notice the complexity of this statement. A business may attract and keep talented people, yet still not fully tap their potential. Organizations that embrace the philosophy of diversity management go further. They seek to understand the unique needs of their workers, and they are willing to help these workers be as productive and fulfilled as possible.

The resource utilization argument deals with inappropriate assumptions managers make about diverse groups of employees and what they expect of them. Tradition-bound managers are often wedded to old attitudes and assumptions about differences. They may assume that members of diverse groups want to and should become like white males. They think the business must find ways to *change people* so they are less different from the norm.[43]

However, noted diversity scholar Roosevelt Thomas suggests that adaptation must be a two-way street, a mutual, give-and-take process between workers and businesses.[44] Individual workers must always adapt to some extent, or a business would have no order or control at all. But the business must also be willing to adjust. Often this means giving workers more options and more discretion rather than rigid systems of rules, policies, and procedures. It means being more flexible about work arrangements, particularly for people with small children or other special needs. It means committing to training, developing, and creating challenging opportunities for bright young workers. Through such approaches, diversity management can build an environment where employee talents are nurtured and used to the fullest.

customer sensitivity
p. 493>

Fourth is the *customer sensitivity* argument, one of the most direct and strongest points in building the business case for diversity. This view contends that a business is better able to understand and respond to the needs of a diverse customer base when the organization contains people who mirror the diversity of that population. This sensitivity may have gender, racial, and ethnic connotations. For example, Avon experienced greater success in its inner-city markets when it started to place racial and ethnic minorities in decision-making positions for these markets. Apparently, a better understanding of customers and their needs allowed these managers to orient their product offerings and service approaches more responsively.

Sometimes the issue is not about gender or minority status. Rather, it is about putting people in key positions who are in touch with the customer. For example,

Maryland National Bank found that its branches that had the best customer retention records recruited and hired locally. This allowed tellers to swap local gossip and made it easy for managers to show interest in local customers. No doubt this led to feelings of comfort and commitment among the bank's customers.[45]

Fifth is the *creativity and innovation* argument. The wide range of attitudes, values, perspectives, and interests a diverse workforce brings with it often results in conflicts and tensions. Yet this diverse mix may be exactly what a business needs as it attempts to find fresh and novel ways to operate and serve customers.

Sixth is the *legal* argument. There is little doubt that some companies' concern for diversity is prompted by a desire to avoid the legal tangles that can arise when diversity issues are left unattended. Research suggests that many diversity efforts are focused on legal concerns. Developing sexual harassment policies, providing access to employees with disabilities, and abiding by equal employment opportunity and affirmative action requirements are often the thrust of the diversity movement. This is particularly true among smaller businesses.[46]

There is nothing wrong with this. Dealing with legal issues proactively is a reasonable and sound advantage of diversity management . Ideally, of course, the company's interest in diversity extends beyond this single issue to embrace some of the other arguments we have noted.

Seventh is the *ethics* argument. In today's business environment, diversity management is simply the right thing to do. All three ethics theories discussed in Chapter 4—utilitarianism, rights, and justice—indicate that diversity management is appropriate. Responsive businesses must take this ethical stance.

Building a Diversity Management Culture

We have identified some of the workforce changes that are facing businesses, defined diversity management , and explained why diversity management makes good business sense. Yet the most critical component of the diversity puzzle is still missing. How does a business respond to the challenges of diversity? How does it build a culture that really values, supports, and manages diversity? There is no easy answer, no blueprint that will work in all situations. Yet some businesses seem to make better strides than others. For example, Motorola, Xerox, Merck, US Sprint, Digital Equipment Co., AT&T, and Stride Rite have all earned reputations for progressively addressing diversity needs. There are certain common actions these businesses take. When we study these businesses, a general strategic approach to diversity management begins to emerge. This strategic approach has four elements:

- Top management champions
- A diversity audit
- Goals and accountability
- Education, training, and support

Top Management Champions

Most businesses that have enacted successful diversity strategies have individuals at the very top of the company who are willing to champion the cause of diversity. At Stride Rite it was Arnold Hiatt. At Motorola it was George Fisher. At Xerox it was vision p. 310>

David Kearns. These leaders were not simply saying the right words at the politically appropriate time. To them, diversity was a value that became part of their vision for the business. As champions, they were willing to take the lead in convincing others that diversity made sense. They actively spread support for the diversity movement throughout the management ranks. Remember, diversity management represents a fundamental cultural change and most people tend to resist change. These changes are generally most effective when they start at the top.

Assessment: The Diversity Audit

Diversity audit
A snapshot of how good a job a business is doing in the area of diversity management.

It is critical for a business to perform a diversity audit as it begins to get serious about diversity management . A **diversity audit** is a snapshot of how good a job the business is doing in the area of diversity management . It should tell the business where its diversity needs exist.

There are three things the audit should reveal. First, it should crunch the numbers to show what sort of representation exists at all levels of the company, especially at the professional and managerial levels. More importantly, these numbers should help managers see the movements and changes that are occurring. In other words, a business may be underrepresented in the number of women and minorities who hold management positions. But if great strides have taken place over the last few years, the trend is positive.

Second, the audit should reveal underlying assumptions and attitudes about diversity within the company. Third, the audit should uncover the actual behavior toward diversity and diverse groups that is occurring. Steps two and three are absolutely critical, yet often avoided. That is not hard to understand; it is considerably more difficult to uncover attitudes and behaviors than to focus on the numbers. Yet the numbers may be meaningless if the attitudes and behaviors do not support diversity.

For example, a business may be meeting its affirmative action numbers. That is, the number of employees of diverse groups is consistent with the proportion found in the general population. Further, there is reasonable representation throughout the various levels of the company. But that does not guarantee that the workplace is "diversity friendly." The numbers alone are not enough. Perhaps the women and minority members in the managerial ranks are quite dissatisfied. They may feel that they do not get much attention from their bosses, are overlooked for the challenging, developmental job assignments, and receive inadequate performance feedback. Further, they may encounter sexism and racism in the workplace.[47] Thus, if one looks only at the numbers, the business may appear quite progressive. However, a closer look at attitudes and behaviors reveals some major concerns.

To uncover attitudes and behaviors, a business may have to rely on written anonymous surveys of employees, focus groups where small numbers of employees are encouraged to discuss their experiences openly, and perhaps even in-depth interviews with some employees to gain further understanding. To reassure employees and reduce their fear about discussing these matters openly, businesses often turn to outside consultants to conduct this portion of the audit. As you can see, the audit is comprehensive and quite detailed. It takes time, money, and a willingness on the part of the business to openly confront what is going on. Yet the audit is the most logical method of determining what issues the business should confront and what approaches seem to be most reasonable.

Goals and Accountability

The audit should point the business in the direction it needs to move in order to build a culture of diversity. The needs and concerns it identifies should be converted to diversity goals. Goals give managers something to work toward and a way of measuring progress. They are tangible yardsticks used to help the business move continually in the desired direction.

Accountability is also a key. Someone, usually someone in management, must be held accountable for meeting the diversity goals that are established. There is evidence that this accountability becomes more meaningful when managers are rewarded for meeting the goals. At Xerox, for example, diversity efforts were greatly advanced and diversity goals were given far greater attention when management compensation was tied in part to success in achieving goals of diversity. There is a basic truism in business life: people do what they are rewarded for doing.

Education, Training, and Support

The diversity audit should help determine the type of education and training the business needs to help deal with issues of diversity. Education and training may take many forms. They may be oriented toward increasing awareness of issues. Training may attempt to provide needed information and guidelines so employees can understand and deal with certain problem areas of diversity. For example, when a business provides training in how to identify and eliminate sexual harassment, the focus is on information and guidance. A business may want to probe further and actually attempt to address attitudes and preconceptions, especially if the audit reveals deep pockets of prejudice or misunderstanding. Obviously, this requires a greater depth of training. Role plays, simulations, and focus groups may be used. Again, the choice of educational and training approach depends on the diversity audit and what it tells us about the needs of the group.

Of course, if a company's diversity management efforts are going to have any real impact, support programs must be put in place. If the audit indicates unmet employee needs, the business must take programmatic steps to meet these needs. It is easy to talk about diversity and espouse all the right positions. It is tougher to walk the talk, to set up the programs that support what you say you want to do. Businesses must be very cautious here. There is often a tendency to want to implement the latest, trendy, high-profile diversity program, but that may not be what the business needs. A program that does not meet the specific needs of the business can become an inefficient expenditure. Good diversity management support programs are tailored to the particular business in question, based on the needs uncovered by the audit.

Consider the following examples. The diversity audit may indicate that one of the major issues facing the business is the need to increase minority representation. Specific programs should be formulated to address this issue, perhaps special recruiting efforts to attract minorities to the business or scholarships or internships that are earmarked for select minorities. If the audit shows that the organization is having difficulty promoting women and minorities, special mentoring programs or the formalization of support groups may help. Perhaps the audit reveals trouble retaining high-caliber women. Further, the audit may suggest this is due in part to work/family conflicts. Flextime, telecommuting, or company-sponsored child care may be the kind of support necessary to address this issue.

All training and education and certainly all support programs take money. That monetary commitment can be hard to sell in a business environment that is overwhelmingly concerned about cost containment. That is why the business reasons for diversity that we developed earlier are so important. A business will commit to training and support programs only when it is convinced that business value will result. The business leaders must recognize they will gain some advantage from diversity management .

Developing Your Critical Thinking Skills

1. If you were the CEO of a business, what would you do to help assure that diversity was being valued and supported in your business?

2. How would you deal with employees who were obviously intolerant of diverse people or cultures?

SUMMARY

1. The concept of diversity is complex. Yet it is an important area for managers to consider.

   ■ What are the dimensions of diversity?

   The six areas considered to be primary dimensions of diversity are age, race, ethnicity, gender, physical abilities and qualities, and sexual and affectional orientation.
   The eight areas considered to be secondary dimensions of diversity are work background, income, marital status, military experience, religious beliefs, geographic location, parental status, and education.

2. As more women, racial and ethnic minorities, and both younger and older workers enter the job arena, the workplace is becoming increasingly diverse.

   ■ How would you define workforce diversity?

   Workforce diversity refers to the movement of people from differing demographic and ethnic backgrounds and value orientations into the organizational mix.

3. Contemporary businesses face a number of opportunities and challenges with the diversity they encounter.

   ■ What are the major diversity challenges facing business?

   Seven major areas of challenge were covered in this chapter: (1) the growing participation of women in the workforce, (2) conflicts between work and family, (3) the growth in workforce participation of racial and ethnic minorities, (4) the impact of diversity issues on white males, (5) age and generational issues, (6) expanded global operations, and (7) the impact of certain social trends (personal and environmental health, emergence of a learning society, tolerance of diversity).

4.   The first step in dealing effectively with diversity issues is for the business to recognize their existence. The next step is to develop and implement a diversity management plan.

     ■ How would you define diversity management ?

     Diversity management is putting together a well-thought-out strategy for attracting, motivating, developing, retaining, and fully utilizing the talents of competent people regardless of race, gender, ethnicity, religion, physical ability, or sexual orientation.

5.   Diversity has important implications for a business. Attention to diversity can also yield favorable outcomes for the business.

     ■ Why should businesses be concerned with diversity management ?

     There are seven reasons why diversity management makes sense. (1) Resource acquisition: With needed skills in short supply, a business must do everything it can to attract the best and brightest minds. (2) Resource retention: To be competitive and successful, a business has to keep that talent. (3) Resource utilization: In a global, competitive environment, a business must use its human resources as effectively as possible in order to succeed. (4) Customer sensitivity: A business is better able to understand and respond to the needs of a diverse customer base when its employees mirror the diversity of that population. (5) Creativity and innovation: A diverse mix of employees helps the company find fresh, novel ways to operate and serve customers. (6) Legal reasons: A diversity management program will help the company avoid the legal problems that can arise when diversity issues are left unattended. (7) Ethical stance: Diversity management is the right thing to do.

6.   Because the issue of diversity is so complex, it is not easy for a company to implement an effective diversity management program. There are no simple models that can be copied from others and be expected to work without difficulties. Instead, diversity management programs must be tailored to the specific situation of each business. To do that effectively, the company must build a culture that values, supports, and manages diversity.

     ■ What are the elements involved in building a strong diversity management culture?

     Four elements are involved in the general strategic approach to building an effective diversity management program. They are (1) the presence of top management champions, (2) the implementation of a diversity audit, (3) the establishment of diversity goals, and (4) the installation of a program of diversity education, training, and support.

Links to future courses

Diversity touches a number of courses you will take in your business program. It has particular significance for courses in:

- Marketing
- Management
- Organizational behavior
- Human resource management
- International business

KEY TERMS

Assimilation, p. 144
Baby boomers, p. 136
Caucus groups, p. 135
Diversity audit, p. 148
Diversity management , p. 144
Dual-career household, p. 131
Employee retraining, p. 138
Flextime, p. 132

Glass ceiling, p. 129
Heterogeneous society, p. 125
Job sharing, p. 132
Stereotyping, p. 126
Telecommuting, p. 132
Work/family conflict, p. 131
Workforce diversity, p. 128

EXERCISES AND APPLICATIONS

1. You work for the marketing department of a large compact disk distributor. Develop ideas on how you will market your CDs to baby boomers. What ideas do you have for marketing them to young adults?

2. Form teams of six people each. Have each team include men and women and people from different racial and ethnic backgrounds, if possible. Your team is advising the marketing department of the CD distributor in Exercise 1. As a team, develop a plan for marketing the CDs to baby boomers and a separate plan for marketing them to young adults. How do the experience and the results of the team exercise differ from what you did when working by yourself?

3. Interview a business owner who is either a woman or a member of a minority group. Ask whether this person has experienced discrimination as he or she pursued a career. If so, how did the business owner respond?

4. Consult the U.S. Census website (http://www.census.gov) and look for the city closest to your university. Check the demographic profile of that city. What diversity challenges and opportunities does it suggest for businesses in the city? How will those challenges differ for large companies versus small businesses?

5. Look at the demographic makeup of your class. What can the university's admissions office do to create a more diverse demographic mix of students? Do you think it is important to have a diverse mix? Why or why not?

6. Regardless of your career, each of you will encounter an increasingly diverse business world. Write a brief position paper (one-half to one page) describing what you can do to embrace and value diversity.

....

CASE: BREAKING THE GLASS CEILING
IN CORPORATE AMERICA

American corporations have made noticeable progress in hiring women for managerial positions. But women managers still find that there is an upper limit or glass ceiling preventing them from rising to the higher managerial positions. A recent article in *Business Week* put it this way: "For all of the bravado of the past decade, women in most organizations aren't much further along." There are two reasons for this. First, government pressures on business to rectify the situation have lessened. Second, it's difficult to implement an effective program to get women into higher levels of management.

In spite of the difficulty, some companies have succeeded. For example, Colgate-Palmolive has increased the number of its female senior executives from 27 to 48 in the last five years, and Motorola has dramatically increased its number of female vice presidents over the past decade.

What have these companies done to get these results? At Colgate-Palmolive, all employees participate in two-day diversity training workshops. High-potential women are cross-trained to make sure they have the background and experience to assume higher-level jobs. After analyzing census data, Motorola developed projections of the demographic characteristics of workers in key technical occupations such as engineering and computer science. It then set a goal of having each population group (e.g., women, blacks, Asians) represented in the same proportion in management as in the technical fields. Motorola also requires all top managers to supply the names of three people who could replace them. One of the three had to be the minority or woman most qualified for the job. The top manager then had to give that person the training and experience necessary to qualify for the position.

Decision Questions

1. Sydney Sherry is a plant manager at Colgate-Palmolive. She recently said, "Colgate let me do things I had no business doing. [The company] bet on me and my abilities." Why is such an attitude sometimes necessary in today's business world?

2. Some diversity management training programs, like those at Colgate-Palmolive, emphasize education and training. What difficulties might participants encounter in diversity training programs?

3. In Chapter 3, we talked about stakeholders. Suppose you have been asked, as a representative of Motorola, to explain to stockholders why the company is investing so heavily in diversity programs. What will you tell them?

SOURCE: Linda Himelstein and Stephanie Anderson Forest, "Breaking Through," *Business Week*, February 17, 1997, pp. 64–70.

REFERENCES

1. Nina Munk and Suzanne Oliver. "Women of the Valley." *Fortune*, December 30, 1996, pp. 102–8.

2. Peter Francese. "America at Mid-Decade." *American Demographics*, February 1995, p. 23.

3. Marilyn Loden and Judy B. Rosener. *Workforce America! Managing Employee Diversity as a Vital Resource.* Homewood, IL: Business One Irwin, 1991.

4. William B. Johnston and Arnold E. Packer. *Workforce 2000: Work and Workers for the Twenty-first Century.* Indianapolis, IN: Hudson Institute, 1987.

5. Richard W. Judy and Carol D'Amico. *Workforce 2020.* Indianapolis, IN: Hudson Institute, 1997.

6. Joseph H. Boyett with Jimmie T. Boyett. *Beyond Workplace 2000: Essential Strategies for the New American Corporation.* New York: Dutton, 1995.

7. Boyett and Boyett, p. 81.

8. D. R. Dalton and I. F. Kesner. "Cracks in the Ceiling: The Silent Competence of Women." *Business Horizons*, March/April 1993, pp. 6–10.

9. Ann M. Morrison, Randall P. White, Ellen Van Velsor, and The Center for Creative Leadership. *Breaking The Glass Ceiling: Can Women Reach the Top of America's Largest Corporation?* Reading, MA: Addison-Wesley, 1987.

10. Dianne Solis. "A Pioneer in the Land of Machismo." *The Wall Street Journal*, July 26, 1995, pp. B1, B12.

11. Valerie Reitman. "She Is Free, Yet She's Alone in Her World." *The Wall Street Journal*, July 26, 1995, pp. B1, B12.

12. Boyett and Boyett, 1995.

13. Johnston and Packer, p. 87.

14. Robert Levering and Milton Moskowitz. *The 100 Best Companies to Work for in America.* New York: Plume, 1993.

15. Michael Selz. "Enterprise: From School to the Doctor's Office to Home; Ride Service Does the Driving for Parents." *The Wall Street Journal*, May 6, 1994, p. B1.

16. Cheryl Russell. *The Official Guide to the American Workplace*, 2nd ed. Ithaca, NY: New Strategist Publications, 1995, pp. 322–323.

17. Ibid.

18. "Diversity: Making the Business Case." *Business Week*, Special Advertising Section, December 9, 1996.

19. Dorothy J. Gaiter. "Black Women's Gains in Corporate America Outstrip Black Men's." *The Wall Street Journal*, March 8, 1994, pp. A1, A6.

20. S. Shellenbarger. "Workforce Study Finds Loyalty Is Weak, Division of Race and Gender Are Deep." *The Wall Street Journal*, September 3, 1993, pp. B1, B8.

21. Valerie I. Sessa. "Managing Diversity at the Xerox Corporation: Balanced Workforce Goals and Caucus Groups," in Susan Jackson and Associates. *Diversity in the Workplace.* New York: The Guilford Press, 1992.

22. Boyett and Boyett, 1995, p. 79.

23. "White, Male, and Worried." *Business Week*, January 31, 1994, p. 50.

24. Ibid., pp. 50–5.

25. Diane Crispell. "Generations to 2025." *American Demographics*, April, 1995, pp. 24–33.

26. Jay Finegan. "Surviving in the Nike/Reebok Jungle." *Inc.*, 15, no. 35 (May 1993), pp. 98–102.

27. Nicholas Zill and John Robinson. "The Generation X Difference." *American Demographics*, April 1995, pp. 24–33.

28. Margot Hornblower. "Great X Pectations." *Time*, June 9, 1997, pp. 58–68.

29. Ibid.

30. Russell, 1995, p. 220.

31. For an excellent discussion of the impact of an aging America, see Judy and D'Amico, 1997.

32. "Diversity: Making the Business Case." *Business Week*, Special Advertising Section, December 9, 1996.

33. Lee Gardenswartz and Anita Rowe. *Managing Diversity: A Complete Desk Reference and Planning Guide.* Burr Ridge, IL: Irwin, 1993.

34. United Way Strategic Institute. *What Lies Ahead: A Decade of Decision.* Alexandria, VA: United Way of America, 1993.

35. Robert Theobold. *Turning the Century: Personal and Organizational Strategies for Your Changed World.* Indianapolis: Knowledge Systems, 1992.

36. Ron Stodghill II. "Get Serious about Diversity Training." *Business Week*, November 25, 1996, p. 39.

37. *The World of Trek,* Trek Bicycle Corp., 1997.

38. Susan E. Jackson and Associates. *Diversity in the Workplace: Human Resource Initiatives.* New York: The Guilford Press, 1992.

39. Linda Himelstein and Stephanie Anderson Forest. "Breaking Through." *Business Week*, February 17, 1997, pp. 64–70; "The Pursuit of Diversity at Motorola." *AAHE Bulletin*, March 1995, pp. 3–7.

40. The Pursuit of Diversity at Motorola." *AAHE Bulletin*, March 1995, pp. 3–7.

41. Nan Stone. "Building Corporate Character: An Interview with Stride Rite Chairman Arnold Hiatt." *Harvard Business Review*, March/April 1992, pp. 95–104.

42. A nice presentation of this argument is offered by Taylor H. Cox and Stacy Blake. "Managing Cultural Diversity: Implications for Organizational Competitiveness." *Academy of Management Executive* 5 (August 1991), pp. 45–56.

43. M. Loden and J. B. Rosener. *Workforce America: Managing Employee Diversity as a Vital Resource.* Homewood, IL: Business One Irwin, 1991.

44. R. R. Thomas. *Beyond Race and Gender: Unleashing the Power of Your Workforce by Managing Diversity.* New York: AMACOM, 1991.

45. Jackson and Associates, p. 14.

46. Charles R. Stoner, Richard I. Hartman, and Raj Arora. "Diversity Management in Small Business: An Exploratory Investigation of Attitudes and Actions." *Journal of Small Business Strategy*, Spring 1996, pp. 37–48; "1993 SHRM/CCH Survey." *Ideas & Trends in Personnel.* Chicago: Commerce Clearing House, 1993.

47. An excellent presentation of approaches to the diversity audit is provided by Lee Gardenswartz and Anita Rowe. *Managing Diversity: A Complete Desk Reference and Planning Guide.* Burr Ridge, IL: Irwin Professional Publishing, 1993.

6

Economic Forces

"**S**einfeld" is easily television's most expensive show. Star Jerry Seinfeld makes $22 million in the 1997–98 season. Jason Alexander, Julia Louis-Dreyfus, and Michael Richards make $13 million each. "Seinfeld" is also the most profitable TV show, making NBC the most profitable network. Advertisers pay a cool $1 million a minute to push their products. Only the Super Bowl brings in that much.

The economic impact of "Seinfeld" goes beyond its cost and revenue. Shows just before and after it consistently rank high in the ratings. Products like Junior Mints, which happen to see air time on the show, reap great rewards. Advertisers willingly buy advertising on less desirable shows just to get on "Seinfeld." The demand even affects the cost of other programs, as actors negotiate their contracts with the "Seinfeld" cast's salaries in mind. In short, the success of "Seinfeld" has caused major changes in the economics of the entertainment industry.[1]

Like the television industry, every business is subject to economic forces beyond its control. Sometimes those forces threaten the profitability of the business. At other times they present the business with unique opportunities. In either case, the challenge facing you as a business manager is to identify the threats and opportunities and take actions to deal with them. This chapter will help you understand how economic forces affect a business. When you finish this chapter, you should be able to:

1. List the major economic forces beyond the immediate control of a business that affect the firm's success.

2. Use simple macroeconomic concepts to explain how growth, inflation, unemployment, and interest rate changes occur and how a business can anticipate their occurrence.

3. Explain the concept of the business cycle and list the threats and opportunities each phase of the cycle creates for a business.

4. Explain how prices are determined and why they change.

5. Explain the concept of price elasticity of demand and demonstrate how a business can use the concept to increase profits.

6. Explain the types of competition a firm may face.

7. Explain the various forms of competition.

Economic forces are the second of six environmental forces that have an impact on business. Like the others, these forces are largely beyond the control of the firm. This means that managers must anticipate and react to changes in the economy, but they have little power to control them. Economic forces include the macroeconomic forces of unemployment, inflation, interest rates, and growth and the microeconomic forces of supply, demand, and competition. We describe each of these forces and give examples of how it can help or hurt a business. As you read this chapter, you need to understand the concepts and how they relate to the model of a successful business you saw in Figure 1–6. More importantly, you need to understand how the economic forces affect businesses. We begin with a discussion of macroeconomic forces.

Macroeconomic Forces

Macroeconomics
The study of the entire economy of a nation.

Macroeconomics studies the entire economy of a nation. Macroeconomics deals with four factors that concern a business: economic growth, inflation, interest rates, and unemployment. These factors affect businesses in general, so a particular business will be affected because all businesses are affected.

For example, suppose you own a retail bicycle store in a suburb of Miami, Florida. How can macroeconomic variables affect you? Certainly, economic growth will have an effect. As the nation's economy prospers, people have more money to spend. They may spend some of that money on bicycles. If inflation increases rapidly, the costs of products in general go up and individuals have less *discretionary income* to purchase leisure goods. If unemployment in the area goes up, people may hold on to their money in case they get laid off. Finally, if interest rates are high, the cost of buying an expensive bicycle will go up for your customers who charge the bike on their credit card. They may want to invest their money instead of spending it. Thus, each of the factors can affect the sales of your bicycles in Miami. They may also affect the cost of the bicycles that you purchase for inventory.

We will discuss the four factors as well as three other concepts of macroeconomics: gross domestic product, monetary and fiscal policy, and business cycles. We begin by defining gross domestic product.

Gross Domestic Product

The modern concepts of macroeconomics originated in the writings of John Maynard Keynes in the 1930s. Keynes, introduced in Profile 6–1, conceived of the entire economy as composed of a limited number of variables. Modern versions of his theory give the

TABLE 6–1   The Value of GDP in The United States
First Quarter, 1997 ($ billions)

1. Personal consumption expenditures	$4,798.7
2. Gross private domestic investment	1,144.0
3. Government consumption expenditures and gross investment	1,273.1
4. Net exports of goods and services	−126.8
Total GDP	$7,092.1*

*Figures do not add precisely because of statistical estimating error.

SOURCE: United States Bureau of Economic Analysis, http://www.bea.doc.gov/bea/niptbl-d.html #realgdp, (accessed August 13, 1997).

Gross domestic product (GDP)
The market value of all final goods and services produced in a country in a given year.

name **gross domestic product (GDP)** to the entire economy. **Gross domestic product** is the market value of all final goods and services produced in a country in a given year. Today it is customary to think of the GDP as consisting of the following four parts:

1. Personal consumption expenditures.
2. Gross private domestic investment.
3. Government consumption expenditures and gross investment.
4. Net exports of goods and services (the value of exports minus the value of imports).

Table 6–1 shows the value of each of the components of GDP for the first quarter of 1997, the latest information available.

Increases or decreases in any of these variables affect the overall GDP. For example, when government increases its spending, GDP increases. When the private business sector increases its investment expenditures, GDP increases. Can you predict what would happen if consumer expenditures increased? If exports increased while imports remained the same? What do you think would happen if investment spending declined? Do you think the same thing would happen to GDP if consumption expenditures, government spending, or exports declined?

In addition to the direct impact of each of the four variables, Keynes suggested that the variables interact and, as a result, have further effects on GDP. For example, Keynes argued that a fall in investment would cause a subsequent decline in consumption. This would result in a further decline in GDP. On the other hand, an increase in investment would cause an additional increase in consumption expenditures, which would cause an additional increase in GDP. Keynes called this interaction the *multiplier effect*. We now know that through the multiplier effect, a given decline in investment can eventually cause GDP to fall by two or more times the original decline in investment.

PROFILE 6–1   *John Maynard Keynes*

The British economist John Maynard Keynes originated the modern field of macroeconomics. He did it with a new theory of economic growth and unemployment, explained in his book *The General Theory of Employment, Interest and Money*, published in 1936. It took another 10 years for his ideas to earn widespread acceptance by economists. But when the U.S. Congress passed the Employment Act of 1946, his ideas became an official part of American policy and economic education.

Keynes argued that recessions are usually caused by declines in investment spending and government should increase spending or cut taxes to fight recession. He also argued that inflation is caused by excessive government spending financed by borrowing. To fight inflation, the government should raise taxes, cut spending, or raise interest rates so that investment spending would decline. These Keynesian viewpoints led to the belief that government can control inflation and unemployment. The Employment Act of 1946 stated that the federal government of the United States could and should fight inflation and unemployment and promote economic growth.

Prior to the Keynesian revolution, economists had concerned themselves with only one macroeconomic issue—inflation. They explained inflation in terms of the *quantity theory of money*. In simplest terms, that theory says inflation is the result of the money supply growing too fast. The policy prescription for controlling inflation was to control the rate of growth of the money supply.

Modern macroeconomics has advanced greatly beyond the basic ideas presented by John Maynard Keynes. Today's models are far more complex and today's policy conclusions sometimes differ from his. Furthermore, today's economists are not nearly as optimistic about government's ability to use government spending and taxes to fight inflation and unemployment. In fact, as pointed out in the discussion of Milton Friedman in Profile 6–2 beginning on page 163, one influential group of modern economists believes that Keynesian thinking is dangerously misleading. Nevertheless, Keynes' idea of a macroeconomic approach to the economy is a major part of modern economics.

One of the problems that inflation causes is job uncertainty—even for professionals. This is especially true in the health industry as hospitals try to stem the rising costs of health care. Are there alternatives to rising costs besides eliminating jobs?

Economic Growth

Economic growth
An increase in total spending in the economy.

Economic growth refers to an increase in total spending in the economy. It shows up as an increase in gross domestic product. Economic growth means more sales for the average business. It means that the firm can produce more, provide more profits to owners, and employ more workers. But economic growth can be a two-edged sword. Too much growth by a firm can eventually lead to problems in production and out-of-control costs. Further, too much growth in the economy as a whole can lead to inflation.

Inflation

Inflation
A general increase in prices or an increase in the prices of most goods and services.

Inflation refers to a general increase in prices or an increase in the prices of most goods and services. The most popular measure of inflation is the *consumer price index* (CPI). Published by the U.S. Department of Labor every month, the CPI measures the prices of consumer goods and services. The overall index represents a weighted average of the changes in prices of a wide variety of consumer goods and services. Table 6–2 gives you an idea of the major categories that are used in the late 1990s and shows how the rate of change differs among the different items in the index.

The impact of inflation on businesses can be severe. As inflation increases, more money is required for consumers to purchase the same amount of goods. (Figure 6–1 shows inflation rates in the United States since 1987.) This can lead to a general decline in consumer spending, which affects the sales of a business. Inflation also means higher costs of doing business, which translates into a need to raise prices. For example, Russia has experienced extremely high inflation during the 1990s. This has made it difficult for Russian businesses to survive because the cost of doing business is going up and the demand for products is declining at the same time.

Another problem with inflation is the uncertainty it causes, especially if inflation rates are high. Because prices are increasing rapidly, managers do not know how to react. Should they buy more inventory now since prices may rise later? Should they

TABLE 6–2   Annual Changes in the Major Components of the U.S. Consumer Price Index, April 1996–April 1997

Item	Percentage Change
Food	2.9%
Housing	2.6
Apparel and upkeep	0.9
Transportation	1.2
Medical care	3.0
Entertainment	2.3
Other goods and services	4.4
Average of all items	2.5

SOURCE: U.S. Bureau of Labor Statistics, http://stats.bls.gov/news.release/cpi.t01.html, (accessed June 4, 1997).

FIGURE 6–1   Inflation Since 1987

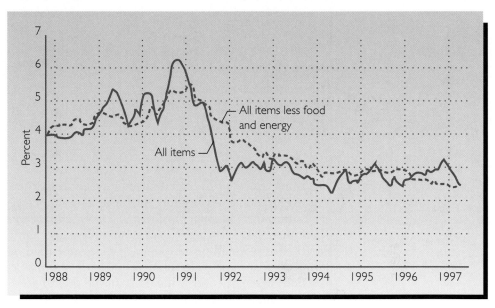

SOURCE: Bureau of Labor Statistics, Consumer Price Index.

buy inventory even if they have to borrow to do it? Should they raise their own prices or try to hold the line? If all businesses raise their prices to offset their own increasing costs, it will cause even more inflation. Should they put any available funds in short-term investments in hope of higher returns, or should they use the same funds to buy capital equipment now rather than pay higher prices later? Since inflation can affect both sales and costs of doing business, an astute manager will watch inflation data closely and be prepared to react when necessary to offset inflationary cost increases.

Unemployment

Unemployment rate
The ratio of the number of people classified as unemployed to the total labor force.

In macroeconomics, unemployment means wanting to work but not having a job. Unemployment is usually measured by the **unemployment rate.** This is the ratio of the number of people classified as unemployed to the total labor force.

There are several types of unemployment, as shown in Table 6–3. One is *frictional unemployment.* This refers to people who are looking for work and will eventually find it because there are jobs available for which they are qualified. These unemployed people will find work if they only keep looking. Suppose that when you graduate from your university, you choose to wait until you return to your hometown to look for a job. If it takes you a few weeks to actually find one, you are an example of frictional unemployment.

A second form of unemployment is *structural unemployment.* This refers to people who cannot find work because the skills they possess are not appropriate for the available jobs. In this case, the unemployed people must learn new skills or relocate in order to get a job. Now suppose that you graduated from college with a degree in special education. There are no openings for special education teachers in the community where you live, but there are vacancies for people with computer science training. Thus, you are structurally unemployed until you get the computer training.

TABLE 6–3   Forms of Unemployment

Form of Unemployment	Cause
Frictional unemployment	The time required to find a job
Structural unemployment	Inappropriate skills
Seasonal unemployment	Seasonal nature of jobs
Cyclical unemployment	Insufficient growth in economy

The ironic aspect of structural unemployment is that some people are unable to find work while companies are searching in vain for employees with the skills they need.

A third form of unemployment is *seasonal unemployment*. This refers to situations where the job is available only at certain seasons of the year. An employee in a construction firm would be an example, since most road or house construction occurs during warmer months. In this case, the employee may earn enough during the construction season to cover living costs during the off-season. Yet, if the person cannot find a job in the winter months, it is an example of seasonal unemployment.

A fourth form of unemployment is *cyclical unemployment*. This refers to people who can't find jobs because a decline in the economy has caused employers to cut back on hiring. Many of these people will have to wait for the economy to improve before they can find jobs.

Some unemployment will always exist because of the combinations of frictional, seasonal, structural, and cyclical unemployment. A certain rate of unemployment is even desirable for the economy at large, since extremely low rates of unemployment can lead to excessive inflation.

Let's consider the impacts of rising unemployment on businesses. Increases in unemployment result in reduced incomes for the unemployed, and that means smaller sales for the businesses that have served them. Higher unemployment rates also mean that people currently holding jobs will be less likely to take a chance on a new, higher-paying job for fear that they might also end up unemployed if the new job does not work out.

The good news is that businesses can take advantage of higher unemployment rates because they can be very selective about who they hire. If many people are looking for work, this gives the recruiter a wide selection of qualified workers.

All of this means that managers should monitor the unemployment rate to see how it will affect both demand for the firm's products and the firm's ability to recruit and hold qualified workers. Structural unemployment may be of concern to businesses that hire large numbers of technical workers or highly skilled workers. Frictional and seasonal unemployment may actually benefit employers, since large numbers of potential workers will be available. Finally, cyclical unemployment will almost always affect a business adversely, since the declining general economy will reduce demand for the firm's products.

Interest Rates

Interest
The price that individuals or businesses pay to borrow money.

Interest is the price paid by individuals or businesses to borrow money. The *interest rate* expresses that price as a percentage per dollar of funds borrowed. Interest rates affect businesses in three significant ways. First, rising interest rates increase the total price customers pay who use credit for products and services. So as interest rates rise, the demand for products will likely decrease.

Second, most businesses borrow money to run their daily business. Higher interest rates mean higher costs of doing business. Managers must either raise the prices of their products to cover this cost of doing business or accept lower profits. To illustrate the impact of interest rates on companies, consider both Motorola and Southwest Airlines. In 1996, Motorola paid $185 million in interest on a total of $3.3 billion in debt. Southwest Airlines paid $59 million on $1.4 billion in total debt. Interest payments are obviously a significant part of each firm's *operating budget.*

budget p. 402>

A third effect of interest rates is on the expansion of a business. Since the firm must sometimes borrow money to finance new equipment, the interest rate is of great concern to the manager. Lower interest rates may mean that it is a good time for the business to borrow to invest in an expansion. Higher rates will make a manager consider delaying expansion until the cost of borrowing decreases. We will discuss this in more depth in Chapter 8.

Business leaders need to know what is happening to the macroeconomic factors of growth, inflation, unemployment, and interest rates. This enables them to take advantage of favorable changes in the economic environment and protect themselves against adverse changes.

Monetary and Fiscal Policy

Keynes' thinking led to a revolution in public policy. His models showed how government could intervene to promote economic growth, reduce unemployment, control inflation, and adjust interest rates. After World War II, most governments established policies to do just that. In the United States, the government agency that implements economic policy is the Federal Reserve Board, often called the Fed. The Fed will be discussed in Chapter 8.

The group of policies emphasized by Keynes involved raising or lowering taxes or government spending in order to influence growth, unemployment, and inflation. Those policies are called **fiscal policy.**

In the 1960s, a movement began among economists to pay more attention to a second group of policies involving the role of money in the economy. This group of policies involves changing the money supply to change interest rates directly, thus influencing inflation, growth, and unemployment. These policies are called **monetary policy.** The leader of that movement was University of Chicago economist Milton Friedman, whose background is shown in Profile 6–2.[2]

Monetary and fiscal policies are now firmly established parts of the macroeconomic environment in which businesses operate. Managers must learn to anticipate the monetary and fiscal policies government will use. This will let them prepare for possible periods of rapid growth, recessions, inflation, and changes in interest rates.

Fiscal policy

Raising or lowering taxes or government spending in order to influence growth, unemployment, and inflation.

Monetary policy

Changing the money supply to change interest rates directly, thus influencing inflation, growth, and unemployment.

PROFILE 6–2   *Milton Friedman*

After World War II, the ideas of John Maynard Keynes became very influential among economists. As a result, American and European economists proposed the frequent use of fiscal policy to improve the performance of an economy. A revolt against this type of thinking arose in the 1960s. The most prominent figure in that revolt was University of Chicago economist Milton Friedman, founder of the Monetarist School of economic thought.

Monetarists believe that the money supply is the most important determinant of the GDP as well as prices. They also believe that a competitive free market economy will naturally tend to produce full employment as long as government does not disrupt the economy with unwise policies. Milton Friedman was especially pessimistic about the ability of government to manage the economy. In his writings and TV interviews, he argued that government decision making tends to be inefficient and ineffective and reduces individual freedom. He therefore recommended that the public sector be made as small as possible and that government avoid trying to manage the economy through monetary and fiscal policy. To learn more about Friedman's views, read *Capitalism and Freedom* and (with Rose Friedman) *Free to Choose*. You will learn more about the monetarists' views on economic policy when you take your first course in economics.

The Business Cycle

One of the major benefits of Keynesian theory was that it told the government how to measure the economy. In the 1930s, the American government began to compile estimates of what was then called the gross national product and its components. Once those numbers became available, economists began to study how GDP changed over time. Soon they discovered a somewhat regular pattern of ups and downs in aggregate production, measured by fluctuations in real GDP, known as the **business cycle.**

Business cycle
A somewhat regular pattern of ups and downs in aggregate production, as measured by the fluctuations in real GDP.

The business cycle has four parts, illustrated in Figure 6–2. One stage is the recession (contraction). This is the time period during which GDP is falling. If GDP falls for at least two quarters (six months), then the U.S. government officially declares that a recession has occurred. Eventually the decline in GDP stops. At that point the business cycle enters the next stage, which is called the trough. This is usually a short stage. It is followed by a period of years during which GDP rises. This period of economic growth is called an expansion. Sooner or later the growth stops and GDP enters the fourth stage, called the peak. The business cycle peak is usually a very short stage and is followed by a recession that marks the beginning of a new business cycle.

FIGURE 6–2   The Business Cycle

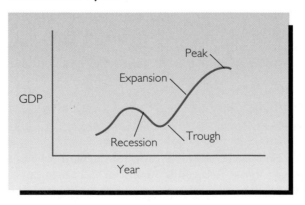

A recession begins when one or more elements of the gross domestic product (GDP) declines. Usually it is investment that falls. Sometimes, however, government spending is cut or taxes are raised, causing consumption expenditures to fall. It is even possible for a drop in net exports to trigger a recession. Once the recession has started, GDP continues to decline for a while due to the multiplier effect.

Since a decline in investment is the most common reason for a recession to begin, it is important to understand why a decline might occur. One major cause is an increase in interest rates. Interest rates naturally tend to rise during an expansion as the demand for loanable funds grows faster than the supply. Sometimes the federal government tries to offset this by increasing the money supply. But that creates the danger of inflation, so sooner or later the government will probably let interest rates rise and risk triggering a recession.

The expansion phase of the business cycle is similarly triggered by an increase in investment spending, government spending, or net exports. That causes an initial increase in GDP, which leads to the multiplier effect. As the process of expansion continues, the economy enters a potential inflationary period.

No two business cycles are identical. Recessions can last for as little as six months or as long as several years. Expansions show similar variations. Table 6–4 shows you the time spans for peaks and troughs in the United States since the 1920s. Figure 6–3 then shows the quarterly detail starting in 1990. Note that there has been only one quarterly decline since the second quarter of 1991, and it was very small.

In order to understand how the business cycle works, consider the following example. A monetary policy action in 1979 caused a recession in the U.S. economy. In October of that year, the Federal Reserve decided to fight a worrisome inflation

TABLE 6–4   Business Cycle Peaks and Troughs in the United States

Date of Trough	Date of Next Peak	Number of Months from Trough to Peak
November 1927	August 1929	21
March 1933	May 1937	50
June 1938	February 1945	80
October 1945	November 1948	37
October 1949	July 1953	45
May 1954	August 1957	39
April 1958	April 1960	24
February 1961	December 1969	106
November 1970	November 1973	36
March 1975	January 1980	58
July 1980	July 1981	12
November 1982	July 1990	92
March 1991	?	

National Bureau of Economic Research, "U.S. Business Cycle Expansions and Contractions," http://www.nber.org/cycles.html (accessed August 19, 1997).

FIGURE 6–3   Gross Domestic Product Quarterly Change, 1990–97
(Percentage change, seasonally adjusted annual rate)

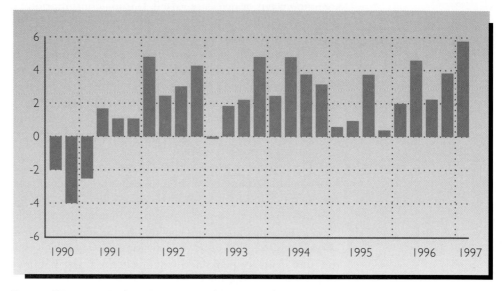

Bureau of Economic Analysis, Department of Commerce, http://www.bea.doc.gov/bea/nipcht-d.html#gdp,
(accessed August 18, 1997).

rate by cutting back the growth of the money supply. That action drove up interest rates and caused GDP to begin falling by the end of January 1980. The decline in GDP was not particularly large, so the inflation problem continued and GDP began to increase at the end of July 1980. Determined to bring down inflation, the Fed continued to reduce the growth of the money supply. Interest rates rose so high that they caused a very sharp drop in investment and consumer installment purchases. GDP fell again beginning in July 1981. This time the drop was quite large and the unemployment rate increased dramatically. But the inflation rate also began to decline.

Then, in the midst of the worst recession since the 1930s, fiscal policy came to the rescue. Ronald Reagan had been elected president in 1980. Once in office, he convinced Congress to enact both tax cuts and increased spending (primarily for military purposes). The result was a sharp increase in *deficit spending* (the government spending more than it was taking in through taxes). Keynesian theory tells us that large-scale deficit spending is the way to pull an economy out of a recession. And that is exactly what happened. GDP began to rise by the end of November 1982 and continued to grow until July of 1990.

That turnaround illustrates some basic features of the role of government policy as it affects the business cycle. Monetary policy was used to attack inflation and in the process caused a recession by driving up interest rates. Fiscal policy was used to pull the economy out of the recession. These are typical developments.

Even though no two business cycles are alike, it is important for business leaders to understand the concept and its history. Knowledge of the cycle can help a business to take actions to minimize the damage done by recessions or inflation. Such knowledge can also be used proactively to take advantage of expansions, inflation and, sometimes, a recession. Managers can use their knowledge of the business cycle concept to prepare themselves for periodic booms and busts.

Developing Your Critical Thinking Skills

1. John Maynard Keynes thought that government should actively try to manage the economy. Milton Friedman disagreed. What do you think?

2. Should top management of a business be more concerned about a rising rate of inflation or rising interest rates?

3. Which seems like the better way to affect the economy, monetary policy or fiscal policy?

Microeconomic Forces

Microeconomics
The study of the behavior of individuals and firms.

Market
The place where buyers and sellers meet and bargain over goods and services.

The previous section discussed the role of forces in the macroeconomic environment that affect businesses. Conversely, **microeconomics** studies the behavior of individual people and firms in particular markets. It studies the interactions of buyers and sellers. The place where buyers and sellers meet and bargain over goods and services is called a **market.** So microeconomics studies how markets work. The two major microeconomics forces that affect business are supply/demand and competition.

Supply, Demand, and Market Price

We introduced the concept of *revenue* in Chapter 1. Remember, a business gains revenue when customers pay for the goods or services the business provides. A business firm's revenue is determined by two factors: (1) the prices customers pay and (2) the total amount of goods and services that customers purchase. This simple but important relationship can be expressed as follows: Price multiplied by the quantity sold equals total revenue, or

$$P \times Q = TR$$
where P = price, Q = quantity sold, and TR = total revenue

Demand curve
A line on a graph that shows how much of a good or service buyers will purchase at each possible price.

Supply curve
A line on a graph that shows the amount of a good or service a business will offer at each possible price.

Equilibrium point
The point on a graph where the demand curve intersects the supply curve.

The price and the quantity sold are determined by bargaining that takes place between buyers and sellers in the market. Buyers are usually willing to buy more of a seller's good or service if the price is lower. Sellers are willing to provide more of the good or service if the price is higher. If the price is too high, the amount the sellers have to offer is greater than the amount buyers will purchase. If the price is too low, the amount the buyers want to purchase is more than sellers have to offer. So the buyers and sellers bargain back and forth until they arrive at a price where the amount sellers have to offer is exactly equal to the amount buyers want to purchase.

Economists explain this relationship between buyers and sellers by drawing demand and supply schedules as shown in Figure 6–4. The curve labeled *D* is called the **demand curve.** It shows how much of a good or service buyers will purchase at each possible price, assuming other factors such as tastes and incomes remain the same. The curve labeled *S* is called the **supply curve.** It shows the amount of a good or service that a business will offer at each possible price, assuming other factors such as technology and the prices of various inputs remain the same. The point where the demand curve intersects the supply curve is called the **equilibrium point.** This is where

FIGURE 6–4   A Supply and Demand Model

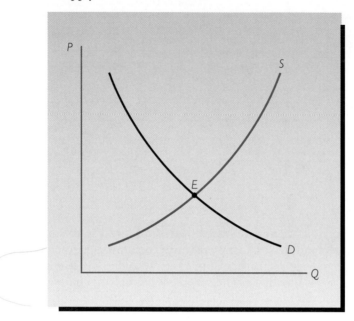

Source: NFIB Small Business Primer, p. 9

the bargaining between buyers and sellers causes the quantity demanded to exactly equal the quantity supplied. This point (*E*) tells us the market price (*P*) and the market output (*Q*). All business firms that serve this market would sell their goods or services at the market price (*P*). All firms together would share in the market output (*Q*). The share of each firm would depend on various competitive factors, which we will discuss later in this chapter.

A typical business firm sells goods or services in more than one market. Thus, its total sales revenue is determined by the prices and outputs in all of the firm's markets.

Price Equilibrium Processes

Equilibrating processes

Processes by which the price moves toward its equilibrium point.

A very important feature of the market is the notion of **equilibrating processes,** which move the price toward its equilibrium point. We explained how demand and supply tend to determine a price in the market. This equilibrium price is a valuable concept because it tells you where the price is heading and where it will settle. However, the market rarely arrives at equilibrium (or stays there) because demand and supply are constantly shifting. In fact, a typical situation is one where the price has temporarily moved away from the long-run equilibrium value and is in the process of moving back. Therefore, the real usefulness of the concept of equilibrium is to tell business leaders where the price is going in both the short and the long run.

The energy crisis of the 1970s and early 1980s illustrates this point. The story began in 1973, when the Organization of Petroleum Exporting Countries (OPEC) succeeded in gaining control of a large percentage of the world oil supply. The cartel proceeded to raise the price to $7.67 a barrel in 1975, $21.59 in 1980, and a peak of $31.77 in 1981. At that time, there was a general feeling that the price of oil would go

When OPEC countries raised the prices of oil, domestic oil companies drilled for more oil while consumers cut back on their use of gasoline. These shifts eventually brought the price of oil down. What other examples can you think of that illustrate shortages or surpluses of a product?

even higher. However, the increase in prices caused oil companies to search for more oil and consumers to be more conservative in the use of energy. That meant the equilibrium price would eventually be much lower than $31.77 a barrel. Sure enough, by 1986 the price had fallen to $12.51 a barrel.[3]

Demand and supply curves shift frequently. As a result, market price and output are always changing. Sometimes these changes are deliberately caused by a business firm. More often, they are caused by forces beyond the firm's control. The macroeconomic forces we discussed earlier are major causes of supply and demand shifts. Shifts in demand are also caused by changes in customer tastes and prices of competitive products. Shifts in supply are also caused by changes in technology and changes in the prices of capital, labor, or raw materials.

Price Elasticity of Demand

Business depends on revenue for survival. As we've seen, revenue depends on market price and the quantity sold. Therefore, business managers must constantly be thinking about price changes and their impact on the firm's future revenue. The concept that explains the relationships among price, quantity, and revenue is the **price elasticity of demand.** Economists measure it by dividing the percentage change in the quantity of a product or service demanded by the percentage change in its price. An elasticity greater than 1.0 is an elastic demand; less than 1.0 is an inelastic demand.

Business history has some exceptionally memorable illustrations of the price elasticity concept. Profile 6–3 describes several of these, and Figure 6–5 illustrates the concept. Note that products that have an elastic demand curve, which is relatively flat, are price sensitive. Examples of price-elastic goods and services are clothes, glassware,

Price elasticity of demand

The percentage change in the quantity of a product or service demanded, divided by the percentage change in its price.

FIGURE 6–5   Elastic and Inelastic Demand Curves

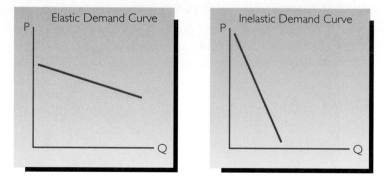

furniture, stereo equipment, restaurants, and relatively low-priced luxury goods. Products that have an inelastic demand curve, which is relatively steep, are not price sensitive. Examples of price-inelastic products include medicine and hospital services, alcohol, legal services, auto repair, and gasoline.

 Let's consider how price elasticity might work for a manufacturer of mountain bikes. Suppose the company is considering whether to raise or lower the price of one of its most expensive bicycles for the next season. Since the bike is at the top of the price line and is purchased by hard-core enthusiasts who are not price sensitive, changing the price is probably not going to affect sales very much. The company has some evidence to support this. Last year it lowered the price of its $2,000 bike by 10 percent. Sales increased, but only by 2 percent. As you can see, the company actually made less money even though it lowered the price, because the demand for this bike was price inelastic. For these expensive bikes, price inelasticity suggests that raising prices may increase total revenues. In fact, this year the company raised the price by 5 percent and saw a reduction in demand of only 1 percent.

Now consider a bicycle at the low end of the price line, one of their cheapest models. This bike is probably of most interest to those just starting out. When the company lowered the price of this $300 starter bike by 10 percent, demand increased by 25 percent. Apparently, customers were very price sensitive, meaning demand was price elastic. For these lower-priced bikes, decreasing the price increases total revenues. Conversely, raising the price would likely decrease demand enough to reduce total revenues.

Keep in mind that price elasticity is not the only factor at work here. Competitors' models and prices are important. Costs of production and marketing capabilities are also important. Managers must balance a number of factors together to reach a final decision on pricing of each model.

PROFILE 6–3   *Historical Examples of Price Elasticity*

Henry Ford. In 1907, most experts thought the demand for automobiles was very price inelastic. But Henry Ford was convinced the demand was highly price elastic. Ford built low-cost cars that he could sell at a lower price. He tapped a huge mass market and the quantity of Ford automobiles demanded skyrocketed.

Steve Jobs. In the mid-1970s, IBM dominated the computer market. Most customers were businesspeople. IBM did not think there was a market for personal computers. Steve Jobs disagreed. He believed the demand for home computers would be price elastic if the computer was also easy to use. He and Steve Wozniak invented just that kind of computer and formed Apple Computer to sell their invention. They were right: demand turned out to be price elastic. Because its prices were so low, the company was able to sell to an entirely new group of people who had never before considered buying a computer. Apple sold millions of home computers and created an entirely new segment of the computer market.

Herb Kelleher. In the 1970s, most airline executives thought demand for their service was price inelastic, so they didn't try to hold the line on airfares. But Herb Kelleher believed that demand was price elastic. He formed a company called Southwest Airlines, which offered extremely low prices. Demand was price elastic; Kelleher's airline became one of the most successful in the industry and is still considered a prime example of good management.

Sam Walton. Sam Walton operated a small chain of variety stores in small towns located in Arkansas, Oklahoma, and Missouri. In 1961, he decided to see if demand for general merchandise was price elastic in those small towns. The experts bet against him. But when he opened his first store with its unbelievably low prices, customers poured in. Total revenue increased because volume was so high. Convinced that demand was price elastic in small towns, Walton opened discount stores in many other communities. Eventually his discount stores spread throughout the country, and Wal-Mart is now the number one retailer in the United States.

Developing Your Critical Thinking Skills

1. Gasoline prices seem to have a habit of going up just before holiday travel begins. Can you explain why in terms of demand and supply curves?

2. Why are many of Southwest Airlines' customers leisure travelers? Why do many airlines have cheaper fares if the customer agrees to stay over Saturday night?

3. Why is the price of strawberries high in early summer?

Competition

We now turn to the second major microeconomic force affecting business, the concept of competition. Most managers can readily give you the names of their major competitors. For example, Table 6–5 shows a partial list of competitors for each of our focus companies. Furthermore, astute managers can tell you what their competitors do well and where they have weaknesses in competing for customers. But there are some difficulties involved in correctly assessing the firm's competitive situation. Sometimes it is hard to define competitors accurately because the industry is quite diversified. The company may have a number of competitors, but each competitor will overlap only a portion of its products or services. Some competitors are fierce competitors, while others are less aggressive. This section discusses the force of competition and how it affects businesses.

TABLE 6–5   Selected Competitors of Focus Companies

Southwest Airlines	Motorola	Brinker International (Chili's)	Mountain Bikes
United Airlines	Wireless Communications	Cheddars	Trek
Delta Airlines	Nokia (Finland)	Perkins Family Restaurants	Cannondale
American Airlines	Emerson	Red Lobster	Specialized
TWA	Sony (Japan)	Applebees	Giant
Continental Airlines	Toshiba (Japan)	Various Mexican restaurant chains	GT
	Semiconductors		Bianchi
	AMD		Mongoose
	Intel		Barracuda
	Cirex Corp.		Raleigh
	AT&T		Schwinn
	Cirrus Logic		Fuji
	Texas Instruments		Gary Fisher
	Services		
	AT&T Wireless Services		
	BellSouth Corp.		
	GTE Personal Communications System		
	United States Cellular Corp.		
	Sorijt Cellular		

Types of Competition

There are two generic types of competition, direct and indirect. The most obvious competitors are direct competitors. These are the firms that sell the same goods and services and compete for the same customers.

Pure (perfect) competition
A market situation where many firms sell nearly identical products and no one firm can raise its price without losing most of its customers.

Monopolistic competition
A market situation where there are many firms but each has a slightly different product.

Direct Competition

Economists group directly competing firms into one of four categories: pure competitors, monopolistic competitors, oligopolies, and monopolies.

Pure competition is a situation where all firms sell identical products and no one firm can raise its price without losing its customers. Since the individual firm cannot raise prices on its own, it has to accept the market price. Agriculture is a good example of a purely competitive industry.

Monopolistic competition is a situation where there are many firms but each has a slightly different product. Each firm can raise its price without losing its customers. Retailing and restaurants typify industries in this category. Brinker International is a good example. Norman Brinker offered *differentiated products* in the crowded restaurant business. Each of his restaurant chains experienced significant

Oligopoly
A situation where a few firms, with or without differentiated products, dominate the market.

Monopoly
A market situation where there is only one firm selling a product or service.

competition. Brinker used particular decors and menu selection to give a unique ambience to each chain. Brinker competed with fast-food chains, even though his prices were higher, by offering full service and a somewhat different product.

An **oligopoly** is a situation where a few firms, with or without differentiated products, dominate the market. The reason for the small number of companies is the extremely high cost of entering the industry. Because there are only a few firms, there is little incentive to compete based on price. Since intense price competition would hurt them all, companies in an oligopoly situation tend to compete in other ways, such as advertising and new product development. The steel and automobile industries are good examples of oligopolies.

A **monopoly** is a situation where there is only one firm selling a product or service. As such, it can set the market price subject to the constraints of the demand curve. Many monopolies are regulated by the government. Electric power companies have traditionally been good examples of a regulated monopoly. Today, their monopolistic position is being challenged. The ability to sell power across geographic areas is now changing the industry from a monopoly toward an oligopolistic situation.

It is important for business leaders to know which category applies to their business situations because the principles for successful competition differ from one category to the next. For example, in purely competitive industries, the firm has to compete strictly in terms of cost. Management must concentrate on lowering costs so that the firm can make a profit at the existing market price. In oligopoly situations, management competes by differentiating the product, perhaps through advertising or new product development.

Indirect Competition

Indirect competitors are less obvious but nevertheless represent serious potential threats. They are usually firms that sell different goods and services but sell to the same customers as your business. In some cases, the firm's indirect competitors sell a *substitute product* or service. For example, during the 1950s the American steel industry lost significant sales to the producers of plastics and aluminum. Similarly, movie theaters have lost much of their business as their former customers stayed home to watch videos. The typewriter industry has lost most of its market to computers with word processing capabilities. Currently, the U.S. Postal Service is encountering substantial indirect competition from the Internet and fax machines (in addition to the direct competition it faces from UPS, FedEx, and others).

The U.S. Postal Service faces direct competition in package delivery from UPS, FedEx, and others. It also encounters indirect competition from fax machines and the internet. Faxing to local recipients is often cheaper, easier, and faster than using mail. What other services might the U.S. Postal Service offer to compensate for this trend?

The Impact of Size and Geography

Other aspects of competition are the size of a market and its geographic spread. Every business has to ask where its customers and potential competitors are located.

Sometimes the market area is restricted to a specific town or part of a town. Sometimes the market covers many towns in a state or a group of states. The market can be the entire nation or even virtually the entire world. It is often difficult to determine a firm's geographic market without substantial experience and research.

The costs of producing and selling increase dramatically as the size and geographic spread of the markets increase. Factors to consider include transportation costs, customer travel time, differences in buyer behavior patterns, and the actual distances that products are shipped. At the same time, larger markets may offer opportunities to save money on a per-unit basis by advertising across different geographic regions and by combining shipments of goods to a variety of destinations.

Forms of Competition

We've discussed different *types* of competition. Competition also takes many *forms*. One of the toughest tasks of management is to choose the combination of ways in which the firm will compete. This section reviews eight ways a firm might compete: price, quality and service, innovation and fashion, selling effort, location, investment in capacity, writing the rules, and cooperating with competitors.

Price

The most obvious, and often the most dangerous, form of competition is price competition. Profile 6–3 identified several firms that made effective use of price competition. The stories of Ford, Apple Computer, Southwest Airlines, and Wal-Mart show how powerful this weapon can be. Note that in all of these examples demand is price elastic.

continuous improvement
p. 448>
efficiency p. 478>

Economies of scale
Lowering a firm's average cost of production by increasing the size of its production facilities and its overall volume of production.

Experience (learning) curve
Lowering a firm's costs by increasing efficiency through experience in making the product.

Price competition is dangerous, however, if demand is price inelastic. Recall that cutting prices in a price-inelastic situation reduces total revenue. Thus, a firm that cuts its price can gain only by taking business away from its competitors and increasing its share of the market. But if the competitors cut prices too, there may be no increase in any firm's market share.

Price competition is most effective and advisable if the firm doing the price cutting is also the *low-cost producer*. In that case, the competitors won't be able to match the price cuts and still stay in business. A firm that wants to be the low-cost producer should be aware of two important economic concepts that govern costs of production. One is the concept of **Economies of scale**. Often a firm can lower its average cost of production by increasing the size of its production facilities and its overall volume of production. It can then offer volume discounts to its customers.

The second cost-related concept is the **Experience curve** (also referred to as the learning curve). Even without increasing the scale of operation, a firm can nevertheless lower costs as a result of increasing efficiencies gained from experience making the product. To take advantage of efficiencies, management has to deliberately try to learn how to cut costs as the company gains experience in producing the product. Later in this textbook, you will learn more about the process of continuous improvement, which is a key to increased efficiency.

Quality and Service

differentiate p. 319> Two major methods whereby a firm can differentiate itself are through the quality of its products and the extra services it offers to customers. Competing on the basis of quality, including superior service, is a popular option for several reasons. One is that it is more difficult for a competitor to match another firm's quality than to match its price. Another is that consumers are willing to pay more for quality. If the firm can establish a quality advantage, it can raise its price and earn a higher profit. To some extent this is the approach taken by Motorola, Brinker International, and some of the high-quality mountain bike companies. Profile 6–4 presents a few additional examples of quality and service competition. Note that one example, Zenith, excelled for 50 years with the quality strategy but then got into difficulty because it neglected other aspects of a healthy business.

PROFILE 6–4   Examples of Quality and Service Competition

Zenith. This company adopted the quality strategy in the 1920s and used it for 50 years to become one of the most successful manufacturers of radios and TV sets. Because customers were willing to pay high prices for high quality, Zenith didn't have to try to be the low-cost producer. That changed in the 1970s when Japanese manufacturers succeeded in matching Zenith's quality while producing and selling at a much lower cost. Zenith's TV business began to incur losses that continued into the 1990s.

Maytag. In the early 1950s, Maytag was just one of a number of good manufacturers of washing machines. Then the company decided to emphasize a quality strategy. A key component of that strategy was the advertising campaign that showed the Maytag repairperson complaining because Maytag machines never required repairs.

Nordstrom's. Nordstrom department stores started as a single retail shoe store in Seattle. The founders emphasized the biggest assortment of footwear in the market and insisted that suppliers provide high-quality shoes. The company made an extra effort to help customers find just the right shoe. Later Nordstrom's branched out into clothing and other lines of business. But it retained the emphasis on a wide selection, strict quality control, and superior customer service. Today Nordstrom's is the acknowledged quality and service leader in its industry.

Companies often compete by providing excellent after-sale service. This gives small businesses an advantage over large discount stores which cannot afford to offer that level of service. Chris Zane of Zane's Cycles continues to be the top bicycle retailer in his area because of excellent after-sale service. Why can small companies often offer more service than large ones?

Quality as a competitive tool is not restricted to large companies. Small companies can also take advantage of quality service to capture and retain customers. An example of this is Zane's Cycles in New Haven, Connecticut. Chris Zane operates in an extraordinarily competitive environment. Large stores and chains, the low-cost leaders, have moved into the retail market, putting small and midsize stores out of business. In New Haven three bike shops went out of business last year alone.

To survive and differentiate himself in this market, Zane has made quality service and customer satisfaction his first priority. Some customer-winning tactics that he either invented or learned are a lifetime free-service guarantee for all his products, a free cellular phone to anyone who buys a bike, and no charge for parts that cost less than $1. Impressive, isn't it? In addition, to attract more customers to his store, Zane added a coffee bar and a play area where kids can stay while their parents are shopping or enjoying the coffee. Zane's strategy has paid off. He is now the largest independent bicycle dealer in New Haven, and his business is growing at a rate of 25 percent per year.[4]

Innovation and Fashion

Some firms find that they can beat the competition by constantly developing new and improved products or services. If the changes represent a new product or a true, verifiable improvement in a product, such as a television set that gives a sharper picture, then the development is an *innovation*. If the changes are largely cosmetic, such as changing the exterior look of a car, then the development is a change in *fashion*. In either case, the firm is competing by giving the customer something new or different. Profile 6–5 provides a few examples of famous innovative firms.

Innovation is a key to the success of all four of our focus examples. The Motorola story is one long example of the development of significant new products, often with patent protection. In the case of Southwest Airlines, the innovations had more to do with operating procedures. In the mountain bike industry, Trek combined new products that had a significant element of fashion with production innovations like its new bonding technology. Finally, Norman Brinker's entire career illustrates the use of innovations in the restaurant business.

PROFILE 6–5   *Examples of Innovative Firms*

3M. Minnesota Mining and Manufacturing, better known as 3M, is famous for inventing thousands of common items, such as sandpaper, Scotch tape and Post-it notes. Every year the company introduces hundreds of new products. The thousands of research workers who come up with the ideas are encouraged to get involved in marketing their ideas within the company. One famous saying at 3M is "Thou shalt not kill a new product idea."

Merck. Arguably the research and development leader in the pharmaceutical industry, Merck plows back 10 percent of its sales revenue into research. During the 1980s its laboratories produced a number of new products, such as Mevacor (the first cholesterol-lowering drug). In 1987 Merck replaced IBM as America's "most admired corporation" (based on an annual survey by *Fortune* magazine).

Du Pont. The leading chemical company in the United States, Du Pont dates back to 1804. It has a tradition of making and commercializing scientific breakthroughs. Among these are such famous products as rayon, cellophane, nylon, and Teflon.

Hewlett-Packard. This company was started in a garage by two engineers. Its first products were innovative electronic testing devices. In 1972 Hewlett-

One of the most recognized products today is Post-it® note pads from 3M Corporation. The product was developed by scientists using glue that was supposed to be super strong. A batch failed but was found to be perfect for removable notes. The product would not have been developed without 3M's innovation-oriented culture. What are the characteristics of firms which encourage innovation?

Packard pioneered the world's first handheld scientific calculator (the HP-35). In the 1980s and 1990s it introduced the famous Laserjet computer printer and the first desktop mainframe computer.

Sony. Sony was founded in Tokyo, Japan, in 1946. The founders' strategy was to invent patentable products that would create new markets. Using this vision, Sony pioneered the development of transistorized tape recorders and radios, (1950s), the VCR (1976), and the famous Walkman (1979). Moving from innovation in product development to innovation in other forms of entertainment, Sony bought CBS Records in 1988 and Columbia Pictures in 1989.

SOURCES: Philip Matter, *World Class Business* (NY: Henry Holt and Co., 1992); Robert Levering and Milton Moskowitz, *The 100 Best Companies to Work for In America*, rev. ed. (Reading, MA: Addison-Wesley, 1994); *Hoover's Handbook of American Companies 1996* (Austin, Texas: The Reference Press Inc., 1995); *Hoover's Handbook of World Business 1995–1996* (Austin, Texas: The Reference Press, Inc., 1995).

Selling Effort

Some of the most famous business success stories are based on superior selling effort. For example, IBM's dominance of the computer industry from 1956 to 1980 was based more on the company's superior sales techniques than on any other single factor. Selling effort encompasses the sales force, advertising, and all of the related activities that persuade the customer to deal with one company rather than another.

Selling can occur at a company store or at the customer's home or place of business. One of the most famous examples of a company excelling in selling at its stores is Nordstrom's. A company whose sales force goes to the customer's residence worldwide is Avon.[5]

Location

retailers p. 282>

This factor is particularly important for retail businesses. Grocery stores, fast-food stores, car dealers and a host of other types of retailers need to choose carefully the places where they will open for business. Shoppers are naturally drawn to some locations but find it hard to go to others. A retail store in a place that shoppers think is out of the way will likely not last long.

The history of Staples, the first superstore to sell office supplies, illustrates the importance of location in retailing. The founder, Tom Stemberg, was a business school graduate with extensive experience in the grocery supermarket business. Stemberg believed there was a huge market for office supplies offered at deep discount prices (he believed that demand was price elastic). He was convinced that he could push prices down and still make a profit by taking advantage of economies of scale. He opened his first superstore in 1986 and quickly set about expanding the chain. Stemberg's primary concern in the early years was to acquire the best retail locations before new competitors copied his concept. As he put it, "Identify the central scarce resource in your business and scrap for it. At Staples, good real estate drives sales growth, protects us from competitors and sometimes acts as a weapon against enemies."[6]

Manufacturers also need to consider location. For them this is more a matter of minimizing costs and speeding up delivery times. If transportation cost is a significant part of the final cost to the customer, then manufacturers need to find locations that minimize transportation cost. If the factory has one major customer that often wants quick delivery on short notice, the manufacturer probably needs to locate close to that customer.

Investment in Capacity

Capacity
A company's ability to produce a good or service.

Capacity is the name given to a company's ability to produce a good or service. For example, if a carmaker has one factory that can produce 200,000 cars per year, the company is said to have a capacity of 200,000 cars per year. If that company builds a second factory that also has the ability to produce 200,000 cars per year, it is investing in additional capacity (and now has a capacity of 400,000 cars per year).

Investment in capacity can be used to combat potential competition. The case of Aluminum Company of America (Alcoa) illustrates how this works. Between 1910 and 1941 Alcoa dominated the aluminum industry with a policy of low prices and innovation. It also fortified its position by investing in new capacity ahead of demand. As demand for aluminum grew, Alcoa expanded capacity to stay ahead of it. All of Alcoa's potential competitors knew that if they tried to enter the industry, they would be adding unneeded capacity.

Writing the Rules

ompetitive advantage
p. 315>

In the competitive technique called writing the rules, a company works with the government or a trade association to establish the technical standards and other rules that will govern competition in the industry. In helping to write the rules, the firm can establish provisions that give it a competitive advantage. For example, a lawn mower manufacturer could help the government write the safety standards for lawn mowers in such a way as to favor the types of mowers being produced by the manufacturer. A trade group of cement manufacturers could *lobby* the state legislature to require the use of cement in all state highway projects.

An important recent example of writing the rules is the case of high-definition television (HDTV). In 1996 the Federal Communications Commission finally adopted the rules for this new high-quality form of TV broadcasting. Making that decision took the commission nine years because a number of private firms were lobbying for standards that would give them a competitive edge. In particular, broadcasters and TV manufacturers wanted the government to mandate a single standard that everyone would have to use. By May of 1996, the commission had arrived at a standard that was acceptable to the American broadcasting companies and TV manufacturers. The proposed system would scan the picture onto the screen in a manner that would make it impossible to use the television set as a computer.

Realizing that this rule would put personal computers at a disadvantage in the American living room, Microsoft's Bill Gates launched a last-minute lobbying effort to stop its adoption. The result? The FCC insisted that the television people negotiate with the computer companies. In November 1996, those negotiations concluded with an agreement that the FCC would not mandate a standard for HDTV reception. That decision kept open the option of developing a HDTV standard that would be compatible with PCs. By his timely action, Bill Gates had prevented future competitors from writing the rules in a way that would put his company at a competitive disadvantage.[7]

Cooperation with Competitors

A final method of competition is actual cooperation with competitors. This method of competition seems at first glance to be at least unethical and perhaps illegal. Indeed, business history is replete with examples of firms that have stepped over the line into activities that break antitrust laws. We will discuss those more fully in Chapter 9. However, there are also many examples of how companies have worked legally with their competitors for their mutual benefit and the benefit of customers.

Two types of cooperation among competing firms are joint ventures and strategic alliances. Both will be discussed further in Chapter 7. **Joint ventures** are separate companies partially owned by two or more firms whose goal is to conduct business they could not do alone. The Alaskan pipeline, for example, was a joint venture among eight oil companies. None of the companies could have afforded the project by itself. Some joint ventures are between companies in different countries or between a company in one country and the government of another country.

Joint ventures
Companies partially owned by two or more firms to conduct business they could not do alone.

The Alaskan pipeline was possible only through the combined efforts of several oil companies. No single company would have had sufficient capital nor would have taken the risk by itself. Is cooperation among competitors good or bad as a general rule? What should be the determining factor in deciding when it should be allowed?

These joint ventures exist because the government of a country insists on either a private or public joint arrangement before it will allow the foreign company to enter its market.

Strategic alliance

Long-term agreements between two firms that benefit both.

Strategic alliances between firms are formal, long-term agreements between two firms for the benefit of both. In some cases, one firm may agree to distribute another's products. In others, they may work together on product development. Still other alliances may be long-term supplier/customer relationships.

Developing Your Critical Thinking Skills

1. Suppose you want to start your own retail bike shop. What types and forms of competition will you expect to encounter?

2. This chapter discussed a number of forms of competition. Successful businesses sometimes achieve a competitive advantage by using two or more of those forms. What do you think are the most effective combinations of forms of competition?

SUMMARY

1. A major responsibility of a manager is dealing with economic forces external to the firm.

   ■ What are the major economic forces that affect a firm's success?

   The two major economic forces that affect how a business operates are macroeconomic forces and microeconomic forces. Macroeconomic forces deal with economic growth, inflation, unemployment, and interest rates. Microeconomic forces deal with supply and demand and competition.

2. It is impossible to forecast changes in the macroeconomic forces accurately. However, business managers can try to anticipate their occurrence by understanding some simple macroeconomic concepts and then using them to interpret economic reports commonly reported in the business press.

   ■ What are the macroeconomic concepts managers should understand?

   Managers should understand the concept of gross domestic product (GDP). This is the market value of all final goods and services produced in a country in a given year. It is the sum of four types of spending: consumption, investment, government, and net exports. Economic growth is measured by increases in GDP.

   The multiplier effect refers to the idea that when one component of GDP increases, that increase causes an additional increase in one of the other components.

   The most popular measure of inflation, the consumer price index, measures the prices of consumer goods and services. Inflation is important because it affects the cost of products or services provided and the demand for the product.

   The unemployment rate is published monthly by the U.S. Bureau of Labor Statistics, which calculates it by dividing the number of people classified as unemployed by the total labor force. Unemployment includes frictional, structural, seasonal, and cyclical unemployment.

Interest is the price paid by businesses to borrow money, and the interest rate measures that price as a percentage of the amount borrowed.

The concepts of monetary and fiscal policy can be used to anticipate possible government actions in response to the most recent reports on GDP growth, inflation, unemployment, or interest rates. Monetary policy refers to government efforts to change the money supply and interest rates. Fiscal policy refers to changes in government spending and taxation.

3. Managers can look at the relative growth or decline in the economy and can watch for changes in government policy that may affect the economy.

    ■ What is the business cycle and how does it work?

    Managers should be familiar with the concept of the business cycle. This refers to the historical fact that GDP exhibits periodic increases and decreases. The business cycle consists of four stages: recession (contraction), trough, expansion (recovery), and peak.

4. Perhaps the single most important determinant of business success is the price received for the company's product or service. If the price is too low, the firm will eventually go out of business or have to abandon the unprofitable product line. If the price is sufficiently high, then the firm can earn profits. If the price is too high, the firm will lose customers. Managers need to be able to forecast the prices they are likely to receive for their products.

    ■ How are prices determined and why do they change?

    Prices are determined by the interaction of demand and supply in the market. Prices may change because of a shift in demand, because of a shift in supply, or because of simultaneous shifts in demand and supply.

5. In the long run, the price of a product or service is determined by the interaction of buyers and sellers in the market. The impact of prices on revenues depends in part on the price elasticity of demand.

    ■ What is price elasticity of demand and how can knowledge of it be used to increase profits?

    Price elasticity of demand refers to how the quantity of a product or service demanded changes in response to a change in price. To measure elasticity, divide the percentage change in quantity demanded by the percentage change in price. If the percentage change in quantity demanded is greater than the percentage change in price, then demand is said to be elastic. If the percentage change in quantity demanded is less than the percentage change in price, demand is inelastic.

    A firm can increase revenues by raising prices in markets where demand is price inelastic or by lowering prices in markets where demand is price elastic.

6. Competition is the key to the success of the capitalist economic system. Society as a whole benefits from the rivalry of business firms. However, firms themselves are under constant pressure to cope with the competition. To do so effectively, managers must first understand what types of competition they are facing.

    ■ What are the major types of competition that businesses face?

    There are two generic types of competition, direct and indirect.

Economists break direct competition into four basic categories: (1) pure competition, in which all firms produce identical products and there are so many firms that no one firm can raise its price without losing its customers; (2) monopolistic competition, where there are many firms but each has a slightly different product, so each firm can raise its price without losing its customers; (3) an oligopoly, where a few firms dominate the market; and (4) a monopoly, where there is only one firm serving the market.

Indirect competition refers to firms that sell different goods or services but sell to the same customers. For example, steel companies face indirect competition from producers of plastic and aluminum.

7. Every business must devote serious thought to how to meet and beat the competition. Managers must consider a variety of ways to compete and then choose those which give the firm the most competitive advantage.

■ What are some of the major forms of competition?

Some major forms of competition are (1) price, (2) quality, (3) innovation and fashion, (4) selling effort, (5) location, (6) investment in capacity, and (7) writing the rules. An eighth way of dealing with competitors is to cooperate with them. This can be done legally through joint ventures or strategic alliances.

Links to Future Courses

Economics forms the basis for many courses you will encounter throughout your college career. Economics affects many areas both within and outside of business. It is relevant to both consumers and business managers. You will learn more and apply economic principles in the following courses.

- Principles of economics
- Principles of marketing
- Principles of management
- Principles of finance
- Business policy
- Not-for-profit management
- Engineering

EXERCISES AND
APPLICATIONS

1. Search the Internet for government sources of economic data. Look up the consumer price index over the past decade and interest rates over the same period. What is the relationship between the two?

2. Working in teams, select one or more products per team. Estimate the relationship between prices and quantity sold. For example, how many PayDay candy bars would your team buy at 60 cents each? 50 cents each? 40 cents each? If your instructor permits, survey your entire class.

3. If you surveyed a large number of people in Exercise 2, now calculate the elasticity of the demand for the product by dividing the change in number sold by the change in price. Was the elasticity greater than 1.0? Remember, elasticity greater than 1.0 is an elastic demand, and elasticity less than 1.0 is an inelastic demand.

4. Interview the owner of an auto repair shop near campus. Ask how sensitive customers are to changes in price. Are they as price sensitive for repairs as they are for a simple oil change? Ask the owner how business has been affected by the advent of the quick-lube businesses. Write up your findings in a one-page paper.

5. In teams of five people, pick a product that is familiar to all of you. Discuss the forms of competition used to sell it. Price? Location? Quality? Others?

6. For the product you chose in Exercise 5, what are the substitutes for it? Who are the competitors?

KEY TERMS

Business cycle, p. 164
Capacity, p. 178
Demand curve, p. 167
Economic growth, p. 160
Economies of scale, p. 174
Equilibrating processes, p. 168
Equilibrium point, p. 167
Experience (learning) curve, p. 174
Fiscal policy, p. 163
Gross domestic product, p. 158
Inflation, p. 160
Interest, p. 162
Joint ventures, p. 179

Macroeconomics, p. 157
Market, p. 167
Microeconomics, p. 167
Monetary policy, p. 163
Monopolistic competition, p. 172
Monopoly, p. 173
Oligopoly, p. 173
Price elasticity of demand, p. 169
Pure (perfect) competition, p. 172
Strategic alliance, p. 180
Supply curve, p. 167
Unemployment rate, p. 161

CASE: THE TEMP POOL IS SHRINKING

Due to recent restructurings and the need to control costs, many businesses have begun to rely more heavily on temporary workers. Consider the logic. Companies can hire temps who have needed skills while avoiding many of the costs of full-time workers, such as health benefits, vacations, pensions, and other perks. This gives firms more flexibility in their staffing needs and better control of costs.

However, these businesses are now experiencing a new problem. There seems to be a shortage of temporary workers nationwide. The apparent culprit is the drastically low unemployment level. In May 1997 the unemployment rate dropped to 4.8 percent, the lowest level since 1973. Even those groups that have historically experienced high unemployment have been more able to get jobs. This low supply of temporary workers is stifling the growth of some high-growth companies, especially financial services, health care, telecommunications, and software companies. And technology-driven organizations are not the only ones being hit. Customer service departments and call centers are feeling the pinch. Some say this temp crunch is part of a national staffing crisis.

Decision Questions

1. If you were the human resources director of a company that was finding it more and more difficult to hire workers, what would you do to make sure your company was continuously well staffed?

REFERENCES

1. Elizabeth Lesly. "Seinfeld: The Economics of a TV Supershow and What It Means for NBC and the Industry." *Business Week*, June 2, 1997, pp. 116–121.

2. Milton Friedman. *Capitalism and Freedom.* Chicago: The University of Chicago Press, 1962; Milton Friedman and Rose Friedman. *Free to Choose.* New York: Harcourt Brace Jovanovich, 1980.

3. U.S. Bureau of the Census. *Statistical Abstract of the United States 1992.* Washington, DC: U.S. Government Printing Office, 1993, p. 692.

4. Donna Fenn. "Leader of the Pack." *Inc.*, February 1996, pp. 30–38.

5. Dyan Machan. "The Makeover." *Forbes.* December 2, 1996, pp. 135–138.

6. Thomas G. Stemberg. *Staples for Success.* Santa Monica, CA: Knowledge Exchange, 1996, p. 62.

7. Frank Rose. "The End of TV as We Know It." *Fortune.* December 23, 1996, pp. 58–68.

7 *Global Influences*

Its population exceeds 1.2 billion people. Those numbers alone explain why China plays an important role in the global economy. In fact, it is difficult for a growth-oriented business to ignore the impact of this huge market. McDonald's is there. Wal-Mart operates a giant Super Center. Business opportunities and staggering growth abound.

In short, the Chinese economy is booming. Twenty years ago, there were perhaps 1 million TV sets in all of China. Today, there are more than 200 million. Consider China's capital city. If the economy of Beijing continues to grow as fast as it has for the past decade, the city's GDP will exceed that of the entire United States by 2010!

Make no mistake, though. China is not just a rich potential market for foreign investors. Today China is a formidable exporter with a massive labor pool. Workers are industrious and wages are low. As a result, many countries, even traditionally low-wage East Asian countries, are losing production jobs to the Chinese. China's trade surplus with the United States approaches $40 billion. China may be about to overtake Japan as America's number one trade rival.[1]

There is no doubt that business has moved into the era of global competition. That movement brings new opportunities and avenues for growth. It also brings enormous complexity to the business landscape. Businesses must be aware of and sensitive to a number of important global forces and influences.

These forces, influences, and business responses are the focus of this chapter. When you finish this chapter, you should be able to:

1. Understand the meaning and implications of globalization.

2. Describe the role of exporting and importing.

3. Explain why globalization is important to today's businesses.

4. Identify and explain a few of the more salient global influences on business.

5. Discuss the major ways in which businesses participate in the global economy.

6. Explain the importance of considering cultural differences when making global decisions.

7. Discuss the ethical issues faced by businesses engaged in global competition.

Consider the following facts:

- Ninety-five percent of the world's population lives outside the United States.
- Today's rich industrialized countries will add fewer than 100 million people to the world's population over the next 30 years. Emerging countries will add 2.4 billion.
- There are 50 million people in China under age 20.
- The top three trading partners of the United States traded over $50 billion worth of goods and services in the month of November 1996.
- World trade was nearly $11 trillion in 1996.
- U.S. exports have approximately doubled in the last 10 years.
- Motorola's sales of pagers in China increased from 100,000 in 1991 to over 4 million in 1993.[2]

Today's businesses operate in a highly competitive global economy. And the level and extent of business' global focus will continue to grow. Businesses are involved in a variety of global activities. For example, manufacturers of complex products like automobiles buy components from all over the world. Just look at Figure 7–1, showing how Ford depends on manufacturers in several countries for the parts it needs to assemble its cars. Most major industries contain competitors from several different countries.

Companies headquartered in one country, such as the United States or Japan, operate manufacturing plants all over the globe. When consumers go shopping in their local communities, they are able to choose products imported from a variety of countries. A company with headquarters in one city may export to or have full operations in a number of countries. We call this globalization. **Globalization** is a way of thinking. It occurs when a business regards its operations all over the world as part of one integrated business system. Global activity is critical to the operations of many businesses. Each of the businesses in Table 7–1 depends on global sales for its existence. Even traditional U.S.-based businesses such as Colgate, IBM, Coca-Cola, and Xerox derive over half of their annual sales from other countries.

There are two approaches businesses take to the issue of globalization: a global strategy or a multidomestic strategy. The distinction between these is important. A **global strategy** occurs when a business sells a uniform product or service throughout the world. The product that is sold in Indonesia is the same as the product that is sold in Brazil. For example, consider a commodity like wheat. A grain marketing company buys wheat from a farm in Kansas and sells that wheat in several different countries. No attempt is made to modify the product from one country to another.

Globalization
A way of thinking in which a business regards all of its operations all over the world as part of one integrated business system.

Global strategy
A strategy where a business sells a uniform product or service throughout the world.

FIGURE 7–1   Assembling a World Car

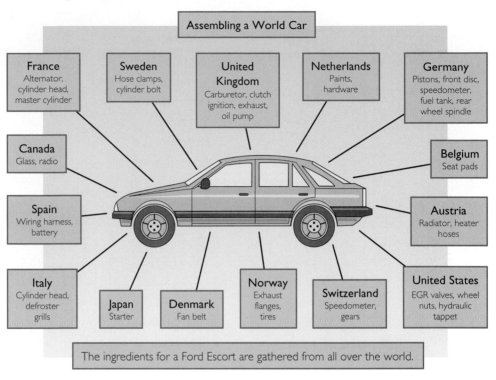

Assembling a World Car

France Alternator, cylinder head, master cylinder

Sweden Hose clamps, cylinder bolt

United Kingdom Carburetor, clutch ignition, exhaust, oil pump

Netherlands Paints, hardware

Germany Pistons, front disc, speedometer, fuel tank, rear wheel spindle

Canada Glass, radio

Belgium Seat pads

Spain Wiring harness, battery

Austria Radiator, heater hoses

Italy Cylinder head, defroster grills

Japan Starter

Denmark Fan belt

Norway Exhaust flanges, tires

Switzerland Speedometer, gears

United States EGR valves, wheel nuts, hydraulic tappet

The ingredients for a Ford Escort are gathered from all over the world.

From Joseph E. Stiglitz, *Principles of Micro-economics*, 2nd ed. (New York: W. W. Norton and Company, 1997), p. 58.

Multidomestic strategy
A strategy where a business modifies its product or service to address the special needs of local markets.

effectiveness p. 478>

ethical issues p. 207>

A **multidomestic strategy** occurs when a business modifies its product or service to address the special needs of local markets. For example, most restaurant chains must adjust their offerings to the tastes and preferences of each area in which they operate. Sometimes the changes are subtle. Sometimes they are striking. When McDonald's entered India, it had to introduce a vegetarian burger to accommodate Indian religious objections to eating beef. We will discuss the need for a multidomestic strategy later in this chapter when we consider the impact of culture on global firms.

For peak effectiveness around the world, many businesses use a combination of both global and multidomestic strategies. They produce a standardized product but make some adjustments for local needs. Consider the automotive industry. Generally, cars are the same throughout the world. Yet in different countries they are driven on different sides of the road. So both left- and right-side driver options must be available.

This chapter will give you an overview of globalization. The chapter contains six sections. The first looks at the role of exporting and importing. The second explains why globalization is important. The third explains some of the important economic and government issues affecting globalization. The fourth explains the various ways businesses participate in the global economy. The fifth focuses on the issue of cultural differences and competitiveness. The sixth points out some important ethical issues related to participating in the world economy.

TABLE 7–1   Highly Internationalized Firms

Company	Headquarters Country	Total Sales ($ billions)	Percent of Sales from Foreign Operations
Nestlé	Switzerland	$45.5	98%
Philips	Netherlands	40.9	95
Volvo	Sweden	23.3	90
Bayer	Germany	32.3	82
Unilever	Britain/Netherlands	52.3	80
Michelin	France	13.9	71
Colgate	United States	8.8	70
Gillette	United States	6.8*	70
Sony	Japan	43.3	70
Coca-Cola	United States	18.6	67
Xerox	United States	17.4	67
Canon	Japan	21.0*	67
IBM	United States	76	64
Daimler-Benz	Germany	69.1	63
Procter & Gamble	United States	35.3	51
Caterpillar	United States	16.5	51
3M	United States	14.2	50
Honda	Japan	39.1	46

*1995

SOURCES: Companies' websites (accessed June 17, 1997).

The Role of Exporting and Importing

Exporting
The situation where a business sells products and services to customers in other countries.

Importing
The situation where customers buy products and services from producers in other countries.

Before we delve into the complexity of globalization, we need to discuss some basic terms that are important when looking at global influences. Some businesses are engaged in **exporting,** which occurs when a business sells its products and services to customers in other nations. Businesses from all over the world are involved in exporting activities. Businesses of all sizes can be involved in exporting. That may surprise you. Yet many small businesses have excellent, high-quality products that are in demand throughout the world.

Other businesses compete with importing rivals. **Importing** occurs when customers purchase products and services from producers in other countries. If you purchase a Canon camera from Wal-Mart, that camera is an import because it was produced in Japan. Canon is a Japanese-based business that sells popular, high-quality cameras in many countries, including the United States. It does so, of course, because consumers in these countries like the features and quality that Canon offers. The number of potential camera buyers in any country is limited. If buyers purchase an import, they have chosen to forgo the purchase of competing products. Thus, importing affects all domestic manufacturers to some extent.

Food producers from California ship their produce to the Orient in refrigerated cargo containers. These exporters rely on others, such as OOCL, for their transportation needs. What other activities are involved in shipping goods from one country to another?

The same reasoning can be applied to businesses of all sizes and even to entire industries. Consider, for example, the consumer electronics industry. At one time, U.S. businesses dominated this field. No longer. Successful imports, often from Japanese firms such as Sony, changed the competitive landscape. Today the United States is a virtual nonplayer in this industry. Even small businesses that sell only within their own

country can be affected by global imports. Few businesses are totally untouched by global competition.

Why Globalization Is Important

Global concerns are a timely issue for contemporary American business. Prior to World War II, most American firms produced primarily for the huge American market. A few manufacturers exported products that they produced in the United States, although their primary market was within the United States. Only a few large companies, such as IBM, actually conducted significant manufacturing operations abroad. Even then, their foreign operations were not integrated with their domestic operations. This has changed. Businesses are going global in their thinking. They are increasingly being involved in world markets, and the American economy is heavily influenced by international trade.

The initial question that must be addressed is why? What prompts a business to take a global perspective? There are three prominent influences. First is the rise of foreign competition. Second is the need to control costs. Third is the opportunity for substantial market growth.

The Rise of Foreign Competition

Increasingly, foreign businesses are competing in American markets. Domestic businesses often see imports invade their home markets. These imports are a concern because they take business away from domestic firms. A classic example of this is the U.S. automobile industry. In the 1970s and 1980s, U.S. manufacturers realized that customers were turning to foreign competitors. Suddenly, Toyota and Honda were no longer minor annoyances. They were capturing market share and threatening U.S. competitiveness. Like it or not, Ford, General Motors, and Chrysler were forced to begin thinking globally.

The Need to Control Costs

Many foreign competitors became strong rivals because they could produce goods much more cheaply than U.S. firms. There may be many reasons for this, but two are prominent. First, low cost-labor was available in their countries. Second, many governments *subsidized* businesses, especially in certain industries. These two factors allowed foreign companies to produce products and ship them to American customers more cheaply than firms in the United States could produce them. For example, Japanese steel firms could import iron ore from abroad, convert it into steel, and ship it to the United States at a lower cost than U.S. steel plants could make it themselves. In addition, Japanese automakers could use that steel to produce cars, transport them to America, and still sell them for less than the Big Three U.S. carmakers could. Thus, U.S. steel and automobile industries were forced to respond to the competitive thrusts of foreign firms.

U.S. businesses had to find ways to get access to cheaper labor and lower costs of production. They could do this by importing raw materials. In other words, they could shop all over the world and purchase supplies wherever they were cheapest.

production p. 464>
outsourcing p. 279>

They could contract part of their production operations to countries with low labor costs. This is an example of *international outsourcing*. They could even locate their own production facilities in the foreign country. Whatever tactic businesses chose, their global movement was motivated by the need to control costs.

Opportunities for Market Growth

The U.S. market for many products is becoming increasingly saturated. Businesses that seek substantial growth may be limited if they confine themselves solely to the U.S. market. There are about 250 million people in the United States. There are about 5.7 billion potential customers in the rest of the world. The world is open for business! The United States will see its population grow by only 21 percent over the next 30 years. By contrast, Indonesia will grow by 50 percent, Pakistan by 125 percent, Nigeria by 156 percent. These and other emerging markets are critical areas of growth.[3]

baby boomers p. 136>

The soft drink industry is a good example. As American baby boomers age, they drink fewer soft drinks. There are also fewer teenagers, the prime market for soft drinks. This is why in the past two decades, major producers have become increasingly aggressive in capturing international markets. They realize that their future growth and competitiveness depends on worldwide sales.

Economic and Government Issues Affecting Globalization

The previous section discussed the importance of globalization. It is important, however, to reconsider the model presented in Chapter 1. Global influences are one of several kinds of influences that affect how a business operates. We discussed economic influences in Chapter 6, and we will discuss other influences in the next few chapters. Global influences are often far beyond the control of individual businesses. Certainly when we eliminate the very largest businesses such as the automobile companies, the oil producers, and a few others, individual firms typically have little effect on global issues. Yet global issues can have a major impact on the competitiveness of U.S.-based firms, especially if they are exporters, importers, or multinational firms.

The following sections discuss a few of the more significant global influences. These include a country's balance of trade and balance of payments, exchange rates, and government involvement through industrial policies such as tariffs and support of a country's global businesses.

Balance of Trade

Balance of trade
The difference between the value of a country's imports and its exports.

Virtually all countries export some goods and import others. As companies produce goods for export and purchase imports for sale to their customers, they are affecting not just their own profits but their country's balance of trade. The **balance of trade** is the difference between the value of exports and imports of merchandise or goods. If exports exceed imports, a country has a favorable balance of trade, or a *trade surplus*. If imports exceed exports, as they have done in the United States for nearly two decades, then we have an unfavorable balance of trade, or a *trade deficit*. Figure 7–2 shows U.S. imports and exports for the past few years.

FIGURE 7–2   Exports and Imports of Goods and Services—United States (billions of dollars)

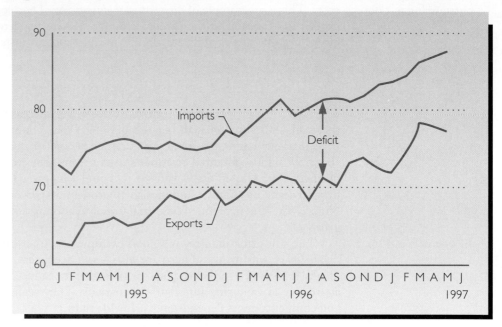

SOURCE: Bureau of Economic Analysis, U.S. Department of Commerce,
http://www.bea.doc.gov/bea/trade-d.html (accessed August 18, 1997).

Balance of Payments

Balance of payments
The difference between
the inflows of money
into a country and the
outflows of money from
that country.

Since customers must pay for everything they purchase, the balance of payments is closely related to the balance of trade. The **balance of payments** is the difference between the inflows of money into a country and the outflows of money from that country. If goods were the only exports and imports, the balance of payments would be the same as the balance of trade. But money flows into or out of a country for other reasons. Income from services such as tourism is one significant reason. Foreign aid is another. Investment income is another. Thus, inflows of capital into the United States come from exports of goods plus the money spent by foreign visitors and any other funds brought into the country from all sources. Outflows include the money to pay for imports, money spent by U.S. citizens in other countries, foreign aid, and other payments for whatever reason. The U.S. government, like all governments, desires a favorable balance of payments. As we will see shortly, governments sometimes take action to help improve both the balance of trade and the balance of payments.

Exchange Rates

Exchange rate
The value of a currency
compared with foreign
currencies.

The balance of trade and balance of payments are important concepts to understand, particularly as they affect the wealth of a country. However, they have a more direct impact on *business* through their impact on exchange rates. Exchange rates are very important to managers making international business decisions. The **exchange rate** is the value of a currency compared with foreign currencies.

International banks, such as the Bank of Tokyo, monitor the exchange rates among various currencies. An important exchange rate is that of the U.S. dollar versus the Japanese yen. What happens to the price of Japanese cameras purchased in the United States if the price of the dollar rises compared to the yen?

As a student of business, why should you be concerned with exchange rates? Why should you be interested in whether the dollar is strong or weak? What is the impact on U.S. companies of a change in the value of the dollar?

A *strong U.S. dollar* benefits companies that import to the United States. A strong dollar is worth more than a weak one, so fewer dollars will buy more products on the international markets. This means that imports are relatively cheap. At the same time, a strong dollar works against exporters because U.S. products are more expensive in foreign markets. That means foreign businesses will be less inclined to purchase from U.S. companies.

Conversely, a *weak dollar* buys fewer imported goods than a stronger one. Thus, it hurts importers by making imported goods and services more expensive. At the same time, however, the weak dollar helps exporters since foreign currencies can buy more U.S. products than they could previously. Now let's look at this in concrete terms.

First, consider Japan. If the value of a dollar rises against the Japanese yen, our dollar will buy more products in Japan than before. Japanese products are, therefore, cheaper in the United States. If, on the other hand, the value of the dollar falls against the yen, it won't buy as many Japanese products because it isn't worth as much.

A second example is Ford. If we assumed that Ford only made cars domestically, managers at Ford might want a low-valued dollar because it would make German cars more expensive and, hence, less competitive. Similarly, if Ford exported cars to Germany, the low-valued dollar would make Ford's exports cheaper relative to German products. The real picture is much more complicated, as you saw in Figure 7–1.

Finally, suppose Trek sells bicycles to distributors of mountain bikes in France in January 1997. Trek, of course, wants to be paid in U.S. dollars, not French francs. So the distributors in France must exchange their francs for U.S. dollars in order to pay Trek. Working with international banks, they trade francs for dollars based on the published exchange rate that day. These exchange rates are always changing. Now suppose that the distributors want to order another batch of bicycles in October 1997.

And suppose that, by this time, the dollar has dropped significantly in value against the French franc. This means that the bicycles are cheaper in France in October than they were in January. The French distributor should be able to sell more bikes at this price than before. As you can see, forecasting exchange rates and their movements is useful for business managers as they make decisions.

Government Involvement in Global Issues

All governments want to increase the wealth, stability, and standard of living of their societies. To achieve this goal, they often implement policies that affect international trade. These policies may consist of tariffs and other trade barriers or of overt support of businesses as they compete worldwide. We will consider some of these policies next.

Tariffs and other Trade Barriers

Free trade

A situation where there are no government-imposed barriers to trade—no tariffs, quotas, or nontariff barriers.

The effectiveness of free trade policies has been debated for decades. **Free trade** refers to a situation where there are no government-imposed barriers to trade—no tariffs, quotas, or nontariff barriers. One of the most common arguments for free trade is that it increases competition. This causes prices and costs to fall, benefiting consumers in all countries. It also encourages firms to develop new products and more productive ways of doing business. Again, consumers in all countries benefit. While many espouse free trade, most governments of the world regularly depart from it to encourage domestic production of goods and services that would be imported under free trade. Further, some *industries* (those that export significant amounts) are more likely to support free trade than industries that must constantly fight imports.

Tariff

A tax on an imported product.

How does the government of a country protect its businesses from imports? The three basic tools are tariffs, quotas, and other non-tariff barriers. A **tariff** is a tax on an imported product. The tax raises the price that customers have to pay for the imported good. If the tax is large enough, it will cause the price of the import to be higher than the price of the locally produced good or service. Accordingly, customers will be more likely to buy the locally produced products.

Nontariff barriers encompass a variety of ways other than tariffs that governments restrict imports. One of the most common nontariff barriers is the use of **quotas,** which are government's restrictions on the amount of specific foreign products they allow into the country. For example, France might impose a quota restricting the number of cars imported from Japan to 10,000 per year. This keeps the French markets from being flooded with Japanese cars without raising the price of the Japanese cars.

Quota

A government's restriction on the amount of a specific foreign product it allows into the country.

There are other nontariff barriers governments can use to protect their home industries. One is for the home government to establish rules and regulations that take away the competitive advantage of the imported goods. Another technique is to use social pressure to discourage local buyers from purchasing imports. Then there is the technique, frequently used by Japan, of requiring a very slow inspection process for imported goods when they arrive at the port of entry.

competitive advantage p. 315>

Free Trade and Free Trade Areas

Since World War II the United States has been the leader of a movement to reduce tariffs, quotas, and nontariff barriers. The long-run goal is to create a world system of free trade.

The United States' primary free trade initiative has been undertaken through an international agreement called the *General Agreement on Tariffs and Trade (GATT)*. GATT is an agreement between the United States and 22 other countries to get together regularly to negotiate the reduction of trade barriers. Over the past four decades, GATT has held a series of negotiations that led most of the nations of the world to agree to make drastic reductions in tariffs and quotas. The most recent of those agreements was completed in 1994 when the U.S. Congress approved it. Called the Uruguay Round, that agreement resulted in an overall reduction in tariffs of 39 percent. It also created a global regulatory body called the World Trade Organization (WTO), which has the authority to determine whether or not a country is violating the terms of the GATT agreements.

The United States has also worked to reduce trade barriers through the North American Free Trade Agreement (NAFTA). In this arrangement, adopted in 1993, Canada, Mexico, and the United States agreed to create a free trade area among the three countries. Free trade areas have also been created in Europe (the European Union, or EU), in the southern part of South America (where Mercosur creates a free trade area among Argentina, Brazil and Uruguay), and in other locations throughout the world. Note that a **free trade area** (or zone) permits free trade among the participating countries but discourages imports from nonparticipating countries. Thus, free trade areas encourage trade within the area while still protecting the group somewhat from outsiders.

Free trade area
A geographic area where free trade is permitted among the participating countries but imports from nonparticipating countries are limited.

What are the implications for businesses of the movement toward free trade and free trade zones? First, managers should be aware of the competitive dynamics caused by free trade. A business that wants to remain globally competitive must sharpen its competitive skills and possibly move production to locations that offer cost advantages. For example, after NAFTA, some U.S. firms moved some of their operations to Mexico to take advantage of the lower wage while being able to import the products back into the United States with little or no tariffs. Similarly, U.S. businesses that export to Canada or Mexico now have fewer restrictions on the movement of the goods between countries. Companies operating in the European Union have similar benefits.

Second, while some businesses benefit from free trade zones and policies, managers should recognize that total free trade is not yet a reality. Thus, managers of internationally oriented firms must be willing to consider establishing plants in countries that restrict normal exporting.

Finally, business leaders should stand ready to work with their governments to assure that foreign companies are not given unfair advantages or to make sure that U.S. firms gain competitive advantages abroad. Lobbying in favor of particular laws—either increasing free trade or protecting home industries—should be the norm for large companies and industry organizations. This leads us to the next discussion, of how government can help businesses in the international arena.

Government Support of Business

The level of government support of business varies from country to country. In command economies such as the former Soviet Union, the government owned virtually all the businesses and dictated how much production would occur and what prices would be charged. Other countries take a more *laissez faire* approach and give businesses much more freedom. The United States has typically been somewhat toward this end of the continuum. Although it regulates anticompetitive actions and has passed a number of social welfare laws, it has traditionally taken a hands-off approach regarding actual support of business.

The government of Japan, on the other hand, openly supports its businesses in their efforts to capture multinational markets. Japan's economic development strategy consists of promoting exports and protecting the home market from foreign competition. The government identifies new industries that have the most potential to stimulate overall economic growth in Japan if the country can only find a way to establish those industries in its homeland. Examples are steel, automobiles, and computers. Then government helps these chosen firms by protecting the Japanese market from import competition and denying foreign firms the chance to locate in Japan. The government also helps by providing various subsidies for exports and by insisting that the protected firms learn to compete successfully in export markets.

The government/business relationship in Japan is an example of what is sometimes called an industrial policy. **Industrial policy** refers to government assistance of various kinds to create a new industry or enable an existing industry to expand more than it could if market forces were the only determinants of output. One of the major issues being debated in the United States today is whether or not the country should have some sort of a formal industrial policy. U.S. companies compete based on their own abilities to forge new markets. The Japanese government's support of business, particularly in regard to global issues, makes competing very, very tough.

Japan is not the only country that influences the United States and world markets. China may be the leading economic player in Asia over the next 20 years. In fact, many people predict China will have the world's strongest economy in just 10 years. It may surprise you to know that there are thousands of Chinese companies in the United States right now, many of them either owned or supported by the Chinese government. By 1996 the U.S. trade deficit with China was a staggering $35 billion.[4]

There have been occasions when the American government has agreed to help a struggling American industry. For example, in the 1960s, it began to restrict the importation of textiles in an effort to protect American producers. In the 1960s and 1970s, it restricted imports of steel. In the 1980s, it convinced the Japanese to "voluntarily" limit their automobile exports to the United States.

In the mid-1980s, the American government began to conceive of another way to help its businesses compete in world markets, especially Japan. The value of Japan's exports to the United States was far greater than the value of imports, and the government believed that a major reason was that the Japanese unfairly restricted imports from America. In 1986, the United States forced Japan to agree to open its home market to American telecommunication equipment. And in 1995, the Japanese agreed to do the same for American cars.

Industrial policy
Government assistance of various kinds to create a new industry or enable an existing industry to expand more than it could if market forces were the only determinants of output.

Developing Your Critical Thinking Skills

1. Explain why it is important for businesses in today's world to go global. Is this more important for some industries than others?

2. We mentioned that some industries are far more eager for free trade than others. Predict how each of the following feels about free trade: (a) airplane industry, (b) textile industry, (c) steel industry, (d) earth-moving equipment industry.

3. China is an emerging economic giant. Some experts argue that China is now the number one trade rival with the United States. Why is China such a force?

How Businesses Participate in the Global Economy

As you saw from our earlier discussion, there are logical, bottom-line reasons why businesses become involved in global activities. This section considers several of the forms businesses can take when they become involved in the global economy.

Domestic Firms that Compete with Imports

We define a *domestic firm* as a firm that does business only in its home country. A domestic firm's involvement with the world economy consists of competing with imports in the home market. Although imports may compete in a number of ways, the strategic approach that is usually most threatening is price competition.

There are three types of foreign price competition. The first is price competition based on the foreign firm's lower costs of production, which we discussed earlier. American firms are particularly vulnerable to this threat because many developing countries have low-wage workers who are as skilled as American workers. It may be difficult for a U.S. firm to compete under such conditions.

The second type of price competition occurs when the value of the home currency increases. We discussed this under the topic of exchange rates. Such a threat was actually faced by American businesses between 1980 and 1985, when the value of the dollar increased by 63 percent. The prices of imported products fell, forcing American companies to make some tough decisions. Some cut their prices and eventually went out of business. Some cut their prices and found ways to cut costs and restore profitability before they went out of business. Some cut their prices and sustained losses until the value of the dollar fell in 1987. One American firm that successfully met this challenge was the motorcycle manufacturer Harley-Davidson. When it was faced with extinction, the U.S. government provided temporary protection and the company used the breathing period to regain its competitiveness. Profile 7–1 summarizes that story.

PROFILE 7–1   *Harley Hogs the Market*

●· · · · · · · · · · · · · · · · · · ·

efficiency p. 478>

In 1903, William Harley and the three Davidson brothers (Walter, William, and Arthur) made and sold their first motorcycle in Milwaukee, Wisconsin. Over the next 60 years, the Harley-Davidson motorcycle became arguably America's most famous brand and the company prospered. Harley-Davidson was acquired by American Machine and Foundry (AMF) in 1969. As a subsidiary of AMF, Harley-Davidson declined in production efficiency and quality, and Japanese imports began to take customers away. AMF finally concluded that Harley-Davidson was no match for the Japanese and put the motorcycle division up for sale.

Surprisingly, a group of top managers in the Harley-Davidson division bought the company in 1981. They were convinced that they could compete with the Japanese imports. Soon after the purchase, the Japanese competitors launched a price war, which threatened to bankrupt the American firm before the new management could turn things around. In desperation, Harley-Davidson appealed to the federal government for temporary relief from imports. In 1983, the government agreed to impose a tariff on imported Japanese motorcycles for

Harley-Davidson was on the brink of disaster in the early 1980s. They received temporary tariff protection which allowed them to regain their competitive position. They are now the number one producer of heavy-weight motorcycles. Do you agree with government protection of industries?

five years. After that, Harley would have to compete without any protection from imports.

Given this opportunity, Harley-Davidson's management completely changed the company by modernizing manufacturing methods, dramatically improving quality, and changing the model line in response to customer demand. That effort was so successful that Harley's management asked the government to remove the tariff on Japanese bikes in 1986, a year before it was set to expire.

Operating without the tariff protection, the revived Harley-Davidson continued to gain market share. In 1985, it had 16 percent of the U.S. market for "heavyweight" motorcycles. By 1987 its share was up to 25 percent; by 1990 it had 45 percent; and by 1994 it had 56 percent. Between 1985 and 1994, the number of employees at Harley-Davidson rose from 2,200 to 6,700, and from 1986 to 1996 revenue grew at an annual rate of 22 percent.

SOURCES: Gary Hammel, "Killer Strategies that Make Shareholders Rich," *Fortune*, June 23, 1997, pp. 70–84; Gary Hoover, Alta Campbell, and Patrick J. Spain, eds., *Hoover's Handbook 1991: Profiles of over 500 Major Corporations* (Austin, TX: The Reference Press, 1991), p. 277; Patrick J. Spain and James R. Talbot, eds., *Hoover's Handbook of American Companies 1996* (Waltham, MA: Little, Brown, 1995), p. 434.

Dumping
Selling imports at prices that are below the cost of production and distribution; illegal in most countries.

The third type of import price competition is lower prices due to a practice known as dumping. Technically, **dumping** occurs when imports are sold at prices that are below the cost of production and distribution. This is really a form of price discrimination. Why would a foreign competitor do this? If a foreign firm can flood a market with very inexpensive products, it may be able to drive local competitors out of business. Dumping is a common practice in international trade, probably because it is hard to determine if a business truly is dumping. U.S. businesses have charged a number of times that Japan engages in dumping. Presumably, Japanese firms could do this because their government subsidized the businesses, which would otherwise have had major losses.

Pier 1 Imports is a chain of retail stores carrying products imported from a number of countries. Its products range from baskets to furniture, but they are all imported goods. What are the advantages of selling exclusively imported products? What are the risks?

Most countries, including the United States, have provisions to stop dumping when it is discovered. Those provisions typically require a complaint from the domestic firms that are being victimized. Of course, the victimized firm has to have enough proof to file a credible complaint. Further, it must have enough resources to survive until the government acts on the complaint.

Import-Oriented Firms

Imports represent an opportunity as well as a threat. A firm that does business in a single country can still take advantage of the world economy by purchasing its supplies from all over the world. As discussed earlier, this approach may be prompted by a need to control costs—though that is not always the case.

retailers p. 282>

Ever since World War II, many American firms have been import-oriented. Nike, discussed in Profile 7–2, built its leadership in the athletic footwear industry on the importation of shoes manufactured in Japan and Korea. The Limited and other retailers built huge retailing empires based on importing clothing manufactured abroad. Pier 1 Imports was built on the concept of importing unusual items produced in other countries.

PROFILE 7–2   *Nike Means Victory*

The world-famous athletic shoe corporation known as Nike was started by Phil Knight and Bill Bowerman in 1964. Knight came up with the idea for the company while writing a paper for a class in the graduate school of business at Stanford University. His strategy was to design unique athletic shoes that could be sold in the United States at very low prices because they would be manufactured in low-cost foreign factories. Bowerman's role was to design the shoes and Knight's job was to handle everything else. Their first shoes were made by the Japanese shoe firm Onitsuka Tiger and were marketed under the Tiger brand. Knight and Bowerman later named the brand Nike after the Greek goddess of victory. Nike also became the name of their company.

Nike and Onitsuka Tiger terminated their relationship in 1972 in a dispute over distribution rights, but Nike continued its strategy of using low-cost Asian labor to manufacture its products for import into the United States. It signed up a new Japanese manufacturer in 1972 and later contracted with a Korean firm.

Nike's growth after 1972 was driven by very effective marketing accompanied by periodic innovations in the product line. It expanded its line of shoes from track to other sports and signed highly visible sports stars for its advertising campaign. Perhaps the most famous example was Nike's introduction of the Air Jordan basketball shoe in 1985, named after basketball star Michael Jordan.

SOURCES: Patrick J. Spain and James R. Talbot, eds., *Hoover's Handbook of American Companies 1996* (Waltham, MA: Little, Brown, 1995), p. 638; Brian Kipp, "The Story of Nike," *The Journal of Business Leadership* 7, Fall 1995, pp. 115–33.

Export-Oriented Domestic Firms

A third way to take advantage of the world economy is to get involved in exporting goods and services that are produced in the home country. Japan's famous big businesses are excellent examples of this. Sony, Toyota, Yamaha, and many other well-known Japanese firms started manufacturing for the Japanese market and then enlarged their scope of activities by exporting to other countries. Their export business has long been a very important part of their total business and a key to their overall success.

Many American firms have also profited handsomely from exporting. Perhaps the most famous is the Boeing Aircraft Corp., headquartered in Seattle, Washington. Exports account for over half of Boeing's sales.

Let's consider two bicycle companies as examples. Trek began exporting in 1987. By 1995, exports accounted for 32 percent of sales. The company achieved that success by establishing wholly owned subsidiaries in Austria, Germany, Japan, Spain, Switzerland, and the United Kingdom and by entering into agreements with 65 international distributors. Trek did undertake some production outside of the United States, but in 1997 over 70 percent of its bicycles were built in the United States. Trek hopes eventually to bring all of its production to Wisconsin and other parts of the United States.[5] The second example is Cannondale, which learned how to export to Japan. Its story is presented in Profile 7–3.

PROFILE 7–3   *Cannondale Learns to Export*

Cannondale was founded in Wilton, Connecticut, by Joseph Montgomery in 1971. At first, the company made bicycle parts. In 1983, it began manufacturing complete bicycles. By 1988, it had reached a sales volume of $30 million and was recognized as a leading manufacturer of high-performance mountain bikes. At that time, 95 percent of Cannondale's sales were in the United States. But Montgomery was convinced that future growth depended on exports, so he and his son

Mario Cipollini, Tour de France stage winner and captain of the Team Saeco pro cycling team.

1997

Alison Sydor,
Olympic silver medalist
and two-time World Champion, of the
Volvo/Cannondale Team.

cannondale®
HANDMADE IN USA

Cannondale used a unique approach to break into the Japanese market. Cannondale was able to use its Japanese subsidiary to sell to Japanese dealers who may have been reluctant to buy directly from a U.S. based company. Why is it sometimes necessary to set up significant operations in another country in order to break into their market?

Scott set out to learn how to export. They were told that in order to export to Japan they would have to work through a local Japanese company.

Scott Montgomery used a different approach. He set up a wholly-owned sales subsidiary in a low-cost location outside of Osaka and hired Japanese-speaking American cyclists to handle sales and promotions. The cyclists would enter races on weekends, generating much free publicity. On weekdays, they would make sales calls on dealers. This approach brought immediate success and Cannondale earned a $60,000 profit in Japan its first year there.

Cannondale also pushed exports to other countries. By 1997, it was exporting throughout the world and even had authorized dealers in nearly 50 countries. Total sales volume to 62 countries was up to $100 million, and exports represented 40 percent of sales.

SOURCES: 1997 Cannondale Product Catalog; Jerry Jasinowski and Robert Hamrin, *Making It in America: Proven Paths to Success from 50 Top Companies* (New York: Simon and Schuster, 1995), pp. 191–3.

Successful exporting can sometimes be profitable immediately, as the Cannondale story in Profile 7–3 illustrates. On the other hand, it may take time for the export effort to become truly profitable. In the early going, it is not uncommon for a firm to experience losses as it tries to achieve market recognition. This is why governments often support the export efforts of their domestic firms.

Multinational Firms

The step beyond exporting is to locate manufacturing facilities in foreign countries. Many businesses have done so, transforming themselves into multinational businesses. **Multinational firms** are businesses that have production and sales operations in more than one country and have a mix of international owners and managers.[6] Profile 7–4 tells the story of how Deere & Co. became a multinational firm. Notice how Deere took a long-run view with respect to the profitability of its foreign ventures. As other chapters in this book point out, the successful business is usually one that plans and organizes with a long-term vision. It may endure short-run losses if it sees them as investments that will lead to long-run profits.

Multinational firms
Businesses that have production and sales operations in more than one country and have a mix of international owners and managers.

vision p. 310>

PROFILE 7–4

Deere & Co. Goes Multinational

Deere & Co. was founded in 1838 to produce the famous steel plow invented by John Deere. For the next 110 years the company expanded its line of products to cover a wide variety of farm implements. In the process, Deere became the number two firm in its industry. Yet until 1955, it remained strictly a domestic American company.

When William Hewitt became chief executive officer, he recognized the need to transform Deere into a successful multinational firm. Hewitt began by sending key executives to Europe to examine the opportunities for Deere to set up manufacturing plants there. The executives returned full of enthusiasm for expansion into Europe, and Deere acquired a German manufacturing firm the following year. Deere's board of directors also authorized Hewitt to build an assembly plant in Monterrey, Mexico. Plans for expansion in Europe continued, and a diesel engine manufacturing plant was established in France in the mid-1960s.

Deere's foreign factories were not immediately profitable because Deere had to learn how to do business in foreign countries. That meant learning what foreign customers needed, how to deal with government regulations in foreign countries, and how to organize foreign operations. Eventually, however, the plants became profitable. Other manufacturing plants were subsequently opened in Mexico, Argentina, France, and Spain. Now Deere generates approximately 20 percent of its sales from production in foreign countries and exports. It is truly a multinational firm.

board of directors p. 64>

SOURCES: Patrick J. Spain and James R. Talbot, eds., *Hoover's Handbook of American Companies 1996* (Waltham, MA: Little, Brown, 1995, p. 295); Richard Hattwick, "William Hewitt: Deere and Co.," *Journal of Business Leadership* 1, no. 2, pp. 23–30.

When American companies like Deere first began manufacturing abroad, their intent was to use their foreign factories primarily to serve foreign markets. In most cases, differences in tastes, high transportation costs, and difficulties of communication made it unprofitable to export from those factories back to the United States. Over time, foreign tastes and American tastes began to become more similar. Transportation costs fell and it became much easier to communicate between U.S. headquarters and the foreign branches. Eventually it became possible to profitably export products or parts from the foreign facility back to the United States. As a result, Deere and a number of other American multinational firms began to regard their production facilities all over the world as part of one interrelated system (the practice of worldwide coordination we have defined as globalization).

MOTOROLA

Motorola is a multinational firm with manufacturing facilities throughout the world. In 1996, Motorola had sales of $20.6 billion, 82 percent of which came from sales outside of the United States. Over two-thirds of its total assets were located outside of the United States.[7]

Another interesting example of an American multinational firm is AMP, which manufactures electrical components for ships, aircraft, and radios. Initially, AMP's international expansion followed a two-step pattern. First it would begin exporting to a foreign country. Then, if AMP was convinced that the country offered a large enough domestic market for a manufacturing plant, it would build a factory in that country. One major advantage of building separate factories in each country was that AMP could excel at adapting its products to the special requirements of that country. It was operating, as you will recall from the introductory section of this chapter, as a multidomestic company.

In its early days, AMP opened factories in Canada, Japan, France, West Germany, and Italy. In fact, the Italian factory was built primarily to provide electrical connectors to the Italian auto manufacturer Fiat. Major expansion in the Far East occurred in the 1980s, when AMP opened factories in South Korea, Taiwan, and Singapore. In the 1990s, manufacturing plants were opened in Brazil, India, Ireland, and Hungary. In 1994, AMP had sales and manufacturing subsidiaries in 35 foreign countries, and foreign sales accounted for 54 percent of its sales of $4.027 billion.[8]

Notice the cleverness of AMP's strategy. It used exports to test out the profitability of each market. Only after it had experienced substantial success in a market did it establish a manufacturing facility there. There is an alternative approach. Rather than build their own facility, some businesses acquire an existing local firm in the foreign country and use that acquisition as the basis for expansion. An interesting example of this is Procter & Gamble's entry into the diaper market in Brazil. Profile 7–5 tells the story of P&G's acquisition of Prebo, a Brazilian firm.

acquisition p. 322>

PROFILE 7–5   *P&G Learns to Sell Diapers in Brazil*

In the late 1980s, Johnson & Johnson controlled 80 percent of the Brazilian disposable diaper market. J & J had chosen to sell diapers at the high price of $1 each, compared to the 14 cents per diaper that prevailed in the United States. As a result, Procter & Gamble saw a huge market to be tapped in Brazil if the price could be lowered. It started by acquiring Prebo, a Brazilian manufacturer of disposable diapers. Then it surveyed Brazilian consumers to find out which features were important in a disposable diaper and which could be eliminated. The result was the introduction of a diaper that was simpler than the American standard but met Brazilian customers' needs. Because the new diaper cost less to make, P&G was able to profitably get the sales price down to 32 cents per diaper.

The new diaper was such a success that it catapulted Procter & Gamble into first place in the Brazilian disposable diaper industry. As a bonus to both P&G and its rivals, Brazilians were willing to buy far more diapers at the lower price. By 1993, total sales of disposable diapers in Brazil were seven times greater than when Procter & Gamble entered the market in 1988.

SOURCE: Luis Nassif, "A abertura e a guerra das fraldas," *Folha de S. Paulo*, January 8, 1996, pp. 2–3.

International Partnerships

Another way of doing international business that has developed in recent years is the international partnership, which can be set up in a number of ways. *International partnerships* are arrangements between two or more businesses from different countries that enable both to do business more successfully.

There are three primary forms of international partnerships. The first type is the *strategic alliance*, a long-term agreement among businesses to work together for the benefit of all. Strategic alliances are becoming popular as manufacturers work more closely with both their suppliers and their distributors. Examples include Nissan distributing Volkswagens in Japan and Volkswagen selling Nissan's vehicles in Germany. In the pharmaceutical industry, America's Marion Laboratories distributes the drug Herbesser, made by Japan's Tanabe, and Japan's Sankyo distributes Squibb's drug Capoten in Japan.

A second arrangement is a special kind of strategic alliance called an international joint venture. A *joint venture* is a partnership among companies for the purpose of achieving mutual success in a particular market or industrial sector, especially to do projects they could not handle alone. For example, Ford has a joint venture with Mazda, as do General Motors and Toyota. In the nuclear power industry, General Electric, Toshiba, Hitachi, ASEA, AMU, and Siemens have joined together to develop an improved nuclear water-boiling reactor.[9]

In some cases, a government will insist that any foreign business selling in the country must work with a locally owned company or the government itself. Russia's recent efforts at free enterprise have relied heavily on joint ventures. A company from the United States, Japan, or Germany may have to partner with a Russian company in order to do business in the emerging Russian market.

Licensing

An arrangement where a domestic manufacturer permits a foreign company to manufacture and sell its unique products.

The third type of arrangement is **licensing,** in which a domestic manufacturer permits a foreign company to manufacture and sell its unique products. The domestic firm shares production specifications and techniques with the foreign firm, which can then build and sell the products in its own home markets. This provides quick access and a friendly and knowledgeable ally as the domestic firm enters a foreign territory. The foreign business gains name recognition and a proven product. Both businesses benefit from the sales that follow.

International partnerships can occur among firms in the same industry or between firms in different industries. Trek offers an interesting example of the latter case. In 1996, Trek and German carmaker Volkswagen collaborated to produce a Volkswagen Jetta that came equipped with a special edition Trek mountain bike.[10]

Trek was able to increase its sales in Germany and Volkswagen was able to offer customers an interesting incentive. This unique arrangement helped both companies.

Developing Your Critical Thinking Skills

price elasticity of demand p. 169>

1. In Chapter 6, we talked about price elasticity. What can you conclude from Profile 7–5 about the price elasticity of demand for disposable diapers in the Brazilian market?

2. Suppose you own a small business. A number of your fbecauseends tell you there are international markets for your products. Which of the approaches we discussed would be the best way to go global? Explain your reasoning.

3. A number of large U.S. companies receive more than half of their revenue from their international operations. What are the risks of such dependency on global markets?

Cultural Differences

Understanding differences among the cultures of countries can be important to a firm that tries to export to or establish a production facility in a foreign country. Problems can arise because of differences in language, customs, values, and lifestyles. Stories of business miscues in the international markets are legend. General Motors' attempt to market the Chevrolet Nova was unsuccessful in South America because GM failed to realize that "no va" means "won't go" in Spanish. Gerber found little success in marketing its baby foods in some third-world countries until it realized that their tradition was to put a picture of the product on the label. This meant that a picture of a baby on the label of baby food was clearly unacceptable. Hand gestures that mean OK or well done in the United States may be obscene in some countries.

Businesses often have to adjust their products and approaches to customers to meet the unique perspectives of foreign cultures. Domino's Pizza has been in international markets since the mid-1980s. However, its one-pie-fits-all approach was modified for the Japanese market. Local franchisees in Japan were permitted to experiment with their own toppings; a popular seller is squid and sweet mayonnaise. The strategy must be working. Foreign sales have grown from $16 million to $503 million over the last 10 years.[11] Pepsi's popular "Generation Next" ads were not used in Japan. The company instead used Pepsiman, a muscle-bound cartoon superhero in a skintight metallic uniform. Pepsiman even whispers, "Shwaah!" —the Japanese onomatopoeia for bubbles fizzing—when he delivers a Pepsi.[12]

Sometimes multinational companies must work with their local counterparts to develop new ways of operating in the local environment. When McDonald's of Canada decided to put its first McDonald's in Moscow, it realized that Russian potatoes were not suitable for making french fries. It had to import potatoes to plant in Russia to assure a continuous supply of french fries. It also had to build huge manufacturing facilities to make buns and process meat and vegetables.

In some cases, a business may attempt to modify some aspect of a country's culture to assure that employee talents are used to their fullest extent. An example occurred when Motorola established a factory in Malaysia. Motorola places heavy emphasis on employee involvement and wanted a group of workers who would speak out when there were problems or opportunities for improvement. However, the Malaysian women employed in manufacturing operations were initially uncomfortable with that approach because the Malay culture does not encourage women to speak out. Motorola had to either adapt to Malaysian ways or change this small part of the culture. Roger Bertelson, Motorola's local manager, encouraged involvement by listening to the women, providing positive reinforcement, and encouraging peer recognition.[13]

In that case it was possible to make modest changes in the local culture. Often it is necessary for the multinational company to adapt to the local culture. An example of this is presented in Profile 7–6.

PROFILE 7–6   *Successfully Adapting to Local Culture*

The following anecdote is from a book on international management. Notice that the reason the French company was more successful than the American one is that it better understood the needs of local workers.

> When a rich vein of ore was found in the Andes, Americans rushed in to develop the mining. But it was hard to get workers. Although the Americans offered all kinds of perquisites—good meals, hot water, housing, movies and so on—workers flocked to the French, who seemed to offer them nothing. The workers for the French lived in the roughest housing, had no movies, none of the comforts offered by the Americans. Baffled, the U.S. company sent in a stream of senior executives and conducted a series of studies, and eventually figured out what was happening. The French offered no perks but paid workers by the hour. The people of the Andes cared more about their time off. It was important for them to be able to come and go without questions. When the Americans switched to an hourly basis they were able to lure the workers.

SOURCE: T. F. O'Boyle, "Bridgestone Discovers Purchase of U.S. Firm Creates Big Problems," *The Wall Street Journal*, April 1, 1991, p. 1, as summarized in Kamal Fatehi, *International Management* (Upper Saddle River, NJ: Prentice-Hall, 1996), p. 241.

Sometimes businesses can take advantage of opportunities created by adjusting to local culture and tastes. For example, Profile 7–7 describes McDonald's willingness to alter its time-honored menu to please the tastes of the Philippine market.

PROFILE 7–7   *McDonald's Targets Filipino Palates*

Business Week recently published the following report on fast-food competition in the Philippines:

> The golden arches of McDonald's Corp. are among the world's best-known corporate symbols, assuring folks that their Big Mac will look and taste the same whether ordered in Manhattan or Malaysia. That consistency has helped McDonald's build the most successful fast-food brand in the world.

> But it has also created an opportunity for the competition, at least in one market. A family-owned chain in the Philippines, Jollibee Foods Corp., has borrowed every marketing

trick in the McDonald's book, from child-friendly spokescharacters to prime locations. But instead of selling a generic burger acceptable in any market in the world, Jollibee caters to a local penchant for sweet-and-spicy flavors, which it incorporates into its fried chicken and spaghetti as well as its burgers. "We've designed these products to suit the Philippine palate," says Menlou B. Bibonia, Jollibee's marketing vice president.

The combination of top-notch service and tailored menus has helped Jollibee become the dominant chain in the Philippines—though laws restricting foreign ownership of businesses have helped, too. . . .

Jollibee's success has not gone unnoticed. McDonald's has introduced its own Filipino-style spicy burgers—one of the few instances in which the chain has changed the actual burger patty.

SOURCE: Hugh Filman, "Happy Meals for a McDonald's Rival," *Business Week*, July 29, 1996, p. 77.   ●

Ethical Issues

Successful competition in the world economy may on occasion create moral dilemmas for business leaders. Of course, ethical concerns and moral dilemmas arise in local competition too, as we discussed in Chapter 4. However, when a company does business in foreign countries, it encounters different cultures. Those cultures may have different standards of right and wrong behavior. Those cultural differences may create unique expectations for business interactions and negotiations. There may even be occasions when a business leader from one country is asked to do something that is considered unethical back home but perfectly acceptable in the country where the request is made.

Ethics, the search for appropriate standards of behavior, can be quite complex in a global environment. It involves some sticky and complex views. Two competing ethical views are relevant when we examine global ethics: cultural relativism and universalism. **Cultural relativism** argues that what is right or wrong depends on the culture of the country where business is taking place. Thus, an act may be considered improper in one culture but quite acceptable in another. By contrast, **universalism** holds that there are commonly shared business standards and principles that are accepted throughout the world. In other words, most people in most places would consider certain actions to be wrong.

An example will clarify the differences between these two views. Sometimes managers may feel pressure to bribe foreign government officials in order to make a sale. Such bribery is a common practice in many countries. Prior to 1977, significant numbers of American firms apparently made such bribes. Most Americans were probably uncomfortable doing so but felt they had to go along with the particular country's customs. They may even have reasoned, from a cultural relativism point of view, that such bribes were acceptable because they were accepted in the host country. In fact, the United States government reported over 400 such bribes in the late 1970s and early 1980s. Examples included a $4 million payment by Gulf Oil to South Koreans and $59 million paid by Exxon to various Italian politicians.

Conversely, universalists argue that bribery is simply wrong. They point out that bribery is "officially" prohibited in nearly every country in the world. The United States provided additional incentive for managers to refuse to make such payments by passing the Foreign Corrupt Practices Act of 1977, which made it illegal to pay bribes abroad.

Cultural relativism
The belief that what is right or wrong depends on the culture of the country where business is taking place.

Universalism
The belief that there are commonly shared business standards and principles that are accepted throughout the world.

The law was subsequently weakened in 1988 because of concern that American firms were being unfairly handicapped in competition with foreign firms that did offer bribes to gain business.[14] Nevertheless, some firms and individual managers refuse to make bribery payments. Of course, they risk losing business to less ethical competitors.

Another common ethical issue involves the working conditions provided by employers. This issue is of particular relevance to American firms because of their high standards of plant safety and protection of workers' health. American standards are normally much higher than those practiced in less developed countries, so American firms locating factories in such countries could get by with much lower expenditures on worker health and safety. Cultural relativists may be tempted to accept the lower standards and enjoy the cost savings. Universalists argue that such actions are clearly unethical. They contend that the truly healthy business will resist those temptations, even if it means not being able to do business in the country in question.

A third common ethical issue is whether or not to reduce employment in the home country and move production to foreign countries with cheaper labor. This is a different twist on global ethics, but it is an issue that faces many firms, including many in the United States. In some cases, the company doesn't really have a choice. To get its costs down to competitive levels, it will have to move production to lower-cost locations. But in other cases, options are available. This is particularly true if the company can differentiate its product so that it doesn't have to match its competitors' lower prices. It is also true if the company can use proprietary technology to offset its higher labor costs. Nevertheless, the decision not to move takes courage. A fine example of such courage is the story of the American clothing company Blue Fish, detailed in Profile 7–8.

PROFILE 7–8   *Blue Fish: The Ethical Small Business that Could*

Blue Fish Clothing, Inc., grew out of Jennifer Barclay's frustration with school. She entered art school in Philadelphia at the age of 16. At 17 she dropped out of school, took a job at a gift shop, and began making artistic dresses in her parents' garage in her spare time. The dresses sold so well at a local art fair that she decided to quit her job and work at her dress business full-time. She received such a large order that she decided to borrow enough money to rent a building and hire a few workers.

Barclay's dresses and other clothing products are made to be objects of art as well as items of clothing. Each piece carries the handstamp of the artist who created it. This concept has attracted such major retailers as Nordstrom's, which began carrying Blue Fish clothing in 1988. Blue Fish sales rose to $9.6 million by 1995 and employment reached 200 people, including 42 artists.

Barclay began selling stock in her company to obtain the funds with which to expand more rapidly. In May 1996 Blue Fish Clothing stock began selling on the Chicago Stock Exchange.

As the company expanded, Barclay was tempted to follow the example of other clothing companies and have the clothing made in foreign countries with low labor costs. That would certainly increase profits, but she refused to do it on ethical grounds. As she put it, "It would be cheaper to go offshore, but people need jobs here."

SOURCE: Barbara Sullivan, "Blue Fish: A Good Catch for Investors?," *Chicago Tribune*, May 29, 1996, sec. 3, pp. 1, 3.

As with any situation that involves ethical issues and moral reasoning, it is impossible for us to prescribe what you should do. It is critical, however, that you think through and understand the ethical implications of each situation. You can use the forms of moral reasoning we discussed in Chapter 4. Moral reasoning does become more complex in the global arena, if only because there are more stakeholders involved.

Developing Your Critical Thinking Skills

1. Do you think a country should discourage its manufacturers from moving manufacturing facilities to another country? Discuss the pros and cons of such a move.

2. If you were the head of a multinational corporation, would you contract with a foreign firm that you knew was going to use child labor to fulfill your contract?

3. Many restaurant chains try to have consistent menus in all their restaurants. This provides them greater control and consistent quality. In this section, we noted that many restaurants must modify their menus to appeal to global markets. What should these chains do to assure continued high quality?

SUMMARY

1. Business managers today must look beyond their domestic borders and see the opportunities of globalization.

   ■ What is globalization?

   In globalization, a business regards its operations all over the world as part of one integrated business system.

2. Two of the most popular methods of global involvement are exporting and importing.

   ■ What is meant by the terms exporting and importing?

   Exporting occurs when a business sells its goods and services to customers in other nations.
   Importing occurs when customers purchase goods and services from producers in other countries.

3. Today's managers enter the global arena for a number of reasons. In some cases, they do so because of opportunities. In other cases, it is a protective or defensive move.

   ■ Why is globalization an important consideration for today's businesses?

   There are three prominent reasons: (1) the rise of foreign competition, (2) the need to control costs, and (3) opportunities for market growth.

4. In order to make effective decisions regarding global operations, business leaders need to be familiar with certain basic economic and government influences.

   ■ What are the most important global influences?

Five major influences were discussed in this chapter:

(1) The balance of trade and the balance of payments. The balance of trade for a country is the dollar amount of goods exported from that country minus the dollar amount imported. The balance of payments is the difference in the inflows of money into a country versus the outflows of money from that country.

(2) The exchange rate. This term refers to the value of a currency compared to foreign currencies.

(3) Tariffs and other trade restrictions. A tariff is simply a tax on an imported good. Other trade restrictions are quotas and nontariff barriers.

(4) Free trade areas. A free trade area involves a geographic territory within which there are no government-imposed barriers to trade.

(5) Government support of business in global competition. One example of this is the so-called industrial policy practiced by Japan. Industrial policy usually involves some protection from import competition plus various subsidies that help reduce the cost of exporting.

5. Once a business recognizes that it must deal with global competition, the company's leadership must still decide how to deal with globalization's threats and opportunities.

■ How might a business deal with the threats and opportunities of globalization?

This chapter highlighted five possibilities for a firm:

(1) Simply compete aggressively against imports.

(2) Become an importer itself. It can search abroad for products that it can bring back to the home country and sell for a profit.

(3) Decide to export from its home base.

(4) Become a multinational firm by establishing production facilities in foreign countries.

(5) Establish international partnerships in the form of a strategic alliance, a joint venture, or licensing.

6. Firms that do business in foreign countries sometimes make the mistake of thinking that what works in the home country will work abroad.

■ What are some of the ways cultural differences might hamper a firm's efforts to compete globally?

Different countries have different customs. The culture of a country influences both what motivates employees and how customers purchase products. Products that appeal to customers in one culture may be totally rejected by those in another.

7. In a global economy, a firm may encounter ethical concerns.

■ What are some basic ethical issues that arise in the context of globalization?

This chapter identified three issues. The first is the question of cultural relativism versus universalism. Cultural relativism argues that what is right or wrong depends on the culture of the country where the business is taking place. Universalism holds that there are commonly shared business standards that should be accepted throughout the world. A second issue is a specific application of the first.

It has to do with whether or not the global firm is ethically obliged to meet the same high standards of working conditions for foreign workers as for domestic workers. A third ethical issue is whether or not to reduce employment in the home country in order to move production to locations abroad with cheaper labor.

Links to future courses

You will encounter international themes increasingly in courses both within and outside of business. You will certainly address these themes in foreign language courses, international studies courses, and even religion courses. Within business, the following courses are particularly relevant.

- Principles of economics
- International economics
- International business
- International marketing
- Business policy
- Business ethics

KEY TERMS

Balance of payments, p. 192
Balance of trade, p. 191
Cultural relativism, p. 207
Dumping, p. 198
Exchange rate, p. 192
Exporting, p. 188
Free trade, p. 194
Free trade area, p. 195
Globalization, p. 186

Global strategy, p. 186
Importing, p. 188
Industrial policy, p. 196
Licensing, p. 204
Multinational firms, p. 202
Multidomestic strategy, p. 187
Quota, p. 194
Tariff, p. 194
Universalism, p. 207

EXERCISES AND APPLICATIONS

1. Form teams and discuss the pros and cons of protectionism versus free trade. Based on your discussion, which argument seems more compelling?

2. Suppose you own a business that makes umbrellas. You think your sales are tapering off, and you are considering exporting them. What do you need to know before you make that decision?

3. Consider the two McDonald's examples discussed in this chapter. Could a smaller company do what McDonald's did to be successful in the foreign markets?

4. Go on the Internet and find the recent exchange rates for the U.S. dollar, Japanese yen, and the Russian ruble. (Several websites provide this information.) Compare these with the rates six months ago. Given our discussion of exchange rates, how is this information important to U.S. exporters and importers?

5. Reread the section on Motorola in Malaysia. Motorola worked with Malay women to change their culture. What are the ramifications of a company's attempt to change part of a country's culture? Are there ethical concerns here? Write a brief report of your assessment.

6. Interview at least two people with different cultural backgrounds from yours (these may be professors, friends, or other students). What frustrates them most about American culture? How can a business use this information to respond better to customers from that culture?

CASE: GLOBALIZATION ON THE MEXICAN-AMERICAN BORDER UNDER NAFTA

Earlier in this chapter, you learned about the North American Free Trade Agreement. Adopted in 1993, it provided for the reduction of trade barriers among Canada, Mexico, and the United States. How have the world's businesses responded to the incentives created by NAFTA? Here is how the May 12, 1997, issue of *Business Week* answered that question.

From deep in Mexico's heartland, hundreds of thousands of job seekers stream northward toward the [U.S.] border every year to live in tarpaper and cinderblock slums near factory gates. They are willing to work hard for low pay. U.S. companies, keen on shrinking costs in the face of international competition, have been setting up assembly plants—*maquiladoras*—on the Mexican side to tap this cheap labor pool. Now totaling 1,500, the maquiladoras may be a key to continued global competitiveness. . . .

It's no longer an American fiefdom, however. Heavy investments are also pouring in from Asia and Europe as well, spurring expansion of the border's economy at close to a 7 percent annual clip. Tijuana [Mexico] has become the world's TV-manufacturing capital, churning out 14 million sets a year. . . . Soaring exports from these plants are helping Mexico pull out of its worst recession in 60 years. And a class of skilled Mexicans . . . is rising to the fore to run the hundreds of new plants. . . .

But there is a dark side to the border's allure as well. When goods and capital can flow freely, so can contraband. . . .

Is the booming border good or bad for the U.S.? Corporate America surely gains, sharpening its competitive edge. . . .

Meanwhile, such Asian companies as Sony Corp. and Daewoo Corp. are building factories to take advantage of Mexico's much touted workforce as well as the tariff cuts provided by NAFTA. That isn't necessarily bad news for U.S. workers. For every factory opened in Mexico, the U.S. wins service, transportation, or distribution jobs. . . .

U.S. suppliers of components are profiting from the rise in border traffic, too. Under NAFTA, the most important components in products such as VCRs must be made in North America to benefit from the treaty's free-trade umbrella. European and Asian companies thus look to U.S. and Mexican suppliers. "Our plan is to buy everything we can in this region," says Dean H. Kim, general purchasing manager at Daewoo's VCR plant in San Luis Rio Colorado, Mexico. . . .

Although the wages are low [in this region], demand for the jobs is high because the pay is better than elsewhere in Mexico. . . . Living standards are slowly improving. . . . Yet the region must grapple with Third World-style woes. Economists estimate that the border needs at least $8 billion just to bring drinking water, sewage treatment, and garbage collection to all its residents.

Decision Questions

1. After reading this case, can you think of any groups that might be worse off because of the NAFTA-inspired rush to the Mexican border?
2. Later in this textbook you will learn about the importance of technology. This case illustrates a technology transfer. Who is transferring the technology? Who is receiving it?
3. When free trade areas are being debated by a nation, one of the major arguments against lowering trade barriers is a loss of jobs in the home country. Based on this case, does it appear that NAFTA is causing a loss of jobs in the United States?

SOURCE: Geri Smith and Elisabeth Malkin, "The Border," *Business Week* May 12, 1997, pp. 64–74.

REFERENCES

1. Bill Powell with Michael Laris, Lynette Clemetson, Melinda Liu, and Michael Hirsh. "A Fast Drive to Riches." *Newsweek*, March 3, 1997, pp. 32–4.

2. American Graduate School of International Management, Thunderbird Faculty Development in International Business Seminar, January 6, 1997; Mort Zuckerman. "Still the American Century." *U.S. News & World Reports*, February 10, 1997, p. 72; William G. Nickels, James M. McHugh, and Susan M. McHugh. *Understanding Business*, 4th ed. Burr Ridge, IL: Irwin, 1996, p. 88.

3. American Graduate School of International Management, Thunderbird Faculty Development in International Business Seminar, January 6, 1997.

4. Marcus W. Brauchli. "Polled Americans, Japanese Have China on Their Mind." *The Wall Street Journal*, June 16, 1997, p. A8; Bruce Einhorn. "The China Connection." *Business Week*, August 5, 1996, pp. 42–5.

5. Trek World (http://home.sportsite.com/trekbikes/world_intro.html), accessed January 1, 1997.

6. Richard M. Hodgetts and Fred Luthans. *International Management*, 3rd ed. New York: McGraw-Hill, 1997, p. 4.

7. Motorola 1996 Annual Report.

8. Patrick J. Spain and James R. Talbot, eds. *Hoover's Handbook of American Companies 1996*. Waltham, MA: Little, Brown, 1995, pp. 94–5.

9. Luis Nassif. "A abertura e a guerra das fraldas." *Folha de S. Paulo*, January 8, 1996, pp. 2–3.

10. Trek World (http://home.sportsite.com/trekbikes/world_time.html), accessed January 1, 1997.

11. "Think Globally, Bake Locally." *Fortune*, October 14, 1996, p. 205.

12. Yumiko Ono. "PepsiCo's Pitch in Japan Has a New Twist." *The Wall Street Journal*, May 23, 1997, p. B10.

13. William Greider. *One World, Ready or Not*. New York: Simon and Schuster, 1997, pp. 82–3.

14. Douglas E. Greer. *Business, Government and Society*, 3rd ed. New York: Macmillan, 1993, pp. 219, 223.

8

The Impact of Financial Markets and Processes

Since it went public in 1990, Cisco Systems' stock has risen more than 8,000 percent. It is the third highest-valued company listed on NASDAQ (the National Association of Securities Dealers' Automated Quotations) behind only Microsoft and Intel. *Financial World* has called Cisco Systems the best growth company in America. Cisco makes routers, networking hardware that allows computer networks in different locations and using different languages to talk to each other. Cisco's goal is to totally dominate that part of the computer industry, and it seems to be on the way toward meeting that goal. The recent acquisition of Stratacom has helped move it deeper into Internet and telecommunications fields. In fact, about 80 percent of the routers directing traffic on the Internet were made by Cisco. The company's management and investors hope the potential of this giant market will justify the $4.5 billion dollars it paid for Stratacom.[1]

Financial markets are the enablers of growth for businesses. Like Cisco Systems, businesses cannot grow substantially without funds available from outside sources. Without access to financial markets, a firm can grow only as far as its sales generate enough funds to support both current and future needs. Financial markets are not important just for big, thriving businesses like Cisco. New, start-up businesses also rely on these markets. Small businesses often need to tap into banks and other financial institutions. Therefore, it is important for you to understand the nature of financial markets and processes. After you have read and studied this chapter, you should be able to:

1. Explain the nature of financial markets and identify the major financial institutions.

2. Describe the major ways in which financial markets affect businesses.

3. Define the concepts of interest and interest rate.

4. Explain why interest rates change over time.

5. Explain how stock prices are determined.

In Chapter 6, you learned about the role that competitive markets play in the daily affairs of business. There the emphasis was on the markets where the business sells its goods or services. In this chapter, you will learn about another set of markets that are vitally important to business firms—financial markets. As the model of a successful business in Chapter 1 showed, financial markets are a major part of the environment.

This chapter will introduce you to three important aspects of financial markets. First, you will learn about the six ways financial markets influence businesses. Second, you will explore the basic features of interest rates. Third, you will become familiar with stock market fundamentals. You will also learn about several types of government policies that have important influences on financial markets. When you finish this chapter you will not be an expert in finance, but you will have a good general understanding of the various opportunities and threats financial markets present to the healthy business.

The Nature of Financial Markets

Businesses need money for a variety of purposes over the course of time. These include money to start the business, to finance expansion, to underwrite day-to-day operations, and to acquire other businesses. Every business hopes to generate money from the sale of its products or services, but in many cases those funds are insufficient. Then the manager must go outside the firm for additional funds. The most likely outside sources are financial markets.

Financial markets
Places where businesses that need to acquire capital are brought together with financial institutions that help provide the funds.

Financial markets are places where businesses that need to acquire capital are brought together with financial institutions that help provide the funds. There are many financial institutions available, including commercial banks, venture capital firms, insurance and pension fund companies, and investment banking houses.[2]

The most common type of financial institution is banks. Commercial banks deal in the lending and borrowing of funds. Banks make loans to businesses and charge interest on the loan. As you learned in Chapter 6, interest is the cost of borrowing money. Banks often require some kind of collateral to guarantee the loan. **Collateral** is any asset owned by the borrower that is pledged to the lender in case the loan is not repaid. If the business defaults on the loan, the bank can take possession of the asset.

Collateral
Any asset owned by the borrower that it pledges to the lender in case the loan is not repaid.

interest p. 225>

Keep in mind that what you and I would consider lending and borrowing are precisely the opposite for banks. Thus, when we make a deposit in a bank, we are actually lending that money to the bank. The money is a liability for the bank. Conversely,

Venture capital firm
A corporation that invests in risky businesses with high-growth potential, usually in exchange for a considerable share of the ownership.

Investment banking house
A financial institution that works with businesses to get large amounts of financing.

Stock
Shares of ownership in companies that are sold to individuals or financial institutions.

going public p. 230>

Corporate bond
A loan sold to the public by a business. Buyers may be individuals or financial institutions.

when we borrow money from a bank, that loan is an income-producing asset for the bank, an asset on which it earns interest. The success of a bank depends on its ability to lend its money at a higher rate than it pays for it.

With deregulation, banks have moved into new consumer services. In addition to the normal checking and savings accounts, certificates of deposits, and a variety of loans, banks can now sell mutual funds, stocks, and other investment instruments.

A second institution is **venture capital firms,** corporations that invest in risky businesses with high-growth potential, usually in exchange for a considerable share of the ownership. They know they will lose money on many of these ventures, but they make high returns on others.

A third financial institution is *insurance and pension fund companies.* Insurance companies allow businesses to shift risk, as we will discuss later in the chapter. Perhaps more important, insurance and pension fund companies invest premiums in stocks and bonds of other companies. Thus, these companies are the largest single owners of many companies, and they can put significant pressure on firms to perform adequately.

An **investment banking house** is a financial institution that works with businesses to get large amounts of financing when they need it. Investment bankers are usually involved in growth-oriented businesses, particularly those that anticipate going public.

In addition to these financial institutions, businesses are also influenced by the stock and bond markets. **Stocks** are shares of ownership in companies that are sold to individuals or financial institutions. Stock ownership gives investors voting rights on certain major issues affecting the business. The nature of the stock market will be covered in more detail later in the chapter. A **corporate bond** is a loan sold to the public by a business. The bonds are sold in an organized market where the buyers are various financial institutions as well as individuals.

Six Ways Financial Markets Affect the Firm

Financial markets and institutions play a variety of roles in the operation of successful businesses. Six of the most important roles are shown in Table 8–1.

Before we study each impact individually, let's look back at Cisco Systems. Cisco was not always the high-flying hero of growth companies. Its beginning, like that of many growth companies, was rough and not without a fair amount of pain to its

TABLE 8–1   The Impact of Financial Markets

1. Providing the funds needed to start a business and expand it.
2. Underwriting the costs of operating the business.
3. Influencing customer demand for the firm's products.
4. Pressuring management to focus on short-term profits.
5. Providing opportunities to reduce operating risks.
6. Providing opportunities to supplement operating earnings by wisely investing the company's surplus cash.

founders. The early Cisco Systems story is presented in Profile 8–1. There you can see how the market made it possible for the founders of Cisco Systems *to obtain the money to start their company.* You can also observe how financial markets made it possible *to expand the company* at critical times in its history. Finally, you can see how the stock market became *a source of external pressure on management.* Such external pressure can sometimes become so strong that the top managers decide to resign or are fired. That is what happened to Cisco's founders. For them, the financial environment of business was both a blessing and a curse.

PROFILE 8–1   *Cisco Systems and Financial Markets*

Cisco Systems is one of the hottest technology stocks in the world today. The company makes devices that allow different computer networks to communicate with one another. Cisco's founders were a husband and wife team, Leonard Bosack and Sandy Lerner. Prior to starting Cisco, Bosack operated the computer services for Stanford University's computer science department and Lerner ran the computer system in Stanford's business school.

As part of Bosack's job at Stanford, he developed the technology needed to allow different computer networks to communicate. He then decided to start a company to sell the concept to other universities and businesses. To get the money to start that company, he and Lerner borrowed from a bank, using their home mortgage as collateral. They also both borrowed against their personal credit cards.

The company opened for business in 1984. By 1987, it had grown to the point where it needed an investment of several million dollars in order to continue expanding. To get that money, Bosack and Lerner sold almost one-third of their stock in the company to a venture capitalist, who bought the stock on the condition that the company would eventually offer its stock to the general public. That required management to devote more attention to producing good financial results so that there would be a demand for the company's stock when it was offered for sale.

In 1990, stock in Cisco systems was offered to the public for the first time through an initial public offering (IPO). Some of the proceeds from the sale were used to finance further expansion of Cisco. Another major portion went to the founders and their venture capital partners, repaying part of their investment.

customer service p. 340> After the public offering, Cisco Systems' management assumed an additional burden. The company had to try to report increased earnings continuously in order to keep the stock price rising. Cofounder Lerner began to feel that this emphasis on good quarterly earnings reports was interfering with the company's focus on quality and customer service. The rest of the management team disagreed, and that difference of opinion finally led Lerner and her husband to leave the company.

SOURCE: Joseph Nocera, "Cooking with Cisco," *Fortune,* December 25, 1995, pp. 114–22.

With the Cisco Systems story in mind, we now discuss the six functions of financial markets. As mentioned in Chapter 1, we are interested primarily in how these

TABLE 8–2   Sources of Funds for Start-ups and Expanding Firms

Start-ups	Expanding Firms
Nonfinancial market sources	*Nonfinancial market sources*
Personal savings	Additional owner contributions
Families and friends	Partners
Partners	Suppliers
Suppliers	
	Financial market sources
Financial market sources	Banks
Banks	Private investors
Personal finance companies	Venture capitalists
Credit card companies	Investment bankers
	Bond market
	Stock market

financial market functions affect a business. We begin with a discussion of *capital funds*, the monies the firm uses to start, operate, or expand its business.

Providing Funds to Start and Expand Businesses

When a business is launched, its founders can raise funds from a limited variety of sources. These are shown in the first column of Table 8–2. Note that, especially for start-up situations, entrepreneurs cannot make good use of financial markets. The most common source for start-ups is personal or family savings. Such funds are relatively easy to acquire, and no formal ties or contracts are needed. The owner may have personal funds or count on family members and acquaintances to contribute the necessary funds, in the form of either a loan or an investment. Sometimes a partner may join the firm and contribute capital. Suppliers may also provide inventory on credit.

These personal sources are not considered financial markets. Remember, financial markets include only those formal financial institutions that provide capital to businesses. Generally, only one common financial institution is relevant for start-ups: a commercial bank. Personal finance companies and credit card companies will sometimes be used if banks will not lend the money. In Cisco Systems' case, the founders pledged their home as collateral. Had they been unable to repay the loan, the bank would have taken possession of their home.

Once firms are launched and are stable, more sources are available to them, as shown in the second column of Table 8–2. As you might expect, growth-oriented firms and relatively large companies that need substantial infusions of capital to achieve their goals are most likely to use financial institutions other than banks.

Profile 8–2 discusses Southwest Airlines' early efforts at financing. Its situation is unusual because of the magnitude of funding required to start an airline. The profile shows how many different financing sources and financial institutions were involved.

PROFILE 8–2   SOUTHWEST FLIES HIGH ON BORROWED FUNDS

The history of Southwest Airlines provides an interesting example of fund-raising in the early stages of a company's growth. The initial capital was provided from personal funds by founders Rollin King and Herb Kelleher, as well as from a group of

Herb Kelleher and his partners used an amazing array of financing in launching Southwest Airlines. Most businesses do not need nor have access to the funds required to start an airline. Spend a few minutes considering a business you might like to start. What kind of financing would be appropriate for it?

investors contacted personally by King and a few other early investors. The total amount raised was $543,000. Most of that was spent fighting legal roadblocks placed in Southwest's way by existing competing airlines. After the legal battles were won, Southwest had $142 left in its bank account—and $80,000 in unpaid bills.

Nevertheless, the company was able to hire a retired airline executive named Lamar Muse as the new CEO. Muse immediately went to work raising the capital needed to get the airline off the ground. He invested $50,000 himself and was able to raise another $250,000 from friends and from contacts in the airline industry. Muse then called on a wealthy business friend who invested $750,000. Next he arranged a public stock offering after finding a brokerage firm that agreed to take a large share. (The first stock was sold on June 8, 1971.)

The public offering, plus the earlier private investments, gave Southwest $7 million of start-up capital. That made it possible for Muse to turn to a supplier for the final slice of funding needed to get into the air. Muse then convinced Boeing to sell Southwest three new jet planes on an installment plan.

SOURCE: Kevin Freiburg and Jackie Freiburg, *NUTS! Southwest Airlines' Crazy Recipe for Business and Personal Success* (Austin, TX: The Bard Press, 1996), pp. 18–22.

If a company tries to raise funds through any of the financial markets except banks, it may need to have one or more financial specialists on staff. The reason for this is that the complicated legal and financial knowledge needed to make key financial decisions may be beyond that possessed by the typical company founder or nonfinancial manager. At this point in their company's evolution, most managers will want to have a top-level management employee who is a financial specialist. Two common titles for such a person are treasurer and chief financial officer (CFO), as discussed in Chapter 3.

One of the most important tasks of the company's top financial manager is to determine the best time and terms for seeking funds from financial markets. Trying to sell stock at the wrong time or for the wrong terms can harm a company's performance. Sometimes bad timing can so cripple a company that it loses its ability to compete effectively.

Consider, for example, the different fates of Hardee's and Sandy's in the early 1970s. Both fast-food hamburger chains had experienced significant growth in the 1960s. Each opened its 100th store in 1967. And the managements of both knew that they needed a huge infusion of outside capital to finance continued growth. So both made plans to sell stock to the general public. There the similarity ends.

Hardee's successfully sold its stock in 1969 at a time when stock prices in general were rising. Sandy's waited a little longer. By the time it was ready, general stock market conditions had become quite bad. It was clear that Sandy's would have trouble selling the stock, so the public offering was canceled. That meant that Sandy's could not raise the funds for the expansion it needed to remain competitive with the larger firms. Sandy's management reluctantly decided to merge with a competitor. On November 30, 1971, Sandy's was sold to Hardee's. Sandy's ceased to exist because it had failed to make its public offering at the right time.

Underwriting the Costs of Operating the Business

Working capital

Money set aside or used for operating a business.

The amount of money available in a business changes continuously. Sometimes a business has more money than it needs, and it invests that money in financial markets. At other times, however, a business needs additional funds from other sources to handle daily operating expenses. For example, the business usually needs money to pay suppliers before customers make their payments to the business. Occasionally the week's or month's sales fail to provide enough cash to pay employees their weekly or monthly salaries. Money set aside or used for operating the business is called **working capital.**

It is possible for the business to generate part of its working capital out of its earnings. But it is also possible to obtain the working capital by taking out a bank loan. The interest rate the company has to pay for its working capital loan depends on several factors. One of the most important is the bank's cost of obtaining the funds it is lending to the business. The bank's cost of funds is determined by the general level of interest rates in financial markets. Since that rate changes frequently, the business can expect its interest expense to fluctuate over time.

There is nothing the business manager can do to change the general rate of interest in financial markets. In a sense, this part of the cost of operating the business is at the mercy of the firm's financial environment. But the manager can try to anticipate changes in interest rates. When managers expect rates to rise, they can reduce their financial costs by borrowing before the rates go up. When they expect interest rates to fall, they can reduce their financial costs by postponing borrowing. It pays for the manager of a business to understand how and why interest rates rise and fall.

Influencing Customer Demand for the Firm's Products

Some businesses sell products that customers purchase using borrowed funds. For example, cars and homes are typically purchased on an installment plan. In such cases, the customer has to consider not only the selling price but also the interest expense to

With the advantages of the Internet, customers can now buy cars and even consider financing them through web sites. Sometimes this can eliminate intermediaries and allow customers to study cars or financing options from their homes. What are the advantages and disadvantages of this method?

be incurred. When interest rates are very high, many households postpone making the purchase in order to avoid the high interest charges on the installment loan. On the other hand, when interest rates are very low, many households are motivated to make the purchase now.

Thus, interest rates become a matter of some concern to those businesses whose customers borrow the funds to make purchases. High interest rates mean that such businesses can expect a drop in demand. Low interest rates usually mean an increase in demand.

As noted earlier, there is not much that a manager of a business can do to affect the market rate of interest. However, the business can avoid the worst effects of high interest rates and take advantage of low ones by anticipating changes in rates. For example, if the business expects an increase in interest rates, it can obtain a loan at current lower rates and use those funds to help customers finance their purchases when rates rise. If the business expects interest rates to drop, it can plan to increase production so that it will have plenty of product to sell when interest rates do fall and customers increase their purchases.

Pressuring Management to Focus on Short-Term Profits

Our discussion of Cisco Systems showed how the stock market puts pressure on the management of a company to increase earnings. You learned that once Cisco offered stock to outsiders, the founders had to pay more attention to increasing short-run earnings. Neither their skills nor their interests were up to the challenge. The founders eventually left the company, and professional managers took over the job of increasing short-run earnings.

Some experts argue that this kind of pressure is good for a company. They say stockholder pressure forces managers to be more efficient and competitive. Managers who don't meet the challenge will be forced out of office and "better" managers will be brought in. This can be done by the existing board of directors, or it can be accomplished through a takeover.

board of directors p. 64>

If a publicly held company consistently performs below its potential, the business becomes vulnerable to a takeover. A **takeover** occurs when investors (including other companies) purchase enough of the company's stock to control the company.[3] In some cases, the price of the company's stock under the old management may fall until it becomes attractive to outsiders. In other cases, the takeover process triggers an increase in the price of the company's stock before the takeover has taken place. This occurs because the takeover group believes the company could be much more profitable than it is, and the outsiders are willing to pay a higher price for the chance to prove they are right. Once the outsiders gain control, they will introduce more efficient methods of operation and make the firm more competitive. This means that earnings will increase, just as the takeover group expected. Again, proponents argue that financial markets can provide a useful public service in this manner.

Takeover
A situation where investors (including other companies) purchase enough of a company's stock to control the company.

But some observers believe financial markets create undue pressure for short-term performance. These critics fear that firms will cut back on R&D expenditures because of the long time it takes for these kinds of investments to produce a profit. Similarly, firms may underinvest in training and in developing new markets if the payoff will be too far in the future. They argue that even though the business may look financially sound, it is not paying enough attention to the other, longer-term measures of business success that we have discussed throughout the text.

training p. 379>

In order to avoid the problem of short-run stock market pressures, many privately held firms adamantly avoid going public. Similarly, publicly held firms may convert to a privately held status. A privately held corporation avoids the pressures by simply not making its stock available on any stock exchange. Take the example of Cargill, Inc., America's largest privately held corporation. In 1996, it employed approximately 79,000 workers and generated revenues of almost $60 billion. It controlled one-fifth of the nation's corn-milling capacity, one-fourth of the oilseed-crushing capacity, and one-fourth of America's grain exports. It slaughtered one-fifth of America's cattle. It operates in almost 100 countries.

One of Cargill's many foreign businesses supplies seed and fertilizer in India and mills flour there. It took the company seven years to earn a profit in India, and company officials doubt that Cargill could have persisted if it had been publicly held. Referring to the Indian situation and numerous other slow-to-develop projects, company president Ernest Micek said, "It takes patience to be in our business. We can't worry about some analyst's expectations for the next quarter." That view is echoed by Thomas Urban, chair of Pioneer Hi-Bred Interval, Inc., a publicly held company. Urban's company had to close a potentially profitable oilseed plant in Egypt because it did not become profitable fast enough. Urban said, perhaps with a touch of jealousy, "Cargill can take risks a publicly traded company can't."[4]

Providing Opportunities to Reduce Operating Risks

We have discussed how financial markets affect the way a business operates on a day-to-day basis. Financial markets can also help managers deal with the risks associated with operating the business. The risks of operating a business cannot be completely eliminated; indeed, risk taking is a primary function of business. Nevertheless, managers use a variety of methods to reduce or shift risks. A few of those are found in specialized financial markets. More specifically, managements can use the following financial markets to reduce risks:

1. Commodity markets
2. Foreign exchange markets
3. Insurance markets

Commodity markets

Financial markets that offer businesses the opportunity to guarantee the future prices of certain agricultural products and raw materials.

Commodity markets are financial institutions that offer businesses an opportunity to guarantee the future prices of certain agricultural products and raw materials. In commodity markets, sellers guarantee that an agreed-upon volume of a particular commodity will be available at a specified price at a future date. Buyers get the right to buy the commodity at that price at that date.

Buying the right to *sell* a product at a set price in the future can be important for an agricultural or raw materials business that wants to reduce the risk of an unexpected fall in the price of a product it is selling. For example, wheat farmers might want to guarantee the price they will get for their next wheat crops by selling a wheat contract in a commodities market. Buying the right to *buy* a product at a specified price in the future can be important to a business that wants to avoid the risk of an unexpected increase in the price of a raw material that is an important input into its production process. For example, a candy company might want to use the commodity markets to guarantee the future price of the cocoa beans that it buys to make chocolate.

Foreign exchange markets

Financial markets that offer businesses an opportunity to avoid potential losses when money earned from foreign sales is exchanged for home currency.

Foreign exchange markets are financial institutions that offer the business an opportunity to avoid potential losses when money earned from foreign sales is exchanged for home currency. Suppose that an American computer maker sells 1,000 computers to a German retail chain, with payment to be made in German marks within 90 days after the computers are delivered to Germany. At the time of the sale, the exchange rate is two German marks for each dollar. The American manufacturer sells the computers for a price of 2,000 marks each and expects to exchange the 2,000 marks for $1,000 when the German buyer pays. Unfortunately for the American firm,

Many managers consider the cost of speculation in foreign currency a normal cost of doing business in international markets. They treat it as an expense just as much as they do advertising. What are the pros and cons of speculating in the currency markets?

when the German retailer pays for the computers 90 days after delivery, the exchange rate is 4 to 1. That means the American firm needs 4,000 marks in order to get $1,000 in exchange. Since the American computer maker received only 2,000 marks, it will get only $500 in exchange for its 2,000 marks. Consequently, the American computer maker loses $500 per computer. This loss is due entirely to the change in the price of the dollar against the mark.

One way for the computer manufacturer to avoid this exchange rate loss is to contract to buy dollars 90 days in the future at a preset rate. That is, the manufacturer could go to the foreign exchange futures market and buy the right to sell German marks at the rate of 2 marks for one dollar. The manufacturer would take the 2,000 marks per computer sold at the end of 90 days and exchange them for $1,000. The exchange rate loss would have been passed on to the speculator who contracted to buy the marks at the 2 to 1 rate. Of course, the manufacturer must pay a fee to a speculator to arrange this futures contract. But many businesses regard this price as a reasonable cost of shifting the risk.

Insurance

A contract in which one party agrees, for a fee, to reimburse the other for financial damages incurred.

Insurance is a contract through which one party agrees, for a fee, to reimburse the other for financial damages incurred. Insurance policies allow a business to shift the risk of losses. If you drive a car you are already familiar with the insurance concept. You know that, for a price, insurance companies will agree to assume the risk of paying the cost of repairing your car if it is damaged in an accident, within certain limits. The fee you pay to shift risk to the insurance company is called a premium. This insurance principle applies to a wide variety of risks. Businesses can buy insurance to protect against losses due to fire, windstorms, flooding, theft, lawsuits by injured workers or customers, and other hazards.

Insurance companies are financial institutions. The fees they collect from policyholders provide funds that can be invested at a profit. They then use these funds to pay claims to those who have incurred losses under the terms of the contract. Insurance companies pool the risk of loss of tens of thousands of businesses, so it is often cheaper for a business to buy insurance than to set aside money to cover its own losses.[5]

Providing Opportunities to Invest the Firm's Surplus Cash

A sixth important function of financial markets is to provide businesses with ways of supplementing earnings by investing a temporary surplus of cash in financial instruments that earn interest or dividends. This surplus cash is money the company is holding temporarily and plans to spend to cover future operating expenses.

Suppose a local furniture store knows that it will have to pay local property taxes in the amount of $48,000 once a year. The store's owner decides to set aside $4,000 per month out of earnings. Thus, nine months before the taxes are due, the company will have set aside $12,000; and six months before the taxes are due, the owner will have accumulated $24,000.

What should the owner do with those funds? The obvious answer is to put them in some kind of income-earning investment. Possibilities include a savings account in a bank, a certificate of deposit (CD), or a six-month U.S. Treasury bill. All of these short-term investments would generate some interest income while at the same time guaranteeing the store owner the ability to get the original investment back in time to pay the taxes. Thus, the financial markets have provided the furniture store with an opportunity to supplement earnings.

Most companies invest their temporary surpluses in this manner. In larger companies there is often so much money involved that the company employs one or more people who specialize in managing investments. In fact, some of you may decide to major in finance and end up doing this type of work for a large corporation or for a financial institution that manages the corporation's funds.

Developing Your Critical Thinking Skills

1. Which is the most important of the six impacts of financial markets on the business firm? Explain your answer.

2. On balance, is our economy better off or worse off because of the short-run pressures that the stock market puts on publicly held companies?

3. How do you as an individual reduce or shift risks? How are your techniques similar to or different from the ways businesses deal with risk?

Interest Rates

By now you know that interest rates have an important impact on the business. You can see why managers need to watch for changes in interest rates. In this section, you will learn some important concepts about interest rates.

Definition of Interest

Interest, as you learned in Chapter 6, is the price a borrower pays a lender in return for receiving a loan. What interest do you pay if you borrow $1,000 for one year and agree to pay the lender $1,100 at the end of the year? The answer, of course, is $100. Another way of expressing the cost to the borrower is as the amount of interest paid divided by the amount of the loan. In our example, this would be the $100 in interest divided by the $1,000 loan, or an interest rate of 10 percent. It is customary to report this interest rate in terms of the annual percentage rate.

TABLE 8–3   Changes in the Prime Interest Rate over Time

Year	Prime Rate Charged by Banks
1977	6.83%
1978	9.06
1979	12.67
1980	15.27
1981	18.87
1982	14.86
1983	10.79
1984	12.04
1985	9.93
1986	8.33
1987	8.21
1988	9.32
1989	10.87
1990	10.01
1991	8.46
1992	6.25
1993	6.00
1994	7.15
1995	8.83
1996	8.27

SOURCE: *Economic Report of the President* (Washington, DC: U.S. Government Printing Office, 1997), p. 382.

There are many different types of loans. For example, there are long-term loans and short-term loans. There are government loans and private loans. There are loans made by banks in return for a signed promise to repay the loan with interest. There are loans made by government agencies and large businesses in the form of bond sales. Just as loans differ, so do interest rates. A large, well-known business may be able to get loans with a low interest rate and with no collateral other than the company's name. A small, start-up business will pay considerably higher rates because of the risk of business failure.

Prime rate
The interest rate that large commercial banks charge their best corporate customers for short-term loans.

One of the most important interest rates is the **prime rate.** This is the interest rate that large commercial banks charge their best corporate customers for short-term loans. In fact, interest rates that business borrowers are charged usually reflect the prime rate. You may know of a small business owner who obtained a loan for "two points over prime." This means that the owner paid two percentage points more than the rate given to the best corporate customers. Table 8–3 shows the prime rate for recent years.

Interest Rate Changes over Time

One of the most important features of interest rates is the way they vary over time. Table 8–3 shows the fluctuations in the prime rate. Over time there is a cyclical pattern. That is, interest rates rise for a period of time. Then they fall for a while. Then they rise again.

Managers know that interest rates fluctuate. How does this knowledge affect their decision making? Keeping in mind that interest is the cost of borrowing money, managers may decide to borrow for expansion now if they anticipate that interest rates will rise later. Conversely, they may decide to delay borrowing if they think interest rates will decline later. The following example illustrates the impact of rate fluctuations.

In 1990, a business owner was considering whether to replace old equipment. She would have to borrow $500,000 to replace the equipment. However, the interest rate in 1990 was 10.01 percent. Thus, the cost of interest payments the first year alone would be $50,050. The old equipment was still operable, however, and the owner was concerned that the interest payment seemed terribly high. She knew the interest rate had already fallen from the previous year, and she expected that it would continue to fall. She decided to wait. Finally, in 1992, the interest rate dropped to 6.25 percent and the owner decided the time was right to purchase the equipment. Now the interest payment for the first year was only $31,250, a savings of nearly $20,000.

The business owner's decision seems logical. Saving $20,000 by waiting only two years makes sense. (In fact, if she had waited one more year, the interest rate would have dropped another 0.25 percent, saving even more money.) However, there are other factors to consider. If the equipment was old, the cost of repairs during the two-year period could eat up much of the $20,000 savings. In addition, the price of the new equipment may have gone up during the two years. Importantly, the business would not have access to the latest technology during the two years. Staying with the old **efficiency p. 478>** equipment may have reduced efficiency, offsetting more of the interest saved. As you can see, business decisions are complex and always involve trade-offs.

One reason for the pattern of rising and falling interest rates is shifts in the demand for and supply of loanable funds. Demand increases periodically when large numbers of businesses decide to borrow to finance expansion of their operations. It falls periodically after businesses complete their expansions or if they experience a widespread decline in the sale of final goods and services. In other words, when the customers of businesses stop buying, the businesses stop borrowing.

Inflation and Interest Rates

A second reason for rising and falling interest rates is inflation. In the long run, interest rates tend to consist of two parts. The first is the amount necessary to cover the risk that the loan will not be repaid, plus an amount necessary to cover the lender's forgone alternative uses of the funds that are loaned. The second is the expected rate of inflation.

An example should make this clear. Suppose a lender needs to earn an interest rate of 5 percent in order to cover the risks and forgone alternative uses of a loan to a particular borrower. If the inflation rate is expected to be 2 percent over the life of the loan, then the lender will require the borrower to pay an interest rate of 5 percent plus 2 percent, or a total of 7 percent. If our lender expects the inflation rate to be 10 percent, then the borrower must pay an interest rate of 5 percent plus 10 percent, or a total of 15 percent.

TABLE 8–4   Real Rates of Interest in the United States

Year	(1) Prime Interest Rate*	(2) Inflation Rate**	(3) Real Rate of Interest (1 – 2 = 3)
1986	8.33%	1.1%	7.22%
1987	8.21	4.4	3.81
1988	9.32	4.4	4.92
1989	10.87	4.6	6.27
1990	10.01	6.1	3.91
1991	8.46	3.1	5.36
1992	6.25	2.9	3.35
1993	6.00	2.7	3.30
1994	7.15	2.7	4.47
1995	8.83	2.5	6.33

*Prime rate.

**Consumer price index year-to-year changes.

SOURCE: *Economic Report of the President* (Washington, DC: U.S. Government Printing Office, 1997), pp. 382, 365.

Real rate of interest
The rate the borrower actually paid minus the rate of inflation.

Table 8–4 gives a few more examples in order to help you understand this point. The examples are taken from the actual experience of the American economy between 1986 and 1995. Notice that we have added a column called the **real rate of interest,** the rate the borrower actually paid minus the rate of inflation. In the table, you can see that the real rate of interest varies over time.

It is important for borrowers to understand the concept of the real interest rate. Otherwise they may be misled by interest rates that seem high because of inflation but are actually low in terms of the real rate.

The Fed, Monetary Policy, and Interest Rates[6]

In a strict economic sense, interest rates are determined by the demand for and supply of loanable funds. Further, the supply of loanable funds is determined by the amount of saving that takes place in the economy and by the government's monetary policy. Accordingly, it is important to take a brief look at how government exercises its influence. It acts primarily through the Federal Reserve Board, which is highlighted in Profile 8–3.

PROFILE 8–3   *The Federal Reserve System and Its Board*

The Federal Reserve System was created in 1913 to stabilize the American banking system. This was to be done by lending money to banks when they needed reserves to meet depositor demands. The Federal Reserve System was also expected to regulate the nation's money supply in order to prevent inflation from becoming a problem.

The Federal Reserve System consists of 12 regional Federal Reserve Banks and a seven-member Board of Governors. Each governor is appointed by the president for a nonrenewable term of 14 years, which gives the Fed a significant degree of independence from Congress and the president.

The most important decision-making body in the system is the Federal Open Market Committee, which consists of the seven members of the Board of Governors plus five of the 12 presidents of the regional Federal Reserve Banks. The Open Market Committee meets regularly to determine whether or not to tighten or loosen monetary policy and thereby push interest rates up or down.

Monetary policy is discussed in Chapter 6. It encompasses the actions taken by the Fed's Board of Governors to influence the economy, primarily by influencing interest rates. The main method the Federal Reserve Board uses to influence interest rates is to increase or decrease the money supply. The primary reasons the Fed takes such actions are (1) to change the rate of growth of the overall economy and (2) to reduce the rate of inflation.

For example, when the Fed believes that the inflation rate is too high, it tries to decrease the money supply in order to bring down the inflation rate, usually causing the general level of interest rates to rise. On the other hand, when it believes that the economy is growing too slowly, it tries to increase the money supply to bring about faster growth. This usually causes interest rates to decline.

We have already seen how our economy goes through alternating periods of growth and contraction as well as alternating periods of lower and higher rates of inflation. So we should expect the Federal Reserve to go through alternating periods of first tightening the money supply and then loosening it. That means we should expect to see interest rates rising and falling in response to the Fed's actions.

Raising or lowering interest rates is a way of controlling the economy. High rates discourage borrowing and encourage saving. But should you borrow if you think the rate will rise? Even if you don't really need to?

Fed Message On Rates Sends Stocks Tumbling

In Blunt Testimony, Greenspan Talks of Inflation Concerns

By Mitchell Martin
International Herald Tribune

NEW YORK — Stock and bond prices tumbled Wednesday after the top U.S. central banker warned that American interest rates would be increased

You may be wondering how this relates to the job of managers of businesses. The answer is that astute managers pay attention to the actions of the Federal Reserve to form a better idea of what is likely to happen to interest rates. For example, if you read the business section of the *Chicago Tribune* on February 24, 1996, you would have learned that Federal Reserve Board chair Alan Greenspan had hinted, in testimony before Congress, that the Fed might reduce interest rates in order to stimulate economic growth. If you were the head of a major corporation, you would take this information to the next meeting of your top executive group and all of you would discuss the likelihood of future short-term cuts in interest rates. If you all agreed that such cuts were likely, you would postpone some of the borrowing you had planned to do in the next few weeks so you could take advantage of the lower interest rates that Greenspan hinted were coming.

The Global Economy and Interest Rates

In the past two decades, the emergence of the global economy has caused two important changes in the interest rate environment in the United States. First, it has become possible for American businesses (and our government) to borrow from foreign lenders or in foreign financial markets. This means that managers can shop around the world for the best possible terms on a loan. If they can get a better deal in London or Tokyo than in Chicago or New York, they will borrow their funds in England or Japan. Of course, their main competitors will be doing the same shopping around. Therefore, companies today need to shop worldwide for loans in order to stay competitive, in addition to reducing their own costs as much as possible.

The second important change is that American monetary policymakers have to pay more attention to the flow of loanable funds into and out of the United States. This is a concern because of the differences between interest rates here and abroad. In essence, if the Federal Reserve allows a large-scale inflow of foreign funds, the demand for the dollar will rise and the foreign exchange rate will rise. This means American businesses will face stiffer competition from imports because imports will be cheaper in terms of the dollar.

This is why the Federal Reserve Board has to be concerned about keeping interest rates at just the right level. The rates need to be high enough to keep the value of the dollar from falling but low enough to keep the value of the dollar from being pushed up by the inflow of foreign investment funds. Once you understand this situation, you will be better able to predict the Fed's moves with respect to interest rates.

By now, you should understand how interest rates are determined, why they are important, and how business leaders can try to assess what is likely to happen to them. You should also be aware of the high degree of uncertainty involved in forecasting future rates. That should lead you to have even more respect for the ability of top-level managers to continue to produce good performance despite the turbulent environment in which their businesses operate.

Developing Your Critical Thinking Skills

1. Why do banks charge higher interest rates for loans to small or new companies than to large established companies?

2. We discussed how interest rates can affect the economy. Suppose a recession occurs. What will the Federal Reserve do to help out the economy?

3. As the owner of a small retail clothing store, you are convinced that interest rates will rise over the next six months. What business decisions can you make to respond to this movement?

The Stock Market

In Profile 8–1 you observed the important roles played by the stock market in the history of successful, healthy businesses. You learned how Cisco Systems first sold stock on a very restricted basis to a venture capital group. Later that group made the stock available to the general public through an initial public offering. You learned that once the stock of Cisco Systems became widely held by public investors, the company was pressured to produce steady and growing profits. We now take a closer look at a few of the basic features of the stock market.

Going Public

Going public
The situation when a company offers to sell its stock to the general public for the first time.

Initial public offering (IPO)
A company's first-time issuance of stock to the public.

Going public has become a very popular practice for growing companies. **Going public** means that for the first time in its history, a company offers to sell its stock to the general public. This first-time issuance of stock is appropriately called an **initial public offering (IPO)**. To go public, the company often hires an investment banking firm to arrange the initial sale. Once the sale has been made, the company's stock can be bought or sold on a daily basis through one of the various stock markets that handle such sales. The three major stock exchanges are the New York Stock Exchange (NYSE), the American Stock Exchange (AMEX), and the over-the-counter market. Table 8–5 gives you a brief introduction to each of them, as well as to the regional exchanges in the United States.

TABLE 8–5   The Major Stock Markets in the United States

The New York Stock Exchange (NYSE). The largest American stock exchange, NYSE is located in New York City. It has 1,366 members and lists over 2,400 common stocks.

The American Stock Exchange (AMEX). The second largest American stock exchange, AMEX is also located in New York City. It lists about 1,000 common stocks.

Regional stock markets. Regional exchanges are located in Chicago, Philadelphia, Cincinnati, Boston, San Francisco, Spokane, and Salt Lake City. Each of these specializes in trading stocks of companies located in its region of the country.

The over-the-counter (OTC) stock market. The OTC is actually an electronic network of several thousand brokers around the country. This network is called the National Association of Securities Dealers Automated Quotation system (NASDAQ). It lists over 4,000 stocks.

SOURCE: William G. Nickels, James M. McHugh, and Susan M. McHugh, *Understanding Business,* 4th ed. (Burr Ridge: Irwin, 1996), pp. 618–20.

The IPO boom is a unique feature of the American economy. No other country has anything like it. That is due in part to the highly developed state of U.S. financial markets. It is also due in part to the flood of money pouring into American mutual funds and pension funds. The managers of those funds need to find a place to invest them. In the 1990s, IPOs were one attractive place for investing them.

There are several reasons for a company to go public. One is to provide new investment funds the firm can use to expand its operations. Examples of this are the Cisco Systems and Hardee's public offerings you learned about earlier.

Norman Brinker's first successful restaurant chain is another interesting example, as described in Profile 8–4.

BRINKER
INTERNATIONAL

PROFILE 8–4   *Brinker's Success with Steak and Ale*

After successfully helping to build the Jack in the Box restaurant chain, Norman Brinker started a coffee-shop business that was not successful. He then decided to develop a new restaurant concept, which he called Steak and Ale. Initial capital for the idea came from Brinker and a friend who became a 50 percent partner. Each put up $5,500 in cash. They also obtained a $60,000 equipment loan from a Dallas, Texas, bank. Finally, they talked a landowner into building the restaurant on his property and then leasing it to Steak and Ale.

That first Steak and Ale opened in 1966. Once it proved successful, Brinker and his partner began the process of expanding the business. To raise funds for the expansion they used an unusual partnership arrangement. Each new Steak and Ale restaurant was a joint venture between Brinker and his partner on the one hand and a new investor or group of investors on the other. The new investor would provide *all* of the equity capital needed to start the new restaurant, but 20 percent of the ownership would be credited to Brinker and his partner. It was expected by all involved that eventually Steak and Ale would go public, at which time the equity in each restaurant would be sold to the new publicly held company.

Brinker was not satisfied with the rate of expansion between 1966 and 1970. So he decided to make an initial public offering and use the funds that generated to speed up expansion. The IPO, made in 1971, was organized by the investment banking firm of Goldman, Sachs, which had an office in Brinker's headquarters city of Dallas. The head of the local Goldman, Sachs office was initially skeptical about its success, but Brinker sold him on going ahead with it. The offering was a success. Steak and Ale grew rapidly after that, partly because Brinker had a concept that appealed to customers throughout the United States, partly because Brinker was an excellent manager with a knack for hiring and motivating the right people, and partly because the company now had enough capital to finance the expansion.

SOURCE: Norman Brinker and Donald T. Phillips, *On the Brink: The Life and Leadership of Norman Brinker* (Arlington, TX: Summit Publishing, 1996).

joint venture
p. 179>

A second reason for going public is to enable the original investors (founders and venture capitalists) to get back their original investment plus some profit. This was also a major factor for Cisco Systems, as well as for McDonald's, whose 1965 initial public offering is discussed in Profile 8–5.

PROFILE 8–5   *McDonald's IPO*

McDonald's was founded by Ray Kroc in 1956 with money he had saved plus personal loans. Initially, he had two partners who could almost be considered co-founders, Harry Sonnenborn and June Martino. He gave each of them a large block of stock in lieu of a decent salary. Up until the time of the public offering, none of these three founders had earned a significant financial return from the business. The public offering was their opportunity to finally get their reward. Here is how that issue was explained in a recent history of the company:

McDonald's did not need new equity capital to fund the company's development. The initial motivation for going public was the desire of the principal owners to sell some of their stock. By 1965, Ray Kroc (with 52.7 percent of the stock), Harry Sonnenborn (with 15.2 percent), and June Martino (7.7 percent) were already millionaires, but their millions were tied up in stock with no public market. While their salaries had recently become respectable, they were far from extravagant: $115,000 for Kroc, $90,000 for Sonnenborn, and $65,000 for Martino. All three agreed that the time had come to convert some of their wealth in stock into wealth they could spend. Sonnenborn says, "Going public was the only way that Ray, June, and I could cash in on our work."

SOURCE: John Love, *McDonald's: Behind the Arches* (New York: Bantam, 1986), pp. 238–9.

A third possible reason for going public is to create the opportunity to institute a profit-sharing plan for employees. Making employees stockholders motivates them; they begin to think and act as owners. Many famous companies have used this tool. Sears, Roebuck did it back in the 1920s. Wal-Mart and Home Depot are more recent examples. One problem with this profit-sharing technique is that it requires a constantly rising stock price. When the price drops, so can employee morale. This happened to both Wal-Mart and Home Depot in 1996.

Factors that Affect the Firm's Stock Price

Once a company has sold its stock to the general public, the firm's environment changes. The new stockholders bought shares in the company with the expectation that profits would grow and the price of the stock would rise over time. If the stock price fails to rise, the stockholders can become quite unhappy. They will show their displeasure by selling the stock. Large-scale sales of the stock will cause its price to fall. If the situation becomes bad enough, the board of directors may even decide to replace the existing management team with a new group of executives. Worse yet, the poor performance of the stock may cause outside groups to attempt a hostile takeover.

top management
p. 65>

Because of the problems that can arise if the stock does not perform adequately, it is important for top management to take preventive measures. "Managing the price of the company's stock" requires a thorough understanding of the forces that influence stock prices, among them earnings, general market conditions, and speculation.

Profit sharing can be an excellent motivational tool because employees are investing in the company by working harder. However, if profits do not continue to move upward, employees can become unhappy. Would you rather work for a company with a profit sharing plan or without one? What else do you need to know in order to decide?

Earnings

The most basic determinant of the price of a company's stock is the company's earnings. In general, stock prices tend to rise or fall with the rise or fall of the company's earnings. Market expectations must also be considered. If earnings rise, but not as much as expected, then the company's stock price may fall. Similarly, if earnings fall, but by less than expected, the stock price may actually rise.

Earnings expectations are influenced by a variety of factors. A few typical examples are rumors of a new product under development, the hiring of a key new manager, the report of a stock market analyst, or a change in the macroeconomic environment such as interest rates or the inflation rate.

Because the price of a company's stock is so sensitive to changes in earnings reports, the top managers of publicly held companies bear a burden they would not have if they were privately held. That burden is the need to try to manage earnings reports so that the price of the stock will neither rise too fast nor rise too slowly (or fall). In the United States, publicly held companies report profits every quarter. This means that managers have to spend time and effort making sure that profit growth is on target every three months.

General Stock Market Conditions

A second factor influencing a company's stock price is the general trend for all stocks. Stock prices tend to go through cycles of increases, called *bull markets,* and decreases, called *bear markets.* Not all stocks follow the trend, but most do. In a bull market, the price of a company's stock may tend to rise faster than earnings increases alone would dictate. In a bear market, the price of the company's stock may actually fall even though earnings continue to increase as expected. There is nothing a company's management can do to influence the general stock market. But fortunately stockholders tend to forgive managers for changes in the company's stock price that appear to be a reflection of the general trend of a bear market.

Speculation

Speculation

A situation where a company's stock is bought or sold on the basis of a belief that its price will soon go up or down.

A third important factor affecting the price of a company's stock is **speculation,** where the stock is bought or sold on the basis of a belief that its price will soon move up or down. This type of investor is called a *speculator.* Speculators have a different investing strategy from most investors, who hold stocks for a significant period of time.

Speculators aim to make a profit by outguessing short-run changes in the market. For example, a group of speculators may suspect that the price of a company's stock will soon fall. They actually borrow a large number of shares, sell those shares at the current price, and plan to buy back the shares after the price falls and return them to the lender. Conversely, if the speculators suspect that a company's stock will soon increase significantly in price, they will buy a large quantity of the stock, wait for the big price increase to occur, and then sell the stock at the higher price.

Speculators add an element of instability to the stock market. An initial speculative sale or purchase can create the belief that the price of the stock will move as they suspect. That can influence many other investors to follow their lead. The result is a self-fulfilling prophecy. That is, the stock price will move as the speculators expected but only because the speculators prompted the followers to make it happen. Once such a movement begins, it can continue until the price of the stock has reached unrealistically high or low levels. Eventually the market will adjust and the stock price will return to a normal level that is justified by earnings.

Developing Your Critical Thinking Skills

1. Many factors affect the price of a company's stock. Will the factors be the same for a discount retailer like Wal-Mart as for a high-tech company like Motorola?

2. Why is it difficult to take small companies public?

3. We noted that initial public offerings are very popular. Why would an investor be interested in placing funds in an IPO rather than in an old, established stock?

SUMMARY

1. It can be argued that the success or failure of a business ultimately depends on its ability to deal with financial markets effectively.

    ■ What are financial markets and what are the major financial institutions that affect business?

    Financial markets are places where businesses that need to acquire capital are brought together with financial institutions that help provide the funds. The major financial institutions that affect business are commercial banks, venture capital firms, insurance and pension fund companies, and investment banking houses.

2. Financial markets affect businesses in many ways. Decisions made by managers are frequently influenced by financial markets.

    ■ What are the major ways financial markets affect a business?

    This chapter discussed six major functions:

    (1) Providing funds to start a business or expand it.
    (2) Underwriting a portion of the cost of operating the business.
    (3) Influencing customer demand for the firm's products.
    (4) Pressuring management to focus on short-term profits.
    (5) Providing opportunities to reduce some operating risks.
    (6) Providing opportunities to supplement earnings by investing the company's surplus cash.

3. Many businesses operate with borrowed money. Consequently, their costs of doing business are influenced by interest rates. Managing those costs of borrowing can be a major management function. In addition, the demand for the company's products is affected directly or indirectly by interest rates. Consequently, managers need to be able to forecast interest rates in order to predict future demand.

    ■ How would you define interest? Interest rate? Real rate of interest?

    Interest is the price a borrower agrees to pay a lender in return for receiving a loan. The interest rate is the amount of interest paid divided by the amount of the loan. This ratio is usually expressed in terms of the amount of interest paid per year as a percentage of the amount of the loan. The real rate of interest is the rate the borrower actually pays minus the inflation rate.

4. One of the key decisions that managers must make is the decision to borrow money and pay the interest that goes along with it. But interest rates go up and down over time. Managers must attempt to forecast changes in interest rates in order to make appropriate borrowing decisions.

    ■ What determines changes in the interest rate over time?

Managers should be familiar with three major reasons for changes in interest rates over time: (1) shifts in demand and supply, (2) inflation, and (3) the federal government's monetary policy.

5.   Many companies are privately held. As companies grow, however, they may realize the benefits of going public. Once a company's stock becomes publicly held, its price becomes an important management issue.

■ What factors determine the price of a stock?

Three basic factors influence the price of a company's stock: (1) the company's earnings, (2) general stock market conditions, and (3) speculation.

Links to future courses

The themes of this chapter affect businesses in a variety of ways. You will explore the topics of this chapter in more depth in the following courses:

- Principles of finance
- Money and banking
- Capital budgeting

- Securities analysis
- Public policy
- Strategic management

KEY TERMS

Collateral, p. 215
Commodity markets, p. 223
Corporate bond, p. 216
Financial markets, p. 215
Foreign exchange markets, p. 223
Going public, p. 231
Initial public offering (IPO), p. 231
Insurance, p. 224

Investment banking house, p. 216
Prime rate, p. 226
Real rate of interest, p. 228
Speculation, p. 235
Stock, p. 216
Takeover, p. 222
Venture capital firm, p. 216
Working capital, p. 220

EXERCISES AND APPLICATIONS

1.   Form teams of five students. Each team is given a hypothetical $100,000 to invest. Choose five stocks to purchase and decide how much of each to buy. Record your decision-making process. Hold your stocks until the end of the semester. Each week, check one of the Internet financial quote services and plot the movement of the stock price. Suggestion: Pick at least one stock that is likely to be highly volatile and one that is considered an established, blue-chip stock.

2.   Remain in teams. Assume that your team is about to start a new restaurant that emphasizes unique vegetarian dishes. Your team is convinced that there is a strong market for your service. You need at least $200,000 to get started in business. Drawing from the individuals on your team, determine how you will secure the needed capital. Write a one-page report of how you will finance the start-up of the restaurant.

3.   From Exercise 2, assume you have been able to secure $100,000 of the needed capital from family and friends. You will need to borrow the additional $100,000 from a commercial bank. Find out what the bank requires to make such a loan (background on the business, collateral, interest rate, and any other relevant information). Will you qualify for this loan?

4. Get a recent copy of *The Wall Street Journal*. On the first page, go to the summary headlines called "What's News." Choose a company of interest. Describe what it is doing and how financial markets are involved.

5. You can buy and sell stock over the Internet. A number of companies such as Charles Schwab & Co., Inc. and Fidelity Investments offer this opportunity. Go to the Schwab home page (http://www.schwab.com) to determine what would be required to buy or sell stocks online. Write your findings in a one-page report.

CASE: WHEN COMPANIES HAVE TOO MUCH CASH

Business profit and cash flow fluctuate in a somewhat unpredictable manner. From time to time, many businesses find themselves with much more cash from earnings than expected. When this happens, top managers suddenly have to decide what to do with the cash.

Such a situation occurred in 1997. The two major causes of the cash buildup were (1) the long, profitable expansion of the American business cycle and (2) the successful restructuring undertaken by many companies.

Just how did U.S. companies cope with the problem of excess cash? To begin with, analysts and managers both agreed that the cash reserves created a problem. As one analyst put it, "Having that much cash is an enormous temptation to waste."

But that's where the agreement stopped. Some companies decided to set the funds aside in safe investments so there would be cash reserves for the next economic downturn. Boeing and the automobile companies did some of this. Managers at Chrysler and General Motors also used some of the funds to finance overseas expansion. Other managers decided to use the cash to acquire other companies. HFS Inc., for example, had $471 million in excess cash, which it used to buy Avis Rent a Car. A fourth approach, used by almost 1,500 companies, was to buy back their own stock. By reducing the amount of stock outstanding, the companies were able to increase the earnings per share of the remaining stock.

Decision Questions

1. From the standpoint of employees, what would be the best use of the excess cash?
2. From the standpoint of stockholders, what would be the best use of the excess cash in the short run? In the long run?
3. What risks are taken by managers that use the excess cash to acquire other companies?
4. What risks are taken by managers that put the excess cash into safe investments like government securities with the idea that they can use those funds when the company runs into financial difficulties in the future?

SOURCE: Andy Reinhardt, Linda Himelstein, and Joseph Weber, "An Enormous Temptation to Waste," *Business Week*, February 10, 1997, pp. 42–3.

REFERENCES

1. Andrew Osterland. "No Kidding. Cisco Isn't Done Yet." *Financial World*, January 21, 1997, pp. 62–6.

2. For a good discussion, see Eugene F. Brigham and Louis C. Gapenski. *Financial Management: Theory and Practice*, 7th ed. Fort Worth: TX: The Dryden Press, 1994, chap. 3.

3. For more information on takeovers, see Arthur A. Thompson Jr. and A. J. Strickland III. *Strategic Management: Concepts and Cases*, 9th ed. Burr Ridge, IL: Irwin, 1996, pp. 192–5.

4. Scott Kilman. "Giant Cargill Resists Pressure to Go Public as it Pursues Growth." *The Wall Street Journal*, January 9, 1997, p. A1.

5. A nice overview is provided by Emmett J. Vaughan in *Risk Management*. New York: John Wiley & Sons, 1997, chap. 10.

6. For a good overview, see "The Structure and Role of the Federal Reserve System." In S. Kerry Cooper and Donald R. Fraser, eds. *The Financial Marketplace*, 4th ed. Reading, MA: Addison-Wesley, 1993.

The Impact of Legal and Regulatory Forces

"On the one hand . . . In March 1989, the Exxon Valdez, an oil supertanker, ran aground in Prince William Sound in Alaska, spilling millions of gallons of oil into the water. Exxon and the oil industry were not prepared to respond to this emergency. The oil eventually contaminated 1,100 miles of shoreline, killing tens of thousands of animals, birds, and fish. The lack of preparedness caused Congress to enact the Oil Pollution Act of 1990. Administered by the Coast Guard, it requires the oil industry to adopt procedures that can more readily respond to oil spills.[1]

On the other hand . . . An employee at Bernhardt Furniture Company in Lenoir, North Carolina, put all the government forms dealing with the disposal of dirty cleaning rags, the company's principal hazardous waste, in a pile and stood beside it for a sardonic photograph. The employee is 6 feet, 2 inches tall, and the stack of forms was slightly taller than he was.[2]

Modern businesses deal with an elaborate system of laws and regulations. Business owners cannot survive without a basic knowledge of these laws and regulations. Therefore, it is important for you to understand the basic legal and regulatory forces that affect business. After reading this chapter, you should be able to:

1. Describe the basic philosophy underlying the legal environment of a capitalistic society.

2. Explain how government regulations actually support business.

3. Explain the various ways government regulates business in the United States, especially the legal and regulatory impacts on the following:

   ■ Monopoly and antitrust issues
   ■ Industrywide regulatory issues
   ■ Employee benefit issues
   ■ Financial and tax issues
   ■ Consumer relations issues
   ■ Environmental issues

4. Discuss the effect of the legal environment on the firm's global competitiveness.

5. Explain the relationship between business ethics and the legal environment of business.

This chapter is divided into five sections. The first helps you understand the basic relationship between government and business. The second explains some of the ways government supports business. The third helps you understand the major ways government regulates business. The fourth points out the relationship between the global environment and government regulation within a country. The last discusses the relationship between the legal environment and business ethics. Together, these elements comprise the legal and regulatory forces that are among the environmental influences on a successful business, as shown in the model in Chapter 1.

To understand the essence of this chapter, consider an analogy between business and a basketball game. The competing business firms are like the competing basketball teams. The CEOs are somewhat like the coaches. The game is played with a number of rules. Many of the rules are well known and cannot be violated, such as the number of minutes in the game, the number of allowable fouls per person, and the dimensions of the court and its markings. Other rules encourage players to act in certain ways even though they do not have to—for example, the three-point line and the opportunity for time-outs. Players do not have to shoot from the three-point arc, but they can earn higher scores if they do. Similarly, the coach does not have to call time-outs but can if desired. Other rules control the flow of the game and the behavior of players. Unwarranted contact between players elicits a foul call from the referee. Taking excessive steps before shooting results in a turnover. However, as long as they operate within the rules, the teams are allowed considerable discretion in how they play the game.

Business operates in much the same environment. Some rules and regulations simply define the nature of business and are freely accepted by all involved. Some regulations penalize businesses for infractions or inappropriate behavior. Other regulations encourage certain types of behavior. For example, tax regulations allow businesses to deduct expenses from their revenues. The managers do not have to deduct the expenses but can reduce their taxes if they do. The government is analogous to the referees. However, you will also learn from this chapter that some of the rules and regulations are designed so businesses can do things without government involvement.

Freedom, Property Rights, Risk Taking, and Responsibilities

Freedom
The power to make one's own decisions or choices without interference from others.

Before we discuss various parts of the legal environment, we will review the basic philosophy of a capitalistic society. Four concepts are important. The first is **freedom,** the power to make one's own decisions or choices without interference from others. Freedom is one of America's most cherished values. The Constitution of the United States and the accompanying Bill of Rights were designed to promote and protect freedom for all individuals and, by extension, for the businesses they choose to operate. Consequently, many of the laws we will be reviewing in this chapter are designed to restrict the actions of the few in order to protect the freedom of the many.

Property rights
The freedom to possess and regulate the use of tangible items (such as land and buildings) and intangible items (such as a copyrighted piece of music or a patented invention).

Second is the concept of **property rights,** the freedom to possess and regulate the use of tangible items (such as land and buildings) and intangible items (such as a copyrighted piece of music or a patented invention). The right to hold and use private property is one of the freedoms protected by the Constitution. Private property is also a key feature of the economic system within which business operates. A major purpose of the American legal environment is the protection of property rights.

Risk taking
The willingness to undertake action without knowing what the result will be.

A third concept is **risk taking,** which means that businesses are willing to undertake actions without knowing for sure what the results will be. Risk taking is necessary for economic growth to take place. Managers are willing to take risks because they are confident that, if their gambles succeed, they will make profits. The legal environment of business has an important role to play in encouraging risk taking through entrepreneurship.

Responsibility
Using one's property (both tangible and intangible) in a manner that does not unduly infringe on the freedom of others.

The fourth concept is responsibility. Along with the property rights of the businessperson is the requirement that the property be used in a socially responsible manner. **Responsibility** means using one's property (both tangible and intangible) in a manner that does not unduly infringe on the freedom of others. Rights and responsibilities go together. Just as the law upholds property rights, it also encourages the property owner to behave responsibly.

Much of this chapter will discuss laws that seem to limit the freedom of business. In a broader sense, however, the law generally encourages managers to behave responsibly so that freedom will be protected in the long run. Furthermore, some laws explicitly expand the freedom of business with the expectation that responsible businesspeople will use that freedom to better serve their customers and other stakeholders.

Government Support of Business

We begin with a discussion of five legal situations that encourage business investment and risk taking. These regulations actually benefit businesses by encouraging them to take risks associated with operating a business. They are shown in Table 9–1.

Supporting Business by Limiting Ownership Liability

Chapter 2 discussed four ways to form companies: the sole proprietorship, the partnership, the limited liability company, and the corporation. Two of these, the limited liability company and the corporation, have as their most salient characteristic limited liability for the owners. You may recall from that discussion that creditors of sole proprietorships and partnerships can seize both business and personal assets of the owners if necessary. However, the LLC and the corporation do not have that risk; the owners can lose only as much as they have invested in the company. This encour-

TABLE 9–1 Ways Government Supports Business

1. Limiting ownership liability
2. Limiting losses through the use of bankruptcy laws
3. Protecting innovation through copyrights, trademarks, and patents
4. Providing structure through establishment and enforcement of rules and industry standards
5. Encouraging competition by limiting monopoly power

ages owners of high-growth or riskier businesses to invest in the business without fearing the loss of their personal assets. Recall, too, that LLCs provide this limited liability protection while allowing the owners to report the business taxes on their own tax forms.

Assisting Business with Bankruptcy Laws

Bankruptcy
A situation where a firm does not have the money to pay its debts.

One of the risks of doing business is the possibility of going bankrupt. In **bankruptcy,** the firm does not have the money to pay its debts. Bankruptcy laws give business owners a second chance to succeed.

There are two major types of bankruptcy provisions. A Chapter 7 bankruptcy (called that because its rules are set out in Chapter 7 of the bankruptcy regulations) frees the owner of a failed business from liability for all debts beyond those that can be paid out of the sale of the firm's assets. The debtor's property is given to a bankruptcy trustee, who sells it and divides the proceeds among the creditors. The debtor is allowed to keep a personal residence, car, personal and household items, and tools of the trade. That makes it possible for the bankrupt debtor to start over in business.

In a Chapter 11 bankruptcy, the business asks the courts for protection against creditors while it attempts to pay off its debts. The business is not forced to cease operations. It continues in hopes of turning the situation around. This approach is possible if the business has a long-term prospect of being able to pay its obligations, even though it cannot do so in the short run. A repayment plan must be approved by the court and the creditors. Some companies emerge from Chapter 11 bankruptcy and eventually become competitive and successful again. Revco Drug Stores is one example. Burdened by enormous debt, Revco filed for Chapter 11 in 1988. The business had to make some tough reorganization decisions. Some of its major creditors even became members of the board of directors. Today Revco is again a major player in the commercial drug industry.[3]

Board of directors
p. 64>

Encouraging Risk Taking with Copyrights, Trademarks, and Patents

We began this chapter by pointing out that risk taking is a major function of the successful business. We also said government reduces risks by providing for organizational forms that limit liability. Copyrights, trademarks, and patents are another method that government uses to encourage risk taking.

Bankruptcy laws assist businesses by allowing them relief from creditors. There are two major types of bankruptcy: Chapter 7 and Chapter 11. What is the primary difference between the two? Which is likely in this photo?

Copyright
The exclusive legal right to the use of intellectual property such as books, photographs, music, or cartoons.

Trademark
The exclusive legal right to the use of a name, symbol, or design.

Patent
A government-protected legal monopoly on a product or product design.

A **copyright** gives the holder the exclusive right to the use of intellectual property such as books, photographs, music, or cartoons. This encourages individuals or companies to produce products without the fear that someone else will duplicate them. A copyright lasts for the life of the author plus 50 years. If the author is a corporation, the copyright lasts for 75 years from the date of publication.

A **trademark** gives exclusive right to the use of a name, symbol, or design. Companies make extensive use of trademarks to identify their goods and services. The logos we have used for our focal examples are examples of trademarks, and we use them with the permission of the companies. Trademarks are good for 10 years and may be renewed for an indefinite number of 10-year periods.

A **patent** is a government-protected legal monopoly on a product or product design. Knowing that their products are protected for an extended period of time and other companies cannot produce identical or virtually identical products encourages firms to engage in research and development. For example, G. D. Searle spent a lot of money developing aspartame, commercially known as NutraSweet. Searle maintained the exclusive right to produce the product for the life of the patent. Beginning in 1995, patents are now valid for 20 years.

Two of our profiled examples, Motorola and the bicycle industry, compete in part with new products and technologies. The existence of patent protection has undoubtedly led them to invest in more R&D than might otherwise have been the case. Patent protection is one of four factors used in determining where and how Motorola invests in technology. The other three are profit potential, development costs, and strategic fit. Even if a proposed product has profit potential and fits with Motorola's plan, the company may question the wisdom of investing if it cannot be convinced of patent potential.[4] Motorola received over 1,000 patents in 1995.

All of our profiled examples use trademarks. All of them have invested heavily in establishing a reputation that customers know and trust. It is important to them that no competitor be able to sell competing products or open a competing airline or run a competing restaurant that uses the same name. This may seem like a trivial point since you probably never see that type of competition. But that is because trademark protection makes it illegal to use a business name or logo that is the same or essentially the same as that of another firm. From time to time you may read about an unknown firm that has been illegally using the name of a well-known trademarked firm. Some firms are absolutely relentless in searching out and stopping such activities. Even when a company accidentally uses a logo or name that is similar to another firm's, it may receive a *cease and desist letter* threatening legal action if the activity is not stopped immediately. Profile 9–1 illustrates the case of Columbia Sportswear, a producer of outdoor wear.

PROFILE 9–1   *Columbia Sportswear and the Copycat Parkas*

Columbia Sportswear of Portland, Oregon, has made clothes for hunting and fishing for decades. In 1986 it introduced its Bugaboo Parka, which became an immediate success. The parka features removable and reversible lining and insulation, making it three or four jackets in one. Columbia sold its one millionth

STAY AS WARM AND DRY AS HER POT ROAST.

The one time you'll enjoy being treated like a piece of meat. Because that's the purpose of Columbia's Spitfire Parka. To make sure you end up like one of Chairman Gert Boyle's pot roasts: comfortably warm and dry as a bone. But on you, these conditions result from the use of superior materials rather than over-cooking. A lining of nylon tafetta quilted to Slimtech keeps the warm in, while a Bergundtal Cloth outer shell keeps the wet out. And fortunately, warm and dry is more appetizing on you than on a three pound slab of beef.

For the dealer nearest you call 1-800-MA BOYLE. www.columbia.com

Columbia
Sportswear Company.

Patents and trademarks help protect products from being copied. Some companies, such as McDonald's, Caterpillar, and Columbia Sportswear, fiercely protect their trademarks and products. Why would a company spend thousands of dollars to fight a copycat product?

Bugaboo Parka in 1992, and the parka makes up a considerable percentage of its total sales.

With success come copycats. While the company's products are protected by registered trademarks, many copycat manufacturers routinely ignore the law, hoping that the original manufacturers won't notice or care enough to search them out and prosecute.

But protection of product designs and names is critical to Columbia. Tim Boyle, Columbia's president, says he spends up to an hour a day addressing knock-off disputes. The company's employees monitor the marketplace closely for copycat parkas and notify Boyle immediately if they find any. In one case, an astute employee noted a copycat parka in a Sears catalog. Boyle immediately called Sears and learned that the goods were still en route from a Taiwanese factory. He got Sears to cancel the order while the ship was still at sea. Boyle will without hesitation bring suit against either a manufacturer or a distributor of copycat parkas. Columbia is letting the industry know that it is one company that will not tolerate competitors trying to overcome its competitive advantage.

SOURCE: Michael Selz, "Columbia Sportswear Tackles Tidal Wave of Copycats," *The Wall Street Journal*, May 24, 1993, p. B2.

Encouraging Business with Rules and Industry Standards

Industry standards can promote business investment by encouraging product standards, process standards, or other rules of competition for a given industry. In Chapter 6, we discussed Bill Gates's involvement in the development of standards for HDTV broadcasting. In this case, industry and government are working together to develop a standard that is acceptable to both the television and the computer industries.

Working relationships between government and industry are not new. Safety standards for many consumer products are a result of cooperation between the relevant industry groups and the *Consumer Product Safety Commission*. These standards are designed to protect consumers and also to give manufacturers opportunities to develop new products that are safe as well as competitive.

It might appear that establishing and enforcing rules and industry standards would not be conducive to business operations, but this may actually be one of the greatest services that government provides. The establishment of clear sets of rules and guidelines, coupled with their fair enforcement, provides a structure much as the rules regarding fouls and substitutions provide structure for a basketball game. When managers know what the rules are and how they will be enforced, they are more likely to continue investing in a given industry. For example, we discussed free trade areas in Chapter 7. The development of rules like NAFTA that govern movement of goods across borders lets businesses know exactly how imports and exports will be handled. It also encourages American businesses to increase production of products for export to Canada and Mexico.

There is, however, a danger with rules. Sometimes they are written in a way that helps some companies in an industry more than others; they may even harm certain companies. You may recall from our earlier discussion that a business can improve its competitive position by encouraging government to write the rules in its favor. Sometimes this puts potential new competitors at a disadvantage.

innovation p. 522>

Southwest Airlines' struggle to get started illustrates both how a set of rules can help a business and also how established firms may use the rules to suppress innovation. As soon as Southwest received its charter from the Texas Air Commission, one of its competitors, Continental Airlines, went to court and obtained a temporary order forbidding Southwest to fly until a trial had been held to determine whether or not a charter should have been granted. The trial took place in the district court in Austin, Texas, and three established airlines—Braniff, Texas International, and Continental—argued that Southwest should be denied the right to fly. Southwest was represented by its cofounder and company attorney, Herb Kelleher. The trial court ruled that there was not enough traffic to support more than the existing carriers, so it denied Southwest permission to fly. Southwest appealed to the appellate court, where it lost. It appealed again to the Texas Supreme Court, and this time Kelleher won. But the established airlines then appealed to the U.S. Supreme Court. That court refused to consider the appeal, leaving Southwest Airlines the winner, with full rights to fly passengers among the three Texas cities.[5]

When Southwest entered the airline business, Kelleher knew the rules of the game well enough to anticipate the possibility of legal opposition by the established carriers. However, he also knew the rules well enough to know he would get several opportunities to present his case in court. He had enough faith in the basic fairness of the process that he expected to win because the economic facts were on his side.

Encouraging Business by Protecting Competition

In the next section, we will discuss how government regulates the behavior of businesses. One important aspect of regulation is the regulation of monopolies. We will see that in some cases monopoly power hinders consumers, while in others monopoly power harms competition among businesses. This can involve a single firm gaining too large a share of the market. Or it may involve several firms trying to eliminate or at least cripple a potential rival. Southwest Airlines faced just such a situation. Even after it won the suit allowing it to fly, other airlines kept up the pressure. Braniff and Texas International Airlines wanted Southwest's underwriters to back out of their agreement to manage Southwest's first public stock offering. Southwest found another underwriter. Next Braniff and TIA obtained a court order to keep Southwest from scheduling flights opposite theirs. Kelleher appealed to a higher court and won. The competitors then attempted to keep Southwest from participating in the airline credit card system, pressured suppliers to refuse to sell to it, and kept it from using the fuel hydrant in Houston. Eventually the other airlines were indicted by the U.S. government for conspiring to put Southwest out of business, and they were fined $100,000.[6]

stock p. 216>

In the Southwest Airlines case, the federal government held that Braniff and Texas International Airlines had conspired to restrict competition. The government used the antitrust laws to punish the rivals. A private firm can use the same laws. Consider Aspen Highlands Skiing Co., one of two that operated skiing facilities in Aspen, Colorado. It had one facility, while its rival had three. For years the two companies cooperated by selling six-day skiing tickets that allowed skiers to use any of the four skiing facilities. The two companies divided the sales revenue on the basis of the actual usage of each company's facilities. But then the larger company tried to force Aspen Highlands to accept a smaller share of the ticket proceeds. When Aspen Highlands refused, the larger company stopped selling the joint tickets. That put Aspen Highlands at risk of going out of business, since most skiers would choose the ticket that gave them access to three slopes. Aspen Highlands filed suit under the antitrust laws—and won.[7]

Developing Your Critical Thinking Skills

1. Many people don't think the government does much good. How would you respond to someone who is critical of the government's role?

2. Government rules and regulations help business because they provide stability and limit business because they impose restrictions. Which is more important?

3. Copyrights owned by businesses last for 75 years. Patents are good for 20 years. Is this too long? Why do you think the government set such long limits?

Government Regulation of Business

Up to this point you have been learning about the ways government and the law make it easier for firms to do business. It is important for managers to recognize this valuable function of government. In practice, however, businesses are more likely to be aware of the ways government and its laws regulate what businesses can do. Let's take a look at some of those regulations.

Regulation of Monopoly

One of the social problems created by some large corporations is monopoly power. All countries show some concern for this problem, but no country has attacked it more enthusiastically than the United States. Table 9–2 presents an overview of some of the key laws in this area.

The most significant monopoly-related regulations deal with *antitrust* issues. The first major American antitrust law was created by the 1890 Sherman Antitrust Act and expanded by the Clayton Act in 1914. These laws are enforced by the U.S. Department of Justice and the *Federal Trade Commission (FTC)*. There have been various changes to the antitrust law over the years, but the basic principles and enforcement agencies have remained the same. Although there are several ways that companies may be affected, two types of fairly common business behavior might run afoul of the antitrust laws—price fixing and mergers and acquisitions.

Many businesses periodically become frustrated by the stiff price competition of their rivals. On occasion, those frustrated businesses consider **price fixing,** which occurs when rival firms agree to charge the same price for their competing products. Their argument is that they all make more money if all competitors agree to raise their prices. Fixing prices, however, hurts customers because they no longer have a choice among variously priced products.

A recent dramatic example of price fixing involved Archer Daniels Midland (ADM), one of the world's leading processors of oilseed and corn. In June 1995, the company announced that it was being investigated for engaging in price fixing in three of its product lines. Various reports that followed indicated that ADM had encoun-

Price fixing
A situation where rival firms agree to charge the same price for their competing products.

TABLE 9–2   Key Laws Regulating Monopolies

Interstate Commerce Act (1887)

- Established Interstate Commerce Commission
- Outlawed price fixing and discrimination practices in the railroad industry

Sherman Antitrust Act (1890)

- The first federal antitrust act (in fact, the term *antitrust* comes from this act)
- Aimed at preventing big businesses from combining, concentrating their power, and blocking the competitiveness of smaller businesses
- Because of vague language and problems with enforcement, the act was not very effective

Clayton Act (1914)

- Prohibits specific actions that hurt competition
- Established remedies, such as injunctions, to stop actions that harm competition
- Allows for remedies, such as suits and damages, for violation of the act

Federal Trade Commission Act (1914)

- Established an independent agency, the Federal Trade Commission (FTC), to enforce antitrust laws

Robinson-Patman Act (1936)

- Strengthened the Clayton Act by prohibiting price discrimination
- Prohibits predatory pricing, specific pricing practices designed to restrict or exclude competition

Wheeler-Lea Amendment (1938)

- Made "unfair or deceptive acts or practices," such as deceptive advertising, unlawful

Cellers-Kefauver Act (1950)

- Prohibits mergers that hurt competition

tered sharp price competition from an oligopolistic rival and had attempted to convince that rival that it was in the best interests of all competitors to agree to refrain from price competition. In October 1996, ADM pled guilty to charges of price fixing in two product areas, citric acid and an animal feed supplement called lysine, and agreed to pay $100 million in penalties for violating the law. That was the largest price-fixing fine ever won by the U.S. Department of Justice.[8]

Although price fixing is illegal, it does still happen occasionally. The government periodically uncovers examples and puts a stop to them. But it is likely that many other cases go undetected. Price fixing is not only a legal matter but an ethical issue. Ethical business managers refuse to participate in price-fixing schemes on both legal and moral grounds.

Another area in which the government antitrust agencies affect businesses is mergers and acquisitions (M&A). A **merger** occurs when two firms join together to

Merger
The joining together of two firms to become a single firm.

Acquisition
The purchase of one firm by another firm.

become a single firm. An **acquisition** occurs when one firm buys a second firm. A merger or acquisition sometimes occurs between two firms that compete with one another. While mergers and acquisitions are ways for a business to expand, they can also be the source of increasing monopoly power. Since antitrust law is designed to prevent monopolization, it is illegal to engage in a merger if the result significantly restricts competition.

Consequently, before a business undertakes a merger or acquisition, its management should seek a legal opinion regarding whether or not the intended action is likely to be challenged by the antitrust authorities. In 1997, Staples attempted to acquire Office Depot. These are the number one and number two providers of office supplies and furniture. The companies agreed on a price of $4 billion. The deal was challenged, however, because of the impact it would have had on the rest of the industry, notably Office Max, the number three company.[9]

Industrywide Regulation and Deregulation

Industrywide regulation
A situation where a local, state, or federal government controls the entry of firms into an industry, the prices they charge, how they operate, and even their exit from the industry.

Industrywide regulation refers to a situation where a local, state, or federal government controls entry of firms into an industry, the prices they charge, how they operate, and even their exit from the industry.[10] In the United States, this form of legal restriction has historically been found in such industries as electrical and gas utilities, telephone service, banking, railroads, trucking, and the airline industry. This kind of regulation began in 1887 when the federal government created the Interstate Commerce Commission to regulate the railroads.

American experience with regulation has produced mixed results. It can be argued that the regulators prevented potential abuses of monopoly power, which some of the regulated firms would have naturally enjoyed. It can also be argued that in some industries, such as trucking, there would not be monopoly power even without regulation. Furthermore, even in those cases where economies of scale or other factors justified monopoly, it often seemed that regulation encouraged inefficient practices by the firms' managers.

Because of these inefficiencies, the U. S. government began a process of deregulation in the late 1970s. Deregulation usually occurred in situations where it was possible to introduce genuine competition. The relatively recent deregulation of the financial services industry affects not only business activities but the services that individuals receive from local financial institutions. Profile 9–2 explains this further.

PROFILE **9–2**   *Deregulation of the Financial Services Industry*

●..........

interest p. 225>

financial markets p. 215>

During the Great Depression of the 1930s, there were so many bank failures that both the federal and state governments passed laws that strictly regulated banks and savings and loan institutions. Those laws dramatically reduced the risk of bank failures and added an element of security and safety to the banking system. However, the regulations also reduced competition. The resulting inefficiency led to interest rates that were generally higher than they should have been.

In 1980 and 1982, Congress passed two banking acts that largely took controls off interest rates in American financial markets. State governments followed, and banking became a very competitive business. American banks tend to give their customers excellent service, and interest rates tend to be as low as is economically possible, though fees for services have risen substantially since deregulation. The separation between banks, savings institutions, and investment brokers has become increasingly blurred. Despite the deregulation, however, federal regulations still greatly reduce the risks of depositors losing money they have placed with a bank. This is done through both regular audits of federally chartered banks and a government-sponsored program of deposit insurance.

In some industries, the expected competition failed to appear or was short-lived, and the possibility of reregulation arose. The airline industry remains deregulated but is now subject to periodic calls for reregulation. In the local cable TV industry, reregulation did occur. Profile 9–3 summarizes that story.

PROFILE 9–3   *Deregulation and Reregulation of Cable TV*

Prior to 1986, local cable television companies were treated as natural monopolies. They received franchises (permission to operate) from the city government, and the city typically regulated the prices they charged customers.

At the height of the American deregulation movement, lobbyists for the cable industry convinced Congress that competition from over-the-air broadcasters would prevent them from price gouging. Congress passed a law forbidding price regulation of local cable companies.

The lobbyists turned out to be wrong. Cable subscription prices rose sharply, generating a consumer backlash. The pressure was on Congress to restore regulation. Before Congress could respond, the *Federal Communications Commission* took matters into its own hands. In 1991, the FCC reinstated local price regulations. It was not a total victory for consumers because the FTC did allow a number of exceptions. For example, cable systems that competed with six or more over-the-air TV stations were exempt from regulation. In retrospect, it appears that by taking undue advantage of their freedom after 1986, many cable companies brought reregulation on themselves.

SOURCE: Douglas Greer, *Business, Government and Society*, 3rd ed. (New York: Macmillan, 1993), pp. 356–7.

Regulation of Employee Relations

Over the decades, the American government has developed an extensive array of laws and regulations that affect companies' relations with their employees. These fall into three broad categories: discrimination, working conditions and compensation, and unionization.

Employment Discrimination

Some laws are designed to prevent employment discrimination. Perhaps best known of these is Title VII of the 1964 Civil Rights Act, which prohibits employment

The Civil Rights Act of 1964 prohibits discrimination based on race, color, sex, religion, or national origin. Affirmative action programs encourage the hiring of minorities and women. Are affirmative action programs still needed today? What will be the effect if affirmative action programs are eliminated?

discrimination based on race, color, religion, sex, or national origin. This law is designed to keep businesses from discriminating in hiring, pay, promotion, or termination procedures. Later equal employment opportunity regulations and affirmative action programs were designed to further discourage discrimination and propose remedies for past injustices. The Americans with Disabilities Act of 1990 deals with employment discrimination against workers who are disabled. Table 9–3 gives an overview of some of the important laws that address discrimination in employee relations.

The purpose of affirmative action programs is to create a level playing field for all individuals regardless of race and gender. However, in recent years, these programs have come under fire because they give preference to women and minorities in hiring decisions. Some states are moving to either remove or reduce the impact of affirmative action programs on businesses. This issue will likely be a topic of consideration for courts and legislatures for a number of years.

benefits p. 433>

Another important issue facing businesses today is sexual harassment. Although it is not specifically covered in Title VII, the courts have since ruled that sexual harassment constitutes a form of sex discrimination that violates Title VII. The most explicit sexual harassment occurs when hiring, promotion, or benefits are contingent upon sexual favors. But sexual harassment also encompasses the presence of a *hostile work environment*. This includes unwelcome comments, conduct, and behaviors that are seen as offensive. As employers are increasingly held accountable for the actions of their employees, they give a lot of attention to creating a harassment-free culture.[11]

Working Conditions and Compensation

Several laws are designed to deal with working conditions and compensation. Table 9–4 gives a brief review of some of the more important laws in this area. Perhaps the

TABLE 9–3   Laws Dealing with Employment Discrimination

Title VII, Civil Rights Act (1964)

■ Prohibits employment discrimination based on race, color, religion, sex, or national origin

■ Covers hiring and firing, compensation, and other benefits or privileges

■ Established the Equal Employment Opportunity Commission (EEOC) to enforce the act

Executive Order 11246 (amended by Executive Order 11375) (1965)

■ Established affirmative action programs to ensure equal employment opportunity

Equal Pay Act (1963)

■ Prohibits a business from using sex alone as a basis for discriminating in pay

Age Discrimination in Employment Act (1967)

■ Prohibits age discrimination against workers over 40

Equal Employment Opportunity Act (1972)

■ Strengthens the power of the EEOC

Americans with Disabilities Act (1990)

■ Prohibits a business from discriminating against an otherwise qualified employee simply on the basis of a mental or physical disability

best-known law in this area is the federal Occupational Safety and Health Act, passed in 1970 to reduce job-related accidents, injuries, and health problems by requiring all employers to institute preventive measures. The act created the *Occupational Health and Safety Administration (OSHA)* to be the watchdog over workplace safety issues.

BRINKER
INTERNATIONAL.

A series of laws attempts to protect the financial security of workers. Perhaps best known is the Fair Labor Standards Act, which, among other things, established that employers must pay their workers a minimum wage and pay higher wages for overtime work. Think of how important the Fair Labor Standards Act is and how it affects organizations. For example, look at Brinker International. In 1996, Congress passed a 20 percent increase in the minimum wage, from $4.25 to $5.15 an hour. Businesses like Brinker employ thousands of minimum-wage employees. Accordingly, a 20 percent increase has a widespread impact on their expenses. They must either suffer lower profits, use fewer workers, or raise prices.

unemployment p. 161>

In addition to these regulations, the federal and state governments require businesses to share responsibility for dealing with certain potential social problems such as injuries on the job, unemployment, medical care, and retirement. They require firms to make payments into funds that are used to help injured and unemployed workers, to provide for medical care, and to make monthly payments to retired workers and/or their dependents. From the standpoint of the business, those payments are part of the cost of employing each worker. These employment costs can be significant. Table 9–5 gives an example that drives home this point.

TABLE 9–4   Laws Dealing with Working Conditions and Compensation

Fair Labor Standards Act (1938)

■ Established minimum wage

■ Guarantees employees overtime pay if they work more than 40 hours a week

Occupational Safety and Health Act (1970)

■ Designed to ensure safe and healthful working conditions

■ Created the Occupational Safety and Health Administration to conduct workplace inspections and protect workers against safety and health hazards

Employee Retirement Income Security Act (ERISA) (1974)

■ Established standards for business retirement, pension, and other employee benefit plans

Family and Medical Leave Act (1993)

■ Requires businesses with 50 or more employees to give unpaid leave for family and medical emergencies

■ Business must offer up to 12 weeks of unpaid leave after childbirth or adoption

■ Business must continue health care coverage during the leave

TABLE 9–5   An Illustration of Mandated Employment Costs

A company going into business in the United States must pay the following government-imposed costs associated with its employees. (The first four items are subject to upper limits not shown here.)

1. 6.2% of wages for Social Security

2. 1.45% of wages for Medicare

3. Between 0.8 and 6.2% of wages for the federal unemployment insurance system

4. Between 2 and 4% of wages for state unemployment insurance programs (some states)

5. Between 0.5 and 1.5% of wages for workers' compensation programs (some states).

SOURCE: Greg Straughn and Charles Chickadel, *Building a Profitable Business* (Holbrook, MA: Bob Adams, 1994), chapter 19, p. 13.

Unionization

In addition to the laws already listed, other important laws allow employees the right to join unions and bargain with employers. Some of the key laws in this area are covered in Table 9–6.

Employees usually join a union for one of three reasons. First, they may be dissatisfied with some aspect of their jobs, such as wages, benefits, or working conditions. Second, they may fear management. They feel the union gives them greater security and protection from arbitrary management actions. Finally, a union often represents employees who feel relatively powerless to deal with problems with the

TABLE 9–6   Laws Dealing with Employees' Rights to Unionize

National Labor Relations Act (Wagner Act) (1935)

- Established the legal right of employees to join unions
- Requires businesses to bargain collectively with unions representing their employees
- Established the National Labor Relations Board (NLRB) to enforce the act
- Prohibits unfair labor practices by employers

Labor-Management Relations Act (Taft-Hartley Act) (1947)

- Prohibits unfair labor practices by unions
- Lists the rights employees have as union members
- Lists the rights of employers
- Gives the president of the United States the right to temporarily stop a strike that will harm the national interest

Labor-Management Reporting and Disclosure Act (Landrum-Griffin Act) (1959)

- Protects union members from abusive activities by their union

employer on their own. They hope the power and clout of the union will get management's attention.

Collective bargaining
The process through which company and union representatives work together to negotiate a labor agreement.

The law gives employees the right to form unions and to engage in **collective bargaining,** the process through which company and union representatives work together to negotiate a labor agreement. That agreement or contract covers many things, including terms of employment, how relationships between employees and the company will take place, and how grievances will be handled. The union represents employees in collective bargaining in exchange for dues the workers pay into the union fund.

Sometimes you will hear of a company and union engaged in collective bargaining but unable to reach an agreement. The collective bargaining process can break down, and unions can go on strike. This right to strike is protected by law. Although strikes get a lot of media attention when they occur, the vast majority of contract negotiations, over 95 percent, reach a settlement without a strike.

Labor–management relations are overseen by the *National Labor Relations Board (NLRB)* which was authorized by the National Labor Relations Act. The NLRB employs a staff of experts who investigate cases where either a union or a company believes the other party has violated the contract. In most cases, it is the union that files an unfair labor practice case with the NLRB on behalf of a represented employee or group of employees. The NLRB also certifies elections conducted by employees who want to form a union for the first time.[12]

Financial Regulation and Taxes

When an American business attempts to raise financial resources, it runs into a variety of laws and regulations. Some make the process of acquiring capital easier or safer; others make it slower and more expensive.

One set of regulations deals with raising capital by issuing stock or bonds. Before a business can offer stocks or bonds for sale, it must satisfy the legal requirements of federal and state security laws. Another set of regulations deals with financial reporting. American businesses are required to report information so that investors in a firm's stocks and bonds can make informed decisions whether to sell or hold the securities. These reporting requirements and provisions are covered by the Securities Act and the Securities Exchange Act. The Securities Exchange Act established the *Securities and Exchange Commission (SEC)*, which oversees the trading of securities. Preparing such reports takes time, but they can be an important factor in potential investors' decisions to provide a business with capital funds.

When American companies enter the global market, operations become far more complex. Laws are different in other countries, so it is difficult to deal with laws and customs in other countries without running afoul of U.S. regulations. A law that was passed to give structure to international business is the Foreign Corrupt Practices Act of 1977, which (among other things) prohibits the payment of bribes to foreign officials in order to get business.

Another important set of regulations deals with the *taxes* that a business must pay. The federal, state, and local governments impose a variety of taxes on business. Minimizing those tax payments is a significant part of business decision making. There are a number of ways to legally reduce the amount of taxes a business must pay. The details are spelled out in the tax law.

Regulation of Consumer Relations

If consumers were all-knowing and all businesses were totally committed to providing information, there would be little need for consumer legislation. Experience shows, however, that consumers do not always have adequate knowledge. Thus, there are situations where legal protection may be justified. Some laws help assure that consumers receive needed information about the products they buy. Others help assure product safety. Still others guard against businesses using deceptive or unfair practices.

As you can see, these laws really address the responsibilities that a business should logically have toward its customers, as discussed in Chapter 4. These topics are governed by state and federal legislation and enforced by agencies within the executive branch of the appropriate governments. With respect to federal laws, the Federal Trade Commission and the Consumer Product Safety Commission are the two most prominent agencies. Table 9–7 contains a partial list of some key laws. Notice that in this area the government's role seems to be to force businesses to tell the truth, the whole truth, and nothing but the whole truth.

Tort
A behavior, either intentional or negligent, that harms another person.

Another area of consumer protection, tort law, is governed by the state and federal court system. A **tort** is either intentional or negligent behavior that harms another person. Tort law makes businesses potentially liable for wrongfully harming a consumer. Under this law, an unhappy customer can sue the seller, and the settlements can be quite large. For example, in May 1996, a California jury decided that Charles Givens, Jr., had defrauded his customers and fined him $14.1 million. Givens had earned a fortune by selling seminars and books that claimed to show customers how they could get rich quickly. One of his customers, after spending over $3,000 on his seminars and materials, believed he had misled her. She sued him, others who also felt defrauded joined the suit, and the jury decided that Givens was indeed guilty.[13]

TABLE 9–7   Highlights of Consumer Protection Laws

Food, Drug and Cosmetics Act (1938) plus amendments

■ Charges the Food and Drug Administration to set and enforce standards for safety, purity, production cleanliness, efficacy, and labeling of drugs, cosmetics, and food products

National Traffic and Motor Vehicle Safety Act (1966) and related acts

■ Gives the National Highway Traffic Safety Administration authority to set and enforce standards for motor vehicle safety and fuel economy

Fair Packaging and Labeling Act (1966)

■ Requires the manufacturer to clearly state the contents of a package in a prominent place and use a unit of measurement appropriate to the product

Truth-in-Lending Act (part of the Consumer Credit Protection Act) (1968)

■ Applies to consumer credit loans; requires the lender to disclose the amount of the finance charge and the annual percentage rate of interest

Consumer Product Safety Act (1972)

■ Gives the Consumer Product Safety Commission authority to set consumer product safety standards, ban hazardous consumer products, and require manufacturers to report defects and dangers in their products

Consumer protection is also provided by the agencies regulating specific industries. In the airline industry, for example, safety is regulated by the Federal Aviation Administration (FAA). The Federal Communications Commission (FCC) regulates the communications industry. The Nuclear Regulatory Commission (NRC) regulates power plants. Transportation is regulated by the Interstate Commerce Commission (ICC).

Regulation of Environmental Issues

By the 1960s, many parts of the United States suffered from air and water pollution. The problem became so serious that the government stepped in with regulations that reduced the pollution and raised the quality of the nation's air and water. Once the public became aware of government's ability to protect the environment, other environmental issues arose. Among those of greatest concern to business are the issues of solid waste disposal and protecting endangered species. Some of the legislation designed to address environmental problems is shown in Table 9–8.

Three areas of environmental regulation—air pollution, water pollution, and toxic substances—affect substantial numbers of businesses. Federal regulation of air pollution began with the Clean Air Act of 1963, which set broad goals for cleanliness. Regulation was substantially toughened by the Clean Air Amendments of 1970. That was the year the federal *Environmental Protection Agency (EPA)* was created to enforce

The government requires producers of food products to put labels on their products which list the ingredients as well as the amount of fat, sodium, cholesterol, and sugars. Why is this important to consumers? Should it be required?

the nation's environmental laws. Water pollution regulation received its first significant federal support with the Water Pollution Control Act of 1972, followed by the Safe Drinking Water Act of 1986. Elimination of unregulated disposal of toxic substances was the target of the Toxic Substances Control Act of 1976. All of these federal laws required businesses to incur the costs of reducing or eliminating the emission of contaminants into the air, water, or land.

City, County, and State Regulations

So far in this chapter, we have discussed federal regulations—regulations either passed by the U.S. Congress or promulgated by the executive branch of the federal government. These regulations generally affect all businesses similarly, regardless of where they are located. However, local and state regulations also affect companies. State regulations may be so severe that the company's managers consider moving to a more *business-friendly* state. We consider here just a few types of local and state regulations that may have an impact on businesses.

Zoning

Zoning laws are normally the purview of city and county governments. These laws are legal restrictions regarding where the business or one of its units can be located. Cities and towns typically reserve many locations for private homes or other nonbusiness uses. They often designate certain areas as high-density residential, light commercial, shopping centers, or manufacturing, among others. The logic is compelling. A business of a significant size operating in a residential neighborhood can damage the physical and psychological appeal of the neighborhood. Even small businesses operating

TABLE 9−8   Highlights of Environmental Laws

National Environmental Policy Act (1970)

- Requires that an environmental impact statement be prepared for business actions that could affect the environment

Clean Air Acts (1963 and 1970)

- Provides broad standards of air quality

Resource Conservation and Recovery Act (1976) and Toxic Substances Control Act (1976)

- Regulates handling and disposal of hazardous waste

Water Pollution Control Act (Clean Water Act) (1972 amended 1977)

- Establishes goals and timetables to eliminate water pollution

Comprehensive Environmental Response, Compensation, and Liability Act (CERCLA) (1980)

- Creates superfund for environmental cleanup of hazardous waste

Safe Water Drinking Act (1986)

- Regulates quality of drinking water

out of a home have the potential to upset the neighbors. Consequently, the typical American city sets aside specific geographic areas where businesses can operate and others where they are barred. Zoning laws provide a sense of order in a community, but they do limit how a business can operate. Although zoning codes can sometimes be appealed, there is no assurance that the appeal will be successful.

City Taxes

Many cities require taxes of one form or another in addition to those collected by state and federal agencies. This may cause an extra burden on some businesses. For example, a city may levy a 2 percent sales tax on restaurants and hotels in order to underwrite the building of a civic center complex. The logic is that hotels and restaurants benefit from the crowds that events at the civic center attract. However, this may encourage businesses to locate just outside city limits in order to escape the tax.

Although cities often make rules or establish taxes that discourage businesses, sometimes the opposite occurs. A large business considering moving into a city may be able to negotiate favorable concessions from the city government. This is especially true if the business intends to hire thousands of the city's residents. In fact, large companies considering building a new manufacturing plant often communicate their intentions to a number of cities. The cities (and sometimes even states) then compete to develop a favorable package, which may include tax relief, the construction of *infrastructure*—roads, sewer lines, and utilities—at no charge, and low-interest loans with favorable payback terms.

FIGURE 9–1   States with Right-to-Work Laws

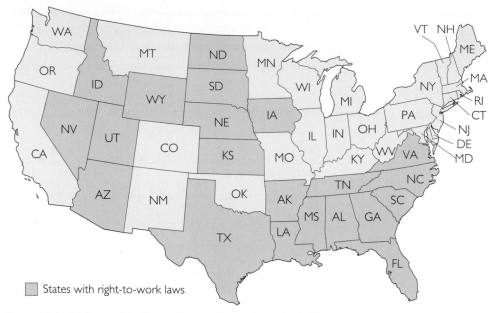

☐ States with right-to-work laws

SOURCE: John M. Ivancevich, *Human Resource Management*, 6th ed. Chicago: Irwin, 1995, p. 562.

Other Regulations

There are many other restrictions that can affect businesses at the local level. Businesses may have to meet stringent health codes when they build and then be subject to periodic inspections. If they fail to pass health inspections, they risk being shut down. Certain types of businesses are often restricted. "Adult" bookstores, nightclubs, racetracks, and other businesses that a city's government disapproves of are often banned.

A state regulation that affects many businesses has to do with unions. We said earlier that laws allow individual employees to join unions. However, 21 states have passed *right-to-work laws* that significantly restrict a union's ability to organize workers. These states are shown in Figure 9–1. Right-to-work laws state that it is against the law to force a worker to be a member of a union as a condition of employment.[14] Industrial states in the northern United States have traditionally not passed right-to-work legislation, preferring a stronger union presence in their manufacturing firms. Other states, especially in the south, have right-to-work legislation. As a result, the last two decades have seen a major migration of plants and entire businesses to the right-to-work states because companies that are not unionized can pay lower wages.

Developing Your Critical Thinking Skills

1. Consider the following philosophical statement: "Companies are supposed to compete aggressively, but if they are extremely successful, they must fear being regulated as a monopoly." How would you reconcile these two ideas?

2. Does antitrust policy really serve a useful purpose? If we did not have such a policy, wouldn't competition eventually break up any monopolies or price-fixing agreements that might develop?

3. Some people contend that government regulation itself is a problem. Present some examples of how this could be true. Is the real problem government regulations or overzealous administration of them?

Global Competition and the Legal Environment

globalization p. 186>

One of the major issues raised by the globalization of the American economy is the differences between the legal environments in the United States and other countries. The basic question is whether or not government regulations in the United States make it overly difficult for American firms to compete. If they do, then the business may find it necessary to move production facilities to countries with less costly legal environments. The company's top executives may agonize over such a decision because of the harm it may do to the American workers who will lose their jobs and the American communities that will lose a valuable taxpayer and community supporter. But in some cases, a failure to move could mean a loss of competitiveness. You could argue that once such competitiveness is lost, the American plant will have to close anyway.

competitive advantage p. 315>

continuous improvement p. 448>

There are two sides to this debate. One side argues that, within limits, a tough legal environment can be a source of competitive advantage, not disadvantage. Professor Michael Porter of Harvard University argues that this is true for two reasons. First, tough standards will force the firm to make continuous efforts to improve its operations to meet the standards. In the process, the continuous improvement habit will spread to other areas of the business. This will give the firm a competitive advantage

Some foreign countries are far more lenient regarding pollution, safety, and other regulations. Some people think this gives companies there an unfair advantage over companies operating in the United States. Do you agree? If so, what should be done?

in terms of operating efficiency and commitment to continuous improvement. Second, tough environmental standards in one location often represent the standards that will eventually become the norm everywhere else. So the firm that learns to meet the standards early will have an advantage when firms everywhere have to meet them.[15]

The other side of the debate views America's legal environment as full of anticompetitive regulations. Here is a recent example of this type of thinking:

> We Americans have amassed plenty of regulatory freight. Amid the pressures of globalization, this hefty cargo of legalities has become less affordable. What social good has been served by the unbounded litigation that inflates the price of some highly tradable products? The notorious assault on the light-aircraft industry is illustrative. In this debacle, an entire U.S. industry was decimated not by "unfair" foreign competition but by liability suits. Before Congress finally got around to enacting some corrective legislation, domestic production, approximately a quarter of which used to be exported, had dwindled. The lawsuits laid out a red carpet for foreign producers to enter the breach; they subsequently snatched a rapidly growing share of the world market for small planes, including commuter airliners.[16]

Which of these views is correct? As is so often the case, the truth probably lies somewhere in between. It may be more expensive in the short run to operate in the American business environment. On the other hand, the firm that is committed to keeping the jobs in the United States can often find a way to do it. In Profile 7–8, you read about a small business, Blue Fish, that did just that. Profile 9–4 gives you an example of a large company that also tried to operate in the competitive global economy while adhering to the high social standards of the American business environment.

PROFILE 9–4   *Levi Strauss Takes the High Road*

takeover p. 222>

stock p. 216>

Levi Strauss is known not only for its leadership in the jeans business but also for its strong sense of corporate social responsibility. The founding Strauss family surely gets credit on both scores.

In the 1980s, company management began to fear that its long-run orientation and commitment to social responsibility would lead to a takeover attempt by outside speculators. The CEO at the time was Robert Haas, a descendant of the founding family and a man with a deep commitment to perpetuating the principles on which the business was operating. In 1985, Haas preempted the potential speculators by taking the company private.

With control of the stock assured, Haas and his management team proceeded to set strict high standards for the working environment. They carefully examined working conditions in all of their foreign facilities and took corrective actions whenever they found failures to meet the company's standards. If correction was not possible, they simply refused to continue doing business there. For example, they canceled $40 million in contracts in China to protest human rights violations.

Keeping jobs in America was an important element of the company's employee strategy. A number of American facilities were closed, but by the mid-1990s, the company still had 34 American production facilities. Haas says none of them would have remained open if the company had evaluated them on strictly economic grounds.

SOURCE: David C. Korten, *When Corporations Rule the World*. West Hartford, CT: Kumerian Press, 1995, pp. 232–3.

Business Ethics and the Legal Environment

ethical issues p. 207>

It is important to end our review of the legal environment of business with a brief consideration of the relationship between ethics and the law. You have already encountered ethical issues in earlier chapters. Here we want to make you aware of the difference between law and ethics.

Lawful behavior represents the minimum standard of conduct that a society finds acceptable. Firms that fail to meet these minimum standards run the risk of being punished. Failure to meet legal standards may even lead to bankruptcy (like Charles Givens, who was mentioned earlier in this chapter). Firms that fail to meet the minimum standards of the law may lose the trust of customers, employees, suppliers, and competitors.

However, the mere fact that some action is not legally required of the business or specifically prohibited by the law does not mean it is right or proper. A firm that is genuinely committed to high ethical standards may do more than the law requires. Sometimes that requires structuring the business so that management has the freedom to operate by high ethical standards. Profile 9–4 demonstrated how Levi Strauss did just that. Sometimes maintaining a high standard of ethics leads to lower profits in the short run. Sometimes a firm may have to pull out of certain markets in order to abide by high standards of ethics.

While ethics is a higher standard of behavior than the law, there is often a close relationship between the two. In a democratic society, laws represent the desires of the people. They map out a collective expression of what is proper and right for that society. Ethics, the search for what is proper and right, is the basis for law.[17] Ethical concerns can lead to the development of laws. In fact, some laws that affect business are responses to alleged or real ethical shortcomings. For example, the National Traffic and Motor Vehicle Safety Act of 1966 was passed after the publication and widespread discussion of the book *Unsafe at any Speed*, written by consumer advocate Ralph Nader. Nader alleged that the carmakers made cars that they knew were unsafe and decided not to take steps to reduce the possibility of serious injuries. The ethical discussions that surrounded this situation raised enough concerns that laws were enacted to prescribe adequate safety in automobiles.

In summary, laws are a minimum foundation. Many businesspeople move beyond that foundation because they feel it is right and proper to do so. These actions, when collectively felt and expressed, can lead to changes in the law to reflect higher standards for all.

SUMMARY

1. Human institutions are based on assumptions regarding the way the world works, or at least ought to work. If the institutions are going to work effectively, the people working in them and with them must understand and accept this underlying philosophy.

   ■ What are some of the basic philosophical concepts underlying the legal environment of a capitalistic society?

   This chapter identified four crucial concepts: (1) freedom, (2) property rights, (3) risk taking, and (4) responsibility.

   Freedom is the power to make one's own decisions or choices without interference from others.

Property rights are the freedom to possess and regulate the use of tangible items such as land and buildings and intangible items such as a copyrighted piece of music.

Risk taking means that businesses (and individuals) are willing to undertake actions without knowing what the results will be.

Responsibility in the business context refers to using property in a manner that does not unduly infringe on the freedom of others.

2. A healthy capitalistic economic system requires a government that not only regu lates but also encourages business investment and risk taking.

■ What are some of the ways government supports business?

This chapter identified five ways in which government encourages business:

(1) Limiting ownership liability.

(2) Limiting losses through bankruptcy laws.

(3) Protecting innovation through copyrights, trademarks, and patents.

(4) Providing structure through rules and industry standards.

(5) Encouraging competition by limiting monopoly power.

3. Most businesses can be counted on to act responsibly most of the time. But there will always be glaring exceptions. And even many basically honorable managers may from time to time be tempted or pressured to engage in socially irresponsible behavior. Consequently, governments in all capitalistic economies find it necessary to regulate business in a variety of ways.

■ What are some of the major ways government regulates business?

This chapter identified the following six forms of government regulation:

(1) Regulation of monopoly.

(2) Regulation of employee relations.

(3) Financial regulation and taxes.

(4) Regulation of consumer relations.

(5) Regulation of environmental issues.

(6) Regulation at the state and local level, such as regulation of location through zoning.

4. All nations engage in government regulation of business, but the regulations differ from one country to another. This creates a potential problem for firms involved in global competition.

■ What is the basic conflict that can emerge between global competition and a nation's system of business regulation?

The basic conflict is that some of the nation's business regulations and taxes may make it difficult for domestic firms to compete in a global economy. If the regulations raise the cost of doing business in the home country, the domestic government may be under pressure to relax its regulations in order to lower the costs of doing business and thereby improve the competitiveness of domestic firms.

5. If all businesses operated on a high ethical plane all the time, there would be no need for many existing government regulations.

    ■ What is the relationship between business ethics and the law?

    Laws represents the minimum standard of behavior a business should maintain. A firm that is genuinely committed to operating by a high ethical standard will do more than the law requires.

Links to future courses

You deal with legal and regulatory issues in many courses. The following courses have direct links to the themes of this chapter.

- Business law
- Public policies toward business
- Small business management
- Principles of management
- Human resources management
- Business policy

- Principles of finance
- Principles of marketing
- Advertising
- Consumer behavior
- Labor–management relations (collective bargaining)

KEY TERMS	Acquisition, 250
	Bankruptcy, 243

Acquisition, 250   Patent, 244
Bankruptcy, 243   Price fixing, 248
Collective bargaining, 255   Property rights, 242
Copyright, 244   Responsibility, 242
Freedom, 242   Risk taking, 242
Industrywide regulation, 250   Tort, 256
Merger, 249   Trademark, 244

KEY TERMS

EXERCISES AND APPLICATIONS

1. Form teams of six people. Half of you take the view that government regulation is basically helpful to business. The other half take the view that government regulation is overly restrictive. Outline your arguments and be ready to present your case to the class.

2. Look up the website for the U.S. Patent Office (http://www.patent.gov). What is required to get a patent? Now do the same thing for trademarks and copyrights. What are the differences? Write your results in a one-page report.

3. Survey 20 of your classmates or residents of your living space regarding their views of government regulation. Use the following scale.

1 = Extremely antigovernment

2 = Believes the vast majority of government regulations are unnecessary

3 = Believes government is necessary to stop businesses from acting illegally

4 = Believes much of what government does is very good for business

5 = Believes the country would be better off if government took a more active role in regulating business

Calculate the responses. Take note of key opinions expressed by your peers. Write up your results in a one-page report.

4. Prepare to debate the following statement: Local and state regulations are more troublesome for most businesses than are federal regulations.

5. Can there ever be a situation where a business or a business manager behaves ethically but illegally? Explain.

CASE: SHINTECH BATTLES LOCALS TO OPEN A NEW PLANT

The following case illustrates one of the most common problems that businesses of all sizes encounter with the legal environment.

Shintech Inc. officials say they will break ground this year on a major PVC plant in Convent, Louisiana, despite local efforts to stop the project on grounds of environmental racism.

The company called the claims "totally groundless" and said the Environmental Protection Agency missed its deadline to halt the project.

The Houston firm was granted air permits on May 23 by Louisiana's Department of Environmental Quality. The permits were issued after state officials determined the proposed plant's emission levels for chloralkyline, vinyl chloride monomer, and finished PVC were within state limits.

However, EPA spokeswoman Cheryl Hoechstetler, in Dallas, said the EPA is reviewing the case after receiving two petitions filed by area residents and Tulane University's Environmental Law Clinic. The petitioners claim the Shintech plant would violate the Clean Air Act. EPA's Washington headquarters has the ability to revoke or revise the permits. . . .

Controversy has centered on the site's proximity to a low-income government housing project that is primarily minority-occupied. Some area residents, as well as representatives of the Tulane Environmental Law Clinic, say the plant will have a negative impact on the community, regardless of the economic growth it is expected to provide.

Lisa Lavie, an environmental law fellow with the law clinic, said Shintech is guilty of "environmental injustice" because the area where it wants to build the PVC plant already is subject to emissions from fertilizer, oil, and grain manufacturers....

[Dick] Mason [Shintech controller and secretary] said ... the company did not take the community's demographics or economic status into consideration because there are only 10 residents within a one-mile radius of the site. (The housing project is about 1.5 miles away.) ...

The Shintech plant will create 165 permanent jobs along with 2,000 construction jobs during the 18-month building process.

Decision Questions

benefits p. 433>

1.   This case illustrates the fact that economic growth has both benefits and costs. From the community's standpoint, what are the benefits and costs of Shintech's proposed plant?
2.   Based on the evidence presented in this case, do you think the residents of the housing project would be better off with or without the Shintech plant?
3.   The complaint uses some colorful language, such as environmental racism and environmental injustice. What do those terms mean? What do they imply about the business ethics of Shintech? Is it fair to use such terms in a disagreement of this sort? Whether fair or not, is it effective?

business ethics p. 108>

4.   What should Shintech do in this case?

SOURCE: Frank Esposito, "Proposed PVC Plant Faces Local Challenge," *Plastic News,* June 9, 1997, p. 5.

REFERENCES

1. Henry R. Cheeseman. *The Legal and Regulatory Environment: Contemporary Perspectives in Business.* Upper Saddle River, NJ: Prentice Hall, 1997, p. 500.

2. Eugene Carlson. "Small Firms Spend Much Time, Money Complying with Environment Rules," In Tony McAdams and Laura Pincus, *Legal Environment of Business: Ethical and Public Policy Contexts.* Burr Ridge, IL: Irwin/McGraw-Hill, 1997, p. 605.

3. Eugene F. Brigham and Louis C. Gapenski. *Financial Management: Theory and Practice,* 7th ed., Fort Worth, TX: Dryden Press, 1994, pp. 1037–8.

4. Adapted from Robert W. Galvin. *The Idea of Ideas.* Schaumburg, IL: Motorola University Press, 1991, pp. 97–8.

5. Kevin Freiberg and Jackie Freiberg. *Nuts! Southwest Airlines' Crazy Recipe for Business and Personal Success.* Austin, TX: Bard Press, 1996, pp. 17–8.

6. Freiberg and Freiberg, pp. 20–5.

7. Douglas Greer. *Business, Government and Society,* 3rd ed. New York: Macmillan, 1993, pp. 151–2.

8. Nancy Millman. "$100 Million Fine in ADM Guilty Plea." *Chicago Tribune*, October 15, 1996, sec. 1, pp. 1, 14.

9. John R. Wilke and Joseph Pereira. "Staples Sets Store Sales to Rescue Merger." *The Wall Street Journal*, March 13, 1997, pp. A3, A4.

10. For an interesting discussion of the logic of regulation and deregulation, see Grover Starling. *The Changing Environment of Business*, 4th ed. Cincinnati, OH: South-Western College Publishing, 1996, chap. 8.

11. Michael Bixby, Caryn Beck-Dudley, and Patrick Cihon. *The Legal Environment of Business: A Practical Approach*. Cincinnati, OH: South-Western College Publishing, 1996, pp. 590–4.

12. Raymond A. Noe, John R. Hollenbeck, Barry Gehart, and Patrick M. Wright. *Human Resource Management: Gaining a Competitive Advantage*, 2nd ed. Burr Ridge, IL: Irwin, 1997, chap. 18.

13. Jane Bryant Quinn. "Jury Rules Against Get-Rich-Quick Pitchman." *Chicago Tribune*, June 2, 1996, sec. 5, p. 3.

14. Ronald A. Anderson, Ivan Fox, and David P. Twomey. *Business Law and the Legal Environment*, 16th ed. Cincinnati, OH: South-Western College Publishing, 1996, p. 737.

15. Michael E. Porter. *The Competitive Advantage of Nations*. New York: The Free Press, 1990, pp. 580–1, 585–6.

16. Pietro S. Nivol. "When It Comes to Regulations, U.S. Shouldn't Cast the First Stone." *The Wall Street Journal*, May 15, 1996, p. A15.

17. Anderson, Fox, and Twomey, p. 25.

10 The Impact of Industry Structure and Dynamics

Ford Motor Co. sells three of the nation's top 10 vehicles—the F-series pickup, the Taurus, and the Explorer. Ford is clearly in the automotive industry, but as you learned in Chapter 2, its reach is far and wide. It is a multinational company with plants in a number of foreign countries. In addition to assembling cars and trucks, it makes many of the components that go into the vehicles. It has strategic alliances with a number of other companies, such as Mazda. Ford and Mercury cars and trucks are sold nationwide through independently owned dealers. Ford recently increased its presence in Japan, which had previously prevented American car companies from competing effectively.

It is important for you to understand how businesses like Ford fit together in industries. It is part of the integrative nature of business to be aware of the links among companies within an industry as well as the links among industries. This chapter will help you understand both the similarities and differences among agricultural businesses, government agencies, manufacturing firms, wholesale and retail firms, service businesses, and not-for-profit organizations. After reading this chapter, you should be able to:

1. Identify major industry sectors.

2. Explain the characteristics of the manufacturing sector.

3. Describe the important characteristics of the distribution sector.

4. Identify the major characteristics of the service sector.

5. Analyze the key characteristics of nonprofit organizations.

This chapter continues the discussion of the environmental influences on a business depicted in Figure 1–6. As we said earlier, managers have little effect on those influences, but the environment in which they exist often has a heavy impact. We bring that environment closer to the actual business in this chapter as we discuss industry structure and dynamics. Large businesses have an impact on the industry because of their size relative to the total industry. Other businesses, especially small ones, have little ability to affect their industry dynamics. Unless they create radically new inventions or dramatically different services, most small businesses have little effect on their industry outside their immediate locale.

This chapter examines how businesses fit within an industry sector and how that industry sector works. We are especially interested in important business concepts that are relevant for an entire industry sector. We will look very briefly at two industry sectors, agriculture and government. We then turn our major attention to three sectors of business: manufacturing, distribution, and service. We will close the chapter with a discussion of the not-for-profit sector.

Before beginning these discussions, however, it is important to note how industries are classified. Thus, we begin this chapter with a discussion of the North American Industrial Classification System (NAICS). You will see the logic of a classification system that helps organize information about industries and businesses.

How Industries Are Classified

On April 9, 1997, the U.S. Census Bureau introduced a new classification system for industries. A classification system is important because it allows for the collection, storage, retrieval, and analysis of millions of pieces of data about business. The new system is readily accessible, so anyone who wants information about businesses or industries can find it. This information can then be used for a vast number of purposes. For example, if you want to know the number of bicycle manufacturers in the United States, you can look into data sources using the classification system.

The North American Industrial Classification System is designed to catalog businesses in the United States, Canada, and Mexico. This gives uniformity among the three countries of NAFTA. NAICS consists of 20 broad categories of industries, shown in Table 10–1. These categories are then broken into more refined classifications until fairly specific industry groups are determined. Each specific industry group has a unique six-digit NAICS number. The new NAICS codes are used in the 1997 economic census, with data reported in early 1998.

The NAICS codes replace the Standard Industrial Classification (SIC) codes developed in the 1930s. The creation of the NAICS codes is significant because, in addition to their NAFTA-wide uniformity, they classify a number of new industries more accurately. Why is this important? How many complete industries can have developed in the 15 years since the last revision of SIC codes? Surprisingly, a significant number have, which demonstrates the dynamic nature of business. Some of the new industries are shown in Table 10–2. Keep in mind that this is just a sample of industries that have developed in the last 15 years.

TABLE 10–1   NAICS Categories

Code	Industry Sector
11	Agriculture, forestry, fishing and hunting
21	Mining
22	Utilities
23	Construction
31–33	Manufacturing
42	Wholesale trade
44–45	Retail trade
48–49	Transportation and warehousing
51	Information
52	Finance and insurance
53	Real estate and rental and leasing
54	Professional, scientific, and technical services
55	Management of companies and enterprises
56	Administrative and support, waste management
61	Education services
62	Health care and social assistance
71	Arts, entertainment, and recreation
72	Accommodation and food service
81	Other services (except public administration)
92	Public administration

SOURCE: U.S. Census Bureau, http://www.census.gov/epcd/www/ naicsusr.html, (accessed June 24, 1997).

Here's an example of how the NAICS classification system works. Suppose you work at Motorola in the semiconductor division. You want to know as much as you can about the industry and the other companies in it. You consult the Census Bureau website, http://www.census.gov/naics. By scrolling down the list of manufacturing codes, you find that semiconductors fall into the manufacturing sector (NAICS 33). But you need to know more than that. Checking further, you find that they are in the industry category of computer and electronic parts manufacturing (334), the subindustry of semiconductors and other electronic component manufacturing (3344), and the specific industry of semiconductor and related devices manufacturing (334413).[1] Once you know this, you can find a substantial amount of information. For example, Dun & Bradstreet, a well-known publisher of industry data, publishes an annual volume called *Industry Norms and Key Business Ratios*.[2] In it you can find how many companies there are that make semiconductors, average financial data for the industry, and even accounting ratios that measure the financial health of companies in the

TABLE 10–2   Sample of New Industries included in NAICS Codes

Semiconductor machinery manufacturing

Fiberoptic cable manufacturing

Computer software reproduction

Compact disk manufacture

Warehouse clubs

Pet supply stores

Cable networks

Satellite communications

Paging

Credit card issuing

Temporary help supply

Telemarketing

Hazardous waste collection

HMO medical centers

Casinos

Bed and breakfast inns

Automotive oil change and lubrication shops

industry. If you want to see how Motorola compares with the industry, the Dun & Bradstreet publications will tell you.

Developing Your Critical Thinking Skills

1. What is the advantage of understanding the North American Industry Classification System? Why is a classification system important?

2. What is the significance of having a classification system that includes both Canadian and Mexican industries as well as U.S. industries?

3. Think ahead to the year 2020. What new industries might be in the next version of the classification system?

Agriculture and Government Sectors

Industry sectors
Major groupings of industries with similar characteristics.

The 20 NAICS codes divide all businesses and government organizations into distinct divisions known as **industry sectors,** major groupings of industries with similar characteristics. We discuss first two industry sectors that are important to the overall economy—agriculture and government (public administration) sectors. Then we turn to

Agriculture consists of crops, livestock, forestry, fishing and hunting, and services. It is increasingly big business as farms get larger and larger, and corporations account for increasing percentages of sales. What accounts for the increase in size of farms? Is this good or bad?

the three primary sectors of interest—manufacturing industries, distribution industries, and service industries. The chapter concludes with a discussion of nonprofit or voluntary organizations, which transcend most industry sectors.

Agriculture

U.S. agriculture entered a new era in April 1996, when new farm legislation was signed into law. This legislation set agriculture on a new course where markets, not government programs, determine how much will be planted and what prices will be paid for products. This replaces 60 years of government involvement in determining the number of acres planted and how much farmers received for their crops. It will be phased in over a seven-year period, during which government subsidies will be replaced by market forces.[3] Projections are that this deregulation of agriculture may cause significant swings in revenues and profits in farm operations as surpluses or shortages of products affect how much farmers plant and what prices they receive for their production.

Agriculture is big business. The agriculture sector consists of five major industry groups: crop production, livestock production, forestry, fishing and hunting, and agricultural services. Two of the most significant of these are crop production and livestock production.

Crop production involves primarily farms that produce a large variety of grains. These farms, like many of the other industries we will discuss, have evolved significantly over time. The number of farms has decreased steadily for decades. The number of acres of farmland, however, has remained essentially constant except for encroaching urbanization. This means that the number of acres per farm has increased dramatically. This trend is driven by two factors. First, the productivity per farm has increased more than tenfold in 30 years. Tractors, combines, and other equipment are larger and far more efficient than their predecessors. This allows farmers to operate larger and larger farms. Second, the cost of farm equipment has risen dramatically, making it difficult for an individual to enter the farming industry. Thus, as farmers retire, their farms are sold to other existing farmers or to *corporate farms*—companies that own thousands of acres of farmland.

Livestock production has likewise evolved over time. The days of small-scale dairy, beef cattle, hog, or poultry farms are limited. Small farms have been replaced by feedlots or egg-producing facilities that are almost fully automated. Computers measure ingredients in feed, cattle are fattened in feed lots holding thousands of animals, and chickens lay eggs in climate-controlled facilities where the eggs move along conveyors to be washed, graded, packed, and shipped without being touched by human hands.

In 1996, the latest year of data available, crop producers had a banner year. Prices were up because of droughts the previous year. As a result, both revenues and profits were up significantly for crop producers. However, since grain to feed animals is one of the biggest expenses of livestock production, the high grain prices depressed profits in the livestock industry. Increases in revenues were largely offset by increases in the cost of production, resulting in limited profits or even losses for many livestock producers. The high grain prices also raised food prices of grain-related foods such as bread, cereal, and processed meat.[4]

Exports of agriculture products remained strong in 1997. Demand has been especially strong in Asia, as well as Mexico and other Latin American countries. Exports of beef, pork, and poultry exceeded $7 billion in 1996, up 13 percent from the preceding year. Exports were expected to increase another 12 percent by the end of 1997.[5]

Government

It may seem strange to think of government as an industry. Yet according to the NAICS codes, there are separate sub-industry codes for executive, legislative, and general government, justice, public order, safety, finance and taxation, human resources, and others. Note that these broad classifications do not separate out levels of government (such as federal, state, and local). Thus, the FBI is in the same NAICS code as your local sheriff or police. We discussed the role of government extensively in Chapter 9.

The Three Primary Business Sectors

Manufacturing sector
The broad group of companies and industries that produce tangible objects.

Manufacturing firms
Companies that convert raw materials or components into products that may be sold to consumers or to other businesses.

Distribution sector
The wholesale and retail firms that move products from the manufacturer to the ultimate customers or users.

We turn now to the three primary sectors of business: manufacturing, distribution, and service. The **manufacturing sector** includes companies and industries that produce things or objects. These objects may be anything from microchips to jet airplanes to nuclear power plants as long as they are tangible objects when completed. **Manufacturing firms** convert raw materials or components into products that may be sold to consumers or other businesses. Thus, manufacturers *add value* to raw materials. Consider the significance of this. Iron ore in the ground has little value. Once it is extracted, it has more value. When it is converted into steel, it has still more value. When it is used to build a vehicle, it has even more value.

Manufacturing is considered here in a broad sense. We include mining as part of manufacturing because it, too, is a value-adding process. We include both drilling for and refining oil, even though drilling only extracts the oil and refining simply changes its nature before passing it down a pipeline as gasoline. We include utilities, which either produce and deliver electricity or distribute other fuels for consumption by businesses and households.

The **distribution sector** involves wholesale and retail firms that move products from the manufacturer to the ultimate customers or users. The distribution sector is the link between the producer and the end user. Without this sector it would be nearly impossible to get products to buyers efficiently.

Service sector
The broad group of companies that provide some sort of service to customers.

The **service sector** includes businesses that provide some sort of service to customers. Even though a service may also bring products to the customer, as in the case of a plumber who installs a new faucet in a customer's home, the primary benefit of the interaction is through the service provided. The service sector includes a wide variety of businesses, from movie theaters to consultants.

We discuss each of the sectors in some depth and cover a number of concepts that are important to that sector. We also profile one or more companies to illustrate the dynamics of that sector.

The Manufacturing Sector

Manufacturing industries generate billions of dollars of products each year. Yet as a percentage of gross domestic product in the United States, manufacturing has declined over the last 40 years. In fact, in 1960 manufacturing comprised approximately 30 percent of GDP. Today it's down to about 20 percent of GDP.[6]

Table 10–3 shows the value of durable manufactured goods, nondurable manufactured products, and services over time. *Durable goods* are those products that have a life expectancy of several years and may be used continuously or with great frequency. Cars, appliances, computers, electrical generating stations, and construction are considered durable goods. Products such as clothing, food, plastics, chemicals, and leather goods are *nondurable goods* because they are either consumed or worn out over a relatively short period of time. Note in the table that services exceeded the total of durable and nondurable goods between 1980 and 1985, and the gap has increased since then.

Who Buys Manufactured Goods?

Manufactured goods may have one of three ultimate destinations. First, they may be purchased by *individual consumers* (those customers who purchase consumer goods for their personal use). Consumer goods include cars, washers and dryers, home construction, apparel, jewelry, and breakfast cereals. Note that there is a great difference between a car and a breakfast cereal, yet both are consumer goods.

Consider, for example, tiremaker BF Goodrich. If you go to a local tire dealer to buy tires for your car, you will have a number of brands from which to choose. These tires are consumer goods because you, the individual consumer, are purchasing them.

TABLE 10–3   Value of Services and Manufactured Goods ($ billions)

Industry	1960	1965	1970	1975	1980	1985	1990	1995
Durable goods	$43.3	$63.3	$85.0	$133.5	$213.5	$361.1	$476.5	$606.4
Nondurable goods	152.9	191.6	272.0	420.6	695.5	927.6	1245.3	1485.9
Services	136.0	189.4	291.1	424.4	851.4	1416.1	2117.5	2832.6

SOURCE: *Economic Report of the President 1997*, U.S. Government Printing Office, p. 300.

FIGURE 10-1   Representative Destinations of Raw Materials

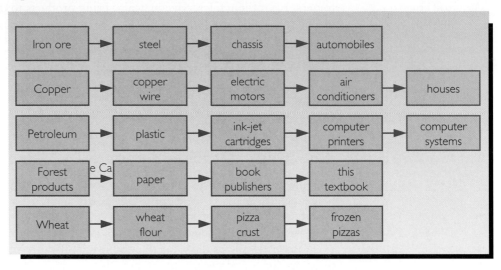

The second destination for manufactured goods is to become *components* of products produced by other firms. For example, sheet steel becomes a component in an auto body. Oil may become a component in chemicals. Copper may become a component in wiring. These components may go through several processes and be considered part of several different industries before reaching the ultimate consumer. Figure 10–1 shows examples of component products.

Original equipment manufacturer (OEM)
A company that makes components for another product.

A term that you hear occasionally in relationship to businesses is **original equipment manufacturer (OEM)**. A company is an OEM if it makes components for another product. Now consider BF Goodrich again. We mentioned that this company makes tires for consumers to buy. It also makes tires for car manufacturers to buy. Thus, BF Goodrich is an OEM for the automotive industry. Goodrich sells tires to General Motors, which puts them on cars as they come off the assembly line.

Capital goods
Machinery and equipment used in the production process.

The third destination for manufactured goods is to become **capital goods,** which are machinery and equipment used in the production process. Note the difference between this and the previous category, even though both are sold to other businesses. For example, Caterpillar Inc. produces truck engines as well as large off-road trucks. The truck engines are often sold for installation in on-road trucks manufactured by Ford, GM, Peterbilt, or Mack. These trucks are then bought by trucking firms to use in transporting all kinds of products. The truck engine is an example of one firm's product being an OEM component in another firm's product.

Caterpillar's large off-road trucks are produced entirely by Caterpillar and are sold to mining companies for use in mining excavation. In this case, the product becomes capital equipment that mining companies use in the extraction process. Individual consumers would never purchase these products; they may routinely cost several hundred thousand dollars and are designed for industrial use. We refer to buyers of either components or capital equipment as *industrial customers*.

Companies in virtually every industry sell consumer goods, component goods, and capital goods. Consider the wood products industry, for example. Georgia Pacific makes paneling that is sold to individual consumers who want to redecorate the family

Capital intensiveness in manufacturing leads to high fixed costs. Most manufacturing plants today are highly computerized, requiring fewer, but more highly skilled employees. What is the relationship between fixed costs and profits?

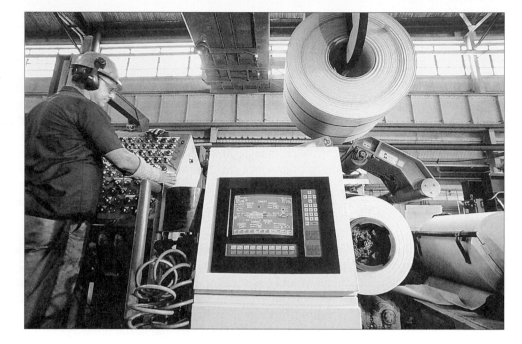

room of their home. It also sells similar paneling to housing contractors to use in new homes. Finally, if the paneling is part of a large office building, it might be considered capital goods.

Motorola is another example. The company produces products in the wireless communications, semiconductors, and advanced electronic systems industries. Many of its products, such as pagers and cellular phones, go to individual consumers who want the products for their own personal use. Motorola also produces components, such as semiconductors, that will go into computers, communications devices, and many other products. And it produces goods that are sold to other companies for use in their operations and to the government, especially in defense and space electronics. As you see, Motorola's products are shipped to all three destinations.

MOTOROLA

Important Concepts in Manufacturing

A number of important business concepts can be illustrated by manufacturing industries. We will discuss a few of these and then show how they apply at Motorola.

Capital Intensiveness   Manufacturing firms often make a significant investment in building and capital equipment as a percentage of their total investment. It is not unusual for a large firm to invest several million dollars to build a new production facility and equip it with high-tech production equipment. Thus, the production of manufactured products is often a *capital-intensive* process. For example, Motorola had fixed-asset expenditures of $2.1 billion in 1996, $4.2 billion in 1995, and $3.3 billion in 1994. This means it spent almost $10 billion in three years just in developing new plants and equipment. Given the changing nature of the technology it uses, Motorola has to spend a lot on new facilities and equipment to remain competitive. Its business is very capital intensive.

The significance of capital intensiveness is seen in the high investment, which can affect both costs and profit. Companies with a lot of capital equipment have ongoing expenditures related to that equipment. For example, they typically make regular interest payments on the equipment and incur regular maintenance costs to keep the equipment working. They have a lot of money tied up in the equipment that cannot be used for other things. Further, these are *fixed costs.* This means the company must pay those costs regardless of its level of sales or revenues. If sales are high, the firm can make substantial profits. But if sales drop, the fixed costs can lead to losses quickly. This is especially important for small businesses. Since their sales are low, managers of small companies must try to keep capital equipment and fixed costs as low as possible. Failure to watch fixed costs can be fatal.

Industry concentration
The number of firms in an industry and their relative size; often calculated by the C-4 ratio (the percentage of total industry sales by the top four firms.

Industry Concentration　　**Industry concentration** refers to the number of firms in an industry and their relative size. Increasing industry concentration means that there are fewer and fewer firms in the industry. Firms either go out of business as they become noncompetitive or are purchased by larger firms. As firms leave the industry, the remaining firms grow still larger. This causes even more problems for smaller firms and causes even more concentration in the industry.

Industry concentration is measured by the *concentration ratio*, sometimes known as the C-4 ratio. This is the percentage of total industry sales accounted for by the top four firms. Some industries, such as home construction, have very little concentration. These industries are highly *fragmented*. Others, such as aircraft manufacturing, are more highly concentrated; there are very few firms and they are extremely large. Table 10–4 shows a few manufacturing industries and their concentration ratios.

Vertical integration
The degree to which a firm operates in more than one level of the overall production chain.

Vertical Integration.　　**Vertical integration** is the degree to which a firm operates in more than one level of the overall production chain. Another way to say this is that vertical integration is the control of two or more sequential processes in the production and distribution of a product. A company that only assembles products is less vertically integrated than one that assembles products *and* produces the components that are assembled. If it also produces the materials that go into the components, it is even

Table 10–4　　Industry Concentration Ratios

Industry	Concentration Ratio
Chewing gum	96%
Household laundry equipment	93
Breakfast cereals	87
Greeting cards	85
Aircraft	72
Tires	69
Motorcycles	66

Source: Campbell R. McConnell and Stanley L. Brue, *Microeconomics: Principles, Problems, and Policies* (New York: McGraw-Hill, 1996), p. 241.

more vertically integrated. Similarly, if a company manufactures products and also distributes them to retailers or to end users, it is vertically integrated. Braum's is a chain of retail stores in Oklahoma that sells ice cream, dairy products, and restaurant fare such as hamburgers and other sandwiches. This chain of stores is highly vertically integrated. It operates its own dairy and meatpacking plant. It also grows its own beef and dairy cattle on land that it owns.

Captive supplier
A supplier that sells all of its output to a single company.

Captive Suppliers   Suppliers are companies that produce products for use by other companies, whether as equipment, components, or supplies. A **captive supplier** is one that sells all of its output to a single company. For example, suppose you own a company that makes automobile mirrors. You could produce mirrors for either the after-sale market or the original equipment manufacturer market. If you produce OEM mirrors, you could sell them to all of the car manufacturers in the United States. Or you could contract with a single carmaker to produce strictly for it. In this case, with only one customer, you would be considered a captive supplier.

There are several pros and cons of being a captive supplier. If you make a quality product at a reasonable price, your customer will continue to use your company as one of its preferred suppliers. Your company can then concentrate on manufacturing processes and not worry about marketing the product to other users. In addition, a captive supplier usually has a close working relationship with the customer, which often shares technology to make the supplier more productive. The downside is that your sales are limited to the amount that one customer wants to buy. In addition, you are vulnerable to the business fluctuations of your customer. For example, if the single manufacturer who is your sole customer should go out on strike, you have immediately lost the entire base of your business.

Quality   We allocate over half of Chapter 15 to the discussion of quality because it is so important. Recall from our model in Chapter 1 that quality is one of the key indicators of business success. This is particularly true in manufacturing businesses. Quality comes from having the best equipment, the best processes, and the best practices. It requires substantial training of the workforce and a major emphasis on empowering individuals and teams to make decisions that improve the quality of the product.

training p. 379>
teams p. 71>

strategic alliance
p. 180>

outsourcing p. 385>
joint venture p. 179>

Strategic Alliances and Joint Ventures   We discussed both strategic alliances and joint ventures in Chapter 7. Perhaps no industry makes better use of strategic alliances than the automotive industry, but they are of importance to virtually all major manufacturing industries. Strategic alliances are long-term agreements between companies to work together. They are often used between major manufacturers and their suppliers as companies move more and more toward outsourcing. Joint ventures are partnering arrangements in which two or more companies own another company. The number of strategic alliances and joint ventures has increased dramatically in the past decade.

Profile 10–1 illustrates the manufacturing concepts discussed here by looking at one of our focus companies, Motorola.

PROFILE 10–1   *Motorola*

mission p. 310>

You know by now that Motorola is a manufacturer of pagers, cellular phones, computer chips, and other technology-driven products. It is also involved in Iridium, the consortium of international firms whose mission is to develop wireless communication around the world. Consider how the manufacturing concepts we discussed apply to Motorola.

We mentioned earlier that Motorola is very capital intensive. It spent nearly $10 billion in three years to enhance its facilities because it is a major producer of many products and is experiencing very rapid growth in most of its products. We also noted earlier how much interest Motorola pays during a year. This interest is necessary to underwrite its capital-intensive operations.

interest p. 225>

The industry concentration in Motorola's industries varies somewhat but is generally very high. In semiconductors, the PowerPC microchip developed by the Motorola–IBM–Apple alliance competes against Intel. These are the only major producers of semiconductors. Motorola's pagers compete against Radio Shack and a few others, but the industry is still highly concentrated. Motorola's other products face similar degrees of concentration.

Vertical integration is illustrated by Motorola's brief entry into the desktop PC business. It already made the PowerPC chip, a major component for PCs. Unfortunately, Motorola had to suspend production of its computers when Apple Computers refused to renew its licensing agreement for its operating system.

Motorola is known for quality in all its products. Its pagers, for example, are so good that they simply are never expected to fail because of manufacturing defects. We will discuss this in more depth in Chapter 15.

Motorola has a number of strategic alliances. Two are notable. First is the Motorola–IBM–Apple strategic alliance, which developed the PowerPC chip. The benefit of the strategic alliance was to have all companies involved in developing the technology competing together against Intel. Each company in the alliance could then use the technology in its own computers. The second is the strategic alliance with international companies in starting Iridium, the company that will help create worldwide wireless communications through the use of low-earth-orbit satellites. ●

Developing Your Critical Thinking Skills

1. Consider the automotive industry. Why might a company want to integrate vertically? Why might it want to decrease the level of vertical integration?

2. What determines whether a manufacturing industry will be intensely competitive or only mildly competitive?

3. Why are strategic alliances more popular today than they were 20 years ago? What do you see happening to the manufacturing sector that would account for this popularity?

The Distribution Sector

The distribution sector consists of businesses that serve as intermediaries or links between the producer and the final customer. It would be difficult and costly for manufacturers of most products to sell directly to the final consumer. It would be equally impractical for final consumers to buy directly from a manufacturer. The distribution sector consists of two subsectors: wholesale and retail.

FIGURE 10–2   The Roles of Wholesalers

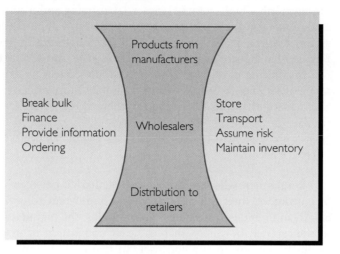

Wholesalers

Wholesaler
A business that serves as an intermediary between manufacturers and retailers.

A category of merchants that is largely invisible to consumers is **wholesalers,** businesses that serve as intermediaries between manufacturers and retailers. Manufacturers typically cannot afford to call on each individual retailer to take orders and transport goods to them. Likewise, most retailers cannot personally contact each manufacturer to find information and order products. This is where the wholesaler comes in.

Think of the typical hardware store. It may stock 10,000 individual products, produced by 2,000 to 4,000 manufacturers. There is simply no efficient way to get the manufacturers and retailers together without the help of wholesalers.

Though unknown to the general public, wholesalers provide major services through their distribution of goods. Figure 10–2 illustrates these important roles. They include storing goods that have been produced by manufacturers, breaking items sent in bulk into smaller shipments for individual retailers or business customers, providing industry and consumer information about products to retailers, providing capital and credit for the purchase of goods, maintaining inventory from which a retailer can draw rather than keeping inventory on site, transporting goods, and ordering goods on behalf of the retailer. As you can see, the wholesaler accepts much of the risk that individual retailers would otherwise assume. Profile 10–2 illustrates the role of wholesalers by looking at the Fleming Companies, a major wholesaler of food and food-related products.

PROFILE **10–2**   *The Fleming Companies*

The Fleming Companies is a marketing and distribution company. It operates primarily as a wholesaler, but it also is a retailer. Fleming markets food and food-related products by serving more than 10,000 stores, including 3,500 supermarkets in 42 states and several foreign countries. It also operates 400 company-owned retail stores. It supplies virtually every national brand of grocery products, plus high-volume private-label items and a full line of perishables including meats, dairy, deli products, frozen foods, and fresh produce. It also provides a variety of general merchandise often found in grocery stores. In 1996, Fleming had approximately $17 billion in sales and 44,000 employees.

In addition to distributing food products, Fleming offers retailers a complete range of services to enable them to compete more effectively. It also has a real estate division that sells stores and commercial real estate.

SOURCE: Fleming Companies, http://www.fleming.com/whoweare.htm, (accessed June 25, 1997).   ●

Remember, wholesalers are intermediaries between manufacturers and retailers or customers. Intermediaries play more important roles in some industries than others. In some industries, such as automobiles, the manufacturer ships products directly to the retailer. In others, such as heavy equipment or machinery, the producer ships products directly to the end user. In many other industries, particularly consumer goods, the manufacturer ships products to a wholesaler, who then ships to retailers. There are exceptions. When the retailer is a large chain such as Wal-Mart, Kmart, or Sears, manufacturers often work directly with the retail headquarter's buyer. This effectively eliminates the wholesaler because the retail chain can perform wholesaler duties. This reduces costs and is one of the key reasons that chains like Wal-Mart can offer lower prices.

Manufacturers' representative
A company or person that sells products to wholesalers or retailers on commission.

Related to wholesalers is the concept of a **manufacturers' representative,** a company or person that sells products to wholesalers or retailers on commission. Think of a manufacturers' representative as the equivalent of a full-time salesperson traveling around the country selling products. The advantage of using manufacturers' reps is that they often represent many manufacturers, each of whom may have only a few products to sell. The rep takes catalogs and order forms and calls on wholesalers and retailers to get orders for the products. The products are then shipped directly to the wholesaler or retailer.

Two key differences between manufacturers' reps and wholesalers is that reps work on commission only, and they do not take possession of the product. They simply take orders and communicate those orders back to the manufacturer. This gives the manufacturer the widest possible coverage for a relatively low cost.

Retailers

Retailer
A store that sells directly to consumers.

The retail industry is the most visible of all industries from the perspective of the individual consumer. **Retailers** are stores that sell directly to consumers. Table 10–5 shows various categories of retail stores.

The competitive structure within retail is continually evolving. Fifty years ago, there were very few large department stores and certainly no malls. Very few franchises existed. Today, every city of at least medium size has one or more malls. Each is anchored by a national department store chain such as JCPenney, Sears, or Montgomery Ward. A second anchor is a regional department store such as Carson Pirie Scott in the Midwest and Dillard's or Foley's in the Southwest. The other stores are likely smaller specialty store chains, which may be either company-owned or franchised. A very small percentage of stores in malls are locally owned and operated.

TABLE 10–5   Selected Types of Retail Stores

Building material and garden supplies	Shoe stores
Grocery stores	Radio, TV, and computer stores
Meat and fish stores	Computer and software stores
New and used car dealers	Eating and drinking places
Boat dealers	Used merchandise stores
Motorcycle dealers	Jewelry stores
Women's clothing stores	Optical goods stores

The retail scene is dominated by large chains of stores. Many of these chains are owned by even larger corporations. Table 10–6 shows the 10 largest retailers, along with their sales, types of stores, and the subsidiaries they operate. Note the subsidiaries. Most of these are well-known names themselves, but it's surprising to see who owns them. For example, did you know that Kmart once owned Waldenbooks, Builder's Square, and Office Max, that Sears owns Western Auto, or that Lord & Taylor, Famous-Barr, Foley's, and Filene's are all owned by the May Department Stores Co.?

As shown in Table 10–6, most of the large retailers are either department store chains or grocery chains. Increasingly, however, chains known as category killers are having a major impact. **Category killers** are large chain stores that specialize in a narrow line of products. They provide great depth in products and offer prices lower than traditional stores can offer. Toys "R" Us in toys, Home Depot in home improvement and hardware, Office Max in office supplies, and others specialize in wide assortments of products within a specific market and sell at deeply discounted prices. As a result, they are formidable competitors within their particular market.

Category killer
A chain store that specializes in a narrow line of products.

While large chains dominate the retail landscape, franchises are almost as significant. As you learned in Chapter 2, a franchise is a business owned by a franchisee that uses the name, standard operating procedures, training, and marketing provided by the franchisor. Over 40 percent of all retail sales are through franchised outlets. Franchises combine the benefits of big business and small business. It may cost only a few thousand dollars to buy a little-known franchise that requires few fixed assets—or over $1 million for a moneymaker like McDonald's, Blockbuster, or Hardee's. A hotel franchise like Holiday Inn costs even more due to the cost of the facility. Table 10–7 lists the top 15 franchises in terms of number of outlets.

The remainder of the retail landscape is populated by numerous small independent businesses. Some consist of a single store, owned and operated by one person with the help of a few full- or part-time workers. Some are multistore chains operating within a relatively small geographic area. Many are specialty stores that cater to particular demographic or customer segments—for example, exclusive gift stores or apparel stores focusing on a particular niche.

Small independent retailers must compete against giants in the industry. Large department stores and category killers can provide much wider selection at a signifi-

TABLE 10–6   The Top 10 Retailers ($ billions)

Rank/Company	1996 Sales	Store Types	Subsidiaries
1. Wal-Mart	$93.6	Discount	Wal-Mart, Wal-Mart Super Centers, Sam's Wholesale Club
2. Kmart	34.4*	Discount	Kmart
3. Sears	38.2	General merchandise	Sears, Western Auto, Homelife, Parts America, Tire America, NTW
4. Kroger	25.2	Groceries	Kroger, Dillon, various convenience store chains
5. JCPenney	23.6	General merchandise	Penney's, Eckerd Drug, Thrift Drug, Fays Inc., Kerr Drug
6. Dayton Hudson	19.4**	Discount, general merchandise	Target, Dayton's, Hudson's, Marshall Field's, Mervyns
7. American Stores	18.7**	Groceries, drugs	Lucky Stores, Acme Markets, Jewel Food Stores, Osco Drugs, Super Saver, Kaps Kitchen & Pantry, Rx America
8. Safeway	16.3*	Groceries	Safeway, The Vons Companies, Casa Ley (a wholesale company in Mexico)
9. May Department Stores	11.6	Department stores	Lord & Taylor, Foley's, Robinson's-May, Hecht's, Kaufmann's, Filene's, Famous-Barr, Meier & Frank, LS Ayres, Strawbridge's
10. A & P	10.1	Groceries	A&P, Waldbaum's, Food Emporium, Super Fresh, Farmer Jack, Kohl's, Dominion

*1995 figures.

**1993 figures.

SOURCES: Companies' websites, accessed July 2, 1997.

cantly lower price. Because of their size and national scope, they can advertise constantly in the media; a small store can afford only a token amount of advertising in comparison. This means the smaller store must compete based on personal service or by serving a small niche of loyal customers.

Profile 10–3 presents the story of C. J.'s Vitesse Cycle, a retailer of high-quality bicycles. Note how C. J.'s compares with other retailers and what allows it to be successful.

TABLE 10–7   Top Fifteen Franchises

Rank	Franchise Chain	Number of outlets
1	McDonald's	16,796
2	Southland Corporation (7-Eleven stores)	15,520
3	Subway Sandwiches and Salads	11,500
4	KFC	8,187
5	Burger King	7,506
6	Tandy Corp. (Radio Shack)	6,600
7	Century 21 Real Estate	6,000
8	Taco Bell	5,644
9	International Dairy Queen	5,347
10	Domino's Pizza	5,300
11	The ServiceMaster Co.	4,408
12	Wendy's International	4,406
13	Baskin-Robbins Inc.	4,404
14	Dunkin' Donuts	4,066
15	Jani-King International (janitorial services)	4,060

SOURCE: International Franchise Association, 1996, quoted in 1997 *Information Please Business Almanac,* Seth Godin, ed. (Boston: Houghton Mifflin, 1997), p. 576.

PROFILE 10–3   *C. J.'s Vitesse Cycle Shop*

C. J.'s Vitesse Cycle Shop is a retail bicycle store owned by C. J. and Theresa Harms. C. J.'s carries a wide assortment of high-quality bicycles, including Trek, Cannondale, Giant, Gary Fisher, and Lamond. It provides service on all makes of

C.J.'s is typical of specialty bike shops. C.J. can give customers personal attention and provide needed information so they can choose the bike that is best for them. Here a customer tries out a Gary Fisher bike that may cost over $1000. What kinds of customers are most likely to shop at a store like C.J.'s? Are there benefits to shopping at a specialty bike shop versus large discount retailers?

bicycles. It has a staff of 10 knowledgeable employees who enjoy biking as a hobby. Some even enter road and mountain bike races. The store is a great source of information on the entire bicycle industry. The expert staff, the wide selection, and the friendly customer service are the keys to C. J.'s success. C. J.'s offers customers a number of benefits—for example, lifetime service on any bike purchased.

C. J.'s Vitesse Cycle competes to a small extent with Wal-Mart, Montgomery Ward, Kmart, Target, and other discounters. Those businesses, however, sell mass-merchandised bicycles and do not provide service. Also competing in the community are two other retailers who specialize in higher-quality bikes, but C. J.'s believes it provides the best service for the money in the area.

C. J's Vitesse Cycle gets its bicycles directly from the manufacturers. The bikes are delivered by common carrier and by UPS.

Multiple Distribution Methods

Some manufacturers have found that they can use multiple methods of distribution. Levi's jeans, for example, are sold in department stores and also in stores owned by Levi's itself. Other companies produce both name brand products and store brand products, giving the manufacturer two different, but similar, products that can be sold at two different prices in retail stores. Profile 10–4 illustrates this with the home appliance industry.

PROFILE **10–4**   *The Home Appliance Industry*

Home appliances are a particular type of retail good—a major purchase that may last 15 to 20 years. These are among the durable goods we discussed under manufacturing. They include refrigerators, dishwashers, stoves, and laundry equipment. Home appliances are produced by relatively few manufacturers, even though the number of brands is large. For example, General Electric makes GE appliances and also Hotpoint. Maytag also owns the Admiral and Magic Chef brands. Some companies make products with their own name on them and also products with competitors' brands on them. Whirlpool, a well-known brand, also makes appliances for Sears, as does Admiral.

The nature of retailing makes home appliance sales complex. It is not unusual for a particular brand of appliance to be sold through both independent dealers and through department stores and discounters. Often manufacturers make slightly different models (with different model numbers) for each outlet type in order to give retailers "exclusive" models to sell and make it harder for buyers to compare prices. They also make models that vary from the basic no-frills appliance to high-end models with numerous additional features. In fact, most brands offer a number of models that vary slightly in features and have incremental price jumps between models.

Competition in the retail home appliance industry is driven by both manufacturers and retailers. Chains like Circuit City, Best Buy, and Lowe's typically sell a number of brands at the lowest possible prices. Independent appliance stores may also sell more than one brand, based partly on the quality of the appliance and partly on the quality of service the store provides. Similarly, some brands tend to focus more on quality than others. In the large appliance market, Maytag and Kitchen-Aid emphasize quality, while Hotpoint and Magic Chef may emphasize price.

You can see that the home appliance retail landscape is a complicated assortment of customer outlets. It is difficult for the typical consumer to know precisely who makes a given model and how it compares with similar models in other stores. Because of the wide range of different features and model numbers, it is hard for customers to differentiate relative price/value relationships. Even the articles in magazines like *Consumer Reports* are sometimes less useful than desired because of the frequency of model number changes and the use of different model numbers for the same product sold in different outlets.

Home appliances are usually distributed via company trucks, unlike clothing, which is shipped either by common carrier or, in the case of small shipments, by UPS or the U.S. Postal Service.

Important Concepts in Distribution

The distribution of products illustrates a number of important business concepts. Some of these concepts are unique to wholesaling, some are relevant to retailing, and some apply to both.

Cost   A manufacturer deciding how to distribute products to the ultimate customer must consider a number of issues. First is the cost of distribution. Indeed, the whole concept of distribution revolves around cost. It is not cost efficient for the manufacturer to attempt to distribute products directly to the final consumer. Cost of distribution is relevant because the cost is ultimately passed on to the customer. For example, if a producer can save 20 percent of total distribution costs by switching distribution methods, then it can reduce the final cost to consumers. With that in mind, let's consider what the distribution-related costs are.

Shipping is one cost. As you might expect, the per-unit shipping cost is much lower if many units are shipped at a time rather than only one or two. Thus, if products can be shipped in bulk to a wholesaler, who then distributes to individual retailers, the net cost to the manufacturer may be less.

Selling is another cost. This includes the cost of manufacturers' representatives, if any. If the products are sold through a wholesaler, the wholesaler marks up the price in order to make a profit when the product is sold to a retailer. The retailer then marks up the price again, often 100 percent, in order to make a profit.

Advertising is another cost. Whether advertising is done by the manufacturer or the retailer or both, someone has to pay for it. In *cooperative advertising*, the manufacturer and the retailer share advertising costs. For example, when the local Ace Hardware store mails fliers to residents, the fliers feature pictures of many products provided by different manufacturers. In most cases, the hardware store and the manufacturer share in the cost of the advertising.

Coverage
The number of customers reached by a distributor.

Coverage   Another key concept in distribution is **coverage,** or the number of customers reached. A manufacturer that chooses to distribute products directly to customers will have difficulty getting wide coverage because of insufficient sales staff. Using a manufacturers' representative and wholesalers ensures far wider coverage. Suppose, for example, that you make superblast water guns. You contract with 10 manufacturers' reps, one in each of 10 regions of the country. Each of those reps calls on 20 wholesalers of toys in his or her region. Each of the 20 wholesalers sells to 50 retailers. You have now reached 10,000 retail establishments.

Coverage and cost may appear to work against each other. Using wholesalers and manufacturers' reps does add a cost to distributing the product. However, the additional cost is far outweighed by the sales generated by the coverage they provide.

Timing   A third important concept in distribution is timing of delivery. This can be especially important in industrial goods distribution if the customer uses a just-in-time inventory system. We discuss JIT in more depth in Chapter 13. The key is that a manufacturer must negotiate with customers to find out how important timing is. For example, if a product must arrive the next business day, either the manufacturer or the customer must pay for overnight shipping of a single product. This may be 10 times the cost of shipping the same product by normal distribution methods. The producer must weigh the cost of timing against the need to satisfy customers.

Transportation   Somewhat related to timing is the issue of transportation. The cost of transportation is directly related to both speed and flexibility of the transportation method. Using overnight shipping is extremely expensive, but it is quick. Using trucks is slower but less expensive. Using train cars or ships for bulk items is even cheaper but even slower.

In some cases, the nature of the product determines the shipping method used. Coal always has to be shipped by rail; its weight and bulk preclude other methods. Produce for grocery stores is normally shipped by refrigerated trucks, which allows distribution to a variety of sites without loss of perishable food. The Fleming Companies, discussed in Profile 10–2, often uses this method.

Contract carrier
A trucking company that specializes in carrying a particular kind of good for a few customers.

Some companies use **contract carriers,** which are trucking companies that specialize in carrying a particular kind of good for a few customers. For example, Asche Transportation has a fleet of refrigerated trucks. Its customers are Jewel Foods, Johnson Wax, Ore-Ida Potatoes, and a handful of other clients. All of these clients need the special handling provided by refrigerated trucks.

Common carrier
A trucking company that transports a wide variety of different products for many clients.

Other trucking companies, called **common carriers,** transport a wide variety of different products for many clients. When you see a truck on the highway with a name like Yellow Freight or Roadway, chances are you are seeing a common carrier. These businesses often transport trailer loads of packages from one point in the country to another. Their loads may differ each trip.

Large manufacturers, wholesalers, and retailers often have their own trucks, which carry only that company's materials. Whirlpool, Deere, McDonald's, Wal-Mart, and Pizza Hut are among the companies that have their own trucks.

The final method of transportation is small-package carriers such as UPS, the U.S. Postal Service, or FedEx. These too are technically common carriers since they carry products for thousands of clients, but because they specialize in small packages, they are considered differently. The price per package may be higher than for other forms of transportation, but since the volume sent at a given time or to a given customer is low, it becomes the most efficient method of delivery. Lands' End, for example, ships all of its clothes to customers around the country via UPS. Because of its volume, it keeps 40 UPS trucks on site, which are loaded during the day and depart each evening.

Lands' End encountered a significant and potentially damaging event in August 1997 when UPS drivers went out on strike. Because Lands' End is totally dependent on single-package delivery, a strike could completely shut them down. Their volume amounts to thousands of dollars of inventory which would sit undelivered in their warehouse. Lands' End countered this threat by immediately contracting with the

U.S. Postal Service to ship packages. As a result, they lost little.[7] Smaller companies, however, were not so lucky.

This section has discussed the distribution function in business. The two parts of it, wholesale and retail, both play extremely important roles in the process of delivering products to customers. We now turn to the service sector, in which businesses provide value through services to customers rather than by making or delivering products.

Developing Your Critical Thinking Skills

1. How does the retail/wholesale sector differ from manufacturing? What are their similarities?

2. Look around the room where you are sitting while reading this chapter. Consider the products in the room—notebooks, computer, microwave oven, bedding, posters, and photos in frames. How did each arrive at the store in which you purchased it?

3. How can a small retailer compete effectively with a giant company such as Sears or JCPenney?

The Service Sector

The manufacturing sector produces products. These are things that we can see and touch. We can consume or use them, or we can return them to the seller if they do not work right. The distribution sector delivers those products to customers. Services, as the name implies, provide intangible benefits to their customers rather than products. In other words, the customer benefits from the service but often has little tangible to show for it. For example, if my attorney meets with me to discuss a contract, I will have benefited from the service, and I will be charged a fee. Yet I have nothing other than the knowledge gained from the meeting and perhaps a few documents. If I go to a fitness center, I may feel better, but (other than possibly sore muscles), I have no immediately tangible benefit from that particular session.

Once a service has been provided, it is difficult to undo it. If I go to the hospital for surgery and I am not happy with it, I may sue the doctor or the hospital, but I can't easily undo the surgery. If I have a bumpy ride on an airplane, I may complain and may even get some restitution, but I still go wherever the plane is going.

Services cannot be either stockpiled or back ordered. For example, if I own a retail business selling apparel, I can have a substantial stock of inventory on hand. If a customer wants a product that I do not currently have in stock, I can order it. Service businesses do not have this luxury. Suppose I own a drain-cleaning business. You call me because your basement is backed up with water from a stopped-up sewer line. If I cannot get to your house today, you will not wait until next week. You will call a competitor immediately. Table 10–8 shows a small sample of the hundreds of services available today.

Employment in the service sector has grown steadily for decades. Figure 10–3 shows employment in the service sector compared with manufacturing and other

TABLE 10–8   Selected Services

Taxicabs	Warehousing	Shipping	Marinas
Airlines	Pipelines	Communications	Hotels
Banking	Sanitary services	Insurance agents	Advertising
Photographers	Real estate brokers	Mailing services	Car leasing
Theaters	Computer services	Car repair shops	Consultants
Hospitals	Physicians	Home health care	Plumbers
Day care	Fitness centers	Vocational schools	Accountants
Attorneys	Employment agencies	Security systems	Dry-cleaning

sectors for the years 1960–96. Note that manufacturing has declined steadily, while mining and construction have stayed essentially steady and agriculture has declined slightly. All indications are that service employment will continue to increase. This shift is due to consumers deciding that it makes more sense to have others provide certain services than to provide those services for themselves. This has usually been the case for essential services like health care, police protection, education, and government. Today, other services are growing as they offer convenience to increasingly busy households, who place a premium on their time. So, it makes sense to have the taxes done by H&R Block, the house cleaned by a maid service, the yard maintained by a lawn service, and routine car repairs and maintenance done by the local garage. Further, computer services are attractive as they offer both speed and convenience. Limited leisure time is used to the fullest extent, fueling growth in travel and recreational businesses.

Service sector industries can be just as competitive as manufacturing even though they provide no product. Hospitals are now among the most competitive industries in existence. Banking and financial services have gone through major industry changes since they were deregulated, as have airlines. Competition has helped keep the service industries efficient and customer focused.

Like manufacturing, service industries vary widely in the cost a firm incurs to produce and market the service. A day care center operator may have to spend only a few hundred dollars to add a fenced yard and meet health regulations. An airline may spend from $38 million for a Boeing 737 to $175 million for a Boeing 747 or 777.[8] A hospital has extraordinarily high fixed costs compared with a consulting firm.

fixed costs p. 278>

A major difference between services and manufacturing is that service businesses do not, as a core part of their business, deal with inventory and cost of goods sold. Thus, the comparison between costs and prices is much different. At the same time, however, service businesses must recognize the need to keep costs at a minimum. Since inventory does not provide a major part of the flow-through of funds for service businesses, these companies must look elsewhere to find avenues for cost containment.

Many service industries are highly labor intensive, so labor costs and fringe benefits form a major portion of a firm's expenses. Business owners must carefully consider

FIGURE 10-3   Private Employment by Sector, 1960–96

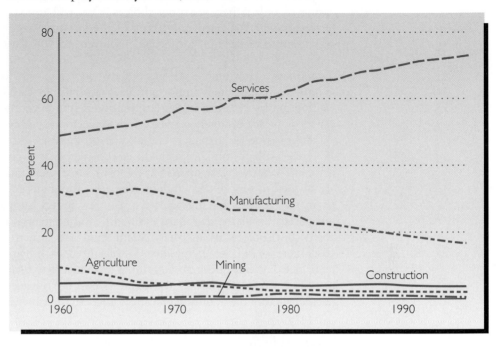

SOURCE: Bureau of Labor Statistics payroll survey (services, manufacturing, construction, mining), household survey (agriculture).

the degree to which controlling the cost of human resources interferes with the effectiveness of those workers.

Important Concepts in Services

Because of the unique nature of services, some concepts are critically important, especially for businesses with a high contact level. We discuss a few of these concepts next.

Cost   We have said cost is a key concern for both the manufacturing and the distribution sectors. Cost is also key in service industries. One reason that costs receive so much attention is that there are fewer opportunities to reduce them. Since there is limited inventory, no manufacturing process, and few suppliers, none of these provide opportunities for cutting costs. Thus, cost reduction must focus on labor costs and the costs of actually providing the service.

Employee Expertise   Since many services depend on interaction between providers and their clients, it is very important to have knowledgeable employees. Few things are more frustrating for consumers than service people who cannot answer their questions. This is also true in manufacturing and distribution, but it is especially important in service businesses because of the close interaction that often occurs between the business and its customers.

Employee Attitude   Today's customers simply will not tolerate a lackadaisical or uncaring attitude if there are other choices. They will go to competitors in search of better treatment. You need only think of the last time you received poor service in a restaurant to realize how important employee attitude is for repeat business.

Timeliness   How much time passes between when a service is requested and when it is rendered is extremely important in service businesses. Waiting in a doctor's office, waiting to be served in a restaurant, waiting in line to get into a movie, or waiting for a car repair—lack of timely service can drive customers away in all these situations.

A key issue for managers is the trade-off between cost and customer satisfaction. We have probably all complained that a bank was irresponsible because not enough drive-up windows were open. But the bank's managers must decide how many tellers are needed to service the windows properly. Too many tellers means that the bank is paying labor costs for idle workers. Too few tellers means that unhappy customers must wait. Similarly, too many trained dental hygienists in a dentist's office can be costly, but too few means that patients must be turned away. Unfortunately, labor costs increase in large increments. For example, each hygienist can clean 20 patients' teeth per day. But hiring an additional hygienist may bring in only five new patients per day because of insufficient demand. Thus, the owner of the dental business must decide whether the additional business is worth the expense.

Changes in Service through Technology

We have emphasized that service delivery depends on customer contact and that satisfaction with that contact is critical. Yet one trend in the service industry seems to be toward less direct contact between the service providers and customers. For example, you probably have little if any contact with your bank other than through the ATM. You probably use a self-service gasoline station, and you may even pay for the gas by swiping your credit card through a reader on the pump. You may check into and out of hotels without talking to a human being. These lower levels of contact are convenient and in some cases allow providers to offer services at lower prices.

Many improvements in service provision are the result of increasing technology. You couldn't have done banking from your computer 10 years ago. Technology even permits some medical services without going to a doctor. Now some doctors' offices allow patients to ask nonemergency questions via e-mail. This saves travel and waiting time for the patients and allows the doctors to use their time and resources more efficiently.

We illustrate the structure and dynamics of service industries by ending the section with a profile of Southwest Airlines. You have already learned a lot about Southwest Airlines. Now observe in Profile 10–5 the important concepts in service that Southwest does well.

PROFILE 10–5   *Southwest Airlines' No-frills Ride*

Southwest Airlines makes a profit based on its ability to maximize revenues on flights while keeping the average passenger-mile cost (the total cost to transport one passenger one mile) as low as possible. Southwest can keep its fares low because it maintains the lowest average passenger-mile cost in the industry. It achieves this cost advantage because it has relatively low labor costs, flies a single type of plane, and uses more efficient scheduling, boarding, and luggage-handling methods than many of its rivals.

Southwest is a no-frills airline. Boarding is on a first-come, first-served basis. Carry-on luggage is limited to what will fit in a rectangular box near the ticket counter. Southwest was the first major airline to adopt ticketless travel, saving the substantial costs of printing tickets for all the passengers, whose reservations are already logged into the system's computer. This use of technology is such a cost saver that it has been adopted by other airlines. Southwest saves money in small ways that reduce costs even more. It reuses boarding passes. Instead of serving hot meals, it serves peanuts or pretzels and soft drinks.

Another important concept for service industries where Southwest excels is in having a knowledgeable staff with a good attitude. Southwest has been listed in *The 100 Best Companies to Work for in America* because it is a fun place to work. The employees have a good time in spite of working many hours. They take care of their customers with spirit and enthusiasm.

CEO Herb Kelleher sets the tone for the entire company. He works 14 hours a day, seven days a week. Southwest's pay scale is comparable to other airlines'. It was the first airline to offer profit sharing, and it puts a lot of money into training. Often Southwest's people work long hours "just for the pride in it."

SOURCE: Kevin Freiberg and Jackie Freiberg, *Nuts! Southwest Airlines' Crazy Recipe for Business and Personal Success* (Austin, TX: Bard Press, Inc., 1996).

Developing Your Critical Thinking Skills

1. Service industries differ from manufacturing in a number of ways. One major way is customer contact. What employee skills are most important for service industries?

2. We mentioned that service industries can be fiercely competitive. What accounts for the differences in the intensity of competition?

3. How can technology be used effectively in services such as real estate sales? Car rentals?

The Nonprofit Sector

This chapter has dealt with different industry sectors in business. We discussed manufacturing, distribution, and service industries. We now turn to the not-for-profit sector, which we discussed briefly in Chapter 2. We return to the topic to illustrate important concepts in this type of industry. Organizations in this sector are known as nonprofit corporations, volunteer organizations, or not-for-profit organizations (NFPs). We use the terms interchangeably.

Table 10–9 shows a number of not-for-profit organizations. Nonprofits are typically in seven industry groups: health services; social and legal services; education and research; religious organizations; civic, social, and fraternal organizations; arts and cultural organizations; and foundations. Health services include hospitals, nursing homes, and drug treatment centers. Social and legal services include nonprofit legal services, family service centers, day care services, and job training. Education and research includes higher education, elementary and secondary education, libraries, and research institutes. Religious organizations include churches, temples, synagogues, and other related organizations. Civic, social, and fraternal organizations include Chambers of Commerce, business clubs, and lodges. Arts and cultural organizations include museums, galleries, symphonies, and not-for-profit theaters. Foundations are established to collect and distribute charitable contributions.

There are two major categories of nonprofit organizations: those that exist to benefit their own members (like professional associations and labor organizations) and those that work to improve the general welfare of the community or society. The organizations in the latter group receive special treatment under the federal tax codes and are known as *501(c)(3) organizations*. A **501(c)(3) organization** is a not-for-profit organization that is authorized to receive tax-deductible donations. Because they are organized to serve a public benefit, nonprofit organizations cannot be owned by individuals or exist for the purpose of making a profit.

Not-for-profit organizations vary almost as much as for-profit businesses. First, they range in *size* from your high school's booster club to large universities. They vary in *missions* from a chamber of commerce to a research hospital. Their *funding* ranges from a few hundred dollars raised by bake sales and car washes to millions of dollars from direct mail and television appeals. Their *beneficiaries* range from the group itself (in the case of a professional organization) to homeless people, disabled people, and other recipients of charitable causes.

As Table 10–9 shows, several organization types may be either for-profit or non-profit. In fact, hospitals and health care organizations are moving toward for-profit status. Humana, Inc. is a large chain of hospitals that are for-profit corporations. Not-for-profit organizations have many similarities with for-profit businesses. The primary differences are that they do not recognize profits or losses and they do not pay income taxes on earnings. You may read of nonprofit organizations discussing surpluses and deficits. These are roughly the equivalent of profits and losses for profit-oriented businesses.

501(c)(3) organization
A nonprofit organization that is authorized to receive tax-deductible donations.

TABLE 10–9   Nonprofit Organizations

Hospitals*	Botanical and zoological gardens
Elementary and secondary schools	Business associations
Colleges and universities*	Professional organizations
Libraries	Labor organizations
Individual and family services*	Civic and social associations
Job training and related services*	Political organizations
Day care services for children*	Religious organizations
Museums and art galleries*	

*May be either for-profit or not-for-profit.

TABLE 10–10   The Magnitude of Volunteering in America

Volunteers (percent of population)	47.7%
Volunteers (in millions)	89.2
Average weekly hours per volunteer	4.2
Average annual hours per volunteer	218.4
Total hours volunteered in 1993 (in millions)	19,481.3
Assigned dollar value at $12.13 per hour*	$182.3 billion

* Average hourly wage for nonagricultural workers.

SOURCE: Virginia Ann Hodgkinson and Murray S. Weitzman, *Nonprofit Almanac 1996–1997: Dimensions of the Independent Sector* (San Francisco: Jossey-Bass Publishers, 1996), p. 24.

The Impact of Nonprofits

It is important to understand the magnitude of nonprofit organizations. In 1994, they employed almost 10 million people. Growth in paid employment in the NFP sector has been 3.4 percent a year, while growth in business and government sectors has been 1.9 percent and 1.4 percent, respectively. In addition, millions of people volunteer in NFP organizations. All nonprofit organizations together bring in contributions of over $500 billion per year for worthy causes.[9]

Volunteers play an extremely important role in nonprofit organizations. According to a Gallup poll, almost half the people in the United States volunteer at least some hours, and they average over 200 hours per year, as shown in Table 10–10. Multiplying all of this by the average hourly wage yields a total contribution from volunteers of over $180 billion a year.

Important Concepts in Nonprofits

We consider here a few concepts that are of importance to nonprofit organizations. Note that due to the great variation in sizes and types of organization, some concepts are more relevant for some NFPs than for others.

The Nature of Competition among Nonprofit Organizations   Nonprofit organizations compete with each other on two separate fronts. The first is competition for customers. The second is competition for funding.

The amount of competition for customers depends on the industry. In the hospital industry, for example, competition is fierce. Universities compete with other universities for students. Even churches compete for members to some extent. In the case of charitable organizations, the competition is less pronounced because each organization has different missions and may serve different constituencies.

Nonprofit organizations compete directly for funding with other organizations within their industry group. They also compete indirectly with all other nonprofit organizations because each relies on individuals and corporations for funding. Charitable organizations like the Salvation Army, Goodwill Industries, Habitat for Humanity, the United Way, the American Red Cross, the American Heart Association, and the American Cancer Society are all very aggressive in their fund-raising.

The Relationship between Revenues and Cost   Nonprofit organizations, especially charitable organizations, have a unique characteristic not shared by for-profit businesses. This is the relationship between the recipients of services and the people who pay for those services. In a for-profit business, the two are typically the same. In other words, the customer pays money and receives a product or service. In nonprofit organizations, a customer receives a product or service that is often paid for or provided by a stranger. For example, a poverty-stricken family receives a food basket from a neighborhood food pantry. The family does not know who provided the food. The staff of the food pantry may be either paid or volunteer. But if they are paid, they are paid by virtue of monetary donations to the organization.

budget p. 402>   Universities also operate in this manner. Even though your tuition may appear to be high, it underwrites only a small portion of the total operating budget of the university. Taxpayers foot much of the bill for state universities. Private universities depend heavily on endowments and other contributions from foundations, alumni, and friends of the university. Thus, students are only partially paying customers and are partially recipients of the contributions of others.

revenue p. 167>   ***Sources of Revenue***   Funding for NFPs comes from three primary sources: earned income, contributions, and grants. Nearly all nonprofit organizations use these three, although the ways they are used may vary.

The first source of funding is *earned income*. The revenue sources may be different for each NFP. For example, a hospital's main source of revenue or earned income is pay-

Habitat for Humanity college chapters exist all over the country. Like these Bradley University students, many chapter members will spend their spring breaks and weekends during school building houses for low income families. The student members gain building skills while working for a good cause. How would you raise funds to underwite a Habitat spring break trip?

ments by patients. A symphony's earned income is primarily from ticket sales and memberships in the organization. A university's earned income is from tuition. Habitat for Humanity's earned income is the sale of the houses that volunteers build or rehabilitate.

**board of directors
p. 64>**

The second source of funds is *contributions from local individuals and corporations.* Often a nonprofit's board of directors includes key employees from major corporations in the area and well-known community residents. These individuals can be counted on for substantial contributions. The nonprofit also sends fund-raising letters to community residents and companies in the hopes of meeting annual fund-raising goals. Cultural organizations depend heavily on advertising in program booklets by corporations in the community.

The third source of funds is *grants* from foundations, the government, arts organizations, and national corporations that have a history of contributions. These sources are extremely important because they often provide large amounts of funding. However, the NFP can be vulnerable if the attitudes or giving patterns of these groups change.

State-supported organizations, such as universities and high schools, receive a considerable amount of their funding through state funds. This source, of course, is not available for the vast majority of organizations.

Cost   Cost is an important concept in every industry we have discussed: manufacturing, distribution, and service industries. It is also important for nonprofits to guard against unnecessary riscs in costs because the relationship between cost and revenues is not close. As we mentioned earlier, much of the revenue in NFPs comes from sources that are not related to their program or mission. Also, many of the managers and staffers in charitable organizations come from disciplines other than business. Their background, experience, and knowledge are often in program-related skills rather than business skills.

Volunteers   Nonprofit organizations live or die by the loyalty of their volunteers. Since the volunteers do a disproportionate amount of the total work in a nonprofit organization, it is imperative for the board and staff to keep the volunteers happy and motivated. This is a key difference between NFPs and for-profit businesses. In businesses, employees are motivated, at least in part, by their paycheck.

In nonprofit organizations, volunteers receive no salary. They contribute their time solely because they want to support the organization. There is little incentive other than personal satisfaction to work diligently. Many volunteers have full-time jobs and volunteer in their spare time. If they are not treated well, they may leave and spend their limited spare time doing other things.

**strategic decisions
p. 77>**

**top management
p. 65>**

Boards of Directors   In Chapter 3, we discussed the role of boards of directors in corporations. We stated that the board makes or approves major strategic decisions, but the day-to-day management of the company is the role of top management. Board members are relatively more important in nonprofit organizations, especially small, local nonprofits.

Nonprofit organizations rely on volunteers to serve on the board of directors. Since the paid staff, such as an executive director, must answer directly to the board, they rely heavily on the board for policy and planning and also for help in running the organization. Thus, board members are often much more active in the affairs of the organization than are board members of a corporation. For example, it is not uncommon for board members of a small NFP to help stuff envelopes for a mailing or to write articles for the quarterly newsletter.

Larger nonprofit organizations function more nearly like for-profit businesses. Your university, for example, may have a board of directors who are volunteers, but the board serves as a governing body much like the boards in large companies. They meet monthly or quarterly and hear reports from the university administrators. They vote on major issues that are brought to the board by the administrators.

As we have done for each of the previous sectors, we illustrate the nature of the industry and some of the important concepts through a profile organization. The Elgin Symphony Orchestra is a good example of how a nonprofit organization works and how the important concepts apply. Note in Profile 10–6 how the organization is structured and how it raises funds for its operations.

PROFILE **10–6**   *The Elgin Symphony Orchestra Makes Music and Raises Funds*

The Elgin Symphony Orchestra was founded in 1950 in Elgin, Illinois, a community of 80,000 residents some 40 miles west of downtown Chicago. It became a professional symphony orchestra, meaning it has paid union musicians, in 1985. It employs 65 musicians each year, many of whom aspire to play in the internationally known Chicago Symphony Orchestra. The orchestra performs about 50 concerts per year, including traditional concerts, holiday concerts, educational concerts for children, summer concerts, and concerts in area schools. It is the largest suburban symphony in the Chicago area, and its patrons come from a number of west suburban communities. Its musicians come from throughout the Chicago area; some drive up to two hours for rehearsals and concerts.

The Elgin Symphony Orchestra is a nonprofit organization that offers classical music and is a source of community pride. What nonprofits in your area offer services that you use? Are you involved as a volunteer in any of these organizations?

In addition to the musicians and conductors, the Elgin Symphony Orchestra has a staff of seven full-time employees: the executive director, a marketing director, a director of development and an assistant, a box-office manager, an operations manager, and a receptionist. The ESO has a board of directors made up of 40 volunteers, and the ESO League has 100 volunteers who help with fund-raising and other activities.

budget p. 402>

The annual budget for the orchestra is nearly $1 million. Funds come from a number of sources. Earned income, primarily from ticket sales, covers about half of the budget. This is about the norm for regional symphonies. Roughly 500 regular donors provide a significant part of the funding. The ESO also receives funding from the city of Elgin, part of which comes from taxes collected from a highly profitable riverboat casino located nearby. The ESO staff also coordinates an annual golf marathon, which brought in approximately $40,000 in June 1997. Golfers collected pledges for the symphony for each hole they played. The golf marathon not only brings in substantial funds each year, but it also develops camaraderie and support for the symphony among the golfers and throughout the community. The 1997 marathon was featured on the front page of the local newspaper.

The symphony also mails and telemarkets solicitations to individual contributors and writes grant requests to agencies that provide funds to arts and cultural organizations. The director of development writes grant requests, coordinates annual giving programs, and works with local corporations to sponsor concerts and provide other types of funding for the symphony. Even in an era of belt-tightening for the arts, the ESO enjoys a healthy balance sheet thanks to its diverse fund-raising activities.

balance sheet, 486 >

Developing Your Critical Thinking Skills

1. For-profit businesses and not-for-profit organizations share many similarities. Which of these is most important when considering the management of the business or organization?

2. Some nonprofits are highly competitive, while others are much more cooperative. What accounts for the difference?

3. We discussed that customers are a prime source of funds for a for-profit business, but they may not be for an NFP. Select a nonprofit organization. Who are its constituents? Who are its benefactors? Why are they different?

SUMMARY

1. All businesses conduct their activities within one or more industries. The nature of the industry represents a key external force a manager must understand and address.

    ■ What are the major sectors of the economy?

    This chapter discussed six sectors:

    (1) Agriculture
    (2) Government
    (3) Manufacturing
    (4) Distribution
    (5) Services
    (6) Not-for-profit organizations

2. The manufacturing sector is the basis of a country's economy. In recent years the impact of manufacturing has declined, but it is still a significant force.

    ■ What are the major characteristics of the American manufacturing sector?

    Manufacturing is the process of building a product or adding value to raw materials. Manufacturing produces either durable goods or nondurable goods. Manufactured goods have one of three destinations—final consumers, components in other products, or capital goods. Some manufacturers (for example, carmakers) practice vertical integration. That is, they control two or more sequential processes in the production or distribution of the product. Some also engage in strategic alliances.

    Important concepts in manufacturing include capital intensiveness, industry concentration, vertical integration, captive suppliers, quality, and strategic alliances/joint ventures.

3. The distribution sector moves products from manufacturers to customers. Many different kinds of distribution are available.

    ■ What are the characteristics of the distribution sector?

    This sector contains two major groups, wholesalers and retailers. Wholesalers are the intermediaries between manufacturers and retailers. Their roles include storing goods, breaking bulk items into smaller shipments, providing industry and consumer information, financing, maintaining inventory, transporting goods, ordering goods, and assuming risk.

    Retailers sell to the ultimate consumer. Retailing companies come in many varieties and represent names familiar to almost everyone, such as Wal-Mart, JCPenney, Sears, Kroger, Safeway, and Home Depot. The competitive structure within retailing is continually evolving. Fifty years ago there were only a very few large department stores and no malls or national discount chains. Today, the discounters and malls are everywhere. The retail scene is dominated by large chains.

    Today's retail scene is also noticeable for its category killers. These large chain stores specialize in a narrow line of goods, provide great depth in product offerings, and offer very low prices. Toys"R"Us and Home Depot are two examples.

    Franchises are also popular today. A franchise is a business owned by a franchisee that uses the name, standard operating procedures, training, and marketing provided by the franchisor.

    Retailing is also characterized by numerous small independent businesses. To be successful they must compete against the chains by offering more personal service or serving a small niche made up of loyal customers.

    Important concepts in distribution include cost, coverage, timing, and transportation.

4. Whereas manufacturing used to be seen as the major source of growth, the service sector is now looked to for both economic growth and employment growth.

    ■ What are the main features of the service sector of the economy?

    Service businesses provide intangible benefits to their customers—for example, taxicabs, airlines, hospitals, attorneys, real estate brokers, computer services, security systems, and dry cleaners. A major difference between services and manufacturing is that services do not typically deal with inventory. Many services are highly labor intensive, so managers must try to control the cost of human resources without compromising on the quality of employees.

In recent years, the service sector has been the largest source of new jobs in the American economy. It has also been the source of some of the most dramatic changes in the nature of competition. A major cause of that change has been deregulation, as illustrated by the case of the airline industry.

Important concepts in services includes cost, expertise, employee attitude, and timeliness.

5. There is a high level of volunteerism in America. Some of that takes place with little formal organization, but today much of it is sponsored by formal nonprofit organizations that engage in businesslike practices.

■ What are the basic features of the nonprofit sector?

Not-for-profit organizations operate similarly to for-profit organizations, except that they do not recognize profits and losses or pay income taxes on earnings.

NFPs are found in a variety of activities, typically in seven industry groups: health services; social and legal services; education and research; religious organizations; civic, social and fraternal organizations; arts and cultural organizations; and foundations. Nonprofit organizations exist to serve either the members of the organization or the general welfare of the community or society.

Nonprofit organizations may have paid employees. They also have unpaid volunteers. It is estimated that almost half the people in America spend at least a few hours volunteering each year. Not-for-profit organizations have a unique characteristic not shared by for-profit organizations; their customer receives a product or service that is often paid for or provided by a stranger.

Important concepts in the nonprofit sector include competition, the relationship between revenue and cost, sources of revenue, cost, volunteers, and the board of directors' role.

Links to other courses

The themes of this chapter are relevant for a number of courses. However, industry themes will receive particular attention in the following courses.

- Principles of economics
- Principles of marketing
- Marketing channels
- Retailing

- Strategic management
- Management of nonprofit organizations

KEY TERMS

Capital goods, p. 276
Captive supplier, p. 279
Category killer, p. 283
Common carrier, p. 288
Contract carrier, p. 288
Coverage, p. 287
Distribution sector, p. 274
501(c)(3) organization, p. 294
Industry concentration, p. 278
Industry sectors, p. 272

Manufacturers' representative, p. 282
Manufacturing firms, p. 274
Manufacturing sector, p. 274
Original equipment manufacturer (OEM), p. 276
Retailer, p. 282
Service sector, p. 275
Vertical integration, p. 278
Wholesaler, p. 281

1. Consider a small retail store in your community. Does it provide better service than department stores? Is this service important?

2. Do you prefer services to be high contact, with knowledgeable, friendly, and attentive service providers, or do you prefer technology-based low contact where you don't have to deal with people? What are the advantages and disadvantages of each? Do you think there is a trend toward less human contact in services?

3. Form teams of six people. Interview the owner or manager of a local restaurant to find out how it gets the supplies it needs. Write a one-page paper discussing the various distribution methods that you identified.

4. How does the Internet help the retail and service industries? How do the two sectors differ in their use of the Internet? Go to the home page of a major retailer and analyze the benefits of the home page.

5. Form teams of six people. Take turns describing the volunteer activities that each of you have done. What benefit did you provide to the organization? What benefit or value did you personally gain from the experience? Do you think young people starting their business careers should spend time volunteering for nonprofits?

CASE: THE LONG ARM OF MICKEY MOUSE

Few companies compete in as many different ways as Disney while staying in a single broad industry—entertainment. Disney sells a wide variety of merchandise, which it either produces or licenses. It produces movies and television shows. It also distributes those movies and TV shows through its networks and movie distribution companies. Its theme parks provide entertainment to millions of eager customers. It also sells services through its training units.

Disney is in the entertainment industry. Yet that industry is broad. It includes manufacturing of products, distribution of those products, and service businesses such as theme parks. Thus, it competes in a number of different industry sectors. Consider a sample of Disney's holdings.

In the film production area, you are well aware of Disney Studios. But did you know that Disney also owns Buena Vista studios and Touchstone Pictures? In fact, Touchstone was started so the company could produce films with PG-13 and R ratings without damaging the family orientation of Disney Pictures. In theme parks, Disney owns Disneyland and Walt Disney World—as well as Tokyo Disney and Disneyland Paris. You may not be aware that Disney is heavily into publishing. These ventures include *Discover* magazine, *Family Fun* magazine, and publications of Disney Press. It also owns the Mighty Ducks professional hockey team. It owns Capital Cities/ABC, which includes ABC, ESPN, A&E, and a number of TV stations. And, oh, yes. It owns the rights to Mickey Mouse.

Decision Questions

1. How many industry sectors does Disney operate in?
2. What are the relationships among all of Disney's holdings?
3. What do you think would be a logical area for Disney to move toward in the future?

SOURCE: Disney website (http://disney.com).

REFERENCES

1. U.S. Census Bureau web site, http://www.census.gov/naics, (accessed June 24, 1997).

2. *Industry Norms and Key Business Ratios, 1996–97.* New York: Dun & Bradstreet Information Services, 1997.

3. Mark Drabenstott. "Will the Wild Ride for U.S. Agriculture Continue in 1997?" *Economic Review* 82, no. 1 (1997), pp. 63–78.

4. Drabenstott, p. 64.

5. Drabenstott, p. 72.

6. *Economic Report of the President.* U.S. Government Printing Office, 1997, p. 300; Gene Smiley. *The American Economy in the Twentieth Century.* Cincinnati, OH: South-Western Publishing Co., 1994, Ch. 11.

7. Susan Chandler, "Hit Hard, Catalog Firms and Retailers Learn to Cope," *Chicago Tribune*, August 20, 1997, sec. 3, p. 2.

8. Boeing, Inc. website, http://www.boeing.com, (accessed August 25, 1997).

9. Virginia Ann Hodgkinson and Murray S. Weitzman, *Nonprofit Almanac 1996–1997: Dimensions of the Independent Sector.* San Francisco: Jossey-Bass Publishers, 1996, p. 24.

Three

Providing Excellence in Goods and Services

MODEL OF THE PATH TOWARD A SUCCESSFUL BUSINESS

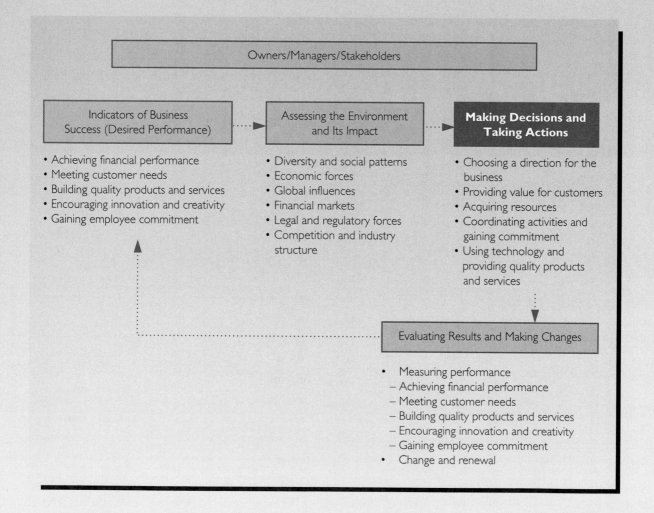

Owners/Managers/Stakeholders

Indicators of Business Success (Desired Performance)

- Achieving financial performance
- Meeting customer needs
- Building quality products and services
- Encouraging innovation and creativity
- Gaining employee commitment

Assessing the Environment and Its Impact

- Diversity and social patterns
- Economic forces
- Global influences
- Financial markets
- Legal and regulatory forces
- Competition and industry structure

Making Decisions and Taking Actions

- Choosing a direction for the business
- Providing value for customers
- Acquiring resources
- Coordinating activities and gaining commitment
- Using technology and providing quality products and services

Evaluating Results and Making Changes

- Measuring performance
  - Achieving financial performance
  - Meeting customer needs
  - Building quality products and services
  - Encouraging innovation and creativity
  - Gaining employee commitment
- Change and renewal

Part Two of the text discussed the environmental forces that affect business. We stressed that managers must be aware of these forces and recognize how they will likely influence business activities. Given this information and perspective, the chapters in Part Three address the decisions that must be made in order for the business to provide its customers with excellence in goods and services. Whether it is deciding the strategic direction for the business, getting the money to start a new plant, using the latest technology to build superior quality products, or working with employees to develop a more motivated and committed workforce, Part Three addresses the actions necessary for business health and competitiveness.

Chapter 11 explores the strategic activities of successful businesses. You will see how businesses establish areas of competence and build these into competitive advantages. The chapter highlights the important foundations of business strategy and describes strategies for international competition.

Chapter 12 examines the comprehensive topic of providing value for the customer. Here, you will learn the dynamics of customer service. You will see how businesses learn about customers and develop products and services that meet customer needs. You will understand the key approaches that are used to communicate value to customers, and you will recognize the importance of receiving and addressing customer feedback.

Chapter 13 discusses how businesses get the resources they need to operate. The acquisition of human, physical, financial, and information resources will all be discussed. You will see that resource acquisition always involves trade-offs, since no business can have all the resources it ideally desires. Deciding how to handle those trade-offs is part of the challenge and excitement of business decision making.

Chapter 14 deals with two important and related issues. The first part of the chapter talks about how businesses try to organize all of their activities into some logical pattern or structure so that they can operate effectively and efficiently. Both traditional and emerging approaches to organizational structure and design are discussed. The second part of the chapter looks at how businesses build strong commitment in their employees. You will learn some important foundations and contemporary ideas about employee motivation.

Chapter 15 looks at how businesses integrate quality and technology in their products and services. You will learn why quality has become so critical in today's business world, and you will learn how business is continually improving its quality. You will understand the dramatic role technology plays in business, and learn of some important ways businesses are using technology to build greater quality, customer service, and efficiency in their operations.

You will enjoy the hands-on tone of Part Three. The chapters in this part look at the things business people do day-in and day-out. You may even see an area of business that appeals to you as a future career as you study the actions discussed in this part of the text.

11

Thinking Strategically about the Business Operation

With a solid reputation for reliable express delivery, Federal Express has become a powerful giant of American business. The company's beginnings are part of business legend. The concept of an all-freight airline with pickup and delivery services focusing on overnight delivery of small packages was the brainchild of Fred Smith. In fact, Smith proposed the original concept in a paper for a college economics class. While he earned only a C– on the paper, he built the idea into a Fortune 500 company. Indeed, FedEx's success has been phenomenal.

Today FedEx faces some of the strongest competition of its history. While FedEx has always emphasized superior service, its feature-rich services raise costs. Competitors are emphasizing two- or three-day deliveries instead of overnight. They are using discounts to lure customers like the federal government to turn business over to them. As a result, competition is gaining market share through price cuts that FedEx simply cannot match.

The picture is equally troubling overseas. FedEx seeks to grow its overseas operations with entry into China and Russia and expansion in Latin America. Efficiency of operations is critical, yet FedEx's system has some serious gaps. And international competitors DHL and UPS are formidable.[1] While opportunities in the delivery

efficiency p. 478>

services industry abound, FedEx faces some critical competitive threats. Indeed, it needs some careful strategic thinking and action.

In Part Two of the book we focused on six key environmental forces: diversity and social patterns, economic forces, global influences, financial markets, legal and regulatory issues, and industry dynamics. With this information in mind, business decision makers must begin to think strategically about their operations. This chapter looks at the ways managers determine where the business is going and how it intends to get there. This chapter will show you how a business strategically plans and positions itself in a competitive market to gain the greatest possible success. You will learn how business leaders think through their environmental readings and put together effective strategic actions to achieve the indicators of business success (as defined in Part One). Most students find the strategic issues and action ideas of this chapter quite interesting. More specifically, after reading this chapter, you should be able to:

1. Establish the importance of the business profile and the role SWOT analysis can play.

2. Show the role and importance of business vision and construct the key parts to the mission statement.

3. Present the concepts of distinctive competence and competitive advantage, understanding why they are critical and how they can be achieved.

4. Gain a sense of business strategy and formulate some of the general strategies that businesses typically pursue.

5. Formulate some of the basic approaches a business might use to pursue a strategy of global operations.

6. Recognize why business objectives are important.

7. Construct categories of objectives and formulate factors to consider in developing them.

8. Demonstrate a working knowledge of the strategic planning process.

9. Recognize the role and significance of business culture within the process of strategic thinking.

diversity p. 125>

financial markets p. 215>

Managers of businesses must be sensitive to changes in any of the six forces in their environment. You will recall that although those six forces have strong impacts on the company, the firm in general cannot exert much influence on them. Diversity and social patterns affect how the company hires and works with its employees and how it interacts with its customers. Economics has a big impact on businesses because of the magnitude and interaction of the economic forces at work. Global issues increasingly influence how a business operates, even if the business itself is not directly involved in foreign markets. Financial markets affect a business as it tries to raise capital, take the company public, or make effective use of its financial resources. Laws and regulations affect many day-to-day operations, since government both encourages and regulates companies in many ways. Finally, the industry in which a business operates can also have substantial influence on how the business competes.

The chapters in Part Two were analytically oriented. That is, they were aimed at analyzing the impacts of the environmental forces. We turn now to chapters oriented toward the actions the company must take to compete in a dynamic marketplace. This chapter discusses the need to think strategically. The first step in thinking strategically is to develop a meaningful **business focus,** the general direction in which top managers plan to take the business. Succeeding chapters will look at additional pieces of the action thrust, as shown in the highlighted portion, "Making Decisions and Taking Actions," in our model of successful business.

Business focus
The general direction in which top managers plan to take a business.

The Need to Look both Outward and Inward

Environmental sensitivity is important for two reasons. First, managers must understand what is happening in the environment. They must recognize changes that are occurring or are likely in the future. Second, they must anticipate how environmental events and anticipated changes are likely to affect their businesses. A firm's environment can hold both opportunities and threats. A manager's task is to identify those opportunities that can be exploited and counter those threats that may do damage.

Simply being aware of opportunities and threats facing the business is not enough, however. Managers must take a hard and objective look at the firm's internal operations and determine how it is positioned to address both environmental opportunities and threats. This process of looking inward is commonly known as developing the business profile. The **business profile** is an assessment of the firm's strengths and weaknesses. For example, a company's strength may reside in the excellent facilities and technology it has available. Its strength may lie in its strong customer orientation and the consumer-focused reputation it has built. Or strength may be in its people, who are both highly skilled and dedicated to their work. A single company may even have all these strengths. Its weaknesses may also cover a range of areas. The company may be experiencing an unstable financial position. Costs may be rising. The possibility of taking on additional debt financing may be quite low. In this regard, the business profile is an internal reality check.

Business profile
An assessment of a firm's strengths and weaknesses.

The business profile suggests two things to management. First, it helps determine what areas of business focus are really possible. Wonderful opportunities for growth or expansion into promising new markets may exist in the environment, but the profile may indicate that the business simply does not have the internal resources to take advantage of these opportunities. Thus, not every environmental opportunity is a real *business opportunity*. Second, the business profile reveals the problem areas that must be addressed if the business is to be competitive and successful.

SWOT analysis
Stands for strengths, weaknesses, opportunities, and threats; an assessment of a firm's key strengths and weaknesses compared with the opportunities and threats it faces.

Many techniques are available for drawing interpretations about the external and internal condition of the business. One of the most direct and most common is known as the SWOT analysis. SWOT stands for *s*trengths, *w*eaknesses, *o*pportunities, and *t*hreats. The **SWOT analysis** provides an assessment of the firm's key strengths and weaknesses compared with the opportunities and threats it faces. The SWOT assessment may be quite basic in a small business; perhaps a group of leaders get together to think through the various areas and assess what has been happening. Or the SWOT analysis can be complex, relying on quantitative analysis of trends and using a variety of sophisticated techniques to project into the future. Regardless of the level and nature of complexity, every business uses some form of SWOT analysis. This gives the business a feel for both movements in its environment and its internal capacity to respond. Many businesses and nonprofit organizations use variations of a SWOT analysis in their planning activities.

The SWOT analysis is the beginning of the firm's efforts to establish a meaningful business focus. Armed with the awareness and sensitivity gained through the SWOT analysis, the manager must decide how to act to best position the business in the environment. Those decisions are never easy. Uncertainty and risk are always involved. Despite these difficulties, the manager must outline a direction for the business.

Let's consider an example of a how a small business used the SWOT approach informally. Bob and Len Gorgan had been operating a small restaurant since they had graduated from college with degrees in restaurant management four years earlier. Located only one block from the main gate of a midsize university, their Handlebar Cafe had experienced modest success at best. The brothers knew that their business had some areas of strength and competence. For example, they were close to campus and no other walk-in restaurant was within a two-block area. Both owners had solid training and backgrounds. There was a ready supply of bright and energetic college students to serve food. The Gorgans were willing to try new things; they were always tinkering with menu items and themes.

Unfortunately, the Handlebar Cafe also had certain weaknesses. The restaurant was in an old building that lacked any real restaurant ambiance. Good cooks were hard to keep and their turnover rate was exceptionally high. The most glaring weakness was money. The business lacked capital. Cash flow was always tight. Any growth opportunity that required much investment would be beyond its capability. The cafe was pretty much tapped out.

One winter morning, the Gorgans were forced to begin to think strategically about their business. On the way to work, Bob walked past the corner vacant lot only a half block from the Handlebar. A gas station had been there but had gone out of business about a year ago. On this morning, Bob was shocked to read the sign on the lot: "Future site of a new 24-hour McDonald's!" As Bob and Len sat at a corner table drinking coffee, they recognized the significance of this threat. McDonald's would be more popular with the students. Its presence could capture Handlebar's customer base and drive it out of business.

In the midst of their discussion, Len brought up an idea he had been thinking about for some time. He knew coffeehouses were growing in popularity across the nation. Could this be an area of opportunity for the Handlebar? The brothers explored this idea. They became convinced that a coffeehouse with a very limited breakfast, lunch, and dinner menu could work. Local performers or students playing music and doing skits in the evening just might be a popular draw with the college crowd. Could they pull it off? Little extra really needed to be done to the cafe. In fact, the old building already had a coffeehouse feel. They had the background, talent, and basic facility to capitalize on this opportunity. In the process, they could sidestep the threat of McDonald's. Within a year, the new Handlebar Cafe had a steady following of loyal customers, with packed houses for the evening performances.

What the Gorgan brothers did was not magical. You might argue that it wasn't even proactive management, since they were literally forced into making a change. But however awkward it may have been, they did do some systematic strategic thinking. They carefully thought through the relevant strengths and weaknesses and opportunities and threats. They performed a basic SWOT analysis.

A Sense of Vision

Here is another entrepreneurial example. Armed with an initial investment of only $48, Ian Leopold established Campus Concepts while he was attending Hobart College. His chances for a successful venture may have appeared slim, but Leopold knew what he wanted to do. Drawing from his personal experiences, he identified a real student need that was not currently being addressed. He had a vision of how that need could be met.

Leopold wanted to create an unofficial guide to the student experience, offering practical information about student life, sports, and off-campus attractions for students at Hobart. The key was that it would be distributed by the college as a free service for its students. The guide worked and students appreciated the information. Soon Leopold transplanted his idea to other colleges around the country. By the mid-1990s, Campus Concepts was distributed to 75 colleges in 35 cities with revenues approaching $5 million.[2]

revenue p. 167>

Leopold did his homework. He assessed the environment. He identified an important need among college students that was not being met. He uncovered a business opportunity. Just as important, he had a clear sense of vision prescribing how his business would address the students' needs. As Leopold demonstrated, a meaningful business focus begins with a sense of vision.

Today, much attention is given to the notion of a vision for the business. A **vision** is some desirable and possible future the business believes in and strives to attain.[3] Although the vision is generally quite brief and is stated broadly, it can provide direction and focus for the business and its stakeholders.

Vision
A desirable and possible future a business believes in and strives to attain.

stakeholder p. 91>

Our definition of vision includes two elements. First, the vision must propose a future that is desirable. In other words, it must suggest a future that will be good for the business and good for the people working in the business. The vision should be phrased in a way that lets employees recognize and accept the value gained by pursuing and achieving it. When this happens, the vision can be a unifying force for the business. Indeed, this may be one of its most important roles. Second, the vision must be possible. If the vision is seen as being too lofty or unrealistic, it has little unifying or motivating effect. Therefore, both desirability and possibility are key to a meaningful vision.

Good vision statements do not come to leaders in a ray of enlightened insight. A vision is the product of knowing the business, knowing the environment, and recognizing real opportunities. It should be clear and succinct. Some business leaders become enamored of creating vision statements that are elaborate and lofty, but this probably is of limited value. Consider the clarity of the following vision statements. "We will be the leading company in our industry in five years." "Over the next three years, our superior customer/quality focus will make us the preferred real estate business in the region." "We will advance our programs to become one of the top 20 colleges of business in the country within five years." A vision may even be as direct as the one President John Kennedy articulated successfully in the early 1960s: "We will put a man on the moon by 1970!" A vision may be as clear as that expressed by Lowe's, the large home improvement chain. "Lowe's is in the business of providing the products to help our customers build, improve, and enjoy their homes. Our goal is to outservice the competition and be our customers' first-choice store for these products."

The Mission

While the vision is a brief statement of direction and intent, the mission goes further. The mission adds substance to the broad theme of the vision. It defines more clearly the aim, scope, and direction of the business.

Lowe's vision is to provide products to help customers build, improve, and enjoy their homes. They rely on good service including help in picking out lighting products. Think of a company in your hometown. What might be its vision statement?

Mission statement
A statement that spells out what a business seeks to do and why it exists.

core values p. 112

customer service
p. 340>

The **mission statement** spells out what the business seeks to do and the reasons why it exists. Notice that the mission statements in Profile 11–1 share certain common themes. In fact, a mission statement generally addresses three areas. First, it defines the company's basic business. In other words, it broadly specifies the activities or services the business provides. Second, it specifies the markets or constituents the business serves. These first two areas are important. In them the business designates not only what it does and who it serves but by implication, the areas it will not serve. Third, the mission statement specifies the basic philosophy of the business. This third area is growing in popularity. More and more businesses are using the mission statement to state their *core values*, as Saturn does in Profile 11–1. These core values are held as standards of behavior for all to see and for all to meet.

Look carefully at the Southwest Airlines mission statement. Since the nature of the business is somewhat obvious, Southwest uses its mission statement to express its underlying philosophy. It emphasizes customer service, warmth and spirit, concern and respect, and strong employee focus. These themes, which are so critical at Southwest, are stated clearly in its mission statement.

PROFILE 11–1   SELECTED MISSION STATEMENTS

Ben & Jerry's

Ben & Jerry's is dedicated to the creation and demonstration of a new corporate concept of linked prosperity. Our mission consists of three interrelated parts.

Product mission: To make, distribute and sell the finest-quality all-natural ice cream and related products in a wide variety of innovative flavors made from Vermont dairy products.

Economic mission: To operate the company on a sound financial basis of profitable growth, increasing value for our shareholders and creating career opportunities and financial rewards for our employees.

Social mission: To operate the company in a way that actively recognizes the central role that business plays in the structure of society by initiating innovative ways to improve the quality of life of a broad community: local, national, and international.

The Leo Burnett Co.

The mission of the Leo Burnett Co. is to create superior advertising. In Leo's words: "Our primary function in life is to produce the best advertising in the world, bar none."

"This is to be advertising so interrupting, so daring, so fresh, so encouraging, so human, so believable, and so well-focused as to themes and ideas that, at one and the same time, it builds a quality reputation for the long haul as it produces sales for the immediate present."

[The company follows this with 10 operating principles covering products, clients, people, environment, organization, markets, new business, reputation, finances, and integrity.]

Saturn

To market vehicles developed and manufactured in the United States that are world leaders in quality, cost, and customer satisfaction through the integration of people, technology, and business systems and to transfer knowledge, technology, and experience throughout General Motors.

[The company follows this with a list of values to which it is committed.]

Intel

To do a great job for our customers, employees, and stockholders by being the preeminent building block supplier to the computing industry.

[The company follows this with six value orientations that emphasize customers, results, discipline, quality, risk taking, and being a great place to work.]

Southwest Airlines

The mission of Southwest Airlines is dedication to the highest quality of customer service delivered with a sense of warmth, friendliness, individual pride, and company spirit.

creativity p. 522>
innovation p. 522>
effectiveness p. 478>

To our employees, we are committed to provide our employees a stable work environment with equal opportunity for learning and personal growth. Creativity and innovation are encouraged for improving the effectiveness of Southwest Airlines. Above all, employees will be provided the same concern, respect, and caring attitude within the organization that they are expected to share externally with every Southwest customer.

SOURCE: Patricia Jones and Larry Kahaner. *Say It and Live It: The 50 Corporate Mission Statements That Hit the Mark*. New York: Currency Books, 1995.

Core Competence, Distinctive Competence, and Competitive Advantage

Core competence
An activity or set of activities that a business performs very well or a quality it possesses in abundance.

Distinctive competence
A skill, activity, or capacity that a business is uniquely good at doing in comparison to rival firms.

The environmental assessment and the business profile provide the background for framing the vision and mission statements. These assessments and business profiles also provide the information managers need to determine the **core competence** of the business.[4] A core competence is some activity or set of activities that a business performs very well or a quality it possesses in abundance. Core competences can cover a number of themes. One business may feel that the way it serves customers is its core competence. It may have an excellent sales force and expert maintenance and repair personnel. A manufacturer may feel that quality and innovation are its core competences. It may hire expert technicians and engineers and use state-of-the-art technology. This is the case with Trek, which uses its expertise and technology to continually develop new designs and models that set the pace for the industry. Trek constantly fine-tunes its designs to offer the most efficient, most comfortable ride possible. This does not mean it forgets about the other areas of business. Trek knows that a successful business must produce while controlling costs. It realizes that catchy advertising is important to success. It does not ignore these or other critical areas; it merely remembers that innovative design is where it really excels. That is Trek's core competence.

There is a fine but important distinction between core competence and distinctive competence. A **distinctive competence** is some skill, activity, or capacity that the business is uniquely good at doing in comparison to rival firms. These are the themes that make the business special and distinguish it from others in its industry. In a competitive market, these themes are used to convince customers to choose one business over another. Like core competences, distinctive competences can cover a number of themes.

It is possible for an organization or business to have a core competence but no real distinctive competence. That may seem confusing, but it really is not. Consider a university. The school may make a concerted effort to hire only those faculty who have considerable experience and who excel in their communication skills. Accordingly, the university boasts that its core competence is excellence in undergraduate teaching. While teaching excellence is important, it is unlikely to be a distinctive competence. A number of competing universities also emphasize excellence in teaching. Although teaching is important and it is done well, it may not distinguish the university from its rivals. On the other hand, perhaps the university has an unparalleled program in international business with a focus on Asian countries. This is a distinctive competence since it does it better than anyone else.

Distinctive competence can be developed. Consider the car dealerships in your community. One may have built a reputation for offering the best deals. In fact, it may even be one of the emerging car dealerships that offers a low, nonnegotiable sticker

Southwest Airlines constantly looks for ways to reduce the cost of operating the airline while still providing excellent service. This gives them a competitive advantage over other airlines. Do you think they can sustain this competency over several years?

SPEND LESS TO FLY FREE ON THE COMPANY CLUB.

Southwest, which ranked first in service quality, also had the best frequent flier program.

The number of dollars spent... to earn a domestic award typically ranges from $3,626 to $6,555. At Southwest the average cost of a free travel award is an exceptionally low $929.

...rather than 20,000 miles...The average frequent flier on Southwest collected his free ticket after only 7,104 miles.

Continental actually provided members with an effective discount of just 4.6 percent, well behind our first place pick: Southwest, with a discount of 6 percent.

Worth Magazine, May 1994

As these quotes from *Worth* magazine show, compared to other airlines' frequent flier programs, Southwest Airlines' Company Club is a greater value faster, because it gives you free travel faster, for much less money. Which is in keeping with the way we do everything at Southwest.

If you're not currently a Member, pick up an application at any Southwest gate or ticket counter today. Fly Southwest Airlines and take advantage of the best frequent-flier program in the country — The Company Club.

SOUTHWEST
THE Low Fare Airline

©1994, 1995 Southwest Airlines

price. Its low price, hassle-free approach to customers may indeed be unique in the community and therefore be a distinctive competence. Another dealership may have a reputation for the excellent service it provides once the purchase has been made. It may even have developed a special set of procedures and services for customers while their cars are undergoing maintenance. To the extent that its approach is unique or special, this business may have a distinctive competence.

Southwest Airlines has carefully crafted a special approach to competing in the airline industry. Its activities are arranged in such an unusual way that many consider its overall approach to represent a distinctive competence. While most major airlines fly into large airports in major cities, Southwest does not. It flies between midsize cities and uses secondary airports in large cities. Most major airlines have various classes of passenger seating. Southwest provides a "no-frills" approach. Most major airlines employ large staffs and use sophisticated equipment to coordinate transfers and plane changes. Southwest avoids these hassles by focusing on shorter routes or what is known as point-to-point service. Recognize a pattern? Southwest arranges its activities so it can provide low-cost travel. You will not waste time waiting for hours at its gates. Its planes fly shorter routes and have more frequent departures. This allows it to have a smaller fleet of planes. In fact, it flies 737s, which are especially efficient at the shorter flights. Put all this together and Southwest is special. It doesn't try to please every possible traveler. It targets customers who need to fly a short route between selected cities. Indeed, on the routes it serves, no full-service airline can offer more convenience or lower cost than Southwest.[5] It is unique. It has built a distinctive competence.

Competitive advantage
An area of competence that consumers value and the business is capable of exploiting.

Ultimately, a business wants to possess competences that are real competitive advantages in the marketplace. A competence becomes a **competitive advantage** when two conditions are met. First, the competence must represent some skill, activity, or capacity that consumers really value and care about. Second, the business must be capable of exploiting its area of competence.

Consider again Trek bicycles. Trek emphasizes quality and craftsmanship. In fact, it believes its focus on these areas provides an advantage over rival businesses, which makes them both a core competence and a competitive advantage. Trek has unique technology and can build and market bicycles that customers want. Profile 11–2 shows how Trek emphasizes its competences through advertising and promotional literature. As Trek continues to tell its story, its reputation grows and its competitive advantage becomes stronger.

PROFILE **11–2**   *"Hands On Steel"*

With more than 20 years of experience behind us, we've elevated the craft of producing custom steel bicycles into an art form. That's how our reputation was made. In fact, nobody else builds more premium Cro-Moly bikes, by hand, right here in the USA. Why steel? First of all, as any experienced rider will tell you, "it works." It's a strength-proven material with a great history of performance. And listen up, here's the most important point: It's not just the material, but what you do with it that creates a great bike. Ultimately, Trek technology and craftsmanship are what sets us above the rest.

There's steel, and there's premium Cro-Moly. We use the premium grade, OX III heat-treated Cro-Moly from True Temper. This stronger material allows us to use less, making durable frames that are also very light. How? Custom butting maximizes strength-to-weight ratio, with tube walls beefed-up near frame joints and tapered near low stress areas to reduce weight.

On the cutting edge of laser perfection. Perhaps what distinguishes our steel frames the most is that we precision-cut our tubes with a laser mitering tool for razor-perfect tube edges, hewn to exact angles. Achieving exact 90 degree cuts makes for ideal welds and super-strong frame joints. This advanced precision means unbeatable strength and smooth riding.

Doing it right is what sequential tig welding is all about. Our frame builders weld only partial sections of frame joints at a time, moving from one joint to another and back again in a predetermined order until all the welds are completed. This careful approach maintains frame alignment during welding and, ultimately, delivers a better ride. "TIG" refers to Tungsten Inert Gas that's flowed over welds to prevent them from oxidizing and weakening during the process. The outcome is super-durable welds and a much stronger bicycle frame.

Extra effort delivers extra strength and performance. Jigs are the structures that hold a frame together during welding. To ensure precise frame alignment and ultimate performance, we design our own custom jigs—one for each frame size and model we build. Our size-specific jigs ensure that each frame angle is welded into correct alignment, for a smooth, straight-tracking ride. Some builders buy adjustable jigs that can be adapted to different frames. It's easier and cheaper. It also leads to errors in frame alignment as jigs are repeatedly moved. At Trek, a final frame alignment step locks in the proper angles. Craftsmanship like this is why we can confidently place a limited lifetime warranty on every steel frame we make.

SOURCE: Trek Bicycle Company Catalog, 1997, pp. 28–29.

Having a competence and being able to deliver on it do not always go hand in hand. Consider the case of EMI, Ltd., which developed the modern CAT (computerized axial tomography) scanner. In fact, the EMI research engineer who invented the CAT scanner won a Nobel Prize for it. Initially, EMI was the only company that knew how to make CAT scanners. Clearly, it had a technological know-how that was special. However, EMI lacked the background to market the product effectively and lacked the service and support staff to build customer confidence in such a complex machine. It had the competence but lacked the capability to bring the scanner to market successfully.

GE took the idea, built an imitator (to avoid patent infringement), and marketed the product successfully. Within eight years, EMI was out of the CAT scanner business and GE was in the driver's seat. Although EMI had a competence (unique technology), it lacked the capability to build a competitive advantage.[6]

You may wonder whether all businesses possess distinctive competences and competitive advantages. The answer is no. Further, you may wonder how important it really is to have these features. That question is not easy to answer. If consumer demand for a product or service far outstrips the available supply, then any business that offers the product or service will make sales and generate revenues. There may be no special competence required. Yet in a competitive market, this condition is likely to be short-lived. Remember the discussion of economics in Chapter 6. If demand outpaces supply and existing businesses are making money, new competitors will seek to enter the market. Eventually the shortage of supply will be eased. In the process, competition will increase. Market battles will occur as businesses try to secure a hold on the market. Some businesses will not survive. Which are most likely to succeed? In all likelihood, it will be those businesses that have established strong competences and competitive advantages.

One final piece that should be considered in this initial look at how a business thinks strategically is the concept of a sustainable competitive advantage. A **sustainable competitive advantage** is one that is not easily duplicated by competitors. It is special and can remain unique to the business for some period of time. Logically, every business would like a sustainable competitive advantage. One way of accomplishing this is to secure trademarks and patents, as we discussed in Chapter 9. These legal means pro-

Sustainable competitive advantage
A competitive advantage that competitors cannot duplicate easily.

TABLE 11–1   Competences and Competitive Advantages

Core competence	A strength; anything that we do very well.
Distinctive competence	A unique core competence; something that we do better than everyone else.
Competitive advantage	A distinctive competence that customers value and that we have the resources to exploit.
Sustainable competitive advantage	A competitive advantage that we can continue to exploit over time.

vide some protection against a rival directly pirating your ideas or technology. Another way to ensure a sustainable competitive advantage is to remain on the cutting edge of the industry, offering the latest and best innovations. As we said, this is exactly what Trek tries to do. Table 11–1 summarizes the concepts we've just discussed. Notice that each concept builds on and is more beneficial than the previous one.

The reality of business is that most competitive advantages are very difficult to sustain. In fact, bright competitors are always looking for ways to invade and minimize another firm's competitive advantage. Of course, in a free enterprise system, this is exactly what we expect.

We now turn to the discussion of business strategies. These are actions business managers take to make their competences successfully reach their vision.

Developing Your Critical Thinking Skills

1. From a recent edition of the undergraduate catalog, find the mission statement of your university. Is it clear? How does it match the criteria outlined in this chapter?

2. Look at your college or university. In your mind, what is the core competence of the school? Do you feel the core competence is a distinctive competence? Is there a real competitive advantage?

3. Consider some of the businesses in your community. Which do you feel have a true distinctive competence? Why?

Foundations of Business Strategy

Competitive strategy
The specific approach a business chooses to pursue for addressing its environment.

In a competitive environment, a business must continuously try to develop ways to compete more effectively. Businesses try to identify strategies that will give them an edge over the competition. The search for strategies for business success is one of the most interesting areas of business.

Some of the early work done in the area of competitive strategy came from Harvard University Professor Michael Porter, who contends that when businesses compete they must pursue some strategic approach to gain an advantage over their rivals.[7] They must use some type of competitive strategy. In other words, **competitive strategy** is the specific approach the business chooses to pursue for addressing its environment. According to Porter, there are three broad and rather basic competitive strategies that can be pur-

Wal-Mart is able to offer brand name items at lower prices than their competition. This is because of their obsession with keeping costs low. What are the tradeoffs between cost and other factors in successful retail stores?

sued: the low-cost leader strategy, the differentiation strategy, and the focus strategy. A business may emphasize one or a combination of these strategies.

Low-Cost Leadership Strategy

Low-cost leadership Finding ways to reduce the cost of providing a product or service and pass the savings on to customers.

The first general strategy that some businesses pursue is known as **low-cost leadership.** Here a business looks for ways to reduce the cost of providing a product or service and pass the savings on to the customer. A business may reduce costs in many ways. It may find more efficient ways of operating, be able to get supplies or products at reduced rates, or find cost-effective ways to distribute its products. One of the best-known companies that pursues a low-cost leadership strategy is Wal-Mart. Its ability to buy name brand products in bulk and pass the cost savings on to customers through lower prices has made it the leading discount retailer in the country.

Both manufacturers and service businesses can pursue a low-cost leadership strategy. When manufacturers use this approach, they attempt to reduce production costs every way possible. All unnecessary steps are eliminated and every phase of operation is made as efficient as possible. H. J. Heinz, which sells everything from canned vegetables to ketchup, uses this low-cost leadership strategy. If it can shave even a fraction of a cent per can off canning operation costs, the benefits can be significant. This allows Heinz to keep product costs low. It relies on high volumes of sales, not price markups, for a competitive edge over the competition.[8]

Southwest Airlines is immensely successful using the low-cost leader strategy. As we've said, it uses a single type of plane that is efficient over short hauls. They use less congested airports than other major airlines. Its employees are more flexible and more productive, thereby reducing labor costs. The efficiency of Southwest's operations allows each employee to handle twenty-three hundred customers a day, which is twice as many as any other airline.

Differentiation Strategy

Differentiation
Providing a product or service that has some unique feature.

The second general competitive strategy is *differentiation*. A business that is pursuing a **differentiation strategy** is providing a product or service that has some unique feature. That unique feature can cover a broad range. Perhaps the company's products are known for being of higher quality than those of competitors. Perhaps the business provides superior service once a purchase has been made. Perhaps the business has such friendly, knowledgeable workers that customers feel comfortable with the help and support they receive.

The competitive strength of the differentiation strategy comes from what the unique feature allows the business to do. In theory, the unique feature should enable the business to sell more of its products because customers value the uniqueness provided. Many companies look for creative ways to differentiate themselves from competitors. For example, New Balance is the only company in the athletic-shoe industry to use width sizing extensively. In many New Balance shoe models, customers have a range of width options, at times from AA to EEE. The extra comfort and fit this feature provides give New Balance an edge over its rivals.

In some cases, a business may even be able to charge higher prices than competitors because the unique feature is valued so highly. Consider the example of Caterpillar Inc. which manufactures off-road earth-moving equipment. The equipment is known for its high quality. The firm is also known for having a superb dealer network, so parts and service are readily available. These features allow Caterpillar to charge a premium over competitors whose reputation and dealer support are inferior.

Let's return to the fiercely competitive restaurant industry. Restaurants are always looking for ways to differentiate themselves. Romano's Macaroni Grill, one of the restaurants in the Brinker International family, uses the differentiation strategy. It patterns itself after restaurants in Italy, with an open-market feel that includes fresh vegetables, choice meats, and various pasta choices. Meals are prepared in full view of customers. Jugs of wine are placed on tables, and customers serve themselves. Customers even report on an honor system how many glasses of wine they have consumed. Macaroni's tries to create a different sort of dining experience for its customers.[9]

Litespeed is also a good example of the differentiation strategy. Its bikes are certainly not cheap; even the lowest-priced models sell for over $1,000. The top-of-the-line model sells for close to $6,000. The company's real strength is in the quality of its bicycles. Through the use of excellent design and titanium frames, Litespeed produces bikes that are in high demand among hard-core riders. Customers are willing to pay the premium price because they know the name and the quality it represents.[10]

Focus Strategy

Focus strategy
Positioning a business to serve the needs of some unique or distinct customer segment that is not being fully served by the competition.

In the **focus strategy,** the business positions itself to serve the needs of some unique or distinct customer segment that is not being fully served by the competition. The market may be segmented in a number of ways. For example, the unique segment may be a distinct group of customers, a geographic area, or some specific need that has not been fully addressed by any other competitor. Often the focus strategy is the natural and most reasonable approach pursued by small businesses and entrepreneurs. These creative people look at the business environment and see areas of consumer need that are not being tapped. They are convinced that if they offer products and services to meet these market needs, they can be successful. They are searching for a gap between what is currently available in the market and what consumers want. They organize their businesses to serve this niche.

The stories of successful focus strategies are legendary. For example, Dave Thomas entered a market that nearly everyone thought was already laden with too many competitors. In many ways, he extended the market by focusing on a unique set of consumers. The hamburger fast-food market was dominated by McDonald's and Burger King. Thomas believed that neither of these competitors appealed directly to the adult consumer. He committed his efforts to providing a quality hamburger for adult customers. This focus paid off, and his company, Wendy's, experienced unprecedented growth in its early years.

Martha Morris focused on parents of young children when launching Play It Again Sports which purchases used equipment and resells it to others. This reduces the cost of sports equipment. Can you think of other products for which reselling used equipment could be profitable?

Martha Morris founded Play It Again Sports because she was sure there was a market for used sporting goods at discounted prices. This unique approach is especially popular with parents of young children, who hate to buy new equipment that their child will probably outgrow by the end of the season. This is particularly troublesome for equipment-intensive sports such as football and hockey. At Play It Again Sports, parents can purchase used equipment they can resell to the business after the season ends. Morris found a unique focus and the business has been a success.

Keys to Success

teams p. 71>

The key to success with each of Porter's three general strategies is in attention to the specific emphasis. In the low-cost leadership strategy, the key is attention to the *production process*. Managers must be singularly focused on how to wring costs out of the production process in order to provide products or services at the lowest possible price. In the differentiation strategy, managers pay attention to how they can improve the *product*. Product teams are charged with finding ways to make the product more valuable to customers. They constantly strive to add visible value that customers will be willing to pay a premium for. In the focus strategy, attention must be given to better serving the *customers*. The managers place great importance on interacting with specific customers, since providing value to that unique customer niche determines their success.

Other General Strategic Considerations

There are many other strategic moves a business can make. You will study these when you take a course in business strategy, probably during your senior year. While certainly not exhaustive, three additional strategic considerations you should understand are diversification, acquisition, and business portfolio management.

Diversification

Diversification
Branching out into an additional area (or areas) of business.

Hit the Road is a retail shop that sells road and mountain bikes. It has an excellent reputation and has been in business about five years. While business is brisk at times, it is seasonal. Sales are high from April through September. October and November see sales taper off, but repair work is strong. Sales rebound in December due to Christmas. The problem occurs in January, February, and March. During these three months, both sales and repair work are limited, so the business records little revenue. How can Hit the Road respond? One of the co-owners suggested that the shop consider going into an additional line of business. Why not sell and rent cross-country skis during the three winter months? This logical move helped the store cope with the downturn that always occurred in the bicycle business. This is an example of **diversification,** which occurs when one business decides to get into an additional area (or areas) of business.

Usually a company diversifies for one of three reasons. First, as you saw in the Hit the Road example, it may diversify to deal with the seasonal nature of its main business. Second, a company may feel the need to diversify if its traditional business is losing market attractiveness. Third, a company may diversify simply as a way to grow and enhance its profits. Businesses often diversify into other businesses that are closely related to their traditional business focus. This was the case when Brinker International, which already owned the strong Chili's chain, acquired Macaroni's. However, some businesses do diversify into completely unrelated businesses. A classic example occurred when RJR (the tobacco company) acquired Nabisco (a consumer food company).

Acquisition

Acquisition
The activity where one company buys another company.

We hear a lot today about **acquisitions**—when one company buys another company. In fact, barely a day goes by without news of some new acquisition or merger that alters the business climate. Consider the Disney–ABC deal described in Profile 11–3. Why would Disney purchase ABC? What is the logic behind this deal? Basically, it did so because there was logic or operational *synergy* to the deal. Let's explore what that means. As the profile points out, Disney's traditional strength has been in production (movies, TV, etc.). ABC's strength has been in distribution. This deal gives Disney ready access to the distribution strength of ABC and thereby gives it control over the entire range of its operations.

Why would Disney acquire ABC rather than simply work to further build its own avenues of distribution? Acquisition allows quicker entry. It takes a lot of time, expertise, and money to build your own, but ABC is already up and running. Also, ABC came with a solid reputation and proven track record, which could take a firm years to develop on its own.

PROFILE 11–3   DISNEY BUYS CAPITAL CITIES/ABC

In the summer of 1995, the announcement of Disney's purchase of Capital Cities/ABC rocked the business world. This deal was particularly intriguing since Disney CEO Michael Eisner had carefully avoided the acquisition route for years. The $19 billion deal was the second largest acquisition in U.S. business history.

For years, Disney's strength was in production. This included movies that were clear winners (*The Lion King*), successful TV shows ("Home Improvement"), and even theme parks worldwide.

ABC's strength was in its delivery. At the time of the sale, it boasted the top-rated TV network. It also owned TV stations, radio stations, interests in several cable networks (e.g., ESPN), and publications (such as *Women's Wear Daily*).

Disney and ABC offered each other valuable opportunities. Disney's strength in production and ABC's delivery meshed and gave each company the chance to do its jobs better. There seemed to be a real fit between these businesses.

SOURCE: Laura Landra, Elizabeth Jensen, and Thomas R. King, "Disney's Deal for ABC Makes Show Business a Whole New World," *The Wall Street Journal*, August 1, 1995, pp. A1, A12.

Business Portfolio Management

BRINKER
INTERNATIONAL.

Often major companies are composed of many businesses. For example, we have discussed the various restaurant chains that are part of Brinker International. Companies like Brinker are always looking at all of their businesses and how they contribute to the profitability of the whole company. In strategy, we refer to this as the company's *business portfolio*. Often the portfolio must be adjusted. For example, in 1995, Brinker's business portfolio included Chili's, Macaroni's Grill, Grady's, On the Border, and Spageddies. However, two businesses in this portfolio, Grady's and Spageddies, were not meeting the company's financial goals. Brinker sold these units in 1996. Later, it added three new businesses to its portfolio: the Corner Bakery, Maggioni's Little Italy, and Cozymel's. As Brinker entered 1997, it owned six businesses and was exploring a new restaurant concept, Eatzi's.[11] Generally, to manage and balance its portfolio, a company wants some businesses that are solid and fairly secure (such as Chili's) and some that are emerging but appear to have strong future growth prospects (such as Eatzi's).

Global Strategic Thinking

In Chapter 7, we discussed the global forces affecting today's businesses. We said competitive forces often encourage a business to go international with its operations. For example, global operations can provide access to cheaper labor, lowering the costs of production and reducing the firm's overall costs. Of course, one of the most basic reasons for going global is purely strategic—the business believes it can expand sales by having access to larger markets and expanded customer bases. In this section, we look at global strategy and explore some specific global entry strategies that businesses pursue.

Competing Globally

The main difference between being globally and domestically competitive is that in the case of global competition the firm's performance is measured against international standards. This means that management must identify the best companies in the world and use their performance as the standards to meet or beat.

In what categories should such comparisons be made? Table 11–2 lists many actions a company can take to improve its global competitiveness.

As you read the list of competitiveness factors in Table 11–2, you'll notice that many of them apply to domestic competition as well. Whether or not it is engaged in competition with foreign firms, the healthy business must adopt an attitude of relentless improvement. It must deliberately seek pressures for innovation. It must monitor **globalization p. 186>** industry change. In these categories of competitiveness, globalization merely forces the firm to broaden its horizons. Profile 11–4 illustrates how this worked for one leading American computer maker.

PROFILE 11–4   *Sun Microsystems Uses Exports to Compete*

One example of global strategic thinking is the experience of Sun Microsystems, the California computer manufacturer that was the number one maker of UNIX-based workstations in 1994. Sun's cofounder and CEO, Scott McNealy, desperately wanted to export to Japan because he feared that if Sun did not do so, the Japanese would eventually develop a competitive advantage over his company. Here is how McNealy put it:

> I said we're not going to stand around and wait for somebody to build up a workstation business and then use that to go dumping offshore and blow us away. We're going to go over there and win. And most important, we said we had to win in Japan. That is the best way to test your level of quality in a world-class way. If we can ship world-quality products to Japan, I'll never hear a peep out of U.S. or European customers.

McNealy reports that learning how to export to Japan was not easy and that Sun had to spend a great deal of time and humility learning how to meet Japanese quality expectations.

SOURCE: Jerry Jasinowski and Robert Hamrin, *Making it in America* (New York: Simon and Schuster, 1995), p. 184.

Global Entry Strategies

While this thinking makes sense, a major issue remains unanswered. Once a business makes the strategic decision to go global, how is it done? How does the business go about moving from a domestic to an international operation? The answer is indeed complex. Here we will address four common entry strategies that a business may use: an export management firm, licensing, foreign sales offices, and manufacture abroad.

TABLE 11–2   How to Become Globally Competitive

I.   Adopt an attitude of relentless improvement

II. Deliberately seek pressures for innovation
  1. Sell to the most sophisticated and demanding buyers
  2. Seek to exceed the toughest regulatory standards
  3. Buy inputs from the most advanced suppliers
  4. Treat employees as permanent
  5. Consider outstanding competitors as motivators

III. Monitor industry change
  1. Identify and serve buyers with anticipatory needs
  2. Investigate emerging buyers
  3. Find localities where regulations foreshadow the rest of the world
  4. Discover and highlight trends in the costs of factors of production
  5. Monitor centers of research and sources of talented people
  6. Bring some outsiders into management teams

IV. Tap selected advantages in other nations
  1. Be prepared to locate production anywhere in the world
  2. Be prepared to buy inputs from anywhere in the world
  3. Search for foreign technology that you can use
  4. Compete directly with the best foreign competitors
  5. Place regional headquarters where the competition is strongest
  6. Make foreign acquisitions to gain skill or market access
  7. Forge foreign alliances

SOURCE: Adapted from Michael Porter, *The Competetive Advantage of Nations* (New York: The Free Press, 1990), pp. 577–615.

Export Management Firms

Some businesses, particularly small and midsized ones, have sound products that sell well in the United States. There may appear to be a market for these products in select foreign countries, but there is a problem. The business and its managers have no idea how to do business in the international arena. In simplest terms, no one in the firm has sufficient expertise to take the firm's products international. This is a real dilemma. The business has a great product with real global potential, but it doesn't have enough skill to make it happen. One answer for such a business is to use an **export management firm,** a company located in the United States that sells products abroad for another business.

Why would a small business use an export management firm? It gives the small business entry to international markets it could not otherwise reach. The export management firm does a lot of the tough work. Of course, the business makes two significant sacrifices. First, the export management firm gets a cut of the profits. Second, the business loses some control, particularly over how the product will be sold.

Licensing

A second entry strategy a business might use is **licensing,** when a U.S. business allows its products to be produced and distributed in other countries by a foreign company. There are many advantages to this approach. Like export management firms, licensing gives a business a fairly easy, low-cost entry into a foreign market. Further, much of the legwork is being done by a business that knows the country and knows the markets it wants to serve. There are two big concerns, though. First, the U.S. business must share its profits with the foreign business. Second—and this can be a major concern—the U.S. business must share certain sensitive information with the foreign business. For example, it must disclose special processes or ingredients so production can take place. This can be dangerous; once the licensing arrangement ends, a possible competitor knows some of the U.S. firm's secrets.

Foreign Sales Office

Some businesses sell in foreign markets directly by establishing **foreign sales offices** in the countries where they operate. The products are not produced in the foreign country, but they are sold and serviced by special operations there. Caterpillar is a good example of this approach. It has an extensive worldwide network of dealers who sell the large earth-moving equipment it makes. Caterpillar produces a machine in Illinois and ships it to its dealer in Lima, Peru. This local dealer handles the sales and service needs of customers in the Peru market. Caterpillar maintains control but works with the local dealer, which facilitates more sensitive and timely responses to the needs of customers in the foreign country.

Manufacture Abroad

Manufacturing abroad can be a demanding entry strategy for a U.S. business to take, so it is generally used by large companies. A U.S. business decides to both produce and sell its products abroad. Sometimes it establishes a separate operation in the desired foreign country and treats it as one of the businesses of the large (parent) company. When the foreign operation is owned as part of the larger business, it is known as a **wholly owned subsidiary.**

A second approach to manufacturing abroad that is frequently used is the joint venture route, which we discussed in Chapter 7. Remember, a joint venture is really a

Export management firm
A firm located in the United States that sells products abroad for another business.

Licensing
An arrangement where a U.S. business allows its products to be produced and distributed in other countries by a foreign company.

Foreign sales office
A special operation in a foreign country that sells and services products that were made domestically.

Wholly owned subsidiary
A business that is owned as part of a larger business; may be a foreign subsidiary of a domestic firm.

joint venture p. 179>

partnership where companies from different countries join together. There may be many strategic reasons for doing a joint venture. It gives companies a chance to share costs and risks, thus taking on projects too big to approach without support (for example, the Alaska pipeline). There are two other important strategic reasons for joint ventures. First, when a U.S. business joint ventures with a foreign business, it gains the knowledge of the market and how to deal with it that the foreign business has. This helps break through some of the bottlenecks and mistakes that companies make when they don't know the people, customs, and markets fully. Second, in some cases joint venture is the only possible route of entry to a country. Some governments demand it as a condition of manufacturing in their countries.

Developing Your Critical Thinking Skills

1. Porter's general strategies apply to businesses as they engage in global operations as well as their domestic ventures. Which strategic approach do you think Sony has taken in the consumer electronics industry? Explain.

2. Which approach has Toyota taken in the automobile industry? How about Mercedes-Benz? Justify your reasoning.

3. When should a company planning a global strategy use a joint venture instead of setting up its own manufacturing facilities without help from a foreign partner?

Business Objectives

Once a business has determined its strategies, it continues to make its planning efforts more detailed by defining objectives. Objectives add greater specificity, precision, and clarity to what the firm wants to do. While many people make a distinction between business objectives and goals, we use these terms interchangeably. Accordingly, **business objectives** are the basic outcomes the business hopes to achieve as it operates.

Business objectives
The basic outcomes a business hopes to achieve as it operates.

Why Objectives Are Important

Objectives are important for at least three reasons. First, they provide the organization and its members with clear action targets. That is, they are outcome expectations or standards that the business can work toward. When a business says its objective is to "increase its share of the market by 2 percent this year" or "reduce industrial accidents by 10 percent this year," people know what is expected and how they must gear their work efforts.

Second, objectives become standards against which a business can measure its success and take corrective action. Suppose the goal is to reduce industrial accidents, but at the end of the year, accidents show no significant decline. Now key workers know that their actions for addressing the accident goal must be modified. They have clear evidence of the need to do something differently.

Third, and quite important, is the motivational impact objectives can have for employees. If objectives are properly developed, they can encourage worker effort that leads to outstanding performance. They can serve as targets that challenge employees and energize their behavior.

TABLE 11–3   Drucker's Key Results Areas

Key Results Area	Objectives
Productivity	"Reduce production costs by 12% this year"
Financial resources	"Secure $25 million for financial campaign this year"
Marketing	"Increase overall market share by 10% this year"
Human resources	"Hire three qualified real estate analysts this year"
Physical resources	"Acquire and integrate two new industrial robots into the manufacturing operation by the end of the year"
Innovation	"Bring multimedia conference center to the business by the end of the year"
Social responsibility	"Support community outreach programs through a 10% increase in United Way pledges"
Profitability	"3% growth in return to stockholders this year"

SOURCE: Adapted from Peter F. Drucker, *The Practice of Management* (New York: Harper & Brothers, 1954), p. 63.

Key results areas
Those areas of a business that are critical to its effectiveness and even its survival.

Categories of Objectives

What categories of objectives should be stated? Basically, objectives should be set for the key results areas of the business. **Key results areas** are those areas of the business that are critical to its effectiveness and even survival. At a minimum, the business must set objectives for each key results area. Business guru Peter Drucker notes eight key results areas: (1) productivity, (2) financial resources, (3) marketing, (4) human resources, (5) physical resources, (6) innovation, (7) social responsibility, and (8) profitability. These key results areas and sample objectives for each are shown in Table 11–3.

Integrating Business Objectives

In businesses, objectives must exist in an organized and integrated manner. Somehow all of the objectives, throughout the whole business, must fit together and support one another. This integrated overview is presented in Figure 11–1. Let's take a careful look at the model and what it tells us about objectives in business organizations.

First, look at the *business-level objectives.* These apply to the entire business. They are the things that the business, taken as a whole, hopes to accomplish. So business-level goals must be set by top managers or owners of the business. Goals should be set for each key results area. However, business-level objectives must be further broken down.

Business-level goals must be translated into goals that apply to each part of the organization. These are known as *unit-level objectives.* For example, if a business-level objective is to increase market share, there will implications for each unit of the business. The marketing unit, the production unit, the finance unit, and in all likelihood the research and development unit will all be affected. Each of these units must establish their own objectives with the business-level objectives clearly in mind. In other words, units establish objectives within the overall framework that is provided by the business level objectives. Admittedly, this is a difficult task. Yet a business and all its units must establish objectives that fit with and complement one another.

FIGURE 11–1   Integrated Model of Objectives

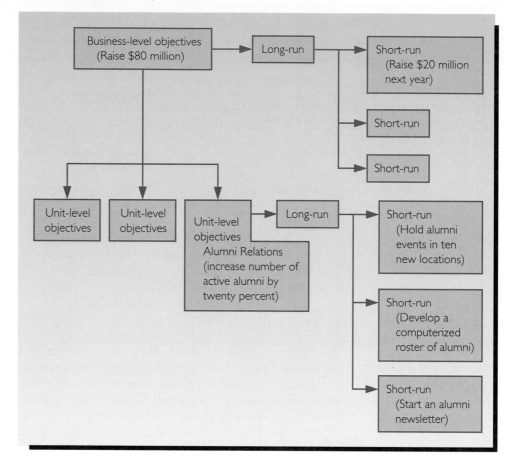

Assume your university is about to embark on a major fund-raising drive that will be used to support the academic growth of the various programs in the university. The administrators look carefully at the university's needs as well as its fund-raising prospects. They decide that its fund-raising campaign, which they call the "Campaign for Creativity," will have a business-level objective of "raising $80 million over the next five years." The only way this overall business-level goal can be met is if every unit of the university pitches in and does its fair share. It affects the development unit, the college relations unit, the publications unit, the alumni relations unit, and so on. Each must establish more limited objectives that are relevant to their areas yet work to help fulfill the overall objective of the business.

Let's concentrate on one unit, the alumni relations unit. To help the university reach its business-level objective, the alumni relations unit sets a unit-level objective of "increasing the number of active alumni by 20 percent over the next five years." The alumni relations people know this is important because the people most likely to contribute to the university are active alumni. You begin to see how all of the objectives must fit together. Unless alumni relations (and other units) meet their objectives, the university is unlikely to meet its overall financial objectives in the Campaign for Creativity.

Objectives are also stated for different periods of time. One of the most basic ways to think of this is in terms of "long-run" and "short-run." The precise definition varies from business to business, depending in part on the nature of the industry and how long it takes to make major changes in it. For general purposes, the long-run looks three to five years into the future and the short-run deals with the next operating year.

It is important to break long-run objectives into smaller, short-run increments. This provides more immediate targets that must be attained on the way to reaching overall long-run objectives. For example, a long-run objective of the overall business might be "to increase growth in market share by 15 percent in the next five years." The accompanying short-run objective may be "to increase overall market share by 3 percent within the next 12 months."

Let's look again at our university example. The long-run objective of the business is "to raise $80 million over the next five years." Accordingly, the short-run objective may be "to raise $20 million in the next year." Of course, each unit takes a similar approach. Since alumni relations has a long-run objective of "increasing the number of active alumni by 20 percent over the next five years," this unit must establish a series of short-run objectives. For example, it may aim to "hold alumni events in 10 new locations within the next year," "develop a computerized roster of alumni within the next year," and "implement an alumni newsletter of campus updates and needs before the end of the year." It is by meeting its short-run objectives that the alumni relations unit expects ultimately to meet its long-run objectives.

Developing Objectives Statements

If objectives are going to be effective standards or targets, be motivational, and be mechanisms prompting control and corrective action, they must be carefully developed. Good objectives statements should meet the criteria noted in Table 11–4. These criteria apply to all organizations, whether businesses, service organizations, or even social groups.

motivation p. 426>   First, objectives should be *clear and specific*. Nebulous "do your best" statements may be easy to set, but they fail as objectives. They provide neither direction nor motivation.

TABLE 11–4   Criteria for Objectives

Objectives should be
■ Clear and specific
■ Stated in observable terms (objective and measurable)
■ Stated in terms of accomplishments (outcomes or results, not activities or processes)
■ Challenging
■ Prioritized (by importance and urgency)

Second, objectives should be *stated in observable terms.* That means they must be measurable. This makes it easy to know when targets have been met. When they have not been met, the corrective action needed is also clear.

Third, objectives should be *stated in terms of accomplishments.* They should focus on outcomes and results, not activities and processes. Activities do not set a direction and do not provide clear targets.

Let's consider these first three points together: good objectives should be clear, specific, measurable, and focused on outcomes and results. Consider Longrane Manufacturing, which is facing a problem in the key results area of productivity. It consistently incurs high costs and excessive scrap in the production process, supposedly due to production inefficiencies and lack of attention to product quality. The business, in addressing these issues, may say, "This year we will work hard to reduce scrap as much as we can." This statement is not clear, it is not measurable, and it focuses on a process (work hard) rather than a measurable outcome. A more complete objectives statement would call for precision and action. "The production shop will reduce scrap by 20 percent by the end of this fiscal year." Now we have a target. That target focuses the production shop on an outcome that is clear and measurable.

Good objectives should also meet two other criteria. They should be *challenging.* This is important for employee motivation. If objectives are too easy to achieve, they require no "stretch" from employees. They neither tap employees' potential nor encourage them to work hard. But if objectives are too lofty, employees may view them as unrealistic. This can reduce motivation. Employees question why they should work hard when they can't meet the goals anyway. Objectives should occupy a middle ground: realistic, but requiring hard, committed work. That is, they must be challenging. Interestingly, research suggests that clear, specific, and challenging objectives enhance employee motivation and lead to better performance.[12]

Finally, objectives should be *prioritized.* There is no way a manager can do everything. Trying to do the impossible leads to frustration and failure. Certain objectives are more demanding than others. Some are more important, while others are more urgent (timely). Managers must take care to prioritize their objectives, highlighting those that are most critical.

Strategic Planning

Strategic planning
A systematic way of analyzing and responding to a competitive environment.

In this chapter, we have discussed a number of important areas of business that must be addressed as decision makers begin to think strategically. We have noted that vision, mission, areas of competence, competitive advantage, strategic approach, and objectives must all be considered. In fact, these areas fit together to form the strategic planning process of the business.

Strategic planning is a systematic method of analyzing and responding to a competitive environment. The need for well-thought-out strategic planning has never been greater than it is in today's dynamic, ever-changing world. Strategic planning should be viewed as an ongoing process. It provides an overview and analysis of the business and its relevant environment. Then it prescribes an outline or action plan of how the business will proceed to capitalize on its strengths and minimize its weaknesses or threats. Figure 11–2 gives a graphic overview of the strategic planning process.

FIGURE 11-2   Overview of the Strategic Planning Process

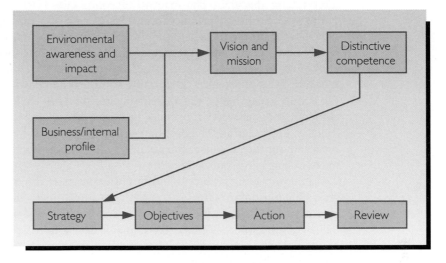

There are numerous advantages to strategic planning. One advantage dominates: As an ongoing and active process, strategic planning keeps the business focused on change. It encourages the business to continually assess its business environment and search for ways to operate more effectively. By its very nature, strategic planning is future-oriented and proactive. While strategic planning helps the business map out a direction for the future, the process is fluid and flexible enough to deal with unpredictable events. In many ways, strategic planning is one of the most powerful tools in a businessperson's arsenal.

You will use this strategic planning framework throughout your business career. You will refine and gain expertise in applying the ideas presented. You will build on the foundations of this model that we have discussed in this chapter.

Who in the business should be involved in strategic planning activities? Certainly, strategic planning is the unique responsibility of upper management. They have the broad, overall view of the business needed to provide a real strategic perspective. However, upper managers are increasingly realizing that they need input from people throughout the business as they develop strategic plans. They need information, outlooks, and insights from those employees who are closest to their customers, products, and services. Further, when employees have a hand in establishing strategic plans, they feel active ownership of the plans. They understand the reasons for objectives and may work harder to achieve them.

Business Culture

Part of the focus of the business comes from its culture. As you learned in Chapter 4, the business culture is an unwritten set of beliefs and values about what is proper, right, and appropriate in the organization. These beliefs and values are well known and accepted by the members of the business. When this culture is consistent with the core values and strategies of the business, it can be a great source of strength. A classic case of such a fit occurred at Johnson & Johnson. In the 1980s, several people died after taking the giant pharmaceutical company's Tylenol tablets. The prospect of pulling this profitable product from the shelves and incurring the loss of public confidence in the product was daunting. Further, such a venture would cost millions of dollars. The company had carefully crafted a culture that focused on consumer safety above everything else. Accordingly, there was little question that it would immediately recall all Tylenol products. Interestingly, rather than destroying customer confidence, the action strengthened it. Consumers (and stockholders) placed even more trust in a company that put safety above profits. Customers stayed with Johnson & Johnson and Tylenol, appreciating the consumer-oriented culture. Their trust was rewarded when it turned out the poisoned Tylenol had been tampered with in the store, not contaminated during the production process.

The prevailing culture does not always support the firm's core values and strategies. When it doesn't, the leaders of the business must consciously attempt to build a new culture. For example, in recent years, many businesses have attempted to move from a culture where bosses make all major decisions to a culture of employee involvement in decision making. This has exposed to scrutiny and change many beliefs and assumptions about the importance of employees, how they should be treated, and how much power they should have. Such transitions take considerable time and dedication. Cultures change slowly. Management has the main responsibility for setting this change in motion. Remember, culture can be a key factor in helping the business zero in on its focus.

Here is the key. It is important for the business culture to support the strategic direction that the business chooses. When the two go hand in hand, the strategy has a much greater chance of succeeding. For example, look at General Electric and its maverick CEO, Jack Welch. Welch has worked to establish a unique set of values and culture at GE. He wants what he calls "the body of a big company . . . but the soul of a small company." In other words, he wants the resources that are available to big businesses but the speed, creativity, and flexibility of small businesses. He reinforces this culture by getting people involved, empowering them, encouraging risks, and promoting open sharing throughout the business. This unique culture has helped the business to pursue its strategic agenda. Even though the company has made nearly $20 billion worth of acquisitions over the past 15 years, it has been able to avoid the excessive bureaucracy that paralyzes some companies. GE remains nimble and responsive—and extremely successful.[13]

Developing Your Critical Thinking Skills

1. Small businesses often do not do enough strategic planning. Why do you think this is?

2. What does an organization gain from having a well-integrated set of objectives?

3. Pick a group with which you are associated, such as a fraternity, sorority, or club. How would you describe the culture of that group?

SUMMARY

1. Successful businesses are those that match the abilities of the firm with the opportunities in the business environment. The business profile and the SWOT analysis are starting points for developing such a business focus.

- What is a business profile?

A business profile is an analysis of the strengths and the weaknesses of the business.

- What is a SWOT analysis?

A SWOT analysis is an assessment of the firm's strengths and weaknesses in comparison with the environmental threats and opportunities it faces. SWOT stands for strengths, weaknesses, opportunities, and threats.

2. A successful SWOT analysis will produce much detailed information. It should also result in a broad understanding of the direction in which the firm should move. Business leaders use terms like vision and mission to refer to this general sense of direction.

- What is a business vision?

A business vision is an image of a desirable and possible future that the business believes in and strives to attain.

- What is a mission statement?

A mission statement spells out what the business seeks to do and the reasons why it exists.

3. A successful SWOT analysis must be brutally honest in identifying ways the firm can realistically aspire to compete. In other words, the analysis must identify the firm's core competence, distinctive competence, and potential competitive advantage.

- What is a core competence?

A core competence is some activity or set of activities that a business performs very well or a quality that it possesses in abundance.

- What is a distinctive competence?

A distinctive competence is a core competence that the business is uniquely good at in comparison with rival firms.

- What is a competitive advantage?

A competence becomes a competitive advantage when consumers value it and the business is capable of exploiting it.

4. After the firm has successfully completed its SWOT analysis, it must determine how best to take advantage of the findings. This requires the development of a business strategy.

- What is a competitive strategy?

A competitive business strategy is the specific approach the business chooses to pursue for addressing its environment.

- What are the basic general strategies a business might pursue?

There are three general strategies: (1) a low-cost leadership strategy, (2) a differentiation strategy, and (3) a focus strategy.

- What other general strategic issues should be considered?

Three common additional considerations are (1) diversification, (2) acquisitions, and (3) business portfolio management.

5. Many companies decide to compete in global markets in addition to their domestic market.

■ How does a decision to compete globally affect the development of a business strategy?

The main difference is that the firm's performance is measured against international standards. Once that comparison has been completed, the firm must choose its global entry strategy. This chapter discussed four possible entry strategies: (1) using an export management firm, (2) licensing, (3) establishing foreign sales offices, and (4) manufacturing abroad.

6. Management is not finished once the strategy has been developed. Many more details need to be worked out before the firm can get down to the business of competing. Working out those details means setting business objectives.

■ What are business objectives?

Business objectives are the basic outcomes the business hopes to achieve as it operates.

■ What are the key result areas for which a business should develop objectives?

This chapter identified eight key areas: (1) productivity, (2) financial resources, (3) marketing, (4) human resources, (5) physical resources, (6) innovation, (7) social responsibility, and (8) profitability.

■ Given the large number of possible objectives, what are the considerations involved in integrating business objectives?

Objectives must fit together and support one another. Objectives that apply to the entire business (business-level objectives) must be translated into goals that apply to each part of the organization (unit-level goals). Long-run objectives must be broken down into smaller, short-run objectives.

7. The ability to develop meaningful objectives statements is one of the skills that successful managers must learn.

■ What are the criteria for good objectives statements?

Objectives should be (1) clear and specific, (2) stated in observable terms (objective and measurable), (3) stated in terms of accomplishments (outcomes/results, not activities/processes), (4) challenging, and (5) prioritized (in importance and urgency).

8. Earlier in this text you learned about the large number of decision makers in business. Top management is one of those groups. Perhaps the most important decision-making role of top management is to direct the development of the SWOT analysis and the resultant strategy and objectives. When those activities are combined with a review of their results, we refer to the entire process as strategic planning.

■ What is strategic planning?

Strategic planning is a systematic way of analyzing and responding to a competitive environment. It prescribes an action plan of how the business will proceed to capitalize on its strengths and minimize its weaknesses.

9. One often overlooked factor that determines the success of a strategic plan is the company's business culture. If the plan fits with the culture, the chances of success are much greater.

   ■ What is a business culture?

   A business culture is a set of unwritten beliefs and values about what is proper, right, and appropriate in a business organization.

Links to other courses

Analyzing the business and its environment to develop a sense of strategic thinking covers a range of activities. Themes from this chapter are covered throughout the business curriculum. However, certain courses emphasize strategic thinking quite extensively:

- Business policy and strategic management
- Principles of management
- Principles of marketing
- International business

KEY TERMS

Acquisition, p. 322
Business focus, p. 308
Business objectives, p. 326
Business profile, p. 308
Competitive advantage, p. 315
Competitive strategy, p. 317
Core competence, p. 313
Differentiation, p. 319
Distinctive competence, p. 313
Diversification, p. 321
Export management firm, p. 325
Focus strategy, p. 320

Foreign sales office, p.325
Key results areas, p. 327
Licensing, p. 325
Low-cost leadership, p. 318
Mission statement, p. 311
Strategic planning, p. 330
Sustainable competitive advantage, p. 316
SWOT analysis, p. 308
Vision, p. 310
Wholly owned subsidiary, p. 325

EXERCISES AND APPLICATIONS

1. Contact the president of a campus fraternity, sorority, or club. Meet with him or her and do an informal SWOT analysis of the organization.

2. Southwest Airlines recently decided to extend its routes nationally. Given our discussion of its strengths, weaknesses, competences, and competitive advantages, what concerns do you have with this move? Write your analysis in a one-page report.

3. Form teams of five people. Brainstorm and choose a business that you think would be fun to start and could be profitable. What environmental and competitive information do you need to know to help assure success?

4. Use one of the Internet search engines to find as much of the information for Exercise 3 as you can. Outline the information and include the address for each website where you found it.

5. Find a small local business in your area that competes with large chains or franchises. Casually visit the business. How do you think it competes in the shadows of the larger firms? In other words, what strategy does it seem to be pursuing? Outline your analysis.

6. Interview the owner of the business from Exercise 5 to determine the impact of the large competitor on the smaller firm.

CASE: **STRATEGIC PLANNING FOR BOOKSELLERS ON THE INTERNET**

For most of its history, the bookstore industry was dominated by tens of thousands of relatively small independent businesses. This began to change when the expansion of shopping malls in the 1960s and 1970s created an opportunity for chain bookstores such as Waldenbooks and B. Dalton. It changed again in the 1980s when the superstore model was copied by a handful of bookselling entrepreneurs. The superstores chose a strategy of large stores with a huge inventory of new books and a pleasant environment for leisurely browsing (espresso bars). The superstore model has become such a powerful strategy that today almost half of all bookstore sales are generated by three superstore chains: Barnes and Noble, Borders, and Crown.

Will the strategy of the book superstores continue to dominate? At least one entrepreneur thinks not. Thirty-two-year-old Jeff Bezos believes that the future of bookselling lies on the Internet, and he has founded a company, Amazon.com, to prove his point. The name refers to his vision of a company that offers the customer every new book in print. In other words, like the world's largest river, Bezos's company will carry much more volume than any other competitor.

Amazon.com opened for business on the World Wide Web in 1995 and had 110 employees by the end of 1996. Customers connecting to Amazon's website find more than a million book titles they can order. When they order over the Web, they can expect the book to be delivered in about five days. Amazon.com takes the order, contacts the publisher or a distributor, and has the book delivered to Amazon's warehouse in Seattle. Then it ships the book to the customer.

Another company that has decided to use the Internet is a well-established independent bookstore that has already figured out how to compete with the superstores. Powell's City of Books in Portland, Oregon, is a huge store with a bigger inventory of books than even the superstores offer. Powell's also differentiates itself from the superstores by offering used as well as new books and by offering several editions of the same book. Like the superstores, Powell's enhances the book-browsing experience by providing a coffee bar.

In spite of its current success, Powell's has decided to expand its business onto the Internet. But it has chosen a strategy that differs from Amazon.com's. Here are some of the basic differences.

Amazon focuses on new books, while Powell's offers both new and used books. Powell's reasoning? Selling both new and used books at the same location is Powell's niche.

Amazon lists all books in print. Powell's lists only books it actually has in inventory. Powell's reasoning? This avoids unfillable orders.

Amazon is committed to heavy promotional spending. Powell's is not. Powell's reasoning? Word of mouth will be more effective.

Amazon attempts to enrich its website with supplemental material such as reviews and chats. Powell's avoids these extras. Powell's reasoning? Focusing on what the customer wants is more effective.

SOURCE: Charles Mann, "Business Volume," *Inc. Technology*, 1997, no. 2, pp. 54–61.

Decision Questions

1. Will either Amazon or Powell's have to change its strategy to compete for book sales on the Internet? Explain your answer and speculate regarding changes both firms will have to make.
2. The three big superstores will eventually open for business on the web. Bezos anticipated that happening and an important part of his strategy was to become a large Web firm quickly so that when the superstores arrive, he can compete with them. Use a SWOT analysis to estimate the likelihood that Amazon.com will be able to survive when Barnes and Noble, Borders, and Crown Books open their competitive websites.
3. Suppose you owned a small independent bookstore today. What strategies could you follow to compete with the superstores on the one hand and the new Web stores on the other?

REFERENCES

1. Jennifer Fischl. "FedEx: Tall Order." *Financial World*, January 21, 1997, p. 20.

2. Christopher Cassiano, Jay Finegan, and Robina A. Gangemi. "Bootstrapping." *Inc.*, August 1995.

3. Some wonderful views and thoughts about vision come from the work of Warren Bennis. See for example Warren Bennis and Burt Nanus. *Leaders: The Strategies for Taking Charge.* New York: Harper & Row, 1985.

4. The concept of core competence is presented in detail by C. K. Prahalad and Gary Hamel. "The Core Competence of the Corporation." *Harvard Business Review* 90, no. 3, May/June 1990, pp. 79–93.

5. Michael E. Porter. "What Is Strategy?" *Harvard Business Review*, November/December 1996, pp. 61–78.

6. Charles W. L. Hill and Gareth R. Jones. *Strategic Management: An Integrated Approach.* Boston: Houghton Mifflin, 1992, p. 104.

7. Michael E. Porter. *Competitive Strategy: Techniques for Analyzing Industries and Competitors.* New York: The Free Press, 1980.

8. Hill and Jones, p. 148.

9. Norman Brinker and Donald T. Phillips. *On the Brink: The Life and Leadership of Norman Brinker.* Arlington, TX: Summit Publishing, 1996, p. 167.

10. Litespeed Titanium Bicycles (http://www.litespeed.com).

11. Brinker International. "Shareholders '96 Presentations," 1996.

12. E. A. Locke and G. P. Latham. *A Theory of Goal Setting and Task Performance.* Englewood Cliffs, NJ: Prentice-Hall, 1990.

13. John F. Welch, Jr. "To Our Share Owners." General Electric Annual Report, 1996, pp. 1–4.

12

Providing Value for Customers

In the ever-expanding world of high technology, Neil Senturia sensed that the needs of business travelers were not being met. His logic was basic and direct. Fewer than one-third of all business travelers carry laptop computers. But between flights, many business travelers would like to send e-mail back to the office, use the World Wide Web to check stock prices, or access other online services. Senturia's business, Atcom/Info, lets them make such connections.

The business concept is unique. Atcom has installed 167 high-speed, public Internet kiosks at airports, convention centers, and hotels all across the country. With the swipe of a credit card and for only 33 cents a minute, the harried traveler can surf the corporate network easily and conveniently. Atcom hopes its public Internet kiosks, or Cyberbooths, will be the high-tech equivalent of the phone booth. Importantly, Senturia recognizes a key to business success: find out what customers need and create products and services that will provide the value they seek.[1]

In Chapter 11, we discussed how businesspeople think strategically and consciously choose a strategic direction for their businesses. We noted that strategic thinking involves careful study and analysis. It allows the business to carve out an approach that it believes will bring competitive success. While it is absolutely critical, strategic thinking alone does not guarantee success. Progressive and truly insightful strategic plans mean nothing until they are translated into actions.

As we have stressed throughout this book, action starts with the customer. This chapter focuses on customers and the ways businesses try to provide value for them. After reading this chapter, you should be able to:

1. Understand the meaning of customer service.

2. Explain the processes involved in customer service.

3. Communicate the basic principles of learning about customer needs.

4. Demonstrate an understanding of product and service development processes.

5. Communicate value to a customer in a business situation.

6. Use the key aspects of product availability to increase the value of a product.

7. Recognize the value of customer feedback and know how to obtain it.

This chapter is about providing value for customers. Our concept of customer value is a broad, encompassing one. Successful businesses understand the needs and expectations of their customers. They build products and offer services that meet or exceed those needs. They provide their customers with consistent quality. They supply service and follow-up in a timely manner. A business provides value for customers by doing all these things and doing them well.

In today's markets, customers are very demanding. Businesses must respond by showing sensitivity and attention to customer needs and expectations. This is a question of exchange and value. If customers are going to surrender their hard-earned dollars, they demand products and services that offer them what they want. In other words, they demand value. The purpose of this chapter is to explore some of the basic ways a business provides value by understanding and meeting the needs of its customers. These actions form the foundation of customer service. This is why "providing value for customers" is an element of "Making Decisions and Taking Actions" in our model of a successful business.

Defining Customer Service

Customer service
Knowing what customers want and seeing that they get it.

Customer service can be thought of as knowing what customers want and seeing that they get it. Sometimes in businesses we think this is solely the job of the marketing department. Indeed, some of the specific activities that are done in the area of customer service are marketing in nature. Yet true customer service is really everyone's job.

For example, Gionne's is a successful Italian restaurant located in the heart of a midsize city. Patrons love the food and the atmosphere. The intimate setting seats only 85 people. Weekend reservations are needed weeks in advance. Leo and Lisa Gionne are enjoying their work and enjoying their success. But the picture has not always been so positive. Ten years ago, the Gionnes operated a sandwich shop at the same location. They catered to the downtown lunch crowd. Their evening clientele consisted of stragglers from downtown events who would occasionally stop in for drinks after a play or sporting event. Gionne's looked like a dozen other restaurants in the area. It was losing money. Leo and Lisa even considered selling the business.

The Gionnes were perplexed. The business, they thought, *should* be more successful. Their location was great. There was plenty of traffic. The downtown area was active with businesspeople during the day and hopping with potential evening customers who attended theater, musical, and sporting events at the Civic Arena only two blocks away. Why aren't we doing better, the Gionnes wondered? In desperation, they began to talk to people who wandered in. They asked simple questions. What are you looking for in a restaurant? What sort of environment do you want? What sort of menu? How expensive? What drink selections are important? They learned that most evening patrons wanted a nice experience to complement their night on the town. While price was not unimportant, most people were willing to pay for reasonable value. They wanted a nice, quaint, intimate atmosphere. They wanted good ethnic food. And, most surprisingly, they wanted a good selection of wines.

The Gionnes listened. They remade their restaurant in the image of the customer wishes they had received. Small tables for two or four were purchased to replace booths. Candlelight dinners became the norm. The menu was limited to a small selection of Italian favorites that Lisa had perfected over the years. Leo began delving into the best selection of moderately priced wines he could find. And he never stopped talking to patrons. You could expect Leo to visit your table once or twice each meal, usually to make sure the wine you selected met your expectations and again to make sure you enjoyed your meal. Leo learned the names of customers. He would greet repeat customers by name and suggest new wine selections they might enjoy. Soon the word was out: the place was intimate and cozy, it had great food, and it offered a super wine list. In a few short months, Gionne's became the place to go. Visiting celebrities would often stop by before or after a performance. A thriving, healthy business had been born.

The Gionnes had tapped the secret of customer service. First, they found out what their customers wanted. Second, they did everything they could to provide products and services to meet customer needs. Third, they went out of their way to keep their customers happy so they would come back and bring others.

Leo is also practicing an aspect of customer service that is quite popular today. It is known as **relationship marketing,** and it occurs when you get to know your customers and establish rapport and long-term relationships with them. Relationship marketing emphasizes meeting customers' needs over time. It rejects the notion of exploiting customers to make quick sales and gain one-time profits. Owners, like Leo and Lisa, would rather build understanding and establish repeat business. This makes good sense. It costs significantly less to keep a customer than to get a new one.

Relationship marketing
Getting to know one's customers and establishing rapport and long-term relationships with them.

In a competitive market, customers simply will not tolerate (at least for any extended period) businesses that are insensitive to their needs. If customers feel they are not being properly served, they will turn from that business and its products and services. Consider the example of Major League Baseball in Profile 12–1. True, baseball may not be the typical business that comes to mind when you think of appealing to customers. Yet look at what has happened. Customers (fans) feel ignored and slighted—and they're staying away from the ballparks.

PROFILE 12–1   *Baseball Strikes Out*

It is America's game, our national pastime. Baseball is played and enjoyed by millions. Boys and girls of all sizes, races, and economic standings play baseball. For adults, it has traditionally been a wholesome sporting event the whole family can enjoy. Through the years, professional baseball has captured the American public. For 160 years, it has sat at the top of the spectator sports world. But recently much of that allure has been lost. Major League Baseball is experiencing trouble. Game attendance is waning; in 1995, attendance was down 26 percent from 1993.

Fewer people are watching at home too. Change and renewal are needed. Let's take a look at what's going on and see if we can figure out a direction of change.

One of the first things you notice when examining the state of Major League Baseball is the escalating costs that fans are asked to bear. The average cost of a day at a major league game for a family of four (including tickets, treats, and parking) is nearly $100. While this is still about half the cost of an average pro football game, the expense can be overwhelming, particularly for lower- and moderate-income families. In fact, these families are less likely to attend games now than they were 10 years ago. Increasingly, affluent families are the most likely to attend pro baseball games.

The second reason behind the plunge in attendance and interest is that fans feel alienated from the game and its players and management. Many fans think players are overpriced. The staggering million-dollar salaries are a far cry from the "working man" image that baseball once sported. Many fans believe owners care little about fan interests. Owners threaten to and at times do leave cities that have supported their teams for years. In short, many feel that both owners and players just don't care about their customers. They seem to be more concerned about TV revenues and multiyear contracts.

The game and its players were tarnished by the bitter strike of 1995 and the hoopla that surrounded it. Many fans had trouble relating to players who wanted more financial concessions when they already earned unbelievable salaries yet they didn't approve of some owners' power plays either. Some high-profile players' on-field antics and shunning of fans have done nothing to help this image.

The game needs a facelift. Rules should be changed. The game needs speeding up to be more viewer-friendly. Interleague play may generate more fan interest, but its impact is most likely only short term. The game needs superstars. But the real bottom line is that Major League Baseball needs to draw its fans closer and to clean up the squabbles that have deflected the focus from the game.

Experts argue that these changes may be difficult without renewed leadership. The top official of major league baseball is the commissioner, but Fay Vincent was fired in 1992 and baseball has been operating without an independent commissioner since. The acting commissioner, Bud Selig, is an owner (of the Milwaukee Brewers). Major league baseball moved to address this leadership void by naming Paul Beeston as its president and chief operating officer in August, 1997.   ●

The Dynamics of Customer Service

Customer service involves five processes, noted in Figure 12–1. First, it involves *learning about customers*. This means that a business must continually study its customers (as well as potential new customers) to find out what they really want and need. Customers are sometimes fickle. Tastes and preferences change. The business must take regular readings on what customers really desire.

Once needs and wants have been identified, the business becomes concerned with a second process, *product or service development*. This means that the business must generate products or services that meet identified customer needs and that provide value for customers. For a manufacturing business, this may mean working in customer-oriented teams of engineers, marketing, accounting, and management personnel to develop new and improved products that are tailored exactly to a client's specifications. In service businesses, it may require focus groups to determine how best to provide

teams p. 71>

FIGURE 12–1   Dynamics of Customer Service

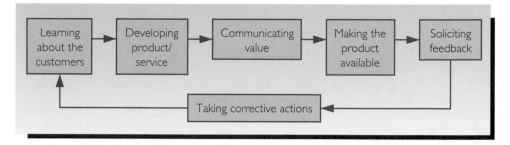

the services customers want. Whatever the business, the goal of product development should be to create new value for the customers.

Once the product has been developed, a third process becomes critical. *Communicating value* means that the business must inform potential customers about its products or services and convince them of the value these products or services provide. Value may be communicated through a number of techniques. This process is not just informational; it also involves persuading customers to select the products of the business over alternatives that may be available in the marketplace. A real challenge of this communication phase is to convince customers that true value exists.

The fourth process is *product availability*. This means that managers must make sure the product is available when and where customers want it. These issues are part of the timeliness theme we emphasized earlier in the book.

The final process in the dynamics of customer service involves soliciting feedback from customers regarding how well the business has met customer expectations. *Soliciting feedback* consists of communicating with customers, as well as those who choose not to be customers, in order to find out what is good as well as bad about the firm's products, services, and activities. This step tells the business where it has fallen short in providing value for customers. This feedback should be the foundation for appropriate corrective actions.

The five processes involve a number of people from different areas of the business. At a minimum, they involve employees from research and development, marketing, and manufacturing. Quality considerations are critical in every area and in every phase of the five processes highlighted here.

Learning about the Customers

The first step in serving customers lies in learning what they really want and need. There are both a short answer and a long answer to the question "How do we find out what the customers want?" The short answer is "Ask them." This, of course, is simplistic, but it captures the spirit immediately. Far too many businesses make a product that they *think* customers will want. Then they build an advertising plan to convince customers that they do, indeed, want what the manufacturer built. It would be much better if managers *first* asked customers what they wanted and *then* proceeded to build it. Then the task would be simply to communicate that the product was available and to accentuate those parts of the product that particularly meet the customer's needs. Learning about customers can involve a number of approaches. Most fall under the heading of market research, which lies at the heart of learning about customers.

Market Research

Market research
Collecting and analyzing information about the market or potential market for a product or service.

Market research deals with the tasks of collecting and analyzing information about the market or potential market for a product or service. Information is critical because it communicates what products are in demand, what features are desirable, and how the product is best delivered to the customer. Whatever form market research takes, it involves the effort to learn about customer needs and how best to meet those needs. This can be done in a number of ways.

First, business decision makers may rely on secondary data. **Secondary data** are any data that have already been published. A number of databases contain excellent information—for example, census data, trade association reports, economic forecasts, online information services, and the vast amount of information on the Internet. Secondary data are relatively easy to find, and they can give a wealth of general information about customers, the economy, and trends.

Secondary data
Any data that have already been published.

Primary data
Data that a business collects directly from customers and potential customers.

Second, customer information may be gained through **primary data,** which are data the business collects directly from customers and potential customers. A popular way to collect primary data is with surveys. You may have participated in a market research survey at some time in your life. Researchers may survey people by telephone, in a mall, by mail, by e-mail, or by visiting with customers in the marketer's store. This kind of information is often more difficult, costly, and time consuming to gather and analyze than is secondary data, but it provides very direct and relevant information if done well. Surveys offer the advantage of tailoring questions to provide specifically needed information and probing for reasons behind the answers.

When developing surveys to collect primary data, managers must first answer the question, "What is it that we need to know, and what will we do with the information?" This information helps managers design the survey and identify the target sample. They can then determine how much accuracy and specificity they need. Are extensive details important, or are general answers acceptable? Should they use a mail survey, which is inexpensive but has a low response rate, or do they want to talk with people personally or by phone to get better response rates and more detailed answers?

Surveys are not the only way to gather primary data. Many companies use their websites on the Internet to encourage customers to provide ideas and thoughts on their products or overall activities. Trek's online website encourages bikers to comment or ask questions. Since starting the website in 1995, Trek has heard from thousands of cyclists from all over the world.[2]

Focus group
A small group of people who are asked to respond to a researcher's questions.

Other businesses gain primary data through **focus groups,** which consist of a small number of individuals who are invited to sit as a group and respond to questions posed by a researcher. For example, a dentist wanted to know whether there was a market for specialized dentistry aimed at senior citizens. He commissioned a consultant to assemble a panel of 10 residents of the community who were between the ages of 55 and 65. The dentist provided a list of topics to cover. The consultant then brought the panel together, provided sandwiches and soft drinks, and led a group con-

ABOUT THE ONLY THING
IT HAS IN COMMON WITH
THE TYPICAL
50-YEAR-OLD
IS THE SPARE TIRE.

F-SERIES CELEBRATES FIFTY YEARS OF BUILT FORD TOUGH

Ford used extensive market research prior to designing its new F-series pickups. Many large companies use similar research in order to learn more about their customers. This is costly, but it usually pays great returns. How can small businesses do market research?

versation in such a way as to collect the information. The consultant videotaped the focus group so the dentist could refer back to it later.

Sometimes a firm gains primary data by involving customers directly with the business and its decision makers. For example, consider a small manufacturing business that builds components that are used by a major manufacturer, such as Caterpillar. It would not be unusual for the small firm to assemble a team that includes Caterpillar people to better understand Caterpillar's needs and how to meet them.

As you can see, market research can be quite broad in its applications. For example, Ford used market research in designing its 1997 F-150 pickup truck. Designer James Bulin created an "automotive anthology" by pinpointing the tastes and characteristics of six generations of American customers. Some of this information came from quite useful secondary data. Some came from various forms of primary data. By using Bulin's *value groups*, Ford was able to tailor the design and marketing of the truck to the baby-boom market. It helped provide ideas for a trimmed-down truck full of family-friendly features, including a rear passenger door that hinges at the back to make entry/exit easier. The approach of looking first at what customers value was a real change for Ford from the more traditional research of adapting existing products or benchmarking competitors' products.[3]

benchmarking p. 450>

Data analysis
The study of information to help a manager reach a conclusion about some aspect of the company.

Throughout our discussion of market research, we have assumed that the data that are gathered can be meaningfully analyzed. This represents an additional step. **Data analysis** is the study of information with the goal of helping a manager reach a conclusion about some aspect of the company. Sometimes in-depth statistical analysis is needed. Sometimes the manager can just look at information and interpret it. Regardless of the method of analysis used, the final result will be a set of data that tells the manager something about how customers think and act, what they like and dislike, and how they perceive the company's products or services.

Developing Your Critical Thinking Skills

1. Why is customer service more critical today than it was 10 years ago?

2. Relationship marketing has been stressed as an important theme for contemporary businesses. How should a business treat its customers to develop the desired relationship?

3. Why do small business owners often fail to do adequate market research?

Developing the Product or Service

Product/service development
A broad term for the creation of a product or service that provides greater value to customers than previously existed.

Before getting into the process of product or service development, we need to first define what we mean. **Product or service development** is a broad term referring to the creation of a product or service that provides greater value to customers than previously existed. There are actually six types of product development.[4]

1. A new-to-the-world product.
2. A new product line.
3. A new product added to an existing line.
4. An improved product.
5. A repositioned product.
6. A lower-priced version of an existing product.

New-to-the-world products refer to totally new products never before seen by humankind. These are actually rather rare. In the vast majority of cases, new products are simply variations on existing products. An example of a new-to-the-world product is the Zip Drive produced by Iomega Corp. It is an external or internal drive for computers that uses a disk that is about the size of a 3.5-inch floppy but thicker and holds the equivalent of 70 normal disks. The clever thing about the external drive is that you can plug it into a computer without even turning the computer off. This gives major flexibility in transporting data and applications from computer to computer.

New product lines are products developed by a company that did not produce them before, even though other companies did. Dickies, a long-time maker of heavy-duty work clothes, has developed a line of work clothes for people who do not work in heavy-duty situations. Such products existed before but they are new for Dickies.

A less radical method is to add a *new product to an existing product line*. This means that a company develops a product it has never had in order to expand its current product line. When General Mills brought out Multi Grain Cheerios, it was adding a new product to go with its regular Cheerios, Honey Nut Cheerios, and Frosted Cheerios products. Thus, it added a new product to the Cheerios line of cereals.

The firm may also improve or revise an existing product to make it more appealing to customers. *Product improvement* does not create a new product, but it makes a significant improvement on an existing product or product line. This includes bringing out new models or adding features that make the product more valuable—for example, a faster, more powerful computer chip.

Sometimes a firm may reposition a current product for a new customer grouping. *Product repositioning* means taking an existing product and finding ways to market it to new customer groups. This is the basis of Levi's efforts to get office workers to wear its Dockers clothes to work, as discussed in Profile 12–2. It has repositioned Dockers as being appropriate for office attire, not just as casual wear.

Finally, the firm may introduce *lower-priced versions of existing products* in an effort to increase sales volume. These versions often have far fewer features than the standard product, but they are considerably less expensive. For example, contemporary remote controls for TVs are complex instruments that can also program the VCR. They have too many buttons that many people simply do not know how to operate them. Now a remote has been introduced that has only a power button and two toggles, one for increasing or decreasing volume and one for changing channels. This remote is substantially cheaper (and easier to use) than the traditional remote.

PROFILE 12–2   *Levi's versus the Dress Code*

Sometimes providing value to customers entails convincing them that the firm's product is in fact valuable. There is perhaps no more brash example of this than Levi Strauss, which is attempting to convince the entire business sector—as well as anyone else who will listen—that suits are unnecessary. This may sound like a daunting task. But suppose there are, say, 1 million companies where people wear suits to work every day. If Levi's can convince even 1 percent of companies to adopt a more casual look, that is 10,000 companies. And if the average business has 100 people who would be affected, that's an extra million sets of casual clothes even if each person buys only one outfit.

Many companies have endorsed the concept of casual Fridays. One staff member said he had to go out and buy a whole new wardrobe because all he owned were suits and sweats. The casual Fridays fad has spread wildly across the country. But the real impact may be that companies are deciding that casual Mondays, Tuesdays, Wednesdays, and Thursdays are also acceptable. Levi's certainly hopes so and is investing millions of dollars to encourage the idea.

SOURCE: Linda Himelstein, "Levi's vs. the Dress Code," *Business Week*, April 1, 1996, pp. 57–8.

Product differentiation
Developing a product that differs enough from existing products that customers can distinguish the new product from existing ones.

Service development is essentially the same as product development even though the base is a service rather than a product. Thus, a service firm may bring out a new-to-the-world service, introduce an entire new line of services, add new services, improve or revise its services so they are more appealing, reposition its services to appeal to other markets, or bring out a similar service at a lower price.

Often at this stage of product development, the business is concerned with **product differentiation.** Product differentiation means developing a product that differs enough from existing products that customers can distinguish the new product from existing ones. Obviously, the hope is that customers will prefer the differentiated product over currently available options. If the product is really different, the business may attract new customers.

Developing Quality Products

Early in the text, we emphasized the significance of product quality. Customers expect quality and demonstrate limited patience when their expectations are not met. Accordingly, an eye toward quality is an essential part of the product development process. However, saying we want product quality is one thing; knowing how to achieve it is more complex and challenging. While we will address the quality theme more fully in Chapter 15, some basic points are relevant to our discussion here.

Product quality
A situation where a product satisfies customers' needs by performing up to their expectations.

A popular way of thinking about product quality is to compare product performance with customer expectations.[5] In fact, **product quality** exists when the product satisfies customers' needs by performing up to their expectations. Assume you need to buy a new car. If you purchase a Hyundai for under $10,000, you have certain expectations of the car, its performance level, and its maintenance. However, if you buy a BMW for over $60,000, you surely have a different and more stringent set of expectations. You expect the BMW to be better made, to perform better, and to perform more consistently (in other words, need less maintenance) than the Hyundai. You judge the quality of the two cars differently because the standards for Hyundai and BMW are dramatically different. Of course, the same ideas hold true for service quality.

The Development Process

At the beginning of this chapter, we said meeting customer needs begins with assessing those needs and then developing services or products that meet them. In many cases, ideas for new products do come directly from customers. However, employees, distributors, and even competitors may generate ideas that seem worthy of development. The specific process companies use when developing products or services involves concept evaluation, business analysis, and development activities (including perhaps test marketing).

Concept Evaluation

Concept evaluation
Analysis to determine if the overall idea fits with the firm's strategy and existing product/service mix.

The first step is to evaluate the concept. **Concept evaluation** means analyzing the overall idea to see if it fits with the firm's strategy and existing product or service mix. In other words, does the concept seem to make sense for the business? Concept evaluation is a broad-brush analysis that is completed before in-depth analysis occurs. It looks at the big picture of how the idea fits with the existing products or services.

Business Analysis

Business analysis
A comparison of projected demand for a product with the firm's ability and cost to produce it.

Once the concept has been evaluated favorably, the idea must be subjected to **business analysis,** which compares projected demand for a product with the firm's ability and cost to produce it. The company considers how the product would affect existing products, what investments in production facilities would be required, and what additional marketing staff might be needed. The analysis is ultimately aimed at predicting how much profit can be expected from the product. A concept may look promising, but if it fails to pass the scrutiny of the business analysis it should not be pursued further.

Development Activities

If a product idea passes all the business analysis tests, then the actual product development begins. Often a development team is used to create the product or service. A **development team** is a group of individuals from various parts of a company who have an interest in the product/service and are selected to develop it into a profitable activity. The best development work occurs when the development team consists of an integrated mix of employees from research and development, engineering, marketing, accounting, production, and perhaps even suppliers. There are a number of reasons to use an integrated development team. One is that the different departments that may be involved in either producing, advertising, or selling the product will be more committed to the product if they have input into its design. Second, the probability of customer acceptance increases if those employees who interact directly with customers are involved. A third reason for integrated development teams is to reduce development time, or cycle time.

Cycle time is the time it takes to develop a new product. It is a key to successful business today. Years ago, development time was not so crucial. Today, however, a product may be obsolete in a year or two, as in the case of the PowerPC computer chips. Further, a firm's competitors may achieve *first-mover advantages* if the business does not move quickly. Cutting cycle time also saves money, since the firm must invest more and more funds into development as time goes on. Firms that use computer-aided design, for example, have been able to cut months off the development time for new products. Using integrated development teams also reduces cycle time by bringing all factors of the production and selling processes together simultaneously to resolve any problems that might occur.

The action stage may involve building a prototype that can be studied to make sure the product is sound and feasible. This stage may also include **test marketing**, which involves piloting a product or service in certain select markets to see what customers think. If customers in the targeted locations do not buy the product or respond favorably, some changes or modifications may be necessary. The entire product idea may even have to be scrapped.

Some businesses do extensive test marketing before introducing products to customers on a broad scale. In 1997, Procter & Gamble began test marketing a new product called *Bibsters*, disposable bibs that consumers use when feeding babies. P&G reasoned that disposable bibs would be just as desirable for today's families as disposable diapers were when they were test marketed 35 years ago. P&G selected cities for the test marketing that met a number of stringent requirements. The cities needed to be medium-sized with fairly defined geographic boundaries so marketing could be pinpointed. They also needed to have demographic characteristics similar to the rest of the country. If Bibsters sell well in the test markets, P&G will have good evidence that they may sell well throughout the country.

Creating Value

Creating value refers to taking actions that make a product or service more useful to customers. Developing new products or product modifications is one example of creating value, but value can be created in less dramatic ways. In some cases, creating value simply means *adding customer-friendly touches* to the services already provided. For example, the new Star Market in Boston offers in-store sushi chefs, a Starbucks Coffee outlet, a bank branch, and—perhaps most appreciated—a child care center where customers can leave their kids while buying groceries. In fact, the Star Market created the kids play area after many focus group participants listed shopping with children as one

Development team
A group of people from various parts of a company who have an interest in the product/service and are selected to develop it into a profitable activity.

Cycle time
The time it takes to develop a new product.

Test marketing
Selling a product/service in certain select markets to see what customers think.

Creating value
Taking actions that make a product/service more useful to customers.

of the greatest hassles of grocery shopping. Value for these customers comes from being able to shop without somebody tugging on their leg.[6]

Elliott Baretz of suburban Philadelphia has a *customer-friendly* store. As Profile 12–3 explains, his computer superstore, More Computers, sells and services computers. But it also provides amenities that customers want, with particular emphasis on allowing customers (even children) to try out machines and software.

PROFILE 12–3   *More Computers Lives Up to Its Name*

Elliott Baretz graduated from college in 1991 with a degree in advertising and political science after "denying for four years that his destiny was to be in business." With some family connections, he landed a job with a brokerage firm and soon became involved with an acquisitions business. One of the companies he purchased was Valens Business Machines, which had begun as a typewriter repair shop in the 1970s and had moved into computer sales in the 1980s. Baretz immediately renamed the firm Valens Information Systems and used it as a base for starting More Computers, a unique computer superstore in suburban Philadelphia.

More Computers in Springfield (Delaware County), Pennsylvania, offers hardware, software, and peripherals for DOS- and Macintosh-based home and office computer systems. Opened in 1995, in an old Boeing helicopter plant, More Computers delivers expert advice in a fun, relaxed, interactive atmosphere. An exciting alternative to the chain superstores that already exist in the Delaware Valley market, More Computers focuses on customer service. Since a computer is often the third-largest purchase a person makes in life, More Computers is designed to offer customers both the small-store attention such a purchase deserves and big-store selection with guaranteed low prices.

The interior layout of More Computers is the creation of Dan Sykes, a design specialist who is responsible for the stylish redesign of Pier 1 Imports, Williams-Sonoma kitchen stores, and Computerware stores in California. More Computers' colorfully decorated warehouse environment invites customers in, shows them exactly where to go, and compels them to come back. Primary colors splash across the 15,000-square-foot warehouse. Patterned floors and industrial paintings add to the decor.

More Computers is divided into several zones, or stores within a store, which appeal to its different target markets. The Play, Work, Compute, Move, and Connect sections each cater to a specific market and can change as technology evolves. Customers can test merchandise in every zone of the store.

Children and adults are invited to have fun and learn in the Play zone, whether they want to page through an encyclopedia on CD-ROM, try out the latest software games, or travel to faraway lands. Since small business customers comprise more than half of today's retail computer shoppers, More Computers created the Work zone to meet entrepreneurs' needs, including multifunctional units, printers, fax machines, and modems.

Most of More Computers' customers enter the Compute zone since all high-profile products, including the powerful systems, scanners, and networks, are located here. Local area networks (LANs) can help link three or four computers with a server or connect people's home computers with their systems at work. Experiencing the network before the purchase reassures customers about compatibility. For people on the go, the Move zone makes finding a laptop computer or other portable, high-tech devices easy.

The Connect zone is the Internet connection. While everyone has heard of the Internet, industry estimates that only 30 percent of people have actually tried it. Large monitors display the latest activity on America OnLine, Prodigy, and Microsoft On-Line. Customers are invited to sit down and surf the net themselves. They can explore online chat rooms, link into the World Wide Web, or check into forums that provide advice on everything from gardening to pets to international travel.

The Ask More and Cafe zones cater to two important customer needs, answers and relaxation. Once in the front doors, customers don't have to walk far to have all their questions answered by helpful staff members at the Ask More information center. They can qualify customers' needs and send them off into the zone of their choice or introduce them to a salesperson. They can also sit at a bistro table in the Cafe zone to review product literature, read computer-related books or magazines, enjoy some coffee or tea, or talk with a salesperson about purchase options. This area is intended to allow customers to relax and carefully consider their anticipated purchases.

The different zones strategically located throughout the store are successful not only because of their accessibility and merchandise selection but because of the knowledgeable, approachable staffers.

SOURCE: Personal interview; company documents.

Oxo's line of kitchen tools have won product design awards because of their thick, soft handles. Based on market research, these tools were created especially for the elderly and handicapped but have been well received by all customers. Can you think of other products that could meet specific market needs?

Discount pricing
Pricing products significantly lower than the same or a similar product at competing stores.

Part of the value that a customer receives is in the *design* of the product or service. Improved product design makes the product more durable, more reliable, easier to use, or easier to maintain.[7] Any time a company can bring more of these into a product, that product will have more value for customers. Many companies are aware of the need for state-of-the-art designs. Some companies are also identifying particular needs of subgroups within a market and adapting products specifically for those subgroups. One company, for example, developed kitchen tools with large handles that are easier for elderly or disabled people to use.

Customers can also receive value through the company's *pricing policy*, especially if the pricing is combined with other sources of value. This is the basis for Wal-Mart, Kmart, and Target's discount pricing. **Discount pricing** is product pricing that is significantly lower than the same or similar product at competing stores. Discounters believe that customers perceive value in the lower prices and are willing to endure the hassle of trekking to the far corners of a mammoth store to get a bargain. These stores generate value for customers in another way: selection. The giant stores prosper in spite of the inconvenience of navigating aisles by providing very large selections at very low prices. Other customers, perceiving value through quality of products or quality of service, shop at stores that admittedly charge higher prices but provide additional service. These customers are quality sensitive, not price sensitive.

Employees who are specially trained to emphasize service are another way to provide value for customers. These employees may include sales clerks in department stores, servers in restaurants, flight attendants on airplanes, telemarketing order takers, salespeople at car dealers, and a host of others. Customers are quick to dismiss employees who provide poor service or who are not knowledgeable. Conversely, those who provide extra service reap greater sales for their businesses. For example, servers in a restaurant provide extra value by getting to know their customers' idiosyncrasies. One server in a restaurant knows that a particular couple who dine there often are particularly fond of iced tea. When she spots them coming in the door, she meets them at the table with two large glasses of iced tea and makes sure the glasses are never empty. This small action creates happy customers who return frequently because of the good service.

Value can be created through *timing*. Providing a service at a specific time for harried customers is important. An example of value through timing is car dealers whose service departments stay open late at night for customers who don't have time to take their cars to the shop during the day.

Value can also be created through *product distribution*, which we will discuss later in this chapter. There are certainly other sources of value that can be added to products or services. The point, however, is that managers must constantly be aware of how their products or services provide value and how that value may be improved.

Developing Your Critical Thinking Skills

1. McDonald's is test marketing its new made-to-order burgers.[8] How will McDonald's use the information gained from its test site in Colorado Springs to determine whether this product will be a winner? Will the test results apply to New England or California?

2. Why do businesses invest so much money in the product or service development process?

3. We discussed a number of ways a company can create value for customers. Which do you think would be most useful for a local independent hardware store that is trying to compete with a large national chain that has just entered the market?

Communicating Value

Communicating value
Informing customers
and potential customers
about how a product can
meet their needs.

The best product in the world is of little value if customers are not aware of it. **Communicating value** means informing customers about how a product can in fact meet their needs. The essence of promotion is communicating value. Managers must ensure that the innate value of their product or service is communicated to customers and potential customers in such a way that customers clearly grasp the intent of the message and are persuaded to buy from the company.

Communicating value to customers is important all the time, but it's especially important at certain specific times, like when a new product is being introduced. Companies spend millions of dollars promoting new products. General Mills, for example, introduced two new cereals in the fall of 1996 using the Betty Crocker brand. It believed that the Betty Crocker brand name had value for customers and decided to extend that value from baking goods to ready-to-eat cereals. It expected the "home-baked" taste of the cereal to be a hit with consumers. But just to make sure, when Cinnamon Streusel and Dutch Apple cereals hit the shelves of grocery stores, they were accompanied by a $40 million promotional campaign.[9]

creativity p. 522>

Value must also be communicated when a firm wishes to significantly increase sales of existing products. It takes a major marketing campaign to ratchet sales up to a higher level. When the product is exciting, generating customer enthusiasm is relatively easy. But when the product is mundane, creativity is needed to develop advertising that captures customers' attention. A product that ranks among the most mundane was the basis for one of the top advertising campaigns in 1995–96, featured in Profile 12–4.

PROFILE 12–4   *The Milk Mustache*

budget p. 402>

There are few products that are less exciting than milk. Milk didn't exactly have a poor image; it just didn't have much of an image at all. Sales of milk had declined for three decades and few people over age 12 drank it. So the National Fluid Milk Processor Board, an industry trade association, contacted an advertising agency to see what could be done to improve the image of milk. What it got was an ad campaign that won first place in an annual survey of memorable ads, beating out ads for Absolut Vodka, Budweiser, Calvin Klein, Revlon, Ford, Philip Morris, Unilever, Nike, and Nabisco. What it got was the milk mustache.

Jay Schulberg of Bozell Worldwide decided to commit the entire $36 million advertising budget to magazine advertising and to enlist numerous celebrities in the milk mustache campaign. His approach was to send the celebrities a picture of themselves with a drawn-on milk mustache. The stars reacted with humor and eagerly signed on. Producing the ads was also a challenge. The task was to apply makeup to the actor's face and then have him or her take a gulp of milk. Unfortunately, the milk didn't always stay right. The mustaches often needed fake touch-ups to look real.

What's a hip drink?
Let me lay some lyrics on you,
man. Hey, *Chocolate* milk.
It's nutty, it's too neat. Get your
nutrients with a koo-koo beat.
Get it lowfat, get it fat free.
It's a swingin' chocolata treat.
Chocolate milk, oh yeah!

MILK
Where's your mustache?

What do Paul Shafer, Wesley Snipes, Cal Ripken, and David Copperfield have in common? All have appeared in Milk Mustache advertisements paid for by the National Fluid Milk Processor Promotion Board. How do these and other celebrities communicate value in a creative way to help promote sales? Will these ads convince you to drink more milk?

The campaign has created national attention. Comedians have joked about milk mustaches, and the campaign even ended up as a question on "Jeopardy," the TV quiz show.

SOURCE: Sall Goll Beatty, "Milk-Mustache Ads: Cream of the Crop," *The Wall Street Journal*, May 20, 1996, p. B6.

TABLE 12–1   THE TOP TEN U.S. ADVERTISERS

Rank	Advertiser	Total Annual U.S. Ad Spending ($ Billions)
1	Procter & Gamble	$2.8
2	Philip Morris	2.6
3	General Motors	2.0
4	Time Warner	1.3
5	Walt Disney Companies	1.3
6	Sears, Roebuck	1.2
7	Chrysler	1.2
8	PepsiCo	1.2
9	Johnson & Johnson	1.2
10	Ford	1.1

SOURCE: *Advertising Age*, September 30, 1996, p. S4.

Communicating Value through Promotional Techniques

Promotion
Actions taken to inform customers about and encourage them to buy a firm's products or use its services.

institutional advertising, p. 355>

Product advertising
Persuasive communications that specifically focus on a particular product.

Institutional advertising
Persuasive communications that promote a company or organization as a whole.

effectiveness p. 478>

Businesses may communicate value to their customers by informing them in a number of ways. One way, as we have noted, is through promotional efforts. **Promotion** is actions taken to inform customers about and encourage them to buy a firm's products or use its services. Although there are many forms of promotion, the most popular is advertising. Over $160 billion is spent annually on advertising.[10]

Table 12–1 shows the top 10 advertisers in the United States. These are all well-known companies with well-known products. Why are they so well known? Because they produce widely used products and commit millions of dollars to communicating with customers. Keep in mind that most of the firms listed in the table include many products in their promotion budgets.

Value may be communicated through advertising in the form of either product or institutional advertising. **Product advertising** is persuasive communications that specifically focus on a particular product. **Institutional advertising** is persuasive communications that promote a company or organization as a whole, not a particular product.

Some companies advertise primarily on television. Others find radio more cost effective. Still others believe that print advertising in newspapers and magazines is most effective. Probably because of its low cost and ability to reach large numbers of customers, newspaper advertising is the most common form currently used.

Some companies are best served simply by advertising in the Yellow Pages of telephone books, which are particularly well suited for small contractors and other service providers. Consider a local plumber, for example. This business owner most likely could not afford TV advertising, and it would be of limited effectiveness anyway because customers don't need a plumber unless they have a plumbing problem. When a problem does arise, they need a plumber immediately, so they grab the phone book and quickly turn to "plumbers" in the Yellow Pages. There they can find a listing of the plumbers in town and see immediately what the plumbers' forte is, where they are

The World Wide Web is increasingly used to advertise products and services. As more and more homes and businesses use computers and the time spent on the web increases, this becomes a natural outlet for advertising. Check out Adobe's web site. Is the information useful?

located, if they are bonded and insured, if they work on weekends and evenings, and whether they offer discounts to senior citizens.

Other methods of promotion exist. Increasingly, businesses are communicating with their customers through electronic media. This occurs, for example, when you are flipping through the TV channels and reach a home shopping network. Yet electronic approaches are becoming more sophisticated—for example, the World Wide

Web. Some companies are supplementing their other communications with home pages that catch the attention of potential customers. Interactive computer communications (and subsequent sales) are growing in popularity. Consider the opportunities. If you want to buy hiking boots from L.L. Bean, you can access its home page to learn about its products and place your order. Companies can also target services. Many of you may have checked out airline schedules and fares and even ordered tickets through the Internet.

Communicating Value through Price

Cost-based pricing
A situation where a company figures all of the costs involved in producing and selling a product and sets a price high enough to cover these costs plus a reasonable profit.

Businesses must always struggle to determine the proper price to set for their products or services. Obviously, as we discussed in Chapter 6, the pricing decision is critical. But how is price determined? In one traditional approach, known as **cost-based pricing,** the business figures all of the costs involved in producing and selling the product and sets a price high enough to cover these costs plus a reasonable profit. The driving force in setting the price is the costs that are incurred.

In other situations, price is affected by the actions of competitors. In a competitive market, this makes sense. For example, in 1997, American Airlines faced the threat of a major strike by its pilots. Customers lost confidence in American and worried that their tickets would be useless if the pilots went on strike and the airline was unable to fly. When the strike was averted at the last minute, American had already lost many of its customers to other airlines. To win them back, American slashed ticket prices by as much as 50 percent. Other major airlines responded by lowering their prices too. Thus, one of the driving forces in pricing is the competition.

Value-based pricing
A situation where a company figures out what customers want, what they are willing to pay, and what price thus seems appropriate.

Today an alternative approach to pricing seems to be gaining favor. **Value-based pricing** determines what customers want, what they are willing to pay, and what price seems appropriate. Rather than setting prices based on costs or competitors' prices, value-based pricing looks first at the customers. This may mean that products or services are designed or modified to meet these needs and prices. Of course, costs and competition are never ignored. Rather, the process focuses first on the customer. In value-based pricing, the business wants the customer to feel that a product's price, given its value, is good when compared to other options that are available.[11]

Recently some fast-food chains realized that the prices of their meals were getting too high. Customers were turning away because for just a little more, they could eat out at a more comfortable, family-style restaurant. In essence, customers were questioning whether the fast-food meal was worth the price they were paying. Burger King responded by introducing its "value meal." Its advertising emphasized that while prices are always escalating and you never know when unexpected expenses will arise, the Burger King value meal is one thing you can count on to stay low in price. Burger King built the meal around its sense of what customers expect from a fast-food establishment and what they are willing to pay for it. It used price as a major way to communicate value to the customer.

Image pricing
A situation where a business sets prices very high to indicate the exclusive or high-status nature of the product/service.

retailers p. 282>

Another approach to pricing that communicates value is **image pricing,** in which a business sets prices very high to indicate the exclusive or high-status nature of the product or service. Upscale, trendy restaurants in major cities often set very high prices with status in mind. Many vacation resorts do the same thing. Some retailers of fine jewelry follow this same practice; customers gain value from being among the few who can afford the jewelry.

Other Ways to Communicate Value

Beyond promotion and pricing, firms can communicate value to customers through the *brand names* they assign to products. In fact, businesses select names for their products that they hope will distinguish them from competing products. The ideal brand name is so well recognized that it suggests value to customers, who think of it when they need to purchase the product. Some companies have been so effective at this activity that their brand names have become almost synonymous with the products they are selling. For example, Kleenex is such a famous brand name that many people don't even realize that the broader product category is facial tissues. The same could be said of Rollerblades, the popular brand of in-line skates.

Functional packaging

Packaging that provides some value beyond simply containing the product.

Companies may also communicate value through effective *packaging*. Products packaged in functional packaging have more value than those with less functional packaging. **Functional packaging** provides some value beyond simply holding the product for sale. A company that sells paint rollers for do-it-yourselfers found that it could add value by packaging a small roller inside a small paint tray. The tray was the package itself, made of clear plastic with a replaceable plastic top. The rollers, which were designed for trim work, did not require the large trays normally used for wall painting. The unique tray/package combination created value for customers who would find it unhandy to have to use and clean a large tray just for trim work.

Some businesses spend considerable money to design packaging so appealing that customers choose one product over another because of it. In these cases, the packaging adds value. For example, a parent is shopping for drinks to include in a child's school lunchbox. Being nutritionally conscious, the parent looks for an orange fruit drink. There are shelves of canned orange drinks available. The cans are heavy, large, and bulky. However, the same juice is available in a boxed version that comes with a straw. The parent quickly grabs the box. Although the content of the juice cans is the same, the box best meets the customer's needs.

Companies may also communicate value through *personal selling and service*. Retail businesses that emphasize quality, for example, almost always have more and better-trained salespeople than firms that emphasize low prices. You may decide to purchase your next computer from a specialty store, such as More Computers in Profile 12–3, because it offers excellent advice and follow-up help. You may find the support worth the extra cost.

Making the Product/Service Available

We have discussed how to provide value by finding out what customers want. Managers then take that information and develop products that best meet those wants. We have discussed how firms must communicate that value to the customer. We now turn to providing value by delivering the service or product to customers *when* it's needed, *where* it's needed, and in the *form* that is needed. A manager's decisions must make sure these three criteria are met. If any of the three is missing, customers will be unhappy, and ultimately the manager will also be unhappy.

Timeliness

We discussed timeliness in Chapter 1 as one of the critical measures of a successful business. We will also treat just-in-time inventory control in detail in Chapter 15. Our interest here is in two areas. First is the minimization of time from placement of order or request to delivery to the customer. Second is the commitment to providing the product precisely when it is promised. Thus, timeliness is the provision of products when promised and in the minimum amount of time. Most industries are becoming increasingly time sensitive, though some find this theme more important than others do.

Mail-order companies especially understand the need for timely shipping of goods; some guarantee arrival in two days. They also know of the need for timeliness in order taking, so many have order takers available 24 hours a day, seven days a week.

Some companies have found that, in today's hectic world, timeliness is even more important than face-to-face communications. Thus, banks have moved heavily toward the use of ATMs, which allow customers to make transactions 24 hours a day.

A few years ago hotels began to allow customers to check out via the TV in their room. Guests check their bill on the TV screen and indicate their acceptance by touchtone telephone or perhaps just by leaving. Some hotels are now using the equivalent of ATMs for check-in in response to studies that found one of travelers' greatest frustrations is waiting in line to register. ATM check-ins reduce the average registration time from many minutes to the seconds required to pass a credit card through a reader and punch in a few keys or touch spots on a monitor. This is particularly handy when many guests arrive at the same time.

Airlines are also discovering the role of timeliness in airport check-in. They too are using the equivalent of ATMs for some departing passengers. Checking bags at curbside eliminates the time standing in ticket counter lines. As noted in Chapter 10, a number of airlines are now using the convenient practice of ticketless travel. Travelers can make their reservations over the Internet, pay for them with a credit card, and go directly to the gate if they have no baggage to check. The gate attendant verifies the traveler's identity and issues a boarding pass.

Managers must guard against going to extremes with automated processing. Customers must be polled to determine which method gives them the greatest value. In most cases, they prefer the option of choosing either automation or face-to-face interaction.

The second issue in timeliness is for companies to provide service precisely when it is promised. This is especially important for service businesses, whether they work with consumers or with other businesses. Consider the following three examples.

Suppose I am the president of a small company and I have just hired a consultant to do a job analysis to see how I can make my workers more efficient. I have arranged for the consultant to interview each of my 50 employees over a one-week period beginning June 10. I have scheduled each employee to visit with the consultant for 30 minutes at prescribed times throughout the week. On June 9, the consultant calls me to tell me he can't start until June 15. As a result, I have to change the entire schedule of appointments. I am not happy, the employees are not happy, the production schedule is wrecked, and my own customers may become unhappy.

Or suppose I am a college recruiter looking for the best talent I can find. I recruit on over 30 campuses and our company hires perhaps 400 graduates each year. I know that during the spring recruiting season, most seniors will interview with six to eight companies. Good students will receive offers from more than one of them. Because of my heavy workload, I am the last recruiter to get back to students with an offer, even though I promised them short turnaround. As a result, potential employees may have offers in hand from other companies while they wait impatiently for my letter or call. I lose many good recruits and cause significant problems for others.

Finally, suppose I have an auto repair garage. I put a customer's car on the rack for a muffler problem. I call my supplier and order new parts for it. The supply house promises me the parts will arrive in 30 minutes. Two hours later, the mechanic calls the supply house back and finds that the delivery truck has not left yet. Not only does this cause my customer unnecessary problems, but it also prevents me from using the rack for other customers' cars.

In each of these cases, someone failed to deliver the service or parts as promised and others were inconvenienced. Even if the problem was beyond that person's control, the failure to deliver in a timely manner detracted from the value normally associated with the product or service.

Location

Creating value through delivery of products to specific locations can be lucrative if done well. Lear Corporation is a supplier of seat assemblies to several carmakers. Customers like Ford and GM are quite demanding. Lear has perfected the value-through-location concept so well that it provides seat assemblies not only to the building where they are needed but to the actual assembly-line position where they are inserted in a car or van.

Providing value through location assures that customers get products delivered in a convenient manner. Lands' End, which we discussed earlier, excels here. They deliver their products to the customer's front door, making shopping a simpler and less time-consuming process.

Companies sometimes have options in how or where products can be delivered. Business supply houses, for example, can deliver supplies to the central receiving station for a company or directly to the office that ordered them. The latter method is more time consuming for the supplier, but it provides better value. The key is making sure that the product is at the desired location.

Form

Form
The specific design, size, or model of a product that a customer needs.

The final way to provide value through product availability is to provide it in the form that is needed. **Form** refers to the specific design, size, or model of a product that a customer needs. The desired form will, of course, vary from situation to situation. An auto mechanic may want to have motor oil delivered in 55-gallon drums rather than in quart cans. That way the mechanic can pump what is needed from the drums and may also be able to get the oil at a lower price. A business may request specially designed invoice forms to bill its own customers rather than using standard forms. A buyer of computer equipment may order the computer with specific software preloaded rather than having to load software after the computer arrives. As these examples show, a company that can customize its products for others can add value to the product through attention to form.

Some progressive and successful companies compete, at least in part, through their efforts to provide value to their customers by emphasizing both form and delivery. For example, Gateway Computers builds quality PCs that many customers, including a number of large businesses, have selected. Customers order Gateways either by calling a toll-free number or through the Internet. Once a customer chooses the basic model desired, he or she selects the features, options, and software needed. All of this is done electronically, without face-to-face contact. Even though each machine is custom built, the company can usually build, ship, and promise delivery within a week of the initial order.

Soliciting Feedback

**customer service
p. 340>**

The very first step in providing customer service is to find out what the customers want. It can also be the final step in the cycle. Managers are well advised to work closely with their customers to assess the quality of their service and how it can be improved.

A restaurant manager (like Leo Gionne early in this chapter) makes a habit of going to each table to ask the customers how they like their food and service. Leo realizes that many people will say things are fine even when they are not, but he is skilled at picking up slight indications of dissatisfaction in customers' voices and then probing to discover if a real problem exists. Then Leo takes the next very important step: he corrects the problem on the spot. He either replaces the food or gives the customer a discount or perhaps a coupon for a free meal at a later date. The process is important for two reasons. First, the manager recaptures a disgruntled customer. Second, the manager identifies problems and can correct them before they make other customers unhappy.

Many service-oriented businesses are using feedback mechanisms to improve their operations. Today it is not unusual to receive a phone call or survey after a hospital stay. Generally, the hospital wants the patient's views of the staff, general conditions of the hospital, and overall satisfaction with the care received. It probes for areas of concern. Importantly, the hospital managers use this information to make changes to ensure better and more sensitive patient care. Many automobile service centers do the same thing. After your car has been serviced, the business calls or writes to ask whether the repairs were satisfactory and the service personnel were friendly and helpful. Again, this feedback allows the repair service to make needed corrections. Customer feedback can also be achieved through comment cards in restaurants or hotels or through registration cards in product packages. The surveys should be direct and make it clear that their purpose is to improve service.

Developing Your Critical Thinking Skills

1. Critically watch at least three TV commercials. What elements of customer value does each one emphasize?

2. When a business actively seeks feedback from its customers, what impression do you think this makes on those customers?

3. Suppose you own a car wash that is located in an older section of town, far away from your desired clientele. How can you overcome the problem of location and reach your target customers?

Examples of Providing Value for Customers

joint venture p. 179>

Two examples may illuminate the overall approach to providing customer value that we have emphasized throughout this chapter. The first example is Eatzi's, a joint venture between Brinker International and Philip Romano, founder of Romano's Macaroni Grill. The second is Camelbak, which takes a unique approach to providing fluids for bikers, runners, and hikers.

Eatzi's

In today's hectic world, customers are always looking for something new and different in the restaurant world. Eatzi's is just that. The concept was born from a perceived need in the market, a one-stop shop and diner. Philip Romano, founder of the Eatzi's concept, says, "It's a throwback to the 1950s–1960s urban market," small in size and big on service.

The concept is positioned between the grocery store and the traditional restaurant. Customers enter the shop, which is designed like a racetrack. Their food options are enormous. There is a bakery with a broad assortment of baked breads. There are fresh fruits and vegetables, prepared salads and entrees, a cheese and meat deli, a salad preparation area, a sandwich station, a short-order cooking area, a coffee shop, and a dessert counter. There are raw products such as stuffed tenderloin and chicken breasts, and there are prepared salads, pizzas, and pasta. Wines and beers are available. In fact, you can even take advantage of Eatzi's innovations like the "create your own sixpack." Customers order meals, fully prepared if they want, and take them home, to work, or wherever. The food is top quality.

Open from 7 AM to 10 PM, the store employs 125 people, including at least 35 trained chefs. Eatzi's hires friendly employees who have what it calls "customer awareness." They interact with customers, Italian opera music plays in the background, and the smell of baking bread permeates the shop. Customers are assured of good service in a pleasant and even exciting atmosphere. They are also assured of a quality meal with no preparation. All of this seems a perfect fit for contemporary lifestyles.

The original Eatzi's was built in the high-traffic, high-income Oak Lawn section of Dallas. Careful attention to customers has been a hallmark of the operation. For example, Eatzi's expanded from four checkout registers to seven because of the traffic during peak periods. It is considering ways to reconfigure the aisle space so it is easier to get around when the store is crowded. Of course, management is always tracking purchases to determine which items are popular and which need to be reevaluated. Pricing seems to be right on the mark, between restaurant and supermarket prices. The average transaction is between $12 and $15, which seems consistent with the value of the food and service provided.

The pilot store has been so successful that the company has opened a second location in Houston and is looking for other locations. Reading emerging customer needs, providing top-notch service to meet those needs, and being open to changes that will improve the overall experience for its customers have been the foundations for success at Eatzi's. It is inventing new ways to provide value for customers.[12]

Camelbak

Camelbak calls its product the "unbottle system." It's designed specifically for bikers who need to hydrate themselves regularly but cannot be bothered with the inconvenience of carrying a bottle. Camelbak is a heavy-duty, insulated bladder that is contained in a backpack strapped around the user's back. A small tube runs from the bladder, carrying liquid to the rider through the patented Bite Valve, which is drip-free and practically indestructible. Particularly during races, riders can drink more often and do not have to risk riding with one hand, as with competing models. A special model that fits around the waist is especially convenient for hikers. Camelbak also sells an IceBak, which straps to the back and helps keeps the user cool during strenuous workouts. Tests at the Olympic Training Center suggest the IceBak can reduce heart rates by 6.5 percent.

The product has been carefully designed and ergonomically built to fit the body without restricting normal movement. Thus, it is ideal for the serious bike customer. Additional options are geared toward a specific market niche of serious or competitive exercisers. While the Camelbak is priced considerably higher than a water bottle, customers pay the premium because of the easy access, convenience, and amount of fluid. In other words, they believe the value received from Camelbak justifies the extra cost. Not surprisingly, Camelbak's advertising is done through specialty magazines, such as those for bike riders and other athletes.[13]

SUMMARY

customer service p. 340>

relationship marketing p. 341>

feedback p. 361>

market research p. 344>

1. No business will survive for long without providing meaningful service to its customers. Long-term success usually comes through establishing long-term relationships with the company's customers.

   ■ How would you define the concept of customer service? Of relationship marketing?

   Customer service can be thought of as knowing what the customers want and seeing that they get it. Relationship marketing occurs when the business gets to know its customers and establishes rapport and long-term relationships with them.

2. Providing excellent customer service is not a simple matter. It requires a variety of skills and tasks.

   ■ What are the five processes involved in providing excellent customer service?

   This chapter described five basic processes:
   (1) Learning about customers.
   (2) Developing the product or service to meet customer needs.
   (3) Communicating the value of the product/service to customers.
   (4) Making the product/service available to customers.
   (5) Soliciting customer feedback.

3. The process of providing customer service has to begin with a clear understanding of what customers want.

   ■ What are the basic principles involved in learning about customers?

   The most straightforward way to find out what customers want is to ask them. This is the essence of market research, which involves collecting and analyzing information about the potential market. The data may be already published (secondary data) or gathered directly from current and potential customers (primary data). Once the data are gathered, they must be analyzed. This process typically involves the use of tools of statistical analysis.

4. Once the firm understands what customers need or value, it can begin to create the product or service that will meet those needs.

   ■ What are the basic kinds of product or service development?

   There are six types of new product development:
   (1) A new-to-the-world product.
   (2) A new product line never before produced by the company, although other companies already offer it.
   (3) A new product added to an existing product line.
   (4) An improved product.
   (5) A repositioned product.
   (6) A lower-priced version of an existing product.

■ What are the basic steps in the development process?

The process used in product development consists of the following steps:
(1) Concept evaluation.
(2) Business analysis.

test marketing p. 349>

(3) Development activities (including test marketing).

■ What are some of the major issues in the development process?

This chapter highlighted two issues:
(1) The desirability of using a development team.

cycle time p. 349>

(2) The importance of minimizing cycle time.

■ What is value and what are some ways the business can build value into its product or service?

Value is any feature that makes a product or service more useful to a customer. This chapter identified the following ways to build value into a product or service:
(1) Customer-friendly stores.
(2) Product designs.
(3) Pricing policies.
(4) Specially trained employees.
(5) Timing.
(6) Product distribution.

5. In addition to creating value for the customer, a company must communicate that value well.

■ What techniques can a business use to communicate value to the customer?

This chapter discussed the following tools of communication:
(1) Promotional techniques, particularly advertising.
(2) Price, particularly value-based pricing and image pricing.
(3) Brand names.
(4) Effective packaging.
(5) Personal selling and service.

6. Increasingly, in today's markets, product and service availability are key parts of the customer value process.

■ How is customer value provided through product or service availability?

This chapter discussed three aspects of product/service availability:
(1) Timeliness—providing the products when promised and in the minimum amount of time.
(2) Location—delivering the goods to the specific locations where customers need them.
(3) Form—providing the products in the design, size, and model customers need.

7. Once the business has successfully delivered the product or service to the customer, the value-creating process is still not complete. The remaining step is to determine if the firm has satisfied the customer.

■ What is the role of soliciting customer feedback in providing customer value?

The process of providing customer service is a never-ending cycle. Feedback from customers who have purchased and used the product can provide extremely useful information that can help improve future products and service.

Links to future courses

You will encounter customer value in many courses, most directly in your marketing courses. The following are some examples of marketing and other business courses that address the themes of this chapter.

- Principles of marketing
- Marketing research
- Advertising and promotion

- Quality management
- Business policy and strategic planning

KEY TERMS

Business analysis, p. 348
Communicating value, p. 353
Concept evaluation, p. 348
Cost-based pricing, p. 357
Creating value, p. 349
Customer service, p. 340
Cycle time, p. 349
Data analysis, p. 346
Development team, p. 349
Discount pricing, p. 352
Focus groups, p. 344
Form, p. 360
Functional packaging, p. 358

Image pricing, p. 357
Institutional advertising, p. 355
Market research, p. 344
Primary data, p. 344
Product advertising, p. 355
Product differentiation, p. 347
Product quality, p. 348
Product/service development, p. 346
Promotion, p. 355
Relationship marketing, p. 341
Secondary data, p. 344
Test marketing, p. 349
Value-based pricing, p. 357

EXERCISES AND APPLICATIONS

market research
p.344>

teams p. 71>

1. You have probably come into contact with several forms of market research. You may have participated in market research efforts. Drawing from your experiences, identify as many forms of market research as you can.

2. Form teams of six students each. The makers of Scope mouthwash have asked your team to create a new 30-second TV commercial. All team members need to play a role in the commercial. It should be creative and should be designed to appeal to the young adult market (18- to 22-year-olds). Each team should present or act out its commercial for the class. If your university has audiovisual capabilities, film your commercial.

3. In the commercial above, how did your team go about creating value for the target customer? Write a one-page paper discussing your approach and why it was selected.

feedback p. 361>

4. Pick a product or service with which you are familiar. Develop a market research questionnaire that could be used to solicit feedback from customers. What questions should you ask to determine how well the product provides value to customers?

relationship marketing
p. 341>

5. How did your university communicate value to you before you chose to attend? Did the admissions office attempt to use relationship marketing? If so, did that continue once you arrived on campus? Discuss this with your friends. Did they have the same experience? Outline your conclusions and be prepared to discuss them in class.

6. Go to the websites of Cannondale and Gary Fisher bicycles. What kinds of value do the messages on their home pages provide? How do they differ? What target base of customers is each trying to reach?

CASE: HOME DEPOT GOES UPSCALE

Home Depot is a chain of 543 stores catering to the do-it-yourself home improvement market. The chain is growing at a strong pace, and expects to have 1,100 stores by the year 2000. It is entering the international market with a joint venture in Santiago, Chile. It provides value to do-it-yourselfers through a wide selection of home improvement products in a one-stop shopping environment.

Despite Home Depot's rapid growth, some analysts fear that the do-it-yourself market is becoming saturated. To further complicate the picture, it faces significant challenges from competitors such as Lowe's, Builder's Square, and Menards. CEO Arthur M. Blank is working to provide value to a new group of customers. Through an upscale chain called Home Depot Expo, he is targeting customers doing major remodeling or renovation projects. He is also moving into the professional contractor market. While the do-it-yourself market is $140 billion a year, professionals spend $220 billion. There is a giant opportunity in this market that has largely been untapped.

Some contractors do not think Home Depot will give them the attention they need. Analysts are concerned that the professional market will be more vulnerable to interest rate changes and fluctuating lumber prices. CEO Blank is not concerned; he believes the do-it-yourself market will offset cyclical worries in the professional market.

Decision Questions

1. What will Home Depot have to do differently in order to provide value for the professional market contractors as opposed to do-it-yourselfers?
2. How will it have to communicate that value to the professional market?
3. How would you go about assessing customer needs in the upscale, large-projects market?

SOURCE: Nicole Harris, "Home Depot: Beyond Do-It-Yourselfers," *Business Week*, June 30, 1997, pp. 86–8.

REFERENCES

1. Shaifali Puri. "Cool Companies." *Fortune*, July 7, 1997, pp. 87–8.
2. The World of Trek, 1997, p. 46.
3. Keith Naughton. "How Ford's F-150 Lapped the Competition." *Business Week*, July 29, 1996, p. 74.
4. Charles W. Lamb, Jr., Joseph F. Hair, Jr., and Carl McDaniel. *Marketing*. South-Western Publishing, Cincinnati, 1996, p. 312.
5. For example, see William M. Pride and O. C. Ferrell. *Marketing: Concepts and Strategies*, 10th ed. Boston: Houghton Mifflin, 1997.
6. Steve Stecklow. "Some Supermarkets Get Kid-Friendly in an Effort to Build Customer Loyalty." *The Wall Street Journal*, June 18, 1996, p. B13B.
7. Lamb, Hair, and McDaniel. *Marketing*, p. 38.

8. Richard Gibson. "Custom Burgers Get Speed Test at McDonald's." *The Wall Street Journal*, June 30, 1997, pp. B1, B2.

9. Richard Gibson. "Can Betty Crocker Heat Up General Mills' Cereal Sales?" *The Wall Street Journal*, July 19, 1996, p. B1.

10. "Leading National Advertisers." *Advertising Age*, September 30, 1996, p. S54.

11. Lamb, Hair, and McDaniel. *Marketing*, p. 265.

12. Ron Ruggles. "Eatzi's: Romano and Brinker's One-Stop Dine 'n' Shop." *National Restaurant News*, May 20, 1996.

13. Camelbak ad. *Mountain Bike 1996 Buyer's Guide*. April 1996, p. 7.

13 *The Acquisition and Use of Resources*

Resources can come from many places. Eric Crown, founder of Insight, graduated from college in 1988, pooled his savings with his brother Tim, got a $2,000 cash advance on his credit card, and started selling computer parts by mail. Today their financial resources come from other places. They bring in $373 million a year selling computers, peripherals, parts, and programs. They have gone public, and their stock was listed on the NASDAQ at $28 a share in the summer of 1997.

Even with their excellent sales and stock prices, Insight's managers are working to conserve the resources they have. They are setting up a website to sell their products interactively. Customers can peruse the listings of equipment and order by entering their credit card number. This reduces the number of phone sales representatives they have to pay, thereby increasing their bottom-line profits.[1]

No business can operate without resources. Resources are the fuel for businesses just as gasoline is the fuel for automobiles. If a business has insufficient resources or an inappropriate mix of resources, it will operate just as poorly as a car with not enough or the wrong kind of fuel. Businesses rely on four major fuels: human resources, physical resources, financial resources, and information resources. Business managers must be able to balance the need for each of the resources, acquire them, and allocate them among the units of the business. This is a challenging responsibility and an important aspect of building a successful business, as you saw in the model of a successful business. Thus, after reading this chapter, you should be able to:

1. Explain the integrative nature of resource acquisition and use.

2. Identify the major challenges a manager must overcome in allocating and using resources.

3. Identify the four major challenges in human resources management and briefly explain some of the issues involved in each challenge.

4. Explain the major issues involved in the acquisition of physical resources.

5. Describe the major characteristics of the acquisition and use of financial resources.

6. Identify uses for and sources of information resources.

7. Explain the role of budgets in allocating resources.

Resources

The people, physical materials, financial assets, and information a firm's managers use to produce a product or service.

Resources are the lifeblood of a company. They provide the basic ingredients it needs to succeed. **Resources** are the people, physical materials, financial assets, and information the firm's managers use to produce a product or service. Either a lack of resources or the wrong mix of resources can spell disaster for a company. Business managers spend much of their time acquiring resources, providing an appropriate mix of resources, managing them, and using them in the firm's operations.

The Integrative Nature of Resource Acquisition and Use

Resource acquisition and use is one of the most integrative topics confronting managers. Resource acquisition demands that managers work with a host of people throughout the company to create an acceptable balance. A manager cannot decide to hire 10 more employees without consulting with those in charge of financial resources. Similarly, acquiring new plants and equipment not only takes financial resources but also may require extra training of employees in order to use the equipment effectively. Even those in charge of financial aspects of the firm cannot simply decide to issue more stock or invest excess cash without checking with managers of other areas.

The integrative nature of resources is evidenced by two sets of relationships. The first is synergy. The second is opportunity cost.

Synergy

Synergy

The combined action of two resources such that their total effect is greater than the sum of the effects taken independently.

If a business adds financial resources, it can purchase new technology-related equipment. In turn, this equipment may help employees work more efficiently. Thus, a change in one resource ripples through the business. It affects physical resources like technology, and it enhances the productivity of human resources. The same is true for other investments. For example, if a business invests capital to increase the number of trained employees, productivity will go up. This illustrates **synergy,** the combined action of two resources such that their total effect is greater than the sum of the effects taken independently. Simply defined, synergy means two plus two equals five.

Consider Jones Electronics, a manufacturing firm. The business has some amount of equipment, a certain number of employees, and certain financial resources. If the managers of Jones Electronics decide to automate part of an assembly process, they will increase their physical resources. In turn, they will make their existing employees more efficient and capable of producing more components each day. If they invest funds to purchase new equipment, the manufacturing process will be more efficient. This in turn will save financial resources, which can then be used elsewhere.

The integration of resources is just as real in service firms as in manufacturing firms. A business that provides a service will likely have fewer physical resources than a goods-producing firm. Still, if managers invest financial resources in the purchase of more technology, that technology may help employees to perform more efficiently and effectively. Since the employees are now more efficient, the business can avoid having to hire additional employees, even as sales grow.

efficiency p. 478>

Consider a small company that does termite inspection and treatment. The owner has 20 technicians who call on customers to inspect their houses. If the owner does nothing more than buy them pagers or cellular phones, efficiency may increase since technicians can now communicate with their boss regarding which house to inspect next. This reduces their time on the road since they do not have to return to the shop for their next instructions. If a handheld computer is added to each truck, technicians can call up the history of a house to see when the last treatment was done and where problems have been in the past. This allows them to provide better service and in-

revenue p. 167>

creases the revenues of the business. Further, because the technicians are more efficient, the increase in revenues need not be accompanied by an equivalent increase in staff.

These examples from manufacturing and service firms illustrate the interrelated nature of resources. Increasing one resource may increase the capacity of another resource. Enhancing technology enables people to operate more efficiently. Business managers look for ways to build synergy and make decisions with it in mind.

Opportunity Costs and Trade-Offs

While the addition of one resource often makes another resource more productive, the integrative nature of resource acquisition also requires trade-offs. A useful concept in understanding the trade-offs that are necessary in resource acquisition is that of opportunity cost. If a manager uses funds for one activity, the manager gives up the opportunity to use those funds for some alternative activity. Some opportunity is forgone, or lost. The value of the activity that a firm sacrifices in order to pursue a different activity is known as the **opportunity cost.**[2]

Opportunity cost
The value of an activity that a firm sacrifices in order to pursue a different activity.

You encounter the idea of opportunity costs and other trade-offs quite often. For example, if you use your discretionary money to buy a car, you will not also be able to buy a computer system. The value you could have received from that computer is your opportunity cost. If your college uses its library funds to purchase books, the funds cannot also be used to order magazines or journals. The value that could have been derived from those magazines and journals is the opportunity cost. If a business purchases a new conveyor belt system to move packaged parts from one part of the plant to another, it will not have funds to replace an aging drill press. The value (such as higher quality and fewer breakdowns) that a new drill press could have provided is the opportunity cost.

It is important for managers to understand the concept of opportunity costs and trade-offs when considering the acquisition and use of resources. For example, a manager may want to hire a new staff person in the training department and also equip a new multimedia training room. Yet the new training facility may cost as much as the annual salary plus benefits of the staff person. The manager must choose between personnel and equipment. Each has value, and either decision will result in some value being forgone. The manager must decide which contributes the greater value as the business pursues its goals and strategies. The manager must balance the trade-offs that occur when he or she chooses resources.

Note that synergy and opportunity cost work against each other. Synergy suggests that adding one resource may make another resource more productive. Opportunity cost, on the other hand, suggests that adding one resource may preclude adding another. Both of these concepts are the result of the interrelatedness of resources.

The Flow of Resources

Another concept that is important for both resource acquisition and use is the flow or movement of resources. For example, in order to operate, a business purchases raw materials. Those raw materials move from suppliers into the operations area of the business. In turn, cash moves from the business to the suppliers as payment for the materials. As the business hires additional employees, the employees enter the firm in exchange for wages or salaries, which leave the firm. As the business adds new equipments, funds leave the business to pay for that equipment. Accordingly, resources are added that increase the capacity of the business to perform. Other resources, in this case money, leave the business.

The movement of resources does not stop here. The materials, people, and equipment that have been gained are used to produce products. Those products leave the business as they are sold to customers. Customers pay for the products, which returns cash to the business. This process of resources moving into, through, and back out of the firm is a dynamic and continual process.

Resource Challenges

There are three important challenges that managers attempt to overcome in dealing with resource allocation and use. The first is to have an adequate *amount* of resources. Second is to have the *right mix* of resources. Third is to have the most appropriate *allocation* of those resources within the organization.

The Total Amount of Resources

Managers virtually never have sufficient resources. Even in the best of times, more staff would be desirable, additional equipment would increase productivity, and more and better raw materials would lead to better products. Consider the class for which you are reading this book. It would be nice if the class were small and were taught in a comfortable classroom with plush seats and state-of-the-art multimedia equipment. If you are indeed in one of these rooms, count yourself lucky.

However, limited university resources often dictate that the course must be taught in large lecture sections. Further, many university buildings are not equipped for optimal learning. If the university had all the resources it desired, it could have excellent facilities and still have funds to offer scholarships and pay faculty members high salaries. Since it does not, university administrators must make trade-offs. Perhaps by keeping the size of your class high and not investing in the latest technology, the university was able to offer additional financial aid packages that permitted you or your friends to attend the university.

Capital is always limited. It must be generated through sales or be acquired from external sources. These sources may not be adequate: Banks may refuse to lend as much as requested, investors may not be willing to underwrite additional equipment, or sales may not reach desired levels. Any of these events may cause the amount of resources available to be less than desired. It is important for managers to understand that funds may be scarce. It is also important for lower-level workers to understand that the firm cannot generate additional funds just by asking someone for more capital.

The Right Mix of Resources

Even though the overall amount of resources is perhaps a more severe problem, a second challenge is to have the right resources in place at the right time. Physical resources, for example, are not easily reallocated from one area to another. Falling demand for a product produced at one plant may suggest that resources should be reallocated to a plant that produces a different product that is in high demand. However, since physical resources are fixed, they cannot be transferred easily from plant to plant. In fact, it may be impossible to get the desired efficiency.

Even human resources can reflect this problem. Suppose the plants are in cities 150 miles apart. The demand for one of the products is decreasing while the demand for the other is increasing. The company would like to move some workers from the low-demand plant to the high-demand plant. But the employees are reluctant to move. Thus, the firm has more than enough human resources, but they are in the wrong place.

production p. 464>

Managers struggle to predict production, marketing, and distribution needs so resources can be available in the proper mix when they are needed. Sometimes they can rely on past trends to help in this determination. However, when they are dealing with new products or new markets or undertaking new strategies, predicting the needed resource mix is very difficult.

The Allocation of Resources

The third challenge is to allocate available resources so they can be used most effectively by the business. **Resource allocation** is the division of authorized resources among the various units under one's command. This problem can sometimes be even more difficult than the others. While obtaining sufficient funds overall is a problem, allocating them to lower-level units can be extremely trying. It is human nature for employees in each department or unit to think that their unit is most deserving of the

Resource allocation
The division of authorized resources among the various units under one's command.

Even though computer systems are expensive and significantly affect budgets, the use of spreadsheets and databases, access to the Internet, interactive web sites, and videoconferencing can save a company considerable money. If you were in charge of setting budgets for your company, how would you respond to the request for computer upgrades for your company?

scarce resources. Claims of favoritism, playing politics, and arbitrariness may occur among lower-level managers who think their colleagues got more than their share of the resources. Thus, a business manager must tread a fine line: help one department without hurting another.

Given an awareness of the basic resource challenges that businesses face, we next consider three primary resources that any business must have: human resources, physical resources, and financial resources. A fourth very important type of resource is information resources, which will be covered briefly in this chapter and in depth in Chapter 15. Keep in mind as you read that these decisions are not made in a vacuum and are heavily influenced by both external and internal forces. Our discussion focuses on the nature of the resource, the importance of planning for its acquisition and use, and its sources.

Developing Your Critical Thinking Skills

1. What are the differences between synergies and opportunity costs?

2. Consider the resource challenges just discussed. How are they interrelated?

3. Are the resource challenges as important for a given type of resource as they are when you consider all types together?

The Acquisition and Use of Human Resources

CEOs and presidents often say their most important asset is their people. Chapter 14 will discuss how to maximize the productivity of workers. Our intent here is to consider how to acquire the quality and quantity of human resources necessary for the efficient operation of a business.

top management
p. 65>

As Chapter 3 said, human resources consist of four groups: top management, middle management and professional staff, supervisory management, and nonmanagerial workers. It is important that each position be staffed with the best people possible given the constraints of budgets. To achieve quality and quantity goals, managers should address five challenges:

1. Accurately forecasting human resources needs.
2. Recruiting potential candidates.
3. Selecting the best talent possible.
4. Training and developing the talent base.
5. Encouraging high performance from employees.

training p. 379>

Forecasting Human Resources Needs

Forecasting human resources needs follows the logical process outlined in Figure 13–1. First, managers must predict where the business is headed and the impact that movement will have on human resources needs. For example, they must decide how many employees the business will need to make its strategies succeed. They must also decide the type of backgrounds and skills those employees will need to possess. Managers ask a basic question: "What type of workforce do we need to reach our goals?"

Second, managers analyze the characteristics of their available workforce. They examine the number of workers they have now, their skills, and their abilities to perform needed tasks. Managers must also determine whether this available workforce will be sufficient to meet the needs of the future. To do this they must predict the number of retirements, promotions, and terminations of employees. They also try to gauge whether the existing workforce can be trained in the needed new skills. Through this process, managers are trying to determine, "Is there a gap between the available employees and skills we have and those we will need?"

Finally managers ask, "If there is a gap, what types of people do we need to bring to the business?" The answer may simply be that we need more people, but increasingly the answer is that the business must bring in people with new talents, skills, and backgrounds.[3]

This forecasting challenge is especially difficult when the business is growing rapidly or is facing a turbulent environment. It is also difficult when technologies are changing rapidly and skill sets must be continually upgraded. Even the task of hiring lower-level workers is more difficult today than in the past because of the changes in equipment, software, and networking among workstations.

FIGURE 13–1   Overview of Human Resource Forecasting

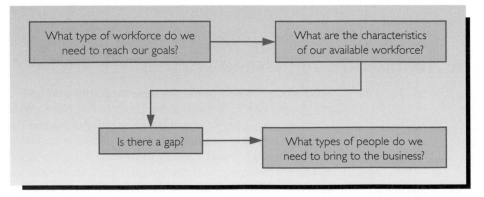

Downsizing
Reducing the number of employees in a business.

Rightsizing
Eliminating those functions and people that are least critical to a firm's success.

Businesses that are experiencing mergers or acquisitions or those facing extremely tough, competitive times may face another forecasting problem. They may find that their current level of business is not sufficient to support the staff that they now have. They may need to **downsize,** or reduce the number of employees in the business. This process is painful for all involved. Accordingly, businesses want to be sure that they not only downsize but rightsize. **Rightsizing** occurs when a business eliminates those functions and people that are least critical to its success.[4] The determination of how rightsizing should proceed depends on the success of the human resources forecasting the business has done.

Recruiting Potential Employees

The challenge of recruiting potential employees changes with the times and industry situations. Changing demographics and economic forces affect the pool of available talent. For example, hiring fast-food workers used to be a simple task when the number of teenagers searching for jobs far exceeded the number of jobs. But now fast-food restaurants are hiring retirees and other older workers because there are simply not enough teenagers around who are willing to work there. In universities, new faculty formerly had their pick of several offers as universities scrambled to meet their staffing needs in periods of growth. But now the number of individuals earning advanced degrees exceeds the number of openings, making it much easier to hire highly qualified professors. College graduates in the early 1990s faced a very tough job market. Graduates in the late 1990s are finding a much more promising market, especially in computer-related jobs.

Employees can be recruited from many different sources. These range from ads in newspapers to employment agencies, trade associations, and other companies. Employees may also come from within the organization when someone is either promoted or transferred to a new position. Table 13–1 illustrates both internal and external sources of employees for a few selected positions. Notice how we have separated the positions into the four categories we discussed in Chapter 3.

Internal sources of employees are individuals within the company who are interested and qualified to fill the job. Note that in virtually every position listed, the internal candidates include others at the same level and employees one level down. This allows for both lateral transfers and promotions. A *lateral transfer* means a transfer from a position at one level in the company to another position *at the same level* but with different responsibilities. Many individuals want this extra experience. Even though the position is not a promotion and does not pay more, the experience often prepares them for later promotions. Filling a position through promotion means advancing one of the people who holds a lower-level position into the open position.

Companies often look for candidates internally before looking externally. There are compelling reasons for filling job openings from within. First, promoting someone from a lower level is very psychologically rewarding. It serves as reinforcement and recognition for good work that person has done. Further, it signifies management's confidence that the employee will continue to perform well. Second, filling the job with someone at the same level (a lateral transfer) has the advantage of broadening an employee's experience base. Third, selecting someone from either the same or a lower level creates an opportunity for someone else to advance. Fourth, an employee promoted or transferred from within already knows the organization, its culture, and its method of operation. This makes training faster and easier.

TABLE 13-1   Sources of Individuals for Selected Positions

Position	Internal Sources	External Sources
Nonmanagerial		
Secretary	Other secretaries or other positions with clerical skills	Newspaper ads, employment agencies, recommendations
Janitor	Other janitors or low-level operative workers	Newspaper ads, employment agencies, recommendations
Machine operator	Operators of similar machines, apprenticeship programs	Newspaper ads, employment agencies, recommendations, trade schools
Salesperson	Production or service workers, professional staff, sales personnel in other territories or products	Newspaper ads, employment agencies, colleges/universities, recommendations
Supervisory		
First-line supervisor	Other supervisors, related staff positions, promotion from nonmanagerial ranks	Newspaper ads, employment agencies, vocational schools, recommendations
Mid-management/professional staff		
Middle manager	Other middle managers, promotion from staff, sales, or production supervisor positions	Newspaper ads, employment agencies, colleges/universities, recommendations
Professional staff	Related professional staff, promotions from lower-level positions in same area	Newspaper ads, employment agencies, colleges/universities, trade associations, recommendations
Top management		
Vice president	Other VPs, high-level managers in headquarters or divisions	Specialized newspapers, trade associations, headhunters, recommendations
Executive vice president	VPs	Specialized newspapers, trade associations, recommendations, headhunters
President	VPs or executive VPs	Specialized newspapers, trade associations, recommendations, headhunters
Board member	Top levels of management, including controller and general counsel	Contacts in high levels of other companies, headhunters

Searching externally is often a wise decision when higher-level positions are being filled. Outside candidates can bring a fresh perspective to the position and may have experience that internal candidates simply do not have. An external search may also be needed if there are no highly qualified candidates inside the firm.

Now look at the external sources of employees in Table 13–1. Note the differences in sources as the positions move from lower to higher levels of responsibility. *Nonmanagerial* candidates are often found simply through ads in the local newspaper or contacts with the local, state, or private employment agency. Companies filling sales positions sometimes find applicants through ads in newspapers, but many companies prefer to recruit on college campuses. Candidates for technical and *supervisory* positions may be found in trade schools. *Managerial and staff* positions are still advertised in newspapers, but other sources such as community colleges and universities are also tapped. *Higher-level management* people, such as vice presidents or presidents, may be located via specialized newspapers such as *The Wall Street Journal* and through contacts in trade associations. Some trade associations even run placement services for their members. Organizations filling the highest-level positions may also use specialized employment agencies that focus strictly on upper-level employees. These agencies are often referred to as *headhunters.*

Each business has its own sense of the type of candidate that is most appropriate for its needs. Brinker International prefers to hire either college students or other young people for Chili's and other restaurants. It finds that these servers interact well with customers and are readily available, particularly if the restaurant is in a college town. On the other hand, Brinker's Eatzi's restaurant hires about 35 trained chefs for each location. These chefs are critical to the success of the restaurant, so Eatzi's management spends considerable time recruiting for the chef positions. Trek takes a different approach. It likes to hire workers who are already heavily into biking in their personal time. Many of them apply to Trek because of their love of biking.

An increasingly popular source of candidates for many jobs is the Internet. For example, you can consult Southwest Airlines' website to find what jobs are open. The listings include the requirements for each position and the benefits offered. Southwest has 25,000 employees, 84 percent of whom are unionized. It receives 138,000 applications a year, and it hired 3,956 new employees in 1996. Table 13–2 shows two positions for which openings often exist.

To assure a broad and diverse pool of candidates, a company should take steps to advertise and recruit candidates in all logical markets. In addition to expanding the pool of candidates, these actions help make sure that the company stays within the legal frameworks dealing with recruiting. The business should generate a set of qualified candidates who meet the needs of the business while reflecting the demographic makeup of the relevant labor market. (For more about the benefits of employee diversity, refer back to Chapter 5.)

diversity p. 125>

Selecting the Best Candidate

Once enough qualified job candidates have been identified, the next task is to identify the best candidates. The selection process must be done carefully. Managers must screen candidates based on predetermined criteria for the job.

customer service p. 340>

Return to the Southwest Airlines listings in Table 13–2. Note that the requirements of each job are listed, as well as its duties. The maintenance instructor is required to have extensive technical skills regarding the Boeing 737 airplanes, along with verbal skills necessary to communicate with trainees. The customer service representative requires a much different set of skills. This person needs to have great interpersonal skills, have a high school diploma, be a team player, be willing to work shifts, and be able to handle emergencies.

Managers must ensure that the business does not discriminate or otherwise violate laws relating to the hiring process. For example, all those who interview candidates must be careful to restrict questions to job-related issues. It is illegal to ask questions on application blanks or in interviews about a candidate's race, gender,

TABLE 13–2   Selected Job Openings at Southwest Airlines

Job title: Technical Instructor

Reports to: Manager, maintenance training

General purpose: Develop and implement training for Southwest Airlines and contract personnel. Remain current on latest technology, equipment, and training procedures as they apply to Southwest Airlines.

Job functions: Provide training to employees of Southwest Airlines and contract maintenance personnel.

Develop and implement training curriculums.
Develop and operate training aids.
Provide assistance with aircraft troubleshooting.
Remain current on all aircraft/systems operated by Southwest Airlines.

Qualification and requirements:
A&P Mechanic Certificate required.
Must have strong aircraft systems and powerplants background.
Previous Boeing 737 technical instructor experience desired.
Must be able to instruct on all aircraft systems and aircraft maintenance-related subjects.
Knowledge of PC and mainframe computer systems preferable.
Must have strong written and verbal skills and ability to speak in a classroom situation.
Must be able to operate visual aids such as video equipment and training simulators.
Must be able to lift and move items up to 50 pounds on a regular basis.
Ability to work in a stressful environment with multiple tasking and tight time constraints.
Ability and willingness to travel extensively for long periods of time.
Must be a U.S. citizen or have authorization to work in U.S. as defined by the Immigration Reform Act of 1986.

For immediate consideration, please submit your resume and salary expectations to: Southwest Airlines Co., People Dept., HDQ 4HR. Attn: DA, P.O. Box 36644, Dallas, TX 75235-1644. Fax: 214-792-5015.

continued

marital or family status, religion, or national origin. In addition, a business should keep its diversity goals in mind when making selection decisions (as we discussed in Chapter 5).

The selection process becomes more rigorous as the business recruits for higher-level positions. Lower-level workers may be given skills tests and then be interviewed by a single manager or by members of the human resources department's recruiting team. Higher-level positions demand more in-depth analysis of the candidate. A number of people may be involved in interviewing and selection decisions. Candidates may be invited back for second or third interviews or may spend a full day or two at the firm to assess whether there is a good match between their qualifications and the needs of the business.

Application blanks routinely ask for references. Managers should always check these references to verify the information provided. This should be done for all positions at all levels. Talking to references will also help determine if there is a good fit between the person and the position.

TABLE 13-2   *(continued)*

Position title: Customer Service Agent

Locations: Kansas City, Birmingham, Houston, New Orleans, Nashville, Baltimore, St. Louis, Oakland, San Jose

General purpose:

Qualifications and requirements:

1. At least 18 years old with a high school diploma or equivalent, college coursework or degree desirable.
2. Natural, national, or intending U.S. citizen as defined by the Immigration Reform Act of 1986.
3. Well-groomed appearance.
4. Team player, able to meet the public and work under stressful conditions.
5. Able to communicate well face to face and via telephone and public address system.
6. Typing skills and/or computer keyboard required.
7. Available to work shifts and overtime.
8. Ability to read documents, write in English, follow instructions, and learn and understand ticketing procedures, rules, and regulations.
9. Height and weight must be proportionate.
10. Must be able to handle emergencies and be aware of hazardous situations.
11. Able to lift and move items of up to 70 lbs. repetitively.

Training: 2 $\frac{1}{2}$ weeks of training

For customer service agent positions in Kansas City, Birmingham, Houston, New Orleans, and Nashville, please fax resumes to (214) 792-5015. Attn: HDQ CMH. Include "Customer Service Agent" and city location preference.

For customer service agent positions in Baltimore and St. Louis, please fax resumes to (708) 458-8422. Include "Customer Service Agent" and city location preference.

For customer service agent positions in Oakland and San Jose, please fax resumes to (510) 633-3064. Include "Customer Service Agent" and city location preference.

SOURCE: Southwest Airlines web site, http://www.iflyswa.com, (accessed July 7, 1997).

After the analysis of the application, the interview, and the reference checks, managers are ready to choose the best candidate. They should consult with everyone who has been involved in the selection process, particularly those who will be working with the successful candidate. Only when all concerned are in general agreement should an offer be made.

Training and Developing Employees

We began this chapter by discussing the acquisition of resources. It is also important for managers to know how best to utilize those resources once they are acquired. Thus, training and development are ongoing activities for successful businesses. Since

High technology occupations require substantial training in order to operate computer-controlled equipment. Some of this training will be on-the-job training and some will be off-the-job training. What are the advantages of each in a situation like the one here?

technology and other forces are constantly changing and creating new challenges, training and development become important ways for the business to keep pace with the dynamics of its environment.

Training

Training of employees involves two tasks, orientation and skills training. *Orientation* refers to making sure employees understand and accept the norms and culture of the organization. Managers must work with new employees to clarify the rules, policies, and values. This is not an easy task, especially if the workers have been accustomed to a different kind of organizational culture. For example, encouraging employees to accept an empowerment-oriented culture can be difficult when they are used to a culture where bosses make all the major decisions. Businesses spend anywhere from a few days to one or two weeks in basic orientation for new employees.

Skills training is undertaken to make sure the employee has the skills needed to perform work in the manner the business desires. For example, Andersen Consulting hires college graduates to do computer-related consulting. However, many of them need to be trained in the specific programs that Andersen's clients use. Thus, the typical new employee spends considerable time gearing up on appropriate computer language skills before being trained in working with clients.

One type of skills training, known as **on-the-job training (OJT)**, occurs when employees are given instructions on how to do a job while they are working at it. Typ-

On-the-job training (OJT)
Instructing employees in how to do a job while they are working at it.

ically, this instruction is conducted by an experienced employee who does similar work. The experienced employee coaches the new employee. One advantage of this training approach is that employees can contribute to the organization while they are being trained. You may have experienced on-the-job training in a part-time or summer job.

A second type of skills training is **off-the-job training,** which occurs when employees are taken away from the job and offered education that will improve their job performance. This training may be done through lectures, videos, or experiential activities that emphasize the development of skills that are important in the job. In many businesses, employees receive numerous hours of off-the-job training each year. They may listen to experts discussing proper safety procedures, watch a film on the proper way to interact with customers, or go to the local college to learn how to use a new computer program.

Decisions regarding the type of training depend on the job being done. Training for some jobs may be technical in nature and aimed specifically toward skills development. Other training may be motivational in nature or aimed at improving interpersonal relations.

Off-the-job training
Taking employees away from the job for education that will improve their job performance.

Development

Development differs from training in one major way. Whereas training is geared to improving employees' skills so they can perform their jobs as well as possible, development focuses on the future. It helps employees acquire the background and skills they will need to continue being successful as their careers progress. Development is more educational than skills oriented. Often businesses spend considerable amounts of money sending their managers to development programs to help them stay apprised of new theories and technologies in their fields. For example, managers may be asked to attend sessions at a local community college to hear speakers discuss the changing economy as it relates to their geographic area.

Motorola is one company that devotes time, energy, and substantial money to its training and development programs. For example, when technology changes, Motorola encourages employee development and retraining. The company even holds training sessions at Motorola University, the training and development arm of the business. Every employee must take at least five days of training each year.[5]

Both development and training are significant challenges in light of the rapidity of changes in technology and obsolescence of equipment. Both are important if the company's workforce is to be up to date and productive. These issues affect the efficiency and effectiveness of employees, as well as their motivation.

effectiveness p. 478>

motivation p. 426>

Encouraging High Performance

Having the right people in the right jobs is a requirement for maximum productivity, but it alone does not ensure productivity. Even adequate training is not enough. Having a skilled workforce only ensures that employees *can* do their job. It does not mean that they *will* do the job. This requires motivated and committed employees who are encouraged by empathetic managers. High performance can be achieved only when employees are both able and *willing* to work hard.

This topic is so important to business that we devote a portion of the next chapter to it. In Chapter 14, you will learn how to develop a loyal workforce that is committed to productivity.

Management Recruiters International provides recruiting services for its clients. It is just one of the many human resource services that can be outsourced. These and other services allow a client to concentrate on its core mission and leave administrative tasks to others. Is this a good idea even if it is more expensive?

Outsourcing Human Resources

In the next section on physical resources, we will note that materials can be either produced in-house or outsourced (purchased from another company). This is also true of human resources. We have discussed obtaining human resources through schools, other companies, employment agencies, and ads in the media. A remaining method is to outsource human resources.

Outsourcing human resources means contracting with temporary help agencies or with consulting firms to provide the people the firm needs. The individuals technically work for the outside company, but they do their work at the host company's location. They are paid by their own company, and the amount of benefits (such as vacations and sick leave) they receive is a function of the company they work for rather than the host company at which they work.

Consider the following example. Nims Associates is a computer consulting firm in the Midwest. It specializes in providing staff to do computer training for large companies. Nims' employees are well-trained college graduates in computer information systems who can communicate well with other employees. Companies contract with Nims to provide training for their workers over an extensive time period. This saves the companies from having to hire their own trainers. When all of a firm's employees have been trained on the prescribed software, Nims' employees move on to the next client—or, as often happens, begin teaching the next version of desired software to the large firm's employees.

The advantage of outsourcing workers is that they are totally contract labor. The company does not have to go through the hiring process, provide benefits, or worry about promotion and retirements. Outsourcing personnel also provides a smoothing effect in regard to the size of the workforce. Since contract labor has no long-term arrangement with the company, outsourced workers can provide assistance only when needed. When the extra workload ends, no permanent employees are laid off.

In addition to outsourcing individual workers, companies are increasingly outsourcing entire functions or departments. The trend in business today is to outsource everything that can be done more efficiently outside the company, including both products and services. For example, many companies—and perhaps even your university—contract out their cafeteria operations. Many companies outsource their maintenance or repair services and their security services. Some even contract out some human resources functions, such as the administration of employee benefits. Profile 13–1 describes Hewitt Associates, which specializes in designing employee benefit systems for clients. If desired, Hewitt can also operate the system.

PROFILE 13–1   *Outsourcing with Hewitt Associates*

Hewitt Associates was begun in 1940 by Edwin (Ted) Hewitt as an insurance brokerage firm. He and his associates soon decided to change from selling insurance to consulting in the area of benefits administration. Today the firm has over 5,000 employees and 65 offices worldwide. Its 3,000 clients include most of the Fortune 500 companies and a host of smaller companies.

Hewitt's activities include two major parts. First is benefits administration consulting. In this part of the company, consultants work with clients to develop administrative systems for their employee benefits. Computer specialists and others work with the client to design an information system that automates as much of the information as possible. They carefully check the system to make sure it works for the client. Once the system is totally operable and has been fully tested, the consultants move on to another client.

The second part of Hewitt Associates' business actually operates the system that the consultants have designed. This group of people will work for a specific client over an extended period of time to answer questions and enter decisions from individual employees in the client company. Employees who need information about their benefits call a number that is answered in Lincolnshire, Illinois, not at their own company. They may not even know that the person on the other end of the line is not in their own corporate headquarters building.

The benefit to the client company of having Hewitt design and operate its benefits administration system is that the company can go about its primary mission and outsource a complex but secondary part of the firm's overall operation.

mission p. 310>

SOURCE: Personal interviews and company documents.

Some companies take outsourcing even further. One company advertises to small businesses that it "wants to become your human resources department." Its ad observes that most small businesses do not have the expertise to handle their own human resources issues. For a fee, the specialist firm will contract with the client to perform all of its human resources activities, from payroll processing to benefits administration to providing temporary employees and helping to recruit employees throughout the firm.

We now turn our attention to the next important resource for a firm, its physical resources. You will see how a business acquires physical resources and some of the key decisions managers must make in the process. As you read the next section, keep in mind our discussion at the outset of this chapter about trade-offs and the interrelatedness of the different kinds of resources.

Developing Your Critical Thinking Skills

1. Why is the geographic labor market so much broader for higher-level jobs than for lower-level positions?

2. What changes in hiring practices might we expect as the baby-boom generation continues to grow older?

3. Why is outsourcing human resources appealing to large companies? To small businesses?

Physical Resources

Physical resources
(1) Fixed assets such as land, buildings, and equipment, (2) raw materials that will be used in creating the firm's products, and (3) general supplies used in the operation of the business.

At the start of this chapter, we noted that businesses use four important types of resources: human, physical, financial, and information resources. This section focuses on the **physical resources,** which include fixed assets such as land, buildings, and equipment. They also include raw materials that will be used in creating the firm's products and general supplies used in the operation of the business.

The key to effective acquisition of all four types of resources is planning. Planning is especially important in the acquisition of physical resources, both fixed assets and the raw materials used in production.

capital intensive p. 277>

Fixed assets are extremely capital intensive. This means that a large amount of capital is required to build or purchase the facilities, and they may be used for more than 20 years. Overestimating or underestimating the amount of fixed assets needed can be a fatal flaw in the operation of a business. Thus, it is extremely important to forecast fixed-asset needs accurately. This is certainly true in manufacturing industries because of the production equipment needed. It is also true for some service businesses. Recall, for example, that Southwest Airlines is considered a service business even though its airplanes may cost over $30 million each. Even a smaller service business such as a doctor's office or consultant will have significant fixed-asset purchases when it is first started.

Careful planning for the acquisition of raw material and other production-related purchases is also important because of the need for scheduling. The production of products can move no faster than the availability of raw materials. Yet too much raw material at one time means excessive inventory, which must be paid for, stored, insured, protected, counted, moved around a warehouse, shipped to other plants, and possibly discarded if the company's needs change. In fact, holding materials in inventory represents a major cost for business.

The Make-or-Buy Decision

Make-or-buy decision
The choice of whether to manufacture a product in-house or buy it from a supplier.

One of the most critical decisions facing firms that produce goods for sale is the **make-or-buy decision.** The managers of a business must decide whether to manufacture a product in-house or buy it from a supplier. There are two types of make-or-buy decisions. First, managers must decide whether to make a given product in-house or have other people make it for them. Second, for any product they do produce themselves, they must decide what percentage of the total process they want to do in-house.

Outsourcing
Purchasing a product or component of a product (or labor) from another company.

A business can make an entire product and package it, market it, and ship it to customers, or it can outsource the product. **Outsourcing** means that the firm purchases a product or component of a product from another company. Thus, the make-or-buy decision is a decision about whether to outsource or not.

If the manager chooses to outsource the product, the business purchases the product already completed and possibly already packaged with the firm's name and logo. In the extreme, managers can arrange to have another firm build a product to their specifications, package it, and ship it directly to their customers. That way, they need not invest in production facilities at all. They can concentrate their efforts on marketing the product. If a business decides to outsource production of a product, they may have to pay more for it than if they made it in-house. However, they do not have to tie up money in capital equipment. In some cases, they may even save money because the other firm can produce the product more cheaply than they can. Many large companies, especially those that are unionized, are finding that outsourcing is both more efficient in the short run and less capital intensive in the long run.

Outsourcing is a good example of the interaction among financial, human, and physical resources. Although outsourcing requires considerably fewer human resources and a smaller investment in physical resources, it does require close cooperation and coordination between the finance department, the human resources department, and the operations area of the firm. Issues of quality, timeliness, and total cost must be resolved before a final decision can be made.

The second type of make-or-buy decision relates to the purchase or manufacture of *components* that go into manufactured products. General Motors, for example, has hundreds of suppliers producing thousands of products that become parts of its cars. These range from seatbelts and windshield wiper blades to tires, batteries, windshields, and seats. It might be possible for GM to make all of these components. Yet it would be economically unwise because of the investment needed to develop the factory capability. Thus, GM outsources about 30 percent of the components that go into its cars. Ford and Chrysler outsource even more.

Ford's experience with outsourcing in 1997 shows the care companies must use in the make-or-buy decision. Johnson Controls makes seat assemblies for the Ford Expedition, a high-demand sport utility vehicle. Unfortunately, Johnson Controls' employees went out on strike. Because Ford uses a just-in-time manufacturing process, it was immediately affected. It began making plans to shift orders for seat assemblies to other suppliers, but not before production of the Expeditions was significantly slowed down.

The component make-or-buy decision also requires interaction among several departments and levels within the organization. Financial managers, production managers, and human resources managers are all involved in determining which components can be outsourced and which should be made in-house.

Acquiring Fixed Assets

Manufacturing firms own millions of dollars of fixed assets. These are the buildings and equipment that are used to produce products. Acquiring major equipment or facilities involves a number of people within a firm. Building a new factory requires the combined efforts of financial managers, production managers, legal staff, human resources managers, site acquisition experts, public relations staff, and many others. Top managers are involved in the decision to build new facilities due to the great cost involved and the impact the building will have on the community. In fact, many people in the community are also involved. Local government must provide *infrastructure*, the combination of roads, sewers, utilities, fire and police protection, and other services necessary to build and operate a plant. Chamber of Commerce representatives may help get tax relief and other enticements to encourage the company to build the plant.

Locating the Facilities

Locating sites for new manufacturing plants—or for other businesses such as retail shopping malls—is a very involved process. Site location decisions must be made at the regional, local, and individual site level. Some factors to consider are the proximity to customers, closeness to suppliers, total cost of construction, available infrastructure, availability of quality labor, government regulation or encouragement, and the overall business climate.[6]

Once a decision has been made to build or expand in a community, managers must decide whether to build on a new site, remodel the current plant, or purchase an existing building. A totally new site is sometimes referred to as a greenfield site. The term *greenfield* comes from the fact that many new manufacturing sites, such as the Mitsubishi Motors plant in Illinois, were literally built where cornfields had been. For new sites, managers must purchase the site and get building permits—an onerous task, to say the least. Residents of the area may resist the company's attempts to purchase or rezone the property. They may fear a decline in their property values and worry about the possibility of hazardous waste production.

Companies may decide to purchase or remodel existing facilities rather than build a greenfield site. This is often faster and may be cheaper, but the decisions are no less critical. If the site is currently being used by the company, arrangements must be made to move production to other facilities while remodeling this one for its new use. That,

The Mitsubishi Eclipse is built in a new manufacturing plant outside Bloomington, Illinois. The plant was originally built by an international joint venture of Mitsubishi and Chrysler which later sold its share of the plant to Mitsubishi. What are the advantages of building a completely new facility rather than adapting an existing facility?

of course, will trigger extensive planning at the other affected site. If the company decides to purchase a plant, then it must negotiate with the current owner to determine the appropriate price, the amount of equipment that stays with the plant, and the method of payment. This again illustrates how interrelated the resource acquisition decisions are.

Building the Facilities

Once the company gets permission to build, the site must be designed, equipment must be purchased and moved in, a parking lot must be built, and a host of ancillary arrangements must be made. Will the cafeteria be run by the company or outsourced? What level of technology will be used in the plant? Will the plant be built for the minimum possible cost and contain the absolute minimum amount of equipment, or will it be built as a state-of-the-art facility with the latest technology and substantial room for expansion? These questions and decisions are complex.

One utility company, for example, built a new generating plant on a greenfield site. It designed the facility in modules. It purchased enough land and received permission to build three modules of generating units. It needed only one module immediately and expected to need the second in a very few years. It completely constructed the first module and made plans to build the second. The third would be built decades later, so no investment in construction was needed at that time.

In some cases, the equipment must be specially designed and made for the particular use at that site. Hence, the company may spend over $1 million on one piece of equipment. Tremendous coordination is required in order for all parts of the facility to be operational at the same time.

The types of decisions made by a manufacturing firm are typically more detailed than those of service firms, but do not assume that the task is easy for service firms. With the growth in service industries, the need for facilities is tremendous. You need only drive along interstates in or around large cities to witness the growth in corporate facilities in recent years. Most of these are service firms. Like manufacturing firms, service firms must give considerable attention to the location, design, technology, parking, and ancillary services to be provided.

Acquiring Raw Materials

Once managers have acquired facilities, they must begin the task of acquiring raw materials to use in the production process. There are many different sources of raw materials. Each has particular benefits, each requires a different type of coordination, and each uses a different type of contractual arrangement. Table 13–3 shows various types of suppliers for manufacturing firms, emphasizing materials used in the production process.

Independent contractors are typically small businesses that may range from a small carpenter business to a machine shop specializing in a few products. This kind of supplier often provides personalized service and may produce for only a very few customers. Sometimes it produces, under contract, for a single large customer. Thus, a small company might make only the cabs for John Deere tractors. In this case, the small company works very closely with the larger manufacturer and is almost an extension of the larger firm. Incidentally, although our focus here is on physical resources, independent contractors are a prime source of services to other businesses.

Regional producers market their goods or services in a larger geographic area which may cover a few counties or perhaps several states. They often have either a single plant or a small number of plants. They usually sell to a number of customers, which may be either industrial or final consumers. Some may have a product line or service that they sell in a limited area plus a small segment of their business that reaches a larger market. An example of this is an architectural firm that designs office buildings in a several-county area but designs hospitals in a multi-state region and designs prisons for construction anywhere in the United States.

TABLE 13–3   Types of Suppliers

Independent contractors	Local producers with only a few customers
Regional producers	Medium-size producers that sell within a several-state region
National or international	Large producers that routinely sell to a large number of customers, often internationally
Specialty goods producers	Producers that make a single product that is used by a number of customers nationwide or worldwide
Foreign producers	Producers in other countries that build under contract for individual companies or sell to a broad market
Competitors	Producers that make a product for other companies but also make similar products to sell under their own brand name.

National and international producers are those companies that typically make a number of products for sale virtually throughout the United States and international markets. Their products may range from components to entire products. An example is Cummins Engines, which produces truck engines that may become part of trucks built by Peterbilt, Mack, GMC, or Ford. Since these companies make major components, they may have plants in a number of states and other countries. Lear Corporation, featured in Profile 13–2, is a supplier that operates in both the domestic and international markets.

PROFILE 13–2   *Lear Seating Is in Your Car*

Regardless of what kind of car you rode in last, the odds are high that you sat on seats made by Lear Corporation. Although Lear Corporation has been in the automotive parts business since 1917, it sold its first automotive seat in 1984. Since then, Lear has provided automotive seats for more than 85 models of cars throughout the world. Through 160 facilities in 23 countries, Lear serves the global requirements of Ford, General Motors, Fiat, Chrysler, Volvo, Saab, BMW, Volkswagen, Jaguar, Isuzu, Subaru, Mazda, Peugeot, Renault, Audi, Mercedes-Benz, and Honda. Lear is the largest independent automotive-seating supplier in North America and Europe. As the leading player in the $45 billion global automotive interior market, it generated revenues of $6.2 billion in 1996.

Lear Corporation now produces components for all portions of a car interior. This includes the seating system, floor, acoustic system, instrument panel, doors and sidewalls, overhead material, and functional equipment systems. Approximately 58 percent of the products go into cars, with the remaining 42 percent going into light trucks such as the Ford Explorer.

globalization p. 186>

Lear's growth, averaging 33 percent a year, has been the result of several trends—outsourcing, globalization, supplier consolidation, greater design and engineering responsibility given to suppliers, and increasing sophistication of seat systems.

In addition to producing car interiors, Lear Corporation is involved in the *design* of the systems and even R&D into ergonomics and passenger safety. Its people work closely with the automotive manufacturers to provide the most appropriate seating.

SOURCES: Lear Corporation 1996 Annual Report; Lear Corporation website, http://www.lear.com, (accessed July 9, 1997).

Specialty goods producers are companies that produce a single product, which may be sold worldwide. For example, Potash Corp. of Saskatchewan Inc., a potash mining company headquartered in Saskatoon, Saskatchewan, Canada, produces 22 percent of the world's potash (which is used in fertilizer). Potash is essentially the only product sold by PCS, but it has customers throughout the world.

Foreign producers make an item and ship it to the United States either for sale to the public or for use in products. Use of foreign suppliers may lower costs since wages are lower in developing countries than in the United States. In some cases, the U.S. company owns the foreign producer and therefore has a direct supply channel. In other situations, the foreign company is separately owned but has contracts with the U.S.- based firm to provide the desired products. Nike, for example, sells a wide range of athletic shoes and apparel. Most of it is made in southeast Asia and shipped to Nike to sell.

A final source of physical resources may surprise you. In several industries, it is not unusual for companies to purchase goods from their *competitors*. For example, in the home appliance industry, Sears does not produce any of its products. Instead, it contracts with suppliers to produce goods for marketing under one of the Sears brand names, like Kenmore. Often the supplier also markets similar products under its own brand. Sears buys its refrigerators from Whirlpool—which also makes refrigerators that it sells under the Whirlpool brand. Why would Whirlpool sell to a competitor? The answer is simple. Sears is an extremely large retailer that sells hundreds of appliances a day. It is a ready market, then, for thousands of units a year that Whirlpool would not be likely to sell under its own brand name.

The Acquisition Process

The process of acquiring physical resources typically takes one of two forms, both of which require negotiation between buyer and seller. These are the traditional bidding system and the increasingly popular just-in-time system.

In the *traditional bidding system*, a manufacturer solicits bids from a number of suppliers to produce desired components. One or more suppliers are selected to provide the needed goods in large batches. The selection is often made on the basis of the lowest-cost bid. In some cases, the company may have a number of suppliers producing the same product for it, so if one supplier cannot provide the product, others will likely be able to take up the slack. The contract is rebid periodically to ensure the lowest possible prices. Suppliers have to keep careful track of their bidding history and also keep an eye out for new customers in case they are underbid by a competitor.

**Just-in-time
production**
An integrated set of ac-
tivities designed to
achieve high-volume
production using mini-
mal inventories of raw
materials, work in
process, and finished
goods.

Companies using the traditional bidding method carefully calculate the order quantity
that will minimize ordering costs while also minimizing the cost of storing materials.

Just-in-time (JIT) production is an integrated set of activities designed to
achieve high-volume production using minimal inventories of raw materials, work in
process, and finished goods.[7] The logic of JIT is that nothing is produced until it is
needed. The supplier provides the component at precisely the time it is needed in the
customer's manufacturing process. This eliminates the need to stock inventory, reduces setup times for assembling the end product, and eliminates waste.

The just-in-time system of acquiring resources changes much of the relationship
between buyers and sellers. Whereas in the traditional philosophy the supplier and
buyer were adversaries, the JIT system develops long-term relationships and strategic
alliances that both create and rely on interdependency between the two companies.

Profile 13–3 continues the discussion of Lear Corporation, emphasizing its relationship with its customers.

PROFILE 13–3   *Lear Corporation (continued)*

As a key supplier, Lear Corporation is responsible to the automotive manufacturers for the design, development, component sourcing, manufacturing, quality assurance, and delivery of interior systems on a just-in-time basis. Now it has taken

Lear Corporation designs and makes seating and other interior systems for most carmakers,
both foreign and domestic. Its just-in-time system provides high quality products precisely
when they are needed. Why would a major manufacturer of automobiles want to outsource
both the production and design of components?

JIT to a higher level. In what is called sequential parts delivery, Lear not only delivers the interior systems to customers just in time, but delivers them to the actual point of assembly in the precise color and trim sequence requested. This means Lear must build high-quality seats and work especially closely with its customers.

teams p. 71>

To provide the highest possible quality in the shortest possible time, interior assembly is performed in modules by highly skilled teams of workers and quality is inspected often. Also, Lear's assembly plants are strategically located within 20 miles of its customers' facilities.

An interior system order is sent from the customer's assembly plant, usually as the vehicle enters the paint department. The order is received by Lear's computers, which signal the sequencing and loading of the component systems. The system is often delivered to the automotive plant within 90 minutes after the customer sends the order.

Our discussion of acquisition of physical resources has keyed on manufacturing firms since they require the most physical resources in order to produce the products. Keep in mind, however, that acquisition of physical resources is also important in service organizations. The resources to be acquired are typically either fixed assets (such as computer systems, furniture, and buildings) or supplies. Even here, JIT and close relationships with suppliers are important. State Farm Insurance, for example, is a service firm; it produces no physical products for sale. Yet because of its size, it requires considerable office space in headquarters and regional offices. Even items like paper and printer toner are consumed in giant proportions. Acquiring those resources requires the full-time attention of many employees, not to mention considerable warehouse space. JIT agreements with suppliers significantly reduce the cost to State Farm.

Developing Your Critical Thinking Skills

1. What is different about the *process* of acquiring fixed assets compared with acquiring inventory or supplies?

2. Why are more and more firms moving toward outsourcing components or products? Is your answer the same for physical resources as for human resources?

3. Describe the relationship between Lear Corporation and its customers. How is it beneficial to both?

Financial Resources

Financial resources are valuable in that they can be used to acquire other resources as well as invested to earn more resources. In contrast, physical resources are used for a single purpose. Further, if they are not being used, physical resources just sit there. Financial resources can be used to purchase equipment, pay workers, buy advertising, or acquire another company. Excess financial resources can be invested to add to the company's earnings. Therefore, the acquisition and use of this type of resource is very important.

TABLE 13–4   Cash Inflows and Outflows

Cash Inflows	Cash Outflows for Operations	Cash Outflows for Financing and Investments
New infusions of equity or debt financing	Production Raw materials Labor Other expenses	Cash to creditors Principal Interest
Revenues Cash sales Payments on accounts receivable	Utilities Supplies Rent Marketing Wages and salaries Taxes	Cash to owners Acquisitions Investments Acquisition of land, buildings or equipment

SOURCE: Adapted from Robert C. Higgins, *Analysis for Financial Management* (Burr Ridge, IL: Irwin, 1995), p. 4.

Cash flow
The movement of cash into, through, and out of a firm.

Financial resources can best be discussed in terms of the concept of cash flow. **Cash flow** refers to the movement of cash into, through, and out of the firm. *Cash inflow* is the movement of cash from somewhere outside the firm into the firm. *Cash outflow* is the movement of cash back out of the company in exchange for services, materials or labor, to pay taxes, to provide a return to owners, or to purchase other companies. Table 13–4 illustrates the inflows and outflows. In between the inflow and outflow, the cash may move from one department to another within the company as one unit in the firm "sells" its services or production process to another. We will discuss inflow, outflow, and intrafirm movement in turn.

Cash Inflow: Acquiring Financial Resources

Cash inflow
Money that moves into the business from owners, lenders, or customers.

Equity financing
Any money invested in a business by the owners.

Debt financing
Money a company borrows from outsiders such as individuals, banks, or other lending institutions or raises by selling bonds.

Cash inflow may come from three primary sources: owners, lenders, and customers. These sources, commonly called equity financing, debt financing, and revenues, are shown in the first column of Table 13–4.

A first source of cash is the owners of the company. Any money invested by owners is called **equity financing.** In small firms, individual owners may put some of their own personal funds into the company. Company owners can also raise equity money by taking in a partner. Corporations can raise cash through selling stock to investors. These stockholders become part owners of the company in exchange for the cash they pay. Companies wishing to raise substantial funds may do an initial public offering. You will recall from Chapter 8 that an IPO offers stock to the public for the first time. Once the IPO is made, the firm can raise more cash by issuing more stock.

The second source of funds is money loaned to the company by outsiders such as individuals, banks, or other lending institutions. Large corporations may also issue bonds, a special type of loan that outsiders buy in much the same way that stockholders buy stock in the firms. Loaned cash is called **debt financing.** There are interest p. 225>

two significant differences between debt financing and equity financing. First, debt financing *requires* the borrower to pay interest on loans to the business. The loan contract is a legally binding agreement that the business will pay back the principal of the loan plus any interest. Equity financing does not require paying back the investment. Second, the providers of debt financing are called *lenders*. These lenders do *not* become owners. Thus, if a bank lends a business $100,000, the bank has a legal agreement with the firm, but it is not an owner of the firm.

Revenue
Cash generated from the sale of goods or services to customers.

The most critical source of funds is revenue. **Revenue** is cash that is generated from the sale of goods or services to customers. As customers purchase goods or services from the firm, they pay for those purchases with either cash or credit that is later turned into cash. Revenues are the most critical source of funding because they are a continual source of new funds. As goods or services are sold, more money flows into the business, money that can then be used to create still more items to sell. If a company is successful, revenue-generated funds will be sufficient to underwrite day-to-day operations. Revenue will also provide returns for the owners and allow excess funds to be reinvested in the business.

Revenue-generated funds may not be enough to keep the firm running at the time of start-up, during seasonal fluctuations, or when the firm is growing rapidly. In these cases, either additional debt or equity financing may be required.

Cash Outflow: Using Financial Resources

Cash outflow
Cash that moves out of the business for any reason.

Cash outflow is cash that moves out of the business for any reason. Outflows may be as simple as dividends paid to stockholders or checks written to a TV station for advertising. Or outflows can be quite complex, such as a combination stock swap and cash purchase of another publicly held company. Generally, outflows fall into two categories. The first is outflows related to the production of the goods or service; we call this simply outflows for operations. The second is outflows for financing and investments.

Cash outflows for operations consist of all those uses of cash that deal with production and sale of the firm's goods and services. These expenditures may be for raw materials or inventory that will eventually be processed or sold. Major amounts go to pay the people who work in the production process. Significant amounts of funds are used to purchase utilities, supplies, and miscellaneous items necessary for the operations aspect of the firm.

Once goods or services are produced, there is still the task of marketing them to customers. This is also a large use of cash. It is not uncommon, for example, for a company to spend $10 million on marketing just to introduce a single new product. In addition to production and marketing, much of a firm's cash outflow goes to the general administration of the firm. If you think of all the clerical staff, accountants, janitorial staff, researchers, and attorneys, it becomes apparent that much of the cash outflow goes simply to pay people. Of course, you must add the computers and communications equipment necessary to operate the firm. Then add in the office furniture, supplies, and travel needed to manage a business. Administrative costs are often 40 percent of the entire cost of the product. In fact, much of the downsizing among large businesses today is the elimination of administrative staff.

The final category of operations-related outflows is taxes. Some taxes, such as sales taxes, are simply pass-throughs from the customer to the taxing bodies. Other taxes, such as income taxes, are a real part of the cost of doing business. Still others, such as real estate taxes in some communities, are an expense the business must incur even though they are not directly related to its operations. The business manager who forgets to include the outflow for taxes in financial planning may make a mistake that is fatal to the business.

Cash outflows for financing and investment include the investment of funds for acquisition of additional fixed assets, the payment of the principal and interest on loans, the payment of dividends to stockholders or returns to the owners (if sole proprietors or partners), and the investment of funds in either typical financial instruments or the acquisition of other companies.

Earlier we noted that land, buildings, and equipment are known as fixed assets. Acquiring these fixed assets requires a major use of funds. For example, General Motors spent over $1 billion just to build and equip its state-of-the-art facility in Spring Hill, Tennessee to produce Saturn cars. We also noted in Chapter 10 that Motorola spent approximately $10 billion over the past three years to expand operations.

We mentioned that two of the three *inflows* of cash deal with debt or equity financing. Similarly, cash *outflows* must be made to return that cash to lenders, bondholders, and owners. In debt financing, the business must pay back the amount borrowed plus interest. Regardless of whether the debt comes from bonds, individuals, or banks, the business still must pay the holders of the debt the agreed-upon interest plus the principal. In equity financing, the business pays the owner or owners part of the profits of the business. In the case of stock companies, the company may pay dividends to stockholders (although many public companies do not pay dividends) plus the occasional repurchase of company stock. In the case of sole proprietorships and partnerships, the payment is that portion of the cash the owners take out of the business.

stock p. 216>

Companies with excess cash would be ill-advised to simply let it sit in the firm's checking account. It is common to invest excess cash beyond what the business needs to reinvest in the company. Excess cash may be invested in any form that an individual might use. Thus, a company's investments could range from certificates of deposit and savings accounts to stocks or bonds of other companies.

BRINKER
INTERNATIONAL.

Profile 13–4 shows the cash flow statement for Brinker International, one of our focus companies. Note that Brinker had both inflows and outflows of millions of dollars.

PROFILE   13–4   *Brinker International's Cash Flows*

The financial document that illustrates the movement of cash into and out of an organization is known as the *cash flow statement*. It is important because it focuses on the movement of *cash* rather than on income and expenses. For many companies, especially small businesses, this movement of cash is more important than income and expenses since it is cash that is used to pay bills. In addition, many purchases and many sales are made on credit. The cash flow statement acknowledges funds movement when the flow occurs rather than when the sale or purchase occurred. Also, some aspects of a company's expenses are noncash expenses. For example, depreciation is an expense related to the declining value of assets as they are used up. That expense is a noncash expense.

This cash flow statement shows the cash inflows and outflows of Brinker International. Note that some of the entries offset noncash expenses. Note also that the statement is broken into cash flows related to operations and cash flows from investments and financing. Finally, some of the entries are clear only in light of the "notes of consolidated financial statements," which we have not included here. Items in parentheses are outflows. Those without parentheses are inflows.

Brinker International, Inc. **Consolidated Statement of Cash Flows, 1996** **($ thousands)**	
Cash Flows from Operating Activities	
Net income	$ 34,381
Depreciation expense (adds back in a noncash expense)	54,138
Amortization of goodwill and other assets (noncash expense)	10,473
Gain on sale of restaurant concepts (noncash income)	(9,262)
Restructuring charges (noncash expense)	50,000
Decrease in accounts receivable (creditors paid their bills)	4,783
Increase in inventories (paid cash to buy food and supplies)	(1,236)
Increase in prepaid expenses (bills paid before they were due)	(3,920)
Increase in other assets (paid cash to purchase goods)	(21,883)
Increase in accounts payable (expenses not yet paid)	1,537
Decrease in accrued liabilities (paid earlier bills)	(1,596)
Decrease in deferred income taxes (paid taxes with cash)	(8,313)
Increase in other liabilities (bills not paid)	3,607
Other	2,220
Net cash provided by operating activities	114,929
Cash Flows from Investing Activities	
Payments for property and equipment	(187,141)
Proceeds from sale of concepts	73,115
Purchases of marketable securities (investing excess cash)	(61,390)
Proceeds from sales of marketable securities (sold other investments)	25,137
Other	375
Net cash used in investing activities	(149,904)
Cash Flows from Financing Activities	
Borrowings of short-term debt	15,000
Payments of long-term debt	(1,530)
Proceeds from sale of common stock (issued more stock)	3,667
Net cash provided by financing activities	17,137
Net cash decrease in cash and cash equivalents	(17,838)

From the cash flow statement, we see that Brinker International had a net decrease in cash of almost $18 million. This is not necessarily bad, especially when $61 million of marketable securities (short-term investments) and $187 million of property and equipment were purchased.

SOURCE: Brinker International web site, http://www.sec.gov/edgar, (accessed September 4, 1997).

A final form of capital outflow in the investment category is the acquisition of other companies. Businesses may use their current cash plus other funding to purchase another company. These acquisitions often add to a company's product line, reduce competition, or allow the company to expand abroad. As Profile 13–5 explains, H.J. Heinz purchased two kinds of companies. It bought pet-food companies from Quaker Oats. It also purchased a number of baby-food companies in other countries, which gives Heinz a bigger presence in the international market.

PROFILE 13–5   *H.J. Heinz: Would You Like Ketchup on Your Kibble?*

How much is a bag of dog food worth? More importantly, how much is an entire dog food company worth to a company best known for producing ketchup?

H.J. Heinz is a household word—providing that the household is discussing tomato-based products. Not many consumers know that Heinz also owns Starkist Tuna, Ore-Ida, Weight Watchers, Earth's Best baby foods, and others. Heinz is in fact a highly diversified company in the food products industry.

Recently, however, Heinz paid $272 million for Quaker Oats Co.'s North American pet-food operations, including such brands as Gravy Train and Kibbles

A major use of finances is the purchase of another company, such as Heinz's purchase of Quaker Oats Co.'s pet food business. Heinz paid $272 million for the business because of the addition it would make to their existing pet food business. What inflows of cash might be necessary to offset this significant outflow? What will Heinz expect from the new business in terms of revenue?

'N Bits. They will become part of its existing pet-food division. In fact, Heinz moved some of the production in the new companies to existing pet-food plants. The company also bought baby-food companies in India, Britain, and the Czech Republic. In 1994, it purchased Borden Inc.'s food-service group, which sells to restaurants, hotels, and other food-service establishments.

Heinz paid for some of the purchases with cash and some with stock. The $272 million represents a significant cash outflow, but Heinz gains a substantial increase in its overall assets as well as its earnings base.

SOURCE: Matt Murray and Christian Duff, "Heinz Agrees to Acquire Quaker Oats' North American Pet Food Operations," *The Wall Street Journal*, February 3, 1995, p. A3.

Intrafirm Cash Flows: Moving Resources within the Firm

Cash can move not just into and out of a company but also within and around the company. The movement of cash within a firm need not involve the physical carrying of cash or writing of a check. Transactions between departments are often simply recorded paperwork that reflects the movement of goods from one section of the firm to another. But that movement of goods means that there is an equivalent movement of "cash" in the opposite direction. Thus, if the research and development department develops a new product, it will be somehow rewarded for that development. Similarly, if one department produces a component of the finished product, it gets "paid" for those components.

Historically, internal transfers of goods or services typically did not affect the overall performance of the company since revenue to one department was an expense to another. However, this is changing as many companies allow their subunits the option of buying from other parts of the company or buying components on the open market. Thus, individual departments feel the pressure of market forces even though their prime customer may be simply another part of the company.

A key to the importance of the internal transfer of cash is the concept of budgets. We mentioned earlier in discussing the challenges of allocating resources that departments or subunits seldom have large enough budgets. Thus, even if a particular unit within a company gets all of its material inputs from other units of the company, its budget may be wrecked by inefficiencies of the other units. If you are the manager of a company unit, your financial resources are, in actuality, a budget allocation from the next higher level in the company. You may have some flexibility in how you use those resources, but you have little flexibility in how many resources you have. So, moving "cash" within a company is a real challenge.

Developing Your Critical Thinking Skills

1. What are the advantages of equity financing compared with debt financing? The disadvantages?

2. What are the impacts of using too much debt? Are there problems with using too little debt?

3. What is the difference between cash outflow for operations and cash outflow for investment?

Information Resources

It is hard to think of information as a resource, but it is one of the fuels that power an organization just as much as human resources, physical resources, and financial resources are. Without sufficient information, managers cannot make appropriate decisions.

Managers need two broad categories of information, strategic and operational. **Strategic information** is information about a firm's competitors, customers, and markets that affects its ability to compete. **Operational information** is information that affects the internal workings of the company and will help it run more efficiently. There is obvious overlap between the two types of information. For example, marketing-related information can be both strategic and operational. So can some financial information. So can some manufacturing information. The difference between the two categories of information is the focus. Strategic information has an external focus while operational information has an internal focus.

Strategic information
Information about a firm's competitors, customers, and markets that affects its ability to compete.

Operational information
Any information that bears on the internal workings of the company and will help it run more efficiently.

Strategic Information

Strategic information consists of information about the firm's environment. The chapters in Part Two of this book all dealt with external information that is relevant to businesses. Table 13–5 lists examples of strategic information. Note that the strategic information parallels our model of a successful business discussed in Chapter 1.

Managers use strategic information to develop strategies that help the business excel in a dynamic marketplace. For example, they need information about their customers to understand the customer trends that will affect their sales. The more information they have, the better they can position their product or service in a way that maximizes their chances for success.

financial markets
p. 215>

Information regarding the economy and financial markets is important for assessing the future demand for products. This kind of information is also useful in making expansion decisions because of the effect of interest rates on a company's expenses.

exporting p. 188>

Information on foreign markets is important if the company plans to enter those markets. Even if the business sells only domestically, information about foreign companies exporting to the United States is also important. Information about the size of competitors, exchange rates, and export procedures is critically important.

Operational Information

Operational information is any information that will make the organization run more efficiently. Operational information encompasses at least the following five categories:[8]

1. Marketing information
2. Manufacturing information
3. Accounting and financial information
4. Quality control information
5. Human resources information

Each kind of information helps managers assess how the company is doing and help it adjust for the future. For example, quality control information allows companies to determine how well they have been doing in terms of product defects. It also

TABLE 13–5   Samples of Strategic Information

Demographic Information

> Age of customers
> Education level of customers
> Income of customers

Economic Information

> Gross domestic product
> Unemployment rate
> Inflation rate
> Industry performance
> Sales compared with price (demand)

International Information

> Global sales of products
> International competitors
> Imports/exports of products
> Currency exchange rates
> Market reports from other countries

Financial Market Information

> Trends in interest rates
> Stock and bond prices
> Amount of consumer debt

Legal Information

> Relevant government regulations
> Trends in industry-specific regulation

points to possible solutions to problems. Human resources information allows managers and employees to assess salaries, benefits, vacation days, bonuses, stock options, and a host of other information.

Sources of Information

In each of the prior sections, we discussed sources of the relevant resource. We named different sources of human resources, sources of equipment and raw material, and debt and equity sources of capital. Here we mention a few of the many sources of information.

The Internet

There may be no better external source of information for businesses than the Internet and World Wide Web. Note, for example, the number of company websites listed in the front and back inside covers of this book. Many of the sources we cite in this book are websites from companies, the U.S. government, or other organizations. The amount of data available from the Internet is simply mind-boggling. The ease and low cost of getting the information also make it a first-choice source. The use of search engines to find information makes data gathering easy from any personal computer connected to the Internet. Government data are particularly useful and easily accessible. Virtually every large company and many small ones have Internet sites. Information can be accessed and then either printed or downloaded into computer files and stored for future use.

Annual Reports

Every publicly held company is required to prepare annual reports, which are routinely sent to stockholders. Publicly held companies are also required to file financial reports with the Securities and Exchange Commission (SEC). These reports are available from the companies, at many libraries, and at most company websites. This allows managers to access significant information about their competitors. Most of the information is provided for multiple years, which lets you see trends or changes in financial conditions.

BRINKER
INTERNATIONAL.

Suppose, for example, that you are either a competitor or a potential investor of Brinker International. You might consult its website to see what information you can find. The Brinker International cash flow statement shown in Profile 13–4 was downloaded from the World Wide Web. If you consult the site, you will find that Brinker International financial reports show its income dropped from $72 million in 1995 to $32 million in 1996. This rather precipitous drop in net income seemed severe, since sales revenue increased from $1.04 billion to $1.16 billion. Further analysis of the reports, however, showed that the cause of the drop was a one-time restructuring charge of $50 million. More information can be gleaned from annual reports and other sources to give additional detail on a company's financial condition.

Trade Association Data

Much information can be gleaned from trade associations, which most industries have. For example, the International Franchise Association has information related to franchises. The American Automobile Manufacturer's Association has information about the automotive industry. Most of this information is available on the Web.

Internal Databases

The best source of internal information is the broad set of company databases that exist in any business. Like Internet information, these are often readily available and accessible from desktop computers. Most companies have databases for financial information, human resources information, marketing information, manufacturing information, and others. Most of this is in searchable form if you have the appropriate authorization. The information is easily retrievable and can be analyzed using statistical software.

We have only skimmed the surface here of information sources. In fact, most managers today have more information available to them than they can use effectively. The key to effective use of information resources is to identify what information is needed, what form it is needed in, and where to find it.

Developing Your Critical Thinking Skills

1. Why are companies eager to put their information on the World Wide Web for all to see?

2. Why do we say that there is an overlap between operational and strategic information?

3. What can you find out about the bicycle industry, for example, by looking at websites of individual bicycle manufacturers?

Resource Allocation

We've said resource acquisition is one of the most integrative of tasks in a company because of the trade-offs between types of resources and the impact that one resource has on another. This same relationship holds in the area of resource allocation.

Budget
A plan for the controlled use of financial resources.

The previous section mentioned the need for budgets. A **budget** is a plan for the controlled use of financial resources. Actually, there are many types of budgets. There are manufacturing budgets, research and development budgets, advertising budgets, capital equipment budgets, and many more. The common theme of budgets is the amount of financial resources allocated to given areas. With this in mind, we can say that resource allocation is also an integrative task in business because of the need to consider impacts throughout the organization of a change in budgets.

You may have wondered why your college can't just add another section of a course when the available sections fill up. The answer has a lot to do with budgets. To add a section of a course would mean hiring another faculty member, finding classroom space, and perhaps adding secretarial support. Unfortunately, people cost money. More significantly, budgets are set months before school starts. Although some departments may have some emergency flexibility, that flexibility is sorely limited because of budgets.

Similarly, managers of businesses as well as not-for-profit organizations work within the confines of a budget. They sometimes have limited input into the size of the total budget. They often have some input into the allocation of the total budget.

Suppose you are the marketing manager for a chain of grocery stores. The president of the grocery store chain must consider the total budget for the chain. Each segment of the budget, usually called *line items*, must be carefully weighed against all the others. The president must determine how much should be allocated to new store development, remodeling and maintenance of existing stores, inventory, employee wages and salaries, and, of course, marketing.

It is not uncommon for managers in charge of each line item in the budget to lobby to get an increase in their particular segment of the chain's operations. Upper management will listen carefully to each manager's appeal for funds and after careful analysis will announce the amount in each line of the budget. Managers may be disappointed at the paltry increase (or perhaps decrease) in their budget. However, they must use the amount they have received as effectively as possible.

For example, as the marketing manager, you must decide how much to spend on radio or TV advertising, how much to put in the standard newspaper ads, and how much to hold back for special event advertising such as Valentine's Day specials on candy. You will consult those who work with you and will carefully analyze the needs in each area. You will study the increase in costs of each type of advertising. You may also consider different forms of marketing, such as doubling manufacturers' coupons or offering store rebates. Eventually, you will arrive at a budget that appears workable.

This example was designed to illustrate for you the complexity of resource allocation. It is certainly not an easy task, especially when the amount of resources is less than optimal.

Developing Your Critical Thinking Skills

1. Why are budgets important?

2. What happens if a unit goes over budget?

3. What is so important about our emphasis on the integration of resource acquisition processes? Allocation processes?

SUMMARY

1. This book emphasizes the importance of integrative thinking in business.

   ■ What are some of the issues of integration you must consider when dealing with resource acquisition and use?

   Resource acquisition demands that managers work with many people throughout the company to acquire and use resources in the most effective and least expensive manner. This is important because changes in one resource can affect the use of others. This is also important because of the concepts of trade-offs. Trade-offs mean that using funds for one thing precludes using them for another. Opportunity costs, the value of activities that are sacrificed, must also be considered. Resource acquisition and use involve the movement of goods, equipment, inventory, money, people, and information from outside the organization to inside and back.

2. Resource acquisition provides three major challenges to a business.

   ■ What are those three major resource challenges?

   The three challenges are (1) acquiring an adequate amount, (2) acquiring the proper mix, and (3) making the appropriate allocation of the acquired resources within the organization.

3. CEOs of most companies are quick to tell you that their people are the key to their company's success. What they do not tell you is how they happen to have such superior employees.

   ■ What are the five challenges of human resources management?

   Successful companies must be able to (1) accurately forecast the company's human resources needs, (2) recruit a pool of candidates, (3) select the best individuals based on the needs of the company, (4) train and develop the employees, and (5) ensure their productivity.

   ■ What are some of the major issues involved with each of the five major human resources challenges?

   (1) Forecasting human resources needs requires managers to predict where the company is going and what kinds and number of employees will be required.

It requires predicting changes in the current workforce, such as retirement, promotions, and terminations. It requires forecasting demographic and lifestyle changes and determining how they will affect the firm's ability to find and attract future employees.

(2) Recruiting candidates involves the use of many different sources, ranging from ads to employment agencies, trade associations, direct hiring from other companies, and internal promotions.

(3) Once candidates are found, they must be carefully screened to make sure their capabilities meet the company's needs. Before actually deciding to hire a new employee, the business should consider the possibility of outsourcing.

(4) Orientation, training, and development are crucial to making sure that new employees integrate effectively with other employees. The task of orientation is to make sure that employees understand and accept the norms and cultures of the business. The task of training is to make sure that employees learn the specific skills needed to perform their job effectively. Development is the provision of educational experiences that will help employees stay successful as their careers progress.

(5) Ensuring high performance is partly a result of doing the first three tasks well. It also involves the motivational themes that will be discussed in the next chapter.

4.   One important determinant of employee productivity is the nature of the physical resources workers use. The right plant, equipment, raw materials, and supplies will enable workers to achieve peak performance. Inadequate or inappropriate physical resources will prevent even dedicated workers from doing their best.

■ What are some of the major issues related to the acquisition of physical resources?

(1) First and foremost, planning is crucial.

(2) Second, a major issue that must be considered in the planning stage is whether to make the product in-house or buy it from a supplier (outsource it).

(3) Third, for fixed assets a major issue is whether to build on a new site, remodel, or purchase an existing building.

(4) Fourth, in choosing suppliers for physical resources, the firm must consider such alternatives as independent contractors, regional producers, national or international producers, specialty goods producers, importers, and competitors.

(5) Fifth, in the process of actually acquiring the physical resources the firm must consider two possible forms of negotiation with the seller, traditional bidding and the just-in-time approach.

5.   Both human and physical resources have to be purchased with financial resources. So acquiring financial resources is also a continuous challenge for the firm.

■ What are some major characteristics of the acquisition and use of financial resources?

Financial resources can best be understood in terms of the concept of cash flow. This refers to the movement of cash into, through, and out of the firm.

(1) Cash inflow refers to the actual acquisition of financial resources. The issue facing the firm is how to acquire the cash. The three major alternatives are equity financing, debt financing, and revenues.

(2) Cash outflow refers to the movement of cash out of the business for any reason. Cash outflows are caused by expenditures for production of the firm's goods and services or by financing activities such as the acquisition of additional fixed assets, payment of dividends to stockholders, and investment of excess cash.

(3) Intrafirm cash flow refers to transactions between departments or units within the company. These are often simply recorded without any actual cash payments being made. Historically, such internal transfers did not affect overall performance since revenue to one department was an expense to another. But that is changing as many companies allow their subunits the option of buying from outside sellers.

6. Information is much more readily available today than it was even 10 years ago.

    ■ What sources of information exist and how can they be used?

    Information is available from a vast array of sources, both inside a business and outside. The most usable source of information today is the Internet, where information from government agencies, other companies, and industry can be found. Company annual reports and information from trade associations also are valuable. Internal information about a company can be gathered from company files and databases.

7. You learned that resource acquisition is one of the most integrative of tasks in a company because of the trade-offs of resources and the impact of one on another. You also learned that an effective way to deal with the trade-off problem is to use budgets.

    ■ What is a budget?

    A budget is a plan for the controlled use of financial resources.

Links to future Courses

This chapter discussed four different types of resources. You will learn more about these in many of your future classes. In particular, you will get more in-depth knowledge in the following courses:

- Human resources management
- Operations management
- Principles of finance
- Working capital management

- Capital budgeting
- Management information systems
- Information technology

KEY TERMS

Budget, p. 402
Cash flow, p. 393
Cash inflow, p. 393
Cash outflow, p. 394
Debt financing, p. 393
Downsizing, p. 375
Equity financing, p. 393
Just-in-time production, p. 391
Make-or-buy decision, p. 385
Off-the-job training, p. 381
On-the-job training (OJT), p. 380

Operational information, p. 399
Opportunity cost, p. 370
Outsourcing, p. 385
Physical resources, p. 384
Resource allocation, p. 372
Resources, p. 369
Revenue, p. 394
Rightsizing, p. 375
Strategic information, p. 399
Synergy, p. 369

1. The Internet sources www.reportgallery.com/bigaz.htm or www.sec.gov/edgar/ can be used to access company annual reports. (Other Internet sources can also be used.) Go to one of these sources and find Motorola's annual report. What kinds of information does the report contain about Motorola?

2. Form teams of six students. Your team is to identify and hire a student to serve as a reporter on the campus newspaper. Outline what must be done to find, interview, and select the best person to fill this job.

3. We discussed outsourcing twice in this chapter and earlier in the book. Assume the role of a staff employee in the manufacturing department of one of the bicycle companies we've highlighted. Prepare a one-page memo to your boss outlining the pros and cons of outsourcing for your particular company. Make sure your memo is specific to your company rather than a generic essay.

4. Suppose you have just started your own business, a small consulting company that focuses on training other firms to be more customer sensitive. Which resources (human, physical, financial, or information) will be most critical for you as you begin the company? Would your answer be the same if your company were five years old? Fifteen years old?

5. You are the president of a firm that manufactures a line of ceramic vases used in floral shops. Because of growth, you need to add $200,000 more capital. Write a two-page report on the benefits of using equity financing rather than debt financing for the $200,000. What sources of equity financing are most likely available?

6. Search the Internet for as much strategic information as you can find about an independent toy store. Now pool your answers with four other students. How many sources did you have in common?

CASE: **SIMPLICITY—HOW GERMANY'S MIDIZE
INDUSTRIAL COMPANIES SUCCEED**

One of the most interesting success stories in global competition is that of a group of midsize manufacturing firms headquartered in Germany. Their superior growth rates, financial performance, and worker productivity were the subject of a McKinsey & Co. study that highlighted a number of resource acquisition and allocations issues.

In the area of human resources, the superior German companies made some interesting decisions. They used only half as many R&D employees and two-thirds as many staff, production, and administrative workers as did their poorer-performing competitors. But the superior companies employed 80 percent more people in sales, marketing, and services than did their weaker competitors.

In the area of supplies, raw materials, and other physical inputs into the production process, the superior companies carefully evaluated the question of outsourcing. They brought the production of those items inside only if the company had strengths allowing it to do a better job. Otherwise they used outside suppliers. But they kept the number of outside suppliers small and worked to integrate those suppliers into their own decision-making processes.

They further reduced the cost of inputs by finding ways to reduce the number of components that had to be purchased and stored. One way was to reduce the number of different models of products being manufactured. Another method was to design new models so that they had more parts in common.

With respect to physical production facilities, the superior companies tended to locate production for each product or product group at a single factory. Their reasoning was that this would allow managers and workers to make decisions and implement changes much more rapidly. The superior companies also tended to build greenfield sites more often than their poorer-performing competitors in order to get better flow of materials and information and to take advantage of favorable labor supply situations.

Finally, resource decisions at the superior firms were made lower in the organization than at less successful competitors.

SOURCE: Gunter Rommel, Jurgen Kluge, Rolf-Dieter Kempis, Raimun Diederichs, and Felix Bruck, *Simplicity Wins: How Germany's Mid-sized Industrial Companies Succeed* (Boston: Harvard Business School Press, 1995).

Decision Questions

1. The title of the McKinsey study is "Simplicity Wins." What are some of the ways these superior companies "simplified" their resource acquisition and utilization procedures?

2. The case says the superior firms benefited from pushing resource decisions lower in the organization. This means that factory managers, supervisors, and even machine operators were expected to make decisions that in other companies were made by higher-level managers. Can you think of any reasons why this might result in improved performance? Can you think of any resource acquisition mistakes that might be made if decisions were made at the lower level?

3. The study found that superior companies got more output with fewer resources in almost every case. One major exception was marketing and sales, where the superior German companies deliberately used more resources than their competitors. Do you think this is a wise decision? Why? (Hint: In developing your answer, you might look back at Chapter 12 for ideas regarding how marketing and sales personnel can add value for customers.)

REFERENCES

1. Jeanne C. Lee. "Cool Companies: Insight." *Fortune*, July 7, 1997, p. 92.

2. Sharon M. Oster. *Modern Competitive Analysis*, 2nd ed. New York: Oxford University Press, 1994, pp. 26, 396.

3. This forecasting approach is adapted from Gary Dessler. *Human Resource Management*, 6th ed. Englewood Cliffs, NJ: Prentice-Hall, 1994, p. 108.

4. See, for example, C. F. Hendricks. *The Rightsizing Remedy*. Homewood, IL: Business One Irwin, 1992.

5. Robert Levering and Milton Moskowitz. *The 100 Best Companies to Work for in America*, rev. ed. New York: Plume, 1994, pp. 318–22.

6. Richard B. Chase and Nicholas J. Aquilano. *Production and Operations Management*, 7th ed. Burr Ridge, IL: Irwin, 1995, pp. 374–78.

7. Chase and Aquilano, chap. 6.

8. Uma G. Gupta. *Management Information Systems: A Managerial Perspective*. Minneapolis: West Publishing Co., 1996, p. 392.

14 *Integrating Activities and Building Commitment*

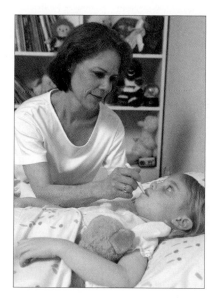

Eddie Bauer Inc. is a successful retailer of casual clothing and other products. It is also a company that believes in supporting its employees (or associates, as Bauer calls them) by building a culture that encourages a balance between home and work. For example, realizing that associates sometimes simply need a break from their work, Bauer instituted a Balance Day that allows associates to schedule a "call in well" absence in addition to normal time off. That is just the beginning. The company's well-designed employee benefits package includes liberal parental leave, on-site mammography, emergency child care services, and elder care services. Its employee assistance program helps associates who need counseling for alcohol or chemical dependency, mental and emotional stress, and other difficulties. It has adoption assistance and group mortgage programs for associates. There are opportunities for job sharing and telecommuting. The list continues to grow as Bauer looks for creative ways to support the needs of its employees.

The employer of 12,000 people worldwide, Bauer takes this worker-friendly approach not just because it's the right thing to do. It also pays dividends for the business, among them fewer sick days, less absenteeism in general, and lower overall health care costs. Sue Stoorgard, director of work/life services, captures the tone when she says, "We want everyone working at Eddie Bauer to feel they're working for the best employer in the country."[1]

As we have noted throughout this text, many interrelated activities must be accomplished if a business is going to be healthy and successful. These activities do not occur in isolation from one another. Rather, as our model of the path to a successful business notes, they must mesh together simultaneously if the business is going to achieve its goals in a timely manner. For example, business leaders and managers must know what is going on in the environment. They must know their own current state of internal affairs. They must choose a direction for the business and select appropriate strategies. They must be attuned to customers and provide quality products and services in a timely manner. There are many things to be done and many decisions to be made.

This chapter emphasizes the way the activities of a business fit together. It looks at how businesses are designed and how managers build commitment from the workforce. Thanks to these activities, the business is able to perform in a successful manner. After you read this chapter, you should be able to:

1. Define the concepts of organization design and organization structure.

2. Illustrate the logical way a successful business builds an organization structure.

3. Explain some of the structural concerns encountered in business.

4. Understand some of the ways that businesses are addressing these issues and concerns.

5. Demonstrate the basic dynamics of employee motivation and commitment.

6. Formulate and apply some of the actions managers can take to build greater commitment among employees.

Important decisions are being made every hour of every day by individuals employed throughout any business. Managers hope that these decisions will move the organization where it wants and needs to go. They hope that everything will fit together properly. This process of decisions and choices is quite complicated because a business is really a set of interrelated parts. That means if one part of the business is changed, it will, to some extent, affect all other parts of the business. For example, if funds are low and a decision is made to reduce budgets by 25 percent, this is not simply a finance decision. The decision is financially based, but everyone is affected. Manufacturing may have to cut back on overtime pay and eliminate the third shift. This affects its capacity to fill special custom orders as quickly as it has in the past. Marketing now has to deal with customers differently since it can no longer promise the same deadlines. It is a fundamental property of a business that a change in one part of the business generally affects other parts.

The concepts of structure and commitment are key to the model we introduced in Chapter 1. Only with committed workers who are organized logically can the business achieve success. In this chapter, we consider the way the parts of the business fit together and operate to gain the best performance possible.

Two key performance themes are emphasized. First, we talk about the overall design or layout of the business. These decisions are important because they affect how work activities are arranged to attain high levels of performance. Second, we talk about building commitment within the workforce. While this theme has always been important, it is all the more significant in today's streamlined, downsized businesses.

Motivated work behavior is critical as managers encourage their workers to do more with less. Importantly, the design and commitment themes fit together. For example, no matter how well jobs are designed, without a committed and motivated workforce, performance will fall short of expectations. Similarly, motivated workers may provide high levels of energy and effort and still fail to meet performance goals if their efforts are frustrated by poorly structured tasks. The good news is that it works both ways. Developing exciting new work arrangements and designs can help build commitment and motivation in the workforce. At Motorola, as you see in Profile 14–1, redesign helped build quality and efficiency. It also fostered employee involvement, an important building block of motivation. The message is clear: effective performance depends on both proper design and commitment.

efficiency p. 478>

MOTOROLA

PROFILE 14–1   *Motorola Redesigns and Builds Employee Involvement*

In the early to mid-1980s, Motorola experienced some troubling competitive struggles. The Japanese were dumping pagers and cellular phones in the United States. Not surprisingly, Motorola rapidly lost market share. But over the next decade it staged a dramatic comeback. Today Motorola is a world leader, recognized for its product quality and efficiency of operations. It is perennially listed as one of the most admired businesses in the country.

The turnaround at Motorola was the result of a number of interrelated components, approaches, and changes. One critical aspect was the effort to redesign operations and involve people. For example, the company reduced layers of managerial and supervisory personnel. It gave the remaining managers broader scope, with many more people reporting to each manager than had been. This meant the workers would have to be more involved in decision making—exactly what Motorola wanted.

teams p. 71>
training p. 379>
cycle time p. 349>

Further, the size of each unit was limited to encourage more interaction and teamwork. The redesign brought different departments together. This allowed the company to break functional barriers, which often constrain large businesses. At the same time, teams were established throughout the company. Team members received extensive training. Teams strove to find ways to improve quality and reduce cycle time. Workers were involved, on a daily basis, with a new streamlined business. Their ideas received attention. They could affect the operations of the business. They saw that their actions and decisions played key roles in the company's quest for quality performance. Motorola boldly undertook a progressive approach to redesigning its business. Quality, efficiency, and employee commitment were the byproducts.[2]

Integration and Organization Design

It is the interrelated nature of business that makes the theme of integration so important. The various parts of the business have to be coordinated in some logical manner. **Organization design** deals with how the various parts of the business are coordinated. Organizing and coordinating everything so that the business operates with efficiency and everything that needs to be done gets done is a daunting assignment. This is why businesses develop organization structures.

Organization design
The way the various parts of a business are coordinated.

In small retail stores, such as this bookstore, there is very little formal structure. The owner may also sell books in addition to running the store. Yet, there is still logic in how work is assigned. Is this lack of structure appealing to you, or would you prefer more defined tasks often associated with larger firms?

Organization structure
A framework that prescribes how a business organizes, arranges, and groups the work that needs to be done.

An **organization structure** is a framework that prescribes the way the business organizes, arranges, and groups the work that needs to be done. It is a pattern of how the business will integrate the various activities. Every organization has a structure. In a very small business, the structure may be informal and unwritten.

For example, Jane Long owns and operates Reader's Cove, one of the few remaining independent bookstores in her city. Her husband, Jeb, works at the business on weekends and handles all of the bookkeeping. Jane employs three part-time salespeople who work in the store at various times throughout the week. Although nothing is formalized, Reader's Cove has a structure. Jane makes all purchase decisions. Jeb takes care of billing and payments and prints the paychecks each week. The sales clerks handle all customer matters and provide full service to customers as they shop in the store. Jane and Jeb meet at least once a day to discuss the business, and Jane meets with the salespeople whenever a need arises. As you can see, there is a definition of duties and there is logic to the way the work is arranged.

Certainly, such informality will not work as a business grows larger. At some point, there must be a formal outline of how work will be arranged and integrated. It is this more formal approach to structure and design that we address in this chapter.

Building Organization Structure

Organization structure is developed in order to integrate the operations of the business in a manner that is as orderly and efficient as possible. Organization structure is really a framework for arranging and coordinating work to use resources when and where they are required and to minimize duplication and redundancy of resources.

market research p.344>

Structure should be built logically as the company's leaders consider the jobs that need to be performed and how these jobs must fit together. Suppose that after careful market research, you decide there is a market demand for domestically built high-performance bicycles. You decide to start such a business. You are the president and you call the business Transit Cycles. From your research, you decide to build two models of bicycles—a road bike and a mountain bike. You will design and build the bikes but will produce none of the component materials.

You decide to assemble a group of people who will design the bicycles. Logically, these people will need to work together in the same area of the business, since much of the information and materials they need for their design work will be shared. These design employees will have engineering backgrounds. They must understand the dynamics of existing competitor bikes and design new ones that will be significant improvements. You decide that initially you will need three designers to work on the road bike and three designers to concentrate on the mountain bike. Logically, these six designers need to report to someone who can oversee their work, provide the resources they need, and coordinate their efforts with other areas of the business. Therefore, you hire an experienced bike designer from a rival firm to manage the design process. This manager will report directly to your plant or facilities manager, who will oversee all production work.

Even at this early stage, an organization structure is beginning to take form. Figure 14–1 portrays the organization structure graphically in an *organization chart*. While the chart is very basic, there is a logic to it. Positions and jobs are arranged in a way that seems to make sense in helping the business meet its design needs.

Once the design work is done, the bicycles must be built (manufactured) and assembled. The manufacturing process is quite complex. Metal alloys (which you purchase from a supplier) must be molded and formed into frames that meet the specifications provided by the design engineers. This involves three distinct manufacturing operations. One operation deals exclusively with the frames, another with the handlebars, and another with the wheels. Each of these manufacturing operations employs five workers. These 15 workers are supervised by a manufacturing manager, who makes sure the manufacturing is done properly and manufacturing schedules are met. She also spends a lot of time with the design manager to be sure that the product being built is consistent with what the designers had in mind. Logically, the manufacturing manager also reports to the plant manager. We now have another structural piece, depicted in Figure 14–2.

Finally, once the various component parts are built, the bicycles must be assembled. This operation is done by teams of workers. On most days, there are three assembly teams working. Each assembly team consists of four employees, who perform all of the assembly operations. They attach handlebars to frames, add the wheels and tires, assemble all cable linkages and derailleurs (which you purchase from an Italian

FIGURE 14–1   Partial Organization Chart

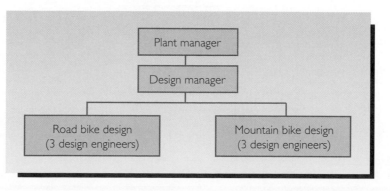

FIGURE 14–2   Partial Organization Chart

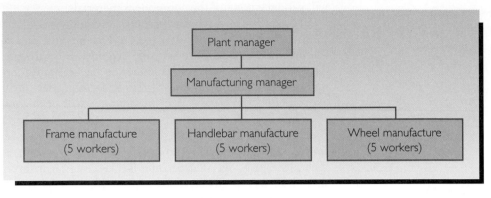

company), and test the final assembled bike to be sure it operates properly. These teams are led by an assembly team manager who checks their progress, coordinates with the manufacturing area to get parts when needed, and helps the teams from time to time. This manager also reports to the plant manager.

Let's take a look at the structure that has developed in our business and talk about what it means. Figure 14–3 shows the structure used to build the bicycles. What does this structure reveal about the business? First, it clearly portrays the lines of authority and responsibility in the business. For example, a worker who manufactures wheels reports to the manufacturing manager, who in turn reports to the plant manager. This line of authority is known as the **chain of command.** Many managers feel strongly that the chain of command must be followed when communication takes place. The chain of command also leads to another concept, span of control. The **span of control** is the number of employees who report to a given manager. This number will vary depending on the skills of the employees, the skills of the manager, and the complexity of the tasks performed.

Chain of command
The line of authority in a business; who reports to whom.

Span of control
The number of employees who report to a given manager.

FIGURE 14–3   Partial Organization Chart

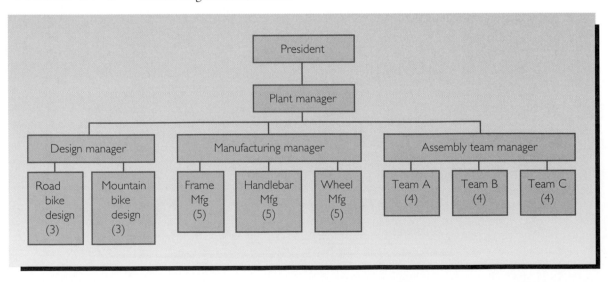

Let's look a bit more deeply at the structure. It also shows how your business divides up the overall work to be done. There are some important points to be made here. Obviously, you do not expect all of your workers to do everything. Frame manufacturers do not have the background and expertise to do design work. Further, design engineers should focus on their specific areas and not dabble in unrelated tasks. To accomplish this end, employees are placed in specific jobs and are asked to perform only those jobs. This process is known as **specialization.** You can see by looking at the organization chart the degree of specialization that exists in Transit Cycles.

The chart also shows that specialized jobs are grouped together in a way that seems to make sense. Design jobs are grouped together, manufacturing jobs are grouped together, and assembly jobs are grouped together. This process of grouping similar jobs is known as **departmentalization.** There are a number of ways that a business can group jobs. Our sample business has departmentalized according to *function.*

Some businesses departmentalize based on the *markets or customers served.* For example, most banks are organized into commercial divisions and consumer divisions. This assumes the needs of commercial markets are different from the needs of everyday consumers. This customer-based departmentalization allows more careful attention to the unique demands of both.

An increasingly popular approach, particularly with global businesses, is to departmentalize into *geographic divisions.* For example, a business with operations in South America, Europe, and Asia may have a separate division for each. Again, the assumption is that these unique geographic areas need more discretion in decision making. This should enable the units to be more responsive to customers than could a large business operating from a single headquarters in another country.

In most situations, where these divisional approaches are being used, certain activities are still *centralized* (Chapter 3). In other words, some activities are done by the firm's headquarters for all divisions rather than duplicated by each division. This is usually the case for expensive services such as computing and financing.

The structure offers further revelations. Even in this relatively small business, there are already four levels of employees. You are the president at the top level. At the next level is the plant manager. The third level is composed of the various area managers from design, manufacturing, and assembly. The fourth level is made up of the workers in each area. In Transit Cycles, three levels of hierarchy are management. The issue of hierarchy is very important. It is easy for businesses to add more and more levels of hierarchy, but this may lead to problems, some of which are discussed in the next section.

It may have occurred to you that the structure in Figure 14–3 is incomplete. Significant areas of the business have been left out. We have included only the activities or jobs that are directly involved in making the bicycles, but a number of additional activities must be performed in order for our business to operate. For instance, some people need to be hired to purchase the raw materials and component parts needed to build the bicycles. These purchasing people will staff the purchasing department, finding the best suppliers, negotiating contracts with them, and seeing that all materials are delivered when needed.

In addition, some people have to deal with various retail outlets, encourage retailers to carry your bicycles, and ship the bikes to them. These people are grouped in the marketing department. Some people are needed to track your finances, extend terms of purchase with retailers, be sure payments are received, and handle the payroll. These people are grouped in the accounting area. People in the human resources department will be responsible for hiring and training employees. You also need people in the information systems department to provide information services and support for all areas of the business.

Specialization
Placing employees in specific jobs and asking them to perform only those jobs.

Departmentalization
Grouping similar jobs together in any of several ways (among them function, markets, or geography).

retailers p. 282>

human resources p. 374>

Line activities
The areas of a business that are directly involved in making or adding value to a product.

Staff activities
The areas of a business that support what the line areas are doing.

Now a more expanded and complete business organization has been defined. This organization structure is presented in Figure 14–4. The areas of the business that are directly involved in making or adding value to the product—areas like design, manufacturing, and assembly—are known as **line activities.** Areas that support what these line areas are doing are known as **staff activities.** Accounting, human resources, purchasing, marketing, and information services are typical staff departments.

The Logic of Structure

As the structure of Transit Cycles unfolded, you began to see the complexity involved. Imagine the complexity of a large business that employs thousands of people and provides a diverse assortment of products or services. Yet the structure of all businesses exists to provide order and efficiency. This cannot be overemphasized. The structure outlines an orderly flow of activities and interactions that keep the business moving toward its goals. The structure is present to avoid the chaos of employees doing their own thing, without any sense of whether it contributes overall value for the business and its customers. The structure should arrange activities and interactions so that the business is operating in the most efficient manner possible. Unnecessary duplication should be avoided. Clear reporting and communication will ensure that no decision maker is taken by surprise. Businesses realize that structure, control, and order are essential in today's tough and demanding business climate.

business culture
p. 114>

BRINKER
INTERNATIONAL.

Consider the need for structure at a large company like Brinker International. Its restaurants are known for establishing a business culture where employees feel comfortable enough to communicate freely. They are encouraged to provide input, and that input is given serious consideration. Brinker wants people to feel excited about their work. It wants them to be entrepreneurial, always looking for ways to serve the customers better. Keeping this spirit and still effectively managing a business with thousands of employees requires a carefully defined structure. In fact, Brinker International, like all successful businesses, puts considerable thought into how the parts of the business should fit together. For example, the employees at each restaurant report to a restaurant manager. The restaurant managers, in turn, report to regional managers, who report to company vice presidents. As Norman Brinker comments, "A precise and logical chain of command gave us a structure that allowed for an orderly and efficient decision-making process."[3]

FIGURE 14–4   Organization Chart for Transit Cycles

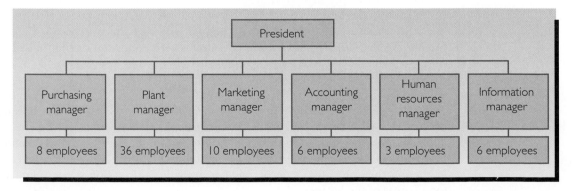

Southwest Airlines has a typical organization structure. Herb Kelleher is the president, chair, and CEO. Three executive vice presidents report to him. A total of 21 vice presidents cover areas such as schedule planning, in-flight service, flight operations, ground operations, and marketing and sales.[4]

Developing Your Critical Thinking Skills

1. Some very small businesses pride themselves on having a very informal structure, with few designated links between activities. Do you think such a loose structure is good for a small business? Why or why not?

2. As the business grows, structure becomes more critical. At what size do you think a business needs to begin formalizing its structure?

3. The next time you visit a fast-food restaurant, observe the activities that are occurring. Sketch the structure that seems to exist. What could you change in the structure to help the restaurant improve efficiency and customer service?

**customer service
p. 340>**

Structural Concerns

Companies have long been structured in a hierarchical, pyramidal shape. As we have seen, this is fine as long as the structure assures order and efficiency and helps the business meet its goals of serving customers and meeting performance objectives. But problems can arise when structures become too complex.

Some large companies have numerous levels of management between the president and the lowest-level nonmanagerial workers. In recent years, some critics argue, these traditional structures have become increasingly unworkable. Led by global competitive pressures and the need for efficiency, companies are trying to do two things—reduce costs and get closer to their customers. They found they could do both by restructuring. The restructuring has gone by many names: downsizing, rightsizing, reengineering, redesigning, rethinking, and a host of other synonyms. While each is slightly different in concept, all are designed to restructure the people and positions in businesses and reconsider relationships both within a company and between the company and its customers.

reengineering, 421>

The result of many restructurings has been a much flatter organization. That means that some of the intermediate levels of management have been eliminated, reducing the number of levels separating top management from customers. At the same time, authority to make decisions has been pushed down in the organization. Now top management must trust lower-level managers and nonmanagerial workers to make decisions that are in the best interest of both the customer and the organization. This is the employee empowerment that we have mentioned throughout the text.

**top management
p. 65>**

Thus far, we have outlined a rather simple organization structure and introduced some fundamental terms and concepts. With this background, we are ready to address some of the structural issues that contemporary businesses are facing.

**customer sensitivity
p. 493>**

True, structure must provide order and efficiency to the complex set of activities the business needs to perform. Yet structure must do more. First, it should encourage integration across departments. Second, it should assure customer sensitivity and

innovation p. 522>
creativity p. 522>

Suboptimization

A situation where one department of a business, acting in its own self-interest, hurts or inhibits the performance of another department, leading to less effective outcomes for the business overall.

timely response. Third, it should foster employee innovation and creativity. Failing to meet these needs is extremely dangerous in today's competitive environment.

Unfortunately, some businesses do ignore this advice. Traditionally, most major businesses in this country have had large, functionally oriented departments that may have hundreds of people in them. These departments are often minibusinesses in and of themselves. While there is not necessarily anything wrong with this structure, it can lead to problems. One common problem occurs when the various departments begin to view themselves as the heart and soul of the business rather than as pieces in the larger organizational puzzle. Employees' loyalty becomes tied to their own department. Department success becomes more important than the success of the business as a whole. Employees begin to make decisions that benefit their department but hurt other departments, which can lead to less effective outcomes for the whole business.

For example, the marketing department of a large business wants to sell as many products as it possibly can. In their zeal to make sales, their reps promise faster delivery than any competitor. Unfortunately, they don't check with the manufacturing people to see if the products can be made within the stringent deadlines. Now the production department is in a bind. Its people work overtime and feel the strain of next-to-impossible deadlines. The accident rate goes up. Quality defects rise. Production runs have to be reworked. Customers become frustrated. In the end, the business may lose an important customer. The situation described here is known as suboptimization. **Suboptimization** occurs when one department, acting in its own self-interest, hurts or inhibits the performance of another department and leads to less effective outcomes for the business overall. When the business becomes too large and extensively departmentalized, the critical holistic focus may be lost and the risk of suboptimization increases.

Another problem is that as businesses grow large, they often add levels of hierarchy, most of them management. Policy and strategy makers become further and further removed from the people who are in direct contact with customers and who are developing and making the products of the business. Control becomes an issue. Upper managers frequently develop rules and procedures to tell employees exactly what they are to do in various situations. The organization now has many levels of hierarchy, a formal set of rules and procedures, and considerable distance between the "thinkers" and the "doers." This type of organization is generally labeled a bureaucracy.

Numerous problems may be present in a bureaucracy. First, as we noted, large, complex organizations may lose touch with their customers. This threatens the essential business outcome of customer sensitivity.

Second, bureaucracies are often slow to change and slow to innovate. With so many layers to move through, communication and decision making simply take a great deal of time. Since quick responses are not part of this organizational package, the business outcome of timeliness is often sacrificed.

Third, bureaucracies are rather inflexible. Certain areas perform certain functions and follow specified procedures. While such rigidity helps ensure consistency and control, it also inhibits quick and flexible responses to changing consumer demands. In today's environment, consumers have little patience and often fleeting brand loyalty. The inflexible business often loses in a competitive marketplace.

Fourth, bureaucracies may be quite frustrating for skilled employees. Rather than fully utilizing their talents, the bureaucratic organization often places these people in specialized jobs with limited variety and autonomy. Instead of encouraging employee commitment, this leads to job dissatisfaction and frustration, especially for highly talented professional employees.

Teams provide many benefits such as motivation, increased communication, and the ability to respond more quickly to customer needs. Some teams are cross-functional. Some are self-directed. Have you worked in a team environment? What was your experience?

Solutions to Structural Concerns

Companies that are concerned about reaction time and employee utilization are exploring a number of solutions. Teams, business units, reengineering, strategic right-sizing, outsourcing, empowerment, project approaches, matrix approaches, virtual organizations, and strategic alliances are being introduced into companies today with varying degrees of success.

outsourcing p. 385>

strategic alliance
p. 180>

Teams

One of the most significant changes in the restructuring era has been the use of teams. Prior to 1990, teams were not extensively used in businesses except for special projects or task forces designed to solve some specific problem. But recently teams have become a major way to help make a business more competitive. This enhanced competitiveness occurs for a number of reasons:

motivation p. 426>

1. Teams are more responsive than hierarchies.
2. Teams' diverse inputs lead to creative decisions.
3. Teams increase members' motivation and commitment.
4. Teams flatten hierarchies, saving time and money.

Teams can break away from some of the limitations and restrictions of the traditional hierarchy. They are much more responsive than the traditional hierarchical structure. In fact, cross-functional teams may be formed around product innovations or new customer needs. A **cross-functional team** may consist of individuals from marketing, production, finance, product development, and human resources who work collectively to bring about the needed change.

Cross-functional team
A group of workers from different departments who work collectively to bring about a needed change.

A *participatory team* addresses an issue or problem and recommends solutions to the appropriate manager. This manager then decides whether and to what extent to use the team's ideas.

Self-directed work teams are the most progressive and extensive use of the team concept. They have changed the face of production activities at companies like Ford.

Self-directed work team

A group of workers given broad responsibility for carrying out tasks on its own.

Self-directed work teams are given broad responsibility for carrying out tasks or jobs on their own. The team typically has the freedom to organize its tasks, perform operations, handle problems that arise, and perform quality assurance checks. Often the team is allowed to make decisions that used to be left up to a supervisor. Accordingly, self-directed teams have permitted businesses to downsize by eliminating some supervisory positions.

Teams of all kinds get input from a variety of people with different skills and different perspectives. This variety often leads to differences of opinion and conflict. Yet as the team discusses the issues, addresses the conflict, and works toward an acceptable consensus, it often finds new ideas and approaches to old problems. If the team works well, it can be a vehicle for making decisions that foster creativity and innovation.

Importantly, teams often allow members more involvement and input, with broader decision-making prerogatives than they have traditionally experienced. Many members find their team activities challenging and motivational. They may feel their unique talents and skills are being better utilized. This may lead to a greater sense of commitment and more interest in their jobs.

Teams are an excellent way to flatten the hierarchy. They are often given the freedom to manage their own activities, so traditional supervisors may not be needed. This not only cuts costs and improves efficiency, but gives workers a greater sense that their decisions are important. Sometimes team results are staggering. Consider the case at Fiat, Italy's largest company. The automaker experienced its worst-ever loss in 1993, but today the company has reversed its slide and has bright prospects for the future. As part of this turnaround, Fiat reorganized, slashing layers between plant managers and workers. It also introduced teams. In fact, the company now has a series of 31 independent teams of workers and engineers. These teams, ranging in size from 31 to 100 people, oversee the entire car assembly from start to finish. As a result, Fiat has cut the time it takes to get new models to market by 40 percent. Revenues are growing and the business is again experiencing healthy profits.[5]

Similar results are reported by other businesses. Cummins Engine used teams comprised of shop workers, foremen, and design engineers to develop new operating practices and a new production floor layout. The innovations were so impressive that the number of assembly hours needed to build an engine was cut by over 25 percent. Goodyear Tire's radial tire plant in Lawton, Oklahoma, has been organized into a series of work teams. The plant produces twice as many tires per day as do comparable facilities and does so with 35 percent fewer managers.[6]

Business Units

There is a growing tendency, particularly among very large businesses, to reorganize their overall operations into business units. For many businesses, this represents a significant change in the way they group their activities. **Business units** are unique product or market groupings that are treated as self-contained businesses. Typically, this means that each business unit has its own performance goals. Accordingly, each business unit can focus careful attention on its products and its customers. This type of arrangement gives the overall business more flexibility and helps assure sensitivity to customers. Look at the Motorola example in Table 14–1. Each of Motorola's seven business units is involved in a different sector of the company's business.

Business unit

A unique product or market grouping that is treated as a self-contained business.

Caterpillar has also organized its company into business units based on the products produced, with areas such as the Track-Type Tractor Division, the Engine Division, and the Industrial Products Division. General Motors years ago established

TABLE 14–1   Business Units at Motorola

Automotive, Energy & Components Sector

Cellular Networks and Space Sector

Cellular Subscriber Sector

Land Mobile Products Sector

Motorola Computer Group

Messaging, Information & Media Sector

Semiconductor Products Sector

SOURCE: Motorola website, http://www.mot.com/General/units/html, (accessed September 6, 1997).

separate units of the company that focused on its various product lines, such as the Pontiac Division, Chevrolet Division, GMC Trucks Division, and Cadillac Division.

Note that in both examples, the various units are given considerable autonomy and are allowed to make decisions on their own. This discretion allows each unit to stay closely focused on its customers and respond to changing needs in a timely manner. Indeed, one of the strengths of the business unit approach is that it helps give a very large business more of a small business feel. The financial and other resource advantages of being big are retained. However, each unit can be creative and responsive. Further, each self-contained unit is less constrained by the conflicting demands of competing departments of large and diverse businesses. Remember that the idea of staying close to the customer is very important here.

Reengineering

Reengineering
A process whereby a business takes a critical look at itself and changes its design and operations in an effort to cut inefficiencies and focus on quality and customers.

In recent years, many businesses have engaged in a self-improvement process known as reengineering, a term popularized by management consulting gurus Michael Hammer and James Champy.[7] **Reengineering** occurs when the business takes a critical look at itself and changes its design and operations in an effort to cut inefficiencies and become more focused on quality and customers. This definition is broad and may encompass a number of activities.

The key to understanding reengineering is to realize that it typically requires a major rethinking about how the business operates. This often produces a radical redesign and other sweeping organizational changes. Reengineering begins with a tough question: "What does the business need to do to create value?" It then focuses on the tough changes that are necessary. Often it has structural redesign implications.

Strategic Rightsizing

Strategic rightsizing
Eliminating functions and positions that are not critical to a firm's strategic success.

In Chapter 13 we talked about the tendency of many businesses to downsize. Strategic rightsizing results in a downsized business, but the approach is more guided and logical than across-the-board cuts. **Strategic rightsizing** occurs when a business eliminates functions and positions that are not critical to its strategic success. First, managers determine the strategic initiatives they wish to pursue. People and positions that are essential to those initiatives are retained, and the nonessential people and positions are considered for elimination. Rightsizing reduces the number of employees, which if done strategically should cut costs while improving efficiency. Structurally, it pares down and reduces the complexity of the structure.

The magnitude of organizational downsizing or rightsizing in recent years has been staggering. In the early to mid-1990s, many thousands of people in the United States were laid off their jobs. Companies like IBM, AT&T, General Motors, and Sears announced downsizings in excess of 50,000 workers each![8] In recent years, an interesting pattern has emerged. While many medium-size and large companies are laying off workers, they are also hiring new ones.[9] This is due to their attempts to rightsize, or get skilled people into the growing areas of the business while cutting back on the dwindling areas.

Outsourcing

The concept of outsourcing was also discussed in Chapter 13. In outsourcing, the business relies on outside specialists to perform functions (jobs or even whole operations) that previously were done in-house. Outsourcing reduces the number of employees the business needs and allows it to remove areas of its structure. This lets it concentrate on what it does best. Generally, cost is the driving force behind outsourcing. The company finds outside businesses that can handle certain activities and processes cheaper than they can be done internally.

Empowerment

Empowerment
Giving employees more responsibility and discretion in decision making.

Another concept in structuring organizations is **empowerment,** or giving employees more responsibility and decision-making discretion. This approach has some important structural implications. Many businesses, particularly large, complex bureaucracies, are highly centralized, as we mentioned in Chapter 3. This means that most of the major decisions are made in higher levels of the business. The opposite of this is a decentralized business, where decision making is increasingly placed in the hands of those at lower levels. Many business leaders today are shifting from a belief in centralization toward an acceptance of decentralization. Empowerment is part of this movement.

A business that decentralizes drives decision-making responsibility deeper in the organization. It delegates more authority to employees and places a broader range of responsibilities in their hands. A business with empowered employees doesn't need as many levels of management. In fact, entire layers of the hierarchy may be eliminated. As the business empowers its people, eliminates layers of management, and streamlines its structure, it addresses many of the concerns we've been discussing.

As you can see, a company's reengineering efforts can produce a more responsive structure that can lead to customer sensitivity, timely response, innovation and creativity, and employee utilization and commitment. Ultimately, the business believes that these outcomes will improve its financial performance.

Project and Matrix Approaches

One of corporate America's success stories was IBM's pioneering of the personal computer in the early 1980s, a story with an important message about organization structure. IBM, as a large business, was organized in a rather traditional functional manner.

In companies such as this computer repair firm, empowering the employees to make decisions without checking with supervisors allows them to interact closely with the customer to find solutions to problems. This speeds service and pleases customers. Can you think of other businesses where empowering employees may help improve customer service?

There were many departments and their structure was complex. Creating new ideas and bringing them to the market in a timely manner was often difficult. A new idea could get lost for years in the structure. Even worse, it could become so politically watered down that by the time it passed through all levels and departments, real novelty was gone. IBM executives, especially CEO John Opel, realized this, so they sought to break the rigidity of the existing structure. They established Project Chess and charged it with developing a new low-cost PC.[10]

Here's the way it worked. Project Chess was headed by a project manager, who was responsible for completing the design. Skilled workers from various functional areas of the business were pulled out of their usual work areas and brought together to work as members of the project team. For example, hardware experts, software experts, design engineers, and manufacturing representatives all came together to work on the PC project. The project manager reported directly to CEO Opel. In essence, the project team functioned as a separate area of the business. It had its own budget. It was removed from much of the complexity and politics of the business. The team's focus was on completing the project—and it succeeded.

budget p. 402>

This example shows a novel approach to structure known as the project organization. The **project organization** is a structural approach that uses teams drawn from various areas of the business to accomplish high-profile tasks. What prompts this structural approach? Usually two concerns are at work. First, when an important, high-visibility project needs to be completed in a limited time, business leaders question whether the existing structure will be able to meet the deadlines. This issue is very important in fast-paced industries where being first to market a product is critical to competitive success. Second, a business may turn to the project structure when it wants innovation and creativity and fears the existing structure is hostile to these qualities. In a departmental structure, people tend to be concerned about protecting their turf and are reluctant to venture too far from the accepted approaches. Bringing people together as members of special projects teams dispels these fears and encourages innovation.

Project organization
A structural approach that uses teams drawn from various areas of the business to accomplish high-profile tasks.

For the project form of business to work, certain factors must be present. First, the business must be willing to commit people and resources to the project for a certain period of time. Second, skilled people from various areas of the business who can work together must be found. Third, the project manager has to have special management skills to deal with people from many different areas and keep the project on target. Finally, and perhaps most significantly, the project team has to be given enough independence and discretion so it can take some risks and be innovative. This usually means the project must be important enough to have solid backing from key leaders in the company.

If the logic of this project approach makes sense, the next extension will be easy to see. Today, many businesses are turning toward the matrix approach, which uses the project idea but takes it a bit further. Businesses in rapidly changing fields need to have a number of projects going on at the same time. This is what the matrix tries to do. The **matrix organization** combines the functional structure with the project structure.

In the matrix structure, people are hired and assigned to a functional area of the business and given assignments to work on. Yet they are moved into special projects when their skills are needed. Thus, an employee contributes to both the functional area and the project. In fact, employees may contribute their skills and perspectives to several high-profile activities at once. The business gains the advantages of a project approach, plus an additional benefit: it is using workers in a highly flexible and efficient manner. Employees often feel good about this too. They enjoy being challenged, and the projects are often exciting. Many businesses in high-technology fields use the matrix approach, among them General Electric, Texas Instruments, Boeing, and Dow Chemical.[11]

Matrix organization
A structural approach that combines the project structure with the functional structure.

Virtual organization
A business that performs a core set of activities and outsources everything else.

distinctive competence
p. 313>

The Virtual Organization

One of the newest structural models is the **virtual organization,** which exists when the business maintains a core set of activities that it does particularly well and outsources everything else.[12] The business concentrates on those areas where it possesses a true distinctive competence. It performs these activities and functions because it is particularly good at them. For example, the business may be very good at assembly work and able to perform assembly operations in an efficient, low-cost way while adding quality and precision. This, then, is where the business focuses its internal efforts and resources. All other activities necessary to operate are contracted out to others. Perhaps the business outsources the manufacture of certain items. Perhaps it develops alliances with other businesses to get the parts it needs. Perhaps it hires contract workers to take care of the information systems and advertising work that must be done.

The advantages to the virtual organization are that the company capitalizes on efficiency and flexibility. It controls costs by getting others to perform where it is not particularly strong. Of course, contracts can be reviewed and modified regularly. The business makes only limited investments in fixed assets, so its options are open and it can change readily. Many businesses are using this philosophy today.

Strategic Alliances

An increasingly popular approach that is consistent with the virtual organization concept is the use of strategic alliances. As we discussed in Chapters 7 and 11, a strategic alliance exists when two (or more) businesses agree to work together to accomplish some task or project. Each business contributes in areas where it is uniquely qualified or competent and relies on others in the alliance to contribute in their areas of strength. This allows businesses to share costs and therefore risks. It also allows all involved to move forward in a highly efficient manner. Obviously, businesses choose to ally with one another when their capabilities complement each other. This works only when each partner brings valued strengths and advantages to the deal and trusts the other participants to do their part.

The Structural Challenge

Managers should always be open to changing existing structures. Indeed, such change may be quite positive. Since business conditions and internal capabilities are always changing, logically, structure must change to meet new business realities. This is a key to successful integration today. Organization structure should be viewed as a tool, not as a limitation. In other words, an existing structure should not stand in the way of what the business needs to do strategically and competitively. A business should first determine its competitive and strategic initiatives and goals. Then it should modify the structure as needed to help meet those initiatives and goals. This focus on structural flexibility will probably be a hallmark of the 21st century.

Developing Your Critical Thinking Skills

1. Why is it sometimes difficult for managers and leaders to break from their established organization structures and try some of the structural ideas we have discussed in this section?

2. If you were an employee of a large organization, what would you be thinking if you had just survived a major rightsizing by the business?

3. Would you like to work in a project or matrix environment? Why or why not?

Building Employee Commitment

As we saw in the previous section, proper design and structure are part of the equation for business success. A creative structure provides a framework that can facilitate desired performance. But it lives up to its potential only when committed and motivated employees are added to the equation.

To accomplish its objectives as quickly and efficiently as possible, a business needs the right people to work within the structure. These people must be both talented and committed. In Chapter 13, we discussed the acquisition of resources. We noted that businesses must hire people who have the skills and expertise to perform necessary competitive tasks. Further, the business must invest in continually educating and training these workers so their skills remain fine-tuned and relevant. To fall short in either acquiring skilled people or supporting the development of their talents is a formula for long-run problems.

However, talent alone is not enough. Somehow that talent has to be energized and committed in order to achieve its full potential. In many ways, this is the most difficult job a manager faces. There is no pat formula. There is no algorithm that always yields a predictable outcome. Each employee is unique. The process of working with people and gaining their commitment to give their all for the business is a perplexing and inexact task.

Understanding Motivation

Motivation

A person's willingness to work hard and expend great effort for the firm.

Gaining commitment is really an issue of **motivation,** an individual's willingness to work hard and expend high levels of effort for the business. Motivation comes from inside. People are usually willing to work hard when they expect to benefit by doing so. In other words, people will expend effort when that effort helps them meet some personal need.

In a most basic sense, every action we take is done to meet some need, whether a very short-run need (such as eating when we are hungry) or a longer-term interest (such as performing well in hopes of getting a bonus).

One of the key theories regarding needs satisfaction was developed over 50 years ago by Abraham Maslow. These needs and the ways a business might respond to meet them are summarized in Figure 14–5.[13] Maslow suggested that individuals have five levels of needs. Each level after the first does not become operative until the preceding need has been essentially satisfied. Maslow's five needs are physiological needs, safety or security needs, social needs, esteem needs, and the need for self-actualization. Thus, an individual who is out of work and has no money for food and shelter will focus on the lower two needs, physiological and safety/security. That person will not be interested in status or self-fulfillment. A person who is financially secure may be far more interested in making some contribution to society or gaining nonfinancial rewards like a plaque that reads, "top sales person." Managers can motivate workers better if they understand where the workers are on the needs hierarchy.

Another useful theory of motivation is Frederick Herzberg's two-factor theory, outlined in Table 14–2 on page 428. Herzberg tried to figure out what really motivated people in work situations. He found that one category of factors, known as hygiene factors, will lead to employee dissatisfaction if they are not present in the workplace. However, the increased presence of the hygiene factors will generally not motivate employees to higher levels of satisfaction and performance. Hygiene factors have to do with the context or the environment in which the job is carried out.

On the other hand, Herzberg identified another set of factors that he called motivators, among them recognition and responsibility. These factors relate to the content of the job. Providing employees with more of these motivators should lead to satisfaction and generate higher levels of performance.

Herzberg's ideas are quite popular. Many experts contend that businesses often spend a lot of money and energy attending to hygiene factors, such as company policies and salary. But they don't pay enough attention to the motivators. They should be creating a work environment that emphasizes the nature of the work itself. When employees receive motivators—such as a sense of achievement, responsibility, and recognition—from their work, they feel satisfaction and are motivated to do even better and keep the positive feedback coming. Therefore managers must be sure that hygiene factors are adequate, but they should concentrate on motivators to attain high commitment from their people.[14]

No manager can command someone to be motivated. All a manager can do is provide conditions that will encourage or lead people to be motivated. A manager can create a climate and provide rewards so workers believe that they will be better off by committing themselves to organizational tasks. In other words, managers create conditions where employees believe they can meet their personal needs by undertaking

FIGURE 14-5   Maslow's Needs Hierarchy

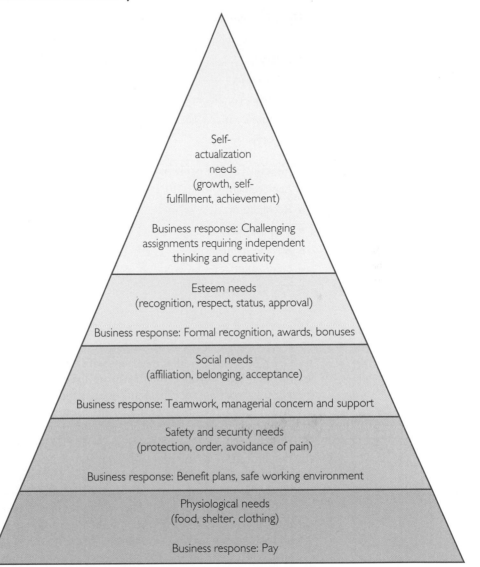

work activities. To understand this process of motivation, let's look at the various decision points that can affect motivation.

Susan Moore works in the computing services department of a large manufacturing business. Susan has excellent technical and excellent interpersonal skills. Her job is basically one of troubleshooting. She handles systems problems for users throughout the company. It is a challenging and ever-changing set of assignments. She is on call 24 hours a day. Generally, she likes her job and is quite good at it. Recently the company installed an advanced computer network for interacting with suppliers and dealers. Clearly, people throughout the business can benefit from the program if they can understand how to access and fully use the program.

Toward this end, the business has plans for Susan. Her boss, Lawanda White, wants her to coordinate and be lead trainer in the software applications. This will

Table 14–2   Herzberg's Two-Factor Theory

Hygiene Factors (context of the job)

- Company policies
- Salary
- Job security
- Working conditions
- Relations with co-workers
- Supervisory style

Motivator Factors (content of the job)

- Achievement
- Recognition
- Responsibility
- Advancement
- Opportunities for growth
- The work itself

involve a series of two-day meetings with small groups of people within the business, as well as a series of meetings with both suppliers and dealers. Given the number of people involved, Susan will spend the next six months in this coordinating and training job. Susan's boss has just met with Susan to outline the new six-month project. Will Susan be motivated? Will she be willing to exert high levels of effort on this project? Since she is temporarily moving from work that she enjoyed and did well, will she be committed to the new job activities?

The answer is, it depends. Let's assume that Lawanda has clearly outlined the demands of the new project and the specific job that Susan is to do. Therefore, Susan is clear about what is expected of her in this new job. Now she is probably running through some questions in her mind. First, she is probably trying to figure out whether she can meet the expectations of the job. She is assessing whether her efforts can lead to the successful performance of the job requirements. If Susan feels that the job demands are so heavy and resources so thin that the probability of being successful is low (or maybe even zero), she will no doubt have little willingness or commitment. Why should she, if the task expectations are impossible?

However, if Susan assesses the job expectations and is confident that she can complete the job successfully, she will feel that her probability of success is quite high. She now probably considers a second question. What's in it for her? What rewards are likely for performing the job? These rewards may come in many forms. They may be monetary. Or they may be nonfinancially based, such as the chance to work in a new area, be part of a new team approach, take advantage of a telecommuting work arrangement, be given more freedom in making decisions, or receive a promotion. For example, Lawanda may indicate that if the job in training is successfully completed, Susan will be able to do more training, even including training for top executives in the company's international operations. This means travel to a number of countries and the chance to meet and work with some of the top people in the business. Lawanda even suggests that such visibility will probably help Susan advance.

At this point, Susan will mentally evaluate those rewards and decide how much value they hold for her. The potential rewards attached to this job include challenging work, interesting people, the chance to travel, visibility, and activity possibly leading to promotion. Will Susan value these rewards? That really depends on her unique needs and whether she feels these outcomes will help fulfill the personal needs that are critical to her. For example, it is possible that Susan does not really want to travel, the thought of meeting corporate leaders strikes fear in her heart, and she does not desire a promotion because of the added responsibility and stress. While these rewards may excite some people, they may not be what Susan is looking for. Logically, she may assign a relatively low value to them. On the other hand, Susan may be an ambitious and energetic woman who enjoys travel and meeting new people. She wants to get ahead and rise in the business. So the promotion opportunity is exactly what she has been hoping for. She places high value on these rewards because they are consistent with her needs and wishes.

There is a third concern affecting Susan's motivation: her belief that management will actually deliver the promised rewards. What is the likelihood that successful performance will lead to the desired reward? This decision is critical. Susan may truly want the promotion. It may be of quite high value to her and therefore potentially motivational. However, if Susan thinks management is unlikely to provide the promotion, her motivation will wane. There may be a number of reasons for this. Perhaps the company has frozen all promotions. Perhaps Lawanda has repeatedly made such promises and then failed to deliver. If Susan suspects the promise of rewards is false, they won't motivate her.

You see how three elements interact to affect the presence and level of Susan's motivation. First is her perception of the likelihood that she can successfully accomplish the required tasks. Second is the value she places on the rewards that are being offered. Third is her perception of the likelihood she will actually receive the rewards if she does complete the tasks. This approach is consistent with the expectancy theory of motivation, which is probably the most popular approach to motivation today.[15] A simplified model of expectancy theory is shown in Figure 14–6.

The Manager's Role in Motivation

It is important for Susan's manager to be aware of what Susan is experiencing. While her manager certainly cannot impose motivation, she can facilitate it. For example, if Susan's belief that she cannot succeed in the intended tasks is due to misunderstandings, Lawanda can add clarification. If her belief is due to her fear of being overworked or given inadequate resources, her manager can respond. However, the most powerful

FIGURE 14–6   Simplified Model of Expectancy Theory

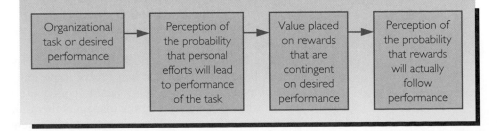

| Organizational task or desired performance | → | Perception of the probability that personal efforts will lead to performance of the task | → | Value placed on rewards that are contingent on desired performance | → | Perception of the probability that rewards will actually follow performance |

Jack Welch, CEO of General Electric, feels that Work-Out sessions—problem solving teams that meet whenever needed—provide the benefit of giving immediate attention to problems and opportunities. What are the advantages and disadvantages of this method of team work? Will it work equally well for large and small companies?

way that managers improve motivation is through the actions they take to build a business culture that promotes employee commitment.

This begins with the assumptions managers make about their employees. Early views of managerial assumptions about employees were popularized by Douglas McGregor.[17] These are known as Theory X and Theory Y assumptions and are outlined in Table 14–3.

Managers who make **Theory X** assumptions believe that workers are naturally lazy, dislike work, shirk responsibility, and will do as little as they can in most work situations. It is not hard to understand the actions of managers who think Theory X assumptions portray their employees accurately. These managers offer workers little autonomy or discretion in their jobs. The resulting culture is boss-centered and control-oriented.

On the other hand, managers who make **Theory Y** assumptions believe that workers can enjoy work. They believe workers desire responsibility and want to accept challenges in their work. Not surprisingly, these managers often provide their employees with a chance to exercise their creativity and to be actively involved in decision making. The resulting culture is more open and involvement-oriented.

Which set of assumptions is correct? There is no doubt that some people are indeed lazy and will do as little as possible. Yet some managers realize that Theory Y assumptions may be more relevant. There are two reasons for this. First, workers often bring important talents and skills to their jobs. To assume that they don't care what happens is probably illogical. Second, astute managers realize that when employees get the opportunity to be involved in meaningful ways, they appreciate it and often rise to the occasion. Making assumptions that are inconsistent with the nature and needs of the workforce can produce frustration, restrict motivation, and threaten a firm's performance potential.

Profile 14–2 describes how General Electric built a special culture of employee involvement. A business culture that helps meet important needs of workers is a key piece in the motivational puzzle. Many factors contribute to a motivational culture, not the least of which is the nature of the managers themselves. So where do we start? How do we figure out how to build a culture of commitment?

Theory X
The belief that workers are naturally lazy, dislike work, shirk responsibility, and will do as little as they can in most work situations.

Theory Y
The belief that workers can enjoy their work, desire responsibility, and want challenges.

TABLE 14-3   Management Assumptions about Employees

Theory X Assumptions
People dislike work and will work as little as possible
People lack ambition and dislike responsibility
People are self-centered
People resist change
People are gullible and not very bright
People by nature are passive and even resistant to organizational needs
People prefer to be led

Theory Y Assumptions
People can enjoy work if the conditions are favorable
People are not by nature passive or resistant to organizational needs
People desire responsibility
People want challenge in their work
People can exercise self-control and self-direction in their work

SOURCE: Douglas M. McGregor, "The Human Side of Enterprise," in Michael T. Matteson and John M. Ivancevich, *Management and Organizational Behavior Classics*, 6th ed. (Burr Ridge, IL: Irwin, 1996), pp. 429–37.

PROFILE 14-2   *Work-Out at GE*

In a recent report to shareholders, Jack Welch, chair and chief executive officer of General Electric, discussed the GE approach to employee involvement. Excerpts from that powerful statement follow.

> The centerpiece of our culture change at GE was one we had to invent ourselves. We called it Work-Out. Work-Out was based on the simple belief that people closest to the work know, more than anyone, how it could be done better. It was this enormous reservoir of untapped knowledge, and insight, that we wanted to draw upon. Across GE today, holding a Work-Out session is as natural an act as coming to work. People of disparate ranks and functions search for a better way, every day, gathering in a room for an hour, or eight, or three days, grappling with a problem or an opportunity, and dealing with it on the spot—producing real change instead of memos and promises of further study. Everyone today has an opportunity to have a voice at GE, and everyone who uses that voice to help improve things is rewarded.

Welch goes on to say the culture created through Work-Out helped "develop a fresh, open, anti-parochial environment, friendly toward the seeking and sharing of new ideas regardless of their source. . . . Ideas around the company began to stand and fall on their merits—rather than on the altitude of their originators."[16]

The outcomes are staggering. People feel needed and important. They know their talents will be put to good use. And GE wins too. It gets fresh and exciting ideas. The company receives an injection of vitality that can be a true competitive edge.

A Culture of Commitment

Remember, commitment comes when workers believe that working for a particular company will somehow meet their needs. Logically, then, an understanding of workers and what they are looking for from their work seems important to building commitment and motivation.

Of course, all workers are different. It is important for managers to know their people and tailor rewards and approaches to their particular circumstances and personalities. Despite this comment, we believe there are generally certain things workers look for, among them fair pay, good benefits, work that is interesting, challenging, and meaningful, growth and development, trust and respect, and a balance between work and family.

Fair Pay

Performance-based pay
Wages that are tied directly to performance.

A common reward for encouraging commitment and motivation is compensation, or the money and fringe benefits that are provided for doing work. In general, workers expect compensation to be adequate, competitive with other businesses, and distributed fairly.

In today's business environment, the emphasis is on **performance-based pay.** That means the pay received should be carefully and directly tied to performance. In some cases, pay is tied to the individual worker's personal performance. For example, at the end of the year, each employee's performance is evaluated against relevant performance measures. Those who perform best get the biggest raises. In other cases, pay is tied to the performance of an employee's team or project group. If the team saves the company money or completes a special project that brings in thousands of dollars of new business, the employees on the team receive some share of the money saved or made. In some cases, pay is tied to the overall performance of the business unit where an employee works, or even to the overall performance of the entire business.

This is the case with Lincoln Electric in Cleveland, Ohio, the world's lowest-cost producer of induction engines. Its pay scheme is unusual. Nonmanagerial workers are paid on a piece-rate basis. That means they get paid for how much they produce. There are no limits or quotas on how much they produce as long as quality is not sacrificed. Piece-rate pay rewards people for their personal effort. In a normal year, about half of a worker's pay comes from this method. However, Lincoln Electric also pays a performance bonus based on the overall profitability of the entire business. If the company makes no profit, the workers don't get a bonus. If the business is highly profitable, they receive big bonuses. Typically workers receive about half of their annual salary from this performance bonus. Workers receive outstanding wages, well above industry standards. What does this pay approach say to the workers? Work hard, work efficiently, cut costs, and profits should flow. When they do, you get more money. Realize the motivational focus of performance-based pay. Better performance, whether at the individual, team, unit, or business level, results in higher pay.

A bold application of the pay-for-performance thinking has surfaced at Levi Strauss, which is known for its innovative, employee-focused approach to business. Levi Strauss told its workers that if the company reaches its financial goals over the next six years (cumulative cash flow of $7.6 billion), all of the company's employees will get a full year's pay as bonus! With 37,500 employees throughout the world, Levi's is probably the "richest and most unusual reward program ever."[18]

In addition to their innovative advertising, Levi Strauss uses a unique long-run incentive plan with its employees. If the company meets its financial goals over the next six years, all employees will get a full year's pay as a bonus! How would that affect your motivation to work? How would it affect your interest in leaving the company?

Adequate Benefits

Compensation really consists of two main areas, benefits and pay. You may not ordinarily think of benefits as part of compensation, but they typically comprise about 40 percent of a worker's compensation package in the United States.[19] Although benefits can cover a range of issues, there are three typical categories. First are "security and health" provisions, such as health insurance coverage and pension plans. Second is "payment for time not worked," including benefits such as paid holidays and vacations. Third are "employee services," such as child care and counseling. Benefits can be quite important and may affect decisions about whether to join or leave a business.

Certain benefits are more relevant for some workers than others. Benefits work best when people have a chance to match them to their specific needs. For example, family health insurance is not relevant for an employee who has neither a spouse nor a child.

Flexible benefits plan
A plan in which workers can select from a menu of benefits the ones they wish to receive.

Some businesses let employees do this matching through a **flexible benefits plan,** under which workers can select from a menu of possible benefits the ones they wish to receive. This approach stands the best chance of assuring the motivational link between the reward (benefits) and the worker's true needs.

Many businesses, such as Southwest Airlines, offer flexible benefits to their workers. At Southwest, employees can buy the benefits that they want, selecting from a menu the ones that meet their needs. Southwest calls its program BenefitsPlus. Employees also have a profit-sharing plan and free travel on Southwest and discounted travel on selected other carriers' routes.[20]

Interesting, Challenging, and Meaningful Work

As important as money can be in motivating workers, most people want work that provides some sense of challenge as well. In fact, many consider challenging and meaningful work even more important than high salary and benefits. Thus, another part of the culture of commitment is the nature of the work itself.[21]

Motivation through challenging work occurs when employees are called on to use their skills and talents. In other words, people want to feel utilized through their work. Many employees feel frustrated when they are slotted into jobs where they have little chance to use the skills they have. You may have experienced this yourself in a summer or part-time job.

Many employees desire some degree of freedom or discretion in their work. They don't want to be tightly controlled, watched over, and constantly told how to do tasks where they have background and knowledge. They want a chance to give input on matters they know something about before final decisions are made. They truly want to have some say. Of course, not only does this make employees feel better, but getting input from skilled people should help the business make better decisions and operate more effectively. Increasingly, skilled and talented employees want to know where the business is headed and where they fit in. This allows them to see that their jobs are important and they make a difference.

In short, workers want interesting, challenging, and meaningful work opportunities. When they get them, they tend to feel better about the work they do. And the work environment tends to energize and motivate them. There are a lot of things companies can do to enhance the levels of interest, challenge, and meaning that employees get from their work. Let's explore just a few of these.

Some companies use participation and employee involvement programs to solicit workers' input on matters that affect them. Others empower workers to make decisions in areas where they have expertise. As we discussed earlier, some businesses empower teams to make decisions. Consider the example of Steelcase, the world's largest manufacturer of office equipment. Work teams are everywhere. Literally hundreds of teams in the various Steelcase plants tap the skills, knowledge, and potential of every employee. Steelcase managers report that "for the first time people feel that they have a say in what's going on." Evidence indicates that the people rise to this challenge and make the right things happen at the company.[22]

Growth and Development

Many businesses demonstrate their commitment to employee growth and development through their support of education and training. This approach makes sense. For the organization, training is really an investment in people to help assure that the business will have the skills and background that it needs. From the employees' point of view, the investment in training helps assure them that they always have cutting-edge skills. This can make them feel needed and important.

MOTOROLA

Companies like FedEx, General Mills, IBM, and Motorola are known for their superb training programs. In Chapter 13 we talked about Motorola's training programs. Because the company operates in an industry where technology changes at a rapid pace, employee skills can quickly become outdated. Motorola counters this obsolescence with its commitment to up-to-date, relevant training and education. Training classes are held regularly throughout the company and thousands of people participate each year. The employees keep their skills focused and current: Motorola gains a workforce with the talents needed to stay on the leading edge of the industry.[23]

Trust and Respect

There are many ways trust and respect for employees can be developed and promoted. Business leaders build trust day in and day out by the way they act. It is important to remember that trust and respect come not from words but from actions. We believe trust and respect occur only when leaders truly "walk the talk."

One of the most powerful action statements regarding trust and respect has to do with empowerment. When a company empowers its workers, it invests high degrees of trust in them to do the work that needs to be done. It depends on them to take proper actions and make proper decisions.

Another way to develop trust and respect is to limit artificial distinctions among people at various levels in the business. Sometimes this is achieved through basic everyday steps. Many companies have reduced or even eliminated privileges for top leaders—for example, big corner offices, reserved parking spots, and executive dining rooms. Many encourage all executives to be on a first-name basis with their people.

nonmanagerial employees p. 70> Some businesses go even further. For instance, Hewitt Associates has no titles on their business cards. A client receiving the CEO's business card would not automatically know that he is not just a team leader somewhere in the organization. Target Stores refers to all nonmanagerial employees as team members and managers as team leaders, and Wal-Mart refers to employees as associates.

Balancing Work and Family

Many workers today are trying to maintain a balance between their work and family (nonwork) lives. Some businesses, however, do much better than others. Although many companies espouse the value of family friendliness, the bottom-line emphasis on profits can hamper the day-to-day implementation of these values. However, a recent *Business Week* survey of the nation's largest businesses named Motorola second in family friendliness. Motorola has built a corporate culture that eases work–family conflicts and consistently meets the approval of Motorola's employees.[24]

There are a number of actions that management can take to help employees reduce the disruptions of work spilling over into the family segment of their lives. In

Chapter 5 we discussed three popular approaches, flextime, telecommuting, and job sharing. Let's take a closer look at their unique advantages.

Flextime is a work arrangement that gives individual employees some discretion to decide when to start and stop their workday. In a typical flextime system, employees are required to work a set number of hours per day (perhaps eight hours) and must be at work during a core period each day, say between 10 AM and 2 PM. Beyond that, they are free to decide when they start and end each workday. For example, a worker may decide to start at 6 AM and leave promptly at 2 PM, having put in an eight hour day.

Think of the advantages. Parents can be home early in the afternoon when their children arrive from school. Other workers, especially those commuting in large urban areas, may choose certain schedules to avoid heavy traffic patterns. Others may simply enjoy the freedom to schedule afternoon activities in the summer.

A second approach is telecommuting. Simply defined, telecommuting is working at a nonbusiness site (usually the home) and using a computer to communicate with the office. (Some employees spend 8 hours a day at the office and work on the home computer another three hours in the evening. That is an example of electronic overtime, not telecommuting.) Telecommuters work at home several days a week and send their work electronically to the business. Most telecommuters spend part of the workweek at the office.

Think of the advantages. Telecommuters have the freedom to schedule work activities to complement other demands on their time. Also, most telecommuters feel they are more productive at home than on the job, probably due to the reduced number of interruptions.

There are some downsides to the telecommuting arrangement. Telecommuters may miss some of the social interaction that goes on at the business. Further, since they are away from the office much of the time, they are out of the mainstream of office events and office politics. This lack of visibility or "face time" may affect their promotability.

Job sharing

A work arrangement in which two or more employees share one job and split all the duties, responsibilities, and compensation of that job.

The third arrangement that can help achieve a work/family balance is **job sharing,** where two or more people split a job and share all its duties, responsibilities, and compensation (both pay and benefits). Normally job sharers split the workweek. For example, one worker does the job on Monday, Wednesday, and Friday, and the other goes to work on Tuesday and Thursday. Consider the advantages to both the employees and the business. Employees now have more flexibility and free time. They can pursue a career without neglecting their families. Employers often find that job sharing allows them to bring talented people into the business who may be reluctant to commit to a full work schedule. Also, each job sharer probably does a bit more than half as much work as one full-time employee. The downside is that no one person has total responsibility for a given set of responsibilities, and coordination can sometimes be onerous.

Building Employee Commitment: Overall Conclusions

We have presented a number of aspects of a culture of commitment, but it is certainly not an exhaustive list. There are as many employee needs and desires as there are employees. Yet we have highlighted some of the more critical needs that workers want their jobs to meet. We can expect these themes to be even more important in the future. Managers must understand these needs and offer work cultures that can meet them if they hope to gain motivation and commitment from their employees.

Developing Your Critical Thinking Skills

1. Herzberg said people are motivated by factors in the content of the job. Why do companies spend so much time and money focusing on hygiene factors if they have little effect on motivation and performance?

2. Of the various rewards and approaches discussed for building employee commitment, which are most important to you personally? Why?

3. Why do you think most managers prefer to have employees on-site rather than as telecommuters?

SUMMARY

1. In virtually every business, important decisions are being made every hour of every working day. The larger the organization, the greater the number of employees making those decisions. The greater the number of decisions, the greater the need for ways to make sure that decisions are coordinated and integrated. Organization design and structure serve that function.

   ■ What is meant by the terms organization design and organization structure?

   Organization design deals with how the various parts of the business are coordinated. Organization structure is a framework that prescribes the way the business organizes, arranges, and groups the work that needs to be done.

2. An organization's structure will change as the organization changes. Small businesses have simple structures, while large businesses have more complex structures. Nevertheless, every business has a structure that provides a common logic—creating order and efficiency within the business.

   ■ What are some of the basic elements of an organization structure?

   An organization chart is the graphic representation of organization structure that shows all employees how work is to be coordinated. Chain of command is the line of authority among employees. Span of control is the number of employees who report to a given manager. Specialization is the placement of employees in specific jobs to which they restrict their work. Departmentalization is the grouping of similar jobs. Hierarchy is the establishment of different levels of employee groupings. Line activities occur in areas of the business that are directly involved in making or adding value to the product (like design, manufacturing, and assembly). Staff activities occur in areas that support the line activities (like accounting, human resources, marketing, and information services).

3. When a business fails to design a good organization structure, problems will arise. Some problems may be unique to that firm, but others occur frequently in the business world.

   ■ What are some of the common structural concerns a business might expect to confront?

   Restructuring is the rearrangement of people, positions, and relationships in order to reduce costs and get closer to the customers. Suboptimization is the result of one department acting in its own self-interest in a way that hurts or inhibits the performance of another department or the whole business. Bureaucracy is the situation where many levels of hierarchy result in a formal set of rules and procedures that can inhibit performance. Flattening the hierarchy reduces the number of levels of management.

4. When a company realizes it has problems with its structure, it should begin its search for a solution by looking at what other companies have done in similar situations.

■ What approaches have been developed for addressing structural concerns?

(1) Teams. Cross-functional teams consist of people from, say, marketing, production, finance, product development, and human resources who work collectively to bring about the needed change. Participatory teams consist of a group of workers who address an issue or problem and recommend solutions to the appropriate manager. Self-directed work teams are given broad responsibility for carrying out tasks or jobs on their own.

(2) Business units. These unique product or market groupings are treated as self-contained businesses.

(3) Reengineering. The business takes a critical look at itself and changes its design and operations in an effort to cut inefficiencies and focus on quality and customers.

(4) Strategic rightsizing. The business eliminates functions and positions that are not critical to its strategic success.

(5) Outsourcing. The business relies on outside specialists to perform functions that previously were done in-house.

(6) Empowerment. The business gives employees more responsibility and decision-making discretion.

(7) Project organization. This structural approach uses teams drawn from various areas of the business to accomplish high-profile tasks.

(8) Matrix organization. This approach combines the functional structure with the project structure.

(9) The virtual organization. The business maintains a core set of activities that it is particularly good at doing and outsources everything else.

(10) Strategic alliances. Two (or more) businesses agree to work together to accomplish some task or project.

5. The best structure in the world won't perform effectively if employees aren't adequately motivated. It is no wonder that most excellent companies point to committed employees as the key to their success.

■ What is meant by commitment and what are its underlying determinants?

Commitment is really a matter of motivation. Motivation refers to an individual's willingness to work hard and expend high levels of effort for the business. People are motivated to work hard when doing so meets some of their needs. A number of motivational theories are available to help managers better understand the motivation process, among them Maslow's needs hierarchy, Herzberg's two-factor theory, and expectancy theory. Managers will do a better job of building commitment among their employees if they understand and use the insights of these theories.

6. In addition to understanding motivation theories, managers must make certain assumptions and take actions to create an environment that encourages motivated employees.

■ What can managers do to build a culture of commitment?

At the most general level, managers make Theory X or Theory Y assumptions about their employees. Theory X assumes that workers are naturally lazy and cannot be trusted to assume responsibility. Theory Y assumes that workers desire responsibility and want challenges. Increasingly, companies realize that employees respond to actions that are consistent with Theory Y assumptions. A manager can also improve commitment by developing appropriate policies in the following areas:

(1) Fair pay.
(2) Adequate benefits.
(3) Interesting, challenging, and meaningful work.
(4) Employee growth and development.
(5) Trust and respect.
(6) Work/family balance.

Links to Future Courses

Integration and commitment themes are seen in a number of courses both inside and outside business curricula. Behavioral concepts are studied in psychology and sociology and many management courses. Among the most relevant are the following:

- Principles of psychology
- Social psychology
- Industrial psychology
- Introduction to sociology
- Sociology of group dynamics
- Principles of management
- Organizational behavior
- Strategic management

KEY TERMS

Business units, p. 420
Chain of command, p. 414
Cross-functional team, p. 419
Departmentalization, p. 415
Empowerment, p. 422
Flexible benefits plan, p. 434
Job sharing, p. 436
Line activities, p. 416
Matrix organization, p. 424
Motivation, p. 426
Organization design, p. 411
Organization structure, p. 412
Performance-based pay, p. 432

Project organization, p. 423
Reengineering, p. 421
Self-directed work team, p. 420
Span of control, p. 414
Specialization, p. 415
Staff activities, p. 416
Strategic rightsizing, p. 421
Suboptimization, p. 418
Theory X, p. 430
Theory Y, p. 430
Virtual organization, p. 424

EXERCISES AND APPLICATIONS

1. Think of a job you have had (perhaps a part-time or a summer job). List the times when you really felt excited and satisfied with your work. Be as specific as possible. What does this reveal about motivation and commitment?

2. At that same job, identify someone who seemed to have a low level of motivation and commitment. Given the motivational ideas presented in this chapter, what are some possible reasons for his or her lack of motivation?

3. Survey 10 of your peers, asking them to rank the following job factors in order of importance:

- Recognition
- Feeling of accomplishment
- Job security
- Intellectually stimulating work
- Comfortable working conditions
- Respect from other people
- Opportunity for learning and growth
- Opportunity for promotion
- Challenging work
- Good pay and benefits

Write a two-page paper summarizing and explaining your findings.

4. Find information on companies that have recently downsized. (Start with the Internet, *Business Week*, or *The Wall Street Journal*.) Explain why the companies believed this form of restructuring was necessary. What are the behavioral impacts on those employees who remain after downsizing has occurred?

5. In teams of three to six people, look at the organization structure of your college or university. What does it tell you about power and decision making in the organization? Consider chain of command, span of control, and other basic elements of structure.

6. Go to the website for Southwest Airlines (http://www.iflyswa.com). Consider the benefits listed for its employees. Which of them appeal most to you? Which do you think would interest someone twenty years older than you?

7. Interview at least one small business owner or manager. How is the task of motivating employees different from what it would be for a manager in a large company?

CASE: A COMPUTER LEADER'S SECRETS OF SUCCESS

The computer industry is arguably America's greatest current business success story, so it seems reasonable to look there for insights into the structural and employee commitment factors that lead to business success. Such insights are provided in a fascinating 1997 report on the views of the industry's leaders. The study is called "In the Company of Giants: Candid Conversations with the Visionaries of the Digital World." One of those leaders is Steve Jobs, cofounder of Apple Computer and the leader of Apple's development of the Macintosh computer. Jobs left the company for a number of years, but he recently returned. Here are some of his views:

> No major work that I have been involved in can be done by a single person, or two people, or even three or four. . . .

> After recruiting [the right people] it's then a [matter of] building an environment that makes people feel they are surrounded by equally talented people and that their work is bigger than they are. The feeling that the work will have a tremendous influence and is part of a strong, clear vision. . . .

vision p. 310>

You must offer them the ability to make larger decisions and to be a part of the core company. That involvement is what drives much of this fun....

You'd better have an open communication policy so that people can know just about everything; otherwise they will make important decisions without the right information. That would be really stupid. Generally technology companies are very open.... They are driven by the meritocracy of ideas, not by hierarchy. If there is someone really good four levels down—and you don't listen to them—they'll go somewhere else that will listen to them....

Part of the CEO's job is to cajole and beg and plead and threaten, at times—to do whatever is necessary to get people to see things in a bigger and more profound way than they have, and to do better work than they thought they could do....

You must play those cards carefully. You must be right a lot of the time, because you're messing with people's lives. But that's part of the job. In the end, it's the environment you create, the co-workers, and the work that binds. The Macintosh team, if you talk to most of them—a dozen years since we shipped the product—most will still say that working on the Mac was the most meaningful experience of their lives.

Decision Questions

1. What organizational and motivational principles do Steve Jobs's views seem to illustrate?
2. Does Jobs seem to be a Theory X or a Theory Y manager?
3. Take a close look at the role that work was supposed to play in the life of an employee when Jobs was leading Apple. Could you work for such a company? Do you think most college graduates today would be willing to make the kind of commitment to work that Jobs demanded of his employees?

SOURCE: Rama Dev Jager and Rafael Ortiz, *In the Company of Giants: Candid Conversations with the Visionaries of the Digital World* (New York: McGraw-Hill, 1997), pp. 12–25.

REFERENCES

1. Leslie Faught. "At Eddie Bauer You Can Work and Have a Life." *Workforce*, April 1997, pp. 83–90.

2. Joseph H. Boyett and Henry P. Conn. *Workplace 2000: The Revolution Reshaping American Business.* New York: Plume Books, 1991, pp. 332–5.

3. Norman Brinker and Donald T. Phillips. *On the Brink: The Life and Leadership of Norman Brinker.* Arlington, TX: Summit Publishing, 1996, pp. 172–4.

4. Southwest Airlines, 1996 Annual Report and correspondence with company.

5. John Rossant. "The Man Who's Driving Fiat like a Ferrari." *Business Week*, January 23, 1995, pp. 82–3.

6. Boyett and Conn. *Workplace 2000*, 1992.

7. Michael Hammer and James Champy. *Reengineering the Corporation.* New York: HarperCollins, 1993.

8. John A. Byrne. "The Pain of Downsizing." *Business Week,* May 9, 1994, p. 61.

9. "Downsizing in America: The Revolving Door." *The Economist,* October 26, 1996, p. 79.

10. Glenn R. Carroll and Michael T. Hannan (eds.) *Organizations in Industry: Strategy, Structure and Selection.* New York: Oxford University Press, 1995.

11. Arthur A. Thompson, Jr., and A. J. Strickland III. *Strategic Management: Concepts & Cases,* 9th ed. Burr Ridge, IL: Irwin, 1996, p. 265.

12. B. J. Hodge, William P. Anthony, and Lawrence M. Gales. *Organization Theory: A Strategic Approach,* 5th ed. Upper Saddle River, NJ: Prentice-Hall, 1996, pp. 202–3.

13. Abraham Maslow. "A Theory of Human Motivation." *Psychological Review* 80, 1943, pp. 370–96.

14. For a discussion of the Herzberg theory, see Richard M. Steers, Lyman W. Porter, and Gregory A. Bigley. *Motivation and Leadership at Work,* 6th ed. New York: McGraw-Hill, 1996, pp. 17–8.

15. Victor H. Vroom. *Work and Motivation.* John Wiley & Sons, 1964.

16. General Electric Co. 1995 Annual Report.

17. Douglas McGregor. *The Human Side of Enterprise.* New York: McGraw-Hill, 1960.

18. Joan O'C. Hamilton. "Levi's Pot of Gold." *Business Week,* June 24, 1996, p. 44.

19. George T. Milkovich and Jerry M. Newman. *Compensation,* 5th ed. Burr Ridge, IL: Irwin, 1996, p. 417.

20. Southwest Airlines Benefits Summary (http://www.iflyswa.com/people/benefits/html), accessed July 14, 1997.

21. Frederick Herzberg. "One More Time: How Do You Motivate Employees?" *Harvard Business Review,* September/October 1987.

22. Robert Levering and Milton Moskowitz. *The 100 Best Companies to Work for in America.* New York: Plume, 1993, pp. 328–32.

23. Levering and Moskowitz, pp. 318–22.

24. Keith H. Hammonds, Roy Furchgott, Steve Hamm, and Paul C. Judge. "Work and Family." *Business Week,* September 15, 1997, pp. 96–9.

15

Integrating Quality and Technology in Products and Services

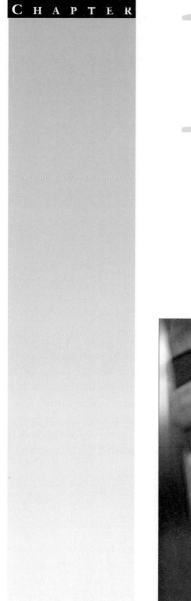

"Quality is Job 1!" "The quality goes in before the name goes on." These phrases may be familiar to you from Ford and Zenith ads. But these are more than cliches or catchy company slogans. They are indicative of the focus on quality that is sweeping the business world. The quality revolution has changed how managers think, just as technology has permeated the business landscape.

Alfonso Cordero came to the United States at age 15 from Mexico City. After finishing high school, Cordero was trained as an engineer by the U.S. Air Force. Later, when working for an electronics firm, he noted how terribly expensive power amplifiers were and vowed to build a cheaper one. He now owns a high-tech company, Powerwave Technologies, Inc., which makes power amplifiers for cellular phones. The power amplifiers boost phone signals and extend the talking range of cell phones. Most of Powerwave's earnings come from South Korea, one of the first countries to implement a nationwide digital cell-phone system. Powerwave has 80 percent of the Korean market. Analysts predict 1997 earnings will reach $12 million, up 58 percent over 1996. Powerwave has built its success by improving cell-phone technology to better meet customer needs.

Technology enhances the transfer of information and the production of products and services. The rapidity of technological change boggles the imagination. It is important for you to understand the basics of quality as they are applied in contemporary business, and it is important for you to have a feel for how technology affects businesses today. After reading this chapter, you should be able to:

1. Describe the meaning and significance of quality.

2. Apply total quality management and continuous improvement to actual situations.

3. Illustrate how quality can be integrated into both products and services.

4. Explain the contributions of some of the quality experts who have influenced business.

5. Demonstrate the role that information technology plays in today's society.

6. Explain the operational and strategic use of information technology.

7. Recognize the importance of modern production techniques such as JIT, flexible production, and lean manufacturing.

effectiveness p. 478>

efficiency p. 478>

mission p. 310>

It should not be surprising to you by the time you have read this much of this book that quality and technology are both important issues. We have referred to quality many times throughout the text. The model from Chapter 1 shows that quality is a prime indicator of business success. In Chapter 11, we emphasized how quality is important as part of a firm's mission and vision statements. In Chapter 12, we discussed quality as a customer need. We have also discussed technology a number of times as it relates to the efficiency and effectiveness of a company's processes. This chapter will look at each of these important topics.

The Role of Quality

Quality
The ability of a product or service to consistently meet or exceed customers' expectations.

Quality is a strategic issue in today's businesses. In fact, the company that does not address quality as part of its strategic planning may well be left behind by more enlightened competitors. Quality is no longer a luxury that some firms can offer as a unique feature of their operations. Rather, it is a basic standard that every business must strive to achieve in order to be successful. Further, that basic standard is constantly being pushed higher and higher. Quality is one of the prime forces in the competitive dynamics of an industry. Customers are increasingly sophisticated and demanding about the products or services they purchase. They expect quality in every experience they encounter. In short, quality is now the norm. Successful companies constantly work to instill more quality into their operations and into the mindsets of their employees.

The Meaning of Quality

Quality is a broad term that encompasses a number of issues. In its most basic sense, quality refers to the ability of a product or service to consistently meet or exceed customer expectations.[1] Quality has seven dimensions, as shown in Table 15–1. *Perfor-*

TABLE 15–1   Dimensions of Quality

1. Performance	5. Durability
2. Special features	6. Perceived quality
3. Conformance	7. Service after sale
4. Reliability	

SOURCE: William J. Stevenson, *Production/Operations Management*, 5th ed. (Burr Ridge, IL: Irwin, 1996), p. 95.

mance relates to how well a product performs or how well a service is provided. *Special features* are those added extras that affect performance but are not standard on all competing products or services. *Conformance* is critical from a customer viewpoint: How well does the product perform compared to consumer expectations? *Reliability* relates to the consistency of performance. Can the product always be expected to perform the way it should? Is the service provided always good? *Durability* relates to the life of the product. Is the life expectancy logical? For the amount of money paid, does the product last as long as customers think it should? The *perceived quality* is almost as important as quality itself. Quality is, by definition, customer focused. However, customers also have a perception of quality based on ads, past experiences, and competing products. The perceived quality is important because it affects customers' expectations. Finally, *service after sale* is the handling of complaints and requests as well as whether the company checks on the customer's satisfaction.[2]

These seven dimensions are important regardless of whether we are discussing products or services, whether we are talking about for-profit businesses or not-for-profit organizations, and whether the customers are end users or other businesses. For example, suppose you take your lawn mower in for service at the beginning of the season, partially because it was not running right when you put it away last fall. You get the mower back. In considering whether you will take the mower back to the same shop next time, you might ask yourself the following questions. Did the mower run right when you got it home? (performance) Did they wash it and clean it up in addition to servicing it? (special features) Was the mower ready when the service manager said it would be? (conformance) Did it continue to run throughout the season? (reliability, durability) Was the shop neat and clean or a junked-up firetrap? (perceived quality) Did the shop owner check back later to see if the service had been provided well? (service after the sale) These dimensions are not difficult to understand, nor are they difficult to implement. They do require time and attention and a focus on quality.

Quality Management Foundations

One way to better understand quality management and many of our current approaches to quality is to look at the thinking of some the world's most prominent quality gurus. W. Edwards Deming, Joseph Juran, and Philip Crosby are recognized throughout the business world for their contributions to the practice of quality.

Foremost among this trio is W. Edwards Deming, an American statistician who proposed innovative views on quality nearly 50 years ago. His ideas were not well received by American business at the time. In fact, it was the Japanese, struggling to re-build after World War II, who took Deming's ideas to heart and applied them to business practice. Deming's methods are credited as one of the major forces behind the rise in Japanese business prominence. Even today, the Deming Award is the highest honor and measure of excellence that a Japanese business can receive. In the 1980s, as American companies struggled with global competition (much of it coming from Japan), American business leaders finally turned to Deming and his quality insights. Deming's message is straightforward and is captured in his 14 points for management, which are featured in Profile 15–1. He emphasizes knowing customers and their needs. He also insists that a firm should improve all phases of operations so that enhanced quality becomes the underlying, guiding philosophy of the business.

PROFILE 15–1   *Deming's Fourteen Points for Management*

innovation p. 522>

1. Establish the objective of constant innovation and improvement.
2. Adopt a new philosophy. We cannot accept the old mistakes and defects.
3. Cease dependence on mass inspection. Require statistical evidence that quality is built in.
4. End the practice of awarding business on the basis of price alone.
5. Improve constantly and forever the system of production and service.
6. Institute modern methods of training on the job.
7. Improve supervision. Do what is right for the company, don't just turn out the required quantity.
8. Drive out fear. Create trust. Create a climate for innovation.
9. Break down barriers between departments and with suppliers and customers so there will be open, effective communication.
10. Eliminate posters and slogans. They don't help people solve problems. Go to work and show people how.
11. Eliminate work standards that prescribe a numerical quota. They disregard quality and put a ceiling on production.
12. Remove barriers that rob people of their right to pride in workmanship.
13. Institute a vigorous retraining program to keep up with changes and new developments.
14. Create a top management structure that will push every day for these points.

training p. 379>

top management p. 65>

SOURCES: Adapted from W. Edwards Deming, *Quality, Productivity, and Competitive Position* (Cambridge, MA: MIT Press, 1982), pp. 16–7; W. Edwards Deming, *Out of the Crisis* (Cambridge, MA: MIT Center for Advanced Engineering Study, 1986).

One of the best-known programs in quality comes from one of our focus companies, Motorola. The company has a highly respected quality program known as Six Sigma, whose goal is to have no more than 3.4 defective parts out of every million parts produced. Essentially, Motorola is aiming for virtually zero defects. That means every part and process must work properly so products are made right the first time and every time. This seems to work at Motorola.

Imagine the advantages the Six Sigma approach brings. First, the company earns a well-deserved reputation for quality. Second, costs are reduced as methods are improved and defects are minimized. Third, employees feel excitement and challenge from striving to improve and do better. All of this together leads to greater customer satisfaction and a more favorable profit picture. Profile 15–2 describes the Six Sigma program.

Profile 15–2   *Motorola's Six Sigma Quality Program*

In 1985, a quality management professional at Motorola gave a presentation on the relationship of a product's early-life reliability (its lack of failure the first few times it is used) and the number of defects repaired during the actual manufacturing process. His discovery was that if you have to find defects during the manufacturing process, you will likely miss some. These defects will cause problems once the product is purchased by a customer. On the other hand, if your designs are robust (that is, they minimize or eliminate defects) and your manufacturing process is highly controlled, then virtually everything should work the first time. The objective is to eliminate the cause of defects rather than to identify and repair the defects. In order to achieve the goal of "doing it right the first time," Motorola established and communicated a program called Six Sigma.

Six Sigma actually refers to a statistical concept used to explain error rates in the production of parts. For Motorola, Six Sigma means no more than 3.4 defects per million parts. From the customer's perspective, this means that a Motorola pager or cellular phone simply will not fail because of defects in design or manufacturing.

The significance of Six Sigma quality is not so much in the statistical measure of quality as in the philosophy behind the drive for quality. The mindset of all Motorola employees is on maximizing quality and continuously improving processes to eliminate errors. This means customers can expect near perfection in Motorola products. The quest for quality spills over into areas of the company beyond manufacturing and design. For example, part of customer service quality is the order entry process, which includes shipping and billing. Even these areas are committed to handling customer orders with virtually no mistakes. Customer service quality also includes intervening with dealers or customers to keep these relationships robust too.

**customer service
p. 340>**

TQM and Continuous Improvement

Two concepts have been popularized in quality management over the past decade. These are total quality management and continuous improvement. These ideas are simply different ways of looking at and achieving the same quality goal.

Total Quality Management

Total quality management (TQM)
A systematic approach to addressing quality issues that involves a total, integrated, companywide commitment to quality.

Total quality management (TQM) is a systematic method for addressing quality issues. TQM programs vary depending on each company's individual approach, but one theme is common to all successful TQM programs. They require a total, integrated, companywide commitment to quality. TQM may begin with careful market research

market research p.344>

to assess customer needs, but quality goes far beyond market research. Designers, development staff, and engineers must be able to take customer desires and translate them into winning, high-quality product designs. Manufacturing must be able to produce these quality products at reasonable cost. Finally, the products must be delivered in a timely and convenient way so customers receive satisfaction.

TQM involves everything the business does from initial customer contact through delivery to customer follow-up. It is a fallacy to assume that quality is the job of any single area or function in the business. In TQM, quality is everyone's job! This is why teams are so often used in TQM. People from different areas of the business come together to address customer needs and learn how everyone can help deliver customer satisfaction.

teams p. 71>

Morton Metalcraft is a midsize metal fabricating business that supplies a number of large customers, including Deere, Caterpillar, and Hallmark Cards. Morton builds the metal racks Hallmark uses to display its cards. Morton pulls together a team of employees that works on the Hallmark account from start to finish. This team includes employees from marketing, manufacturing, engineering, and accounting. They work closely with the Hallmark people and collectively decide how all areas of the company can best respond to meet Hallmark's needs as efficiently as possible. This team approach allows Morton to provide excellent customer service and to address quality issues. In fact, quality is so important at Morton Metalcraft that it has a vice president for quality assurance. (The head of quality assurance is at a lower level in most companies.) This VP oversees quality engineering, safety, and quality control.

Continuous Improvement

Continuous improvement
A process where a firm and all of its people continually look for ways to change and improve all facets of the business.

The second quality management concept, **continuous improvement,** is a mandate to the business and all of its people to continually look for ways to improve everything. Continuous improvement truly covers all facets of the business, and all employees should be involved in the effort. Production methods, work flow, equipment, and procedures are all examined and altered where appropriate. Relationships with customers and suppliers are explored to see where changes can be made to improve the contacts and interactions. Again, teams of employees from different areas of the business are used to help meet this need. Even upgrading employee skills and developing new training opportunities may be areas to target. The possibilities for improvement are endless.

You now have a general sense of what continuous improvement is all about. However, a practical question remains. How do businesses actually go about achieving continuous improvement? What strategies and techniques do they use? Two of the most popular techniques are statistical process control and benchmarking.

Statistical Process Control

In the past, products were tested for quality as they were completed. For example, consider a business that produces metal alloys to sell to large car manufacturers as raw materials. The alloys must be of a certain composition, texture, and strength to be acceptable to the carmakers. Alloy composition, texture, and strength were tested only once—at the end of the process. If the finished alloy product was defective, it would have to be scrapped or reworked. Think of the implications. First, either scrapping or reworking is quite costly to the business. Second, it may delay deliveries, which can affect relations with the auto companies. Finally, it can be demoralizing for employees.

Statistical process control is used to increase quality in the manufacture of cars and many other products. Inspection is done throughout the process rather than waiting until the end of the process. How does this improve the overall process?

Statistical process control
Checking quality at regular intervals in the production process and taking corrective action when necessary.

They have worked hard only to find that their efforts have not produced a successful product.

Statistical process control refuses to wait until the end of the alloy run to test for quality. Instead, quality is checked at regular intervals in the production process, and corrective action is taken when necessary. Statistical checkpoints are used to determine whether each phase of the production process is performing as it should. Employees are trained to measure progress, identify problems, and take corrective action *throughout* the production process. The product is refined and perfected as it flows through the various stages of production. This idea of giving operating employees responsibility for quality inspection is a key part of continuous quality improvement thinking. Some experts refer to this as "quality at the source," meaning that quality improvements are made at the source of the problem by employees who understand and regularly perform the tasks, not by some inspector who only views the finished product.

In our metal alloy example, early in the production process, large vats of molten compound are prepared and treated. This compound will be poured to form the alloy components that the auto manufacturers desire. With statistical process control, employees take samples of the molten compound at regular intervals and measure its composition using computer technology. If the composition differs from the standards that are in place, the employee alters the batch to correct the problem. For instance, if the batch is short on potassium, the computer reading specifies exactly how much potassium is needed. The employee adds the necessary potassium to the compound. Once the correction is made, more testing is done at established checkpoints throughout the process.

Consider what statistical process control adds to the business. First, it assures a better and more consistent quality of output. Second, it eliminates costly production runs that fail to meet final quality standards. Third, it involves employees in the process of improving quality. They take action to *build* quality in rather than waiting for an inspector to *inspect* quality in. This makes their jobs more important and more interesting. Fourth, statistical process control allows the most timely solution to the problem, since those best able to resolve problems address them early in the manufacturing process. Finally, the technique reinforces, on an ongoing basis, the importance of continuous improvement.

Benchmarking

Benchmarking
Comparing one's practices to those of recognized leaders to see where and how improvements can be made.

A second approach to continuous improvement for overall total quality management, benchmarking, has become very popular in the past few years. In **benchmarking,** managers compare their practices to the practices of recognized leaders to see where and how improvements can be made.

As a continuous improvement technique, benchmarking follows a three-step process. First, management identifies and studies quality leaders to see what they are doing. Eaton Corp. is a midsize manufacturer of meters and circuit breakers. A few years ago, it decided to take a careful look at its manufacturing process in an effort to increase quality and reduce costs. Eaton identified companies known for their innovative and successful manufacturing activities. One of these companies was Harley-Davidson, the motorcycle manufacturer. Eaton representatives visited Harley, toured its plants, talked to people, and learned as much as they could.

From these observations, Eaton was able to identify the Harley success practices that seemed most relevant to its situation. These *critical success factors* represent the second step in the process. In Eaton's case, one of the critical success factors identified was Harley's unique use of manufacturing teams.

The final step is forming goals and plans for implementing the critical success factors in the benchmarker's own facilities. Eaton got some good ideas from Harley about how teams should be used in the manufacturing process, so it developed a detailed action plan for bringing teams into the work process. Through this three-step process, Eaton has built quality improvements by borrowing relevant techniques and methods from proven quality winners.

You may wonder why one business would be willing to share its insights with another. Isn't it afraid of losing its competitive edge? Not really. Since these businesses are in completely different industries, Eaton has no competitive impact on Harley. Such benchmarking is an accepted practice.

Recognizing and Certifying Quality

Baldrige Award
The highest quality recognition that an American business can receive, earned by at most six companies each year.

We have said there are real business advantages to having a quality focus that emphasizes continuous improvement. There are also advantages to a business in being recognized for its quality leadership. The highest quality recognition that a U.S. business can receive is the **Malcolm Baldrige Award,** given by the federal government. To give you an idea how good a business has to be to win the Baldrige Award, a maximum of six U.S. businesses win it each year. It is a tremendous honor and a real spark to a company's reputation. Motorola received the first Baldrige Award in 1988. The Baldrige Award is so important that we list its criteria in Profile 15–3.

PROFILE 15–3   *The Baldrige Award*

In 1987, Congress passed the Malcolm Baldrige National Quality Improvement Act, named after the late Malcolm Baldrige, an industrialist and former secretary of commerce. The legislation was designed to inspire quality efforts by businesses in the United States. The award is great publicity for the winning companies. A maximum of two winners are allowed each year in each of three categories: manufacturing, service, and small businesses. The award is administered by the National Institute for Standards and Technology. Companies that compete for the award must submit an in-depth application covering seven main categories of quality. The categories and selected components are shown here, along with the highest possible scores for each.

human resources
p. 374>
training p. 379>

Category	Points
1. Leadership Includes senior executive leadership, quality values, management for quality, and public responsibility	100
2. Information and analysis Includes management of quality data and information, competitive comparisons and benchmarks, and analysis of information	70
3. Strategic quality planning Includes strategic quality control process and quality goals and plans	60
4. Human resources utilization Human resources management, employee involvement, quality education and training, employee recognition, employee well-being and morale	150
5. Quality assurance of products and services Design and introduction of quality products, continuous improvement of process, quality assessment, documentation, business process and support service quality, supplier quality	140

6.	Quality results	180
	Product and service quality results, business process, operational and support service quality results, supplier quality results	
7.	Customer satisfaction	300
	Determining customer requirements and expectations, customer relationship management, customer service standards, commitment to customers, complaint resolution for quality improvement, determining customer satisfaction, customer satisfaction results, customer satisfaction comparison	
	Total points possible	1,000

SOURCE: Adapted from William J. Stevenson, *Production/Operations Management*, *5th ed.* (Burr, Ridge, IL: Irwin, 1996), p. 108.

Although companies that enter the Baldrige Award competition must do extensive analysis and paperwork, it can be well worth it. The award has had a dramatic impact on awareness of the need for quality. It has also provided examples of how quality can be achieved. Adding to the award's significance is information suggesting that high-quality companies also perform better financially. In a recent survey, companies that had won the Baldrige Award outperformed the Standard & Poor's 500 (a list of typical publicly held industrial companies) by a magnitude of 4 to 1. Even those companies that competed but did not win outperformed the S&P by 2 to 1. This suggests a very strong relationship between high quality and high performance.[3]

ISO 9000

Quality management and assurance standards published by the International Standards Organization; a common denominator of business quality accepted around the world.

Another quality designation we hear a great deal about is ISO 9000. **ISO 9000** certification is really a "stamp of approval" indicating that the business has documented procedures to ensure the highest standards for quality. To earn ISO 9000 status, the business is visited by an outside certifying agency, which conducts a detailed, comprehensive on-site audit of the business, carefully scrutinizing every aspect of the quality process. Often the agency notes changes and improvements that must be made before it will grant certification.

Much of the effort to increase quality requires studying past performance. Teams, such as this, study performance charts and set goals for future improvements. How can studying the past lead to improved performance in the future?

Today many businesses have received ISO 9000 certification, and many others are working toward it. This certification is important for reasons beyond image. ISO 9000 lets all customers know that the firm has the highest quality standards. Many companies prefer dealing with businesses that have achieved ISO 9000 certification. Many large businesses that have already been certified demand certification (or a plan of progress toward certification) from their smaller suppliers. This makes sense. The larger business figures its quality is only as good as the quality of the input it receives from its suppliers. It wants the best quality assurance possible from these suppliers. Accordingly, ISO 9000 certification tends to snowball in actual practice.

ISO 9000 is a worldwide set of standards administered by the International Standards Organization (in which 91 countries participate). These standards are critical to doing business in international markets; most overseas manufacturers require their suppliers to be ISO 9000 certified.[4]

Developing Your Critical Thinking Skills

1. Define quality. What is the real significance to a business of receiving the Baldrige Award? Of receiving ISO 9000 certification?

2. Total quality management is both a process and a philosophy. What is the difference between these two approaches to TQM?

3. Define continuous improvement. How does it relate to TQM?

Quality in Service Industries

Opportunities to improve quality may be greater in manufacturing firms since they deal with a tangible product and a definitive process that produces the product. However, quality is also important in service firms. The differences between the two types of firms are shown in Table 15–2 (which summarizes the discussion in Chapter 10).

Because services are partly intangible, it is more difficult to measure or assess service quality than product quality. Since products are tangible, defective products can usually be easily identified, but service quality is based on customer perceptions. One person may feel that service is inadequate while another may find the same level of service acceptable. Also, some customers are more likely to complain than others who are as displeased. This means it can be difficult to know whether high-quality service has been provided or not. Unless communications between the provider and the customer are excellent, the business may not even know when there is a problem.

For example, if a movie theater is dirty or patrons are noisy, the vast majority of customers will not complain to the management. They will, however, complain to each other and go to a different theater next time. The theater management may be unaware of the magnitude of the problem and may even think the few people who do complain are simply whiners. How many times have you gone to a restaurant, had less than desirable food or service, and said nothing to management? Perhaps you left no tip or left a token tip for the server, but you probably did not complain to the very people who could affect the quality of the service.

TABLE 15-2   Differences between Manufacturing and Service Firms

Manufacturing	Service
Product is tangible	Service consists of both tangible and intangible components
Customer acceptance of the product is easily quantifiable	Customer satisfaction is difficult to quantify because of behavioral component associated with delivery of the service
Back orders are possible	Services cannot be stored; if not used, they are lost
Producer is the only party involved in making the product	Producer *and* customer are both involved in delivery of the service

SOURCE: Adapted from Amitava Mitra, *Fundamentals of Quality Control and Improvement* (New York: Macmillan, 1993), p. 563.

Another difference between manufacturing and services is the inability to store services. If the service is not provided at the time requested, it often cannot be provided at all. If an airplane is grounded, many of the passengers will choose another airline, take other means of transportation, or not go at all. Thus, the provider of a service often has only one chance to perform the service. Therefore, quality is critically important in every interaction.

A final quality-oriented difference is that the service provider and the customer interact, which gives service providers the opportunity to build rapport with customers—who become repeat customers if the service is provided well. Of course, the service provider must be willing to listen carefully to the customer and respond to specific requests. If good rapport is not established, interaction can become strained and the customer's specific needs are ignored.

Clearly, it can be hard to achieve a quality focus in service industries. How can companies build better quality into the services they provide? Table 15–3 lists some of the key areas to address.

Consider the hotel industry. A hotel can enhance service quality in a number of ways. The attitude of the front-desk personnel (human factors), time standing in line to check in or out (timeliness), the number of times an error is made in a customer's

TABLE 15-3   Areas of Service Quality

- Human factors and behavioral characteristics
- Timeliness characteristics
- Service nonconformity characteristics
- Facility-related characteristics

SOURCE: Adapted from Amitava Mitra, *Fundamentals of Quality Control and Improvement* (New York: Macmillan, 1993), p. 565.

bill (nonconformity), and the cleanliness and overall condition of the room (facilities) all affect the customer's perception of service quality. In a bank, the willingness of a teller to make an exception in order to better serve a customer (human factors), the time waiting in line (timeliness), the ability and willingness to correct an error (nonconformity), and the number of times the ATM machine is out of order (facilities) affect quality perceptions.

In a restaurant, indicators of quality could include the friendliness of the table server (human factors), the length of time from when the order is placed until the food arrives (timeliness), the correctness of the food compared to the order (nonconformity), and the cleanliness of restrooms (facilities). An airline could have the willingness of flight attendants to assist in storing carry-on luggage (human factors), the length of time to load a plane and take off (timeliness), the number of lost pieces of luggage (nonconformity), and the number of flights canceled because of equipment (facilities). A hospital could use the completeness with which a nurse attends to a patient's needs (human factors), the time from the push of a call button until a nurse arrives (timeliness), the number of errors in administering medicine (nonconformity), and aesthetics of the patient's room (facilities).

As we said, providing service quality is complicated by the interactions between the customer and the provider. For example, a disorderly airline passenger can cause problems not only for the flight attendants but also for other customers. A diner in a restaurant who gives an incorrect order and then blames his mistake on the server can affect both timeliness and human factors. Emergencies on a hospital floor may confuse staff to the extent that they make an error with another patient. Thus, managers studying quality of service must do careful analyses.

You may have heard the cliche that there are only two rules in customer service. "Rule 1: The customer is always right. Rule 2: If the customer is not right, see Rule 1." This suggests that the customer calls the shots in anything relating to customer service. Many companies have this policy and would rather lose money on a transaction than have an unhappy customer. They reason that the unhappy customer will tell a number of friends and may cause other problems for the company that outweigh the loss it incurs by giving in.

On the other hand, sometimes a customer is simply wrong. Sometimes the customer is either intentionally or accidentally taking advantage. This creates a dilemma for the company. Should it give in when it is obvious that the customer is wrong or should it hold its ground? There is no right answer here, but often communication is the key. If the server (clerk, nurse, flight attendant, bank teller) can pleasantly but completely communicate the issue to the customer, that may resolve the misunderstanding and satisfy the customer.

The key to solving customer problems is to address the human factors involved, usually communication, and make every attempt to solve the issue immediately before it gets out of hand. Many companies empower their customer representatives to solve problems, within limits, without needing approval from a higher authority. This makes customers happy and gives the employee responsibility and control over their own job.

Developing Your Critical Thinking Skills

1. Is timeliness more important for some service businesses than for others?

2. What are some of the human factors that affect the level of service quality?

3. Why are human factors so important in service quality compared to manufacturing quality?

The Role of Technology

Technology
The use of machines, tools, and information in the production of goods and services.

We define **technology** as the use of machines, tools, and information in the production of goods and services. Machinery is both increasingly complex and increasingly efficient. Many manufacturing tools today are at least partially operated by computers, and robots have taken the drudgery out of many tasks. The key to operating automated machines is information. Computerized information often tells a machine precisely what cuts to make, holes to drill, or material to move. We will discuss two primary types of technology as they affect companies today, information technology and production technology.

Information Technology (IT)

Information technology (IT)
The use of electronic devices to collect, analyze, store, and transmit information.

Information has been available since the first humans learned to communicate. Written information dates back at least to the cave age. Information has been widely disseminated since the printing press was developed over 500 years ago. But the concept of **information technology (IT)**—the use of electronic devices to collect, analyze, store, and transmit information—is a relatively recent phenomenon, available only in the last 50 years and used extensively only in the past couple of decades.

Profile 15–4 describes Cerner Corp., an excellent example of the contemporary use of information technology. Cerner develops clinical and management information systems for health care organizations that assemble *all* information about a patient—administrative information, health history, and current care information—into a single record. This is clearly superior to prior systems, in which health care professionals could not track needed information about their patients across different databases.

PROFILE 15–4   *Cerner Corp.'s Healthy Information Systems*

stock p. 216>

As a self-proclaimed "farm boy" from Manchester, Oklahoma, Neal Patterson didn't know what he wanted to be when he grew up. For now, he's content being the chair and CEO of Cerner Corp., the top stock performer on the Forbes honor roll of the "best small companies" in America.

Cerner is the leading supplier of clinical and management information systems to the health industry, including hospitals, HMOs, clinics, physicians' offices, and integrated health organizations. Cerner believes that the key to success for the future of health care is the strategic use of an interrelated information system.

Cerner provides the information architecture that automates the clinical and management processes across a health system. Founded in 1979, Cerner initially designed and developed a comprehensive information system for laboratory clinicians, called the PathNet Laboratory Information System. Since then, Cerner has

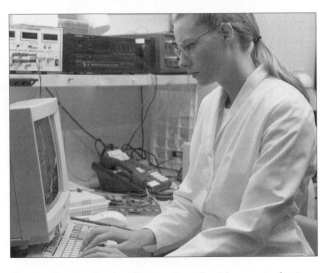

Cerner Corporation's software allows health care professionals to access all data about a patient rather than just the most recent medical records. How is this additional data useful to hospital staff working with a patient?

designed and developed more than 200 clinical applications for use throughout the health care enterprise. Today Cerner is the leader in the market for clinical information systems that address the needs of clinical laboratories, pharmacies, radiologists, internal medicine departments, direct care providers, and clinical repositories. These are combined into what Cerner calls Health Network Architecture.

Cerner has over 1,000 client sites across the United States and around the world. It went public in 1986 and now has over 33 million shares outstanding. Its sales for the first six months of 1997 were over $114 million, a 15% increase over the first 6 months of 1996.

SOURCE: Cerner Corporation web site, http://www.cerner.com, (accessed September 17, 1997).   ●

Operational and Strategic Use of Information Technology

Operational use of IT
The use of information to make a company more efficient or effective in communication and internal operations.

Strategic use of IT
The use of information to better position a company to compete within its industry.

Companies can use information technology operationally, strategically, or both. **Operational use of IT** is the use of information to make a company more efficient or effective in communications and internal operations. **Strategic use of IT** is the use of information to better position the company to compete within its industry. These two uses overlap. That is, companies that use technology to become more efficient in internal operations may use the same information for communicating with current or potential customers, thereby improving their competitive position.

Consider a technology as basic as e-mail. It lets people within the business communicate quickly. Information can be shared and decisions made that involve many people. The information flow permits people to play a role even if they are geographically separated from one another. This is an operational use of information technology, and operational efficiency is the outcome. The same technology can also play a strategic role. The business that uses the internet to place employment notices, engage customers in dialogue regarding products and services, and gain information regarding market trends is using information technology to make strategic gains over rivals.

Some businesses convert operational information into a strategic use. Owens Corning's research department collected substantial information on the energy efficiency of various house designs as part of its research into different insulation materials. The company then developed programs that could evaluate the energy efficiency of house layouts and offered builders a free analysis of their designs if they bought their insulation from Owens Corning. Thus, although the information on energy efficiency was developed for internal use, it was converted to the strategic use of developing new customers.[5]

American Airlines and United Airlines each operate computerized reservations systems that assist in their own operations and are also leased to other airlines. For instance, American maintains information on virtually every flight and every passenger and their baggage for any plane at any time. The systems were developed for use by the airlines and by over 24,000 travel agents and 99,000 terminals. Newer versions can be accessed by anyone with a PC and a modem. If you want to check the status of a particular flight that is due to land in Tulsa at 8:00 PM tonight, you can do it on your home computer.[6]

Southwest Airlines is one of the first users of Ticketless Travel. A potential traveler accesses the Southwest Airlines home page, clicks on Ticketless Travel, then clicks the departure city, the destination city, and the date and approximate time of desired flights. The website responds with flight availability and fares. The customer can enter a credit card number to reserve a seat and then simply show up for the flight.

Selling Products via Information Technology

Increasingly, firms are using information technology to sell products. For example, many companies have electronic catalogs. Customers can browse, make their selections, and enter their account or credit card number to expedite the order. Lands' End provides information about much of its inventory, including overstocks and specials, on its website. Customers can scan the site weekly for different products available at reduced prices. They can order via e-mail, phone, or fax. Lands' End competitor L.L. Bean also sells clothes and outdoor products through its website.

American Airlines also uses the Internet for strategic advantage. In the summer of 1996, American announced its NetsAAver Fares. On Wednesday of each week, it sends subscribers an e-mail notice of deep-discount fares for the coming weekend to selected cities. Flights must originate the following Friday evening or Saturday with return on Monday or Tuesday. This is American's way of filling seats that were not booked with the normal seven-day advance tickets. Since the additional cost of those seats is negligible, it makes good strategic sense to provide extra income while not giving up any flexibility in traditional pricing.

Encyclopaedia Britannica recently announced that it is discontinuing its door-to-door sales in favor of direct mail advertising, TV commercials, and a website. It is also using money saved from the door-to-door operation to develop Britannica OnLine and its CD-ROM edition.[7]

Lands' End and L.L. Bean sell clothes via the Internet. American Airlines sells airplane seats. Britannica sells encyclopedias. All three sell products or services that might otherwise go unpurchased.

Using Information Technology for Customer Service

Companies that use information technology for customer service are using it as a communication device. Electronic information is easily disseminated to customers via telephone hot lines, Internet addresses, and interactive websites.

One of the best examples of Internet-focused customer service is Federal Express, the world's largest express transportation company. FedEx delivers more than 2 million items to 211 countries each business day. It employs more than 124,000 people worldwide and operates 563 aircraft and more than 37,000 vehicles in its integrated system. It has almost 41,000 pickup stations and handles 2.5 million packages a day. Its 1996 revenues were $10.3 billion.

FedEx's use of technology is awesome. It sends over 45.5 million electronic transmissions per day. Its website gives customers a direct window into its package-tracking data base. Thousands of customers a day click their way through web pages to locate their packages instead of calling a human operator. Customers feel that they are receiving better service because they know where their parcel is at any given moment.[8] FedEx's IT system helped it handle millions of extra packages each day during the UPS strike in the summer of 1997.

Using Information Technology for Internal Communications

Internal communications are critical for managers in organizations. Effective communications motivate workers and ensure that all departments are working toward the same goals as the overall organization. Internal communications are also important to coordinate the efficient production of goods and services.

The information system at FedEx is a key not just to customer service but to the operation of the entire company. The tracking system enables the efficient and timely delivery of parcels. FedEx uses an **intranet,** which is essentially the same thing as the Internet except that it is designed for use totally within a particular company.

Companies are finding that an intranet solves many of their communications problems. It lets computers in one part of the company talk to computers in another part (even if different kinds of computers are used). It lets users throughout the company access databases, substantially reducing the need for paper while permitting continuous updating of information. Whereas paper-published information may be obsolete as soon as it is printed, an internal website can be updated instantly and be immediately accessible to large numbers of people. Financial reports, supply catalogs, employee benefits, corporate phone books, company policies, training manuals, requisition forms, and a host of other information can be stored on web servers for browsing by employees. Intranets are secure from outsiders and from insiders who should not have access to confidential information.[9]

With the vast array of electronic communication (including e-mail, voice mail, faxing, video conferencing, and intranets), the whole concept of office space is changing. Telecommuting and hoteling are becoming more prevalent in today's business world. In telecommuting, which we discussed in Chapters 5 and 14, an employee works either full- or part-time from a home office, connected to the company by modem, fax, and phone. In some cases, this is a permanent arrangement, with the employee seldom if ever going to an actual office. An example is people who do extensive amounts of data entry into a computer. They can work just as well at home as they can at the office. Even if they must spend time with clients on the phone, the client is unaware that the account rep is not in a plush office downtown. In other cases, the arrangement may be temporary. A recent college graduate got a job with an Internet

Intranet
A version of the Internet designed for use inside a particular company.

benefits p. 433>

service firm. Unfortunately, he slipped on the ice and ended up with his leg in a cast up to his thigh, which made driving his stick-shift car in city traffic difficult. The company set him up with a modem and software so he could continue to work from his home.

Hoteling is both caused by and facilitated by the increased use of cross-functional teams in businesses. **Hoteling** is the creation of temporary rooms for meetings of people who do not have an office in the area.[10] Many people today work either out of their home or out of their suitcase, accompanied by a cell phone and a laptop computer with e-mail and fax capabilities. These workers, whether they are executives, account reps, or marketing, engineering, or design employees, may not have a permanent office. They may be assigned a small cubicle for those days when they do happen to be in town. However, these people need an occasional meeting room for in-person conferences and access to the data and communications relevant to their project. These alternative-office strategies go by various names, but the idea is to promote better coordination among workers who may be working on a variety of different projects in different locations and with different team members on each project.

Using Information Technology in Market Research

Any healthy company must spend time and effort learning what customers want, what trends are occurring, and what its competitors are doing. Failure to study both customers and competitors inevitably leaves a firm left behind in a competitive market. In fact, competitive intelligence is important to discover what actions competitors are taking and also how customers are reacting to those actions. Gathering information on customers and competitors can range from person-to-person interviews in a mall to disassembling a competitor's product to see how it is made to conducting full-scale marketing research that costs thousands of dollars.

Information technology makes data gathering less onerous. Considerable information about competitors can be gained on the Internet. Most large companies now publish their annual reports and other information on the Web. They also often have detailed discussions about their products and services. Of course, this information could be found elsewhere, but the Web is a single, easily accessible source.

In addition to finding out specific information about another company, it is possible to find information about existing products. Profile 15–5 shows how easy it is to find product information.

PROFILE 15–5   *A Sample Internet Product Search*

A reporter for *Inc.* magazine decided to see how much information she could find about left-handed kitchen tools and how long it would take. She accumulated substantial information in a matter of minutes and at near zero cost. This is an excerpt from her account of her search.

So you're thinking you could make a killing selling left-handed cooking gadgets. Why not? Cocooning is a national trend, as more and more baby boomers entertain at home and develop their gourmet skills. And if the rule of thumb holds true, 13 percent of them are southpaws. Well, as your on-staff, on-line guru, let me check out the information the Internet has on this niche market:

Hoteling

Creating temporary meeting rooms for people who do not have an office in the area.

baby boomers p. 136>

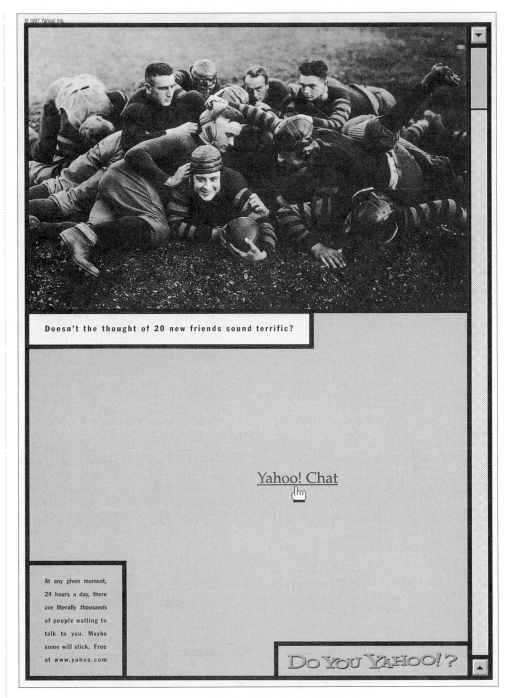

Yahoo! is one of many search engines that can help find information on the web. By typing in a word or phrase, you can use the search engine and find web sites where that information is stored. Check out your university or college web site. Is there information on the site that would be valuable for someone thinking about enrolling at your school?

Monday, 4:40 pm: Online newsgroups. I have to search through the Usenet listings by keyword. I try *cooking, gourmet,* and *left.* There are only two discussion groups with *cooking* in the title, and none with *gourmet.* While I'm searching, however, I notice several that list *food* in the title. I search under that and find 72 different groups, ranging from "alt.food.grits" to "rec.food.sourdough," and several regional food groups in between. I post a quick message to a busy discussion group called "rec.food.cooking," asking people what left-handed tools they'd like to see, what they use, and where they buy them. Under *left,* I find several political groups listed, along with "alt.lefthanders." I post the same message in that group. It will take a while for the message to post (anywhere from 15 minutes in the best case to two or three days at the outer limits of the Internet galaxy) and for others to read and respond, so it's time to move on.

Monday, 4:53 pm: Yahoo!'s search engine. I stop here and type in the keyword *left* to see what's available. That gives me 64 matches, most with political connotations. So I narrow down my search and type in the keyword *left-handed.* That turns up five matches, including a left-handed golf-equipment retailer, two left-wing political websites, and an informational site on left-handedness. The big score is Southpaw Pineapple, a left-handed gift shop. I decide to check out the potential competition and click on the link that sends me to its website.

Although the store does list kitchen aids in its online catalog, the site is probably still under construction; there's no link to product listings. I browse around, clicking on links, but can't find those kitchen gadgets listed anywhere. Finally, I file the URL on my internet browser's "hot list" (a standard feature of browser software) so that I can come back to it easily later on and keep checking to see if those products show up.

Tuesday, 9:30 am: Back to the newsgroups. Checking in, I find three responses to my message in "rec.food.cooking." (When you post a message with a newsgroup, it always comes up the next time you log on, with any responses appended to it.) One woman tells me she used to own a left-handed specialty shop, and she lists those products that sold well and those she still has boxes of. She also lists the names of several lefty shops across the country for me to check out. Another person pleads for a left-handed can opener. The third asks for left-handed oven mitts and lists a few more lefty specialty stores. There aren't any responses yet in "alt.lefthanders."

Time spent:	48 minutes
Total cost:	About $2 per hour for Internet service
Info found:	Product suggestions from potential customers, the names and locations of competitors, and one website that appears to be selling the exact product line I'd want to sell

SOURCE: Phaedra Hise, "Getting Smart On-Line," *Inc. Technology* 18, no. 4 (1996), p. 65.

Using Information Technology to Communicate between Suppliers and Customers

In Profiles 13–2 and 13–3, we discussed Lear Corporation, which is connected electronically to the carmakers it sells to. Lear receives information literally minutes before a given seat assembly is required in a car. It produces the seat assembly and ships

Electronic data interchange (EDI)
A system that converts most if not all of the paper communication between a supplier and another business into electronic form.

it so that it arrives precisely when and where it is needed. This would not be possible without the computer communications concept known as **electronic data interchange (EDI),** which converts most (if not all) of the paper communications between a supplier and another business into electronic form.

There are at least four advantages to EDI. First, it eliminates the lag time needed to update data. Since the data are electronic, changes are instantaneous. Second, EDI makes available processed, accurate data, since it eliminates the errors that occur when data must be rekeyed or reentered. Third, EDI increases customer service efficiency. Paperwork is eliminated, and unique customer needs can be addressed immediately. Finally, EDI links production and marketing systems electronically, which ensures that both departments are using the same information. As you can see, each of these advantages helps improve service and reduce costs. Sears, for example, cajoled its suppliers to convert to EDI by offering free software and training to bring suppliers online. With EDI, Sears can ship merchandise directly from the supplier to the customer without routing it through Sears.[11]

Developing Your Critical Thinking Skills

1. Why is the Internet useful in selling the same products that could be sold through catalogs or in stores?

2. What is the difference between an intranet and the Internet?

3. How can information technology improve customer service?

Production Technology

Although quality affects all areas of the business, attention often focuses on how businesses actually go about building quality products. This means managers must take a careful look at the way they manufacture their products. Let's take another look at Transit Cycles, the company whose structure we created in Chapter 14. As you recall, Transit builds road bikes and mountain bikes. Transit has studied the market. It believes it has a special product that a unique set of customers wants. As mountain biking has grown in popularity among riders from their late teens to late thirties, Transit's business has grown too.

Transit now produces three models of bikes. Each is geared to the needs of its target market. The Transit Deluxe carries a retail price of $525, the Transit Professional sells for $660, and the Transit Elite sells for $840. Although Transit builds and assembles these bikes, it buys many of the parts and raw materials it needs from other businesses. The lightweight aluminum that is used to mold frames is purchased from one company. The metal used for the seat posts is purchased from another company. The acrylic foam for the hand grips and the synthesized rubber for the brake pads are purchased from other companies. Some items are even purchased in their final form. For example, Transit buys its seats from a Canadian business that supplies seats to a number of bicycle builders. Likewise, it purchases derailleurs from an Italian business known for superb quality. It is Transit's job to take all these materials and use its own machinery, equipment, and people to build the final product—a Transit bike. This, of course, is what production is all about.

Production
The process that uses machinery, equipment, and people to create valued goods and services from raw materials or components.

Production is the process that uses machinery, equipment, and people to create valued goods and services from raw materials or components. There are many ways a business can go about doing this. Sometimes the equipment and machinery are highly automated; sometimes they are not. Sometimes the company buys raw materials from other businesses, as Transit does. Sometimes the company makes its own.

For most businesses today, the production process is guided by two concerns. First, the business is looking for ways to *boost the quality* of the products it makes. Second, the business is looking for ways to *lower the costs* of production. Techniques that address these concerns include just-in-time inventory control, flexible manufacturing, and lean manufacturing.

JIT Inventory Control

Transit Cycles depends on various suppliers when building its bikes. Transit has to be sure that it has the parts and materials from these suppliers when they are needed. Making sure this happens is known as *inventory control*. A business faces two conflicting forces in inventory control. On one hand, it must have enough inventory on hand, or the production flow is disrupted, which is costly. On the other hand, the business never wants to have too much inventory on hand. It is simply too expensive. In fact, the cost of holding inventory is one of the major costs of production. Thus, the business needs the right parts and materials at the right place and at the right time, but it wants to avoid having excess inventory that is expensive to store.

A popular response to this problem is just-in-time inventory control. As we said in Chapter 13, JIT requires suppliers to deliver parts and raw materials "just in time" to go into the production process. The supplier delivers the right parts at the right place at the right time. Production flows smoothly and inventory holding costs are dramatically reduced.

To reap the benefits of the JIT approach, close links must exist between the business and its suppliers. First, the firm must do careful planning and scheduling. Then the suppliers must know precisely when and where parts are needed. Finally, responsibility for just-in-time delivery resides with the supplier. Of course, much of the communication between the business and suppliers is computer-linked to facilitate the exchange of information.

Flexible Manufacturing

Flexibility is another hot topic in business today. The traditional approach to manufacturing came from mass production, where machines were set to produce single operations on a large scale. This approach works well when the business is mass producing a highly standardized item. This yields large quantities of output at lower costs. In the past, this was the approach used by car makers and other large manufacturers on their assembly lines.

As you can see, there are real advantages to mass production. A company can produce a lot, do it efficiently, and therefore keep costs down. However, there are also real problems. For example, once a machine was programmed, or tooled, it was rarely changed. It was simply too expensive to do so. Consequently, businesses that were locked into mass production thinking were often reluctant to change. But resistance to change simply will not work in most industries today. To compete, businesses must be flexible. They must respond to changes in customer preferences and demands, and they must do so quickly. Mass production thinking can be out of sync with the needed focus on customer sensitivity and service.

customer sensitivity
p. 493>

Again the business faces conflicting forces. It needs the efficiency of mass production thinking but cannot afford to alienate customers by being slow and inflexible. One response to this problem is a set of processes known as flexible manufacturing. Flexibility is a key to production in most contemporary businesses. **Flexible manufacturing** is the reliance on highly automated machinery that can be changed quickly and can perform multiple tasks. Thus, a given machine may be able to produce a variety of product options. This highly automated equipment is often smaller and more portable than mass production machinery.

Flexibility is important because it allows the business to customize its manufacturing to closely meet the needs of its customers. For example, Transit Cycles' road bikes and mountain bikes are sold to the public by a number of retailers throughout the world. One of these retailers is Hit the Road, a retail store that is quite popular with bicycle enthusiasts. A customer enters Hit the Road looking for a new mountain bike. She test rides a number of bikes. She is most impressed with the Transit Professional. She likes the ride and the feel, and the price is within her target range. She wants the bike, but only if certain features can be added. First, due to her height, she needs an 18-inch frame. Second, she wants the derailleur and brake package upgraded. Third, she wants an extended front suspension because of the rough terrain she intends to travel. Finally, she is particular about color. She wants the bike only in crimson and gray.

The employees at Hit the Road fax these special requirements to Transit, which builds a bike that meets the customer's special requirements and still promises delivery in less than a week. Flexible manufacturing has allowed Transit to give the customer exactly what she wants. This satisfies the customer. It satisfies Hit the Road because it makes the sale. Of course, it also benefits Transit because it receives a nice shot of revenue.

Lean Manufacturing

Lean manufacturing is a production trend that involves streamlining of every aspect and phase of the production process, enabling the business to produce while using less of everything. This means the business is looking for ways to use less space for its actual production, use fewer or more efficient machinery and tools, and tap the potential of its people. The reason for this is usually twofold. First, the business wants to save money in the long run. Second, it wants speed and flexibility.

Lean manufacturing typically involves the extensive use of technology. Specifically, computer technology is usually integrated throughout the production process. Computer technology is expensive. The business must make a significant initial payout to purchase this technology and build it into the production process. However, once in place, the technology offers many opportunities for cutting costs and operating more efficiently. Over time, it will probably be quite cost effective.

Let's look at some examples of lean manufacturing applications. Industrial robots often perform tasks with greater efficiency and accuracy than people, particularly repetitive activities that people find boring. It is not just big businesses that make use of robotics. Many midsize and even some small businesses use robots to help with part of their operations.

Another common technique is **computer-aided design (CAD).** Just as the name implies, computers are used to help in the design and development of new products. The applications and the cost savings are unbelievable. For example, new cars today are almost always designed on CAD systems. Features can be changed. New looks can be tried out. Aerodynamics of various design options can be tested. The creativity and

---

Flexible manufacturing
Manufacturing with highly automated machinery that can be changed quickly and can perform multiple tasks.

retailers p. 282>

revenue p. 167>

Lean manufacturing
The streamlining of every phase of the production process, enabling the business to keep producing while using less of everything.

Computer-aided design (CAD)
A system that uses computers in the design and development of new products.

creativity p. 522>

Most large companies and many small ones use computer-aided design and computer-aided manufacturing to speed the design and manufacture of new products. They can cut years off the process of designing products and eliminate the need for expensive prototypes. Can you think of other products where CAD techniques could be used?

flexibility gained are wonderful, and expensive prototypes do not have to be built. The CAD system shortens the time a product needs to travel from concept to production, so it improves a company's ability to compete.

The Role of People

Throughout this chapter we have discussed three separate but related topics—quality, information technology, and production technology. In each of these areas, the key to high performance is people. People must design the production systems even if they are highly automated. People must assess a firm's need for information and determine how much, how fast, and in what form that information must be presented. Finally, people, through their decisions and actions, ultimately determine the level of quality of a company's products or services.

Successful businesses are always searching for ways to best utilize their people and assure productivity and quality. For example, much of the actual operation of the lean manufacturing approach is facilitated by the use of work teams, which we discussed in Chapter 14. Teams are often an excellent way to bring people from different areas together to work on problems and get things done. This often reduces duplication and overlap. Further, as teams are empowered, administrative layers can be reduced and efficiency increased.

Developing Your Critical Thinking Skills

....

1. Why is flexible production significant in today's world?

2. What are the risks of just-in-time inventory policies?

3. Can lean manufacturing be applied to every manufacturing firm?

4. Why is technology viewed as a tool to help people perform better?

SUMMARY

1. Stiff competition from Japanese imports prompted American business to pay increased attention to the issue of quality beginning in the 1970s. This focus on quality continues today.

   ■ What is quality?

   In its most basic sense, quality refers to the ability of a product or service to consistently meet or exceed customer expectations. More specifically, quality can refer to any of the following characteristics of a product: (1) performance, (2) special features, (3) conformance, (4) reliability, (5) durability, (6) perceived quality, and (7) service after the sale.

2. When the quality movement began, it centered on the thinking of a few well-known quality experts such as W. Edwards Deming. Deming was an American statistician who is credited with helping the Japanese learn quality management principles. In the 1980s, American managers turned to him to learn how to improve quality. Two concepts emerging from the quality movement are TQM and continuous improvement.

   ■ What is total quality management?

   TQM is a systematic approach for addressing quality that requires a total, integrated, companywide commitment to quality.

   ■ What is continuous improvement?

   Continuous improvement is a mandate to the business and all of its people to continually look for ways to improve everything.

   ■ What are some techniques for achieving continuous improvement?

   In this chapter you learned about two techniques:
   (1) Statistical process control. Quality is checked at regular intervals in the production process and corrective action is taken when necessary.
   (2) Benchmarking. Managers compare their practices to those of recognized leaders to find out where and how improvements can be made.

3. The quality movement has progressed to the point where businesses can obtain outside recognition and certification of their achievement of high quality standards.

   ■ What is the highest quality recognition that a U.S. company can receive and what are the criteria for winning it?

   The Malcolm Baldrige Award is the highest recognition for quality achievement awarded to businesses by the federal government of the United States. The award is based on performance in seven areas: (1) leadership, (2) information and analysis, (3) strategic quality planning, (4) human resources utilization, (5) quality assurance of products and services, (6) quality results, and (7) customer satisfaction.

■ What is the most prominent international program for certifying a company's dedication to high quality standards?

The ISO 9000 certification program is the largest and most prominent international quality certification program. It consists of a worldwide set of standards developed and evaluated by the International Standards Organization.

4. Quality applies to both manufacturing and service businesses. Because service businesses differ from manufacturing businesses, service quality categories differ somewhat from product quality categories.

■ What are some major categories of service quality and how can they be measured?

In this chapter you learned about four areas of service quality and how they can be achieved. They are human factors and behavioral characteristics, timeliness, service nonconformity, and facility-related characteristics.

5. The quest for quality, efficiency, and effectiveness usually leads a company to adopt new technologies. Some deal with information, while others involve production.

■ What is information technology?

Information technology involves the use of electronic devices to collect, analyze, store and transmit information.

■ What are some of the operational and strategic uses of information technology?

Operational use of technology makes a company more efficient or effective in its communications and operations within the company. Strategic use of information technology helps the company to better position itself within its industry.

■ What are some uses of information technology?

In this chapter you learned about the following five uses of information technology: selling products, improving customer service, communicating internally (via an intranet), market research, and communicating between suppliers and customers (via EDI).

Companies must do everything they can to make their production processes as efficient and effective as possible. This includes using production technology.

■ What is production? What is production technology?

Production is the process that uses machinery, equipment, and people to create valued goods and services from raw materials. Production technology is used to raise the quality or lower the costs of production.

■ What are some current uses of production technology?

In this chapter you learned about three current uses of technology in the production process: inventory control through JIT, flexible manufacturing, and lean manufacturing.

Links to Future Courses

Quality, information technology, and production technology are intertwined in courses throughout your academic career, regardless of whether your major is business or not. Courses are increasingly using information technology in both the presentation of lectures and student assignments and projects. Businesses are moving rapidly into the use of all kinds of technology. In particular, the following courses will emphasize themes addressed in this chapter:

- Operations management
- Information technology
- Quality management
- Strategic management
- Marketing research
- Management information systems

KEY TERMS

Baldrige Award, p. 451
Benchmarking, p. 450
Computer-aided design (CAD), p. 465
Continuous improvement, p. 448
Electronic data interchange
  (EDI), p. 463
Flexible manufacturing, p. 465
Hoteling, p. 460
Information technology (IT), p. 456
Intranet, p. 459

ISO 9000, p. 452
Lean manufacturing, p. 465
Operational use of IT, p. 457
Production, p. 464
Quality, p. 444
Statistical process control, p. 449
Strategic use of IT, p. 457
Technology, p. 456
Total quality management
  (TQM), p. 447

EXERCISES AND APPLICATIONS

1. Choose a fast-food restaurant in your area. Visit it and analyze the level of service quality you see there. Use the criteria for service quality discussed in this chapter as the basis for your evaluation. Prepare a one-page report of your findings.

2. Form teams of four people. Each of you name a product that you have purchased but with which you have been dissatisfied. Compare your experiences. Which dimensions of product quality were missing?

3. In teams of four people, discuss a restaurant or other service in which you experienced problems. What was your response to the bad service? Did you complain to managers? How many people did each of you tell about your bad service? What business impact or lesson can be gained from your reaction?

4. Pick a career that interests you. Use one of the Internet search engines to find as many sources as possible that relate precisely to that career.

5. Find examples from magazines or on the World Wide Web about JIT. How do they relate to the topics discussed in this chapter?

6. As businesses move more fully into using information technology to serve customers and improve organizational effectiveness and efficiencies, what problems can arise for the customer-oriented business?

7. Form teams of six. Prepare a summary of the role of information technology. Present the overview to the class using as many forms of IT as possible. The team that demonstrates the most creative use of technology in its presentation is the winner.

CASE: **INNOVATION AT RUBBERMAID**

One of the world's most innovative companies is Rubbermaid. CEO Wolfgang Schmitt is proud that his company has been ranked among the 10 most admired companies for decades. Following are a few of his comments.

We attribute that remarkable record to both instincts and culture. We characterize our success as a combination of the Five Ts: trends, teams, training, technology, and creative tension....

Which trends do we consider? We track such conspicuous currents as demographic swings, changes in fashion, and market fluctuations as well as the less apparent psychographic trends ... and regulatory developments.... [For example,] recent years have witnessed continued growth in day care centers.... Our Little Tikes unit responded to their need with the PlayCenter, a sturdy, mostly plastic playground structure....

From color to product design to pricing, Rubbermaid's team-matrix structure balances our innovation groups' entrepreneurial approaches with their access to the resources of a $2.3 billion company. Every core team includes one member from each of four areas: marketing, design, finance, and manufacturing/engineering....

While it is true that we don't spend a lot of time doing pure scientific research, don't make the mistake of thinking we ignore current technology. Even our simplest items comprise an infusion of advanced techniques to achieve the best total value. An extensive array of computer-aided processes speeds up virtually every aspect of our value chain: procuring materials ...; designing ... products; controlling manufacturing particulars such as how much molten plastic should flow in our molds ... and monitoring retailers' scanner data to follow consumer purchases and continually replenish our customers' inventories....

Of course, none of that works well unless we invest in continuous learning.... We cultivate a learning environment in which the sky's the limit. We encourage associates to log onto our internal networks to share information on process improvements, and through a variety of programs we provide opportunities for continuous improvement, which we expect of all associates....

I expect every member of every team to make a personal commitment to superior performance and quality. Because there must be no doubt about Rubbermaid's commitment to superiority, we distribute a copy of our company's Statement of Management Philosophies to each associate who joins our company.

In addition to quality, our total-value focus extends, of course, to service and market performance. Salaries and bonuses rise and fall, and people win and lose assignments and responsibilities, all on the strength of their support for that standard....

Technology paves the highway to perpetual innovation.... Using computer models we define our products' physical properties and specifications, test their structural integrity, and develop the packaging, including the photographically realistic images of products that are still under development. Our aggressive use of technology allows us to dispatch our sales force even before we have the actual products to show the retailers. . . .

Last December marked a Rubbermaid milestone: our Global Leadership Development Program graduated its first class of new hires who had on-the-job training in our company business teams. The three year program brings people from diverse cultures around the world into our midst. It's part of our strategy for globalizing Rubbermaid from the inside out. We recognize that to sell products to the world, our workforce must mirror the world. . . . The international background of the participants will help us consider different ways to market our products around the world. . . .

[O]ur research laboratories direct their attention to the very specific concerns of our customers. Business teams from our commercial products division, for instance, regularly spend time with restaurant owners who use such Rubbermaid products as serving containers and cleanup containers. . . . Team members actually flip burgers and bus tables in order to gain real—and sometimes gritty—experiential data. During a stint working in a restaurant kitchen, one of our teams saw that the chef preferred to use synthetic-rubber scrapers instead of metal spatulas whenever he cooked in no-stick pans. The synthetic rubber didn't scrape the pans' surfaces, but after repeated use, the scrapers warped and lost their shape. The result of that discovery was [our] new high heat scraper made of pliable synthetic rubber . . . [that] can withstand temperatures of up to 500°F without melting. . . .

[We take a long-term view]. When the cost of plastic resin, our major raw material, doubled in less than a year, it affected our short-term results. One decision we had to consider was where to cut back, at least temporarily. Sure, we could have cut some training investments. But it's my belief that we should not dilute our commitment to those activities, because, like our globalization and technological programs, training programs are the fuel of our long-term quality growth.

Decision Questions

1. What is the relationship between people management and technology management at Rubbermaid?
2. This case illustrates a number of the features of the model from Figure 1–6. Can you identify examples of each feature in the case?
3. How does Rubbermaid define quality?

SOURCE: Wolfgang Schmitt, "Technology Paves the Highway to Perpetual Innovation," in Rosabeth Moss Kanter, John Kao, and Fred Wiersema, eds., *Innovation: Breakthrough Thinking at 3M, DuPont, GE, Pfizer and Rubbermaid* (New York: HarperCollins, 1997), pp. 147–75.

REFERENCES

1. William J. Stevenson. *Production/Operations Management*, 5th ed. Burr Ridge, IL: Irwin, 1996, p. 94.

2. Stevenson, p. 95.

3. National Institute for Standards and Technology Stock Investment Study 1996, http://www.nist.gov/quality/qualstok.htm, (accessed July 16, 1997).

4. A good discussion of ISO 9000 certification is provided by Richard B. Chase and Nicholas J. Aquilano. *Production and Operations Management: Manufacturing and Services*, 7th ed. Burr Ridge, IL: Irwin, 1995, pp. 190–6.

5. Antone F. Alber. *Interactive Computer Systems: Videotext and Multimedia*. New York: Plenum Publishing Corp., 1993, p. 15.

6. Alber, pp. 370–5.

7. "Britannica Drops Door-to-Door Salesmen in Favor of the Web." *Web Week*, May 20, 1996, p. 23.

8. FedEx http://www.fedex.com, (accessed July 16, 1997).

9. Joan O'C. Hamilton. "The New Workplace." *Business Week*, April 29, 1996, pp. 106–17.

10. Richard Pastore. "The High Price of Nice." *CIO*, February, 1992, pp. 56–63.

11. Pastore, pp. 56–63.

MODEL OF THE PATH TOWARD A SUCCESSFUL BUSINESS

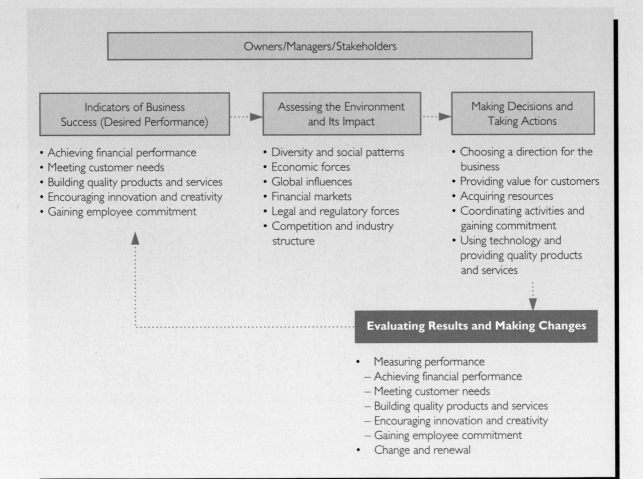

Owners/Managers/Stakeholders

Indicators of Business Success (Desired Performance)

- Achieving financial performance
- Meeting customer needs
- Building quality products and services
- Encouraging innovation and creativity
- Gaining employee commitment

Assessing the Environment and Its Impact

- Diversity and social patterns
- Economic forces
- Global influences
- Financial markets
- Legal and regulatory forces
- Competition and industry structure

Making Decisions and Taking Actions

- Choosing a direction for the business
- Providing value for customers
- Acquiring resources
- Coordinating activities and gaining commitment
- Using technology and providing quality products and services

Evaluating Results and Making Changes

- Measuring performance
  - Achieving financial performance
  - Meeting customer needs
  - Building quality products and services
  - Encouraging innovation and creativity
  - Gaining employee commitment
- Change and renewal

As we start the last part of this textbook, it is important to pause a moment and consider where we have been. We began this text by introducing the concept of a successful business. We then spent time discussing the kinds of decisions a manager needs to make and the types of information needed to make those decisions. Part Two looked at different forces outside the business that affect how it operates. These include social patterns and diversity, economic forces, global influences, financial markets, laws and regulations, and competition and industry structure. In Part Three, we presented key decisions and actions the firm must take to perform well. These processes include determining the direction of the business, providing value to customers, acquiring and using resources, gaining commitment from workers, and integrating technology and quality initiatives to achieve excellence in products and services.

In this final portion of the book we turn to the assessment of performance and the need for change. A business cannot be truly successful unless it can assess its own performance. As you will see, this includes far more than just bottom-line financial performance. Further, a business must constantly adapt to changes in its environment and make changes in its strategies and internal operations to maintain its success. We focus on assessment in Chapter 16 and on change and renewal in Chapter 17.

Again we call your attention to the model on the preceding page. Note that the highlighted box deals with assessment and change. Note also that an arrow goes from that box back to the indicators of business success, showing that the entire process is a circular one.

16 *Measuring Performance*

Coca-Cola held the number one spot in *Fortune*'s "Most Admired Companies" for the second year in a row. More importantly, it scored at the very top of five of *Fortune*'s eight measures of reputation: financial soundness, quality of management, quality of products and services, value as a long-term investment, and community and environmental responsibility. It scored second in two more: ability to attract, develop, and keep talented people, and use of corporate assets. Few could quibble with these. The company's profit for 1996 was $3.5 billion, a 17 percent increase over 1995, and its return on investment for 1996 was a whopping 43.3 percent. The late Roberto Goizueta, who was Chair and CEO, attributed Coca-Cola's quality to dedicated employees. Goizueta said, "Employees with integrity are the ones who build a company's reputation. Working for the Coca-Cola company is a calling. It's not a way to make a living. It's a religion."

Other companies in *Fortune*'s top 10 included Mirage Resorts, Merck, United Parcel Service, Microsoft, Johnson & Johnson, Intel, Pfizer, Procter & Gamble, and Berkshire Hathaway. The measures of reputation included innovativeness, three financial measures, two management and employee-related measures, a measure of quality of products and services, and an indicator of social responsibility.[1] These are very similar to the measures we use in this chapter.

Two statements set the tone for this chapter: "You can control only what you can measure" and "You can reward only what you can measure." Managers of businesses must constantly be alert to how the business is doing. They must be able to objectively measure the firm's progress toward its goals. This chapter brings us back to the indicators of business success we discussed in Chapter 1. We now look at ways to actually identify results that help assess how successful the firm is. After reading this chapter, you should be able to:

1. Describe some major cautions that managers must keep in mind when dealing with measurement.

2. Identify and explain the basic measures of business success in terms of a conceptual model of performance.

3. Explain the primary measures of success from the accounting and financial perspective.

4. Discuss the measures of performance from the customer perspective.

5. Describe the measures of quality and value that can be used in a business.

6. Explain the measures of innovation and creativity.

7. Discuss the most important measures from the employee perspective.

Measurement of performance is essential. Managers spend the bulk of their time planning, making decisions, acquiring resources, developing and implementing strategies, and working with employees to make sure those strategies and decisions are carried out. It is important, however, for managers to also spend time studying performance in order to check the progress of the business. Performance must be compared with the goals set by the firm and the relevant indicators of success. Only when the performance is carefully measured will managers know whether or not corrective action should be taken. This is the circular aspect of the model in Figure 1–6 which we have repeated at the beginning of each part of the text.

Measurement Caveats

Before addressing the measures individually, we note some important caveats or cautions that pervade each of the measures we will present throughout the chapter.

1. Measurements are interrelated and are not done in a vacuum.
2. Managers must measure both efficiency and effectiveness.
3. Companies must measure processes as well as results.
4. Dynamic measurements are more useful than static ones.
5. Measurement must foster communication.[2]

Interrelatedness of Measurements

Managers do not measure performance in unrelated assessments. It is not as if they have unique containers into which they put different kinds of material and then measure how full each is. How well a business does in one instance affects how well it does in others. For example, innovation and creativity are important not only be-

Integrated assessment
The simultaneous measurement of variables in different parts of an organization.

cause they result in new products or services for customers, but also because employees may be happier and more challenged, and owners may ultimately be wealthier. **Integrated assessment** refers to the simultaneous measurement of variables in different parts of an organization. Performance must be measured by an integrated set of assessment variables and techniques so overall effectiveness of the firm's decision makers can be fully grasped.

Effectiveness and Efficiency

Two overriding issues in measuring business performance are effectiveness and efficiency. These important concepts are different but easy to confuse. Look carefully at the differences between the two.

Effectiveness
A measure of the degree to which a business achieves its goals.

innovation p. 522>

Efficiency
A measure of the relationship between inputs and outputs.

Effectiveness is a measure of the degree to which a business achieves its goals. These may be financial goals, customer goals, employee performance goals, quality goals, innovation goals, or any other outcome that the business deems critical. The key is that a business is effective if it reaches its goals. When a business sets a goal of increasing market share by 10 percent this year and does indeed do that, it has been effective in meeting its market share goal. If the business sets a goal of reducing employee turnover by 15 percent and achieves that goal, it has been effective.

Efficiency is a measure of the relationship between inputs and outputs. A business may be effective in meeting its sales goals—but only by committing excessive amounts of human and financial resources to its sales effort. In this case, the business is effective (at least in the short run), but it is inefficient. If the business can reach its sales goals while committing fewer human and financial resources, it becomes more efficient. Improved efficiency saves the business money and conserves its resources. As we have noted throughout this text, businesses are increasingly concerned with finding ways to enhance their efficiency.

We measure efficiency by calculating the ratio of outputs to inputs. Businesses may measure efficiency by looking at sales per person, costs per unit, sales per advertising dollar, sales per square foot of retail space, and other output/input measures. It is important to measure efficiency because it gives us a feel for how well the business is using its resources. It tells us if we are being wasteful or investing unnecessarily in plant and equipment or human resources.

Both efficiency and effectiveness are important, and up to a point they are related. For a while, the more efficient a business becomes, the more it eliminates waste, and the more effective it is. After some point—and this point differs for each company—the quest for efficiency may adversely affect the quest for effectiveness. This can occur if the business strips resources so much that it reduces its ability to perform. Recently some critics have argued that this condition may have occurred with corporate downsizing. No one would argue that many organizations have some fat in them, but after a point, downsizing may jeopardize effectiveness. Efficiency and effectiveness may begin to move in opposite directions.

Processes and Results

Profit is a result, and a very important one. Defects per million is a result. Employee turnover is a result. These results are important and must be measured. However, it is also important to measure processes. Teamwork is a process. Developing new ways to satisfy customers is a process. Reducing the time it takes to develop new products is a process. We cannot abandon measurement of results, but we must also pay attention to processes.

Dynamic versus Static Measures

balance sheet, 486 >
benefits p. 433>

Dynamic measurements
Measures that include some time element, often comparing results in different time periods.

The company's balance sheet at the end of the year is a snapshot of the firm's financial health at that moment. It is a static measure. Financial ratios by themselves are static measures. Payroll, benefits paid, the number of days lost to accidents, and the number of customer complaints are all static measures. **Dynamic measurements** are those that include some time element, often comparing results in different time periods. When we compare this week's measures with last week's, or this quarter's measures with last quarter's or the equivalent quarter from last year, the measures become dynamic. We look at historical trends and project them into the future to help predict what will happen. Thus, measurement must be an ongoing, dynamic process. We must continuously collect information for measurement, analysis, and comparison.

Fostering Communication

Effective measurement requires information from various sources throughout the organization. The results of measurement should also be communicated back throughout the organization. Disseminating results to the lowest ranks will help motivate and focus employees. Thus, the measurement process becomes an integrating device that links units together and fosters communication among them. As results are discussed in management forums, they become a central part of the management process. Communication is essential throughout the entire process of measuring performance and making changes.

Developing Your Critical Thinking Skills

1. Why is measurement important? How does it relate to good management?

2. We suggested five caveats regarding measurement. Add some of your own.

3. Are some of the caveats more important than others? If so, which ones are most important?

The Measures of a Successful Business

In Chapter 1, we presented five indicators of a successful business, which we defined as one that continues to survive and grow and provide value for its various stakeholders. As we turn to analyzing the firm's success in creating value, it is important to compare how we are doing with the goals we have set. Figure 16–1 illustrates the relationships among the five categories, using a model adapted from the "balanced scorecard" developed by Harvard University professor Robert S. Kaplan and consultant David P. Norton.[3]

FIGURE 16–1   A Model of Performance Measures

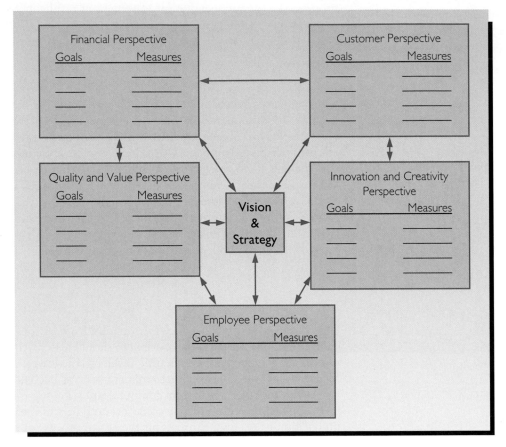

vision p. 310>   As shown in Figure 16–1, evaluation and measurement revolve around the vision and strategy developed for the company. Thus, the goals in each box reflect the vision and strategies that the firm's owners or managers developed. Note that the boxes are interconnected. This means that measurement, like strategies, is an integrated activity and must be done with the whole organization in mind. This is the concept behind the balanced scorecard.

There are two other considerations as we begin the measurement process. First, it must include both cost-oriented and noncost measures. Cost-oriented measures are those items on which a dollar value can be placed. Examples include research and development expenditures, supplier costs, design costs, and distribution costs. There are also a number of noncost-related measures of performance. These items are measurable, but not in terms of dollars. These include market share, complaints, repeat customers, and quality, among others. They may be measured in terms of percentages, numbers of customers, or some technical measure of quality. They are just as important as the cost-oriented measures.

The second consideration is that measurements may be either internal or external. Some measures of performance are clearly in-house. These include number

production p. 464>

of new products, number of production costs, and quality measurements. Other measures, however, are outside the organization. External measures include competitor performance compared with ours, market share, image, and customer complaints.

The following sections will look at each of the broad performance areas shown in Figure 16–1. Little you will see throughout this chapter is new; we set the stage for these topics in Chapter 1 and addressed each of them in previous chapters. But the perspective is different here. In earlier chapters we looked at how to create performance. Here we look at how to measure it.

Developing Your Critical Thinking Skills

1. How are the five areas of measurement related? How does a change in one area affect another?

2. How does changing the vision or strategy of an organization affect how we measure success? Think of an example.

3. Why are both cost-oriented and noncost measures of success important? Are the two related?

4. Will internal and external measures usually support each other, or will they sometimes contradict each other?

The Financial Perspective

Financial performance is one of the most important areas of measurement. Fortunately, it is also one of the most objective measures of the firm's overall performance. Accounting-related measures have the advantage of being comparable both to industry norms and to historical performance. Financial performance should always be measured using generally accepted accounting practices. Accounting-based measures are also more objective than others because they use a common denominator for most measures—dollars. We can measure sales, net cash flow, net profit, and net worth in dollars. Even those measures that are stated in terms of percentages are calculated with dollars. The following paragraphs consider three important measures of financial performance: net profit, cash flow, and net worth.

Profit

Profit
Total revenues minus total expenses.

Perhaps the most common and simplest measure of financial performance is net profit, or net income. In the most basic sense, **profit** is total revenues minus total expenses. In *Business Week* magazine's list of the top 50 businesses each year, one measure of success is the growth in profits. Table 16–1 shows the top ten in the *Business Week* 50 for 1996. Note that the table focuses on *growth* in profits rather than actual profits for the year. Actual profits would yield a different listing that would include large international firms such as General Motors and General Electric.

TABLE 16–1   Top Ten Companies in Profit Growth, 1996

Rank	Company	Percent Growth	Industry
1	Kimberly-Clark	4,128%	Paper and forest products
2	Boston Scientific	2,495	Health care
3	Consolidated Natural Gas	1,297	Utilities
4	Armstrong World Industries	1,112	Consumer products
5	ITT Industries	960	Leisure-time industries
6	Darden Restaurants	671	Leisure-time industries
7	AMR	476	Airlines
8	CIGNA	400	Nonbank financial
9	Burlington Northern Santa Fe	349	Railroad
10	Hemerich & Payne	348	Fuel

SOURCE: "Business Week 50," *Business Week*, March 24, 1997, pp. 19–90.

Return on equity (ROE)

The amount of profit the firm makes for each dollar it invests.

Profit is an absolute figure rather than a relative one. We need to add a few more variables to the analysis to get a better picture. It is often useful to look at the amount the owners have invested in the business. Thus, a second meaningful profit-oriented measure of financial performance is profit divided by investment. This is commonly referred to as **return on equity (ROE),** or the amount of profit the firm made for each dollar the owners invested. Another of the *Business Week* 50 measures is growth in return on equity. The top 10 companies in ROE growth are shown in Table 16–2. Other related measures are return on sales and return on assets, which measure the amount of profits compared with the firm's actual sales or total assets.

TABLE 16–2   Top Ten Companies in Growth of Return on Equity, 1996

Rank	Company	Percent	Industry
1	Avon Products	222%	Consumer products
2	General Mills	186	Food products
3	US Airways	179	Transportation
4	UST	146	Consumer products
5	Tupperware	69	Consumer products
6	Coca-Cola	56	Consumer products
7	Schering-Plough	54	Health care
8	Dell Computer	49	Office equipment and computers
9	Ceridian	49	Office equipment and computers
10	McGraw-Hill	46	Publishing and broadcasting

SOURCE: "Business Week 50," *Business Week*, March 24, 1997, pp. 79–90.

stock p. 216>

Earnings per share
A company's earnings divided by the number of shares of stock outstanding.

Another measure of performance for publicly traded businesses that eases comparisons with other firms is known as earnings per share (EPS). Earnings is another word for net income or profit. **Earnings per share** is earnings (profit) divided by the number of shares of stock outstanding. This measure allows analysts to compare one publicly held firm with another. One business might have more profits than another but have considerably lower earnings per share. The *Wall Street Journal* and other financial reporting services report the EPS of companies in their listings.

Cash Flow

Although net income, return on equity, and earnings per share are extremely important measures of success from a financial perspective, cash flow is also a critical measure. Cash flow is especially important when we consider smaller companies over a shorter time period, such as one year or perhaps a single selling season. We discussed cash flow in Chapter 13 under resources. Cash flow is important because it involves the actual cash coming into or going out of the business. Many of a typical firm's sales are on credit. Customers may buy products or services from a business but not pay for them for perhaps 60 to 90 days. The sales are counted when they are made, but the actual cash is not received until much later. Therefore, cash is not received or does not flow into the business for a while. Smaller companies with limited financing must be particularly sensitive to cash flow. It is not uncommon for a business to be making a profit but be strapped for cash.

Cash is also important due to the seasonal and cyclical nature of business. Suppose you own a toy store. Stores order toys for the Christmas season as early as February. Christmas toys begin arriving in late summer, which is a slack time as far as actual sales go. The firm may have to borrow funds now to pay for products that are sold months later. This problem is even more complicated if the firm's customers buy on credit. The business may have to pay for goods several months before they are sold and then wait several weeks more before it is paid. Thus, the firm's financial health is highly dependent on how well its managers measure and manage cash flow. The importance of cash flow is illustrated in Profile 16–1.

PROFILE 16–1

The Rollerina: Not Rolling in Cash

Beth Jacobson decided that the midsized East Coast city she lived in needed and could support a roller rink focusing on in-line skating. She reasoned that there were few activities available in the city for teenagers and others who liked skating. She capitalized on the resurgence of skating sparked by the introduction of in-line skating. Jacobson and a partner invested much of their personal capital. They also received loans from banks and the Small Business Administration for a total package of debt and equity amounting to $1.5 million.

The rink was scheduled to open in late summer to take advantage of Labor Day and to capture the attention of students and their parents, who would sign them up for roller hockey, a burgeoning sport. Unfortunately, construction delays pushed back the opening until early December. Still, things went well throughout the Christmas holidays and spring. Then came summer. Although Jacobson was counting on summer roller-hockey leagues to keep her going, it finally became clear that there simply were not enough customers for summer leagues. Revenues were substantially lower than projected. But loan payments still had to be made. Utility bills for the large rink, pro shop, snack bar, and other entertainment areas were enormous.

The decline in cash flow caused strain among the investors, who were concerned about their investments, and creditors, who were not being paid. By midsummer of the very first year, Jacobson was already considering closing the business and cutting her losses.

Net Worth

Net worth

The value of a business. For a publicly held firm, its stock price times the number of shares outstanding; for a private firm, its assets minus its liabilities (or its future income projected in today's dollars).

The final financial measure of performance is the value, or net worth, of the business. The **net worth** of a publicly held firm is simply its stock price times the number of shares outstanding. The net worth of a privately held company is much more difficult to assess. To estimate the net worth of a private firm, analysts subtract its liabilities from its assets to obtain its *book value*. Or they may project future income in today's dollars to get a good estimate of the firm's net worth.

Regardless of whether it is a publicly held corporation, a privately held corporation, a sole proprietorship, or a partnership, a healthy firm is one whose net worth continues to increase over time. The amount that the net worth increases from year to year is very much a function of the owner's desire for growth, the environment the business operates in, and how successful management decisions are over time.

Analyzing Financial Reports

Income statement

A financial statement that shows a firm's performance over the course of a specific time period, such as a quarter or a year.

Some of you reading this book may plan a career in accounting or finance. If so, you will learn how to create and analyze financial reports. Others will learn enough in your basic accounting courses to study a few of the major reports and draw some basic conclusions regarding a firm's financial health. Among the concepts you will learn is the need to compare a company's performance both with the industry and with its own historical performance.

Tables 16–3 and 16–4 show two very important financial statements, the income statement and the balance sheet, using Motorola as an example. An **income statement** shows the performance of a company over the course of a specific time period, such as a quarter or a year. It is also known as a profit-and-loss statement, a statement of earnings, or an operating statement. It focuses on sales or revenues and on expenses. As we said, subtracting all expenses from total revenues gives profit (net income or net earnings).

Table 16–3 shows Motorola's income statement for year-end 1996 and 1995. Note that it is called a statement of consolidated earnings, meaning that it is the income statement for the entire company. Each division or profit center of a large company usually has its own financial statements, which are then consolidated into the parent company's statements. Note also that figures are given in millions, which means you should add three zeros at the end of any number to read it accurately.

Table 16–3 shows that Motorola's sales increased approximately $900 million between 1995 and 1996, but earnings before taxes actually decreased by a bit over $1 billion. This means that although sales revenue increased, expenses increased more, giving Motorola and its investors some cause for concern. Part of that expense, however, was an increase in depreciation expense for the 1996 year, which is a *noncash*

revenue p. 17>

TABLE 16–3   Motorola, Inc., Statement of Consolidated Earnings ($ millions)

	Dec. 31, 1996	Dec. 31, 1995
Net Sales	$27,973	$27,037
Manufacturing costs (cost of goods sold)	18,990	17,545
Selling, general, and administrative expenses	4,715	4,642
Depreciation expense	2,308	1,919
Interest expense	185	149
Total costs and expenses	26,198	24,255
Earnings before income taxes	1,775	2,782
Income taxes	621	1,001
Net Earnings	$ 1,154	$ 1,781
Segment Sales		
General systems products	$11,324	$10,660
Semiconductor products	7,858	8,539
Messaging, information, and media products	3,958	3,681
Land mobile products	3,986	3,598
Other products	3,560	3,346
Adjustments and eliminations	–2,713	–2,787
Total Sales	$27,973	$27,037

TABLE 16–4   Motorola, Inc, Consolidated Balance Sheet ($ millions)

Assets	Dec. 31, 1996	Dec. 31, 1995
Cash and cash equivalents	$ 1,513	$ 725
Short-term investments	298	350
Accounts receivable (net)	4,035	4,081
Inventories	3,220	3,528
Other current assets	2,253	1,826
Total current assets	11,319	10,510
Property, plant, and equipment (less depr.)	9,768	9,356
Other assets	2,989	2,872
Total assets	$24,076	$22,738
Liabilities and Stockholders' Equity		
Notes payable	$ 1,382	$ 1,605
Accounts payable	2,050	2,018
Accrued liabilities	4,563	4,170
Total current liabilities	7,995	7,793
Long-term debt	1,931	1,949
Other liabilities	2,355	2,011
Stockholders' equity	11,795	10,985
Total liabilities and stockholders' equity	$24,076	$22,738

expense resulting from increases in the amount of plant and equipment. Motorola's industry segment sales are shown in the bottom half of the table. This is a breakdown of total sales into the various product lines. Note for example, that though total sales went up, one segment—semiconductor products—went down. This may have been partially because one of Motorola's major customers, Apple Computer, had hard times in 1996.

Balance sheet

A financial statement that shows a company's assets (what it owns), liabilities (what it owes), and net worth at a specific point in time.

Table 16–4 shows Motorola's balance sheet. A **balance sheet** lists a company's assets (what it owns), its liabilities (what it owes), and its net worth (owners' equity) at a specific point in time. Note that Motorola's total assets increased by $1.3 billion during 1996, while total liabilities (current liabilities plus long-term debt plus other liabilities) increased by only about $500 million. Thus, the net worth of the company increased by over $800 million during 1996.

Large companies typically send press releases to the media when their financial reports are completed. Analysts and other interested individuals can then seek additional information from the companies, including their annual reports and other financial statements. Profile 16–2 is the press release prepared by Southwest Airlines in January 1997 to publicize its 1996 performance. As is typical, the press release gives financial information plus brief explanations for changes.

PROFILE **16–2**   *Southwest Airlines Reports Record 1996 Earnings*

Dallas, Texas—January 23, 1997. Southwest Airlines' net income for the year ended December 31, 1996, was $207.3 million, as compared to 1995's net income of $182.6 million, an increase of 13.5 percent. Net income per share was $1.37 in 1996 versus $1.23 in 1995.

Southwest's net income for fourth quarter 1996 was $28.2 million ($0.19 per share), compared to fourth quarter 1995 net income of $43.4 million ($0.29 per share). The decrease in earnings was primarily due to a 25 percent increase in jet fuel prices.

Total operating revenues for fourth quarter 1996 increased 11.1 percent to $831.8 million, compared to $748.6 million for fourth quarter 1995. Revenue passenger miles (RPMs) increased 20.9 percent in fourth quarter 1996 as compared to a 9.7 percent increase in available seat miles (ASMs), resulting in a 6.2 point increase in load factor to 68.0 percent. Operating revenue per ASM increased 1.3 percent to $0.0797 in fourth quarter 1996.

Operating expenses per ASM for fourth quarter 1996 increased 5.6 percent to $0.0750, compared to $0.0710 for fourth quarter 1995, primarily due to significantly higher fuel prices.

Herbert D. Kelleher, Chairman, President, and Chief Executive Officer, said: "1996 represents another year of record earnings and our 24th consecutive year of profitability, achieved despite dramatic increases in fuel costs and a 12.6 percent increase in capacity. As expected, our fourth quarter 1996 earnings of $28.2 million fell below last year's record earnings of $43.4 million, in large part due to significantly higher fuel prices.

"Demand for our low-fare, high-quality product was exceptionally strong during fourth quarter 1996, resulting in an increase in unit revenue from year-ago levels. Traffic remains robust and we expect January 1997's load factor to exceed our January 1996 performance. Thus far bookings for February and March are also strong.

"The 5.6 percent increase in our unit cost was primarily due to a 25 percent increase in jet fuel prices, which increased our operating costs by approximately $28 million in fourth quarter 1996. Excluding fuel, our unit costs were up 2.2 percent. Based on current average jet fuel prices of $0.78 per gallon, we expect unit cost growth again in first quarter 1997.

"We initiated service to Providence, Rhode Island on October 27, 1996, and Jacksonville, Florida on January 15, 1997, and are enjoying an extremely positive customer response. Initiatives to control costs are proving successful and, as a result, our earnings outlook is favorable, at this juncture.

"We ended the year with $581.8 million in cash on hand plus our available and unused bank credit line of $460 million.

"Our Board of Directors, at its meeting held January 16, 1997, increased our regular dividend 5 percent in declaring a quarterly dividend of 1.155 cents per share on all shares currently issued and outstanding. This 82nd consecutive quarterly dividend will be paid on March 25, 1997 to shareholders of record at the close of business on February 28, 1997. The 5 percent increase in the dividend is in recognition of our record 1996 financial performance and a promising future for Southwest Airlines."

This press release as well as past releases can be accessed on the Southwest Airlines Internet site at: http://www.iflyswa.com.

The Need for a Long-Term Outlook

As we evaluate the financial health of a company, we need to look at two comparative pieces of information: (1) How has the business done in the past and how is it projected to do in the future? (2) How has it performed or is expected to perform compared with its industry in general?

The Firm Over Time

Determining the value of a business on a given day is important. But more important is looking at how it has done over time. Thus, one measure might be the average value of the firm's stock over a period of several years. This would offset the inevitable peaks and valleys in the value of the stock. A significant event in the industry, the economy, or the company can affect the stock price dramatically. It is not uncommon to see a particular stock drop in value by 20 percent over the course of a week. That drop is usually a reaction of the marketplace to some event.

Consider the situation at Borland International, Inc.,[4] a large maker of database software. Like all software companies, Borland is a high-tech growth company that has high swings in stock prices throughout any given year. In December 1991, Borland's stock closed at $82 per share. Because of the competitive dynamics of the industry, Borland's stock closed at $22 per share in December 1992. It would never see anything near $80 again. It generally stayed in the teens to low 20s until mid-1996, when it dropped to a low of approximately $5 per share at year-end. By mid-1997, its stock was creeping back up to $8 per share. The fluctuations of Borland stock from 1993 to 1997 are shown in Figure 16–2. Who knows where it will go next? It may go back up to its high levels of the early 1990s, or Borland may be acquired by another firm.

The Borland discussion illustrates that assessing the financial health of a firm is a tenuous process. Is Borland financially healthy in 1997? Clearly, more information is needed.

FIGURE 16-2   Borland Stock Prices

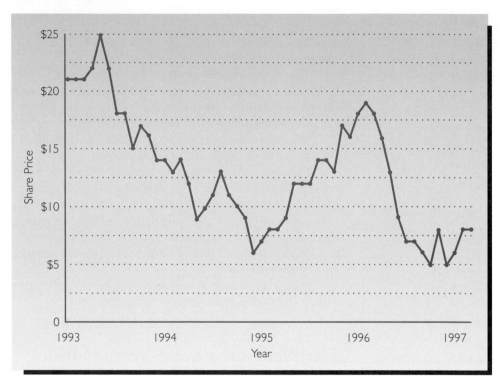

The Firm and Its Industry

The second comparative information we need to assess the true value of a company is how it has performed or is projected to perform compared with the industry it is in. A firm may appear to be doing either well or poorly, but its performance may be viewed much differently depending on the rest of the firms in the industry. In the Borland case, analysts project a growth in earnings per share of 17 percent over the next five years. This sounds reasonable and perhaps even good until you learn that the prediction for the industry as a whole is 21 percent. Borland may not be performing poorly, but apparently other firms in the industry are doing better.

The benefit of a long-term outlook is that it forces us to look at the business as it changes over time relative to the rest of the industry. While this is particularly true in regard to financial measures of performance, it is also true when we look at some of the softer measures like meeting customer needs, which we discuss next.

Before leaving the financial perspective, consider again the need for integrative measures. In this section we have discussed profit, return on equity, cash flow, net worth, and stock prices. Many more elements could be included. The key to good financial analysis is thoroughness. Emphasizing one or two variables to the exclusion of others always leads to erroneous conclusions. It is not uncommon for a company to have a very good return on equity, for example, yet have a low rate of sales growth or perform poorly on other measures of financial performance.

Developing Your Critical Thinking Skills

1. Financial measures include profit, cash flow, and net worth or value of the company. What is the best way to measure each of these?

2. What is the difference between net income and net cash flow? Why is this distinction important?

3. The balance sheet shows the net worth of a company to be its assets minus its liabilities. Can you think of any reasons why this measure of value may not be the most accurate?

4. Why are stock prices on a single day typically not a good measure of the financial success of a company? (Look at the Borland stock prices for a clue.)

The Customer Perspective

The second indicator of success that must be measured is the customer perspective. This aspect of measuring performance includes three subareas: meeting customer needs, customer sensitivity and service, and timeliness.

Meeting Customer Needs

Healthy financial performance can come only if the business successfully meets its customers' needs over time. The difference between a high-quality growth company that perseveres over time and one that struggles continuously is often the degree to which the firm commits to meeting its customers' needs. Assessing performance in meeting customer needs is far more complicated than assessing the firm's financial performance because there are no easily calculated figures measured in a recognized unit such as dollars. Further, it is nearly impossible to compare one firm's performance with another because of the lack of a standardized measure. In spite of these problems, some companies are well known as highly customer-oriented firms—while others are not held in such high esteem.

The importance of measuring how well a given product or service meets customer needs is that the unmeasured problem will never be corrected until it is too late. Consider a restaurant in your community. The restaurant's food is acceptable, and its ambience is good. But if the service is poor or of erratic quality, customers will not come back. More importantly, they may never tell the owner of the restaurant that they are displeased with the service. They simply do not return. The owner doesn't know what the problem is until it is too late. Word of mouth has done more damage than advertising can correct, and the restaurant slowly dies.

Gap analysis
The study of customers' satisfaction with a firm's product or service compared with their expectations.

Gap Analysis

A key to assessing performance in meeting customer needs is a **gap analysis,** which is the study of customers' satisfaction with a firm's product or service compared with their expectations.[5] This is shown in Figure 16–3.

FIGURE 16–3   Gap Analysis of Customer Needs

Step 1: Determining gap
Customer expectations minus customer perceptions equals gap

Step 2: Identifying source and cause of gaps

Source of Gap	Possible Causes
Incorrect expectations	Miscommunication, overpromising
Incorrect performance	Inappropriate design, defective product
Inadequate follow-up	After-sale communication, warranty/repair problems

Step 3: Taking corrective action
Commitment to solving problem
Communication
Reassessment of gap

Determining the Gap

The first step in gap analysis is to determine whether there is a gap between customer expectations and perceptions. This entails communicating with customers to determine precisely what their expectations were and how their perceptions of the firm's performance compared. Care must be taken to determine what customers' expectations *really* are, not what the firm's managers think customers' expectations are. Continuous improvement must aim at closing the real gap rather than what management thinks is the gap.

continuous improvement p. 448>

Consider the experience of United Parcel Service. Management thought the primary gap between consumer expectations and its performance was in the timeliness of deliveries. So UPS spent considerable time and money to make sure packages were delivered on time. It analyzed how long it took drivers to get the package out of the truck and how long it took them to get the package to the door and return to the truck. It took actions to make the delivery service faster and faster. As UPS analyzed customer expectations, however, it found that what customers wanted was more face-to-face interaction with the delivery person. This was more important to customers than the speed of delivery. Not only had UPS been working to close the wrong gap, but the actions it had taken had widened the real gap by rushing the drivers.[6]

Identifying the Source and Cause of the Gap

The second part of gap analysis requires deeper study to determine the sources and causes of the gap. Gaps between expectations and perceived performance may come

UPS has long worked toward making their delivery system increasingly fast and efficient. Customers appreciated the efficiency but also wanted to be able to talk to the delivery person. How would you measure customer satisfaction at a company like UPS, FedEx, or DHL?

from either incorrect expectations, inadequate performance, or inadequate follow-up. Managers must identify the source because each requires a different kind of corrective action.

Sometimes the gap is caused by nothing more than incorrect expectations. Perhaps the company communicated inappropriate expectations in the first place. The problem may stem from faulty communication in which customers became confused over what to expect. It may stem from a company's management promising more than it can deliver. For example, if a car manufacturer claims that its sports car can go from zero to 60 miles per hour in 7.5 seconds, a buyer may purchase the car and then find that it can achieve that performance only in the most controlled situation. Under normal conditions, the car can be expected to take 9.5 seconds to reach 60 mph. Thus, the company communicated unrealistic expectations for its high-performance car. Interestingly, a buyer of a more traditional car would not have those expectations and therefore would not be displeased by slower acceleration. So the key is to match communicated expectations with the logically expected performance. It is not uncommon today to hear executives telling their employees to "underpromise and overdeliver." This simply means they do not want an expectation gap to occur.

Another source of gaps is in the design and manufacture of a product or in the development of a service. In this case, customer expectations are assessed correctly, but

training p. 379>

the product design team develops a product that does not do what it is supposed to do. In service businesses, the equivalent of product design flaws is the failure to develop a system to ensure good service. The equivalent of a defect might be insufficient training of service providers.

The remaining source of gaps between performance and expectation is in the after-sale service or follow-up. Regardless of whether the business sells a service or a product, after-sale service is critical. Perhaps the epitome of after-sale service is that of Carl Sewall, a well-known car dealer in the Dallas area and co-author of the book *Customers for Life*.[7] For example, Sewall doesn't just provide loaner cars to his customers who are having their car serviced. He sends an assistant to the customer's home with the loaner car for the customer to use while the assistant drives the customer's car to the garage, gets it serviced, and returns it to the customer's home.

After-sale service includes warranties and willingness to accept returned merchandise or redo work. Managers should periodically consult with their customers to assess how well the warranties are meeting the customers' needs. Sensitivity to customers who have warranty calls not only builds loyalty, but it also encourages customers to communicate even more with the business to let them know how their perceptions match their expectations.

Taking Corrective Action

Taking immediate action will remove gaps between expectations and performance that may have developed accidentally. Most customers accept the fact that companies occasionally make a mistake. Suppose, for example, that you always take your film to a local drugstore chain for processing because it has quality developing and a one-day turnaround.

Once when you returned to pick up your photos, you found the store had lost them. The degree to which you were irate depended partially on how critical the pictures were. Perhaps more important, however, was the store's response to its mistake. Although the pictures would be lost forever, the store manager could give you free film and other goodies to assuage your disappointment. If the manager tried hard enough, the store would not lose you as a customer.

However, it is important for a business to ensure that the problem does not recur. Carl Sewall suggests that a long history of providing good service is what allows you to forgive the store. He warns against taking advantage of customers by making a second mistake.[8]

We have mentioned the importance of communication several times in this chapter and, indeed, throughout the book. Communication is perhaps nowhere more important than in removing gaps between performance and expectations. It assures customers that they are important and their concern is a high priority. It helps managers know precisely what the problem is and whether the solution implemented did, in fact, solve the problem. Managers should communicate with their customers, their employees, and their other stakeholders every day. Then when performance gaps do occur, all parties feel comfortable discussing problems and solutions.

Finally, managers must constantly reassess performance and expectations. Continuous improvement truly is a continuous process. It should become a routine task for decision makers to be constantly collecting information, constantly assessing, and constantly improving performance.

Measuring Sensitivity and Service to Customers

The managers of a healthy firm know that meeting customer needs is a key to being financially sound. Managers need to be in touch with customers to assess their needs. The gap analysis is a measurement tool for customer service.

A related but different concept that must also be measured is sensitivity to customers, or how well the business reacts to customer communications. How does the business respond to customer requests and complaints?

Gap analysis is insufficient for this measurement because it assumes a level of customer expectations and company performance. Sensitivity to customers, on the other hand, is often an impromptu action. It involves reacting, on the spot, to accommodate customers. It may even require empowering front-line employees to react immediately to a shifting customer need and then report that shift to higher levels in the organization for further study.

feedback p. 361>

Monitoring customer sensitivity is important because it builds increasing loyalty in customers. It also gives the business powerful feedback from its customers, which can be used for competitive purposes. For example, a computer maker receives a note from a customer saying it would sure be nice if its computer monitors had a little container built in or attached to hold pens and sticky notes. The manufacturer's representative responds immediately by sending the customer a container she found at a supply store that is held on by Velcro. But the rep also passes the suggestion on to the monitor design department, which redesigns the monitor case so the container is a built-in part of the monitor that doubles as a carrying handle.

A number of manufacturers have telephone hot lines specifically to receive complaints and comments from their customers. Whirlpool dubs its toll-free number its "cool line" because having someone listen to their complaints keeps the customers cool. The cool line is also a ready source of new ideas for the firm's appliances.

Since customer sensitivity is often a one-on-one action, it is difficult to measure how well the company does. Still, indicators like letters of appreciation provide a clue. Interestingly, customers will often let the company know when it has done an unusually outstanding job in serving them one way or another. This is above and beyond their response to the normally expected excellent service.

The opposite of the letter of appreciation is of course the complaint letter. These must be not only answered but also studied carefully to determine precisely what the problem is and what caused it.

Second-level communications

Communication that customers make only when their first attempt to gain satisfaction proves fruitless.

A second measure of customer sensitivity (or lack thereof) is **second-level communications,** those communications that customers make only when their first attempt at gaining satisfaction proves fruitless. Suppose you have a complaint about the answering machine you recently purchased. You take the machine back to the store where you purchased it, and the salesperson tells you they cannot fix the equipment because it is no longer under warranty. Feeling that you were treated unfairly, you then contact either the store manager or the manufacturer. This contact is second-level communications. The more sensitive a company is to its customers, the fewer second-level communications they should have.

Sometimes companies receiving second-level communications really cannot help the customer. Sometimes the customer's complaint is unjustified, and sometimes it is beyond the company's control. For example, the government shutdowns in 1996 caused a massive delay in processing student loan requests. Many university presidents received calls from concerned parents when the financial assistance office literally could not help them in expediting the paperwork to determine eligibility for financial

Whirlpool has a 1-800 number that customers can call with questions or complaints. This helps solve problems before they become big problems. What other businesses do you know that have a formalized communications system in which customers can register their opinions?

assistance. Unfortunately, the presidents couldn't help either (although some universities finally took creative and somewhat risky actions to guarantee financial assistance without fully processed paperwork).

Even when a company cannot do anything to resolve a problem, the second-level communication must receive high priority as a way to minimize damage. These communications should be recorded to determine if the problem is unique or common. Both corrective action and preventive action should be taken when possible.

Measuring Timeliness

There are virtually no areas where timeliness cannot be measured. Measuring timeliness is an important efficiency measure. It is also an important customer service measure.

Manufacturers can measure the time it takes to produce a product after the order is received. Suppliers measure how long it takes to make a delivery. Product development departments measure how long it takes to develop and test a new product. Service companies measure how long it takes to provide a service to their customers. Banks and fast-food restaurants measure how long customers stand in line.

Measuring response time is particularly important when the service is being provided on site. This lets customers plan their own activities around the arrival of the service personnel. Measuring timeliness is important, whether the company is a Fortune 500 multinational providing a multimillion-dollar installation or a small clothing store whose owner wants to have the right number of employees on the floor.

Chili's restaurants measure their timeliness in seating customers. When customers come in, the host records the time they entered, the wait time promised, and the time they were seated. This does two things. It tells the restaurant managers if the customers were seated in less time than promised—a measure of customer service relating to delivering what you promise. It also gives the managers information about the relative supply and demand for tables in their restaurant. Managers know roughly how long the average customer is willing to wait to be seated rather than going to a competitor. By recording the wait times as well as the number of would-be customers who left, the manager can get a feel for how severe the loss of customers is.

Adjusting performance based on the timeliness measure is a judgment call. Having the absolutely fastest service does not necessarily mean that a business will capture market share, but having the slowest service will often cause the business to lose market share when customers have other choices. Managers must determine the trade-offs between timeliness and costs. If response time is at least adequate, the manager may not want to add personnel or change the operating system because the change might be more costly than the benefit of quicker response time. For example, a nice sit-down restaurant might have somewhat slow service. However, if the patrons do not mind and even enjoy the ambience while waiting for their food, the problem may not warrant additional cooking or table service staff. By contrast, if customers at a fast-food restaurant wait more than three minutes, they become upset.

Measuring Quality and Value

Assessing the third indicator of success, quality and value, is difficult because it is something of a moving target. We mentioned that financial performance must be measured in comparison with other firms and with its own performance historically. The same holds true for quality. We can get a better picture of the quality of our service if we benchmark it with others. As Table 16–5 shows, at least four indicators of quality exist for products and four for services.

TABLE 16–5   Indicators of Quality

Product Quality	Service Quality
Reliability	Knowledgeable staff
Durability	Responsiveness
Ease of maintenance	Empathy
Ease of use	Tangibles

SOURCE: Adapted from Charles W. Lamb, Jr., Joseph F. Hair, Jr., and Carl McDaniel, *Marketing*, 3rd ed. (Cincinnati: South-Western Publishing Co. 1996), pp. 38, 262–3.

Motorola's pagers virtually never have defects. Few products of any kind have such a high reliability as the pagers do. What other products can you think of that are known for quality?

Product Quality Indicators

Indicators of product quality include reliability, durability, ease of maintenance, and ease of use. Businesses concentrate on all of these as they attempt to improve their quality performance.

Reliability relates to the frequency of breakdown or need for repair. We have often mentioned Motorola and its commitment to quality. Due to its Six Sigma quality program, which we described in Profile 15–2, its pagers are calculated to fail on the average of once every 150 years. In other words, if your pager has a problem, it is probably not with its design or manufacture. We return in Profile 16–3 to Motorola's Six Sigma program to illustrate the need for measurement as part of the process.

PROFILE 16–3   *Six Sigma Quality at Motorola: Measuring Success*

Sigma is a statistical term just as *pi* is a mathematical term. If you have not had a basic statistics course, the concept of standard deviations, or sigmas, may not be familiar to you yet. What Six Sigma means at Motorola is that there will be no more than 3.4 defects per million parts. Another way of saying this is that the product will be right no less than 99.99966 percent of the time.

At the three or four sigma level, most companies can make an improvement just by thinking about the problem and making a few changes to fix obvious problems. But moving toward five sigma and on toward six sigma quality requires a planned improvement system, including statistical analysis of processes and a total commitment to quality. Casual interest in improving quality is not enough at this level.[9]

Improvement becomes more difficult at higher levels. For example, most of us could make perhaps 20 percent of our free throws in basketball after a little practice. Those who want to be better could, with some effort, get up to 40 percent. But to make 75 percent of your free throws, you must commit a major effort specifically to shooting free throws. Now suppose you set the goal of making *all* of your free throws—or 99.99966 percent of them. Now you must practice constantly. But you must also analyze every aspect of the shot: the stance, how you hold the ball, the movements made in shooting, the follow-through, eye focus on the rim, maybe even how many times to bounce the ball before shooting. And you must record every shot to identify which actions are most successful. You watch other top stars shoot and adopt those movements that work for you. But most importantly, you constantly look for ways to improve your percentage.

Durability refers to how long a product will last and how resistant it is to abuse. Durability is different from reliability. Reliability measures frequency of failure. Durability measures length of product life and resistance to abuse. Thus, a Motorola pager is almost certain not to fail because of defects. It is *not* guaranteed to continue working if dropped on the sidewalk. It will break if run over by a car. The pager is extremely reliable, and it is durable enough for most uses. On the other hand, some products are known for their durability. Caterpillar equipment has a reputation for lasting almost forever, even in adverse conditions such as coal mines or the North Slope oil fields. It is not uncommon to see Caterpillar equipment being operated 30 years after it was first put in service.

Products vary considerably in their life expectancy. Refrigerators commonly last 20 years. Washer/dryers often last 15 years. Microwave ovens may last only five to seven years. Statistics abound for these kinds of products, so it is easy to compare projections for one product against those of the industry.

Ease of maintenance refers to how easy it is to service a product as well as how often the product needs servicing. Products today are far more complex than those made a decade or so ago, but servicing them may now be a matter of simply replacing modules rather than repairing actual parts. Some washing-machine manufacturers now put most serviceable parts just inside the front panel so that the machine does not have to be pulled out from the wall to service.

Related to ease of maintenance is frequency of maintenance. Cars are a good example of improvements in quality. Ads for today's cars extoll the virtues of not needing a tuneup for 100,000 miles. Tires last 80,000 miles. Even motor oil needs changing far less often than before.

Ease of use refers to how easy a product is to operate. The phrase *user friendly* is used for products ranging from computers to copiers to kitchen appliances to manufacturing equipment. Great strides have been made in user friendliness in recent years. It's simple to benchmark ease of use against competitor products. Focus groups with users of the product and users of competing products are also informative. Customers in focus groups are quite willing to share their frustrations about product use with researchers.

Service Quality Indicators

Indicators of service quality include knowledgeable staff, responsiveness, empathy, and tangibles. As businesses become more consumer oriented, they focus both time and training on increasing their performance on these indicators of quality. As with product quality, managers must benchmark their quality of service against competitors, other companies known for their excellence, and their own performance in the past.

Knowledgeable staff are employees with sufficient training and expertise to respond to customers' questions and concerns intelligently and properly. Knowledgeable employees are critically important, given the limited time customers have to interact with service providers. This is especially true now since much interaction is electronic rather than in person. Companies can assess and improve their employees' knowledge through in-house programs or by sending them to specialized training schools to learn the needed information.

Responsiveness refers to how quickly a customer receives service or information. Some movie theaters, for example, give free soft drinks if customers wait in line for more than four minutes. Wal-Mart promises to open a new cash register line if more than three people are in line. Some appliance repair businesses guarantee service within 48 hours. Dry cleaners respond to busy customers with an "in by 9:00, out by 5:00" policy. Lands' End puts orders in the mail within 24 hours (48 if they have to be monogrammed).

Some retail companies have found that computers maximize responsiveness. In Wal-Mart's automotive department, for example, a customer can use a touch screen to enter a car brand, year, and model and whether the desired parts are lights, windshield wipers, or oil filters. The computer then prints out a list of part numbers the customer can find on a nearby shelf. Department stores use similar equipment in their bridal registries. Customers touch the first few letters of the name of bride, the groom, or their parents, and the equipment will print out a list of what they want and which items have already been purchased by other customers.

Empathy measures how much the company cares for the customers. It means employees can see the customer's point of view. It means they remember a new customer's name. It means they pay attention and learn about the customer. The better employees can understand a customer's thought process, perspective, and idiosyncrasies, the better the business can build quality into the service it provides.

It seems strange that we can increase a trait as subjective as empathy by measuring something, but it can be done. First, we record any information we do have about the customer. Preferably we record it in a database so that other employees can access it in case the primary server is not available. But recording it anywhere—in a notebook, in a day planner, or scratched on the back of the customer's business card—is better than nothing. Then the next conversation with the customer might include that information if appropriate.

Beyond recording information, managers want to analyze it and compare it with past data. For example, suppose I sell and service copiers. I know from the automatic counter in your copier how many copies you made last month, last quarter, and even since you bought the machine. I can use that information to discuss your emerging copying needs with you. I can suggest ways you can save money by changing the copy cards or improve efficiency by moving the copier. That is part of empathy.

Tangibles are those objects or services that a business can provide its customers to make their lives easier. The ATM machine is a tangible service item. The machine that prints out the bride and groom's wish list is a tangible in a department store. Even the magazines in a barbershop can be tangibles if they are magazines the shop's customers enjoy. Tangibles include those loaner cars at the auto repair shop or at least a ride to work for customers who drop off their car.

Emphasis on Measurement

We began this chapter with the statement "You can control only what you can measure." We have suggested here several good indicators of quality and value, some of which were discussed in more detail in Chapter 15. The key is that you must be able to measure quality and you must be able to affect it.

Let's consider how to measure quality. First we must define what we mean by quality in our particular business. Then we ask customers what they mean by quality. What is important to them? What aspects of the service or product do they like? What do they want to avoid? Blending our definitions and the customers' definitions gives us an idea of what is really important. Next we set out to find ways of measuring those items. We may want to measure defects. We may measure the number of phone calls we get from irate customers. Perhaps we measure the number of thank-you notes from happy customers. We could measure the number of repeat customers. We probably should measure the number of lost customers. We measure how long it takes to return a customer's computer. We measure how long restaurant patrons must wait to be seated. We measure the amount of food left on their plates.

We measure anything under our control, but we also collect information on those things that are not currently under our control. Then we see if we can find a way to control them, or at least to overcome the problem.

Developing Your Critical Thinking Skills

1. We have emphasized meeting customer needs throughout the text. How would you measure whether or not you are meeting customer needs?

2. Why is it important to distinguish customer sensitivity from just meeting customer needs?

3. Define timeliness. How would you measure timeliness at McDonald's? At IBM? At your university?

Measuring Innovation and Creativity

creativity p. 522>
innovation p. 522>

As we mentioned early in this chapter, it is important to measure processes as well as results. Creativity is a process. Innovations, the new products or services that come from creative efforts, are results. Both are important. Innovation is the fourth area in Figure 16–1 that should be measured. As the figure suggests, we should have goals for and measurements of innovation.

It can be difficult to measure innovation. It is easy to say, "We have a very innovative firm," or "Our people are creative visionaries." It is much harder to prove that. Thus, the measures of innovation and creativity are partially objective and partially subjective.

Objective Measures

Rubbermaid and 3M are noted as two of the more creative and innovative firms in the United States. They are known to encourage creativity and innovation among their employees. Both companies insist that new products—those developed in the last five years—make up a high percentage of their total product line. Thus, one measure of innovation for them is the number of new products introduced each year. But they have other measures. Growth oriented firms keep track of the length of time to develop a new product, the number of patents held by the company, and the number of new patent applications each year.[10] Mine Safety Appliances, an innovative company in Pittsburgh, measures 54 variables oriented toward innovation. The nine that deal with product development are shown in Table 16–6.

Subjective Measures

In addition to the objective measures of innovation and creativity, there are subjective measures. These deal to a large extent with the ambience of the workplace. The number of researchers who receive bonuses for inventions can be a measure of how creative the workforce is. The number of new product ideas submitted can also measure creativity.

Many new product ideas never see the light of day. Yet the business must encourage new ideas so that employees continue to be creative. The Post-it Note is a classic example of innovation. This interesting story from 3M includes developing glue that was supposed to be very strong but wouldn't stick, finding ways to trim a micro-thin slice off the paper to make room for the glue, and even selling the concept in an innovative way. But the product would not exist were it not for 3M's innovative culture. We will discuss more ways a business can foster creativity and innovation in the next chapter.

Firms can also measure innovation subjectively just by assessing the excitement of workers. Typically, innovative companies have very low turnover, low absenteeism, and employees who choose to work beyond the hours for which they are paid. But sometimes innovation actually leads to turnover—for example, in high-tech companies. Employees invariably develop ideas or products that the company, because of its limited financial position, cannot pursue. Thus, some employees may leave to start their own business, often with the blessing of their former employer.

TABLE 16–6   Mine Safety Appliances' Measures of Innovation

- Average time to market for new products
- New product sales dollars as percentage of total sales dollars
- R&D investment as a percentage of sales
- Concept-to-customer time milestones met
- Planned and actual return on investment from new products
- Design for manufacturability (how easy is it to make the product)
- Number of part numbers per product (lower is better)
- Number of engineering changes after production release
- Target product cost achievement

SOURCE: The Price Waterhouse Change Integration Team, *The Paradox Principles* (Burr Ridge, IL: Irwin, 1996), p. 250.

3M is noted as having one of the most innovative cultures of any company. This culture helped create the Post-It™ Note and the Buf-Puf™ Facial Sponge. How does innovation become a part of a company's culture?

Developing Your Critical Thinking Skills

1. How will innovation in an accounting firm differ from that in a manufacturing firm?

2. Why is innovation difficult to measure objectively?

3. If innovation is difficult to measure, how does a business go about rewarding it?

The Employee Perspective

The final perspective on measurement deals with employees. A business needs to be able to measure how well it utilizes its workers, how good their performance actually is, and how committed they are.

Workforce Utilization and Productivity

Workforce productivity is relatively easy to measure as long as the workers are producing tangible products for which their individual input is both identifiable and controllable. Unfortunately, this leaves out almost all management jobs, most staff positions, and research. It even leaves out most assembly-line jobs, since the rate of efficiency is not individually controllable. It also leaves out maintenance work and other jobs that are not tied directly to production. Thus, it is really quite difficult to assess the utilization of most employees.

Yet analysis of workforce utilization and productivity is important for efficiency reasons. We measure productivity by dividing total sales or total profits by the number of workers in the company. If a firm can eliminate 10 percent of its workforce and still maintain the same level of sales, it will increase productivity. If it maintains the same number of workers but can increase their output, it will increase productivity.

Workforce productivity involves more than simply dividing numbers. It involves having the right people in the right jobs. It involves having motivated, well-trained employees supervised by effective managers. It involves having sufficient equipment so that employees can do the jobs they are assigned.

benchmarking p. 450>

A firm can measure underutilization by observing worker behavior, looking at the total output per employee, and benchmarking with other departments or other companies. Sometimes colleagues or even the workers themselves complain that they are not being well used. It is, of course, difficult to get an accurate assessment of underutilization because of workers' ability to hide idleness and management's inability to really measure output of staff positions.

Overutilized workers can also hurt the firm. Overworked employees may seem to be more efficient since they produce more output than others. However, they may eventually become unproductive or *burn out* if they are continually asked to do too much. One of the problems with downsizing has been that the remaining employees work excessively long hours to make up for the loss of their colleagues. Overutilization is easier to measure because of the visible evidence. Stressed-out employees, defective work, obvious fatigue, absenteeism, and other indicators can give managers a feel for the amount of overutilization.

training p. 379>

A third situation facing managers is the inappropriate mix of workers and jobs. In this situation, the company has approximately the right number of employees, but they are misallocated. Thus, one department may have several underutilized workers while other departments are scrambling to keep up with their demands. Sometimes individual workers are simply in the wrong job. They cannot function properly because either they have insufficient training or they somehow got assigned a job that just does not fit their personality. A highly innovative employee stuck in a routine, control-oriented job is an example.

Unfortunately, managers may have little discretion in solving either underutilization, overutilization, or misallocation of workers. For example, budgetary constraints or the inability to reassign work from one person to another may limit the manager's ability to address these issues. Still, measuring the utilization of workers can be useful in assessing the overall health of the company.

Performance Appraisal

Performance appraisal
The process a company uses to measure employee productivity.

Performance appraisal is the process the business uses to measure employee productivity. Performance appraisal may be approached in a number of ways. The intent is to measure how well the employee is doing and communicate that assessment to the employee so that improvements and corrective actions can take place.

Performance appraisal should focus on those activities and outcomes that are critical for performing the job. Both objective and subjective performance outcomes are usually assessed. Subjective assessments, such as "works well with team members" or "provides timely information" may be difficult for any one person to assess properly, so some companies use what is known as *360-degree appraisal.* This means employees are assessed or rated by everyone with whom they have key interactions. Co-workers, outside customers, key people in other departments, the boss, and subordinates may all evaluate the employees and offer their sense of whether individuals provide timely information, for example. The range of perspectives should offer a more complete picture of how employees are doing on each performance factor.[11]

Employee Satisfaction and Commitment

business culture
p. 114>

Healthy businesses must have a sense of how employees feel about their work. For these companies, assessing employee satisfaction is fundamental for building the business culture they desire. For example, L.L. Bean thinks of its employees as customers. L.L. Bean's statement of corporate objectives includes, "At L.L. Bean, we consider employee satisfaction to be a valued end in itself. It is simply better that people enjoy what they are doing. Good managers treat their employees with the consideration they would like for themselves. They monitor their employees' level of satisfaction and take appropriate measures to maintain high levels of morale within their work units."[12]

How do businesses measure employee satisfaction and the level of commitment? A number of approaches are possible. First, managers can infer employee satisfaction and commitment by looking at the levels of absenteeism and turnover in the business.[13] **Absenteeism** occurs when employees do not show up at work when they are scheduled to be there. In general, higher levels of absenteeism suggest higher levels of employee dissatisfaction with the business or their particular jobs. However, a caution should be noted here. Sometimes people are absent from their jobs for uncontrollable reasons, such as personal or family illnesses. These have nothing to do with their satisfaction or attitude toward the job. It is controllable absenteeism, where employees simply decide not to come to work on a given day, that can be an indicator of employee dissatisfaction.

Absenteeism
A situation where an employee does not show up at work when scheduled to be there.

Turnover
The rate at which employees leave a company.

Turnover occurs when employees leave the company. Turnover can be affected by many factors, including the range of other employment opportunities available. In general, high levels of voluntary turnover suggest that employees are dissatisfied with some important aspects of the job. A manager must be careful with assessments in this area. Some turnover is natural in any business. However, if six of the 10 employees in information services have left in the past year, some aspect of dissatisfaction is likely present. Because of the high cost of replacing skilled employees, the causes of turnover should be identified and addressed.

Some companies conduct *morale* or *opinion surveys* periodically to assess employee satisfaction and overall attitudes toward the business. Some use outside consultants to conduct these surveys to help assure objectivity and confidentiality. Morale and opinion surveys can be quite detailed and can point out specific areas or practices that employees object to. These surveys may reveal employee views that managers had already suspected—for example, frustration about heavy workloads or disappointment with low pay raises. However, surveys can reveal important employee insights that surprise managers. For example, in light of downsizings, employees may say that they distrust management and feel that communication and respect are poor in the business. While such feedback may be tough to accept, the enlightened manager takes it seriously and searches for ways to improve.

Many companies do *exit interviews* of employees who are leaving the company. It is unfortunate that the information is gained after the fact in these cases, but it is still good information. In fact, exit interviews can be extremely accurate and insightful. Since the interviewees are severing ties with the business, they may be willing to share views or concerns they were reluctant to express while they worked there.

Other indicators of employee commitment and satisfaction exist. The number of formal complaints or grievances lodged against management or other employees, attempts to unionize nonunion firms, and strikes or walkouts by unionized firms are all measurable statistics that can give a clue whether employees are satisfied with their workplace.

In addition to these objective measures, a number of more subjective approaches are available. Regular staff meetings to discuss employee problems, recruitment and retention committees, employee focus groups, open door policies, specific opportunities for employees to discuss problems, and even suggestion boxes can all indicate levels of employee satisfaction.[14] An excellent indicator is the second-level complaint. Just as customers who are willing to take their complaints to higher levels usually indicate a significant customer relations problem, employees who are so concerned that they are willing to take their complaints to higher levels are usually good indicators of problems with employee relations. Some companies use hot lines or other confidential approaches to encourage their employees to offer their frank input. IBM's SpeakUp program allows employees to asks questions and register complaints or concerns anonymously.[15]

One subjective measure of employee commitment is how willing employees are to do things above and beyond the call of duty. At Southwest Airlines, it is common for employees to work long hours. It is also common to see them helping co-workers with tasks that are not in their own job description. This loyalty is enhanced, of course, when employees see Herb Kelleher serving drinks and snacks on a plane when he flies. It is easy to be loyal when the CEO of the company takes that kind of interest. The giant pharmaceutical firm Merck & Co. is another example. When its plant in Virginia that was being built to produce an AIDS-fighting drug became buried under four feet of snow in 1996, the employees—from managers to lab workers—rushed in with their snow shovels to help dig out and keep the process on schedule. In fact, the overall loyalty of Merck's employees had much to do with bringing Crixivan to patients nine months ahead of schedule.[16]

Southwest Airlines thrives on its dedicated and loyal employees who are willing to work long hours because the company is a fun place to work. How can Southwest identify potential employees who may develop into hard working, loyal employees? What criteria do you have in selecting a company and a career?

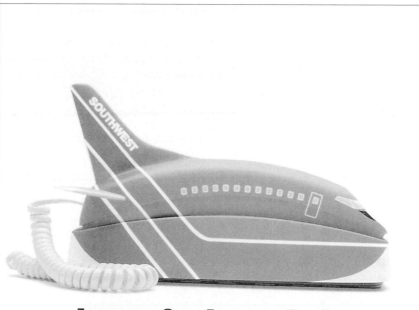

ANYBODY CAN ANSWER THE PHONE.
WE WANT PEOPLE WHO ANSWER THE CALL.

At Southwest Airlines, we believe the people who answer the phones in our Reservations Sales Centers are every bit as important as the folks who maintain our fleet, pilot our planes, or handle our Customers' baggage. After all, they're the first contact for positively outrageous service–"The Voice" of our airline. And we're now hiring for both fulltime and parttime positions. If your time is flexible, allowing you to work rotating shifts and hours (bid on a seniority basis), come talk to us about a career that will let you take off!

There's lots of potential for growth at Southwest. And we offer great incentives, including a flexible medical/dental plan, matching 401(k), Profit$haring, job stability, and financial security, not to mention those terrific travel privileges. Just a few of the many reasons why we were named one of the top ten companies to work for in America.

Just pick up an application at any Southwest Airlines airport ticket counter, complete it, and mail it to Southwest Airlines at P.O. Box 36644, Dallas, Texas 75235-1644.

An Equal Opportunity Employer

Reservations Sales Centers are located in Albuquerque, Chicago, Dallas, Houston, Little Rock, Oklahoma City, Phoenix, Salt Lake City, and San Antonio. Starting salary is $7.00/hr., $7.50 after six months, $8.00 second year, with annual increases thereafter. ©1996 Southwest Airlines Co.

Other companies may have innovative ways of measuring employee satisfaction and commitment. How these employee concerns are measured is not nearly as important as the fact that they are measured and acted on. Companies must constantly be assessing their performance in employee commitment and satisfaction as indicators of business health.

Developing Your Critical Thinking Skills

1. Often the most important indicators of employee performance are quite difficult to measure. How does the 360-degree appraisal approach provide a better measurement of employee performance than a manager alone could provide?

2. Which is worse, workforce underutilization or overutilization? What are the impacts of each?

3. Define employee satisfaction. Now apply your definition to an actual company situation. Does your definition work?

SUMMARY

1. Daily newspapers make it look easy to measure the performance of a business. They present reports on profits and sales and leave the reader with the impression that everything important has been covered. But measurement is much more complicated. To begin with, a number of important caveats must be kept in mind with any attempt to measure business performance.

   ■ What are some of the important cautions that should be considered in the measurement process?

   In this chapter you learned about five caveats:
   (1) Measurements are interrelated and not done in a vacuum.
   (2) We must measure both efficiency and effectiveness.
   (3) We must measure processes as well as results.
   (4) We must measure dynamically, not just statically.
   (5) Measurement must foster communication.

2. Another aspect of the complexity of measurement is the fact that it involves far more than simply looking at the financial performance of a company.

   ■ What are the elements of a comprehensive model of performance measurement for a business?

   In this chapter you learned that a comprehensive model of measurement revolves around the company's vision and strategy and consists of measurements in the following five areas of concern:
   (1) Financial perspective
   (2) Customer perspective
   (3) Quality and value perspective
   (4) Innovation perspective
   (5) Employee perspective

3. The accounting and financial perspective usually receives the most attention. People not familiar with business probably think of this as a simple matter of reporting sales or profits. But financial performance is more complex than that.

   ■ What are the major measures of financial performance?

   In this chapter you studied the following measures:
   (1) Profit. In the most basic sense, profit is total revenue minus total expenses. A second important measure of profit is return on equity investment (defined as

profit or net income divided by investment by the owners). A third important measure is earnings per share (determined by dividing net earnings or net profit by the number of shares of stock outstanding).

(2) Cash flow. This concept measures actual cash coming into and going out of the business. Cash flow differs from profit because some revenue items do not come in the form of cash and some expense items do not involve cash outlays.

(3) Net worth. This is the value of a company. For publicly held firms, analysts measure it by multiplying the stock price times the number of shares outstanding. They can also measure it by subtracting liabilities from net assets.

■ Where does one find measurement information for a company?

Three primary sources were explained in this chapter:

(1) The income statement. This shows the performance of a company over the course of a specific time period, usually a quarter of a year or a year.

(2) The cash flow statement. This shows the amount of cash that comes into and leaves the company over time.

(3) The balance sheet. This shows a company's assets, liabilities, and its net worth at a specific point in time.

4. Financial measurement is important and basic. Nevertheless, it tells only part of the story. Businesses occasionally show excellent financial performance at a time when trouble is on the horizon because of a failure to adequately meet evolving customer needs, develop new products and services, or cultivate employee relationships.

■ What are the major considerations involved in measuring performance from the customer perspective?

Customer satisfaction involves meeting customer expectations in three areas, each of which needs to be measured. These areas are:

(1) Meeting customer needs. This can be measured with a gap analysis, which involves comparing customer expectations with customer satisfaction.

(2) Customer sensitivity and service. This can be measured by complaints and by communication with higher levels of management.

(3) Timeliness. This applies to virtually all areas of the business. It can be measured with such indicators as length of time to produce a product and length of time a retail customer has to wait before being served.

5. Another area that requires measurement is the company's progress in meeting its quality and value goals.

■ How does a company measure quality?

Product quality indicators include reliability, durability, ease of maintenance, and ease of use. Service quality indicators include knowledgeable staff, responsiveness, empathy, and tangibles.

6. In today's world, businesses must continually adapt and innovate. Some companies are known for their innovations.

■ What are the major considerations involved in measuring performance from the innovation perspective?

This area involves both objective and subjective indicators.

(1) Objective indicators include average time to market for new products, new product sales dollars as a percentage of total sales dollars, and R&D expenditures as a percentage of sales.

(2) Subjective measures include the ambience of the workplace and the number of new ideas submitted.

7. Organizations cannot be successful over time without committed employees. Measuring commitment and satisfaction is important for building work environments where employees feel motivated.

- What are the major considerations involved in measuring performance from the employee perspective?

Three themes must be considered. These are:

(1) Workforce utilization and productivity. We can measure productivity by dividing total sales or total profits by the number of workers. We can measure utilization by observing worker behavior and by benchmarking with other departments and companies.

(2) Performance appraisal. Appraisals are used to assess the productivity of individual employees.

(3) Employee satisfaction and commitment. This can be measured by such techniques as employee surveys, employee focus groups, and employee complaint records.

Links to Future Courses

While measurement is discussed in many courses, a few take a more in-depth look at measurement issues and practices. Among them are the following:

- Principles of accounting
- Principles of finance
- Human resources management
- Marketing and marketing research
- Operations management
- Strategic management

EXERCISES AND APPLICATIONS

1. Most large businesses include their annual reports on their websites. These annual reports contain both balance sheets and income statements. Divide the class into four sections. Students in each section will examine the balance sheets and income statements of one of the following four businesses: Apple Computer, Southwest Airlines, AT&T, and Kodak. Each group should provide an assessment of the business they have examined by looking at the financial measures.

2. Form teams of five students each. As a team, identify five important measures of customer satisfaction. Then select a business with which you are familiar. How does it rank on your five measures?

3. Remain in the same teams. Using the measures of service quality discussed in the chapter, evaluate the service quality of your university's food-service provider.

4. List as many measures of employee satisfaction as you can. Brainstorm in your teams to see how many you can develop. Then discuss how easy each is to measure and how accurate the measure might be. Write up your results.

5. As this chapter has noted, measurement must look at a number of factors. In your teams, discuss how this course should be evaluated. Prepare a one-page paper out-

lining the measures you would use to determine whether the class has been successful.

6. Interview one manufacturer and one service business in your community. How does each measure quality? Compare your two answers in a two-page paper.

KEY TERMS

Absenteeism, p. 503
Balance sheet, p. 486
Dynamic measurements, p. 479
Earnings per share, p. 483
Effectiveness, p. 478
Efficiency, p. 478
Gap analysis, p. 489
Income statement, p. 484

Integrated assessment, p. 478
Net worth, p. 484
Performance appraisal, p. 503
Profit, p. 481
Return on equity (ROE),
   p. 482
Second-level communications, p. 493
Turnover, p. 503

CASE: NEW JAPANESE MANAGEMENT TIGHTENS
             MEASUREMENT AT 7-ELEVEN

Your neighborhood 7-Eleven store may soon feature a new Japanese export: a system that allows the company to monitor store managers' every keystroke. Ito-Yokado Co., the Japanese company that controls 7-Eleven, wants to ship its philosophy of strict discipline and control to the United States. The computerized cash registers embody that discipline. The company also plans to impose a version of the just-in-time inventory control that helped cut costs in Japanese auto factories.

To understand just what may be in store for U.S. managers, consider the life of Michiharu Endo, who operates one of the nearly 7,000 7-Eleven stores in Japan. When Endo quit his job marketing office supplies three years ago to buy a 7-Eleven franchise in Tokyo, he looked forward to being his own boss.

It didn't quite work out that way. Like every other 7-Eleven franchise in Japan, he uses a point-of-sale (POS) computer that lets headquarters know every time he makes a sale. POS systems are used in the United States, but what makes this one different is how 7-Eleven uses it to schedule Endo's activities. Headquarters monitors how much time he spends using the analytical tools built into the cash register to track product sales. He is expected to spend his days poring over sales data, demographic trends, and local weather forecasts graphed out on the computer screen.

Endo uses all this information to fine-tune orders to a daily deadline. The POS system is central to 7-Eleven's just-in-time delivery of fresh food like sandwiches, box lunches, rice balls, and deli dishes. Japanese outlets receive deliveries three times a day to ensure that there's just enough food and none is wasted. "Sometimes I don't know who's really running the store," says Endo as his back-office computer beeps a high-pitched alarm that warns him it's 15 minutes before the 10 AM deadline for ordering. However, Toshifumi Suzuki, Ito-Yokado's chief executive, argues that such discipline has helped him double sales for an average 7-Eleven in Japan over two decades and dramatically cut inventory costs.

An Ito-Yokado executive says American 7-Eleven stores, if run the Japanese way, would double daily sales. But in America, the notion has run into resistance from the start. Many U.S. franchisees believe that veteran managers know from experience how to stock their shelves and make adjustments for changes in weather or special events like a local basketball tournament. Some think the Japanese system links orders too tightly to current sales; they fear they would be criticized for stocking things like candles, which may not show any sales for months and then sell out in a weather emergency.

SOURCE: Norihiko Shirouzu and Jon Bigness, "7-Eleven Operators Resist System to Monitor Managers," *The Wall Street Journal*, June 16, 1997, p. B1.

Decision Questions

1. Assume for the moment that the Japanese measurement process consists of only the indicators described in this case. What aspects of measurement are overlooked (or at least not mentioned)?
2. How does the Japanese system for running 7-Eleven stores relate to our discussion of employee motivation and commitment? What effect do you think the Japanese system would have on morale if it were imposed on U.S. franchises?
3. What does this case tell us about the impact of globalization on American businesses?

motivation p. 426>

globalization p. 186>

REFERENCES

1. Edward A. Robinson. "America's Most Admired Companies." *Fortune*, March 3, 1997, pp. 68–76.

2. Information for this section was adapted from The Price Waterhouse Change Integration Team. *The Paradox Principles*. Burr Ridge, IL: Irwin, 1996, chap. 12.

3. Robert S. Kaplan and David P. Norton. "Using the Balanced Scorecard as a Strategic Management System." *Harvard Business Review*, January/February 1996 pp. 75–85; "Putting the Balanced Scorecard to Work." *Harvard Business Review*, September/October 1993, p. 147; "The Balanced Scorecard—Measures that Drive Performance." *Harvard Business Review*, January/February 1992, pp. 71–9.

4. Borland website (www.borland.com), accessed 7/29/97.

5. This discussion was drawn from John E. G. Bateson. *Managing Services Marketing*. Fort Worth: The Dryden Press, 1992, chap. 10.

6. David Greising. "Quality: How to Make It Pay." *Business Week*, August 8, 1994, pp. 54–9.

7. Carl Sewall and Paul B. Brown. *Customers for Life*. New York: Pocket Books (Simon & Schuster, Inc.), 1990.

8. Sewall and Brown, p. 165.

9. Lloyd Dobyns and Clare Crawford-Mason. *Quality or Else*. New York, Houghton-Mifflin, 1991, p. 137.

10. Price Waterhouse Change Integration Team, p. 240.

11. See, for example, George T. Milkovich and John W. Boudreau. *Human Resource Management*, 8th ed. Burr Ridge, IL: Irwin, 1997, pp. 112–3.

12. Quoted in Barbara A. Pope. *Workforce Management*. Homewood, IL: Business One Irwin, 1992, p. 17.

13. For a good discussion, see Stephen P. Robbins. *Organizational Behavior*, 7th ed. Englewood Cliffs, NJ: Prentice-Hall, 1996, pp. 26–8.

14. Pope, p. 20.

15. Gary Dessler. *Human Resource Management*, 7th ed. Upper Saddle River, NJ: Prentice-Hall, 1997, pp. 590–1.

16. "The Business Week 50." *Business Week*, March 24, 1997, p. 79.

17 *Promoting Change and Renewal*

When you think of Huffy bicycles, what comes to mind? For most people, Huffy suggests a bike that is solid and reliable but lacks flair and cutting-edge performance. Huffy dominates the mass-market bike business, selling its rather traditional models at Wal-Marts and Kmarts. Yet Huffy's leaders know they cannot rest on past success because the bicycle industry is changing. The BMX segment of the industry is hot and sales are booming. Unfortunately, BMX riders do not turn to Huffy. BMXers, mostly teenagers, demand upscale, high-performance bikes that can take punishment. They prefer brands like GT and Mongoose that are sold in specialized bike shops. As one advertising executive says, "Huffy is the first bike a kid gets rid of when he turns to BMX."

Huffy is feeling the winds of change and the challenges this change brings. Should it rely on the strength of its past image or should it adapt to meet new demands? Huffy has opted for change. It decided to transform its 105-year heritage to include the BMX market. Accordingly, Huffy has developed 16 BMX models and is using creative advertising to promote them. It also hopes that the young, cool image of BMX bikes will help sales of all Huffy products.[1]

As Huffy has seen, the competitive business environment never stands still. A business that experiences glowing profits one year may find itself threatened by a flood of new competitors the next year. A unique product that captures a select market niche one year may be cast aside the next if consumer tastes and preferences shift. Expansion opportunities that appear promising may be dashed by a sudden economic downturn and skyrocketing interest rates. Environmental threats and opportunities are always emerging and demanding action. Importantly, any change ripples through the business system, affecting a series of interrelated moves. This is the nature of business.

This is part of the excitement, challenge, and risk that exist in contemporary business. Indeed, the successful business manager understands that change and renewal are facts of business life.

This final chapter restates the theme of innovation and change that we have explored throughout this book. Further, it offers you a glimpse into the study of change that is critical for progressive leaders of the future. After studying this chapter, you should be able to:

1. Describe Lewin's three stages of change.

2. Establish the nature and meaning of planned change.

3. Construct the main features of the planned change process.

4. Define creativity and innovation.

5. Formulate some of the common sources or opportunities for innovation.

6. Describe some of the actions that healthy businesses take to promote creativity and innovation.

7. Apply some of the popular approaches to strategic change and renewal.

Throughout this book, starting with the model in Figure 1–6, we have emphasized the topics of business change and renewal. Environmental forces and impacts are dynamic and moving. Customer preferences and demands are always shifting. Existing competitors are always fine-tuning their challenges, and formidable new rivals are arriving on the competitive scene at a dizzying rate. Without a doubt, contemporary business faces a turbulent environment that makes change and renewal a necessity of business operations. Indeed, as we have stressed since the first chapter, innovation and change are hallmarks of the successful business.

In fact, in the rapid-fire world of business, innovation and change are required for survival. If a business does not change over time, it will slip, lose its competitive edge, and eventually struggle to keep from dying! Problems may not be apparent today or tomorrow or even in the next five years. Yet the business that arrogantly assumes it need not change is headed for disaster. To illustrate this, Specialized Bicycle, Inc., has among its assets an old black hearse. Emblazoned across each side of it are the words "Innovate or Die."

No business, no matter how big or how successful, is immune to the need for change. Consider Sears, the retail giant that grew and prospered during the 1950s, 60s, and 70s. For the next 15 years, Sears was rocked by new competitors and new approaches to the retail industry. Discount retailers like Wal-Mart and Kmart redefined the industry, while Sears was caught doing things as it always had. Then specialty niche stores, like Circuit City, Toys "R" Us, and Home Depot ripped even further into Sears' traditional markets. Despite years of dominance in the retail industry, Sears lost market share and struggled in the 1990s to redefine itself and change with the times. Sears CEO Arthur C. Martinez admitted that Sears had lost sight of its customers and was unsure who it really wanted to serve. Out of necessity, Martinez implemented a major

retailers p. 282>

"I went in for insulation."

"And left with a warm fuzzy feeling."

Come see the softer side of SEARS

Sears has taken major steps to improve its ability to meet customer needs. The changes have been instrumental in returning Sears to a major force in the retail industry. What do you think of when someone says the word "Sears"? How would you rank Sears now compared to other major retail stores?

change in strategy and approach at Sears.[2] Today Sears is back as a force in the industry. Interestingly, Kmart has lost much of its luster and even Wal-Mart has recently experienced some rough times.

The message is clear. It does not matter how big you are, you still must change and innovate. In some ways, change can be more difficult for large and highly successful businesses than for smaller and less successful firms. The successful business can easily become a victim of its own success and the closed thinking that success often spurs. "Why should we change when we're the market leaders?" This is a short-sighted and dangerous stance.

Forty years ago, the Swiss virtually dominated the world timepiece market. Nearly 90 percent of all watches produced throughout the world came from Swiss companies. Today the Swiss are minor players whose total share of world markets is less than 15 percent.[3] The international watch industry is now dominated by Japan and the United States. Much of this is due to new technology, notably the quartz watch. The Swiss were so successful and comfortable with their traditional mechanical watches that they were unwilling to adapt to the advances of the newer quartz technology. In their hesitation, they lost market share, and they are unlikely ever to recover. The odd side to this story is that quartz technology did not come from the United States or Japan. It came from the Swiss themselves. They simply did not accurately assess the impact it would have. Their traditional success paralyzed their movement. They wanted to keep things the way they were.

A small retail department store sold a variety of goods, including toys. Its selection was adequate and its prices were relatively high, so the store prospered—until a new competitor came to the community. Unfortunately, that competitor was Toys "R" Us. The small store's owners knew that Toys "R" Us was coming. Yet they did little to change their merchandise mix or their mode of operations. They finally reoriented their product mix toward craft supplies, but the restructuring came too late and the store failed. The store's managers knew change was critical, but they did not respond.

The Nature and Struggles of Planned Change

There are many ways to think of change. Some change is random and chaotic. It is thrust upon us and forces us to alter our intended course of action. For example, as you and your roommate jump in your car to take off for a spring break skiing trip in Colorado, the car won't start. You have to change your travel plans, unpack the car, and get a rental car instead. Such random change is part of life. While it can be frustrating, there is little we can do except cope with such annoyances as best we can.

The same randomness occurs in business. One of the things that makes managing a business so difficult is that unexpected and unforeseen events are always occurring. Some of them are simply minor annoyances; others are major and can have a dramatic impact. For example, as owner of a small manufacturing shop, you employ only 80 people and produce specialized parts that are purchased by a number of larger businesses. This morning your most experienced information systems employee enters your office and declares that she must take an immediate leave of absence. She is visibly upset and barely able to speak. Her 75-year-old mother, who lives 1,000 miles away, has just suffered a stroke. Your employee is the only close family member. There was little prior warning of poor health. There is no way to predict how long your employee will have to be gone. Undoubtedly, her absence will necessitate some significant shuffling of people and will be a major inconvenience for the business. You will probably have to put the morning's planned activities on hold and address this pressing new crisis. Such *crisis management* is part of business life. Through careful planning, you can minimize crises, but you can never eliminate them.

However, in this chapter we are addressing a different kind of change—planned change. Unlike random and unforeseen events, planned change is intentional. It has been thought through and decisions have been made about how to deal with it. With this perspective in mind, we define **planned change** as the intentional process of movement from the present state toward some future state. This is not nearly as confusing as you might think. To explore this notion of change, consider Figure 17–1.

Planned change
The process of intentional movement from the present state toward some future state.

FIGURE 17–1   The Stages of Planned Change

Present state → Change → Future state

Planned change is systematic. In fact, there are three stages of planned change. First there is the *present state*. Then there is the *actual change*, an alteration of that established present state. The movement or change is toward some new set of activities, events, and outcomes known as the *future state*. This present state–movement–future state way of looking at change is fairly direct and often used.

You have experienced this process of planned change. You entered this semester's classes with certain knowledge, skills, attitudes, and outlooks. That was your present state. Presumably you desired a different state or you wouldn't be in college. You desired a future state where your knowledge and skills were fuller and more consistent with the demands of prospective employers. To reach this future state, you engaged in the process of movement. You attended college, studied, reflected on assignments, and paid attention in class (note our heroic assumptions). Without these movements, the desired future state of increased levels of marketable skill and knowledge would not be possible.

Yet these movements were not always easy. Leaving home and coming to college was difficult for some of you. Disciplining yourself to study was rarely easy. Learning and challenging established views probably took courage. Change implies movement and that movement, even for exciting and desired changes, is often trying.

This same sense of planned change holds for business. The present state is of course the business as it exists today. This present state is made up of existing technology, existing reward systems, existing jobs and activities, and existing structure and design. It also comprises existing views of the market and existing competitive strategies. Planned change occurs when the business takes well-thought-out actions to move from this present state to some desired future state.

Often planned change is prompted by efforts to avoid a crisis. The business realizes that the present state simply is not getting the job done. Without change in that present state, the business will slip competitively. Some businesses are truly innovative. They begin the change movements when things are still going well because they realize that change must be ongoing. They also realize that it is easier and ultimately less painful to change before they have to contend with crisis.

Resistance to Change

Resistance to change
The strong tendency in businesses (and people) to maintain the present state, to keep things the way they are now.

As basic as this need for change is, we often resist change. **Resistance to change** refers to the strong tendency in businesses (and people) to maintain the present state, to keep things the way they are now. Why is this so? Change implies uncertainty. The status quo represents stability and consistency and, to some extent, security. Change implies the unknown, with all of the fears any unknown carries. The status quo builds on foundations and sources of past strengths and past success. Change implies risk, stress, and the burning question of whether things really will be better.

Studies indicate that people resist change for very logical and understandable reasons. We emphasize five key reasons why many employees resist change.[4]

First, they are not convinced of the need for change. They do not understand why the prevailing system or approaches need to be altered. To them, the change just does not make much sense. In many cases, this lack of awareness occurs because they are not involved in the process of change.

Second, they do not want to lose something of value. This may include their current job status, known work, or even security.

Third, they don't really understand the change and its implications, so they assume they will be much worse off as a result of the change. Generally this occurs when people are not given enough relevant information to understand what is really going on. Poor communication and low trust levels increase the likelihood of resistance due to misunderstanding.

Fourth, many people fear failure. They may be afraid they will be unable to develop the new skills and behaviors the change will require. Often they fear they will be less effective with change than they are now.

Fifth, some employees have a low tolerance for change. Their personalities value consistency, order, and structure. They find flexibility and uncertainty quite discomfiting.

One thing should be clear: people who resist change are normal. They are not bad people. They are not malcontents. They are neither slow nor inferior employees. They are people responding naturally to the pressures and difficulties that go with change. And they exist at all levels of the business. It is often against this backdrop of resistance that businesses must struggle with the process of planned change.

The Underlying Philosophy of Change

There are a number of models of change that businesses use today. Interestingly, most are derived from the work of a single scholar, sociologist Kurt Lewin. Years ago Lewin noted that successful change involves the three stages of unfreezing, moving, and refreezing.[5]

Unfreezing
The first stage in successful change; breaking away from one's current thought patterns and behavior.

Lewin said that before meaningful change can take place, people have to go through an **unfreezing,** or breaking away from their current thought patterns and behavior. He contended that this happens only when people become convinced that their present views and approaches are not the best. They must believe that greater success for them and the organization could be achieved with different approaches and behaviors. Remember, one of the key reasons for resistance to change is simply not being convinced of the need for change.

Moving
The second stage in successful change; the actual change of thought patterns and behavior from the old way to the new.

The second step of the process is **moving,** or the actual change of behavior and thought patterns from the old way to the new. This means adopting new attitudes, values, and approaches. This step is difficult, but if the unfreezing was successful, moving is easier to achieve. It is important to help employees understand what movement is desired.

Refreezing
The third stage in successful change; reinforcing the new behaviors with evidence of the promised advantages.

Lewin's final step is refreezing. This is a reinforcement notion. If you have convinced people there are important advantages in changing, then the business must deliver. **Refreezing** means presenting evidence of the promised advantages in order for the new behaviors to remain. In other words, good results or rewards are critical for solidifying and maintaining the change.

The Process of Planned Change

Given the basic philosophy presented in Lewin's model, let's consider its application for the process of *planned* change. Oticon, a Danish-based company, specializes in making and distributing hearing aids.[6] With an international reputation for quality and a strong distribution network, Oticon was the undisputed world leader in hearing

FIGURE 17–2   The Process of Planned Change

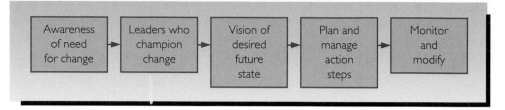

aids. Its system was strong, its returns were lucrative, and its market share was dominant. Consequently, new ideas and approaches for change were often thwarted or ignored. The logic was basic: The present state looks pretty good, so why change?

The "why" began to creep into the industry in the early 1980s, but it went nearly undetected. All of Oticon's hearing aids (and the industry standard at the time) were behind-the-ear models. But competitors began pushing a new technology, hidden-in-the-ear aids. While the components for these aids were mass-produced, each was custom-fitted to the wearer's ear. This product innovation was so popular that over the next few years, Oticon's market share fell by half. By the late 1980s, a crisis was looming and Oticon was in need of change. The present state had slipped in effectiveness. A new future state was imperative for the business to regain its healthy status. Movement (change) had to occur.

effectiveness p. 478>

Though the need for change at Oticon was obvious, change does not magically and spontaneously arise. The inertia of the present state is tough to alter. Thus, a process of planned change must be used. This process is outlined in Figure 17–2.

The first step in the process of planned change is generating an *awareness of the need for change* throughout the business. This idea is used by today's business consultants as the starting point in the process of change. This awareness is not too difficult to build when results have turned bad; it is considerably more challenging to create when the business appears to be productive. Remember, the successful business tries to build the case for change *before* things get bad. Only after this unfreezing takes place is the organization ready to move or change.

In Oticon's case, awareness of the need for change was slow in coming. The impact of new technology and the need to meet the consumer's response to hidden-in-the-ear aids could have been recognized years earlier. Of course, by the late 1980s, sagging profitability brought the need for change into clear focus.

The second step in the process of planned change is the presence of *leaders who will champion change*. These leaders must step forward and guide the business and its people toward change. Sometimes businesses that face difficult but needed change will look for new leadership to champion the cause. Lars Kolind was hired from outside the business to lead Oticon through its needed changes.

This step is critical. Generally, change is most effective when it comes from the top of the business. Leader behavior shows everyone in the organization how important the change really is. Thus, top managers must promote needed changes. This means they must step forward through their speeches, written pronouncements, and reward policies to provide clear, strong support of change. Particularly during the early stages of changes, the leaders may spend large chunks of their time championing change. Lars Kolind devoted nearly a third of his time to the dynamics of change during the early phases.

vision p. 310>   The third step is also significant. Leaders must provide a clear *vision of the desired future state* so everyone knows where the business is headed and what it intends to accomplish. People in the company need this vision if they are to understand and support the change. The vision becomes a rallying point for bringing people into the change process. To inject needed innovations into Oticon, Kolind envisioned a new headquarters without the boundaries and politics that had always existed. He envisioned a headquarters without offices and partitions. There would be no formal titles, departments, or even job descriptions, which often divided and segregated the talent pool. He envisioned using groups of people who would come together quickly to address needed concerns and then move on to other groups and issues. In short, he envisioned a fluid, team-focused culture at corporate headquarters. His vision was radical and even a little strange. It was also the "shot in the arm" the business needed.

As you can see from both steps two and three, the impact of leadership on change cannot be overemphasized. While leaders often use differing approaches to change, the good ones always help their people understand the nature and direction of change, accept risks, and overcome resistance.

The fourth step in the process is to *plan and manage the necessary action steps*. These action steps are the specific things that must be done for the vision to be achieved. At Oticon, Kolind used a variety of techniques to bring the new vision to life. For example, to help build management commitment, there were off-site workshops that explored the details of the future design. Special seminars were held to help people get ready mentally for the changes taking place. Since it was clear that the new organization would depend on full computer literacy, 130 state-of-the-art IBM PCs were purchased. For about $15 a month, employees could rent these computers for their personal use at home. All the company asked was that each employee become proficient at the computer. Counseling sessions were even held with those who expressed resistance to the change. These are just a few of the action steps Oticon engaged in to make the vision and change successful.

The final step in the process of change is to *monitor and modify*. No planned change goes completely as planned. There is never a completely smooth transition to the future. The implementation of successful change is a process of refining and finetuning. This does not mean that the original thinking was poorly conceived; it simply recognizes that adjustments are always needed.

Profile 17–1 describes successful change at Gibson Guitars. Note the action steps the CEO took to turn around the business. These actions changed the business from a stodgy, outdated, enterprise to an innovative, up-to-date, and profitable business. As you look at the change at Gibson Guitars, realize that there is probably no single action that accounts for its remarkable reversal of fortune in a relatively short period of time. Rather, many interrelated actions collectively added up to success.

PROFILE **17–1**   *Gibson Guitar Finds Magic in the Name*

Nashville-based Gibson Guitar Corp. is as formidable as the 40- by 260-foot mural of a Les Paul Gibson Guitar that adorns the Nashville Hard Rock Cafe. Throughout its history, Gibson has been synonymous with quality and craftsmanship. The legends of country and rock music, from Chet Atkins to Jimmy Paige to Keith Richards to Paul McCartney, have played Gibsons.

Gibson Guitars was on the brink of bankruptcy when new management turned it around. They cut costs, updated processes, and hired new workers who had an affinity for guitars. Consider jobs you have had. What could you do to make your job or company better?

Surprisingly, only a decade ago Gibson was barely clinging to life, poised on the brink of bankruptcy. That was before the company was rescued by three young Harvard Business School grads who engineered a turnaround so startling that company sales have risen tenfold over the last decade. How did they do it? **vision p. 310>** What was their vision? And what were their action steps?

The three young entrepreneurs were led by Henry Juskiewicz, only 32 years old when he became CEO. They took over a business where morale was low, equipment was old, and productivity was poor (only about 75 guitars were produced each day). Formidable competitors, such as Yamaha and Ibanez, had blitzed the market. Perhaps most distressing, quality was dismal. But the partners saw glimmers of hope too. They saw a company with great name recognition and image. As Juskiewicz says, "We found young guitarists didn't know there was a problem. They still thought Gibson was the best. The company was putting out some bad guitars, but the magic was still in the name." That became the vision—capitalize on the name while rebuilding quality.

Juskiewicz and his partners began by cutting costs and streamlining the business. For example, they replaced the aging $500,000 data processing system with a $15,000 microcomputer. They updated the company and in the process quadrupled the workforce. The turnaround involved a unique combination of mass production thinking with good old-fashioned craftsmanship. They studied the design and engineering of their classic guitars. From this they totally retooled the factory, committing the money and machines needed to build the product right. Now computerized routers with intricate blueprints digitized on software are being used.

At the same time, the role of experienced crafters has been reemphasized. Gibson began hiring employees who played guitars (many in local bands) and recognized the feel and tone of quality. Knowledge and pride in workmanship became important features. As one manager noted, "You just figure out what tasks machines can do as well as hands, and what demands a human touch."

Juskiewicz and his partners made some astute decisions. For example, they promptly stopped the policy of selling Gibson "seconds" at a discount. "I don't feel anything with the Gibson name should be a second," Juskiewicz argued.

The retooled Gibson produces over 300 guitars a day. Industry experts contend the quality is as good as ever. From all indications, Gibson is a bustling and healthy business. Juskiewicz says it best. "We've improved our equipment and specifications almost to the point of lunacy. Today I'll guarantee every one of our guitars [is] 'cherry.'"

SOURCE: Bruce Watson, "How to Take On an Ailing Company—and Make It Hum," *Smithsonian*, July 1996, pp. 53–62.

Developing Your Critical Thinking Skills

1. Since business leaders recognize that change is important, why is it so difficult for successful businesses to be proactive in changing before they face problems?

2. Think of a change (perhaps with your family or some organization) that you actively resisted. After reading this section, why do you think you resisted the change?

3. Consider the same change that you resisted in Question 2. How could the approach to planned change have been used to facilitate the necessary change in your situation?

Building Innovative Organizations

Creativity is a pattern of thinking and behaving that emphasizes new and different ideas. Innovation deals with the results, or what is produced through these creative activities. In short, innovation is the successful implementation of these creative ideas within the business.[7] As we said in Chapters 1 and 3, creativity is the process; innovation is the outcome. Businesses encourage creativity in order to achieve innovation. For example, Microsoft produced an innovative product with Windows 95. That innovation was possible because of the creative thinking and work of many talented people.

Despite what many people think, most businesses are potential hotbeds of creativity. People are often quite creative if they are given the chance. Unfortunately, all too often that chance is not provided. This is one of the dilemmas of modern business life. Often businesspeople become so concerned with "turf protection," office politics, and formalizing operating procedures and guidelines that true creativity is dampened. This can be deadly. It is also one of the reasons we have focused this book on an integrative view of business.

Businesses must find ways to encourage and even stimulate creativity to gain competitive innovations. A **competitive innovation** is a change so important that it allows the business to distinguish itself and gain an advantage over its competitors. Let's look at some of the ways businesses can generate creativity and gain real competitive innovation.

Competitive innovation
A change so important that it allows the business to distinguish itself and gain an advantage over its competitors.

Sources of Innovative Opportunity

Peter Drucker, an influential business philosopher, identified seven sources for innovative opportunity, which are presented in Table 17–1. Some of these sources are outside the business and some are internal. Think of these as changes that present opportunities for innovation.

First among the external sources of innovation is *demographics*, or basic changes in the population. For example, the population is aging, educational levels are increasing, and income levels are rising. What will these facts mean for businesses? What will they demand from businesses? What new opportunities for innovation will be possible because of these new demographic realities?

Consider the baby diaper industry. What names come to mind? Probably Huggies (made by Kimberly-Clark) and Pampers (made by Procter & Gamble). While

TABLE 17–1   Sources of Opportunities for Innovation

External Sources	Internal Sources
Demographics	The unexpected
Changes in perception	The incongruous
New knowledge	Process need
	Changes in industry or market structure

SOURCE: Peter F. Drucker, *Innovation and Entrepreneurship: Practice and Principles* (New York: Harper & Row, 1985).

Microsoft is one of the most innovative software producers. Their software is used on almost every personal computer including Hewlett Packard's palmtop computer. What accounts for Microsoft's creative abilities?

these two products capture nearly 60 percent of the U.S. diaper market, there are many other firms and products in this industry. Most are scurrying to find innovations. Why? The demographics of their target market are changing. With fewer babies being born, the diaper market is stagnating. Demographic statistics suggest that the birthrate will continue to decline for several years. Due to their size and market shares, Pampers and Huggies will survive. Without innovation, many of the smaller diaper makers may not. Drypers Co. is innovating with an odor-controlling diaper. It claims that putting baking soda in the diapers reduces odor by 77 percent. Obviously, Drypers hopes this innovation will lead to the sweet smell of success.[8]

Cozymel's provides Mexican food in a fiesta-like setting. This makes dining out an experience rather than just a meal. How important is atmosphere in the dining experience? How important is "an enjoyable evening" in today's fast paced world?

BRINKER
INTERNATIONAL.

budget p. 402>

The second external source is *changes in perception*. Drucker says, "When a change in perception takes place, the facts do not change. Their meaning does." The fast-food restaurant business is experiencing such a shift. Some of it is due to a change in customers' perceptions, attitudes, and perhaps even values. Concern about health and fitness has forced many traditional fast-food establishments to focus on healthier options. It has also sparked a shift in competition and many innovations. For example, Kenny Rogers Roasters restaurant chain started as an effort to provide healthier fast-food options.

Health consciousness is not the only shift affecting the restaurant industry. The people at Brinker International recognize another significant change in perception. They believe customers today do not just want the convenience of dining out. Many are looking for unique dining experiences within a reasonable budget. Brinker has responded innovatively with new restaurant concepts. One of these is Cozymel's, which offers authentic Mexican food in a fiesta-like atmosphere that is a different, exciting escape for patrons. The mood is set as soon as you drive in the parking lot. Music is playing. There are the lights and sounds of a festive occasion. As John Miller of Brinker International says, ". . . [Customers] take a mini vacation. . . . You put your cares behind you and enjoy the evening."[9]

The third external source of innovation is *new knowledge*, or new awareness and techniques that allow us to do things we could not do before. New technology is a common example here. Just think of the innovations derived from new technologies in the medical and pharmaceutical industries. Companies battle to be leaders in exploiting emerging technology to bring new life-enhancing and lifesaving products to consumers. For example, in recent research, protease inhibitors in combination with AZT and 3TC have led to remission of the AIDS virus. Pharmaceutical giants such as Merck, Abbott Laboratories, and Roche Holding now offer innovative medicines that capitalize on this research breakthrough. Not surprisingly, demand is high. New knowledge is leading innovation.

In addition to these three outside sources, at least four sources of innovation lie within the organization. First is what Drucker calls *the unexpected*. These can be unexpected successes that are exploited to build competitive strength. Or they can be unexpected failures that help the business understand its customers more fully.

The second internal source of innovation is *incongruities.* While this sounds rather heavy, the idea is simple. An incongruity occurs when there is a gap between what the business expected or was hoping for and what occurs. As with the unexpected, this gap is an invitation to innovate.

Let's consider an example of how unexpected outcomes and incongruities can lead to innovation. As the Internet gains in popularity and business use of computer interactions spreads, computer viruses are also spreading at an unbelievable rate. Today there are over 5,000 known virus strains. This has created a unique business opportunity for Trend Micro, based in Taipei. Over 7 million computer users rely on Trend's protective software. Even Intel motherboards get a protective chip from Trend, known as ChipAway Virus, that checks for viruses before the computer fully boots up. Trend's new protective program for Microsoft's Windows 95, PC-cillin, is sold in 18 languages. Trend Micro has taken a performance difficulty or gap and built a thriving business in response.[10]

The third internal source of innovation is based on *process need.* As the business operates, people become aware of processes that need improving. These needs are the pockets of innovation. Process needs and related innovations are part of the successful company's focus on quality and continuous improvement, as discussed in Chapter 15.

continuous
improvement p. 448>

Drucker's fourth and final internal source of innovation comes from *changes in industry or market structure.* In recent years, there have been some dramatic examples of this source. The breakup of the Bell system and the deregulation of the telephone industry created enormous opportunities for innovation. Hundreds of new businesses entered the industry. Most have been searching for new approaches or new niches that will give them a competitive edge.

Drucker's list is certainly not exhaustive, but it does provide a good sense of some key changes and awarenesses that *can* lead to innovation. These sources have that potential, but enlightened managers must act on the potential before innovation can be realized. With that in mind, let's examine some of the actions successful businesses take to foster innovation.

Actions for Building Innovation

Creativity and innovation flourish when they are supported through the actions and attitudes of the leaders and managers of the business. These actions provide the foundations that enable the creative and innovative efforts of employees. We will look at six of the many actions that are important.

diversity p. 125>

1. Encouraging risk and experimentation.
2. Tolerating and learning from mistakes.
3. Embracing diversity and differences.
4. Promoting boundaryless behavior.
5. Maintaining close contact with customers.
6. Investing in training.

Encouraging Risk and Experimentation

If organizations are going to innovate and change, they must gain creative new ideas. The organization's leaders must be receptive to these new ideas. They must encourage their people to take risks, experiment with new ideas, and break the established

Dairy Queen adopted the Blizzard franchise-wide only after one of their franchisees in St. Louis convinced them to try it. Many ideas come from employees in stores. How can managers ensure that those ideas are heard?

pattern. Profile 17–2 describes how McDonald's, Moto Photo, and Dairy Queen gained important new ideas that led to profitable innovations for their businesses. These creative ideas came from encouraging franchisees to try something different—and from carefully listening to and respecting their ideas.

PROFILE 17–2   *Grassroots Creativity*

Despite its size and success, McDonald's is always looking for new ideas and new products. Some of its best ideas come from franchisees. These are not corporate headquarters people. These are the people in the field who know the customers and what the customers want. In fact, McDonald's best-known product, the Big Mac sandwich, originated with one of its franchisees.

The story is similar for the Egg McMuffin. This English muffin with egg, Canadian bacon, and cheese was developed by Herbert R. Peterson, Sr., a franchisee in Santa Barbara, California. He introduced the product to Ray Kroc, the force behind McDonald's. Kroc liked the Egg McMuffin, and soon it was a mainstay of McDonald's breakfast menu.

Staying tuned into the ideas of franchisees is important at Moto Photo, a franchiser of 450 photographic stores in the United States, Canada, and Norway. For example, the idea of selling annual memberships to customers to spur repeat business came from a franchisee. Today these memberships account for over half of the chain's sales.

One of the most interesting cases of franchisee innovations came from Dairy Queen. Sam Temperato, a 72-year-old St. Louis DQ franchisee, developed a strange concoction. He mixed fruit, nuts, and other ingredients into a vanilla frozen dessert. He called the product a Blizzard. Today, Blizzards are the best-selling product in the Dairy Queen chain.

SOURCE: Jeffrey A. Tannenbaum, "Role Model," *The Wall Street Journal*, May 23, 1996, p. R22.

It is not always easy for people lower in the organization to push for change. Sometimes their innovative ideas are blocked by business leaders who have a lot invested in the status quo. Consider the example of Sam Temperato, whose Blizzard dessert we discussed in Profile 17–2. Temperato had a hard time getting Dairy Queen executives to accept his idea. The headquarters-based committee that screens new products was afraid that preparing Blizzards would be too much work for the individual stores. The committee did not champion the change. Rather, Temperato had to sell the committee members on the product. In a bold move, he brought them to his St. Louis store, at his expense, so they could see how popular Blizzards were with his customers. Only then were they convinced.

There is a basic message here. When a business is in trouble or experiencing a crisis, leaders often look for change. Under these trying conditions, they recognize that the status quo simply is not good enough. But when things are going well, it can be difficult for leaders to champion change. Intellectually, they realize how important it is. Yet resistance to change and that gnawing tendency to maintain the status quo can thwart needed movement.

Tolerating and Learning from Mistakes

It is one thing to encourage risk and experimentation. It is quite another to accept the downside of that risk and experimentation. That downside is the mistakes and missteps that undoubtedly will occur when people are trying new things. Leaders should realize that the only way to avoid mistakes is to never take a chance. They must view mistakes as a natural part of the creative process and as learning opportunities.

A classic story may illustrate this point. Some years ago, a young manager was called to the office of IBM founder Tom Watson. The young manager had misread a risky venture, costing the company over $10 million. Certain that he was about to be fired, the manager fidgeted nervously. "I guess you want my resignation," he blurted. "You can't be serious," Watson said. "We've just spent $10 million educating you."[11]

This is precisely the attitude toward innovation that successful businesses try to promote. The young manager made a mistake that he could have prevented only by playing it safe. He had to take a risk. He had done his homework. He was prepared. His strategies made sense when they were initiated; they simply did not work out over time in an extremely uncertain and volatile environment. Watson was sure the manager would learn from his mistakes and be better prepared to handle such issues in the future.

Mistakes are part of the learning and development that occurs in an innovative organization. However, it's important to note that certain types of mistakes should not be tolerated. If a mistake is made because of a lack of preparation, faulty analysis, arrogance, or other preventable causes, then negative consequences should follow. Further, making the same mistake over and over again is not excusable. In short, tolerance for mistakes and experimentation does not mean it is OK to be sloppy or unprepared.

Embracing Diversity and Differences

One way to foster a climate of creativity and innovation is to encourage diversity within the business, as we discussed in Chapter 5. Innovative businesses actively build diversity into their activities and operations. Although this can occur in a number of ways, two themes seem particularly important.

First, bringing people of different genders, races, and cultural backgrounds into the business is a foundation of creativity. In fact, diversity of talent can often provide the information, perspective, and sense that businesses need as they consider changes and innovations. Consider the case of JCPenney, the giant retailer. In recent years, Penney has shifted its strategic focus from being a mass merchandiser to being a retailer emphasizing women's fashions. It has facilitated that process by moving more women into key decision-making positions where they could address fashion and style issues.[12]

This example is a reminder of issues that must be addressed for diversity to actually lead to innovation. People with differing views and outlooks must be accepted and their ideas given a fair hearing when decisions are being made. Such an approach to diversity can lead to tension and uneasiness. But sometimes this is exactly what a business needs to break out of its stagnating *comfort zone*.

teams p. 71> The second diversity theme deals with the use of teams. As you learned in Chapter 14, teams can bring people from different backgrounds and different areas of the business together to solve problems. For example, a small family-owned investment company sees a need for innovation in the wake of the industry's dramatic changes. The firm's president, a 35-year-old who has just accepted the leadership reins from his recently retired father, is concerned that the business may not be setting the pace given the emerging directions of the industry. He decides that a top-executive team should be organized to identify the strategic moves the business needs to make. This team practice is drastically different from the dictatorial approach of his father. A team is assembled that includes the managers from all the key areas of the business. Most of the members of this executive team think in a similar manner. They are logical and analytical and carefully assess all risks before committing to action. Their tendency is to follow traditional paths of operation.

One member of the team, though, is different. The financial services manager is always thinking up new ideas, reading and studying new approaches, and considering different ways of serving clients. As she tosses her ideas into the team mix, others are often bothered. She looks at things differently. She forces the rest of the team to consider a different view. She challenges others' approaches. While she does not often win the other team members over to her way of thinking, she usually prompts them to extend their thinking. There is no doubt the team comes up with novel ideas because of her influence. Many of these ideas make good business sense and result in increased revenues.

Once more we see diversity leading to conflict that can spark creativity and innovation. Again this presumes that differences on teams are not only viewed as legitimate but encouraged. We do need to be cautious here: It will not surprise you to learn that diverse or heterogeneous teams usually take longer to make decisions than do individuals working alone or teams without diversity. Yet most diverse teams, over time, provide better answers to problems and offer more creative solutions.

Promoting Boundaryless Behavior

Organizations have boundaries. To some extent, these boundaries are necessary to prevent chaos. As people specialize in different tasks, boundaries exist between various functions of the business. Levels of authority create boundaries between managers and other employees. People who work in the business perform different activities from suppliers, again creating boundaries. People work in different locations, perhaps even in different parts of the world—more boundaries. If creativity is going to flow, the business must be structured in such a way that people are free to share ideas across boundaries and call on one another for assistance.

One popular approach to create such an environment of open communication and exchange is known as boundaryless behavior. This does not mean that boundaries are eliminated, just that the links between boundaries are made more open and permeable.[13]

Boundaryless behavior

Behavior that seeks to eliminate unnecessary barriers that limit the flow of information and ideas.

In essence, **boundaryless behavior** means that the business seeks to eliminate unnecessary barriers that limit the flow of information and ideas. Vertical barriers are removed as people are empowered to take action and not feel restricted by the lines of authority that often serve to prevent new ideas from seeing the light of day. Horizontal barriers are removed when teams are used to bring people from various units of the business together to develop new and unique responses to business issues and concerns. Businesses even seek to remove barriers between themselves and key external constituents. This may involve closer contact with suppliers and customers. Boundaryless behavior is usually facilitated by networked computers so people can readily communicate across different levels and units of the business as well as across broad geographic areas.

The term *boundaryless behavior* was coined by Jack Welch, the well-known chair and CEO of General Electric. Welch says boundaryless behavior has "developed a fresh, open, anti-parochial environment, friendly toward the seeking and sharing of new ideas, regardless of the source. It also encouraged looking outside the traditional boundaries that shackle thinking and restrict vision." He further comments that "the sweetest fruit of boundaryless behavior has been the demise of 'Not-Invented-Here' and its utter disappearance from [the] company."[14]

GE is far from the only business to embrace the philosophy of boundaryless behavior. Motorola is also known for its boundaryless approaches, such as the one mentioned in Profile 17–3. As you can see, the boundaryless organization is fertile ground for promoting creativity and innovation.

MOTOROLA

PROFILE 17–3   *Boundaryless Behavior at Motorola*

Motorola encourages boundaryless behavior in many ways. One of these is its cross-functional training approach. This means that people from different disciplines, areas of expertise, and units of the company are brought together to train and learn. Typically, these efforts are facilitated by the premier training center, Motorola University, where people with differing outlooks and perspectives exchange ideas, share experiences, and present approaches. Through these open processes, people from various functional areas of the business become aware of others' operational needs and strategies of action. Unique awarenesses, opportunities, and solutions may arise.

For example, when Motorola wanted to expand its operations to China, the company brought together people from various areas of the business who had some unique understanding of the situation and special views to contribute. All had something to add in deciding the approach that would be selected. Managers representing product areas that would be sold in the China market were there. So were managers with experience in entering new global markets. Managers who were experienced in working in China were added to the mix. Collectively these managers crossed traditional boundaries, sharing views and exploring creative ways to make the China entry as successful as possible. Importantly, it worked. Today, Motorola is a leading supplier of advanced telecommunications and electronics equipment in China with combined annual sales to China and Hong Kong of over $3 billion.[15]

SOURCE: Ron Ashkenas, Dave Ulrich, Todd Jick, and Steve Kerr, *The Boundaryless Organization: Breaking the Chains of Organizational Structure* (San Francisco: Jossey-Bass Publishing, 1995), pp. 165–166.

Maintaining Close Contact with Customers

customer sensitivity p. 493>

One key way for a business to stay on the creative cutting edge is to maintain close contact with its customers. Throughout this book we have heralded customer sensitivity as being essential for competitive success. We have said that healthy businesses understand and address the shifting preferences of their customers. It may be somewhat less obvious, but customers are also excellent sources for new areas of innovation. Of course, this source has no meaning unless business employees listen carefully to what customers have to say.

Sometimes customers point to the need for innovation through their complaints and dissatisfaction with existing products. Ford learned this lesson by listening to both its dealers and eventual car buyers. As the company received comments and explored service records, areas that cried out for change became apparent. It addressed these needs through model redesigns. Some of these innovations were quite small (larger trunk space and more headroom in the backseat). Yet collectively, such design changes represented meaningful innovations that better addressed the customers' wishes.

Sometimes staying tuned in to customers suggests totally new directions. Here is an example that may be relevant for you. Many college students are frustrated as they attempt to track and monitor their finances. Think of all that is involved. You have a meal card, a monthly allowance, and a bank account to handle regular bills. You have a charge card, which (under penalty of death) you have been sworn to use only in the direst of emergencies. Really big expenses, like tuition and books, may be handled separately by your parents. Confusing? Complicated? There must be a better way.

The answer appears to be electronic money, an idea being pursued by giants like Microsoft, Xerox, and Visa. Students register for classes, pay their tuition, get textbooks, go through the campus cafeteria, do their laundry, and even order late-night snacks from the local pizza parlor—all with one electronic smart card. Yes, rest assured, that card can be linked to your parents' bank account.[16] Some universities have already installed the smart card on campus and report excellent response.

baby boomers p. 136>

Consider another example. There is a lot of complaint and debate about the spiraling costs of health care. A simple visit to your doctor to conduct even the most basic tests can run into hundreds of dollars. These concerns will become even more pronounced as baby boomers age. Of course, this frustration becomes fertile territory for innovation, and some creative businesspeople are targeting it. One response is the development of home health monitors. These minimachines are easy to use and relatively inexpensive. As the name implies, they let people monitor their health at home. Only when the monitor registers a problem requiring a doctor's attention does a physician have to enter the picture.

The technology is already available. By using a home monitoring machine to analyze urine or breath, a health-conscious consumer can track many physical functions, from cholesterol to triglycerides to hormonal fluctuations to a host of additional variables. Eventually these machines will even recommend corrective programs, such as exercise, diets, and lifestyle changes. In short, they will do much of what doctors currently do—at a fraction of the cost and inconvenience.[17]

Investing in Training

Jerre Stead has had a stellar business career. He has led six businesses, including AT&T Global Information Solutions and Square D. In his speeches, Stead praises the value of training: "If I only had one dollar left in my business, I would spend it on training."[18] Stead believes that people are the source of business success because they are the engine of creativity. Training is the fuel that people need to generate innovation. Innovative businesses realize that investing in training is critical to sustaining creativity and innovation.

Training should be ongoing and include all levels of the organization. Too often, training is geared toward those at lower levels and ignores managers and executives. Innovative businesses make sure their training encompasses all employees. Training helps people remain competent in new and emerging fields. This ever-expanding approach to learning provides the foundation for creative thinking.

Sometimes the training itself is novel. Brinker International wanted to find a meaningful way to teach teamwork to managers from different disciplines at its restaurant operations. So Brinker concentrated on a series of training exercises, each designed to help build skills and instill a sense of accomplishment. In one exercise, managers form teams. Each team member rides in a bumper car, carrying a Wiffle ball in the basket of a lacrosse-type stick. The object is for the team members to position themselves so they can heave the ball through a goal and score points. This game, known as whirly ball, is fun and teaches valuable lessons about teamwork. Another Brinker exercise builds confidence and encourages managers to take risks. A manager climbs a telephone pole. Standing at the top, high off the ground, he or she is secured by a seat and chest harness. From that position, the fun really begins. The manager jumps about seven feet from the pole to grab a trapeze bar![19]

What do such games and experiences have to do with serious business? Well, creative thinking and innovative action are often exactly what it takes to succeed at these games. Such training also reinforces the philosophy of going beyond the expected and working "outside the box."

BRINKER
INTERNATIONAL.

teams p. 71>

The Creative Personality

All of this talk about the importance of creativity and innovation may be a bit unsettling for some of you. Perhaps you do not think of yourself as creative. Indeed, while some people do seem to be creative thinkers, others—no matter how hard they try—just do not seem to generate much creativity. Maybe some people just have a more creative personality. This idea is both interesting and potentially dangerous. Let's examine it more closely.

Table 17–2 presents a creativity style assessment based on the work of Michael Kirton. Kirton identifies two styles of creativity, which he labels adaptors and innovators. Both are creative, but in different ways. **Adaptors** try to figure out how things can be improved. They tend to feel comfortable working within existing boundaries and systems to push for changes that will make these systems better. They change

Adaptors
Creative people who try to figure out how they can improve things by working within existing systems.

TABLE 17–2   Creativity Style Assessment

Circle *a* or *b*, depending on which is generally more descriptive of your behavior.

1. When I am working on a task, I tend to

   a. Go along with a consistent level of work.

   b. Work with high energy at times, with periods of low energy.

2. If there is a problem, I usually am the one who thinks of

   a. A number of solutions, some of which are unusual.

   b. One or two solutions that are methods other people would generally accept.

3. When keeping records, I tend to

   a. Be very careful about documentation.

   b. Be more haphazard about documentation.

4. In meetings, I am often seen as one who

   a. Keeps the group functioning well and maintains order.

   b. Challenges ideas or authority.

5. My thinking style could be most accurately described as

   a. Linear thinker, going from A to B to C.

   b. Thinking like a grasshopper, going from one idea to another.

6. If I have to run a group or project, I

   a. Have the general idea and let people figure out how to do the tasks.

   b. Try to figure out goals, time lines, and expected outcomes.

7. If there are rules to follow, I tend to

   a. Generally follow them.

   b. Question whether those rules are meaningful or not.

Innovators
Creative people who are catalysts for new ideas that challenge the existing system and the accepted ways of doing things.

cautiously and in small steps. **Innovators,** on the other hand, are more likely to challenge the existing system and the accepted ways of doing things. They are catalysts for new ideas, often discovering new problems and novel solutions. They are always "pushing the envelope" of change. Importantly, innovators challenge rules, break customs, and rarely feel constrained by the existing system.

Businesses need both types of people. They need innovators to shake things up and break from established approaches. The need adaptors to bring stability and order to the confusion that the innovators can create. Innovators give you the outrageous twists that can be truly groundbreaking. Adaptors have the political sensitivity to take these twists and turn them into acceptable ideas that can actually be implemented.

Developing Your Critical Thinking Skills

1. Look again at Drucker's sources of opportunities for innovation. What do you think the managers of a business need to do to be sensitive to these opportunities?

TABLE 17–2   *(continued)*

8. I like to be around people who are

a. Stable and solid.

b. Bright, stimulating, and change frequently.

9. In my home or office, things are

a. Here and there in various piles.

b. Laid out neatly or at least in a reasonable order.

10. I usually feel the way people have done things in the past

a. Must have some merit and comes from accumulated wisdom.

b. Can almost always be improved upon.

Scoring:

Count one point if you answered as follows:

1. b	6. a
2. a	7. b
3. b	8. b
4. b	9. a
5. b	10. b

Add the total number of points. This is your I score (innovator style). Next, take 10 – I score. This is your A score (adaptor style).

SOURCE: Michael J. Kirton, "Adaptors and Innovators: A Description and Measure," *Journal of Applied Psychology*, 61, no. 5, 1976.

2. Which of the actions for building innovation do you think is probably the most difficult for a business to put in place? Why?

3. What do you think would happen in a team if all the members were strong innovators? What if all were strong adaptors?

Thinking Strategically about Change and Renewal

Interrelatedness
The concept that a change in any part of a business system affects all other parts of the system.

Increasingly, successful businesses are recognizing that change and renewal are strategic issues. That means that change must be planned and it must be integrated, covering all areas and phases of the business. In fact, the integrative nature of change and renewal deserves special attention.

To fully understand the organizational impact of change and renewal, consider the concept of **interrelatedness,** which proposes that a change in any part of a business system affects all other parts of the system. Throughout this book, we have been discussing the various parts of the business system, and we have been building the case for interrelatedness.

Let's review some of that thinking. In Part Two of the text, we studied the impact of the business environment. We recognized that environmental shifts affect the business and its operations. The presence of a more diverse workforce, a rise in interest rates, the emergence of promising global markets, the possibility of increasing governmental regulation of business, and the threat of a powerful new competitor are all environmental changes that alter the landscape of business operations. To respond to them, healthy and proactive businesses contemplate making some changes in the status quo.

In such an increasingly complex environment, the successful business faces a series of tough decisions. The business must consider whether it needs to change some phase of its actions and operations (discussed in Part Three of the text). Of course, the performance measures we examined in Chapter 16 suggest the nature and extent of the necessary changes.

financial performance
p. 481>

Financial performance and customer needs and values are typically the factors that stimulate change. That is not hard to understand. If a business feels threatened financially, it must change. If customer value is being threatened (perhaps by new competitors), ultimately financial performance will decline.

Consider the small bicycle manufacturer, Terry Precision Bicycles for Women, which we introduced in Chapter 2. Terry's strategy has been to fill a unique niche in the bike market. Its high-quality product is specifically engineered and designed to fit a woman's body better than bikes that competitors offer. Larger competitors have traditionally ignored this niche, presumably thinking that structural differences along gender lines were not overly important. Yet Terry is betting on a niche strategy to compete in the very competitive high-end bicycle market. This approach makes sense for a start-up business in an extremely competitive field.

Since Terry is a new business concept, we can only speculate on what may occur in the business and the changes that may need to be considered. But let's think about some of the possibilities. Perhaps in its first few years of operations, sales will be exceptional and profits will be surprisingly high. While satisfying, that success may also be problematic. If Terry is successful enough, other bicycle companies may enter this previously ignored niche and flood the market. Terry may decide that its comfortable niche strategy will no longer work. It may need to become much more cost focused. Further, as the environment becomes increasingly competitive, Terry may feel the need to serve customers better and offer even greater customer value than before. In short, Terry may need to change a strategy that was initially successful.

efficiency p. 478>

Consider another scenario. Perhaps some of Terry's large competitors will change their advertising focus to try to convince women riders that their products offer every bit as much design quality and efficiency as does Terry. Terry may need to alter or increase its own advertising to blunt the competitors' impact. Of course, many other possibilities and combinations may occur.

The point is basic. Changes in strategic thinking and customer orientation are prompted by shifts in the competitive environment in which the business operates. Such changes are not unusual. They are not signs of failure or poor decision making. They are simply the changes a business must make over its history. Some of them can be planned, some cannot. A firm's success depends in large part on how effectively it is able to read the need for change and act in a timely manner. The words of Norman Brinker ring true here. "Increased competition necessitates constant tinkering, con-

BRINKER
INTERNATIONAL

stant change. We must stay at least half a step ahead of the competition. We should always be asking ourselves: What can we do better, quicker, and with more imagination?"[20]

All changes must start someplace. There must be some point of entry or initial focus of change. Typically, that change will affect one of the key parts or subsystems of the business. For example, the business may focus change around the people subsystem. We see this all the time. When Apple Computer announces, in the face of declining profits, that it has decided to scale back its workforce by 30,000 people, the people part of the business is being affected. Perhaps change will focus on the organizational design and structure of the business. This may mean that the business reorganizes into teams, moves to a project structure, looks for ways to partner with other businesses, or seeks other creative ways to streamline operations and strive for greater overall efficiency. Or perhaps the business will focus change on technology and information. New technology and information sources may be used to help the business be more responsive to customers. The Internet may be used to market items directly to potential customers. Just-in-time inventory practices may be implemented. Outsourcing may be considered to enhance efficiency and reduce costs.

outsourcing p. 279>

Regardless of the point of entry, change is never isolated in one part of the business. Changes are always interrelated. When a company changes strategy to enhance customer service and improve financial performance, people, design, technology, information, and other processes will change too. If the business downsizes, it will restructure and implement new processes. It will probably have to use information and technology in new ways. If the business decides to reorganize into teams, people will probably be more empowered. Further, information and technology will probably be modified to support the needs of the teams and ensure proper coordination. Due to their awareness of interrelatedness, successful businesses approach change by looking at all the parts of the business together.

customer service p. 340>

Two strategic approaches to change that are popular today are reengineering and learning organizations. Both of these approaches view change as interrelated. Both look at change as a total organizational approach.

reengineering, 421>

Reengineering

A popular approach to change that has touched many businesses in recent years is reengineering, which we mentioned in Chapter 14. It is one of those themes that are relevant to a number of issues facing today's businesses. The idea of reengineering was introduced by management consultants Michael Hammer and James Champy.[21] The impact of their ideas has been sweeping and dramatic. In fact, *Time* magazine named Hammer one of the most influential people in America.

Reengineering was defined in Chapter 14 as the process of systematically changing and redesigning a business to cut inefficiencies and focus on quality and customers. Reengineering asks the business to break from traditions, to redesign and rethink itself totally, as if it were just starting out. This notion of reengineering is a dramatic *process* of total business change. In fact, the term is often used to describe the interrelated process of organizational change.

From heavy manufacturing to retailing to utilities, businesses of all sizes and in all industries are reengineering. Reengineering has become part of everyday business life. Reengineering can deal with a number of change themes and actions. Some of the most common approaches, such as continuous improvement, outsourcing, teamwork

empowerment p. 422>   and empowerment, and redesigning the structure of the business, were discussed in some detail in previous chapters.

Learning Organizations

Learning organization
A business that not only adapts to change but creatively searches for new and better ways of operating and meeting its customers' needs.

In the 1990s, Peter Senge encouraged businesses to operate as learning organizations.[22] **Learning organizations** not only adapt to change, but creatively search for new and better ways of operating and meeting the needs of their customers. Learning organizations are proactive. They are always adapting and transforming themselves to improve.

The key to a learning organization is that it encourages change and renewal as part of its philosophy, its values, and its very culture. Imagine a business that is progressive enough to say, "The strongest component of our corporate culture is our commitment to continually reshape ourselves and our culture." This is done by promoting, on a businesswide basis, many of the actions and approaches we have discussed in this chapter. In learning organizations, leaders are visionaries, sources of innovation are recognized and exploited, and innovative actions are supported as part of "the way things are done." The learning organization philosophy prevails among successful businesses.

Developing Your Critical Thinking Skills

1. Is there really interrelatedness to all business decisions? How does a relatively basic decision, like which technical support employee is hired in the information services department, affect other areas of the business?

2. While many business managers recognize the need for reengineering, employees often shudder at the thought. Why do you think this resistance may occur?

3. Given everything you have learned in this course, why do you think it is important for a business in today's competitive world to behave as a learning organization?

SUMMARY

1. Understanding change is necessary in today's environment. Changes will occur in organizations whether managers plan for them or not. Some changes are forced on a company from external forces. Thus, managers must introduce change into their organizations.

   ■ What are Kurt Lewin's three stages of change?

   Lewin proposed that achieving change is a three-step process. First, people must unfreeze existing behavior patterns. Second, they must move. That is, the change or movement must be made. Third, there must be refreezing, meaning that positive results will solidify the new behavior.

2. Throughout this textbook you have encountered examples of businesses that have devised highly effective methods of competing. Yet the best of them deliber-

ately changed their successful formulas. Instead of waiting for change to catch them by surprise, these leaders anticipate it and plan for it.

■ What is the nature of planned change in business?

Planned change is the intentional process of movement from the present state toward some future state. Planned change can be viewed as consisting of three stages: the present state, movement, and the future state. Planned change often faces resistance due to the strong tendencies in business to maintain the present state, to keep things the way they are now.

3. Each business approaches planned change in a somewhat unique manner because each business has its own particular strengths and weaknesses. Nevertheless, some common features are usually observed in firms that effectively engage in planned change.

■ What are the main features of the process of planned change?

In this chapter you learned about a five-part process that is common in planned change.
(1) Awareness of the need for change.
(2) Emergence of leaders who champion the change.
(3) Development and acceptance of a vision of the desired future state that will result from the change.
(4) Development of an actual plan for change, followed by the management of action steps to implement that plan.
(5) Monitoring of the plan's implementation and modification based on feedback.

4. Businesses that are successful in planning change are innovative. In today's business environment, any organization that intends to survive over the long run must learn how to innovate.

■ What is an innovation? What is a competitive innovation?

Innovation is the successful implementation of creative ideas. A competitive innovation is a change so important that it allows the business to distinguish itself and gain an advantage over its competitors.

5. Many opportunities for innovation are available to businesses.

■ What are the sources of innovative opportunities?

In this chapter, you learned about three external sources and four internal sources of innovation. The external sources are (1) demographic changes, (2) changes in perception, and (3) new knowledge. The internal sources are (1) the unexpected, (2) an incongruity, (3) process needs, and (4) changes in industry or market structure.

6. Innovation does not simply occur. It takes concerted attention and action by businesses to build and support innovation.

■ What are some of the practices that help a business to be innovative?

In this chapter, you learned about the following practices:
(1) Encouraging risk and experimentation.
(2) Creating a culture that tolerates and learns from mistakes.
(3) Encouraging diversity and embracing differences.

(4) Promoting boundaryless behavior.
(5) Maintaining close contact with customers.
(6) Investing in training.
(7) Employing creative personalities, both innovators and adaptors.

7. Change and renewal must cover all areas and phases of the business. Changes in the various areas are interrelated and must therefore be integrated. This means that business leaders must think strategically about change and renewal.

   ■ What are some of the currently popular strategic approaches to change in business?

   In this chapter you learned about two approaches.
   (1) Reengineering involves systematically changing and redesigning the business.
   (2) Creating a learning organization involves developing an organization that not only adapts to change but creatively searches for new and better ways of operating and meeting the needs of customers.

Links to Future Courses

Since change is an interrelated concept, business change affects all areas of study. However, certain courses are more likely to give special attention to the process of change. These courses include the following:

■ Psychology
■ Principles of management
■ Principles of marketing

■ Organizational behavior
■ Business policy and strategic management

EXERCISES AND APPLICATIONS

1. Pick an organization with which you are familiar—perhaps a social group, a fraternity or sorority, or a small business where you have worked. What changes do you think would benefit this organization? Outline the steps you think would be necessary to make these changes happen.

2. Think of businesses you have patronized. Identify one or two you think are the most innovative. What do you see them doing that helps them innovate?

3. Form teams of six. Each team should be provided with a copy of *The Wall Street Journal*, a role of adhesive tape, a ball of string, and 10 paperclips. Using only these materials, each team is to construct a tower, which will be judged on three factors: height, strength, and aesthetic appeal. Teams should be given 5 minutes to meet and plan their tower and 20 minutes to actually construct it. Each team should present a one-page paper on what its members learned about creativity through this exercise.

4. Think of a business where you have worked. Drawing from this chapter, what do you think that business could do to generate more creativity and innovation?

5. Go to Trek's home page on the Internet (http://www.trekbikes.com). Trek prides itself on being an innovative business. What evidence can you find that suggests it really is innovative?

6. Find an example of a business that has recently come up with an innovative product or service. (Look in local newspapers, magazines, and business publications such as *The Wall Street Journal* or *Business Week*). Find out as much as you can about the history of the innovation. See if you can identify actions the business took to support and reinforce creativity and innovation.

KEY TERMS

Adaptors, p. 531
Boundaryless behavior, p. 529
Competitive innovation, p. 522
Innovators, p. 532
Interrelatedness, p. 533
Learning organization, p. 536
Moving, p. 517

Planned change, p. 515
Refreezing, p. 517
Resistance to change, p. 516
Unfreezing, p. 517

CASE: TOYOTA PLANS TO CHANGE—AGAIN

In the 1970s and 80s, Japan's Toyota Motor Corp. changed the recipe for success in the automobile industry with its lean production methods and superior quality standards. As a result, Toyota is widely considered to be the most successful automobile manufacturer in the world today. Yet the company's new president, Hiroshi Okuda, is in the process of making major changes in Toyota's methods and strategies.

Why is Okuda changing a business that is performing so well? For one thing, he sees new opportunities in the external environment. A huge automobile market is emerging in Asia. Furthermore, the fall in the value of the yen has made it profitable for Toyota to export to the United States again. The cheaper yen did cause American automakers to ask the U.S. government to put a 100 percent tariff on Japanese luxury car imports back in 1995. Okuda personally defused that effort by disclosing plans to buy huge quantities of U.S. automobile parts.

tariff p. 194>

Okuda also sees external threats. One of those is the increasing competitiveness of American and Korean carmakers. Another is the technological possibilities for customized production of cars to fit regional differences in tastes in the United States, Europe, and Asia. As *Business Week* recently put it, if Toyota implements its change wisely, it can "create the industry's first real globally organized player, a company that can use its vast manufacturing clout to customize vehicles for regional markets. Manufacturing hubs in Asia, North America, and Europe will rely on locally based suppliers and design teams to tailor vehicles to local tastes. Not only will Toyota be able to pounce faster on consumer trends and bypass regional trade barriers, it will rely on its network of cheaper dollar-denominated parts and materials when the yen is strong and stoke up its exports when it is weak."

Okuda's strategy relies on Toyota's technological and financial strengths. On the technological side, Toyota already leads the world in high-speed, flexible manufacturing. On the financial side, the company has accumulated huge cash reserves of $20 billion. That should support Okuda's plan to spend $13.5 billion on the planned changes.

Toyota's planned change is also designed to address some weaknesses that the company has spotted, including the company's "insular, consensus-driven culture." Okuda wants to make the company more multinational in outlook, reduce the levels of management at headquarters, and move from pay based on seniority to rewards for performance.

Success in making the planned changes will be measured in a number of ways. Customer satisfaction levels will be monitored by, among other things, the percentage of buyers who return to Toyota when they buy their next car. Technological performance will be measured by, among other things, the number of months needed to develop a new car. (Toyota's current 24–month product development cycle is the industry standard, but Okuda is shooting for a 15-month cycle. Toyota actually achieved that with its recently launched Ipsum model.) Overall success will be measured by world market share. Toyota currently holds about 9.5 percent of the world market, compared with 17 percent for GM and 13 percent for Ford. According to analyst Christopher Cedergren, "Okuda's intent, by the middle of the next decade, is to see Toyota with 10 to 15 percent of the global auto market."

SOURCE: Brian Bremner, Larry Armstrong, Kathleen Kerwin, and Keith Naughton, "Toyota's Crusade," *Business Week*, April 7, 1997, pp. 104–14.

Decision Questions

1. What do you think of Okuda's proactive approach to change?
2. Japanese business has been quite successful in using consensus-style decision making and pay and promotion based on seniority. Yet Toyota is talking about moving to an American style of decision making and rewards. Do you think this change will work? What kinds of resistance is Okuda likely to encounter?
3. Do you have any direct experience with Toyota vehicles and dealerships? If so, how do you compare Toyota's ability to provide value to customers with that of its American rivals? What changes do you think the American firms should make?

REFERENCES

1. Raju Narisetti. "Peddling BMX Bikes, Huffy Turns Cool." *The Wall Street Journal*, July 10, 1997, pp. B1, B5.

2. John A. Byrne. "Strategic Planning." *Business Week*, August 26, 1996, pp. 46–52.

3. Glenn R. Carroll and Michael T. Hannon. *Organizations in Industry: Strategy, Structure, and Selection.* New York: Oxford University Press, 1995, p. 12.

4. This is drawn, in part, from the work of J. P. Kotter and L. A. Schlesinger. "Choosing Strategies for Change." *Harvard Business Review*, March/April 1979, pp. 106–14.

5. Kurt Lewin. *Field Theory in Social Science.* New York: Harper & Row, 1951.

6. This example is drawn from "Oticon" in Nick Obolensky. *Practical Business Reengineering*. Houston, TX: Gulf Publishing Co., 1994, pp. 250–262.

7. Teresa Amabile, Regina Conti, Heather Coon, Jeffrey Lazenby, and Michael Herron. "Assessing the Work Environment for Creativity." Working paper, July 1995.

8. Raju Narisetti. "Diaper Makers Face a Maturing Market." *The Wall Street Journal*, July 8, 1996, p. B4.

9. Ron Ruggles. "Hot Concepts: Cozymel's." *Nation's Restaurant News*, May 22, 1995.

10. Louis Kraar. "A World of Cool Companies: Trend Micro." *Fortune*, October 28, 1996, pp. 162–3.

11. Warren Bennis and Burt Nanus. *Leaders: The Strategies for Taking Charge*. New York: Harper & Row, 1985, p. 76.

12. Linda Himelstein and Stephanie Anderson Forest. "Breaking Through." *Business Week*, February 17, 1997, pp. 64–70.

13. Ron Ashkenas, Dave Ulrich, Todd Jick, and Steve Kerr. *The Boundaryless Organization: Breaking the Chains of Organizational Structure*. San Francisco: Jossey-Bass Publishers, 1995.

14. John F. Welch, Jr. "To Our Share Owners." General Electric Annual Report, 1996.

15. "Motorola in China–Facts '96," http://www.motorola.com/General/China/facts96.htm (accessed 9/11/1997).

16. Stephen Miller and William Koop. "The Top 10 Innovative Products for 2006: Technology with a Human Touch." *The Futurist*, July/August 1996, pp. 16–20.

17. Ibid.

18. Jerre Stead. "Values-Based Leadership: The Real People Power." McCord Lecture, Peoria, IL: Bradley University, April 3, 1996.

19. Charles Forman. "Training Is Fun." *Cheers*, March, 1996, pp. 65–7.

20. Norman Brinker and Donald T. Phillips. *On the Brink: The Life and Leadership of Norman Brinker*. Arlington, TX: Summit Publishing, 1996, p. 169.

21. Michael Hammer and James Champy. *Reengineering the Corporation: A Manifesto for Business Revolution*. New York: HarperBusiness, 1993.

22. Peter M. Senge. *The Fifth Discipline: The Art and Practice of the Learning Organization*. New York: Doubleday/Currency, 1990.

A

Preparing a Business Plan

Many of you who are reading this book may have thought of owning your own business someday. Others of you have worked for small companies. Some of your parents may own their own companies. Still others of you have worked for larger companies whose customers are smaller businesses. After reading this book, you are aware of the complexity of running a business. This complexity underscores the need for planning.

The business plan is a tool that helps guide the strategies of the firm. However, a frequent use of business plans is to acquire funding to underwrite the company's operation and growth. We discussed acquisition of resources in Chapter 13. Recall that capital can be either debt capital which must be paid back with interest or equity capital which includes some ownership in the company. Acquiring additional capital of either kind requires a well-written business plan.

In the paragraphs that follow, you will see a number of tasks that must be done in order to do a good business plan. Once these tasks are completed, the writing of the plan is a matter of putting the information in a form that is succinct, appealing, and convincing. A well-written plan does not guarantee that lenders or investors will give you money. However, a poorly-written plan will certainly reduce the odds of gaining the needed capital.

All of the work in producing a business plan is aimed at convincing lenders or investors that the ideas proposed are worth the risk. It is the writer's job to convincingly present information that shows that the company will, indeed, make money. As we discussed in Chapter 1, this means simply that the revenues must exceed the expenses. Thus, two tasks that must precede the writing of any business plan are to show that significant demand exists and to show that revenues generated more than offset expenses. We look first at forecasting demand.

Forecasting Revenues

One of the most difficult tasks for any business owner is the forecasting of revenues. If the business is a new business, that task is doubly difficult. If the business is not only new, but is selling a totally new product or service, the task becomes almost impossible. Still, the owner must attempt to make a forecast or estimate of what sales will be in the future. That estimate should be made on a monthly basis for at least two years, followed by quarterly or annual estimates for three or more additional years.

If the business is an existing business, the first step in the research is to consider past sales. In fact, most lenders want to see three years of past financial records to show what sales were and how they compared with expenses. Historical information on revenues can then be projected into the future. It may then be adjusted based upon information such as competitors leaving the industry, comparisons of the product or service to competitors, changes in the economy and industry, and other information that may impact the firm. Consider the information provided in Part Two when estimating future revenues.

New businesses or businesses producing new products have a more difficult time. Making an accurate forecast is hard because the company has no track record regarding the product. Thus, historical data is nonexistent. Forecasting sales in this case requires estimating the number of customers who might buy the products and multiplying the number of customers by the amount each customer is likely to spend. Identifying potential customers is, of course, the key to the forecast. Sometimes similar products have been sold in the past which can provide a hint about potential sales. If other competitors have similar or substitute products, then total sales must be divided by the appropriate amount depending on the impact competitors will have.

Forecasting Expenses

Once an estimate of revenues has been developed, the next task is to determine what the expenses will be. Expenses will be in two groups. Fixed expenses are those which do not change directly with sales. Examples of fixed expenses are rent, insurance, utilities, advertising, and salaries. Variable expenses change with the amount of production. Cost of materials, direct labor, and distribution costs are variable costs. There are a number of sources of information in your local library that provide information about costs. Since a new business will not have a history of costs, industry information can sometimes be used to estimate what expenses will be. This information is often presented in ratio form. Thus, the cost of goods sold which includes labor and materials might be 65 percent of sales. Salaries might average twenty percent of sales. Total expenses might be 90 percent of sales leaving an industry average for profit of ten percent of sales. These industry averages can be applied to your forecasted revenues to give you a rough estimate of profits for your company.

Once the revenues and expenses have been estimated, the owner is ready to start assembling the plan. The following is a suggested format for a business plan, along with a brief discussion of what each section includes. Following this is a sample plan which was adapted from a plan prepared by a team of students in an entrepreneurship course.

Assembling the Management Team

A common statement from investors is that they would rather fund a Grade B idea with a Grade A management team than a Grade A idea with a Grade B management team. It is important for a business to have a good and balanced management team. If you are thinking of starting your own business, do not simply select a good friend or a neighbor just because they are handy. Select partners based on what they can offer the business. Often it is good to find partners that complement your skills and weaknesses. Thus, if you have good marketing skills, it may be wise to find someone with good financial or accounting skills. If you like to spend time outside the business soliciting customers, you may want to find a partner who likes to stay in the store and control operations. This balance keeps the company from being pulled in the wrong direction.

Format of a Business Plan

Figure A1–1 shows a suggested outline for a business plan.[1] If you look at books on business plans, you may find other possible outlines. The specific outline used is not critical as long as the necessary information is included. Let's consider each of the parts of the business plan.

Executive Summary

The Executive Summary appears first, but it is the last part of the plan written. This is simply because it summarizes everything that follows in the plan. It normally takes no more than two pages and must be compelling enough to get readers to look at the rest of the plan. Accordingly, it is one of the most important parts of the plan. If the Executive Summary does not "reach out and grab" potential investors, they will not read the rest of the plan. It must be letter perfect and well-written. If not, readers will assume that whoever wrote it did not give sufficient attention to the plan and probably would not give adequate attention to their business.

Nature of the Business

This section discusses the background of the business idea, the nature of the product or service, and the location of the business. It gives the reader a good feel for the business and the product or service being proposed. It provides a brief history of the business and why the writer developed the idea.

Description of the Market

This very important section discusses the trends affecting the product or service, demographics of the target market, competitors, and a comparison with competing products. The point of this section is to convince the potential investor that market conditions will support the proposed venture. It is important to draw out and highlight key aspects of the market including the types of customers targeted, reasons why customers would desire the product, and the growth in the size of the market.

Description of the Product/Service

This section discusses the uniqueness of the product, why it is superior to all others, what value it provides to customers, and what alternative uses exist for the product. The focus here should be on why the product or service is better than competitors' offerings. Investors must be convinced that the new product or service is good enough to draw customers away from their existing habits.

The Management Team

This section is critical. Even though investors want to know what the financial projections are, almost all lenders and investors will say that the strength of the management team is key to the success of the business. A management team that is experienced in the industry and has considerable managerial experience will have a tremendous advantage over one that has little business experience or little experience in managing an enterprise.

Objectives and Goals

Both short-term and long-term goals must be included to let investors know where the business is headed. Short-term goals may be something like "to reach the breakeven point in the third month" or to "establish the firm and gain a one percent share of the market within two years." Long-range goals may include expansion plans, profitability goals, or even a long-range goal of selling the business at a hefty profit.

Business Strategies

Each of the functional area strategies must be included. These are the marketing strategies, human resource strategies, production strategies, financial strategies, and an overall strategy for growth. These strategies should be thorough but avoid so much detail that the reader is bored with reading about minuscule parts of strategies that may or may not affect the venture's success.

Financial Information

This information, often in appendices, must give investors an idea of how profitable the company will be and how much cash will be generated. This data should include historical financial statements if available, projected income statements, cash flow statements, and balance sheets. Income statements and cash flow statements should be projected monthly for at least two years and quarterly or annually for at least three more years. Balance sheets typically include a start-up or beginning balance sheet, followed by balance sheets for the end of each fiscal year.

A final item to consider in developing a business plan is the appearance of the plan and the presentation of the plan to potential investors. The plan should be no more than forty pages long and should be in an attractive cover. Those who will be making the presentation to investors must be absolutely familiar with the plan and all of its contents. Nothing is more embarassing than having a potential investor ask a question about something in the plan that cannot be answered. Thus, even though companies or entrepreneurs often have outside help in preparing a plan, it is imperative that the owners be totally involved in the process.

FIGURE A–1   Outline of a Business Plan

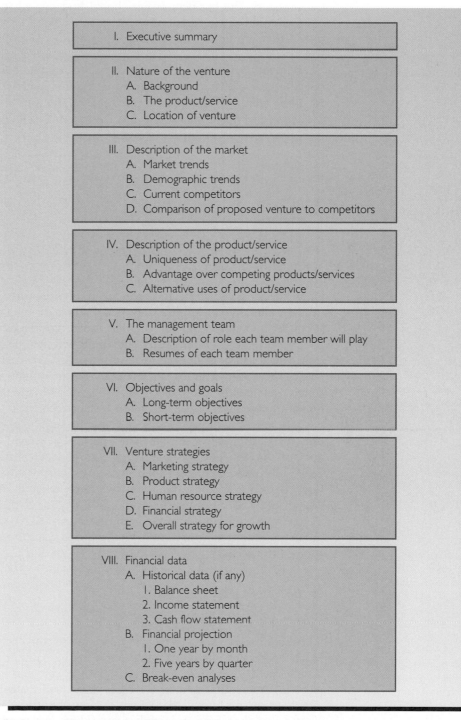

I. Executive summary

II. Nature of the venture
   A. Background
   B. The product/service
   C. Location of venture

III. Description of the market
   A. Market trends
   B. Demographic trends
   C. Current competitors
   D. Comparison of proposed venture to competitors

IV. Description of the product/service
   A. Uniqueness of product/service
   B. Advantage over competing products/services
   C. Alternative uses of product/service

V. The management team
   A. Description of role each team member will play
   B. Resumes of each team member

VI. Objectives and goals
   A. Long-term objectives
   B. Short-term objectives

VII. Venture strategies
   A. Marketing strategy
   B. Product strategy
   C. Human resource strategy
   D. Financial strategy
   E. Overall strategy for growth

VIII. Financial data
   A. Historical data (if any)
      1. Balance sheet
      2. Income statement
      3. Cash flow statement
   B. Financial projection
      1. One year by month
      2. Five years by quarter
   C. Break-even analyses

The format used is adapted from Fred L. Fry, *Entrepreneurship: A Planning Approach*, Minneapolis/St. Paul: West Publishing Company, 1993, p. 103.

The presentation itself is important. When making an appointment with potential investors, the business owner should find out what kind of media is available. Computer-aided presentations are extremely helpful in making a favorable presentation if they are done well. On the other hand, a poorly done presentation detracts from the impression intended even if the owners are competent business managers.

The following business plan is based on an actual business plan which was developed by a team of students for an entrepreneurship class. You should note the format used, the relative lengths of each section, and the tone of the plan. At the same time, recall that every plan is different. The key to a successful business plan is that it is done well, not that it uses a particular format or media.

Conveniesse, Inc.
An Upscale Convenience Store[1]

Executive Summary

Conveniesse, Inc., will be an upscale convenience store located in an office building near the Buffalo Convention Center and hotels. It will feature relatively high-priced products including over-the-counter drugs, cosmetics, hosiery, high-quality soft drinks, beer, wine, and imported liquors. It will include a high-quality deli and offer freshly baked pastries during the morning hours. Limited grocery goods will be available to those who wish to purchase items on the way home at the end of the day. Attractive features of Conveniesse include an ATM machine, a copier, a fax machine, notebook computer rental, and a floral referral service.

There are two target markets for Conveniesse. The first is workers in and around the office building in which Conveniesse is located. The second target market consists of hotel guests in the area. The two target markets are generally distinct and nonoverlapping.

Conveniesse, Inc., will be a New York corporation owned by Sarah Tondeur (forty percent), Yolanda Williams (forty percent), and Jason Stone (twenty percent). The three owners will invest $60,000, $60,000, and $30,000 respectively for a total of $150,000. This business plan seeks the infusion of $310,000 of debt and/or equity capital to underwrite startup costs of Conveniesse.

Nature of the Venture

Background

There is currently not a convenient place in the convention center area of Buffalo for office workers to buy deli sandwiches, over-the-counter drugs, and other necessities during the day. Similarly, hotel guests in the convention center area do not have a place to buy necessities or to purchase high-quality alcoholic beverages. Some hotel gift shops carry a limited assortment of items, but these are primarily gifts and magazines rather than food and drink items. There is a need for an upscale convenience store that is easily accessible by office workers and by hotel guests.

---

1. Fred L. Fry, *Entrepreneurship: A Planning Approach*. Minneapolis/St. Paul: West Publishing Co., 1993, pp. 458–471.

Nature of the Product/Service

Conveniesse will provide a wide variety of products and services in an upscale environment. Products will include bakery goods during the morning hours, deli salads and sandwiches for lunch or for carryout in the evening, a variety of grocery goods, cosmetics, hosiery, and over-the-counter drug items, and a variety of soft drinks, beer, wine, and imported liquors. Soft drinks will include the more exotic juice-based drinks, mineral waters, and seltzers. Services will include an ATM cash machine, a fax machine, notebook computer rental, a floral referral service, and the provision of local area information and directions. All workers in the store will wear distinctive uniforms that will include the Conveniesse logo. The floral service will consist of a catalog of bouquets and other flowers that may be delivered. Conveniesse has an agreement with a local florist who will give Conveniesse a 20 percent commission for all orders called in. A small inventory of popular flowers will be maintained on site for immediate purchase. Hours for Conveniesse are 7 A.M. to midnight.

Location of the Venture

Conveniesse will be located in an office complex approximately two blocks from the Buffalo Convention Center. There are two hotels within two blocks of the building. The ground floor of the office building is open twenty-four hours a day.

Description of the Market

Market Trends

There are two distinct target markets for Conveniesse. The first is office workers in and around the building in which Conveniesse is located. The building itself is twelve stories high and houses nearly eight hundred workers. These are almost evenly divided between male and female. Two office buildings within one block are somewhat smaller, but they do not have a convenience store. Thus, at least some of those workers would come to Conveniesse during their lunch hour or on the way to or from work. Customers from this target market will typically come to Conveniesse early in the morning, during the lunch hour, or at the end of the workday.

The second target market is hotel guests at the two hotels within two blocks of the store. This target market would come to Conveniesse for those items not available in the hotel gift shops. This market will primarily patronize Conveniesse in the late afternoon and evening. The two hotels together can house up to twelve hundred guests per night.

A third, and obviously secondary, market is those individuals attending convention center activities. Those customers may stop by either before or after events to pick up needed merchandise or use the ATM machine.

The first target market, office workers, is stable. Conveniesse will reap significant sales from this market, and it will grow until all those in the building and surrounding area are familiar with the store. Once Conveniesse has fully tapped that market, the customers should be stable, but loyal. The hotel market will obviously be a function of the hotel business. As convention center activities increase, this will have some impact on hotel guest listings. The growth in this market is expected to be low to moderate. Overall, the growth is expected to rise significantly during the first few months and then grow at approximately five percent per year.

Demographic and Economic Trends

Changes in demographic trends are not likely to be significant within any foreseeable time period. Since the two markets are either business or hotel related, demographic changes within the area will have little direct impact. Economic trends, on the other hand, can have an impact on the extent that companies choose to send employees to Buffalo for meetings or individuals choose to come to Buffalo hotels in order to see convention center events. The office worker market would be affected by the economy only to the extent that vacancies occur in the office suites.

Current Competitors

There are currently no direct competitors. A liquor store exists three blocks from the Conveniesse location. However, it tends to serve a much different target market than Conveniesse does. Hotel gift shops provide some of the same products, but they tend to have a much more limited selection. Further, they carry none of the food products that Conveniesse carries, and they provide few services.

Description of the Product and Services

The unique aspect of Conveniesse is the selection of products and services that it will offer. Fresh-baked goods will be offered in the mornings, deli salads and sandwiches will be sold around lunch, and either deli or other food products may be purchased by office workers on their way home at the end of the day. The real uniqueness of Conveniesse lies in the services to be provided. The ATM machine will draw significant numbers of customers into Conveniesse. A fax machine will be useful for some office workers and will appeal to hotel guests away from their home offices. Laptop computers will be available for rental. These will have the latest software on them including presentation software. These will be appealing to conference participants or others who have to make a presentation and find that they have forgotten their computer or it has broken down. A floral referral service will be offered. It should be appealing to both the office workers and the hotel guests who want to send flowers either within Buffalo or elsewhere in the nation. A small inventory of fresh flowers will be maintained for immediate purchase. The advantage of the referral service is that customers can choose flower arrangements from a catalog rather than either calling a florist to send flowers sight unseen or going to a florist.

The employees will enhance the upscale image of Conveniesse as they will be highly knowledgeable about Conveniesse products and services as well as about locations and happenings in Buffalo. For example, the combination greeter/security guard will also be the source for information regarding the area. All employees will be impeccably dressed in uniforms with the Conveniesse logo prominently displayed.

Management Team and Ownership

Conveniesse, Inc., is owned jointly by three individuals. Sarah Tondeur will serve as president and will also be responsible for the accounting tasks for the corporation. She owned her own accounting and tax service in Montreal for ten years. She merged it with another firm and later sold out to her partner. She owns forty percent of the stock of Conveniesse.

Yolanda Williams will be a vice president and will be responsible for marketing activities for Conveniesse. She is a product manager for a major pharmaceuticals firm in New York. Williams has a B.S. in marketing from State University of New York at Buffalo with a minor in French. She has been with her current employer for eight years. She will continue in her present job for now and will commute to Buffalo on weekends for Conveniesse planning meetings. She will also work in the store on weekends as time permits.

Jason Stone will be a vice president and will be responsible for public relations and customer relations and interaction with members of the financial community. He has a B.S. in English with a minor in business from the University of Texas at Arlington. He is currently employed by a public relations firm in Detroit, but will leave that job once funding for Conveniesse is approved.

Objectives and Goals

Short-Term Goals

The major short-term goal of Conveniesse is to gain funding for the upscale convenience store, launch the venture, stabilize the operations, and manage its growth. Financially, Conveniesse has the goal of breaking even within the first three months and increasing profitability each month until sales growth stabilizes during the second year. Profits will be sufficient to pay off debt within ten years while returning twenty percent to owners' investments.

Long-Term Goals

The long-term goal of Conveniesse is to make the Conveniesse store increasingly profitable and to consider adding additional stores in the future.

Strategies

The overall strategy of Conveniesse is to maintain and enhance the upscale image of the store through decor, products, services, pricing, and highly-trained employees.

Marketing Strategy

Conveniesse will use constant but limited advertising. The office target market will initially be attracted through flyers and other information provided to offices in the building and surrounding area. The specific products and services, such as the ATM machine, will be highlighted and are expected to draw office workers to the store. Advertising to the hotel and convention market will consist of advertisements in hotel brochures, convention and tourism booklets, the Buffalo airport, and at the Buffalo Convention Center. These methods should reach the majority of visitors to the downtown part of Buffalo.

Other marketing activities will include the distinctive logo of Conveniesse, which will appear outside and inside the store and on all cups, bags, and other carry-out products. Conveniesse will also be a participant in downtown activities such as parades, trade shows, and other visual events.

Pricing at Conveniesse will be high but bearable. Prices will be significantly higher than grocery or drug stores and somewhat higher than suburban convenience stores. This is justified by the relatively captive market and because many of the products are not price sensitive. Customers will expect to pay higher prices due to the convenience and the upscale ambience of the store. This pricing strategy will allow Conveniesse to have an excellent return.

Conveniesse will offer a wide breadth of products rather than a depth of selection. It will carry only one brand of any given product, which typically will be a well-known brand. The exception to this is in the imported and specialty alcoholic beverages and soft drinks where a wide choice of brands and flavors will be available.

Human Resource Strategy

A key to the success of Conveniesse is the highly-trained and knowledgeable employees. As a result, it is imperative that employees be motivated, conversant, and possess a wealth of information regarding both Conveniesse and Buffalo. Therefore, Conveniesse will hire only experienced employees who already have knowledge of the convenience store business. Floor managers will be hired from among managers or assistant managers of local convenience stores. Employees must be local and have positive and outgoing personalities. Conveniesse will pay higher than the prevailing rates in order to attract and retain excellent employees.

Financial Strategy

Conveniesse is currently totally owned by three individuals, Yolanda Williams (forty percent), Sarah Tondeur (forty percent), and Jason Stone (twenty percent). They would prefer to maintain complete ownership control of Conveniesse. If possible, they prefer that initial outside funding be totally debt financing. If equity funding is required, it will be limited in such a way that the three primary owners retain financial and managerial control of Conveniesse. Future funding should be available primarily through the retained earnings of the corporation.

Financial Information

CONVENIESSE, INC.

Estimated Startup Costs and Six Months Operating Costs

Desired minimum cash balance		$ 30,000
Initial inventory plus net additions		150,000
Rent (six-month lease)		50,000
Prepaid insurance		1,500
Salaries and wages (first six months)		
Salaries (Stone, Tondeur)	$37,500	
Salaries (asst. managers)	24,000	
Wages	17,500	
Total salaries and wages		$ 79,000

Miscellaneous prepaid expenses

Supplies	$ 1,000	
Advertising	2,500	
Legal fees	1,500	
Licenses	2,000	
Total miscellaneous expenses		$ 7,000

Building and equipment

Leasehold improvements	$30,000	
Equipment	97,500	
Fixtures	15,000	
Total building and equipment		$142,500
Total startup costs		$460,000
Owner equity		150,000
Additional funding requested		$310,000

CONVENIESSE, INC.
Opening Day Balance Sheet (projected)

Assets

Current assets

Cash	$134,000	
Inventory	125,000	
Prepaid rent	50,000	
Prepaid insurance	1,500	
Prepaid expenses	7,000	
Total current assets		$317,500

Long-term assets

Furnishings and equipment	112,500	
Leasehold improvements	30,000	
Total long-term assets		142,500
Total assets		$460,000

Liabilities and owners' equity

Liabilities

Notes payable-bank	$310,000	

Stockholders' equity

Common stock	$150,000	
Total liabilities and owners' equity		$460,000

CONVENIESSE, INC.
Proforma Income Statement, End of Year 1

	Jan	Feb	Mar	Apr	May	Jun
Sales	$ 50,000	$75,000	$95,000	$110,000	$125,000	$125,000
Cost of goods	32,500	48,750	61,750	71,500	81,250	81,250
Gross profit	$ 17,500	$26,250	$33,250	$ 38,500	$ 43,750	$ 43,750
Operating expenses						
Salaries (owners)	$ 6,250	$ 6,250	$ 6,250	$6,250	$6,250	$6,250
Salaries (managers)	4,000	4,000	4,000	4,000	4,000	4,000
Wages	2,916	2,916	2,916	2,916	2,916	2,916
Rent	8,333	8,333	8,333	8,333	8,333	8,333
Telephone and utilities	200	200	200	200	200	200
Insurance	300	300	300	300	300	300
Advertising	750	750	750	750	750	750
Maintenance	200	200	200	200	200	200
Legal Fees	200	200	200	200	200	200
Licenses	150	150	150	150	150	150
Depreciation	2,375	2,375	2,375	2,375	2,375	2,375
Net operating profit (loss)	$ (8,174)	$576	$7,576	$12,826	$18,076	$18,076
Interest expense	2,583	2,566	2,547	2,530	2,512	2,493
Net profit (loss)	$(10,757)	$ (1,990)	$5,029	$ 10,296	$ 15,564	$ 15,583
Taxes						
Net profit after taxes						

Assumptions

Assume that sales will increase during the first several months and then stabilize. Sales will be lower in December, January, August, and September. Cost of goods sold is 65 percent of sales. Salaries and wages will increase by 5 percent in the second year, and all operating expenses will increase by 5 percent in succeeding years. Equipment is depreciated over five years with a straight line depreciation. The loan request assumes a 10 percent interest rate for $310,000 to be paid off in eight years. Salaries are for two owners (Stone and Tondeur) and for two assistant managers.

Jul	Aug	Sep	Oct	Nov	Dec	Totals
$115,000	$115,000	$125,000	$125,000	$120,000	$95,000	$1,275,000
74,750	74,750	81,250	81,250	78,000	61,750	828,750
$ 40,250	$40,250	$43,750	$43,750	$42,000	$33,250	$446,250
$6,250	$6,250	$6,250	$6,250	$6,250	$ 6,250	$75,000
4,000	4,000	4,000	4,000	4,000	4,000	48,000
2,916	2,916	2,916	2,916	2,916	2,924	35,000
8,333	8,333	8,333	8,333	8,333	8,337	100,000
200	200	200	200	200	200	2,400
300	300	300	300	300	300	3,600
750	750	750	750	750	750	9,000
200	200	200	200	200	200	2,400
200	200	200	200	200	200	2,400
150	150	150	150	150	150	1,800
2,375	2,375	2,375	2,375	2,375	2,375	28,500
$ 14,576	$14,576	$18,076	$18,076	$16,326	$7,564	$138,150
2,475	2,456	2,438	2,419	2,400	2,381	29,800
$ 12,101	$12,120	$15,638	$15,657	$13,926	$5,183	$108,350
						30,338
						$78,012

CONVENIESSE, INC.

Proforma Income Statement, End of Year 2

	Jan	Feb	Mar	Apr	May	Jun
Sales	$95,000	$105,00	$110,000	$120,000	$132,000	$132,000
Cost of goods	61,750	68,250	71,500	78,000	85,800	85,800
Gross profit	$33,250	$36,750	$ 38,500	$ 42,000	$ 46,200	$ 46,200
Operating expenses						
Salaries (owners)	$ 6,560	$ 6,560	$6,560	$6,560	$6,560	$6,560
Salaries (managers)	4,200	4,200	4,200	4,200	4,200	4,200
Wages	3,062	2,062	3,062	3,062	3,062	3,062
Rent	8,333	8,333	8,333	8,333	8,333	8,333
Telephone and utilities	200	200	200	200	200	200
Insurance	300	300	300	300	300	300
Advertising	780	780	780	780	780	780
Maintenance	200	200	200	200	200	200
Legal fees	200	200	200	200	200	200
Licenses	150	150	150	150	150	150
Depreciation	2,375	2,375	2,375	2,375	2,375	2,375
Net operating profit (loss)	$6,890	$10,390	$12,140	$15,640	$19,840	$19,840
Interest Expense	2,361	2,342	2,322	2,302	2,282	2,262
Net profit (loss)	$4,529	$ 8,048	$ 9,818	$13,338	$ 17,558	$ 17,578
Taxes						
Net profit after taxes						

CONVENIESSE, INC.

Proforma Income Statement, End of Year 3

	Qtr I	Qtr 2	Qtr 3	Qtr 4	Totals
Sales	$325,500	$403,200	$394,800	$380,100	$1,503,600
Cost of goods	211,575	262,080	256,620	247,065	977,340
Gross profit	$113,925	$141,120	$138,180	$133,035	$ 726,260
Operating expenses	83,034	83,034	83,034	83,034	332,136
Net operating profit	$ 30,891	$ 58,086	$ 55,146	$ 50,001	194,124
Interest expense	6,283	6,086	5,883	5,676	23,928
Net profit	$27,296	$55,536	$53,641	$47,541	$170,196
Taxes					47,655
Net profit after taxes					$122,541

	Jul	Aug	Sep	Oct	Nov	Dec	Totals
	$122,000	$122,000	$132,000	$132,000	$128,000	$102,000	$1,432,000
	79,300	79,300	85,800	85,800	83,200	66,300	930,800
	$ 42,700	$ 42,700	$ 46,200	$ 46,200	$ 44,800	$ 35,700	$ 501,200
	$6,560	$6,560	$6,560	$6,560	$6,560	$6,560	$78,720
	4,200	4,200	4,200	4,200	4,200	4,200	50,400
	3,062	3,062	3,062	3,062	3,062	3,062	36,744
	8,333	8,333	8,333	8,333	8,333	8,337	100,000
	200	200	200	200	200	200	2,400
	300	300	300	300	300	300	3,600
	780	780	780	780	780	780	9,360
	200	200	200	200	200	200	2,400
	200	200	200	200	200	200	2,400
	150	150	150	150	150	150	1,800
	2,375	2,375	2,375	2,375	2,375	2,375	28,500
	$ 16,340	$16,340	$19,840	$19,840	$18,440	$9,336	$184,876
	2,242	2,221	2,200	2,180	2,160	2,137	27,010
	$ 14,098	$14,119	$17,640	$17,660	$16,280	$7,199	$157,866
							44,202
							$113,664

CONVENIESSE, INC.
Proforma Income Statement, End of Year 4

	Qtr I	Qtr 2	Qtr 3	Qtr 4	Totals
Sales	$341,775	$423,360	$414,540	$399,105	$1,578,780
Cost of goods	222,154	275,184	269,451	259,418	1,026,207
Gross profit	$119,621	$148,176	$145,089	$139,687	$ 552,573
Operating expenses	87,186	87,186	87,186	87,186	348,744
Net operating profit	$ 32,435	$ 60,990	$ 57,903	$ 52,501	$ 203,829
Interest expense	5,463	5,245	5,022	4,793	20,522
Net profit	$26,972	$55,745	$52,881	$47,708	$ 183,307
Taxes					51,326
Net profit after taxes					$ 131,981

CONVENIESSE, INC.

Proforma Income Statement, End of Year 5

	Qtr I	Qtr 2	Qtr 3	Qtr 4	Totals
Sales	$358,863	$444,528	$435,267	$419,061	$1,657,719
Cost of goods	233,261	288,943	282,924	272,389	1,077,517
Gross profit	$125,602	$155,585	$152,343	$146,672	$ 580,202
Operating expenses	91,545	91,545	91,545	91,545	366,180
Net operating profit	$ 34,057	$ 64,040	$ 60,798	$ 55,127	$ 214,022
Interest expense	4,558	4,317	4,070	3,817	16,760
Net profit	$29,499	$59,723	$56,728	$51,310	$ 197,262
Taxes					55,233
Net profit after taxes					$ 142,029

CONVENIESSE, INC.

Balance Sheet, End of Year 1 (projected)

Assets

Current assets

Cash and investments	$256,281	
Inventory	131,250	
Prepaid rent	8,333	
Prepaid insurance	1,500	
Total current assets		$397,364

Long-term assets

Building and equipment		$114,000
Total assets		$511,364

Liabilities and owners' equity

Liabilities

Notes payable-bank	$283,352	

Stockholders' equity

Common stock	$150,000	
Retained earnings	78,012	
Total liabilities and owners' equity		$511,364

CONVENIESSE, INC.

Balance Sheet, End of Year 2 (projected)

Assets

Current assets

Cash and investments	$392,748	
Inventory	137,812	
Prepaid rent	8,750	
Prepaid insurance	1,575	
Total current assets		$540,885
Long-term assets		
Building and equipment		$ 85,500
Total assets		
		$626,385

Liabilities and owners' equity

Liabilities

Notes payable-bank	$253,914	
Stockholders' equity		
Common stock	$150,000	
Retained earnings	222,471	
Total liabilities and owners' equity		$626,385

CONVENIESSE, INC.

Balance Sheet, End of Year 3 (projected)

Assets

Current assets

Cash and investments	$503,861	
Inventory	144,703	
Prepaid rent	9,188	
Prepaid insurance	1,653	
Total current assets	$659,405	
Long-term assets		
Building and equipment	$ 57,000	
Total assets		
		$716,405

Liabilities and owners' equity

Liabilities

Notes payable-bank	$221,393	
Stockholders' equity		
Common stock	$150,000	
Retained earnings	345,012	
Total liabilities and owners' equity		$716,405

CONVENIESSE, INC.
Balance Sheet, End of Year 4 (projected)

Assets
Current assets

Cash and investments	$620,639		
Inventory	151,938		
Prepaid rent	9,647		
Prepaid insurance	1,736		
Total current assets		$783,960	
Long-term assets			
Building and equipment		$ 28,500	
Total assets			$812,460

Liabilities and owners' equity
Liabilities

Notes payable-bank	$185,467		
Stockholders' equity			
Common stock	$150,000		
Retained earnings	476,993		
Total liabilities and owners' equity			$812,460

CONVENIESSE, INC.
Balance Sheet, End of Year 5 (projected)

Assets
Current assets

Cash and investments	$743,296		
Inventory	159,535		
Prepaid rent	10,129		
Prepaid insurance	1,823		
Total current assets		$914,783	
Long-term assets			
Building and equipment		0	
Total assets			$914,783

Liabilities and owners' equity
Liabilities

Notes payable-bank	$145,761		
Stockholders' equity			
Common stock	$150,000		
Retained earnings	619,022		
Total liabilities and owners' equity			$914,783

B *Careers: Planning Your Future*

It is never too early to begin thinking about careers. While some of you may have a clear career direction in mind, many of you will have little clue as to which career is best for you. Even if you are a freshman or sophomore, now is the time to begin thinking about your time beyond college.

Each course you take, both within and outside of business, helps you decide which fields seem most appealing. If you love chemistry and detest English, you file that in your mind and almost subconsciously gravitate more toward science courses. If you really like working with people and have good communication skills, then marketing or human resources may be appropriate. Some of you may have found that you like everything equally well. Others may have found no area that seems terribly interesting. This is not a problem and is not that unusual, especially if you still have a few years to go in your college career.

If you are a freshman or sophomore, we encourage you to explore. Take courses that interest you even if they do not seem career-oriented. Carefully plan your schedule each semester to include different kinds of courses. Most colleges and universities allow a certain amount of flexibility in selection of general education courses and free electives; take advantage of that freedom to explore a number of options. As you take these courses, ask yourself if the material is interesting and could be applicable to a future career.

We encourage you to always remain open to information about industries and career paths. Talk with roommates. Visit with faculty members. Go to your career center (yes, even as a freshman) and look through their materials. Attend presentations given by business speakers to get a better sense of what they do. Wander through the magazine section of your library and look at articles about industries that might interest you. In short, gather as much career information as you can.

Self-Assessment

Throughout this book, we have discussed the need for managers to continually assess the impact of environmental forces on their businesses and to analyze the strengths and weaknesses of the business. We recommend that you do the same for yourself as an individual.

You should begin a program of conscious self-assessment. What are your strengths? What do you do well? What do you like to do even if you currently have few skills in the area? Remember that most of you have three or four years left to build skills, but you need to know where you want to focus.

Think about your values. Are you a hard-working, super-competitive individual? If so, some careers will be much better for you than others. Stock brokerage, for example, is known for requiring high-energy, intensely focused employees. Some consulting firms look for similar types of people. Are you happiest when you are around people? If so, a sales career can be both psychologically and financially rewarding. Do you quickly become bored with people and find enjoyment in solitude? There are many careers that take advantage of that value system. Do you enjoy working with computers and staying up with the newest in information technology? If so, you may have a future in one of the fast-growing computer and information technology fields. On the other hand, if staring at a computer screen is torture for you, do not force yourself into a career that you will dislike just because it pays well.

Look at your past experience. What jobs have you had? What responsibilities have you assumed? What technical skills have you developed? Do you have good interpersonal skills? Can you handle conflict? In addition, consider your grade-point average in high school and so far in college. Some companies simply will not consider individuals with a GPA less than 3.0 on a 4.0 scale. Other companies and other careers may make use of individuals who may have excellent social and leadership skills even though their academic record is not as stellar. Remember that the self-assessment should not establish barriers or limitations. The assessment provides a sense of the areas that seem closest to your interests and talents.

The Need for a Resume

It may seem strange to talk of the need to develop a resume early in your college career, but it is important. A resume is a snapshot of your skills, experience, and career interests. It lists your past activities and accomplishments, your educational experience, and your career goals. It is the initial key to getting interviews for jobs. Thus, it can be one of the most important documents that you will ever produce.

Because it is so important, you need to start developing your resume now. Build a resume file on your computer and, if possible, get one of the resume software programs that guide you in the process. Add to your resume as significant experiences or changes occur that may affect your personal snapshot. You should revise your resume at least once every semester.

You may find that you want to create two or more versions of your resume. For example, if you think you want to go into a sales-related career, you may create a resume that highlights your interpersonal skills and previous sales experience. At the same time, if you also have good computer skills, you may want a second resume that focuses on information technology. In this resume, you highlight your technical skills by listing the kinds of computer software you know and discussing the experience you have had in computer-related activities.

Sources of Information about Careers

There are many sources of information about careers. Additionally, there is much information available about how to find jobs, write resumes, handle an interview, and locate specific jobs. As a student, you have two great sources of information that are free. The first is your college career center. Career centers have a number of different names on different college campuses, but these can be easily found in your college's phone directory or internet home page. The second source of information is the internet.

Career Centers

The career center in your college has a wide assortment of information and also provides valuable services. Even though many of you will find your first post-college job through sources other than your career center, the center can still provide you with a host of information and training in the skills needed to get a job.

One source of valuable information is the career center library, which typically contains information on hundreds of companies and thousands of jobs. Assistants can show you how to search that information. In addition to the hardcopy brochures and information, they will also be able to point you toward the home pages of companies which may interest you.

Career centers can also help you decide which jobs seem best suited to your skills, interests, and personality. For example, almost all centers will have vocational interest inventories and personality testing software available. These may require up to two hours to complete, but the results tell you much about yourself. Do not discount this information. The information provided by the software or other testing mechanisms helps you firm up your own self-assessment and can point you toward attractive careers.

Most career centers will provide training in resume development. Some have resume software which may be purchased as a freshman and used to develop resumes which can be updated easily and entered into the career center's database. This information can then be forwarded to potential employers who contact the center looking to fill internships, co-op positions, or permanent positions. Career center staff will also provide classes or individual help in writing resumes and cover letters.

Career centers also help in developing interviewing skills. Written information is typically available, and videotapes about interviewing are almost universal. In addition, some centers will provide opportunities for mock interviews. These practice interviews, often including actual recruiters from companies, provide excellent experience in handling an interview. They help identify specific weaknesses—avoidance of eye contacts, overuse of expressions such as "cool" and "like," rambling monologues, and slouching posture. They also help you strengthen your skills such as establishing rapport with the interviewer, asking intelligent questions, and showing interest in the job and company.

Career centers can help you find part-time jobs, internships, and co-op positions. Traditional part-time jobs provide you with experience and cash. While the cash is helpful, the experience may be more important. Part-time jobs can help you decide what kind of career you may want. They also give you experience in working with others. Finally, from a resume and interview standpoint, they give you experience to list on your resume and a topic of conversation in an interview. Internships and co-op jobs (these terms are used somewhat interchangeably at different schools) provide the benefits of part-time jobs with the added benefit of being career-related. Some internships pay a wage or salary; some do not. Some provide academic credit; some do not. In addition, the internships provide potential employers the chance to observe these employees over an extended time. Some employers give preference to candidates who have had internship or co-op experience with them. In fact, it is not unusual for students to finish their college careers and move directly to permanent jobs with the companies where they had previously held internship or co-op positions.

The Internet

College career centers should be your number one source of career information because of the vast amount of information and services they provide. An additional source of career information is available from the internet. Typing the word "careers" on Netscape's search icon found 608,257 sites related to careers. Typing "service-careers" located 3,200 sites. Typing "sales-careers" located 393 sites. One site that is especially useful is the U.S. government's Bureau of Labor Statistics' *Occupational Outlook Handbook* found at http://stats.bls.gov/ocohome.htm. This site has a listing of hundreds of occupations along with job descriptions, skill requirements, and salary ranges.

In addition to doing general surfing of the internet for career information, you can contact company sites. Try any of the sites listed on the inside front and back covers of this book. Almost every company will have a link to employment at that company.

Selecting a Career

Which career should you seek? The information from your self-assessment should help guide you. In addition, you should look for career fields which are growing. The following information is provided by the Bureau of Labor Statistics' *Occupational Outlook Handbook*, which looks at trends in jobs between 1994 and 2005.[1] Note that we are approximately halfway through that time period now, but the projections appear to be accurate. You can find more detailed information by accessing their website listed above.

- Employment growth is projected to be highly concentrated by industry. The services and retail trade industries will account for 16.2 million out of a total projected growth of 16.8 million wage and salary jobs. (See Figure B–1.)
- Business, health, and education services will account for seventy percent of the growth—9.2 million out of 13.6 million jobs—within services.
- Healthcare services will account for almost one-fifth of all job growth from 1994–2005. Factors contributing to continued growth in this industry include the aging population, which will continue to require more services, and the increased use of innovative medical technology for intensive diagnosis and treatment. Patients will increasingly be shifted out of hospitals and into outpatient facilities, nursing homes, and home healthcare in an attempt to contain costs.

FIGURE B – 1   Occupations projected to grow the fastest, 1994–2005

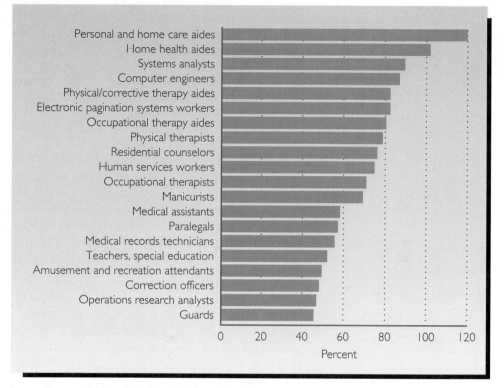

Source: Bureau of Labor Statistics, 1996. http://stats.bls.gov/images/ococ06.gif (accessed 11/20/97).

- The personnel supply services industry, which provides temporary help to employers in other industries, is projected to add 1.3 million jobs from 1994 to 2005. Temporary workers tend to have low wages, low job stability, and poor job benefits.
- The goods-producing sector faces declining employment in two of its four industries—manufacturing and mining. Employment in the other two industries—construction and agriculture, forestry, and fishing—is expected to increase.
- Employment in manufacturing is expected to continue to decline, losing 1.3 million jobs over the 1994–2005 period. Operators, fabricators, laborers, and precision production, craft, and repair occupations are expected to account for more than one million of these lost jobs.
- Among the major occupational groups, employment in professional specialty occupations is projected to account for the most job growth from 1994 to 2005. Professional specialty occupations—which require high educational attainment and offer high earnings—and service occupations—which require lower educational attainment and offer lower earnings—are expected to account for more than half of all job growth between 1994 and 2005.
- Many of the fastest growing occupations are concentrated in health services, which is expected to increase more than twice as fast as the economy

as a whole. Personal and homecare aides, and home health aides, are expected to be in great demand to provide personal and physical care for an increasing number of elderly people and for persons who are recovering from surgery and other serious health conditions. This is occurring as hospitals and insurance companies mandate shorter stays for recovery to contain costs.

■ Employment of computer engineers and systems analysts is expected to grow rapidly to satisfy expanding needs for scientific research and applications of computer technology in business and industry. Systems analysts and other computer-related occupations in manufacturing are expected to increase.

■ Occupations which require a bachelor's degree or above will average twenty-three percent growth, almost double the twelve-percent growth projected for occupations that require less education and training. Occupations that pay above average wages are projected to grow faster than occupations with below average wages. Jobs with above average wages are expected to account for sixty percent of employment growth over the 1994–2005 period. Jobs with higher earnings often require higher levels of education and training.

As you look at this brief selection of possible careers that follows, note the typical job responsibilities, the education required, and the salaries. Keep in mind that the salary ranges are for the lowest decile to highest decile. Thus, the range is quite large. The median salary is given when it was available. This is a better estimate of what you might make. These are also starting salaries, so it does not reflect what you might make in five to ten years. It also is salary only and does not reflect overtime pay or benefits. Finally, the data is for 1994. Thus, the salaries are likely to be fifteen to twenty-five percent higher by 1999 and could be another ten to fifteen percent higher by the time you graduate.[2]

Job Title	Responsibilities	Education/Salaries
First line supervisor, manufacturing	Monitors production, schedules work, writes reports, motivates nonmanagerial employees.	High school or college degree, depending on industry. $18,720 to $56,160, Median = $31,720.
Manufacturer's representative	Visits with new and existing clients discussing customer needs, describing products, and taking orders.	College degree or previous sales experience. Technical degrees in some industries. $15,500 to $69,200, Median = $32,600.
Accountants	Accountants and auditors prepare, analyze, and verify financial reports and taxes, and monitor information systems that furnish this information to managers in business, industrial, and government organizations.	Bachelors or Masters degree. Entry-level accountants: $23,000 to $35,000, Median = $27,900 (B.S.), Median = $31,500 (M.A.). Senior accountants: $31,000 to $47,600.

Buyers/purchasers	Buyers purchase inventory for resale. Purchasers buy industrial supplies and raw materials. They attempt to buy the best products for the lowest price.	College degree or experience in the industry. $18,000 to $57,000, Median = $31,700.
Budget analysts	Analyzes revenues and expenditures and compares these figures with budgeted amounts. Plans future expenditures, finds ways to increase efficiency. Works in business, nonprofits, or government agencies.	College degree. $23,500 to $27,000 in small companies. $26,000 to $30,800 in large companies. Salaries somewhat lower in government and nonprofit organizations.
Marketing, advertising, and public relations	Prepares marketing strategies, advertising plans, and public relations policies.	College degree. Starting salaries, Median = $25,000. Manager salaries, $21,000 to $98,000, Median = $44,000.
Human resource specialists, labor relations managers, benefits plan administrators, compensation managers, training specialists	Wide variety of duties within human resources. In large companies, duties will be very narrow; in small companies, wide responsibilities are common.	HR specialist, Median = $25,800. Managers, Median = $52,000. Salaries vary widely depending on size of company and type of position.
Restaurant & food service managers	Restaurant and food service managers supervise the kitchen and the dining room. They oversee food preparation and cooking, examining the quality and portion sizes to ensure that dishes are prepared correctly and in a timely manner. They also investigate and resolve customers' complaints about food quality or service.	College degree or experience in food service. Training in specific type of restaurants. $11,400 to $46,000, Median = $21,900.
Financial managers	Positions include treasurers, controllers, credit managers, or cash managers. They prepare the financial reports required by the firm to conduct its operations and to ensure that the firm satisfies tax and regulatory requirements. Financial managers also oversee the flow of cash and financial instruments, monitor the extension of credit, assess the risk of transactions, raise capital, analyze investments, develop information to assess the present and future financial status of the firm, and communicate with stockholders and other investors.	At least a bachelors degree in accounting or finance; often an MBA is required. $20,200 to $77,800, Median = $39,700. Salaries will be higher in larger firms than in small ones.

Hotel general manager, assistant manager	The general manager has overall responsibility for the operation of the hotel. Within guidelines established by the owners of the hotel or executives of the hotel chain, the general manager sets room rates, allocates funds to departments, approves expenditures, and establishes standards for service to guests, decor, housekeeping, food quality, and banquet operation. Assistant managers head one of the departments.	College degree in hotel or restaurant management preferred. General manager: $40,000 to $81,000, Median = $57,000. Assistant manager: $30,000 to $44,000, Median = $40,000.
Management consultants	Work with clients to improve the operation of their businesses. Consultants often work in teams to propose solutions to business problems.	College degree or MBA. $30,000 to $53,900, Median = $41,300.
Production manager	Plans production schedules within budget constraints. Responsible for staffing, equipment, quality control, inventory control, and the coordination of production activities with those of other departments.	College degree, or MBA, but may have substantial experience instead. Median = $64,000 (with experience).
Retail sales employees, managers	Assist customers in making their selection, open and close the store, arrange displays.	Entry level: no prescribed education. Minimum wage and up, Median = $20,800. Managers: college degree $12,480 to $47,164, Median = $23,140.
Information systems manager	Supervise data processing employees, help design information systems for companies.	College degree in information technology related major, plus experience as systems analyst or programmer. $35,000 to $80,000, Median = $52,000.

REFERENCES

1. Bureau of Labor Statistics. *Occupational Outlook Handbook.* http://stats.bls.gov/oco-home.htm (Accessed 8/4/97).

2. Ibid.

Glossary

360-degree appraisal   Employee assessment or rating by everyone with whom they have key interactions.

501(c)(3) organization   A nonprofit organization that is authorized to receive tax-deductible donations.

absenteeism   A situation where an employee does not show up at work when scheduled to be there.

acquisition   The purchase of one firm by another firm.

adaptors   Creative people who try to figure out how they can improve things by working within existing systems.

affirmative action   A set of laws requiring businesses to take positive steps in hiring and promoting minorities and women.

antitrust   Laws that prohibit companies from unfairly restricting competition.

assimilation   The assumption that women and minorities should blend in and learn how to work within the existing organization and its culture.

baby boomers   The generation of Americans born between 1946 and 1964, comprising three out of every 10 people in the United States today.

balance of payments   The difference between the inflows of money into a country and the outflows of money from that country.

balance of trade   The difference between the value of a country's imports and its exports.

balance sheet   A financial statement that shows a company's assets (what it owns), liabilities (what it owes), and net worth at a specific point in time.

Baldrige Award   The highest quality recognition that an American business can receive, earned by at most six companies each year.

bankruptcy   A situation where a firm does not have the money to pay its debts.

benchmarking   Comparing one's practices to those of recognized leaders to see where and how improvements can be made.

board of directors   Individuals elected by the stockholders to oversee the management of the firm. May be inside directors (employees of the firm) or outside directors.

book value   The net worth of a company arrived at by subtracting liabilities from assets.

boundaryless behavior   Behavior that seeks to eliminate unnecessary barriers that limit the flow of information and ideas.

brainstorming   A technique for looking at problems and generating many alternatives without judging or selecting among the alternatives.

budget   A plan for the controlled use of financial resources.

business   An organization that strives for profits for its owners while meeting the needs of its customers and employees and balancing the impacts of its actions on other stakeholders.

business analysis   A comparison of projected demand for a product with the firm's ability and cost to produce it.

business culture   A set of unwritten values and beliefs about what is proper, right, and appropriate in a business.

business cycle   A somewhat regular pattern of ups and downs in aggregate production, as measured by the fluctuations in real GDP.

business ethics   The search for and commitment to meet appropriate standards of moral conduct in business situations.

business focus   The general direction in which top managers plan to take a business.

business-level objectives   The achievements that the business hopes to accomplish, as set by top managers or business owners.

business objectives   The basic outcomes a business hopes to achieve as it operates.

business profile   An assessment of a firm's strengths and weaknesses.

business unit   A unique product or market grouping that is treated as a self-contained business.

capacity   A company's ability to produce a good or service.

capital goods   Machinery and equipment used in the production process.

capital intensive   A business that depends heavily on equipment and machinery to produce its products.

captive supplier   A supplier that sells all of its output to a single company.

cash flow   The movement of cash into, through, and out of a firm.

cash flow statements   The financial document that illustrates the movement of cash into and out of an organization.

cash inflow   The movement of cash from somewhere outside the firm into the firm.

cash outflows   Cash that moves out of the business for any reason.

category killer   A chain store that specializes in a narrow line of products.

caucus groups   Groups of employees who get together to address key concerns relating to members of their particular group.

centralized   Decision making retained at the top levels of the business.

chain of command   The line of authority in a business; who reports to whom.

chief executive officer   Individual responsible for the long-range, strategic direction of the company.

chief financial officer   Individual responsible for the overall financial health and strategy of a company.

chief operating officer   Individual responsible for a company's internal day-to-day operations.

code of conduct   A formal, written statement specifying the kinds of things a business believes should be done and those that should be avoided.

collateral   Any asset owned by the borrower that it pledges to the lender in case the loan is not repaid.

collective bargaining   The process through which company and union representatives work together to negotiate a labor agreement.

commodity markets   Financial markets that offer businesses the opportunity to guarantee the future prices of certain agricultural products and raw materials.

common carrier   A trucking company that transports a wide variety of different products for many clients.

communicating value   Informing customers and potential customers about how a product can meet their needs.

competitive advantage   An area of competence that consumers value and the business is capable of exploiting.

competitive strategy   The specific approach a business chooses to pursue for addressing its environment.

competitive innovation   A change so important that it allows the business to distinguish itself and gain an advantage over its competitors.

computer-aided design (CAD)   A system that uses computers in the design and development of new products.

concentration ratio (C-4)   A percentage of total industry sales accounted for by the top four firms.

concept evaluation   Analysis to determine if the overall idea fits with the firm's strategy and existing product/service mix.

consumer price index   The most popular measure of inflation.

continuous improvement   A process where a firm and all of its people continually look for ways to change and improve all facets of the business.

contract carrier   A trucking company that specializes in carrying a particular kind of good for a few customers.

copyright   The exclusive legal right to the use of intellectual property such as books, photographs, music, or cartoons.

core competence   An activity or set of activities that a business performs very well or a quality it possesses in abundance.

core values   Those specific beliefs that a business makes part of its operating philosophy.

corporate bond   A loan sold to the public by a business. Buyers may be individuals or financial institutions.

corporation   A separate business entity owned by stockholders. Maybe privately held by a few stockholders or publicly held by thousands of stockholders.

cost-based pricing   A company figures all of the costs involved in producing and selling a product and sets a price high enough to cover these costs plus a reasonable profit.

coverage   The number of customers reached by a distributor.

creating value   Taking action that makes a product/service more useful to customers.

creative decision making   The process of developing new or different ways to solve problems or capture opportunities.

creativity   New and different patterns of thinking and behaving.

crisis management   Decision making in response to a crisis the business is facing.

critical success factors   Successful business practices that are most relevant to a company's situation.

cross-functional team   A group of employees who are selected from various areas of the business and brought together to make collective decisions.

cultural relativism   The belief that what is right or wrong depends on the culture of the country where business is taking place.

customer sensitivity   The awareness of customer desires and needs.

customer service   Knowing what customers want and seeing that they get it; taking actions to meet customer needs and preferences.

cycle time   The time it takes to develop a new product.

data analysis   The study of information to help a manager reach a conclusion about some aspect of the company.

debt financing   Money a company borrows from outsiders such as individuals, banks, or other lending institutions or raises by selling bonds.

deficit spending   Government spending more than it takes in through taxes.

demand curve   A line on a graph that shows how much of a good or service buyers will purchase at each possible price.

demographics   Categorizing people (according to age, gender, etc.) in order to study changes in the population.

departmentalization   Grouping similar jobs together in any of several ways (among them function, markets, or geography).

development team   A group of people from various parts of a company who have an interest in the product/service and are selected to develop it into a profitable activity.

differentiation   Providing a product or service that has some unique feature.

discount pricing   Pricing that is significantly lower than that for the same or a similar product at competing stores.

distinctive competence   A skill, activity, or capacity that a business is uniquely good at doing in comparison to rival firms.

distribution sector   The wholesale and retail firms that move products from the manufacturer to the ultimate customers or users.

diversification   Branching out into an additional area (or areas) of business.

diversified business   A business that is involved in more than one type of business activity.

diversity audit   A snapshot of how good a job a business is doing in the area of diversity management.

diversity management   Putting together a well-thought-out strategy for attracting, motivating, developing, retaining, and fully utilizing the talents of competent people regardless of their race, gender, ethnicity, religion, physical ability, or sexual orientation.

diversity manager   The individual who coordinates all efforts to help build a culture of diversity.

domestic firm   A firm that does business only in its home country.

downsizing   Reducing the number of employees in a business.

dual-career household   Family in which both partners are actively pursuing full-time careers.

dumping   Selling imports at prices that are below the cost of production and distribution; illegal in most countries.

durability   How long a product will last and how resistant it is to abuse.

durable goods   Products that have a life expectancy of several years and may be used continuously or with great frequency.

dynamic measurements   Measures that include some time element, often comparing results in different time periods.

earnings per share   A company's earnings divided by the number of shares outstanding.

economic growth   An increase in total spending in the economy.

economies of scale   Lowering a firm's average cost of production by increasing the size of its production facilities and its overall volume of production.

effectiveness   A measure of the degree to which a business achieves its goals.

efficiency   A measure of the relationship between inputs and outputs.

electronic data interchange (EDI)   A system that converts most if not all of the paper communication between a supplier and another business into electronic form.

employee retraining   Regularly providing the education and training workers need to expand their base of skills so they can meet the needs of business.

employee stock ownership plan (ESOP)   An arrangement in which employees buy ownership in the company.

empowerment   Giving employees more responsibility and discretion in decision making.

environment of business   Factors or influences that affect the business but over which the firm has little control.

environmentalism   Efforts and actions to protect the natural environment in which a business operates.

equilibrating processes   Processes by which the price moves toward its equilibrium point.

equilibrium point   The point on a graph where the demand curve intersects the supply curve.

equity financing   Any money invested in a business by the owners.

exchange rate   The value of a currency compared with foreign currencies.

executive director   The chief administrative officer of a not-for-profit organization.

expenses   Money a business must pay out in order to make its products and provide its services.

experience (learning) curve   Lowering a firm's costs by increasing efficiency through experience in making the product.

export management firm   A firm located in the United States that sells products abroad for another business.

exporting   A business sells products and services to customers in other countries.

factors of production   Critical input resources needed to produce goods and services, consisting of human, physical, financial, and information resources.

financial markets   Places where businesses that need to acquire capital are brought together with financial institutions that help provide the funds.

first-line supervisors   The lowest level of management directly responsible for overseeing the work of employees.

fiscal policy   Raising or lowering taxes or government spending in order to influence growth, unemployment, and inflation.

flexible benefits plan   A plan in which workers can select from a menu of benefits the ones they wish to receive.

flexible manufacturing   Manufacturing with highly automated machinery that can be changed quickly and can perform multiple tasks.

flextime   Work arrangement that allows employees to adjust work hours, often to meet other responsibilities.

focus group   A small group of people who are asked to respond to a researcher's questions.

focus strategy   Positioning a business to serve the needs of some unique or distinct customer segment that is not being fully served by the competition.

foreign exchange markets   Financial markets that offer businesses an opportunity to avoid potential losses when money earned from foreign sales is exchanged for home currency.

foreign sales office   A special operation in a foreign country that sells and services products that were made domestically.

form   The specific design, size, or model of a product that a customer needs.

fragmented industry   Companies which have very low concentration, often populated by many small firms.

franchise   A business that grants the exclusive right to another individual or business to use its name and sell its products or services.

franchisee   The person or business purchasing a franchise.

franchisor   The business that sells the franchise.

free trade   There are no government-imposed barriers to trade—no tariffs, quotas, or nontariff barriers.

free trade area   A geographic area where free trade is permitted among the participating countries but imports from nonparticipating countries are limited.

freedom   The power to make one's own decisions or choices without interference from others.

functional packaging   Packaging that provides some value beyond simply containing the product.

gap analysis   The study of customers' satisfaction with a firm's product or service compared with their expectations.

General Agreement on Tariffs and Trade (GATT)   An agreement between the United States and 22 other countries to regularly negotiate reduction of trade barriers.

Generation X   Young adults in the 19–30 age group.

glass ceiling   A barrier that is so subtle it is transparent, yet so real and pervasive that it effectively blocks upward mobility.

global strategy   A strategy where a business sells a uniform product or service throughout the world.

globalization   A way of thinking in which a business regards all of its operations all over the world as part of one integrated business system.

going public   A company offers to sell its stock to the general public for the first time.

greenfield site   New manufacturing facilities built from scratch, often on existing farm land.

gross domestic product (GDP)   The market value of all final goods and services produced in a country in a given year.

heterogeneous society   A society composed of many dissimilar people with a varied mix of backgrounds, values, needs, and interests.

hostile work environment   A work environment which includes unwelcome comments, conduct, and behaviors seen as offensive.

hoteling   Creating temporary meeting rooms for people who do not have an office in the area.

image pricing   A business sets prices very high to indicate the exclusive or high-status nature of the product/service.

importing   Customers buy products and services from producers in other countries.

income statement   A financial statement that shows a firm's performance over the course of a specific time period, such as a quarter or a year.

industrial consumers   Buyers of either components or capital equipment which are used in producing other goods or services.

industrial policy   Government assistance of various kinds to create a new industry or enable an existing industry to expand more than it could if market forces were the only determinants of output.

industry concentration   The number of firms in an industry and their relative size; often calculated by the C-4 ratio (the percentage of total industry sales by the top four firms).

industry sectors   Major groupings of industries with similar characteristics.

industrywide regulation   A situation where a local, state, or federal government controls the entry of firms into an industry, the prices they charge, how they operate, and even their exit from the industry.

inflation   A general increase in prices or an increase in the prices of most goods and services.

information technology (IT)   The use of electronic devices to collect, analyze, store, and transmit information.

infrastructure   Roads, sewer lines, and utilities that are necessary to build facilities.

initial public offering (IPO)   A company's first-time issuance of stock to the public.

innovation   New approaches and options that are the result of creative activities.

innovators   Creative people who are catalysts for new ideas that challenge the existing system and the accepted way of doing things.

institutional advertising   Persuasive communications that promote a company or organization as a whole.

insurance   A contract in which one party agrees, for a fee, to reimburse the other for financial damages incurred.

integrated assessment   The simultaneous measurement of variables in different parts of an organization.

interest   The price that individuals or businesses pay to borrow money.

interrelatedness   The concept that a change in any part of a business system affects all other parts of the system.

intranet   A version of the Internet designed for use inside a particular company.

inventory control   Making sure materials and supplies are on hand when needed.

investment banking house   A financial institution that works with businesses to get large amounts of financing.

ISO 9000   Quality management and assurance standards published by the International Standards Organization; a common denominator of business quality accepted around the world.

job sharing   Work arrangement in which two employees share one job and split all the duties, responsibilities, and compensation of that job.

joint ventures   Companies partially owned by two or more firms to conduct business they could not do alone.

just-in-time delivery   The delivery of components for producing a product just as the components are needed for the production process.

just-in-time production   An integrated set of activities designed to achieve high-volume production using minimal inventories of raw materials, work in process, and finished goods.

key results areas   Those areas of a business that are critical to its effectiveness and even its survival.

labor intensive   A business where people are key to supplying products and services.

lean manufacturing   The streamlining of every phase of the production process, enabling the business to keep producing while using less of everything.

learning organization   A business that not only adapts to change but creatively searches for new and better ways of operating and meeting its customers' needs.

lenders   The providers of debt financing, typically banks.

licensing   An arrangement where a domestic business allows its products to be produced and distributed in other countries by a foreign company.

limited liability Business owners are liable for the firm's debts only to the extent of their investment in the business.

line activities The areas of a business that are directly involved in making or adding value to a product.

LLC A form of ownership that combines the advantages of partnerships and corporations without the limitations imposed by subchapter S.

low-cost leadership Finding ways to reduce the cost of providing a product or service and passing the savings on to customers.

low-cost producer The firm with the ability to produce products cheaper than all competitors.

macroeconomics The study of the entire economy of a nation.

make-or-buy decision The choice of whether to manufacture a product in-house or buy it from a supplier.

managers The decision makers of a business.

manufacturers' representative A company or person that sells products to wholesalers or retailers on commission.

manufacturing firms Companies that convert raw materials or components into products that may be sold to consumers or to other businesses.

manufacturing sector The broad group of companies and industries that produce tangible objects.

market The place where buyers and sellers meet and bargain over goods and services.

market research Collecting and analyzing information about the market or potential market for a product or service.

matrix organization A structural approach that combines the project structure with the functional structure.

merger The joining together of two firms to become a single firm.

mergers and acquisitions Two ways that one business combines with another business.

microeconomics The study of the behavior of individuals and firms.

middle managers Managers who work below the vice president down to just above first-line supervisor, responsible for translating broad policies into doable tasks.

mission statement A statement that spells out what a business seeks to do and why it exists.

monetary policy Changing the money supply to affect interest rates directly, thus influencing inflation, growth, and unemployment.

monopolistic competition A market situation where there are many firms but each has a slightly different product.

monopoly A market situation where there is only one firm selling a product or service.

moral dilemma A conflict of interests involving ethical choices.

motivation A person's willingness to work hard and expend great effort for the firm.

moving The second stage in successful change; the actual change of thought patterns and behavior from the old way to the new.

multidomestic strategy A strategy where a business modifies its product or service to address the special needs of local markets.

multinational firms Businesses that have production and sales operations in more than one country and have a mix of international owners and managers.

multiplier effect An additional increase in GDP caused by the interaction of increased investment and increased consumption expenditures.

net profit Total revenues minus total expenses.

net worth The value of a business. For a publicly held firm, its stock price times the number of shares outstanding; for a private firm, its assets minus its liabilities (or its future income projected in today's dollars).

niches Narrow segments of a market that larger firms choose to ignore which are often served by small businesses.

nondurable goods Products that are either consumed or worn out over a relatively short period of time.

nonmanagerial employees   Employees in a business who are actually involved in producing or selling products and providing services.

nontariff barriers   Ways that government restricts imports other than by using tariffs.

not-for-profit organization   An organization that provides benefits to a set of constituents. Also known as nonprofit organizations.

off-the-job training   Taking employees away from the job for education that will improve their job performance.

oligopoly   A situation where a few firms, with or without differentiated products, dominate the market.

on-the-job training (OJT)   Instructing employees in how to do a job while they are working at it.

operational decisions   Decisions that affect the day-to-day actions of the business.

operational information   Any information that bears on the internal workings of the company and will help it run more efficiently.

operational use of IT   The use of information to make a company more efficient or effective in communication and internal operations.

opportunity cost   The value of an activity that a firm sacrifices in order to pursue a different activity.

organization chart   A graphic portrayal of an organization showing positions and jobs.

organization design   The way the various parts of a business are coordinated.

organization structure   A framework that prescribes how a business organizes, arranges, and groups the work that needs to be done.

original equipment manufacturer (OEM)   A company that makes components for another product.

outsourcing   Purchasing a product or component of a product (or labor) from another company.

owners   People who have invested money into the business with hopes of receiving a return for their investment.

parent company   Any company that owns one or more subsidiaries.

partnership agreement   A document that prescribes the responsibilities and privileges of each business partner.

partnership   A business owned by two or more individuals.

patent   A government-protected legal monopoly on a product or product design.

performance appraisal   The process a company uses to measure employee productivity.

performance-based pay   Wages that are tied directly to the employee's performance.

physical resources   (1) Fixed assets such as land, buildings, and equipment, (2) raw materials that will be used in creating the firm's products, and (3) general supplies used in the operation of the business.

planned change   The process of intentional movement from the present state toward some future state.

price elasticity of demand   The percentage change in the quantity of a product or service demanded, divided by the percentage change in its price.

price fixing   A situation where rival firms agree to charge the same price for their competing products.

primary data   Data that a business collects directly from customers and potential customers.

primary stakeholders   Those stakeholders whom a business affects and interacts with most directly.

prime rate   The interest rate that large commercial banks charge their best corporate customers for short-term loans.

private morality   Our personal moral standards.

privately held   A business that has a few stockholders and the stock is not open for public sale.

proactive   Anticipating changes and making decisions based on what is likely to occur.

problem solving   Decision making aimed at correcting an adverse situation that has developed.

product quality A situation where a product satisfies customers' needs by performing up to their expectations.

product advertising Persuasive communications that specifically focus on a particular product.

product/service development A broad term for the creation of a product or service that provides greater value to customers than previously existed.

production The process that uses machinery, equipment, and people to create valued goods and services from raw materials or components.

productivity The ratio of goods and services provided to resources used.

professional staff Employees who make decisions within their area of specialty that assist others in doing their jobs.

profit The amount of money left over after the business records all its revenues and subtracts all its expenses.

project organization A structural approach that uses teams drawn from various areas of the business to accomplish high-profile tasks.

promotion Actions taken to inform customers about and encourage them to buy a firm's products or use its services.

property rights The freedom to possess and regulate the use of tangible items (such as land and buildings) and intangible items (such as a copyrighted piece of music or a patented invention).

proxy Voting for company officers or major issues in absentia, usually by mail.

publicly held A business with stock that is open for public sale.

pure (perfect) competition A market situation where many firms sell nearly identical products and no one firm can raise its price without losing most of its customers.

quality The ability of a product or service to consistently meet or exceed customers' expectations.

quota A government's restriction on the amount of a specific foreign product it allows into the country.

real rate of interest The rate the borrower actually paid minus the rate of inflation.

reengineering A process whereby a business takes a critical look at itself and changes its design and operations in an effort to cut inefficiencies and focus on quality and customers.

refreezing The third stage in successful change; reinforcing the new behaviors with evidence of the promised advantages.

relationship marketing Getting to know one's customers and establishing rapport and long-term relationships with them.

reliability The low frequency of breakdown or need for repair.

resistance to change The strong tendency in businesses (and people) to maintain the present state, to keep things the way they are now.

resource allocation The division of authorized resources among the various units under one's command.

resources The human skills, physical materials, financial assets, and information a firm's managers use to produce a product or service.

responsibility Using one's property (both tangible and intangible) in a manner that does not unduly infringe on the freedom of others.

retailer A store that sells directly to consumers.

return on equity (ROE) The amount of profit the firm makes for each dollar it invests.

revenue The amount customers pay for goods and services they purchase.

rightsizing Eliminating those functions and people that are least critical to a firm's success.

right to work laws Laws which significantly restrict unions' ability to organize workers.

risk taking The willingness to undertake action without knowing what the result will be.

second-level communications Communication that customers make only when their first attempt to gain satisfaction proves fruitless.

secondary data Any data that have already been published.

secondary stakeholders Those stakeholders whom a business affects in an indirect or limited way.

self-directed work team   A group of employees who supervise their own work and are given broad discretion over the direction of their work.

service sector   The broad group of companies that provide some sort of service to customers.

silent partners   Business partners who typically contribute money instead of being involved in day-to-day operations.

small business   Any business that is independently owned and operated, is not dominant in its field, and meets size standards that vary depending on the industry.

sole proprietorship   A business that is owned by one person.

span of control   The number of employees who report to a given manager.

specialization   Placing employees in specific jobs and asking them to perform only those jobs.

speculation   A company's stock is bought or sold on the basis of a belief that its price will soon go up or down.

staff activities   The areas of a business that support what the line areas are doing.

stakeholders   People or groups who have some claim on or expectation of how the business should operate.

statistical process control   Checking quality at regular intervals in the production process and taking corrective action when necessary.

stereotyping   Placing people in broad social groups, then generalizing about and labeling them because they are part of a given group.

stock   Shares of ownership in companies that are sold to individuals or financial institutions.

stockholder   Any person who owns at least one share of stock in a corporation.

strategic alliance   Long-term agreements between firms that benefit all involved.

strategic decisions   Decisions that have a major impact on the general direction of the firm.

strategic planning   A systematic way of analyzing and responding to a competitive environment.

strategic information   Information about a firm's competitors, customers, and markets that affects its ability to compete.

strategic rightsizing   Eliminating functions and positions that are not critical to a firm's strategic success.

strategic use of IT   The use of information to better position a company to compete within its industry.

suboptimization   A situation where one department of a business, acting in its own self-interest, hurts or inhibits the performance of another department, leading to less effective outcomes for the business overall.

subsidiary   Any business that is wholly or partially owned by a parent company.

substitute product   A product which fulfills the same customer needs as another product even though it is not a directly competitive product.

successful business   Any business that excels over a long period of time.

supply curve   A line on a graph that shows the amount of a good or service a business will offer at each possible price.

sustainable competitive advantage   A competitive advantage that competitors cannot duplicate easily.

SWOT analysis   Stands for strengths, weaknesses, opportunities, and threats; an assessment of a firm's key strengths and weaknesses compared with the opportunities and threats it faces.

synergy   The combined action of two or more resources such that their total effect is greater than the sum of the effects taken independently.

takeover   Investors (including other companies) purchase enough of a company's stock to control the company.

tariff   A tax on an imported product.

technology   The use of machines, tools, and information in the production of goods and services.

telecommuting   Workers spend part of each week working at home and communicating with the office via computer.

test marketing Pilot testing a product/service in certain select markets to see what customers think.

theory of justice An approach to ethical decision making that assumes decisions should be guided by equity, fairness, and impartiality.

theory of rights An approach to ethical decision making that assumes there are certain individual rights that must always be protected.

theory X The belief that workers are naturally lazy, dislike work, shirk responsibility, and will do as little as they can in most work situations.

theory Y The belief that workers can enjoy their work, desire responsibility, and want challenges.

top management The officers of a business who make major decisions for the company and are responsible for the company's performance.

tort A behavior, either intentional or negligent, that harms another person.

total quality management (TQM) A systematic approach to addressing quality issues that involves a total, integrated, companywide commitment to quality.

trademark The exclusive legal right to the use of a name, symbol, or design.

trade deficit An unfavorable balance of trade when imports exceed exports.

trade surplus A favorable balance of trade when exports exceed imports.

turnover The rate at which employees leave a company.

unemployment rate The ratio of the number of people classified as unemployed to the total labor force.

unfreezing The first stage in successful change; breaking away from one's current thought patterns and behavior.

unions Formally recognized organizations that represent a company's or industry's workers.

unit-level goals Goals that apply to each part of the organization.

universalism The belief that there are commonly shared business standards and principles that are accepted throughout the world.

utilitarianism An approach to decision making that assumes that decisions that produce the greatest good for the greatest number of stakeholders are ethical.

value-based pricing A company figures out what customers want, what they are willing to pay, and what price thus seems appropriate.

value/price relationship A relationship in which customers get the best possible value from the products they purchase, given the price they pay.

venture capital firm A corporation that invests in risky businesses with high-growth potential, usually in exchange for a considerable share of the ownership.

vertical integration The degree to which a firm operates in more than one level of the overall production chain.

vice president A top manager who is responsible for a specific area of the company.

virtual organization A business that performs a core set of activities and outsources everything else.

vision A desirable and possible future a business believes in and strives to attain.

wholesaler A business that serves as an intermediary between manufacturers and retailers.

wholly owned subsidiary A business that is owned as part of a larger business; may be a foreign subsidiary of a domestic firm.

work/family conflict The sense that work and family demands interfere with each other.

workforce diversity The movement of people from differing demographic and ethnic backgrounds and value orientations into the organizational mix.

working capital Money set aside or used for operating a business.

working partners Business partners who play a role in day-to-day operations.

Photo Credits

Chapter 1
p. 4, © Photodisc;
p. 6, John Thoeming;
p. 20, Courtesy of Trek Corporation;
p. 22, Courtesy of Compaq Computer Corporation;
p. 23, Courtesy of L. L. Bean, Inc.;
p. 24, Courtesy of KMart Corporation;
p. 26, Courtesy of Ford Motor Corporation

Chapter 2
p. 32, © Photodisc;
p. 39, Courtesy of Trek Bicycle Corporation;
p. 42, Charles Stoner;
p. 44, Courtesy of McDonald's Corporation;
p. 45 Fred Fry;
p. 49, Courtesy of United Parcel Service, Inc.;
p. 52, Courtesy of Iridium Corporation

Chapter 3
p. 61, Courtesy of WFLD, Fox Television Inc.;
p. 66, Duane Zehr;
p. 70, Fred Fry;
p. 75, Zigy Kaluzny/Tony Stone Worldwide;
p. 76, Jon Riley/Tony Stone Worldwide;
p. 82, Walter Hodges/Tony Stone Worldwide

Chapter 4
p. 90, John Thoeming;
p. 94, Chicago Tribune photo by Charles Osgood;
p. 99, John Thoeming;
p. 100, John Thoeming;
p. 102, Courtesy of Lands' End, Inc.;
p. 106, Courtesy of Trek Bicycle Corporation

Chapter 5
p. 124, © Photodisc
p. 130, © Photodisc;
p. 132, © Photodisc;
p. 136, Courtesy of Smith Barney, Inc.;
p. 140, Courtesy of the United States Postal Service;
p. 141, Courtesy of The Body Shop, Ltd.

Chapter 6
p. 156, John Thoeming;
p. 159, Leonard Lessin/Photography Alliance;
p. 169, Keith Wood/Tony Stone Worldwide;
p. 173, John Thoeming;
p. 175, Earl Colter Studio;
p. 177, John Thoeming;
p. 179, Ken Graham/Tony Stone Worldwide

Chapter 7
p. 185, © Photodisc;
p. 189, Courtesy of Orient Overseas Container Line;
p. 193, Mike Blank/Tony Stone Worldwide;
p. 198, John Thoeming;
p. 199, John Thoeming;
p. 201, Courtesy of Cannondale;
p. 205, Courtesy of Trek Bicycle Corporation

Chapter 8
p. 214, Susan Van Etten/Photo Edit;
p. 219, Courtesy of Southwest Airlines Company;
p. 221, Courtesy of Auto-By-Tel Corporation;
p. 224, © Photodisc;
p. 229, Leonard Lessin/Photography Alliance;
p. 234, Courtesy of Home Depot

Chapter 9
p. 240, © Photodisc;
p. 244, Rhoda Sidney/Photo Edit;
p. 245, Courtesy of Columbia Sportswear Company;
p. 252, Bruce Ayres/Tony Stone Worldwide;
p. 258, John Thoeming;
p. 261, Tompix/Peter Arnold

Chapter 10
p. 269, Michael Rosenfeld/Tony Stone Worldwide;
p. 273, © Photodisc;
p. 277, Alan Levenson/Tony Stone Worldwide;
p. 285, Charles Stoner;
p. 296, Sarah Severson;
p. 298, Dave Reeser Photography

Chapter 11
p. 306, Courtesy of Federal Express;
p. 311, Courtesy of Lowe's Home Improvement Warehouse, Inc.;
p. 314, Courtesy of Southwest Airlines Company;
p. 318, Courtesy of Wal-Mart Company;
p. 320, John Thoeming

Chapter 12
p. 339, © Photodisc;
p. 345, Courtesy of Ford Motor Corporation;
p. 351, John Thoeming;
p. 354, Courtesy of National Fluid Milk Processor Promotion Board;
p. 356, Courtesy of Adobe Systems Inc.

Chapter 13
p. 368, © Photodisc;
p. 373, Dan Bosler/Tony Stone Worldwide;
p. 380, Tom Raymond/Tony Stone Worldwide;
p. 382, Courtesy of MRI Inc.;
p. 387, Courtesy of Mitsubishi;
p. 391, Courtesy of Lear Corporation;
p. 397, John Thoeming

Chapter 14
p. 409, © Photodisc;
p. 412, John Thoeming;
p. 419, Tom McCarthy/Photo Edit;
p. 423, Charles Gupton/Tony Stone Worldwide;
p. 430, Courtesy of General Electric;
p. 433, Courtesy of Levis Corporation

Chapter 15
p. 443, © Photodisc;
p. 449, Michael Rosenfeld/Tony Stone Worldwide;
p. 452, Courtesy of Miliken Corporation;
p. 457, © Photodisc;
p. 461, Courtesy of Yahoo;
p. 466, Andrew Sacks/Tony Stone Worldwide

Chapter 16
p. 476, John Thoeming;
p. 491, John Thoeming;
p. 494, Courtesy of Whirlpool Corporation;
p. 496, Courtesy of Motorola Corporation;
p. 502, Courtesy of 3M Corporation;
p. 505, Courtesy of Southwest Airlines Company

Chapter 17
p. 512, © Photodisc;
p. 514, Courtesy of Sears Roebuck and Company;
p. 520, Courtesy of Gibson USA;
p. 523, Courtesy of Microsoft Corporation;
p. 524, John Thoeming;
p. 526, John Thoeming

Index

Company Name Index

Name Index

A

Alber, Antone F., 472
Alexander, Jason, 156
Allen, Paul G., 97, 98
Allen, Robert, 111, 112
Amabile, Teresa, 541
Anderson, Ronald A., 268
Anthony, Barbara, 98
Anthony, William P., 442
Aquilano, Nicholas J.
Armstrong, Larry, 540
Arora, Raj, 155
Ashkenas, Ron, 530

B

Barad, Jill, 66
Barclay, Jennifer, 208
Baretz, Elliot, 350
Barneby, Mary Rudie, 130–31
Bateson, John E. G., 510
Beatty, Sally Goll, 31, 354
Beck-Dudley, Caryn, 268
Beeston, Paul, 342
Bennis, Warren, 337, 541
Bertelson, Roger, 206
Bezos, Jeff, 336
Bibonia, Menlou B., 207
Bigley, Gregory A., 442
Bigness, Jon, 510
Bixby, Michael, 268
Blake, Stacy, 155
Blumenstein, Rebecca, 95
Boroughs, Don L., 99
Bosack, Leonard, 217
Boudreau, John W., 510
Bowerman, Bill, 199–200
Boyett, Jimmie T., 128, 153, 154
Boyett, Joseph H., 89, 128, 153, 154, 441
Boyle, Tim, 246
Brauchli, Marcus W., 213
Bremner, Brian, 540
Brigham, Eugene F., 239, 267
Brinker, Norman, 105, 121, 172–73, 175, 232, 337, 441, 541, xxxviii
Brown, Paul B., 510
Bruck, Felix, 407
Brue, Stanley L., 278
Buffett, Warren, 98
Bulin, James, 345
Burnett, Leo, 112
Byrne, John A., 442, 540

C

Campbell, Alta, 198
Carroll, Archie, 120
Carroll, Glenn R., 442, 540
Cassiano, Christopher, 337
Chambers, Ann, 98
Champy, James, 421, 442, 535, 541
Chandler, Rick, 73
Chandler, Susan, 289
Chase, Richard B., 408
Chickadel, Charles, 254
Choi, Audrey, 31
Christian, Nichole M., 95
Cihon, Patrick, 268
Clare, David R., 65
Clemetson, Lynette, 213
Cohen, Ben, 119–20
Collins, Marva, 58–59
Conn, H. P., 89
Conn, Henry P., 441
Conti, Regina, 541
Cook, David, 6
Coon, Heather, 541
Cooper, S. Kerry, 239
Cordero, Alfonso, 443
Corning, Owens, 458
Cox, Taylor H., 155
Coy, Peter, xxxix
Crawford-Mason, Clare, 510
Crispell, Diane, 154
Crosby, Philip, 445
Crown, Eric, 368

D

Dalton, D. R., 154
D'Amico, Carol, 128, 153, 155
Davidson, Wallace N., III, 121
Davidson, Linda, 184
Deere, John, 202–3
Deming, W. Edwards, 445–47
Dennis, William J., Jr., 60
Dessler, Gary, 407, 510
Diederichs, Raimun, 407
Dobyns, Lloyd, 510
Dooley, Tom, 7
Drabenstott, Mark, 303
Drucker, Peter F., 327, 522, 524–25
Dubinsky, Donna, 124
Duff, Christian, 398

E

Ellerman, Gary, 143
Ellison, Lawrence J., 98
Esposito, Frank, 267

F

Faerman, Sue R., 89
Fallesen, Gary, 60
Fatehi, Kamal, 206
Faught, Leslie, 441
Fenn, Donna, 184
Ferrell, O. C., 367
Filman, Hugh, 207
Finegan, Jay, 154, 337
Finkle, Todd A., 31
Fischl, Jennifer, 337
Fisher, George, 147
Flynn, Gillian, 114
Ford, Henry, 170
Forest, Stephanie Anderson, 153, 155
Forman, Charles, 541
Fox, Ivan, 268
Francese, Peter, 153
Fraser, Donald R., 239
Freedman, Alix M., 121, 267
Freiberg, Jackie, 120, 218, 267, 293
Freiberg, Kevin, 120, 218, 267, 293
French, Warren A., 121
Friedman, Elyse M., xxxix
Friedman, Milton, 97, 120, 159, 163–64, 184
Fuller, H. Laurance, 65
Furchgott, Roy, 442

G

Gaffka, Douglas, 25
Gaiter, Dorothy, 154
Gales, Lawrence M., 442
Galvin, Chris, xxxvi, 64
Galvin, Paul, xxxvi, 64
Galvin, Robert, xxxvi, 64, 267
Gangemi, Robina A., 337
Gapenski, Louis C., 239, 267
Gardenswartz, Lee, 155
Gates, Bill, 97, 98, 179, 246
Gerhart, Barry, 120, 268
Gibson, Richard, 367
Gionne, Leo, 340–41, 361
Gionne, Lisa, 340–41

Subject Index